Life in Revolutionary France

Life in Revolutionary France

Edited by
Mette Harder and
Jennifer Ngaire Heuer

BLOOMSBURY ACADEMIC
LONDON • NEW YORK • OXFORD • NEW DELHI • SYDNEY

BLOOMSBURY ACADEMIC
Bloomsbury Publishing Plc
50 Bedford Square, London, WC1B 3DP, UK
1385 Broadway, New York, NY 10018, USA

BLOOMSBURY, BLOOMSBURY ACADEMIC and the Diana logo are trademarks of Bloomsbury Publishing Plc

First published in Great Britain 2020

Copyright © Mette Harder and Jennifer Ngaire Heuer, 2020

Mette Harder and Jennifer Ngaire Heuer have asserted their right under the Copyright, Designs and Patents Act, 1988, to be identified as Editors of this work.

Cover design: Tjaša Krivec
Cover Image: Family Going to the 'Guinguette'
(© Archives Charmet/Bridgeman Images)

All rights reserved. No part of this publication may be reproduced or transmitted in any form or by any means, electronic or mechanical, including photocopying, recording, or any information storage or retrieval system, without prior permission in writing from the publishers.

Bloomsbury Publishing Plc does not have any control over, or responsibility for, any third-party websites referred to or in this book. All internet addresses given in this book were correct at the time of going to press. The author and publisher regret any inconvenience caused if addresses have changed or sites have ceased to exist, but can accept no responsibility for any such changes.

Every effort has been made to trace copyright holders and to obtain their permissions for the use of copyright material. The publisher apologizes for any errors or omissions and would be grateful if notified of any corrections that should be incorporated in future reprints or editions of this book.

A catalogue record for this book is available from the British Library.

Library of Congress Cataloging-in-Publication Data
Names: Harder, Mette, editor. | Heuer, Jennifer Ngaire, 1969– editor.
Title: Life in revolutionary France / edited by Mette Harder and Jennifer Ngaire Heuer.
Description: London ; New York : Bloomsbury Academic, 2020. |
ncludes bibliographical references and index. |
Identifiers: LCCN 2020020650 (print) | LCCN 2020020651 (ebook) |
ISBN 9781350077300 (HB) | ISBN 9781350077294 (PB) | ISBN 9781350077317 (ePDF) |
ISBN 9781350077324 (eBook)
Subjects: LCSH: France–Social life and customs–1789–1815. | France--History--Revolution, 1789–1799–Influence. | France–History–Revolution, 1789–1799–Social aspects. | France--Social conditions–18th century.
Classification: LCC DC159 .L54 2020 (print) | LCC DC159 (ebook) | DDC 944.04–dc23
LC record available at https://lccn.loc.gov/2020020650
LC ebook record available at https://lccn.loc.gov/2020020651

ISBN: HB: 978-1-3500-7730-0
PB: 978-1-3500-7729-4
ePDF: 978-1-3500-7731-7
eBook: 978-1-3500-7732-4

Typeset by RefineCatch Limited, Bungay, Suffolk
Printed and bound in Great Britain

To find out more about our authors and books visit www.bloomsbury.com and sign up for our newsletters.

CONTENTS

FIGURES

MAPS

ACKNOWLEDGMENTS

We would like to thank the many people who provided support and advice as this volume progressed.

We are particularly grateful for those who commented on drafts of the introduction, including Alyssa Sepinwall, Meghan Roberts, Anna Taylor, and Brian Ogilvie.

We would also like to thank the anonymous readers for Bloomsbury for their encouraging feedback, the editors at the press, particularly publisher Rhodri Mogford and editorial assistants Beatriz Lopez and Laura Reeves, for their support, Ronnie Hanna for the careful copy-editing, and Merv Honeywood at RefineCatch Limited for turning our manuscript into a book.

Mette Harder would like to thank Heather Beach at SUNY Oneonta Milne Library for her help with scanning antique maps for this volume, as well as Ambrogio Caiani, April Harper, Phil McCluskey, and, of course, Bianca Tredennick. In sincere gratitude to Stephen Clay, Alan Forrest, and Mike Rapport for years of teaching and support.

Above all, we would like to thank the authors in this volume for sharing your research and knowledge of the Revolution with us, and for your great patience with our repeated queries and suggestions. We learned so much from your contributions and it has been a delight to work with you all.

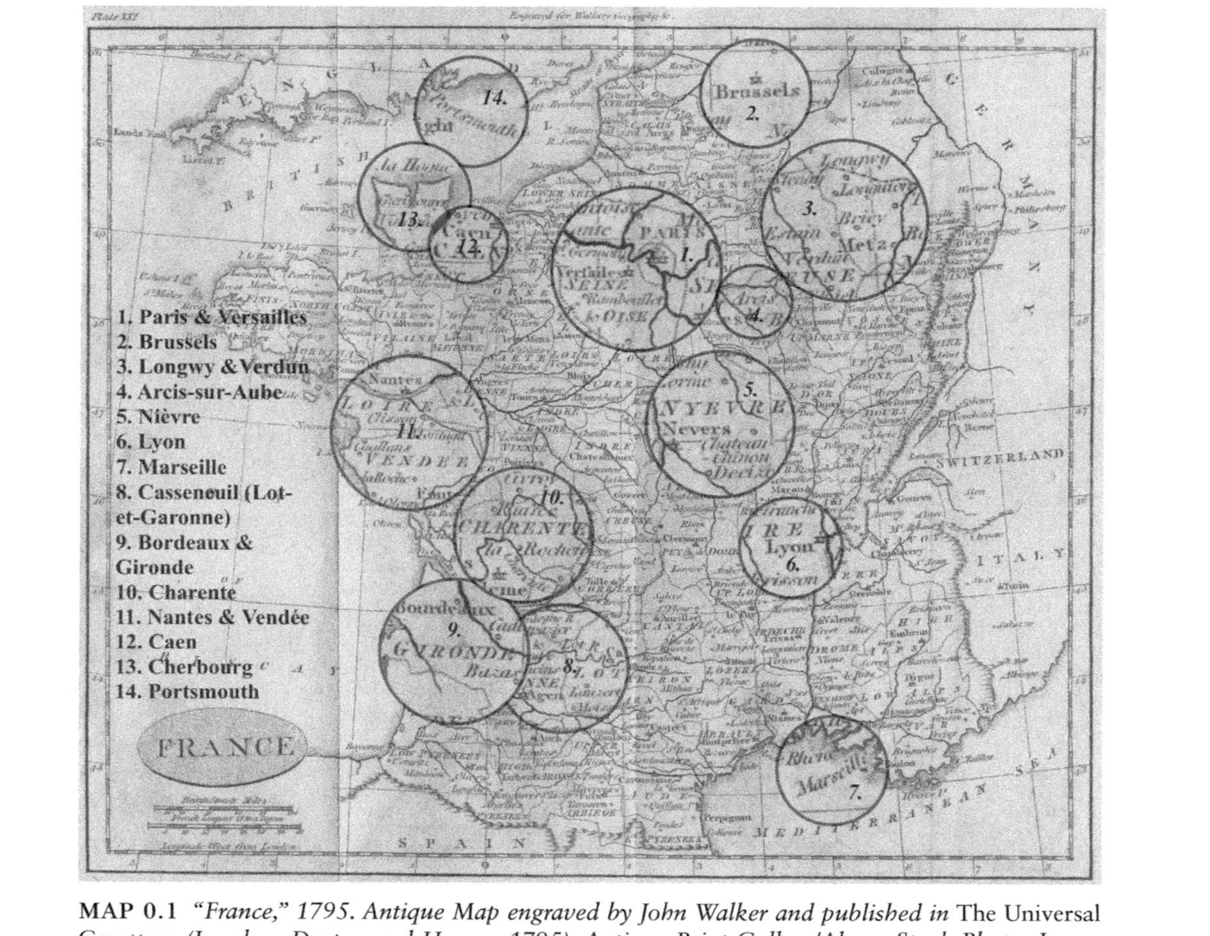

MAP 0.1 *"France," 1795. Antique Map engraved by John Walker and published in* The Universal Gazetteer *(London: Darton and Harvey, 1795). Antiqua Print Gallery/Alamy Stock Photo. Image ID: FPX6DK.*

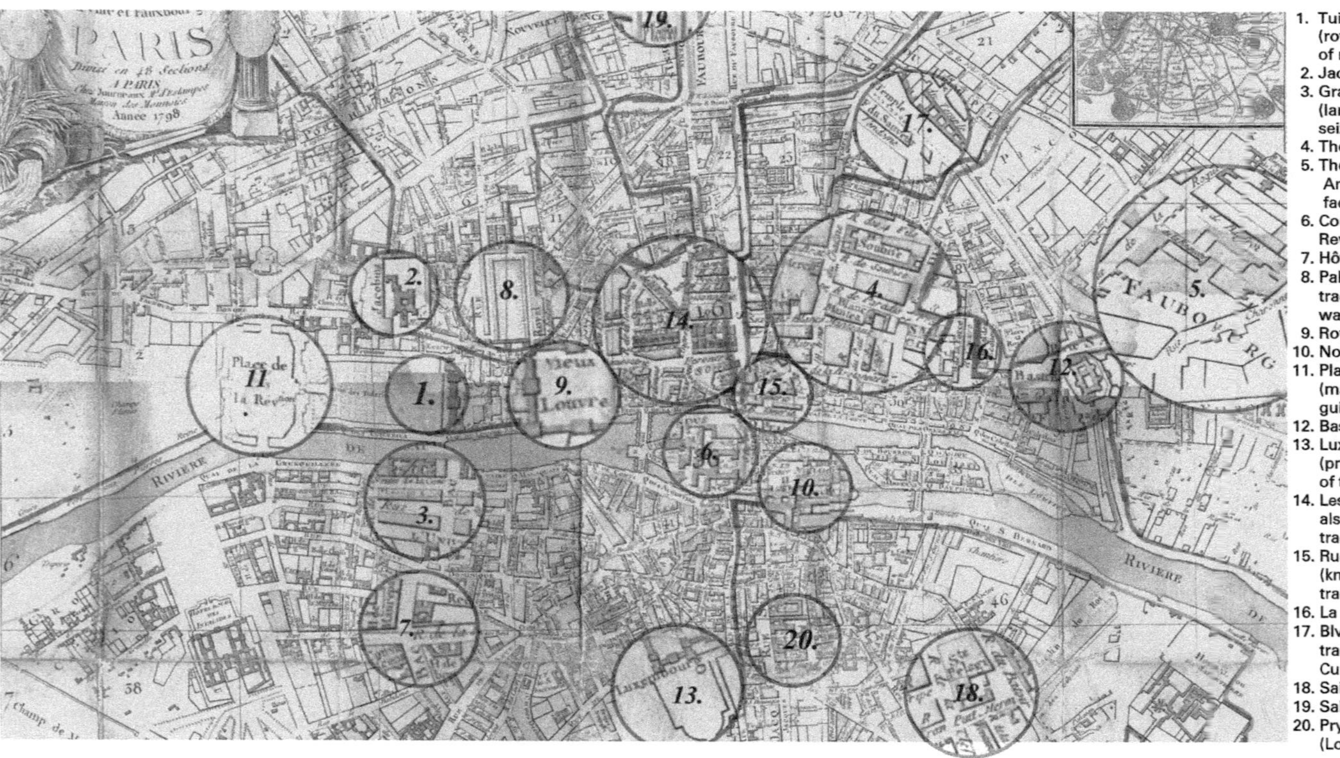

1. Tuileries Palace and Garden (royal residence and loc. of rev. gov.)
2. Jacobin Club
3. Gray Musketeers Market (large rental property seized by rev. state)
4. The Marais
5. The Faubourg Saint-Antoine (wallpaper factory; furniture makers)
6. Conciergerie Prison and Revolutionary Tribunal
7. Hôtel Galliffet, rue du Bac
8. Palais-Royal ("infamous" trades; loc. of Curtius's wax museum)
9. Royal Society of Medicine
10. Notre-Dame Cathedral
11. Place de la Révolution (main loc. of the guillotine in Year II)
12. Bastille
13. Luxembourg Palace (prison, then seat of the Directory)
14. Les Halles (com. district, also known for "infamous" trades)
15. Rue de la Vannerie (known for "infamous" trades)
16. La Force Prison
17. Blvd. du Temple ("infamous" trades; loc. of another of Curtius's wax museums)
18. Sainte-Pélagie Prison
19. Saint-Lazare Prison
20. Prytanée français (Louis-le-Grand) School

MAP 0.2 *Nouveau Plan Routier de la Ville et Fauxbourgs de Paris. Divisé en 48 sections (Paris: Chez Journeaux, 1798). Out of copyright. In the collection of Mette Harder.*

Introduction:

Rethinking the Revolutionary Everyday

Mette Harder and Jennifer Ngaire Heuer

The French revolutionaries led extraordinary lives, shaped by unprecedented opportunities to remake politics, society, and themselves, the stresses of political upheaval and war, and a strange revolutionary "fever" that, according to some who survived those years, almost consumed them.[1]

The French archives, however, contain many tangible reminders of the more mundane aspects of the revolutionaries' existence: a half-moon-shaped stain where Maximilien Robespierre set down his coffee cup on a denunciation sent to him; the stitched image of a flower amongst the papers of Lucile Desmoulins, who paid with her life for protesting the arrest of her husband Camille, outspoken critic of the Terror; a receipt for purchases the legislator Jean-François Escudier made at a draper's shop in the fashionable rue Saint-Honoré in 1792; or a complaint by Antoine Saint-Just's former landlady about rent the permanently cash-strapped revolutionary still owed, made on the day that he was executed.[2]

The archives also reveal much about the everyday lives of less famous people. There are intriguing bundles of private and political correspondence, records of arrests and incarcerations, and endless numbers of newspapers and petitions, all suggestive of how French people responded to the Revolution and how it impacted them. Making sense of these materials is not always easy. As Jill Walshaw explains in this volume, "it takes careful attention" to "tease [people's] experience out of the mountains of revolutionary documents that remain of that decade." But doing so can be hugely rewarding. It allows us to "meet" the people who experienced and carried out revolution on the ground, and to uncover previously untold, silenced, or invisible stories.

People used to see historical analyses of everyday life as trivial; they can appear descriptive, anecdotal, or, in certain historical contexts, even inappropriate.[3] But scholars have shown how important it is that we do this work. Historians have long noted the French Revolution's pervasive and radical nature, and its ambition not just to challenge the political order but also to remake society on public and private levels.[4] The Revolution touched almost every aspect of everyday life. It altered street names and house numbers, calendars and clocks, clothing, artwork, songs and theatrical repertoires, the production and consumption of food, and merchants' ability to make small change, the sizes of measuring spoons and the availability of critical ingredients—from sugar coming from Caribbean colonies to salt from metropolitan hinterlands.[5] It also reshaped human relationships—including those within the family and between friends—introduced new morals and beliefs, questioned long-held notions of race and gender, reformed education and healthcare, and profoundly changed the rules surrounding property, the workplace, the economy, and finances.[6]

Exploring everyday life in the Revolution thus offers us a valuable mode of historical analysis. It particularly highlights the ways in which the revolutionaries politicized people's "private" choices and habits.[7] Politics might not always have "invaded the attic of the servant girl and the apprentice" or the "innumerable furnished rooms on seventh floors," to use the formulations of Richard Cobb, a well-known historian of ordinary people in the Revolution.[8] Recent studies on family relations and friendship, however, have shown how profoundly revolutionary ideas often impacted domestic lives, and to what extent private choices could become political.[9] Looking at the everyday offers important insights into how the revolutionaries infused quotidian life with politics, as well as the ways that even those who sought to avoid political choices or actions often became entangled in them. It shows how many aspects of people's daily existence were affected by revolutionary change. Fastening a cockade to a hat or deciding how many buttons to put on a waistcoat, for example, were not simply questions of personal adornment but also ways of marking adhesion or resistance to the revolutionary order.[10] Writing the date in the "old" or new "republican" style was similarly laden with political meaning, as were hairstyles, footwear, forms of address, and the food one consumed.

In the sense that it politicized, surveilled, and policed private actions, the Revolution could be seen to have anticipated later regimes' "totalitarian" intrusions into people's everyday existence. At the same time, the contributions to this book make a case for viewing the Revolution in its own historical context and considering how people were also able to appropriate or resist changing forms of power. Whether it came to negotiating with tenants in government-owned buildings, policing prostitution, or controlling the

Church—some of the activities contributors explore here—the revolutionary State was neither a cohesive nor all-powerful force in people's everyday lives.

This volume thus has multiple goals. We want to introduce non-specialists to the French Revolution and explore how studying everyday experiences, choices, and objects, from doctors' prescriptions for an ideal diet for regenerated citizens to automata displays of the king's execution, can reveal the Revolution's power to affect people's lives. We also want to orient readers to some of the big themes of the period, including equality, citizenship, justice, and violence. In particular, we wish to highlight how thinking about space and identity, experience and emotion, helps us research and write about the revolutionary everyday. For instance, multiple contributions in this book push us to consider the Revolution as a sensory event, or explore politicized spaces such as villages, urban neighborhoods, battlefields, or prisons, and how they shaped, and were shaped by, people's experiences of revolutionary change. By bringing together international experts trained in different disciplines and schools of histories, we also hope to invite specialists to discover some of the latest sources, methodologies, and topics related to revolutionary history. Many chapters notably resonate in surprising ways with contemporary concerns such as workplace surveillance, carceral communities, transgenerational trauma, or the policing of women's bodies, prompting us to reflect on the Revolution's enduring ability to speak to the new challenges each generation faces.

Contributors to this collection help us see our way over the "mountains of revolutionary documents" available and discover what insights they hold. A remarkable number of materials are still accessible only as manuscripts, the documents that often most viscerally show us people negotiating their lives during the Revolution. Still, many printed sources, including digitalized ones, have contributed to the research in this collection. Most of the Revolution's parliamentary and legislative output is now online, as are thousands of pamphlets, petitions, tracts, and memoirs, including those published in document collections.[11] As several contributions to this volume explore, the Revolution also left us striking visual sources, including caricatures, paintings, waxworks, and other representations, illuminating people's views on contemporary events. Finally, material remnants of the revolutionary everyday, including briefcases, inkwells, cutlery, and clothing, are available in collections like those of the Musée Carnavalet in Paris and the Musée de la Révolution française at Vizille.[12]

Some of the earliest collectors of the Revolution's material culture had themselves lived through the revolutionary decade.[13] By the late nineteenth and early twentieth century, historians began to use their collections to analyze everyday life during these extraordinary times. Jean Robiquet, who was curator at the Carnavalet museum in the early 1900s, wrote one of the first books on this subject, subsequently translated as *Daily Life in the French Revolution*. He described the Revolution's impact on both individuals and society, by focusing on cultural life as expressed in public spaces, fashion, leisure, and language.[14] Since then, a variety of works have explicitly taken everyday life in the Revolution as a topic, including Jean-Paul Bertaud's 1983 study and James M. Anderson's 2007 *Daily Life in the French Revolution*.[15]

Other historians have incorporated everyday life into more general studies of the French Revolution. Sometimes this has been associated with particular approaches or ways of doing history, like the Annales School—an influential group of historians who explored long-term social history—or the history of "mentalities," especially associated with Michel Vovelle's pioneering work.[16] It has also been connected to uncovering the lives and experiences of "ordinary" people—like workers, peasants, and soldiers—who often appear in the historical record only in times of social and political upheaval like the French Revolution. A small sampling of such approaches includes Arlette Farge's 1992 *Fragile Lives*, David Garrioch's 2002 *The Making of Revolutionary Paris*, and Alan Forrest's books on the lives of the poor and soldiers in the revolutionary armies.[17] The 2018 translation into French of Richard Cobb's *Death in Paris* (1978) highlights continued—or perhaps renewed—interest in such explorations. In this classic investigation into the bodies of suicides and murder victims that washed up in the Seine in the waning years of the republic, Cobb focused on the many individuals for whom life and the Revolution were daily struggles for survival.[18] His related research into subjects such as loneliness, alcoholism, domestic violence, and suicide has remained important for the history of the revolutionary everyday.[19]

Historians have also investigated the experiences of particular groups of people during the Revolution, including those of women activists, urban workers, youths, religious minorities, free people of color, and foreigners living in France in the 1790s.[20] Doing so can illuminate not just how individuals experienced this tumultuous period, but also how we understand the dynamics of gender, race, age, religious identity, and citizenship in the Revolution, and how we gauge the opportunities and limits of people's political agency and activism. Recent texts looking at these issues include, for instance, Michael Rapport's study on foreigners in revolutionary France (2000), Ian Coller's *Arab France* (2010), and Clyde Plumauzille's *Prostitution et révolution* (2016).[21] Classic works such as Albert Soboul's *The Parisian Sans-Culottes* (1964) and Dominique Godineau's *The Women of Paris* (1998) inspired more recent studies that highlight the ways in which people expressed their demands vis-à-vis the revolutionary State, such as Micah Alpaugh's investigation into non-violent protests (2015) and Katie Jarvis' *Politics in the Marketplace* (2019).[22] With his *Parlez-vous sans-culotte* (2009), Michel Biard has provided the equivalent of an urban dictionary to decode the imaginative language used in the revolutionary newspaper *Le Père Duchesne*, which was hugely popular amongst contemporaries and helped shape public opinion.[23]

If researchers of daily life in the Revolution have tended to focus on "ordinary" people, some have also examined the experiences of France's elites to understand the intensity and dynamics of political, social, and personal change in the period. Edna Hindie Lemay's work on the daily lives of deputies and Timothy Tackett's *Becoming a Revolutionary* both follow the Revolution's first legislators as they gained power, uncovering their political apprenticeships and the practical details of their new lives as revolutionaries.[24] R. R. Palmer's classic *Twelve Who Ruled* (1941) asked how the members of the "Great" Committee of Public Safety coped with the enormous pressures of governing France during the Terror, a question also addressed by Marisa Linton's more recent work.[25] Countless studies of individual revolutionaries, including radicals such as Robespierre, Saint-Just, Théroigne de Méricourt, Bertrand Barère, or Léonard Bourdon, have given keen insights into their political motivations but also the private challenges they faced before, during, and (in the case of some) after the Revolution.[26] Finally, Linda Frey's and Marsha Frey's *The Culture of French Revolutionary Diplomacy* (2018) has shown how the profession of the diplomat changed with the Revolution, which affected etiquette, language, and dress. An individual diplomat's experience of working in revolutionary Paris is traced in Thomas A. Foster's work on Gouverneur Morris, American Minister to France, in "Disability and Manliness in the Life and Legacy of a Founding Father."[27]

A number of historians have explored how losing power affected the pre-revolutionary elites. Ambrogio Caiani's *Louis XVI* (2012) uses changes in the daily routines of court ceremony to analyze the extent to which the Bourbon monarchy was able to adjust to revolutionary circumstances.[28] Emmanuel de Waresquiel takes a fresh look at the trial of Marie-Antoinette, diving deeply into the sources in order to trace how the queen, and those around her, experienced her ordeal.[29] Patrice Higonnet's influential *Class, Ideology, and the Rights of Nobles* (1981) as well as William Doyle's more recent *Aristocracy and its Enemies* (2009) look at the impact of the Revolution on former nobles who lost their titles, homes, and lives to political change.[30] Similar lines of investigation have been continued by Ronen Steinberg and Hannah Callaway, who research the practical and psychological consequences of persecution, exile, and property confiscations for those who were, or were perceived to be, the Revolution's chief enemies.[31] Concentrating on the later Revolution, Anne Forray-Carlier's and Jean-Marie Bruson's 2005 study on Parisian society at the turn of the century provides anecdotal insights into a moment when some of the émigrés were able to return to France.[32]

Contributors to this volume build on this, and much additional, research on everyday life in revolutionary France. They also bring new questions, sources, and methodologies to explore how changes affected both ordinary people and elites. They address topics ranging from women's political activism to revolutionaries' belief in the "right to health," from the treatment of prisoners of war to the impact of surveillance on daily lives, and from religious freedom to the controversial use of guillotine displays to bring revolutionary "news" to Atlantic audiences. In addition, and to highlight the richness of sources on the Revolution and the creative ways that contributors have used them in their research for this book, a primary document accompanies each chapter. Directly related to the chapter contents, these documents (of which many are previously untranslated) encourage readers to discover for themselves revolutionary speeches, deliberations, and legislation, excerpts from sedition trials, letters written from prison, contemporary advertisements, prints, and portraits.

Revolutionary Identities and Spaces

Our first section looks at revolutionary identities and spaces. The Revolution offered people the potential for personal and political self-realization. But it also tended to categorize, record, and surveille them, and to demand conformity to a new form of national oneness. How did people reconcile their "old" and new identities in the Revolution, and what roles did contemporary ideas of nation, gender, sexuality, and race play in this process?

In order to show the vital importance of space in defining and shaping revolutionary identities, the chapters here draw on theoretical works like Michel de Certeau's *The Practice of Everyday Life* (1984) and on ways of approaching history that some have called the "spatial turn."[33] They look especially at spaces that may be less familiar to modern readers. Events in Paris, of course, shaped the course of the Revolution in dramatic and crucial ways; Michael Rapport has shown that the city itself can be seen as a revolutionary actor.[34] (For a map of Paris, see Figure 0.2.). But Paris's importance means that historians have paid less attention to events elsewhere. Combining a close look at neighborhoods and social relations in Paris with views from village inns and other major cities like Marseille and the wider Atlantic world reveals how people in different circumstances lived and became involved in the Revolution—or in opposing it—and what their experiences and activism meant to them personally.

Thus in our first chapter, "Republicans and Royalists: Seeking Authentic Rural Voices in the Sources of the French Revolution," Jill Walshaw uses, amongst many other documents, the records of seditious speech trials to explore political mobilization and resistance in the French countryside. Local archives highlight the misgivings of many revolutionary authorities towards rural political participation as well as the political views of villagers themselves. They reveal how, in a country that was still predominately rural, peasants helped launch the Revolution and then either supported or opposed it. The archives also draw our attention to the changing dynamics between grassroots politics, freedom of speech, and democracy as the Revolution progressed.

Historians of the French Revolution have been often been innovative in showing its participants' ability to redefine, repurpose, and remake spaces.

They have analyzed attempts to turn France's patchwork of regions into homogenized and uniform *départements* and to establish a tangible presence of the Revolution on public streets and squares as monuments were erected, destroyed, or renamed.[35] Looking at how people inhabited, shaped, and participated in public spaces can help us understand how they experienced the events of the Revolution and their own place in it. Laura Talamante's "Mapping Women's Everyday Lives in Revolutionary Marseille" thus illuminates the dynamics of politicization during the Revolution in an urban arena. She looks at the southern port city of Marseille (see map of France in Figure 0.1), where women claimed rights as citizens even as some disavowed models of citizenship associated with the most famous women's groups, like the Parisian-based Society of Republican Revolutionary Women. Using new mapping techniques, she highlights the changing social identities of women who publicly participated in the Revolution, the opportunities and challenges they faced, and their influence and visibility in politicized urban spaces.

In "Emigration, Landlords, and Tenants in Revolutionary Paris," Hannah Callaway takes us to the capital city and into the private spaces of people's homes. The chapter focuses both on specific spaces—rented apartments—and on a key consequence of revolution: the mass-emigration of France's former elites as they were classified and persecuted as suspects. Callaway poses an obvious question, but one that has not previously been considered: what happened to the tenants who lived in buildings owned by émigré landlords and that were subsequently seized by the revolutionary State? Here, records of property transactions reveal important aspects of social relations and State control in the Revolution. She also helps us understand the role of intermediaries, from concierges to neighbors, in controlling information about absentee landlords and their tenants—data that was relevant not only for pragmatic questions of rent-collection, but also for testing citizenship and trustworthiness.

From 1792 onwards, the outbreak of the Revolutionary Wars and the territorial and political changes they brought caused many French people to take on new professional roles and to cross and re-cross shifting borders. Christopher Tozzi's "Home Fronts and Battlefields: The Army, Warfare, and the Revolutionary Experience" provides an overview of the militarization of French society during the Revolution. It exposes the limits of thinking about the dynamics and experiences of revolution without also thinking about war. Can the home front (to use an expression first popularized by American wartime propaganda in 1918) and the battlefield really be seen as disconnected spaces? Tozzi argues that while the military did not impinge on the daily lives of most inhabitants of France in the earlier eighteenth century, it came to do so intimately during the Revolution—not just for combatants and veterans, or draft-dodgers and deserters, but even for civilians who never took up arms.

Revolution combined with war to remake space in other ways, challenging national borders and how ideas and people moved (whether willingly or under coercion) across those borders. Historians of the Atlantic world and the "global turn" have been particularly innovative in thinking about how the French Revolution interacted with other contemporary movements, and in identifying the practical impacts of distance and travel for news, commerce, and war.[36] Abigail Coppins and Jennifer Heuer's chapter on "Race, Freedom, and Everyday Life: French Caribbean Prisoners of War in Britain" builds on this work. They take us to an unexpected space for reconsidering the French Revolution: the cells of Portchester Castle in Britain. There, about 2,000 black and mixed-race men, women, and children from the French Caribbean were incarcerated as prisoners of war in 1796. Their stories show the potentially startling mobility of the period; some had been taken from Africa to the Caribbean as enslaved individuals, taken up arms to fight for freedom, crossed the Atlantic to Britain as POWs, and, in some cases, would later cross it again as re-enlisted French soldiers. Coppins and Heuer reveal how sources relating to the POWs' arrival and lives in Britain—including administrative reports, correspondence, and ships' passenger manifests—allow us to uncover contested meanings of freedom, captivity, race, and national identity.

The Right To?—Revolutionary Justice at Work

Part Two of this volume examines how some of the Revolution's key ideas and ambitions affected people's daily lives. It focuses especially on radical redefinitions of the ideas of rights, crime, and justice in the 1790s. The chapters in this section consider these issues from multiple angles, including the relationships between "ordinary" and political crime, and issues of privacy, transparency, and surveillance.

We often think of revolutionary justice in its most dramatic form: the tribunals and executions of the Terror.[37] Yet the "Terror" was more complicated and less consistent than people often assume; several historians have recently challenged the term, especially when spelled with a capital "T." They have done so not to minimize or excuse the violence revolutionaries committed. Instead, they question whether September 1793—when terror was supposedly made the "order of the day"—and Robespierre's fall on 9 Thermidor Year II (July 27, 1794) can be seen as definitive starting and ending points for that violence.[38] In his seminal *Violence et Révolution* (2006), Jean-Clément Martin queried the traditional "definition of the Terror" and proposed to "read" the Revolution through the wider phenomenon of violence.[39] Other researchers have since emphasized victims' agency, and tracked the ways in which the Thermidorians constructed a vision of the "Terror" as a "system."[40] Finally, historians have looked at the extent to which the French Revolution should be seen as unique in terms of its political violence, especially compared to that of other contemporary upheavals or civil wars.[41]

The contributors to this book revisit questions of revolutionary violence, justice, and their repercussions. They show how difficult it is to separate "ordinary" from "revolutionary" crime and consider to what extent all crime was politicized by revolution. Claire Cage opens our investigations into "revolutionary justice at work" by exploring the relationships between "ordinary" crimes, including fraud, theft, and everyday violence, and "revolutionary" crimes. She reminds us how much the revolutionaries sought to improve France's justice system. Questions of individual and human rights were critical, even as people struggled to decide what constituted justice and who should benefit from it. The revolutionaries instituted sweeping legal and juridical changes, including promulgating France's penal code, abolishing *lettres de cachet* (ways of imprisoning individuals without trial), reorganizing the courts, and introducing trials by jury. They also decriminalized some religious and sexual offenses.[42] At the same time, they invented and prosecuted new categories of criminal acts, from emigration (leaving the revolutionary nation without official permission) to draft-dodging. Men and women outside of the revolutionary government instituted their own forms of popular justice, from the infamous "September massacres" to protecting non-juror priests and others the State considered threatening. By considering these different visions and practices, Cage encourages us to reflect on what justice actually meant for people living through the Revolution.

Ralph Kingston's "Surveillance at Work: A Theft on the Rue du Bac" looks at a case where "ordinary" crime became entangled with revolutionary justice. In August 1800, an archives clerk named Louis Bonnet was convicted of stealing valuable boxes used to protect seals on international treaties. Acting as a historian-detective, Kingston investigates the case against Bonnet and his arguments that he had been set up. Competing testimony shows how people had learned during the Revolution to behave as if they were constantly under scrutiny—but also how they could use that surveillance to promote their own interests. Using the model of "place-ballet," Kingston explores the—sometimes self-imposed—restrictions on people's movements in the workplace, what this tells us about changing notions of privacy, surveillance, and suspicion in the Revolution, and how justice became closely connected to people's sense of self and space.

Revolutionary justice found expression in a developing and changing body of laws, and sometimes in popular violence. Yet, for those who demanded greater social equality, emancipation, relief, release from prison or restitution of property, it remained a key philosophical and political ideal. Several authors in this section turn their attention to forms of justice that we see in new ways from our vantage points in the twenty-first century—including social justice and women's and health rights.

Clyde Plumauzille's "Sex as Work: Public Women in Revolutionary Paris" explores one of the offenses that revolutionaries decriminalized in 1791: prostitution. For the first time in French history, authorities officially tolerated the activity. Plumauzille examines prostitution to investigate women's roles in the labor market of the revolutionary era and to analyze questions of policing and public scrutiny. Selling sex is often described as the world's oldest profession, but Plumauzille challenges this platitude by showing that the practice took on new meanings as the Revolution changed ideas of sexuality, gender, citizenship, and community health. Drawing on police archives, decrees, and letters, she seeks to restore agency to young women who mobilized their bodies as an economic resource in public spaces and who, when harassed by the authorities, petitioned the government for their rights.

In "Doctors, Radicalism, and the Right to Health: Three Visions from the French Revolution," Sean Quinlan introduces us to doctors who sought to heal, shape, and transform the human body, and who articulated new visions of medical justice. Their careers show them combining radical ideas about nature, science, politics, and society in order to free people's bodies and minds from the sufferings of the past. Quinlan uses their writings to explore both the "medical revolution" of the Paris hospitals and the radical articulation of every citizen's basic "right to health."

Revolutionary Experiences, Practices, Sensations

Part Three turns to a new (or renewed) interest in revolution as a sensory, aesthetic, emotional, and spiritual event. Here we build on recent work that has revealed how much the Enlightenment and the Revolution, which claimed to be rational enterprises, were also dependent on sentiment and sensation.[43] We focus less on what people did than on what they felt and believed, and on how living through these times affected their understandings of revolution and of themselves. As such, we draw on works emphasizing the process of revolution and the ways that living through it could affect how people made sense of social, political, and other change.[44]

In the section's first chapter, "Tasting Liberty: Food and Revolution," E. C. Spary takes us beyond thinking of food as a basic necessity, or revolution as primarily a struggle for bread and other essentials, to the intense experience of eating a "revolutionary diet." She looks at the "nutritional economy" of the Revolution, which included new ideas about food production and consumption, including making potato bread, canning, breastfeeding, and vegetarianism. Food, Spary shows, was closely tied to powerful ideas about national identity and survival. At the same time, by turning our attention to contemporary caricatures of revolutionary butchers, pies, and cannibals, she shows how hunger, gluttony, and bloodletting could become powerful metaphors used across the political spectrum.

In "Spectacles of French Revolutionary Violence in the Atlantic World," Ashli White turns from caricature to another form of visual culture:

waxworks. She examines how life-sized wax models of French revolutionary figures circulated in Britain and the United States. White focuses particularly on recreations of Louis XVI's execution and Jean-Paul Marat's assassination to explore how Anglophone audiences experienced two of the most iconic deaths of the French Revolution. Audiences encountered this violence physically, emotionally, and in visceral ways, through realistic wax automata that differed substantially from the events they represented and from two-dimensional print culture. People's reactions to these spectacles had political import in this age of revolutions. Considering these exhibitions provides us with a better appreciation of the power of objects; it allows us to think about the connections between violence, leisure, spectacle, and news, and to consider revolutionary violence as an Atlantic phenomenon. Jonathan Smyth takes us to the realm of spirituality in "Practice and Belief: Religion in the Revolution," reminding us that religion did not disappear with the Revolution. Building on earlier scholarship that contests simplistic dichotomies between religion and revolution, Smyth shows us how much both religious practice and experience shaped the revolutionary decade. He explores why and how, despite the efforts of the reformers of 1789 to 1791, the de-Christianizers of 1793 to 1794, and the attempts to replace the Christian faith with a combination of Deism and republican philosophy, the Church survived all efforts to remove it from public and private life. People also experienced new forms of spirituality through participation in revolutionary festivals, new revolutionary rituals and morals, and new religions like the short-lived sect of theophilanthropy.

Historians have also begun to think systematically about the relationships between emotions and politics in the period, not only as responses to events but also as ways of shaping and understanding political power.[45] Our last two contributions explore the question of emotions by looking at how prisoners and their loved ones responded to incarceration, and at how children confronted the trauma of quite literally losing their parents to revolutionary politics. In "Facing the Unknown: The Private Lives of Miniatures in the French Revolutionary Prison," Sophie Matthiesson returns us to visual culture, specifically to prison art as a special kind of object and emotional experience. Her chapter offers an intimate look into the emotional and material lives of imprisoned artists, their clients, and their families, and into the support structures and mechanisms that carceral communities developed during the Revolution. She looks at the crucial roles that miniature portraits, incorporated into small objects and jewelry, played in the lives of revolutionary prisoners, and she enquires into the commission and production of the so-called "last portraits" during the Terror. Her chapter helps us think more profoundly about the power of love and art to intervene in environments dominated by violence, repression, and isolation.

In our concluding chapter, "Revolutionary Parents and Children: Everyday Lives in Times of Stress," Siân Reynolds considers the experiences of the children of revolutionaries, using prosopography for tracing their fates after losing one or both parents. Many leading revolutionaries (including political representatives, activists, and ministers) also had young children. These often found themselves in challenging circumstances, negotiating interrupted educations and parental absence or death. Much depended on networks of support from family and friends. Reynolds explores the immediate experiences, memories, and traumas these children confronted as a consequence of revolutionary violence and asks what the subsequent actions and choices of this second generation can tell us about the complex legacies of revolution.

We invite readers to look for connections and conversations between the different chapters and sections in this volume, which cross-cut and echo each other. Some of the leading themes of the book transcend its three-part structure. For example, although Part One focuses most centrally on how the Revolution politicized and transformed everyday space, chapters in other sections also engage related questions, from an investigation of revolutionary surveillance in the workplace in Part Two to an exploration of how miniature portraits could help connect prisoners and their families in Part Three. Similarly, while Part Two focuses most on questions of revolutionary justice, other chapters equally allow us to explore the connected theme of revolutionary violence. Our contributors especially reveal the far-flung reverberations and consequences of such violence—not just in the courts of the Terror, but also in relation to new forms of conscription and wartime violence against civilians, spectacles of violence exported across the Atlantic world, and traumas that affected children long after the Revolution ended.

Other themes weave through the book. Many chapters touch on the history of the body, race, and gender, showing how physical concerns—such as what to eat or how to stay healthy—could become intensely meaningful in the context of nation-building. We see such issues, for example, in E. C. Spary's reflections on "Tasting Liberty" and Sean Quinlan's uncovering of reformers' visions of a "right to health," as well as in Coppins and Heuer's investigations of why British authorities were concerned with the diet, clothing, and lodging of French Caribbean prisoners of war. Similarly, multiple contributors across this book push us to consider how individuals made choices even within the euphoria, turmoil, and uncertainty of the Revolution.

From villagers in the Southwest negotiating revolutionary politics to the challenges facing the women who worked the galleries of the Parisian Palais-Royal, this is a collection of stories of individual and collective experience in the Revolution. There were many ways in which the revolutionary "everyday" escaped the reach of, or existed in parallel to, the government's official vision for a new France. By following groups and individuals to different spaces— from the bureaucrats watching each other in Paris to French Caribbean soldiers held as prisoners of war in Britain—we hope to illuminate how contemporaries drove, responded to, and subverted the changes of the French Revolution.

Notes

1 The former revolutionary Marc-Antoine Baudot recalled having had this "fever" in later conversation with contemporaries. Preface to Marc-Antoine Baudot, *Notes Historiques sur la Convention Nationale, le Directoire, l'Empire et l'exile des votants* (Paris: D. Jouaust, 1893), vi.

2 Stain on a letter and envelope addressed to Maximilien Robespierre from Tours on 28 Germinal Year II, containing a denunciation against "a number of individuals jealous of his glory" in the Jacobin Club of that city. Archives Nationales (henceforward A.N.) F/7/4436/1 (Papiers de la Commission des 21), Pl.4, Piece 144; receipt for items purchased by the Conventionnel Jean-François Escudier "Au Cheval Noir, Rues Saint-Honoré et du Roule, Lemor, Marchand Drapier" on September 25, 1792, A.N. F/7/4435 (Papiers de la Commission des 21), Pl.2, Piece 22; stitched flower amongst the papers of Camille and Lucile Desmoulins, Bibliothèque historique de la ville de Paris (BHVP), Doss. 2, Rés. 25 (MS 986) Desmoulins; statement by Elizabeth Pierret, Veuve Verrier, to the Comité Révolutionnaire, Section Lepeletier, 10 Thermidor Year II, A.N. F/7/4775/11. On Saint-Just's rented accommodation in Paris, see also Louise Ampilova-Tuil and Catherine Gosselin, "Les Logements Parisiens de Saint-Just," *Société des Etudes Robespierristes* (2017), http://etudesrobespierristes.com/recherche.

3 See, for instance, this discussion of *Alltagsgeschichte* —the history of the everyday—when applied to Nazi Germany. In Paul Steege et al., "History of Everyday Life: A Second Chapter," *Journal of Modern History* 80, no. 2 (2008): 359–60.

4 Among other works, see Robert Darnton, "What was Revolutionary about the French Revolution?," in *The French Revolution in Social and Political Perspective*, ed. Peter Jones (London: Arnold, 1989), 18–29; Lynn Hunt, "The Unstable Boundaries of the French Revolution," in *A History of Private Life*, ed. Michelle Perrot (Cambridge, MA: Belknap Press, 1990), 13–45.

5 On house numbers, see Vincent Denis, "Les Parisiens, la police et les numérotages des maisons, du XVIIIe siècle à l'Empire," *French Historical Studies* 38, no. 1 (2015): 83–103; on clocks and calendars, Matthew Shaw, *Time and the French Revolution: The Republican Calendar, 1789–Year XIV* (Martlesham, UK: Boydell and Brewer, 2011); on art in the context of the everyday, Richard Taws, *The Politics of the Provisional: Art and Ephemera in Revolutionary France* (University Park: Pennsylvania State University Press, 2013); on songs, Laura Mason, *Singing the French Revolution: Popular Culture and Politics, 1787–1799* (Ithaca, NY: Cornell University Press, 1996). The historiography on theater in the Revolution is vast; starting points are Susan Maslan, *Revolutionary Acts: Theatre, Democracy, and the French Revolution* (Baltimore, MD: Johns Hopkins University Press, 2005), and Paul Friedland, *Political Actors: Representative Bodies and Theatricality in the Age*

of the French Revolution (Ithaca, NY: Cornell University Press, 2002); on food, see E. C. Spary, *Feeding France: New Sciences of Food, 1760–1815* (Cambridge: Cambridge University Press, 2014); on small change, see Katie Jarvis, "Exacting Change: Money, Market Women, and the Crumbling Corporate World of the French Revolution," *Journal of Social History* 51, no. 4 (2017): 837–68.

6 On the family, see Lynn Hunt, *The Family Romance of the French Revolution* (Berkeley: University of California Press, 1992); Suzanne Desan, *The Family on Trial in Revolutionary France* (Berkeley: University of California Press, 2004); Jennifer Ngaire Heuer, *The Family and the Nation: Gender and Citizenship in Revolutionary France* (Ithaca, NY: Cornell University Press, 2005); Anne Verjus, *Le bon mari: une histoire politique des hommes et des femmes à l'époque révolutionnaire* (Paris: Fayard, 2010), and Marie-Françoise Lévy, ed., *L'enfant, la famille et la Révolution française* (Paris: Olivier Orban, 1990). On friendship, see especially Marisa Linton, "Fatal Friendships: The Politics of Jacobin Friendship," *French Historical Studies* 31, no. 1 (2008): 51–76, and Marisa Linton, *Choosing Terror: Virtue, Friendship, and Authenticity in the French Revolution* (Oxford: Oxford University Press, 2013). On education, see Adrian O'Connor's recent *In Pursuit of Politics: Education and Revolution in Eighteenth-Century France* (Manchester: Manchester University Press, 2017). On health and hygiene, see, for instance, Sean M. Quinlan, *The Great Nation in Decline: Sex, Modernity and Health Crises in Revolutionary France c. 1750–1850* (Aldershot: Ashgate, 2007), and the work of Colin Jones, including his most recent *The Smile Revolution in Eighteenth Century Paris* (Oxford: Oxford University Press, 2014), which includes discussions of dentistry. On property, the workplace, economy, and finances, see, amongst others, Rafe Blaufarb, *The Great Demarcation: The French Revolution and the Creation of Modern Property* (Oxford: Oxford University Press, 2016); Rebecca Spang, *Stuff and Money in the Time of the French Revolution* (Cambridge, MA: Harvard University Press, 2015); Ralph Kingston, *Bureaucrats and Bourgeois Society: Office Politics and Individual Credit in France, 1789–1848* (London: Palgrave Macmillan, 2012).

7 See, for instance, Leora Auslander, *Cultural Revolutions: The Politics of Everyday Life in Britain, North America and France* (Oxford: Berg, 2009).

8 Richard Cobb, *Reactions to the French Revolution* (London: Oxford University Press, 1972), 132.

9 See especially Lindsay Parker, *Writing the Revolution: A French Woman's History in Letters* (New York: Oxford University Press, 2012), and Anne Verjus and Denise Davidson, *Le roman conjugal, chroniques de la vie familiale à l'époque de la Révolution et de l'Empire* (Seyssel: Champ Vallon, 2011).

10 Lynn Hunt, "Freedom of Dress in the French Revolution," in *From the Royal to the Republican Body: Incorporating the Political in Seventeenth- and Eighteenth-Century France*, ed. Sara Melzer and Kathryn Norberg (Berkeley: University of California Press, 1998), 224–49; Richard Wrigley, *The Politics of Appearance: The Symbolism and Representation of Dress in Revolutionary France* (Oxford: Berg, 2002); and Jennifer Heuer, "Hats on for the Nation! Women, Citizens, Soldiers, and the 'Sign of the French'," *French History* 16, no. 1 (2002): 28–52.

11 For French readers, the *Archives Parlementaires* and the *Moniteur ou Gazette Nationale* provide standard starting points. See the French Revolution Digital Archive: https://frda.stanford.edu/en/. Some frequently used document collections in English include Keith Michael Baker et al., eds., *The Old Regime and the French Revolution, Vol. 7 of University of Chicago Readings in Western Civilization* (Chicago: University of Chicago Press, 1987); Paul H. Beik, ed., *The French Revolution* (New York: Walker, 1971); Philip Dawson, ed., *The French Revolution* (Englewood Cliffs, NJ: Prentice-Hall, 1967); Philip G. Dwyer and Peter McPhee, eds., *The French Revolution and Napoleon: A Sourcebook* (London: Routledge, 2002); John T. Gilchrist and William J. Murray, eds., *The Press in the French Revolution: A Selection of Documents Taken from the Press of the Revolution for the Years 1789–1794* (New York: St. Martin's Press, 1971); Lynn Hunt, ed., *The French Revolution and Human Rights: A Brief Documentary History* (New York: Bedford/St. Martins, 1996), and, with Jack R. Censer, *Liberté, Egalité, Fraternité: Exploring the French Revolution*: http://chnm.gmu.edu/revolution/; Beatrice F. Hyslop, ed., *A Guide to the General Cahiers of 1789, with the Texts of Unedited Cahiers* (New York: Octagon Books, 1968); Darline Gay Levy, *Women in Revolutionary Paris, 1789–1795: Selected Documents Translated with Notes and Commentary* (Urbana: University of Illinois Press, 1979); Laura Mason and Tracey Rizzo, eds., *The French Revolution: A Document Collection* (New York: Houghton Mifflin, 1999); Jeremy D. Popkin, ed., *Facing Racial Revolution: Eyewitness Accounts of the Haitian Insurrection* (Chicago: University of Chicago Press, 2007); John Hall Stewart, ed., *A Documentary Survey of the French Revolution* (New York: Macmillan, 1951); Reay Tannahill, ed., *Paris in the Revolution: A Collection of Eye-witness Accounts* (London: Folio Society, 1966); and see Micah Alpaugh, ed. *The French Revolution: A History in Documents* (London: Bloomsbury, forthcoming 2021).

12 For an overview of the Carnavalet, see Jean Tulard, *The French Revolution in Paris: Seen through the Collections of the Carnavalet Museum* (Paris: Paris-Musées, 1989); on Vizille, Philippe Bordes and Alain Chevalier, *Catalogue des Peintures, Sculptures, et Dessins, Musée de la Révolution Française* (Vizille: Musée de la Révolution Française, 1996).

13 See Tom Stammers, "The Homeless Heritage of the French Revolution, c. 1789–1889," *International Journal of Heritage Studies* 25, no. 5 (2017): 478–90, and Gilles Bertrand et al., eds., *Collectionner la Révolution française* (Paris: Société des études robespierristes, 2016).

14 Jean Robiquet, *Daily Life in the French Revolution*, trans. James Kirkup (London: Weidenfeld and Nicolson, 1964). This work was preceded by Gosselin Lenôtre's also interesting but more geographically focused *La Vie à Paris pendant la Révolution* (Paris: Calmann-Lévy, 1936).

15 Jean-Paul Bertaud, *La vie quotidienne en France au temps de la Révolution: 1789–1795* (Paris: Hachette, 1983); James M. Anderson, ed., *Daily Life in the French Revolution* (Westport, CT: Greenwood, 2007).

16 See, in particular, Fernand Braudel, *Civilization and Capitalism: 15th–18th Century*, trans. Siân Reynolds, 3 vols. (London: CollinsFontana, 1981–4); Michel Vovelle, *Ideologies and Mentalities*, trans. Eamon O'Flaherty (Cambridge: Polity, 1990), and *The Revolution against the Church: From*

Reason to the Supreme Being, trans. Alan José (Cambridge: Polity, 1991), as well as *La Découverte de la Politique: Géopolitique de la Révolution Française* (Paris: Éditions La Découverte, 1993). See also Georges Lefebvre, "The Place of the Revolution in the Agrarian History of France," in *Rural Society in France: Selections from the 'Annales, économies, sociétés, civilisations'*, ed. Robert Forster and Orest Ranum, trans. Elborg Forster and Patricia M. Ranum (Baltimore, MD: Johns Hopkins University Press, 1977), 31–49.

17 Arlette Farge, *Fragile Lives: Violence, Power and Solidarity in Eighteenth-Century Paris*, trans. Carol Shelton (Cambridge, MA: Harvard University Press, 1993); David Garrioch, *The Making of Revolutionary Paris* (Berkeley: University of California Press, 2002), and "The Everyday Lives of Parisian Women and the October Days of 1789," *Social History* 24, no. 3 (1999): 231–50; Alan Forrest, *The French Revolution and the Poor* (Oxford: Basil Blackwell, 1981).

18 Richard Cobb, *Death in Paris: The Records of the Basse-Geôle de la Seine, October 1795–September 1801, Vendémiaire Year IV–Fructidor Year IX* (Oxford: Oxford University Press, 1978); recent translation: *La Mort est dans Paris: enquête sur le suicide et la mort violente dans le petit peuple Parisien au lendemain de la Terreur*, trans. Daniel Alibert-Kouraguine (Toulouse: Anacharsis, 2018).

19 See Richard Cobb, "The Rise and Fall of a Provincial Terrorist," and the section "La Vie en Marge: Living on the Fringe of the Revolution" in *Reactions to the French Revolution*. Some of these essays are also reproduced in Richard Cobb, *The French and Their Revolution*, ed. David Gilmour (London: John Murray, 1998). On suicide, see also Dominique Godineau, *S'abréger les jours: le suicide en France au XVIIIe siècle* (Paris: Armand Colin, 2012).

20 It is impossible to cite here the historiography of women in the Revolution, but a few classic works include Joan B. Landes, *Women and the Public Sphere in the Age of the French Revolution* (Ithaca, NY: Cornell University Press, 1988); Olwen Hufton, *Women and the Limits of Citizenship in the French Revolution* (Toronto: University of Toronto Press, 1992); Godineau, cited below; Sara E. Melzer and Leslie W. Rabine, *Rebel Daughters: Women and the French Revolution* (New York: Oxford University Press, 1993); Lisa DiCaprio, *The Origins of the Welfare State: Women, Work, and the French Revolution* (Urbana: University of Illinois Press, 2007), and works cited above and below. For recent research of how a particular group of women negotiated the Revolution, see, for instance, Kate Marsden, "Married Nuns in the French Revolution: The Sexual Revolution of the 1790s" (Ph.D. diss., University of California Irvine, 2014). On young people, see François Gendron, *The Gilded Youth of Thermidor*, trans. James Cookson (Montreal: McGill-Queen's University Press, 1993); on foreigners, see Rapport, cited below, and also Heuer, *The Family and the Nation*. For a discussion of foreign, black, and Jewish soldiers in the revolutionary era, see Christopher Tozzi, *Nationalizing France's Army: Foreign, Black, and Jewish Troops in the French Military, 1715–1831* (Charlottesville: University of Virginia Press, 2016), and his chapter in this volume; some of the most recent works on the Haitian Revolution (including primary source collections) include Laurent Dubois, *Avengers of the New World: The Story of the Haitian Revolution* (Cambridge,

MA: Harvard University Press, 2005); John D. Garrigus, *Before Haiti: Race and Citizenship in French Saint-Domingue* (New York: Palgrave Macmillan, 2006); David P. Geggus, *The Haitian Revolution: A Documentary History* (Indianapolis, IN: Hackett Publishing Company, 2014); Jeremy D. Popkin, *A Concise History of the Haitian Revolution* (Malden, MA: Wiley Blackwell, 2012), and *Facing Racial Revolution.*

21 Michael Rapport, *Nationality and Citizenship in Revolutionary France: The Treatment of Foreigners 1789–1799* (New York: Oxford University Press, 2000); Ian Coller, *Arab France: Islam and the Making of Modern Europe 1798–1831* (Berkeley: University of California Press, 2010), and "Citizen Chawich: Arabs, Islam and Rights in the French Revolution," *French History and Civilization* 5 (2014): 42–52; Clyde Plumauzille, *Prostitution et révolution. Les femmes publiques dans la cité républicaine (1789–1804)* (Paris: Champ Vallon, 2016). There is still a shortage of works on sexualities in the Revolution, but relevant chapters in Jeffrey Merrick's and Bryant T. Ragan's, eds., *Homosexuality in Modern France* (Oxford: Oxford University Press, 1996), and Ragan's very recent "Same-Sex Sexual Relations and the French Revolution: The Decriminalization of Sodomy in 1791," in *From Sodomy Laws to Same-Sex Marriage: International Perspectives since 1789*, ed. Sean Brady and Mark Seymour (London: Bloomsbury, 2019), 15–30 serve as great introductions.

22 Soboul, *The Parisian Sans-Culottes*; Dominique Godineau, *The Women of Paris and their French Revolution*, trans. Katherine Streip (Berkeley: University of California Press, 1998); Micah Alpaugh, *Non-Violence and the French Revolution: Political Demonstrations in Paris, 1787–1795* (Cambridge: Cambridge University Press, 2015); Katie Jarvis, *Politics in the Marketplace: Work, Gender, and Citizenship in Revolutionary France* (Oxford: Oxford University Press, 2019).

23 Michel Biard, *Parlez-vous sans-culotte? Dictionnaire du Père Duchesne (1790–1794)* (Paris: Tallandier, 2009). See also other works on the press, such as Jeremy D. Popkin, *Revolutionary News: The Press in France, 1789–1799* (Durham, NC: Duke University Press, 1990).

24 Edna Hindie Lemay, *La vie quotidienne des députés aux Etats généraux* (Paris: Hachette, 1987); Timothy Tackett, *Becoming a Revolutionary: The Deputies of the French National Assembly and the Emergence of a Revolutionary Culture (1789–1790)* (Princeton, NJ: Princeton University Press, 1996).

25 R. R. Palmer, *Twelve Who Ruled: The Year of the Terror in the French Revolution* (this ed., Princeton, NJ: Princeton University Press, 2005); Linton, *Choosing Terror.*

26 Peter McPhee, *Robespierre: A Revolutionary Life* (New Haven, CT: Yale University Press, 2012); Norman Hampson, *Saint-Just* (Oxford: Basil Blackwell, 1991), and *Will & Circumstance: Montesquieu, Rousseau and the French Revolution* (London: Duckworth, 1983); Élisabeth Roudinesco, *Théroigne de Méricourt. Une femme mélancholique sous la Révolution* (Paris: Albin Michel, 2010); Leo Gershoy, *Bertrand Barère: A Reluctant Terrorist* (Princeton, NJ: Princeton University Press, 1962); Michael J. Sydenham, *Léonard Bourdon: The Career of a Revolutionary, 1754–1807* (Waterloo, ON: Wilfrid Laurier University Press, 1999).

27 Linda Frey and Marsha Frey, *The Culture of French Revolutionary Diplomacy: In the Face of Europe* (Cham: Palgrave Macmillan, 2018); Thomas A. Foster, "Recovering Washington's Body-Double: Disability and Manliness in the Life and Legacy of a Founding Father," *Disability Studies Quarterly* 32, no. 1 (2012); http://dx.doi.org/10.18061/dsq.v32i1.3028.

28 Ambrogio Caiani, *Louis XVI and the French Revolution, 1789–1792* (Cambridge: Cambridge University Press, 2012).

29 Emmanuel de Waresquiel, *Juger la reine: 14, 15, 16 octobre 1793* (Paris: Tallandier, 2016).

30 Patrice Higonnet, *Class, Ideology, and the Rights of Nobles during the French Revolution* (Oxford: Clarendon Press, 1981); William Doyle, *Aristocracy and its Enemies in the Age of Revolution* (Oxford: Oxford University Press, 2009).

31 See Hannah Callaway in this volume and Ronen Steinberg, *The Afterlives of the Terror: Facing the Legacies of Mass Violence in Postrevolutionary France* (Ithaca, NY: Cornell University Press, 2019).

32 Anne Forray-Carlier and Jean-Marie Bruson, *Au temps des merveilleuses: La société parisienne sous le Directoire et le Consulat* (Paris: Association Paris-Musées, 2005).

33 Michel de Certeau, *The Practice of Everyday Life* (Berkeley: University of California Press, 1984), 117–18; Ralph Kingston, "Mind over Matter? History and the Spatial Turn," *Cultural & Social History* 7, no. 1 (2009): 111–21; Beat Kümin and Cornelie Usborne, "At Home and in the Workplace: A Historical Introduction to the 'Spatial Turn,'" *History and Theory* 52 (2013): 305–18.

34 Michael Rapport, *The Unruly City: Paris, London and New York in the Age of Revolution* (New York: Basic Books, 2017).

35 Michel de Certeau, *The Practice of Everyday Life* (Berkeley: University of California Press, 1984), 117–18; on departments, see especially Marie-Vic Ozouf-Marignier, *La formation des départements: La représentation du territoire française à la fin du 18e siècle* (Paris: Editions de l'Ecole des hautes études en sciences sociales, 1989), and William Sewell, "The French Revolution and the Emergence of the Nation Form," in *Revolutionary Currents: Transatlantic Ideology and Nationbuilding, 1688–1821*, ed. Michael Morrison and Melinda Zook (Lanham, MD: Rowman & Littlefield, 2004), 91–125; James Leith, *Space and Revolution: Projects for Monuments, Squares, and Public Buildings in France, 1789–1799* (Montreal: McGill-Queen's University Press, 1991); Mona Ozouf, "Space and Time in the Festivals of the French Revolution," in *The French Revolution and Intellectual History*, ed. Jack Censer (Chicago: Dorsey Press, 1989), 186–200, and Erin-Marie Legacey, *Making Space for the Dead: Catacombs, Cemeteries, and the Reimaging of Paris, 1780–1830* (Ithaca, NY: Cornell University Press, 2019).

36 Among other works, see Alan Forrest and Matthias Middell, eds., *The Routledge Companion to the French Revolution in World History* (London: Routledge, 2015); Bryan A. Banks and Erica Johnson, eds., *The French Revolution and Religion in Global Perspective: Freedom and Faith* (Basingstoke, UK: Palgrave Macmillan, 2017); Suzanne Desan et al., eds., *The French Revolution in Global Perspective* (Ithaca, NY: Cornell University Press,

2013); David Bell, "Questioning the Global Turn: The Case of the French Revolution," *French Historical Studies* 37, no. 1 (2014): 1–24, and also "Global Conceptual Legacies," in *Oxford Handbook of the French Revolution*, ed. David Andress (Oxford: Oxford University Press, 2015), 642–68; and Paul Cheney, "The French Revolution's Global Turn and Capitalism's Spatial Fixes," *Journal of Social History* 52, no. 3 (2019): 575–83.

37 Because of the pervasiveness of the theme, the relevant literature is huge. The vast historiography of the Terror cannot be captured here, but those new to the subject might begin by consulting David Andress, *The Terror: The Merciless War for Freedom in the Revolutionary France* (New York: Farrar, Straus, and Giroux, 2007); Keith Michael Baker, ed., *The French Revolution and the Creation of Modern Political Culture, Vol. 4: The Terror* (Oxford: Pergamon, 1994); Hugh Gough, *The Terror in the French Revolution* (Basingstoke, UK: Macmillan, 1998); Palmer, *Twelve Who Ruled*, and Timothy Tackett, *The Coming of the Terror in the French Revolution* (Cambridge, MA: Belknap Press of Harvard University Press, 2015). A few recent works specifically on criminal justice in the Revolution include Robert Allen, *Les tribunaux criminels sous la Révolution et l'Empire: 1792–1811* (Rennes: PUR, 2005); Emmanuel Berger, *La justice pénale sous la Révolution* (Rennes: PUR, 2008); Jean-Claude Farcy, *Histoire de la justice en France: De 1789 à nos jours* (Paris: La Découverte, 2015); Paul Friedland, *Seeing Justice Done: The Age of Spectacular Capital Punishment in France* (New York: Oxford University Press, 2012); on human rights, see Lynn Hunt, *Inventing Human Rights* (New York: W. W. Norton, 2007). See also works cited in subsequent notes.

38 See Françoise Brunel, *Thermidor, la chute de Robespierre, 1794* (Brussels: Editions Complexe, 1989), 73; Annie Jourdan, "Les discours de la terreur à l'époque révolutionnaire (1776–1798): Etude comparative sur une notion ambiguë," *French Historical Studies* 36, no. 1 (2013): 51–81; Stephen Clay, "The White Terror: Factions, Reactions, and the Politics of Vengeance," in *A Companion to the French Revolution*, ed. Peter McPhee (Chichester, UK: Blackwell, 2013), 359–77, and "Vengeance, Justice and the Reactions in the Revolutionary Midi," *French History* 23, no. 1 (2009): 22–46; Howard Brown, *Ending the French Revolution: Violence, Justice, and Repression from the Terror to Napoleon* (Charlottesville: University of Virginia Press, 2006); Marisa Linton, "Introduction," Michel Biard, "Remplacer *la Terreur* par la 'terreur' pour mieux comprendre l'une et l'autre?," Carla Hesse, "Terror and the Revolutionary Tribunals," Ronen Steinberg, "The Terror as a Difficult Past," and Mette Harder, "Habitual Terror and the Legislative Body in the Revolution," in "Rethinking the French Revolutionary Terror?", *H-France Salon* 11, no. 16 (2019), ed. Marisa Linton, https://h-france.net/h-france-salon-volume-11-2019/#1116.

39 Jean-Clément Martin, *Violence et Révolution: essai sur la naissance d'un mythe national* (Paris: Seuil, 2006), 11–12.

40 See Alex Fairfax-Cholmeley, "Creating and Resisting the Terror: The Paris Revolutionary Tribunal, March–June 1793," *French History* 32, no. 2 (2018): 203–25; Michel Biard, "Après la tête, la queue. La rhétorique antijacobine en fructidor an II et vendémiaire an III," in *Le tournant de l'an III. Réaction et Terreur blanche dans la France révolutionnaire*, ed. Michel Vovelle (Paris: Éd.

du CTHS, 1997), 201–13; Ronen Steinberg, "Trauma before Trauma: Imagining the Effects of the Terror in the Revolutionary Era," in *Experiencing the French Revolution*, ed. David Andress (Oxford: Studies on Voltaire & the Eighteenth Century, 2013), 177–99.

41 See, for instance, Andress, *The Terror*, 2.

42 See Michael David Sibalis, "The Regulation of Male Homosexuality in Revolutionary and Napoleonic France, 1789–1815," in *Homosexuality in Modern France*, 80–101.

43 See Carolyn Purnell, *The Sensational Past: How the Enlightenment Changed the Way we use our Senses* (New York: W. W. Norton, 2017); Andress, ed., *Experiencing the French Revolution.*

44 Timothy Tackett's work has been particularly influential in regard to encouraging this approach. See Tackett, *Becoming a Revolutionary*, and "Becoming Revolutionaries: Papers in Honor of Timothy Tackett," *H-France Salon* 11, no. 2 (2019), ed. Micah Alpaugh, Robert Blackman, and Ian Coller, https://h-france.net/h-france-salon-volume-11-2019/#1101.

45 Recent works include Tackett, *The Coming of the Terror*; Guillaume Mazeau, "Emotions politiques: la Révolution française," in *Histoire des émotions: Des Lumières à la fin du XIXième siècle*, ed. Alain Corbin and Jean-Jacques Courtine (Paris: Seuil, 2016), 98–142; Pauline Valade, "Public Celebrations and Public Joy at the Beginning of the French Revolution (1788–1791)," *French History* 29, no. 2 (2015): 182–203; Lindsay Parker, "Veiled Emotions: Rosalie Jullien and the Politics of Feeling in the French Revolution," *Journal of Historical Biography* 13 (2013): 208–30; Meghan Roberts, "Laclos's Objects of Affection: Venerating the Family during the French Revolution," *Eighteenth-Century Studies* 51, no. 3 (2018): 289–330; Thomas Dodman, *What Nostalgia Was: War, Empire, and the Time of a Deadly Emotion* (Chicago: University of Chicago Press, 2018). On the history of emotions more generally, see William M. Reddy, *The Navigation of Feeling: A Framework for the History of Emotions* (Cambridge: Cambridge University Press, 2001); Jan Plamper, *The History of Emotions: An Introduction* (Oxford: Oxford University Press, 2015); Rob Boddice, *The History of Emotions* (Manchester: Manchester University Press, 2018); and Barbara Rosenwein and Riccardo Christiani, eds., *What is the History of Emotions?* (Malden, MA: Polity, 2017).

PART ONE

Revolutionary Identities and Spaces

1

Republicans and Royalists: Seeking Authentic Rural Voices in the Sources of the French Revolution

Jill Maciak Walshaw

On a warm summer evening, Jeanne Floissac, known affectionately to locals as *La Floissaquette*, was serving customers at the inn she managed with her husband in the village of Casseneuil in the south-western department of Lot-et-Garonne (see map of France in Figure 0.1).[1] It was July 1793, and France was in the fourth year of Revolution. The king was dead and the queen was in prison, awaiting trial. The new government, the National Convention, had been elected by near-universal male suffrage; Robespierre led the radical faction known as the Mountain, and the Terror had begun. France had been at war with Austria and Prussia for about a year, and just six months prior, the republic had announced that 300,000 young men would be conscripted to march under the tricolor banner.

In such turbulent times, inns like the one run by Jeanne and her husband were places where country people would gather, to relax and socialize, but also to hear the news and share their opinions. On this particular evening, some of la Floissaquette's customers were talking, and some were playing a game of "sizette" (a card game played by two opposing teams of three players); all were drinking. When a rival innkeeper, Antoine Barroussel, came to pay his tab with two municipal vouchers worth 20 *sous* and 10 *sous* respectively, Jeanne refused them, saying that they were no longer legal tender. "No matter," replied Barroussel; "I can use them to pay the *taille*," referring to the main tax on land and wealth that had been assessed before the Revolution. Witness testimony was conflicted on what happened next: some, including two weavers, one tailor and two farmers, said that Jeanne retorted, "since we no longer have a king, we shouldn't have to pay taxes," while a third weaver, twenty-four-year-old Pierre Tonbat, added that she had said, "I don't like the Republic; you people like it if you want." Barroussel brought an accusation to local officials and Jeanne was arrested on the charge of *provocation au rétablissement de la royauté*—verbally attempting to bring about the return of the monarchy—the penalty for which was death by guillotine.

Jeanne Floissac successfully defended herself: in the interrogations that followed, she clarified that she had said "since we no longer have a king we don't pay the *taille*, but we do pay the [Republican] property taxes," and she produced three new witnesses who confirmed her version. When she was asked about her opinion on the Revolution—whether she had ever rejoiced at the setbacks of the French army or at resistance to the new regime—she responded evenly that "she had always been happy when the affairs of the Republic were going well." In the end, all witnesses—even those who had initially supported Barroussel—agreed that Jeanne had spoken in a calm way, and that they hadn't perceived any intention, in her words or body language, to inspire hatred of the republic or to discourage them from paying their taxes; they had left her establishment, they said, without having been scandalized by what she'd said. Not only was Jeanne acquitted, but Barroussel was fined 300 *livres* in damages for malicious intentions.[2]

What can this story—and the trial documents used in its telling—teach us about rural responses to the French Revolution? Clearly, political issues were front-of-mind not only for Parisian sans-culottes but also for citizens in the provinces. The Revolution affected everyone, both positively and negatively, and country dwellers were not shy about voicing their opinions. The latter was true from the earliest days of the Revolution, and arguably, before. What had changed by 1793 was that the republic was on shaky ground: threatened by external enemies and domestic ones, its elected body deeply divided, the government issued law after law prohibiting seditious actions or words that might shake people's faith in the regime. Possibly, Barroussel's denunciation was a complete fabrication, aimed at ousting his competition in Casseneuil. Or perhaps Jeanne Floissac had spoken carelessly, expressing what many were feeling: frustration with war, requisitions, and taxes, and a Revolution that seemed increasingly directed from Paris.

The Revolution did not come out of the blue, nor was it a completely modern event imposed on a backward society. True, the Third Estate delegates to the Estates-General and the later governments were largely members of an educated, wealthy, and more urban elite, but the peasants were not as unprepared for the Revolution—or as uninvolved in it—as we might imagine. It takes careful attention to tease their experience out of the mountains of revolutionary documents that remain of that decade.

The basic narrative of the rural response to the French Revolution is familiar. In broad terms, villagers initially supported the gains achieved in

1789 and 1790, such as the abolition of the feudal regime and the administrative revolution that gave more power to local municipalities, but they became a conservative and even counter-revolutionary force as the Revolution diverged from rural values and interests. The split in the Catholic Church resulting from the Civil Constitution of the Clergy in 1791 and the arrest and eventual execution of Louis XVI disrupted two key pillars of rural society, while the relentless demand for recruits and supplies after the declaration of war in 1792 and the radicalization of the political landscape in the spring and summer of 1793 aggravated the situation. Yet while these sweeping brushstrokes are accurate in a general sense, the picture does not allow for the many ways in which villagers engaged with the events and political culture of the Revolution, often enthusiastically and with originality.

In this chapter, we will tackle the thorny problem of how we, as students of history, can uncover the rural experience of Revolution, with little in the way of unfiltered source material. After a brief orientation to the historiography, we will look at a series of moments when the peasantry participated in political affairs on both the left and the right. "If there was a rural popular movement during the Revolution, then it was counter-revolutionary, Catholic and royalist," one scholar has claimed,[3] yet some peasants were decidedly pro-revolutionary. Villagers enthusiastically discussed new laws and announcements in municipal assemblies which had existed before 1789 and which the Revolution infused with new political importance. With a wave of anti-seigneurial uprisings in the summer of 1789, they pushed middle-class deputies to abolish not only the feudal regime but all unredeemed dues, changing forever the social fabric of the countryside.[4] They formed National Guard units and political clubs modeled after the Jacobin Club in Paris, they wrote petitions to the National Assembly, and voted in elections. Villagers also made political statements—often, but not always, expressing apathy, disgust, or outright hostility—which have been recorded in hundreds of trials for sedition and seditious speech. Despite the barriers of language, culture, and more than 200 years that separate us from those who lived through the Revolution, engaging with these raw local sources brings us to a deeper, more nuanced understanding of how the Revolution was experienced in the countryside.

Describing Rural Experience: Approaches and Challenges

In 1993, Vivian Gruder asked the provocative question, "Can we hear the voices of peasants?" Her answer was yes: teasing out questions of local dialect, political awareness, and the divide between peasant spokespeople and literate intermediaries, Gruder argued that the rural views expressed in two 1788 pamphlets could be considered not only authentic but strikingly perceptive. Appearing in the midst of political upheaval, but before their input was formally sought via the *cahiers de doléances*, these two texts reveal that peasants knew something of pre-revolutionary politics and that they acted on their own political beliefs in an attempt to effect change.[5]

Approaching the Revolution as "lived experience"—to attempt to place ourselves in the shoes of historical actors and imagine their reactions to it—is a powerful idea, but a relatively recent one, at least where the peasantry is concerned. The attempt to understand how rural communities experienced the Revolution has most often taken the form of localized studies; some of these are the work of amateur historians exploring the history of their village, while others are by scholars drawing broader links and analytical conclusions.[6] Two creative projects stand out. In *Liberty and Locality in Revolutionary France*, Peter Jones took an original approach in constructing a comparative microhistory of six villages from 1760 to 1820, while, in a smaller thought-piece on the department of the Aisne, Laurent Brassart contended that there were twenty distinct political positions amongst peasants in that department alone.[7] Both emphasized the tremendous variety of rural political responses to the revolutionary endeavor, making national-scale works of peasant life in the 1790s, such as Jones's earlier *The Peasantry in the French Revolution* and Peter McPhee's *Living the French Revolution*, remarkable achievements.[8]

Early twentieth-century scholars were interested in the foundations of peasant activism. Following research by Albert Mathiez and others into economic factors precipitating the Revolution and determining its course, Georges Lefebvre's groundbreaking 1924 study of the peasants of the department of the Nord put forward a variation on the then-fashionable Marxist framework. In addition to the nobility, the bourgeoisie, and the proletariat, Lefebvre argued, there had been a fourth actor on the stage: the peasantry had acted with originality and self-interest, accepting some aspects of the Revolution while rejecting others. Lefebvre's explanation of the origins of the "peasant revolution" inspired generations of historians of rural France.[9]

The shift towards a "history of the people" and "history from below" in the 1960s and 1970s represented the greatest surge in studies of the rural population during the Revolution. George Rudé, writing on the crowd and then the Great Fear, and Richard Cobb, whose intimate knowledge of the police archives of Paris and Lyon allowed him to paint a nuanced picture of individual choice and experience, inspired many working on the lower classes.[10] Historians such as Paul Bois took the economic framework of rural society and attempted to parse out why certain groups had sided for or against the Revolution, inspired by the Annales school and its new "*longue durée*" approach.[11] In the 1980s turn towards culture as a category of enquiry, the interest in popular politics was expanded yet again.[12] Historians looked beyond formal political events and structures to investigate political practice and culture. The bicentenary in 1989 brought an explosion of research on French revolutionary history, not least in the study of rural society, where a combination of broad overviews and narrow investigations gave us a wealth of information while highlighting a perennial truth of French rural society: its diversity.

Indeed, one of the challenges of this topic is the bewildering variety of the French countryside. Even in modern times, France is delightfully and sometimes frustratingly diverse. Until the effects of universal secular education began to be felt towards the end of the nineteenth century, scholars identified about fifty-five major dialects and hundreds of subsidiary tongues. Other variations have persisted even longer, and President Charles de Gaulle might be forgiven for his famous remark in 1962, "How can you govern a country which has 246 varieties of cheese?" From the cereal plains of the north to the winding hills and river valleys of the southwest, from the wooded *bocage* of the west to the Mediterranean littoral by way of the craggy Massif Central, from low-lying swamp to high mountain pastures, those who worked the land faced a staggering number of different environments and conditions.

The status and land-tenure relationships of the rural population varied tremendously from place to place. The "peasantry" might refer to those whose livelihood stemmed from agriculture, and who shared a common outlook. Yet there was a great deal of difference between a prosperous peasant farmer who owned his land and a poor day-laborer who worked for wages and maintained a small cottage garden with a few vegetables. In every rural setting, the population was distributed across a broad social spectrum, including rural artisans and others who had greater connections to the outside world, and whose interests were different from small farmers. To add a level of complexity, the terms used to describe different types of "peasant" varied from region to region; in northern France, for example, a "laboureur" was a large-scale farmer who owned the land he worked; he would have been the neighbor who loaned out tools or plough animals, and who had enough to live comfortably. In parts of the southwest, "laboureur" referred to agricultural wage earners, who elsewhere were called "journaliers," "brassiers," "manoeuvriers," "locataires" or "travailleurs de terre."[13] In sum, factors such as terrain, climate, and social structure strongly characterized rural society in each region, reminding us to avoid assuming that "the peasantry" was a homogenous group of like-minded actors on the political stage.

Although such regional disjointedness meant that local issues tended to loom large, rural communities were not isolated from the outside world; for centuries, news and ideas had been shared when villagers came together at markets, fairs, and inns such as Jeanne Floissac's, and traveling pedlars and soldiers brought new material by word of mouth. Moreover, the events of the Revolution were momentous, exciting, and difficult to ignore. Peter Jones's simile is apt:

> The limitations upon peasant political awareness have been compared to the plight of a man trying to survey the sky while imprisoned at the bottom of a well. Yet seismic events of the magnitude of the Revolution could push back the sides of the well: squabbles over pews became part of a nation-wide campaign of anti-seigneurialism; on-going quarrels over the commons acquired strange new ideological reference points.[14]

We will not dwell on some of the more famous moments when the peasantry took the stage—the Great Fear, the abolition of feudalism, and the division of the commons, for example—as these have been expertly described by other scholars.[15] Instead, the pages that follow explore the rural response to the Revolution through peasants' involvement and engagement in its political culture. By seeking out archival sources which reveal some of this experience—taking care to note when the peasantry was being spoken for or reported on by others—we can uncover some of what it might have been like to live through these exciting and tumultuous events.

Enthusiasm and Engagement: Studying Peasants in Revolutionary Political Culture

In the spring of 1789, a very special call went out from the king of France to his people. The problems facing the kingdom were many: the national debt had reached unsustainable levels, and the privileged classes who sat in the supreme court known as the Paris *Parlement* had blocked legislation which would have put the considerable wealth of the elite within the reach of the tax collectors. In order to break the deadlock, there would be a meeting of the Estates-General—a time-honored ad-hoc representative institution which brought together deputies from all three estates to advise the king in times of crisis, but which had fallen into disuse for a 175-year period which marked the rise of absolutist monarchy in France. The king's subjects had two tasks: to elect representatives to attend the Estates-General, and to draw up *cahiers de doléances*—lists of grievances, or suggestions for improvements to the political, economic, and social fabric of the country—which would then be synthesized and brought to the king's attention in Versailles.

The resulting documents, of which approximately 40,000 have made it down to us today, form, in some ways, the first public opinion poll of the modern era, and they are tremendously revealing—not only of the issues that mattered to French men and women, but of the degree to which they were interested in, and ready for, political change. As a source on the perspectives of the rural population, they are virtually unparalleled, and they hint at the social, regional, and political complexity of the relationship between the peasantry and the State. For while many village *cahiers* addressed traditionally "rural" issues such as the burden of seigneurial demands, better access to land and resources, and their own tax burden, they also spoke out on topics of national import, sometimes with ingenuity and insight. The inhabitants of Bonnac, for example, who lived in the foothills of the Pyrenees, wrote that the provincial estates should be abolished unless they could be replaced with a fairer and more representative body, and twice they reiterated that, until the State got its financial house in order and individual freedoms and property were guaranteed, there would be no further discussion of taxation.[16] While describing the world in which they lived and offering recommendations for solving its problems, villagers also demonstrated that they were capable of discussing broader topics.[17]

In addition to being a unique source of peasant views, the *cahiers* are, paradoxically, also a classic example of the lack of transparency and authenticity in sources to do with the peasantry. Given high rates of illiteracy, many cahiers would have been penned by an intermediary—often the parish priest, a large landowner, or a literate notable from the nearby town. At best, community grievances might have been framed differently by a well-intentioned scribe, a process which would have been compounded by the need (in many locations) to translate from local patois into French. At worst, where the intermediary was (for example) a powerful seigneur or his agent, villagers might not have felt comfortable expressing their true concerns. In addition, "model" *cahiers* from the towns were in circulation, suggesting articles for inclusion which might not otherwise have been central for country dwellers.

Yet while it is important to be conscious of these potential problems, the *cahiers* bear signs of villagers' ability to get around them. For example, in a sample of *cahiers* from the Gironde in the southwest, the parishes were clearly working with a model document, but, in one covering letter, explained, "We are making use of the report in order to strengthen what we have already said in our own."[18] In the *cahier* of nearby Saint Petronille, the stock request for "a general survey of land that has been evaluated" then continued, "*and for us*, a quittance of the remaining sum owed for the new high road, for which we've been paying the taille and the vingtième for the last 25 years."[19] As for coercion, Peter McPhee cites the case of the impoverished village of Erceville, north of Orléans, where the Third Estate meeting was presided over by an agent of the seigneur, a powerful member of the Paris Parlement who owned most of the land in the parish. True, his actual tenants did not attend the meeting, but their neighbors spoke up, demanding that "without any distinction of title or rank, the said seigneur be taxed like them," and that all taxes should require "the consent of the whole Nation assembled in Estates-General."[20]

The parish assemblies that met in spring 1789 to draft the *cahiers* had, in many parts of France, existed for decades, with all heads of household meeting periodically to divide up the tax roll and to make communal decisions such as the start of the harvest or the adjudication of a land dispute. The formal enfranchisement of these assemblies as municipal councils was key in fostering early enthusiasm for the revolutionary endeavor, as it appealed to villagers' desire, so evident in the *cahiers*, to have a hand in resolving the frustrations of the *ancien régime*. Larger villages and bourgs had maintained registers before 1789, but all municipalities were required to do so by the law on municipal government of December 1790. While the minutes can be formulaic (merely listing the decrees received from the government in Paris could take many pages), at other times—particularly in the early years of the Revolution—they give a sense of sincere excitement about the political process. In one village in the Lot-et-Garonne, the secretary wrote on September 19, 1790 that a number of notices had been received from the district "on important questions, such as indigence, local roads, and agricultural reports." Since the council could not answer all of the queries without help, they immediately appointed four delegates to do the work.[21] A moving scene is related in the deliberations of the community of Saint-Lary, in the Hautes-Pyrénées, on the first festival of Federation, July 14, 1790. All the active citizens were brought together, in family groups, to swear an oath of loyalty to the nation, after which the meanings of the oath and of the new regime were explained; the sense of pride and hope for the future is palpable. At times we see purely parochial matters juxtaposed with issues of regional or national importance, revealing the organic nature of politics at the local level. The very next entry in the minutes of Saint-Lary, for example, consists of a fast-paced description of the arrest of a "garden thief," caught red-handed with a plate of cooked onions.[22]

The formation of local National Guard units, modeled on the bourgeois militia that formed spontaneously in Paris in mid-July 1789, represented another conduit by which villagers came into contact with revolutionary politics and culture. Relatively little work has been done on village National Guard units, but a survey in one department suggests that the institution existed in virtually every rural community and involved a large majority of adult males—artisans and peasants, literate and illiterate.[23] For those dressed in the colors of the Republic and defending its aims, the experience of participating in the National Guard was an early instance of the politicizing and nationalizing effect that would later be fostered by conscription into the revolutionary or Napoleonic armies.[24] Yet forming a militia for mutual protection was an ages-old activity, and therefore familiar and easily accepted. The enthusiasm with which men enrolled is telling of their optimism and engagement with the early Revolution, and—given the frequent complaints from local government bodies regarding the autonomous actions of rural guard units—was also adapted to local political culture.[25]

National Guard units provided one of the earliest infusions of politicized revolutionary content into the village, but they were not the only one. Political sociability—"clubs" modeled on the Jacobin Club in Paris, in which members would gather to read news and laws, to discuss political change, and to take action on issues of local relevance—spread from towns into the countryside. In their study of political societies, Jean Boutier and Philippe Boutry suggest that 14 percent of municipalities, in a national average, saw the formation of a political club.[26] The southwest saw a higher rate of implantation, reaching 20 to 30 percent in some departments, and the urbanized and strongly politicized villages of southeastern Provence embraced the movement wholeheartedly.[27] Even for areas where numbers were somewhat lower, such as the Massif Central and the western provinces of Maine and lower Normandy, scholars have emphasized club formation as an indication of rural interest in political culture and as a conduit of pro-revolutionary material.[28] Moreover, even more so than with National Guard units, villagers adapted urban institutions and infused them with local flavor. The Jacobin Club in Toulouse, for example, a major center in the southwest, followed predictable lines in its interests, position, and initiatives, but the political society in the tiny village of Mourvilles-Hautes valiantly defended their parish priest, allowed female members, and paused their meetings for the harvest, all the while engaging with issues of national political importance.[29]

Everyday life was infused with republican symbolism and ceremony. Villages planted liberty trees, appropriating the republicanized version of an originally rural tradition,[30] and paid a varying degree of attention to the formalities of revolutionary oath-swearing ceremonies and festivals. Certain features of political culture fell flat in the countryside. The imposition of the republican calendar, for example, with its rejection of traditional religious and cultural reference points, and its seasons more appropriate to the north of France than the south, was widely seen as further evidence of the Paris-centered nature of the Revolution.[31] The dechristianizing movement was also largely unsuccessful in the countryside: few village cemeteries inscribed their gates with the deist inscription, "Death is an Eternal Sleep," and the later replacement of Catholic worship with the Cult of the Supreme Being was not widely accepted. Yet rejection in these cases does not imply a counter-revolutionary population so much as it highlights choices in adapting aspects of revolutionary political culture.

Finally, if we are looking for documentary sources which indicate revolutionary engagement in the countryside, we cannot ignore elections, both for what they do show us and what they do not.[32] Local elections for municipal government in January and February 1790 produced a high turnout, particularly in rural areas, and the first major national elections came close to drawing a majority of the electorate. By the legislative elections of 1791, participation had fallen, although rural areas in some provinces still remained more strongly engaged than their urban counterparts, which undermines common assumptions about the lack of political "modernization" in the countryside.

From a twenty-first-century perspective, the fact that rural inhabitants participated widely in these elections would seem to be the quintessential indicator of revolutionary engagement. In many ways, they were; the institution of near-universal male suffrage by 1792 marks, along with that of the early American republic, the early history of modern representative democracy. Scholars have unearthed touching vignettes of peasants proudly casting their votes, imbued with a sense of honor at being asked for the first time to weigh in on the political direction of their country. True, later elections were marred by high abstention rates, but we can identify many reasons for this: polls were often conducted during harvest time and sometimes required several days of missed work due to travel or complicated voting procedures. And countryfolk understandably began to close their doors to political violence and civil war under the National Convention. Together with the drafting of the *cahiers*, formation of municipal councils, National Guard units, and political clubs, and the infusion of the everyday with political imagery, participation in formal elections represented yet another means of political engagement by a rural population that was anything but ignorant and unaware.

The Battle for Public Opinion

In part, this political engagement was courted by the revolutionary elite. From the very beginning of events in 1789, deputies were attentive to the reception of the Revolution in the countryside and worked to bring the peasantry onside. The members of the National Assembly held generally conservative views about the role of peasants and their fellow villagers in the political sphere. Dominated by the educated elite, those who had traveled to Versailles as representatives of the Third Estate perfectly fit the social profile of the Enlightenment public, an audience sympathetic to those who worked the land in theory, while exclusionary and condescending in practice.[33]

Despite this, or perhaps because of it, the *bon cultivateur* soon emerged in an idealized form, emblematic of the French nation. Antoine de Baecque's work on revolutionary imagery shows that for at least the first few years of the revolutionary decade, rural citizens were depicted in peaceful country scenes, holding agricultural tools and evoking usefulness and productivity. Drawing similarly on visual representations, Liana Vardi writes that in 1789 the peasant emerged as "a fitting citizen of the state . . . virtuous, hard-working, and . . . anxious to learn and to be guided."[34] Yet most emblematic depictions of revolutionary activities, such as Jean-Baptiste Le Sueur's watercolors of oath swearing and other forms of political participation, focus on sans-culottes, not cultivators; very few pictorial representations of European villagers showed them positively engaged in political activity before the late nineteenth century. During the Revolution, when it came time to determine what place the rural lower classes should have in the new nation, notions of social exclusion persisted. Initially the distinction between "active" and "passive" citizens excluded not only all women but also the poorer classes, both urban and rural; in the constitution of 1791, only about 60 percent of adult males were given the vote.[35] A young Camille Desmoulins expressed his disgust with suffrage restrictions in 1789, when he wrote that "the true active citizens are those who stormed the Bastille, those who bring the land under cultivation."[36] The deputies would continue to idealize the good citizen farmer, establishing the *Comité d'agriculture et de commerce* on September 2, 1789 in order to support the foundation of France's wealth, and substituting neutral terminology, *cultivateur* or *agriculteur*, for the less complimentary *paysan.*[37] Yet real farmers would prove to be considerably more opinionated and three-dimensional than allowed for by the image of the *bon cultivateur*.

As early as the summer of 1789, a shift took place in attitudes towards the inhabitants of the countryside. As news of peasants' attacks on manor houses and emblems of the seigneurial regime arrived in Versailles, deputies listened with shock while arguing that those who had risen up were victims themselves, seeking only "to shake off, at long last, a yoke that has been weighing on their shoulders for centuries."[38] At the same time, legislators speculated that rural insurgents were ignorant of the import of their actions; an early report from the town of Vesoul asked the National Assembly to produce a decree "that would bring public order among the people of the countryside, who seem to doubt the truth of recent notices." Such a decree, it was thought, would calm "those of most sound judgement among the countryfolk" given the events of the early months of the Revolution.[39] As the months wore on, the primary response to resistance (such as unwillingness to pay taxes or to redeem feudal dues, unrest, and outright violence) or—on the other end of the spectrum—disinterest in the revolutionary process, was to focus on better communication: it was assumed that rural communities were simply ignorant of their rights and responsibilities and easily led astray. "By perfecting communication," suggests Emmet Kennedy, "it was believed that misunderstandings and mistrust would disappear. And malevolence—a sin against the *patrie*—would be unmasked, punished, or corrected through education."[40]

This battle for rural public opinion took multiple forms. One of the first initiatives was to ensure that decrees and other texts being sent out from the government were reaching their destination. Given that the postal system was in its infancy and that the road network was deplored by administrators and engineers alike as being in the worst possible state, timely delivery of political missives was far from guaranteed. The National Assembly endorsed multiple initiatives to solve the problem, surveying and improving roads in distant provinces, expanding the postal service to handle a far greater volume and to deliver to many more locations, and relying upon virtual brigades of foot-messengers to bring packets of notices from distribution centers to every village and hamlet.[41] With such a lofty goal—successfully delivering dozens of printed notices to France's 40,000 communes every month—it is unsurprising that the reception of revolutionary material remained a thorny issue throughout the era. Yet as the members of the National Assembly soon realized, the real problem was less straightforward than simply assuring the arrival of mail. Bertrand Barère, a deputy of the Hautes-Pyrénées, explained from the tribune of the National Convention in 1794, "You have decreed that the laws should be sent to all the communes of the Republic, but the benefit is lost . . . the bright light carried at great expense to the farthest reaches of France goes out as soon as it arrives, because the laws are not understood."[42]

As Barère and his colleague, the Abbé Grégoire, had realized, not only was a significant proportion of the French population illiterate, but a large number did not understand French. Inhabitants of the periphery—the Breton peninsula, the departments closest to the eastern borders, and virtually all of the southern Midi spoke a foreign language (such as German, Italian, Catalan, or Basque) or a dialect (including Occitan and Provençal). While the model of a literate, bilingual intermediary reading aloud and explaining government decrees to the population had held under the Old Regime, the volume and complexity of political communication produced by the Revolution had stalled the system. The first impulse to resolve the problem came very early, in a decree dated January 14, 1790: "The executive authority will be responsible for translating the decrees of the Assembly into the different dialects," read the announcement, but despite a series of attempts over the following several years, the task proved overwhelming in both time and expense.[43] Eventually, the decision was reached to focus on the five languages most removed from French—Breton, Basque, Italian, German, and Catalan—and to leave the problem of other "dialects" up to bilingual local administrators. Such languages were acceptable because they had not, according to Barère, prevented the population from embracing French; Occitan, in fact, was quite close to French. The legislator needed to adopt a bird's eye view, Barère concluded, and focus on regions where the exclusive use of a language or dialect with pronounced difference from French had led them to become "separated from the happy family."[44]

The presumption that lack of understanding of revolutionary maxims (and not a lack of interest or agreement) had led to apathy or resistance was part of a broader aim of civic education. On the eve of the ratification vote for the 1793 constitution, the Committee of Public Safety expressed concern that "lack of education is the main reason that a part of the population is led into error in a few departments," through the "pernicious efforts . . . of the enemies of liberty . . . to divide us and make us lose sight of the public interest."[45] During the years of the National Convention (1792–5), various initiatives were undertaken, including sending "patriotic missionaries" (and later the more aggressive and well-known representatives on mission) into the countryside, establishing the *Bureau d'esprit public* whose mandate was to produce enlightening texts and work directly with local administrators, and, through the *Comité de l'instruction publique*, fostering compulsory primary education with a focus on the teaching of French, civic virtue, patriotism, and republican zeal at the expense, potentially, of independent political thinking.[46]

Passionate proponents of the Revolution embraced the challenge of combating resistance and counter-revolution through instruction aimed at the peasantry. Innovators created newspapers designed specifically for the rural population. Some, such as the *Feuille du cultivateur*, contained primarily agricultural information,[47] but most included at least some material designed with political education in mind. The number of such papers testifies to the general acknowledgment of a need to bring the peasants on board, even if most publications were short-lived.[48] The *Feuille Villageoise*, on the other hand, ran for five years and aimed to "provide a civic instruction for country-folk in order to solidify the new regime"; the idea was that their 16,500 subscribers would be members of the literate rural elite who would act as a conduit.[49] "Common sense is in the very nature of the people," intoned the editors; "the disturbances that occurred in the villages could only have come from ignorance. The peasant felt the impulse of freedom before understanding its maxims."[50]

Yet there was a certain irony, even an audacity, in the use of printed material to communicate with a largely illiterate audience. Joseph-Marie Lequinio, a deputy from western Brittany where he had been a landowner and a lawyer, pointed out in February 1792 that the National Assembly could realize the benefits of reorganizing public education ten years sooner by publishing a weekly newspaper "in simple language" to bring knowledge and—notably—obedience to the countryside.[51] Front and center in this battle were provincial Jacobin clubs, who began reaching out to their "brothers in the countryside" long before the government enlisted their aid. By 1791, texts with titles such as "Adresse aux habitants des campagnes" authored by urban club members proliferated. Written in simple language, and sometimes published in local dialects, they covered topics club members believed were of interest to villagers, including the religious settlement, the 1791 constitution, and participation in elections. These tracts were thinly veiled propaganda that aimed both to instruct and to convince a potentially reticent and disinterested population.

The tone of such pamphlets varied from educational to jovial, as members of the social elite worked to befriend local villagers so that their ideas would be more readily accepted. One of the earliest tracts concerning the Civil Constitution begins colloquially, "Really now, has religion been destroyed because we no longer see bishops with two to three thousand *livres* in income?" The 1792 *Almanach du Père Gérard* used similar exclamations as well as jokes, anecdotes and dialogue to popularize its message of support for the Revolution:

A Peasant Well, it's better than it was before, when there were all sorts of different taxes.

Father Gérard And the heaviest ones were on objects of basic need. Anything that was used for clothing, or for shoemaking, was taxed; and also anything that was useful for your house, such as wood, salt, oil, soap . . .

A Peasant And tobacco too, Father Gérard, tobacco! Because of the Revolution, I'm saving at least thirty francs a year on it, not counting the maintenance of my pipe.[52]

A later text aiming to convince peasants to follow the revolutionary calendar used similar rhetoric: "What! They are still trying to lead you astray. Amidst the abundant harvests that you gather in your fields, the enemies of equality, who can disguise themselves in many ways, are trying ... to prevent *la fraternité* from taking root in your hearts."[53] Seeking to be perceived as empathetic allies in a confusing world, the texts assured readers of their value while gently indicating the "correct" political path.

Seeking Out Rural Voices: Unpacking Trials for Seditious Speech

Were peasants as ignorant and easily "led astray" as pamphlets and newspapers suggested? Or did they resist the Revolution also because the republicans had killed their king, removed their priests and their holidays, and then conscripted their sons into the army? Studying the rural response to the Revolution is a classic case of the challenges posed by "history from below," in which the subject population has left only indirect indications of its views and has most often been spoken for by others. In many cases, these "others" were members of the elite who observed the peasantry from afar and put little stock in their potential for political contributions. The primary reason for dwelling on revolutionary authorities' views of the peasantry is that this is largely what we, as historians, have to work with.

As we have seen, rural enthusiasm for the revolutionary endeavor can be read in the *cahiers de doléances*, in the rosters of the village National Guard units and patriotic clubs, and in strong turnout for the elections of 1790 and 1791, yet even these sources are ripe with pitfalls. The National Guard units might be the most comprehensive, and yet apart from profession and height, associated records tell us little about the participants; their motivation for joining, their level of commitment, and the nature of their experience remain question marks. With the *cahiers* and minutes of political clubs (as well as municipal council deliberations and petitions), membership and authorship of the group being spoken for is not certain; the texts might faithfully represent the views of a cross-section of rural society, but they might just as easily describe the views of a rural elite, potentially even one which was hostile to their poorer neighbors. Electoral results are unevenly helpful: strong turnout suggests enthusiasm, but there were many possible reasons for poor turnout, and the statistics are silent on which ones are most pertinent. When the peasantry appears as subject in the archives of administrators and judges, it is usually as a social (indeed, almost racialized) Other to be brought into line, through persuasion or repression. By the time federalism was in full swing and the west had exploded into outright counter-revolution, the discussion over communication with rural populations had changed from the translation to the eradication of foreign dialects; in Bertrand Barère's rhetoric, "Bas-Breton is the language of federalism and superstition; Italian is the language of counterrevolution."[54]

The fear that the rural population was either easily led astray or irreparably reactionary gave rise to a series of laws against seditious speech which, ironically, gives us a glimpse into some of the peasant voices. The archive of seditious speech is vast and rich, touching on a range of rural conversation topics, social dynamics in villages as revealed in denunciations and witness accounts, and judicial developments such as juries and extraordinary courts. Sedition trials have been discussed at length and the document included with this chapter indicates how historians might use components of a trial to learn about the rural revolutionary experience.[55] If early attempts to control public opinion in the countryside focused on the usual suspects—parish priests, in particular, were frequently indicted for their disparaging comments about the Civil Constitution of the Clergy, and former nobles were suspected of sedition of all types—by the end of the second year of Revolution, people of all social groups and classes were being arrested on charges of seditious speech. From the Penal Code of 1791 to the anti-royalist law of December 4, 1792 (drafted in the context of the king's trial) and the laws of March–April 1793 which sought to protect military recruitment and stave off counter-revolution, and culminating in the all-encompassing Law of Suspects passed in September of that year, legislation which was drafted with deliberate conspiracy and counter-revolutionary action in mind was worded in such a way that it could apply to simple verbal statements, such as the ones made by Jeanne Floissac in 1793, discussed at the beginning of this chapter.

The following examples are taken from a sample of 148 seditious speech trials involving peasants and rural artisans in five southwestern departments. Early in the decade, commoners were frequently arrested for "false announcements" or seditious speech regarding taxes and seigneurial dues. In the summer of 1790, for example, Sicaire Linard, a farmer and secretary of the hamlet of Léguilhac de l'Auche (Dordogne), falsely announced to an assembly of villagers that new decrees had arrived prohibiting sharecroppers from paying the dues that they owed their landlords. In nearby Milhac, the farmer Lalbas and his cousin, Mathieu Pebeyre, were accused of saying that "they did not want to pay the dime or the taille . . . the first tax collector or syndic who came to ask for their payment, they would shoot him with a pistol."[56] All three were arrested: the authorities did not want ill will towards the tax regime to spread. As time went on, the topics of seditious speech trials matched issues of political debate in the public sphere. After the deportation of non-juring priests in 1792–3, insurgents in the Ariège were arrested for having told their neighbors that "the constitutional priest's Masses are worthless; he breaks his fast and gets drunk before saying them."[57]

Conscription efforts were met with resignation in some villages and with anger in others. In March 1793, *cultivateur* Gaspard Rousse from Arconac (Ariège) complained that "the nation has begun to lay its hands on our persons." When a bystander, Paul Vidal, responded that "we must all rush to help the nation," Rousse retorted that "since he was speaking that way, they should send *him*."[58] In another case, Barrot and Chaveroche, two sharecroppers, told volunteers that France's enemies "were angry at the *Bourgeois*, not at the peasants," and that they should go to the district "to make the office holders march off to war."[59]

Statements that could shake the people's faith in the Revolution's economic policies came under direct scrutiny during the Terror. Peasant communities tended to be divided on their opinion of the price maximum, but grain requisitions and particularly the *assignats* were universally hated. Jean d'Argelès, a *laboureur* in Villefranque (Hautes-Pyrénées), complained that "the grain he had left was not even sufficient for his household," and two enterprising village butchers in the Lot-et-Garonne traveled the countryside offering to purchase livestock, saying that their owners might as well get some money for their animals rather than wait and be forced to give them up to the requisitions.[60] In the fairs and markets, informants kept their ears open for bargaining on a two-price system, as sellers demanded a higher price in unstable paper *assignats* and a lower price in hard currency; and the words of Jean Bernard, *dit* (*known as*) Biotte, were passed by word of mouth through the town of Verteillac (Dordogne) after he said loudly to a crowd in the square that "the *assignats* are no longer worth anything, they're just damned papers that are good for nothing, and those who keep them will be ruined."[61] Such topics frequently led to more general statements on the political regime: Jean Boué of Sauveterre (Lot-et-Garonne) was arrested for saying, "There's quite a lot of rabble in the government. They've taken all of our grain. Wouldn't it be better to be governed by just one person?"[62] As political instability increased and support for the regime waned, scores of peasants found themselves before a judge on charges of having shouted "merde à la loi" ("to hell with the law"), "à bas la République" (down with the Republic"), "ça n'ira pas" ("it *won't* all work out," a play on the revolutionary anthem "ça ira"), or simply for having expressed, often wistfully, the desire to be governed by a king again. Attached to this chapter are parts of a trial of Thomas Bordas, a weaver from a small village, who was indicted for just that.

For all their flavor and originality, these sources are not without their caveats. Edward Muir and Guido Ruggiero note that "Criminal records can never be simple windows into the past; . . . everyone who speaks during a criminal procedure does so under the constraints of authority, which means that all speech has been conditioned by threats of punishment, the fear of torture, the influence of well-connected persons, and the need of the regime to make criminal sentences exemplary."[63] Yet, as Peter Burke comments, "the point . . . is not that [these sources] are worthless, but that they are distorted, and distortion can be allowed for—indeed, it is the historian's traditional business to do so."[64] Seditious trial records can be read for the authorities' changing attitudes towards rural political opinions, and also to tease out the varied nature of those opinions, providing a personal connection and an immediacy to our knowledge of rural experience during the Revolution. The unsolicited statements of villagers represent a broader cross-section of rural society than, for example, political club membership, both among defendants and through the involvement of dozens of witnesses and passers-by, giving us more qualitative data. By paying close attention to those trials in which witnesses (such as Paul Vidal, above) engaged directly with the views of the defendant or in which juries and local officials thwarted legislation or undermined the judicial process in the attempt to bring about a fair outcome, we can avoid reproducing a formulaic narrative of rural reaction to the Revolution.

Conclusion

There is an ongoing debate, among historians of rural France, as to the timing of the politicization of the French peasantry.[65] Some place it in the late nineteenth century, long after the French Revolution. Historians of the Second Republic, including Maurice Agulhon, Ted Margadant, and John Merriman, have argued that rural involvement in the events of 1848–51 marked the "dramatic entry" of villagers onto the national political scene.[66] And in *Peasants into Frenchmen*, Eugen Weber argued that, as late as the 1870s, economic and cultural isolation prevented peasants from taking a serious interest in politics; it was only the advent of railways, universal conscription, and improvements in education that integrated rural France, and brought politics from an "archaic stage" to a modern one.[67]

Many of the key changes that Weber identifies—the growing influence of market towns and of local cultural intermediaries, and the spread of word-of-mouth news—had begun many decades earlier. More importantly, definitions of rural politicization that prioritize modernization—where political integration is seen as part of a larger transition to a modern, national economy during the nineteenth century, in which politics cannot be local or simple, but must be abstract, national, and characterized by the systems and processes of modern liberal democracy—are problematic. Those who point to 1789 as instrumental in the politicization process, in contrast, are working with different parameters. Melvin Edelstein defined politics as "the possibility for people to participate or influence decisions that are within the public sphere," declaring that "the French Revolution marked the start of peasants' apprenticeship as citizens, and accelerated it." Catherine Duprat and Michel Vovelle use a similar language of initiation, writing of "political acculturation," a "collective realization" (*prise de conscience*), and "the conditions for an awakening of political behaviors."[68]

In seeking to understand the rural experience of Revolution, we should seek out those political and cultural behaviors. The grand narrative—that peasants were initially enthusiastic but then turned firmly and permanently away from the Revolution after certain key events—needs nuancing, not only in timing and details but in its applicability to a rural world characterized by diversity. "Peasants," if we choose to use such a term, were neither wholly on board—the *bons cultivateurs* imagined by Parisian deputies—nor were they universally the counter-revolutionary fanatics of the demonized western departments. At the beginning of the third century of scholarship on the French Revolution, today's students have at their disposal more resources than ever before—millions of pamphlets and obscure treatises have been digitized through the *Bibliothèque nationale de France*'s Gallica collection, and primary sources in translation are increasingly available through print and internet sources alike. More so than with literate subjects, the rules of stringent source-criticism apply: we must pay close attention to the authorship (or transcription) of rural ideas, linguistic and social divides between speaker and scribe, and the paternalistic gaze of an élite that at times considered the peasantry to be both childlike and backward. Yet the hard work of teasing out rural voices from the archive is amply rewarded, for no textbook can communicate the experience of Revolution like imagining ourselves in Jeanne Floissac's tavern in the summer of 1793.[69]

Source: Trial of Thomas Bordas, a weaver from Segonzac, department of the Dordogne, accused of having publicly stated that he wanted to be governed by a king. 28 pluviôse–12 prairial year IV (February 17, 1796–May 31, 1796): Evidence, Interrogation, Witness Accounts, Jury Deliberation and Trial Verdict

Document 1: Minutes from the Municipal Council meeting of 28 pluviôse year 4

Today . . . the members of the administrative council for the canton of St Vincent de Connezac, department of the Dordogne, have met . . . to swear an oath of Love for the Republic and of Hatred of Royalty, which was decreed by order of the Directory on 22 nivôse of last year . . .

. . . the members arrive at the public square with their president at the front, all dressed in costume and with the most peaceful and orderly demeanor; once there, the president of the administrative council . . . gave a speech commensurate to the occasion and swore, before all those present, love for the Republic and hatred of royalty. He then called upon the citizens individually . . . to swear their love for the Republic and their eternal hatred of royalty.

At that moment, Thomas Bordas of the village of La Fayardie (commune of Segonzac) came forward and said to us, what does swearing an oath like this mean? It is only the municipal council that is enforcing it. What is needed is to ask the assembled citizenry who among them want a Republic, and who a king, and then we would know where the majority lies.

At this, the government commissioner working with the administrative council called Thomas to order, but he continued to speak in the same way. The commissioner then asked his name and place of residence . . . and asked him to clearly state what he had to say. Bordas responded that he wanted a king, and that things would go better if they had one; that before, when only one person controlled the public funds, we were better off, given that under the current regime, our hands are full of *assignats* that we can't do anything with . . .

Document 2: Interrogation of the defendant

Today, 4 germinal year 4, at 10 o'clock in the morning, appearing before myself, Joseph Savy, justice of the peace and officer of the judiciary police of the canton of St Vincent . . . is citizen Jean Arvingeas, police sergeant stationed at Périgueux, who informed us that he was bringing Thomas Bordas to appear . . .

Upon being questioned, the defendant stated that he is Thomas Bordas, weaver by profession, about thirty years of age, born in the commune of St Jory de Chalaix, department of the Dordogne . . .

Asked with whom he traveled to St Vincent on the day in question, and what conversation took place during the voyage;
Replied that he traveled with Louis Paleix, Jean Coudert, another Jean Coudert, Jean Dupuy the former mayor, and Raymond Mansy, and as for the conversation it turned to various unrelated topics.

Asked which citizens were with him at the covered market when he took the liberty of speaking in such a way, and before, and whether they had said that he was right and that he did well to speak that way;
Replied that he was with Jean Dupuy "Terrasse" and Joly Labroussas, both of whom are from the place known as La Foret, and many others he didn't know, and that they said we will benefit if we support a bid for to have peace.

Asked if there had not been any who shared his way of thinking, or who had induced him to speak that way;
Replied that many people told him to speak that way but that he didn't recognize them . . .

Reminded him that it is only by telling the whole truth, and especially telling us who might have advised or induced him to speak that way, that he might lighten the gravity of the crime of which he is accused;
Answered that he cannot give any further information.

Asked if, on 29 pluviôse, the day after the assembly, he had not said to several citizens that they were cowards, that they had put him up to it, but that he would have been better to bring a barrel of wine to the church at Chanterac where 3,000–4,000 souls gather for mass, and as they are coming out, invite those who want a king to drink, and those who want a Republic will not;
Replied and admitted the first part of the question but denied the second, indicating that Louis Palleix, stonecutter, and Etienne Chabanes, weaver, were present when he said those words.

No further questions were asked. Bordas was read the above and he confirmed his responses, and, when asked, did not sign the document, indicating that he does not know how.

Whereupon ... considering that according to the minutes of the administrative council dated 28 pluviôse it is evident that Thomas Bordas had the audacity to openly show his desire to be governed by a king . . . that his intentions were clearly to attack popular sovereignty by destroying the government elected by the people and reinstituting the monarchy . . . that, apart from the facts contained in the minutes, in the days following this atrocious affair the defendant demonstrated a most steadfast determination and appears to have planned to gather public support for his position, and in this way seek to pit one section of the population against the other . . .
In accordance with article 70 of the Penal Code, we have decided to issue an order for the transfer of the defendant to the prison . . .

Document 3: Witness accounts (representative sample)

Heard before the Justice of the Peace, 9 germinal year 4

Antoine LaCour Lagilardie, health officer, local resident, 61 years old, said that he is neither a relative, ally, servant or domestic of either the informants or the defendant, and declares that on 28 pluviôse, when citizens were swearing the oath of hatred of Royalty, he heard Thomas Bordas interrupt the process and say that they needed to divide the people into two columns, in order to know which group was larger, those who wanted a king or a Republic; and that as for him (Bordas), he had been happier before, and that he had assignats that he couldn't do anything with. (Signed his declaration.)

Guillaume Fargeot tailor, 51 years old . . . declares that on 28 pluviôse, as he was leaving St Vincent, he heard Thomas Bordas say that the assignats were worthless and that six-franc *écus* were still valuable because they had the king's face on them . . . (Unable to sign his declaration.)

Jean Coudert, 56 years old, farmer . . . declares that Thomas Bordas said in the presence of a number of people, notably Louis Paleix, that he had not benefitted from the Constitution and that he wanted a king. (Unable to sign his declaration.)

Louis Palleix, stonecutter by profession, 45 years old . . . declares that on the morning of 29 pluvîose, as Thomas Bordas was walking near him and Jean Lacheze "Pelletou," he said you are all Jack-Asses, you people didn't support me, I was the only one who stood my ground. (Unable to sign his declaration.)

Jean Cotinal, tailor by profession, 34 years old . . . declares that a citizen from Ribérac named Soullier, having missed that Bordas had been criticizing the assignats, said to him, "on the other hand, you don't want to give them up," to which Bordas replied that he'd prefer to keep them to wipe his arse with . . . (Unable to sign his declaration.)

Raymond Maury, farmer, 58 years old, declares . . . that several days ago, he heard Thomas Bordas say that he wanted to bring a barrel of wine near the exit of mass at Chanterac, that those who wanted a king would drink and those who wanted the Republic would not; adds that on another occasion Bordas told him, I know that people want to give me trouble for this, but I have a pound of gunpowder, two pistols and some bullets—and I know how to defend myself. (Unable to sign his declaration).

Document 4: Jury deliberation and trial verdict, 12 prairial year 4

By my honor and conscience, the declaration of the jury is that it is consistent

1 That there was an incitation to re-establish the monarchy
2 That Thomas Bordas is convicted of being the author of that incitation
3 That he acted with intention to commit a crime
4 That there are attenuating circumstances in this case

That it is also consistent:

1 That there was violent opposition and unlawful acts against national police officers who were responsible for carrying out the arrest

warrant ordered by the justice of the peace against Thomas Bordas, even after these officers had spoken the formula: "you are reminded to obey the law."

2 That Thomas Bordas is convicted of having committed this violent opposition and unlawful acts
3 That he did not act with intention to commit a crime.

Thomas Bordas was released.

Notes

1 Portions of this text appeared previously in Jill Maciak Walshaw, *A Show of Hands for the Republic: Opinion, Information and Repression in Eighteenth-Century France* (Rochester, NY: Rochester University Press, 2014).

2 Archives Départementales (hereafter AD) Lot-et-Garonne, E dépôt Monflanquin 1J1 (Police locale); 2L17-8 (Tribunal de district), 2L97-22 (Tribunal révolutionnaire). Trial of Jeanne Floissac for inciting a return to royalist government and anti-patriotic speech, 29 July–28 Aug. 1793. See also Marcel Massip, "Scènes et types de l'époque révolutionnaire: La 'Floissaquette,' aubergiste à Casseneuil, avait-elle commis le crime de provocation au rétablissement de la royauté?," *Revue de l'Agenais* 83, no. 3 (1957): 169–84.

3 Donald Sutherland, paraphrased in Noelle Plack, "Making and Ending the French Revolution: Nobility, Bourgeoisie and 'the People,'" *European History Quarterly* 39, no. 1 (2009): 100.

4 Peter Jones, *The Peasantry in the French Revolution* (Cambridge, MA: Cambridge University Press, 1988), xii.

5 Vivian Gruder, "Can we Hear the Voices of Peasants? France, 1788," *History of European Ideas* 17, no. 2/3 (1993): 167–90.

6 For example, Liana Vardi, *The Land and the Loom: Peasants and Profit in Northern France* (Durham, NC: Duke University Press, 1993); Jean-Pierre Jessenne, *Pouvoir au village et Révolution: Artois, 1760–1848* (Lille: Presses Universitaires de Lille, 1987).

7 Peter Jones, *Liberty and Locality in Revolutionary France: Six Villages Compared, 1760–1820* (Cambridge: Cambridge University Press, 2003); Laurent Brassart, "'Plus de vingt paysanneries contrastées en Révolution.' De la pluralité des dynamiques sociales du politique en milieu rural pendant la révolution," *AhRf* 359 (2010): 53–74.

8 Jones, *Peasantry*; Peter McPhee, *Living the French Revolution, 1789–1799* (New York: Palgrave Macmillan, 2009).

9 Georges Lefebvre, *Les paysans du Nord pendant la Révolution française* (Paris: Armand Colin, 1972/1924).

10 George Rudé, *The Crowd in History: A Study of Popular Disturbances in France and England, 1730–1848* (New York: Wiley, 1964); Richard Cobb, *The*

Police and the People: French Popular Protest, 1789–1820 (Oxford: Clarendon Press, 1970).

11 Paul Bois, *Paysans de l'ouest* (Le Mans: M. Vilaire, 1960); Peter Burke, *The French Historical Revolution: The Annales School 1929–89* (Stanford, CA: Stanford University Press, 1990); and Lynn Hunt, "French History in the Last Twenty Years: The Rise and Fall of the Annales Paradigm," *Journal of Contemporary History* 21, no. 2 (1986): 209–24.

12 Keith Michael Baker, *The French Revolution and the Creation of Modern Political Culture*, 4 vols. (Oxford: Pergamon Press, 1987–94); Lynn Hunt, *Politics, Culture and Class in the French Revolution* (Berkeley: University of California Press, 1984).

13 Jones, *Peasantry*, 910.

14 Jones, *Peasantry*, 208.

15 Clay Ramsay, *The Ideology of the Great Fear: The Soissonnais in 1789* (Baltimore, MD: Johns Hopkins University Press, 1992); John Markoff, *The Abolition of Feudalism: Peasants, Lords and Legislators in the French Revolution* (University Park: University of Pennsylvania Press, 1996); Noelle Plack, "Agrarian Individualism, Collective Practices and the French Revolution: The Law of 10 June 1793 and the Partition of Common Land in the Department of the Gard," *European History Quarterly* 35, no. 1 (2005): 39–62.

16 AD Ariège 169E dép AA1, *Cahier de doléances*, Bonnac, 1789.

17 On the cahiers, see John Markoff and Gilbert Shapiro, eds., *Revolutionary Demands: A Content Analysis of the* Cahiers de Doléances *of 1789* (Stanford, CA: Stanford University Press, 1998).

18 AD Gironde, Cahiers de doléances, Sénéchaussée de Bazas, document 34, Monségur.

19 AD Gironde, Cahiers de doléances, Sénéchaussée de Bazas, document 48, Saint-Pétronille, my emphasis.

20 Cited in McPhee, *Living the French Revolution*, 13–14.

21 AD Lot-et-Garonne E dép Galapian 1D2, Délibérations du conseil municipal, Sept. 19, 1790, fol. 6–7.

22 AD Hautes-Pyrénées E dép Saint-Lary, Délibérations du conseil municipal, July 14, 1790, fol. 7.

23 Data for the department of the Dordogne are discussed in Walshaw, *A Show of Hands for the Republic*, 125 and 248, n. 149.

24 Alan Forrest, *Conscripts and Deserters: The Army and French Society during the Revolution and Empire* (Oxford: Oxford University Press, 1989); Serge Bianchi and Roger Dupuy, eds., *La Garde nationale entre nation et peuple en armes: Mythes et réalités, 1789–1871* (Rennes: Presses Universitaires de Rennes, 2006).

25 Bianchi and Dupuy, *La Garde nationale*, 11. See also Raymonde Monnier, "La politisation des paroisses rurales de la banlieue parisienne," in *La Révolution française et le monde rural* (Paris: Éditions du CTHS, 1989), 425–41.

26 Jean Boutier and Philippe Boutry, *Atlas de la Révolution française, t.6: Les Sociétés politiques* (Paris: Éditions de l'É.H.É.S.S., 1989), 14.

27 Michel Vovelle, *La Découverte de la politique: Géopolitique de la Révolution française* (Paris: Éditions La Découverte, 1993), and also, especially, "Formes de politisation de la société rurale en Provence sous la Révolution française: Entre jacobinisme et contre-révolution au village," *Annales de Bretagne* 89 (1982), 367–80. See also Jean-Françoise Dubost, "Le réseau des sociétés politiques dans le département de l'Hérault pendant la Révolution française (1789–1795)," *A.h.R.f.* 61, no. 4 (1989): 374–416.

28 Philippe Bourdin, "Le recrutement des sociétés populaires du Puy-de-Dôme," *A.h.R.f.* 64, no. 4 (1992): 491–516; Christine Peyrard, *Les Jacobins de l'Ouest: Sociabilité révolutionnaire et formes de politisation dans le Maine et la Basse-Normandie* (Paris: Publications de la Sorbonne, 1996).

29 AD Haute Garonne L4559-60, Délibérations de la société de Mourvilles-Hautes. See Jill Walshaw, "L'adaptation du jacobinisme au monde rural: la politisation populaire dans les villages de la Haute-Garonne, 1790–1795," *Annales du Midi* 127, no. 291 (2015): 369–90.

30 Michel Duval, "Les arbres de la liberté en Bretagne sous la Révolution (1792–1799)," in *Les Résistances à la Révolution: Actes du colloque de Rennes (17–21 septembre 1985)*, ed. François Lebrun and Roger Dupuy (Paris: Imago, 1987), 55–67; Mona Ozouf, "Du mai de liberté à l'arbre de la liberté: Symbolisme révolutionnaire et tradition paysanne," *Ethnologie française* 5 (1975): 9–32.

31 Matthew Shaw, *Time and the French Revolution: The Republican Calendar, 1789–Year XIV* (Woodbridge, UK: Royal Historical Society, 2011).

32 The literature on elections is vast. In English, two good starting points are Malcolm Crook, *Elections in the French Revolution* (Cambridge: Cambridge University Press, 1996), and Melvin Edelstein, *The French Revolution and the Birth of Electoral Democracy* (Farnham, UK: Ashgate, 2014). Students who can read French should also consult Serge Aberdam, Bernard Gainot, Serge Bianchi, Emile Ducoudray, and Claudine Wolikow, eds., *Voter, élire pendant la Révolution française (1789–1799): Guide pour la recherche* (Paris: CTHS, 2006), and Patrice Gueniffey, *Le Nombre et la raison: la Révolution française et les élections* (Paris: Éditions de l'École des hautes études en sciences sociales, 1993).

33 See Timothy Tackett, *Becoming a Revolutionary: The Deputies of the French National Assembly and the Emergence of a Revolutionary Culture, 1789–1790* (Princeton, NJ: Princeton University Press, 1996).

34 Jean-Pierre Jessenne, *Les campagnes françaises entre mythe et histoire: XVIIIe–XXIe siècles* (Paris: Colin, 2006); Antoine de Baecque, "Figures du paysan dans l'imagerie révolutionnaire," in *La Révolution française et le monde rural: Actes du colloque tenu en Sorbonne les 23, 24 et 25 octobre 1989* (Paris: Éditions du CTHS., 1989), 477–82; and Liana Vardi, "Imagining the Harvest in Early Modern Europe," *American Historical Review* 101 (1996): 1357–97.

35 Crook, *Elections*, chapter 2, esp. 39.

36 *Les Révolutions de France et de Brabant*, no. 3, Nov. 1789, cited in Crook, *Elections*, 32.

37 James Livesey, *Making Democracy in the French Revolution* (Cambridge, MA: Harvard University Press, 2001), chapter 3.

38 From the speech of the Duc d'Aiguillon, August 4, 1789; *Archives Parlementaires* 8:344.

39 *Archives Parlementaires* 8:278, July 25, 1789.

40 Emmet Kennedy, *A Cultural History of the French Revolution* (New Haven, CT: Yale University Press, 1989), 293.

41 See Jill Maciak [Walshaw], "Of News and Networks: The Communication of Political Information in the Rural South-West during the French Revolution," *French History* 15, no. 3 (2001): 273–306, and *A Show of Hands for the Republic*, 100–13.

42 *Archives Parlementaires* 83:715, 8 pluviôse II (Jan. 27, 1794).

43 Cited in a later discussion; see *Archives parlementaires* 54:340, Dec. 4, 1792.

44 *Archives Parlementaires* 83:713–17, 8 pluviôse II (Jan. 27, 1794).

45 AN AF II 60, Comité de salut public, dossier 437, document 9, "Draft of an order regarding the establishment of a Translation Office . . .", June 20, 1793.

46 These texts are available in Bronislaw Baczko, ed., *Une éducation pour la démocratie: Textes et projets de l'époque révolutionnaire* (Geneva: Droz, 2000). Woloch provides a clear overview of the revolutionary deputies' projects for education in *The New Regime: Transformations of the French Civic Order, 1789–1820s* (New York: W.W. Norton, 1994), 177–83; see also Amy Wyngaard, *From Savage to Citizen: The Invention of the Peasant in the French Enlightenment* (Newark: University of Delaware Press, 2004).

47 Even so, the *Comité de salut public* authorized its distribution on 9 germinal II (March 29, 1794): AN AF II 66, Comité de salut public, Intérieur, Esprit public, dossier 484 document 31. Dubois de Jancigny, Lefebvre, Broussonnet, Parmentier, and Calvel, *La feuille du cultivateur* (biweekly), 1, no.1 (Oct. 1790); 9, no. 10 (December 1800). See also Festy, "Agriculture pendant la Révolution française."

48 On other papers for rural audiences, such as the short-lived *Journal des campagnes* and *Code des cultivateurs*, see Éric Wauters, "La presse départementale de l'an II," *A.h.R.f.* 68, no. 1 (1996): 1–35, and Melvin Edelstein, *"La feuille villageoise": Communication et modernisation dans les régions rurales pendant la Révolution* (Paris: Bibliothèque nationale, 1977), 29.

49 This figure comes from Jacques Godechot, *Histoire générale de la presse française* (Paris: Presses Universitaires de France, 1969), 493–4.

50 Cerutti's article in 1791, cited in Beatrice Didier, "*La feuille villageoise:* Un dialogue Paris–Province pendant la Révolution?", in *Aux Origines provinciales de la Révolution*, ed. Robert Chagny (Grenoble: Presses Universitaires de Grenoble, 1990), 269.

51 See Lequinio's speech of February 19, 1792, in AP 38:647; as well as similar discussions later that year. AP 53:682–83, November 30, 1792. Lequinio was the author of several pamphlets designed to inform villagers of political affairs,

as well as the editor of *Le Journal des laboureurs*, published in Vannes from 1790 into early 1792; see Edna Lemay, *Dictionnaire des Législateurs (1791–1792)*, 2 vols. (Ferney-Voltaire: Centre international d'étude du XVIIIe siècle, 2007), 497.

52 J. M. Collot-d'Herbois, *L'almanach du Père Gérard* (Paris: Buisson, 1792), 58–9. See also Michel Biard, "*L'almanach du Père Gérard*, un exemple de diffusion des idées Jacobines," *A.h.R.f.* 63, no. 1 (1991): 19–29.

53 Bibliothèque municipale de Toulouse, BrFaC 1394, "Adresse de la Société populaire épurée de Toulouse, aux habitants des campagnes," 15 messidor II (July 3, 1794).

54 *Archives parlementaires*, 83:713–17, 8 pluviôse II (Jan. 27, 1794), citation 715.

55 See, in particular, my *Show of Hands for the Republic*, chapters 4 and 5. Comparable work on English sedition trials can be useful; for example, Joel Samaha, "Gleanings from Local Criminal-Court Records: Sedition Amongst the 'Inarticulate' in Elizabethan Essex," *Journal of Social History* 8 (1975): 61–79.

56 AD Dordogne B843-2 (Trial of Linard, Aug. 15, 1790), and B1600, trial of Lalbas, Pebeyre et al., July 3, 1790.

57 AD Ariège 8L35-2, trial of Layrix et al., August 25, 1793.

58 AD Ariège 8L33-5, trial of Anel and Dedieu, August 18, 1793.

59 AN W 347-686, trial of Barrot and Chaveroche, August 4, 1793.

60 AD Hautes-Pyrénées, Justice 2L, trial of d'Argelès, 20 floréal II (May 9, 1794); AD Lot-et-Garonne 2L105-5, trial of Lacombe and Cazès, 12 pluviôse II (Jan. 31, 1794).

61 AD Dordogne 24L42, Trial of Bernard, dit Biotte, 9 pluviôse II (Jan. 28, 1794).

62 AD Lot-et-Garonne 2L105-15, trial of Boué, 8 nivôse II (Dec. 28, 1793).

63 Edward Muir and Guido Ruggiero, eds., *History from Crime* (Baltimore, MD: Johns Hopkins University Press, 1994), ix.

64 Peter Burke, *Popular Culture in Early Modern Europe* (Aldershot: Ashgate, 2008), 77–8.

65 For a more thorough analysis, see Walshaw, *A Show of Hands for the Republic*, 5–13.

66 Maurice Agulhon, *La république au village: Les populations du Var de la Révolution à la Seconde République* (Paris: Plon, 1970); Ted Margadant, *French Peasants in Revolt: The Insurrection of 1851* (Princeton, NJ: Princeton University Press, 1979); and John Merriman, *The Agony of the Republic: The Repression of the Left in Revolutionary France, 1848–1851* (New Haven, CT: Yale University Press, 1978); the oft-cited phrase "dramatic entry" is from Margadant, *French Peasants in Revolt*, xxii.

67 Eugen Weber, *Peasants into Frenchmen: The Modernization of Rural France, 1870–1914* (Stanford, CA: Stanford University Press, 1976). See also André Armengaud, *Les populations de l'Est-Aquitain au début de l'époque contemporaine: Recherches sur une région moins dévelopée (vers 1845–vers 1871)* (Paris: Mouton, 1961), and Alain Corbin, *Archaïsme et modernité en Limousin au XIXe siècle (1845–1880)*, 2 vols. (Paris: Marcel Rivière, 1975).

68 Melvin Edelstein, "La place de la Révolution française dans la politisation des paysans," *A.h.R.f.* 62, no. 2 (1990): 135–49; Vovelle, *Découverte de la politique*; Catherine Duprat, "Lieux et temps de l'acculturation politique," *A.h.R.f.* 66, no. 3 (1994): 387–400.

69 While local material like the sedition trials discussed here is unlikely to be digitized in its entirety, students can find excerpts or descriptions of such sources in published document collections. A good place to start is the website edited by Jack Censer and Lynn Hunt, *Liberty, Equality, Fraternity: Exploring the French Revolution*, http://chnm.gmu.edu/revolution/.

2

Mapping Women's Everyday Lives in Revolutionary Marseille

Laura Talamante

In 1973,[1] Michael Kennedy began *The Jacobin Club of Marseilles* by describing 25 rue Thubaneau as "a narrow, seamy, thoroughly disreputable little street adjoining an Arab quarter in central Marseilles" where "[f]ew pedestrians notice the small, weather-stained plaque beside the doorway" that once held the meeting place of the most powerful Jacobin Club in the Midi.[2] Then, as now, the building is memorialized as the first place in France where "La Marseillaise" was sung. Shortly thereafter the brave men of Marseille marched to the capital, joined the Parisians in their August 10, 1792 attack on the Tuileries, and brought down the French monarchy.

In 2011, the city opened Le Mémorial de la Marseillaise on this now somewhat gentrified street. The museum celebrates revolutionary patriotism and includes animated Disneyesque-busts of Marseille revolutionaries and of a royalist lynched in February 1792 for critiquing patriots. Immortalized as *la Cayole*, she sits apart from the other busts, with the museum unintentionally recreating the nineteenth-century stereotype of women as more susceptible to counter-revolutionary influence. However, the museum also includes two ardent female revolutionaries: an unnamed peasant and Madame Brard, "a Marseillaise committed to the Revolution." The museum succeeds in literally putting the Revolution on the map for locals and tourists, in a city where strangely no other revolutionary monument exists, and highlights women's important roles in revolutionary politics.

This chapter builds upon previous analyses of women's contributions to Marseille's revolutionary politics, using mapping as a tool to provide a broader geographic understanding of their creation of, and participation in, new political spaces.[3] Michel Vovelle's *La Découverte de la Politique: Géopolitique de la Révolution Française* (*Discovery of Politics: Geopolitics of the French Revolution*) employs comparative geography and quantitative analysis for understanding the creation of a national revolutionary consciousness and the transition to modern democratic practices.[4] Through mapping and the synthesis of major revolutionary studies, including his own impressive array of works, Vovelle shows the geopolitical dissemination, reception, and adaptation of revolutionary culture and politics across France. He demonstrates how different local and regional histories and politics accounted for variations in creating revolutionary consciousness, culture, and practices. Influenced by Vovelle, the conceptual framework of this chapter is to map Marseille women's revolutionary political experiences from 1789 to 1794. I use part of his model of analyzing particular moments, "stresses, aggressions, stages in what one can call a collective awareness," to investigate the development of a national political consciousness, networks, and concerted political action amongst women in Marseille.[5] I have chosen discrete moments with national and regional implications: the development of the patriot movement, the municipal revolution, a *Bastille marseillaise* (where inhabitants captured the city's three forts and wrested control from royal troops), the Festival of the Federation, the regional expansion of Jacobin Club power, the Federalist Rebellion, and the Terror.

Mapping allows for understanding revolutionary uses and transformations of space in one of France's largest urban environments and shows how women contributed to such transformations. I am influenced by Daniel Smail's cartographic analysis of medieval Marseille, which demonstrates that despite the absence of formal maps, "the city was mapped in diverse ways by its citizens."[6] He uses notarial records to show that linguistic differences for describing property locations depended on the context of who was making the reference and suggests the existence of "a certain degree of collective consciousness or group consensus on cartographic practice."[7] While his overall goal is to demonstrate the role of notarial culture in the movement to "a universal cartographic language," his work also presents the idea of the way ordinary people such as artisans created mental maps of the city through their Provençal linguistic practices. The Revolution created a disruption in cartographic practices that eventually appeared on revolutionary maps of the city through the formal renaming of streets and public spaces; however, before this occurred, the Revolution altered ordinary citizens' use of space and consequently their mental map of the city. I investigate multiple spaces in the cityscape and beyond where revolutionary power relations transpired. I demonstrate how women from various social milieus used their familial, social, and economic networks to influence the development of revolutionary consciousness, culture, and practices: from the patriot movement and the creation and rise to dominance of Marseille's Jacobin Club to the sectional movement of the Federalists. Women contributed to Jacobin and Federalist coalition building in Marseille's local and regional politics. Alongside men, they transformed public spaces such as churches, markets, boutiques, and the streets into political ones, creating a new mental map of the city and the region based on revolutionary practices.

The new institutional and formal spaces the revolutionaries created, however, often excluded women, for example, by limiting Jacobin Club membership or attendance in the sectional assemblies to men.[8] Women therefore developed practices that paralleled men's political opportunities by creating their own political associations, contributing to revolutionary projects, symbolically taking up arms, or becoming communal enforcers of political power to mediate those limits.

Simple mapping techniques render visible the breadth of women's political engagement in the city. Marseille was divided into thirty-two section assemblies, which originally convened as the primary assemblies for elections to the Estates-General in 1789 and became active in 1790 as general debating assemblies. The first two parts of this analysis use a choropleth map with an overlay of the sections' boundaries on the historical map of Marseille to highlight areas where women's participation is noted in revolutionary pamphlets, petitions, and journals, municipal and Jacobin Club records, and nineteenth-century contemporary accounts, which allows for geographic representations of women's experiences. In the later two parts, a proportional symbol map is used as a form of heat mapping to provide comparative data visualization from court records in both the region and in the city's sections, illustrating the repercussions women faced during major shifts of political power in revolutionary Marseille during 1793.

The Crowd, the Patriot Movement, and Revolutionary Democracy in 1789

The calling of the Estates-General triggered political, social, and economic tensions as well as a series of protests and riots. It did so not only in Paris, but across the country, including in Marseille, the second largest city in France with a population of roughly 106,000 inhabitants, compared to Paris's population of 650,000[9] (see Marseille on the map of France in Map 0.1). Marseille, the largest port of the Mediterranean, held one of Europe's largest markets for foodstuffs, supported a significant shipbuilding industry, and brought in large numbers of colonial products, such as sugar, coffee, and cacao. It traded in critical materials for French manufacturing, including many foreign textiles such as cotton, wool, and sheepskins, products for dying fabrics, and olive oil for soap factories.[10] These commercial enterprises helped shape early revolutionary agendas and actions. "In Marseille, like so many other commercial places," notes Paul Masson, "one of the preoccupations of the merchants was not having enough representatives in the Estates."[11] Crowds challenged orders and arrests emanating from representatives of the crown and the Parlement of Aix throughout 1789. Those challenging Old Regime authority adopted a revolutionary mentality in favor of democratic reform and defined themselves as "patriots."

As in other parts of France, Marseillaise women joined the crowds that helped create and radicalize the forces of democratization in 1789 and 1790. Rioting was not new. In her study of women's involvement in uprisings in Provence from 1715 to 1789, Monique Cubells highlights their roles in riots regarding subsistence, municipal taxation, contraband items, and religious conflicts. Women protested alongside men for common causes, but generally did not instigate riots. In 1789, overall percentages for women's participation in riots throughout Provence rose.[12]

John Markoff's research on peasant violence during 1789 highlights that violence served as a strategic and effective means of moving revolutionary democracy forward. Peasant anti-seigneurial violence, argues Markoff, "was not merely a ritualized form of violence but exhibited choices of targets and tactics guided by reason." It also achieved more egalitarian democratic reforms than elite reformers had originally intended.[13]

The case of Marseille illustrates that rioting in 1789 took on a new political character. In the subsistence and tax riot on March 23, the crowd challenged Old Regime power using a geopolitical strategy when they protested outside the Hôtel de Ville and attacked the homes of a rich tax farmer and of the intendant (sent by the crown to enforce royal authority). The mayor and several other municipal officials fled the city. The riot achieved three major concessions from the magistrates fearful of popular violence: the promise to lower the price of bread and meat; the formation of the Council of Three Orders composed of the members of the municipal council and representatives from all three estates; and the abolition of the detested tax farms.[14]

Of women identified by contemporaries, market women are most associated with protests and riots in 1789, especially those from the Saint-Jean quarter in section 17 at the extremity of the old port, where many fishermen, sailors, female fishmongers, and other market women lived. For example, the only group identified with women during the March 23 riot was made up of men, women, and children from the Saint-Jean quarter who joined the protest at the Hôtel de Ville. After the March riot, citizens organized a revolutionary militia, which was open to all categories of male citizens.[15] The subsequent creation of the Bourgeois Guard—with the captains chosen only from the privileged ranks of the nobility, the notables, and the merchants of the first order—was seen as an attack on emerging democratic practices.[16] Citizens labeled those who acted against their militia as traitors. On May 15, rioters gathered as they had in March at the Plaine Saint-Michel, a field just outside the city walls, and marched to the building of the *poids de la farine* (where wheat was weighed), looking for the former employees of the municipal tax farms and breaking into the building. Women armed with sticks patrolled the Cours Belsunce.[17] Jean-Louis Laplane recollected in the nineteenth century that there had been "a lot of people from the lower orders, especially women from the Saint-Jean quarter, fish mongers, sellers of herbs or fruits . . . They ran the streets armed with

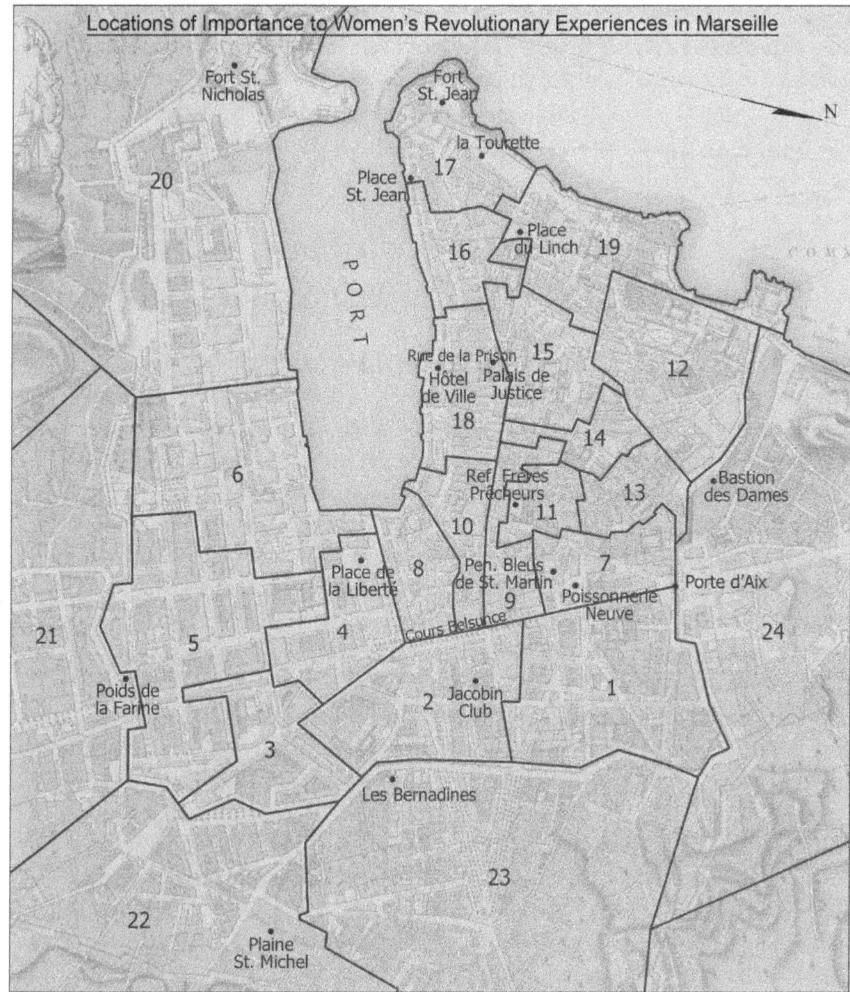

MAP 2.1 *Historical map of Marseille, 1791.* Plan routier de la ville et faubourg de Marseille/Levé par Campen en 1791; Et Gravé par Denis Laurent en 1792. *Bibliothèque nationale de France, https://gallica.bnf.fr/ark:/12148/btv1b53099684g.r=cartesmarseille1791%20marseille%201791?rk=21459;2.*[18]

kitchen knives, sticks and stones, in order to hunt . . . the guards of the [tax] farms, which had again been placed at the Porte d'Aix."[19]

The location of the main market near the Porte d'Aix allowed the market women to use their social networks and geopolitical positioning to organize their role in the riot. In the Saint-Jean quarter "groups of women gathered to march, batons in hand and aprons full of sand . . . to throw in the eyes of the traitors" who had signed a mémoire to the king against the Citizen's Militia in April.[20] The women in the Saint-Jean quarter's support for the Citizen's

Militia and its inclusive membership tied their actions to democratizing forces in the city. The role of women from section 17 in the March and May riots also indicates a heightened political awareness and coalition building in the use of market and neighborhood social networks to coordinate attacks against perceived traitors to the growing patriot movement.

Revolutionary Democracy and Women's Political Transformation of Space in 1790

By the spring of 1790, patriots had created a new political landscape for democratic practices through the municipal revolution in February, the creation of the Jacobin Club, and the success of the *Bastille marseillaise*, dramatically impacting the everyday life of men and women. The patriot movement of 1789 and responses by the authorities gave momentum to the municipal elections in 1790 that brought the city's merchants to power, upending its Old Regime political structure. Patriot men, many released from prison by the new municipal authorities, created the first political association in Marseille and allied themselves with the emerging leadership of the Parisian Jacobin Club (see map of Paris in Map 0.2).

Amongst the patriots, the royal troops' occupation of the city's three forts had become a major point of contention and anxiety. Two of these forts guarded the entry into the port and there were rumors of aristocratic plots to admit foreign troops in order to stop the Revolution.[21] On the night of April 29, the National Guard captured the forts. Madame Brard, a volunteer's wife (likely celebrated in the *Memorial to the Marseillaise*), played a key role. She kept watch through the night for the prearranged signal and apprised the mayor, who then sent a deputation to the forts.[22] Unidentified women participated in crowd violence the following day, when Beausset, the commander of the Fort Saint-Jean, refused to acknowledge the National Guard's victory.[23] The National Guard tried to rescue him:

> But Beausset escaped and took refuge in a wigmaker's shop. The crowd was furious, convinced that the guard had let him escape and that he would elude punishment . . . They seized him, beat him, and hauled him through the mud. Like de Launay in Paris, [they] cut off his head. An exalted crowd . . . paraded it on the end of a pike in triumph throughout the city.[24]

The occupation of the forts symbolized the patriots' own *Bastille marseillaise*, solidifying the power of the municipal authorities and the local Jacobin Club. Donald Sutherland highlights how "[t]he seizure and attempted demolition of the forts was . . . instructive of a style of democratic practice. The seizures were the result of mass action."[25] Women's contributions to this form of democratic practice should not be underestimated even if their participation is not always highlighted in the historical record.

Bringing the forts down served as a symbol for the leveling of tyranny and the rise of revolutionary democracy. Thus, the demolition of the forts became a patriotic project. Women from divergent economic and social milieus contributed, revealing widespread participation across the city that paralleled men's patriotic contributions. The Jacobin Club's campaign to pay workers was well received, "raising 16,574 livres from sources as widely divergent as the shoemakers' guild, the Chamber of Commerce, and the bishop of Marseilles," with donations as low as two livres and as high as 96 livres from religious associations, 600 livres from the corporation of key makers, and 1,245 livres from the Saint Ferreol section.[26] Records for contributions let us map the range of women's participation and reveal that eight women's religious associations, both formal orders (bound by their professional vows to the Catholic Church) and lay orders (with the freedom to live within religious communities or the secular world), contributed:

1 Les Petites Maries (section 1) = 3 livres
2 Les Dames Dominicaines (section 11) = 12 livres
3 Les Dames des Grandes Maries (section 12) = 12 livres
4 Les Dames Sainte-Claire (section 13) = 3 livres
5 Les Dames du Saint-Sacrement (section 19) = 3 livres
6 Les Dames Bernardines (section 23) = 24 livres
7 Les Dames Lyonnaises (section 23) = 24 livres
8 Madame l'Abbesse de Saint-Sauveur (section 20) = 24 livres.

Les Dames Bernardines and Les Dames Lyonnaises were located in section 23, "a very modern and fashionable area" and the "newest quarter of all, outside the town walls."[27] Their contributions alongside those of the Abbess of Saint-Sauveur indicate women of more means than those of Les Dames Sainte-Claire, whose very modest contribution aligns with the popular ranks of those living in section 13. Market women represented less affluent social groups in Marseille, yet they donated as substantially as some women's religious associations located in affluent areas. Les Dames Poissonnières de Saint Jean from section 17, for instance, donated 22.18 livres—approximately 18 months' wages for a day laborer.[28] Their strong presence and personal investment in challenging Old Regime authority in 1789 likely explain their willingness to donate at a higher level than some of the religious associations. Les Dames de la place aux Fruits (49.8 livres) and Les Dames de la Halle (24 livres), whose market women lived in section 17 and other sections, also made substantial contributions.[29] Women from sections 1, 11, 12, 13, 17, 19, 20, and 23 donated to Marseille's first formal patriotic project. Despite not knowing their individual identities or the exact numbers of women represented, mapping allows us to visualize the breadth of their political investment across the city.

With the creation of the Jacobin Club, a new model for political space and networking emerged. Women created parallel political spaces, using neighborhood religious spaces and transforming existing social networks into political ones. Geographical proximity to revolutionary political centers may have influenced the development of two women's political groups. The Dames heroïnes lived in section 11 of the old town at the geopolitical center for the elections of deputies to the Estates-General.[30] The women met in the refractory of the Frères Prêcheurs, which underscores women's roles in the revolutionary transformation of religious space for political purposes. Meanwhile, proximity to the new geopolitical space created by the Jacobin Club in nearby section 2 likely influenced the formation of the Dames citoyennes. The women met in the Chapelle des Pénitents Bleus de St. Martin in section 7 and identified themselves with reference to the religious space in revolutionary publications. Both women's clubs took advantage of the ways religious space had until recently worked to connect people in the community. Prior to the Revolution, churches occupied a central place in the public sphere and served as a shared space for men and women. As men and women transformed religious spaces for the purposes of the Revolution, they extended the formal political sphere beyond Old Regime institutions. Women originally in the Dames citoyennes continued to transform religious space for their political activism when thirty of them came forward at the October 3, 1792 Jacobin Club meeting to support the war effort and request a workspace in the former Bernadine's convent.[31]

Publications from both the Dames citoyennes and the Dames heroïnes demonstrate that women formulated their identities as *citoyennes* based on social and political neighborhood connections, their roles as wives and mothers, gender stereotypes, and historical images of Marseille's sixteenth-century heroines. By formally obtaining permission to assemble from the municipal authorities and highlighting this right in their first published documents, the women created physical and mental spaces to represent their voices in the political sphere. Those reading their publications would visualize the city's new political landscape as including women's political spaces. As part of the success of the patriot movement, the geopolitical locus of revolutionary discourse and power now had to be mediated between the Hôtel de Ville, the Jacobin Club, and to some extent the meetings of the Dames citoyennes and the Dames heroïnes, who, beyond their actions in the public sphere, exerted influence through published petitions and denunciations to local and national authorities. The sixty-six members of the Dames heroïnes claimed their inspiration from the celebrated heroines of Marseille, who, in 1524, defended the city from siege. They elected Madame Bourgain as president and Madame Ponsin-Tourtera as secretary, both of whom were wives of senior officers of the National Guard.[32] Another member, Madame Lieutaud, was married to the commander of the National

Guard. The Dames citoyennes had 105 members, including the mayor's wife, Madame Escalon Martin.[33] However, familial connections to male patriot leaders were likely only one influence; records for the Dames citoyennes reveal familial connections between mothers, daughters, and sisters also motivating political participation in 1790.

While sources indicate the presence of elite members, leadership also emerged from the artisanal ranks in the Dames citoyennes. Yvonne Knibiehler describes the Dames citoyennes in section 7 as coming from the upper middle class (*moyenne bourgeoisie*). Madame Escalon Martin and the mayor, who was a merchant trader, for example, "had a house in the nearby rue du Tapis Vert," close to the affluent area of the rue de Noailles.[34] However, the club secretary, Marie-Jeanne Boude, whose husband was a tailor, came from the less affluent artisanal ranks.[35] Another member, Françoise Mauran, described herself as a clothes maker.[36] William Scott notes that significantly fewer *propriétaires* (property owners) and *bourgeois* (legal privileged fiscal category) lived west of the rue d'Aix than the *propriétaires* and *bourgeois* who lived east of it.[37] Both women's clubs were situated in areas of the city with citizens of mixed social and economic backgrounds. Women living in section 11, as listed in the census of 1793, identified as servants, workers, skilled trades, artisans, shopkeepers/merchants, property owners and *bourgeois*.[38]

While barred from military service, both the Dames citoyennes and the Dames heroïnes used martial imagery of armed female action in defense of the country and its revolutionary principles. Women's participation in the *Bastille marseillaise* became symbolic of their roles as patriots and of their willingness to arm themselves to defend the nation. The Dames heroïnes' President Bourgain emphasized that Marseille had already witnessed women's eagerness to seize "the first sparks of the sacred fire of love for the country and to defend with a male strength the illustrious youth, which is devoted to the destruction of the leeches of the people and of the foreign brigands, who infested this important city."[39] As the *Bastille marseillaise* itself became a symbol of patriotic pride, women included themselves among the conquerors and defenders of the forts and the nation and, in the process, contributed to the creation of a revolutionary map of the city with new symbols of participatory political power.[40]

The Dames citoyennes, in their published call for municipal authorities to include women in the nationwide celebration of the Revolution at the Festival of the Federation, claimed the right to share in the political space created in the act of swearing the civic oath.[41] Voting as an "Assembly of *Citoyennes*" they vowed to march under the flag of *Liberté* to swear alongside their husbands, children, and brothers an oath of fidelity to "the Nation, the Law, and the King," and to defend the Constitution with a "male courage."[42] Although excluded on the day the oath was taken throughout France, a separate ceremony on July 15 allowed women to take center stage.[43] A municipal proclamation legitimated their participation, linking it to Marseille's reverence for its sixteenth-century heroines: "Heiresses of patriotism, which has always distinguished the *Heroïnes Marseillaises*, the *Citoyennes* of this City, having wished to be admitted individually to the Civic Oath, the Municipality willingly adhered to their petition."[44] History credited women with saving the city at a moment when all seemed lost, and the city map of 1791 highlighted the Bastion des dames along the city walls.[45]

The Dames heroïnes built upon the historical precedent and their familial connections to the National Guard and decided to swear the oath organized as a battalion, emphasizing that they "preferred death to the humiliation of chains."[46] They assumed symbolic military ranks: the commander of the National Guard's wife became "General Lieutaud"; the wives of the senior officers became "Major Ponsin-Tourtera" and "Captain Bourgain," while others took the ranks of lieutenants and ensigns. The Dames heroïnes, "dressed in white with a tricolor belt representing the nation and a national cocarde on their left arm," joined with "their sister battalions no 7 and 12" at the Hôtel de Ville, where the mayor, the municipal officers, and the commander of the National Guard awaited.[47] Representation from section 12 indicates that participation included women from the artisanal and workers' population who lived "at the extreme north-west of the town, [which] included many of the most characteristic industries of Marseilles—tanning, dying, soap and starch manufactories—and their workers naturally liv[ing] nearby, as well as a few fabricants and a host of cobblers and humble tradesmen."[48] Madame "General" Lieutaud and Madame Martin led the women through the streets. The choice to have the wives of the mayor and of the commander of the National Guard lead the procession created a parallel female leadership and may have also been an attempt to allay recent tensions between their male counterparts.[49]

A detachment of the National Guard and a battalion from the navy escorted the female "battalions" to the Place Saint-Louis, where the mayor gave a speech, comparing the women to the heroines of the siege of Marseille.[50] The mayor, however, also attempted to redirect the women's focus away from direct political action towards maintaining liberty and peace by raising the next generation of citizens:

> *Mesdames*, Marseille sees with joy that the patriotism of the *Dames Marseillaises* has not deteriorated. History cites our Heroines with the greatest praise; your zeal proves to us that you are capable of the same efforts, if we found ourselves in the same circumstances. We are happy enough not to have to arouse your courage. The use of your talents for persuasion, your care in developing citizens who [will follow in] your footsteps, are the most useful services that you can render to the country today. It is no longer a question of conquering liberty but of conserving it. The oath that you are going to take imposes the obligation of working with us to maintain the public peace, no less than the maintenance of the constitution.[51]

Women's violent participation that May, first in the occupation of the forts and then in a protest led by market women outside the local prison that forced municipal authorities to institute martial law, likely informed the mayor's appeal for peace.[52]

The Dames citoyennes maintained the strongest political presence throughout the summer and fall of 1790 and would become known as the Dames patriotes and active participants in the Jacobin Club. The women continued meetings and weighed in politically via publications regarding ongoing tensions between the municipality, the National Guard, and those associated with Old Regime authority and corruption. They did so, for example, when the capture of the forts pitted the royal Minister, d'André of Aix, against the municipality. On May 13, 1790, d'André denounced the municipal authorities and those who had seized the forts to France's National Assembly. He also complained about the municipal authorities' removal of Lieutaud as commander of the National Guard.[53] The Jacobin Club required members to sign an address against d'André and stated that failure to do so could result in removal from the Club. Using a military identification, the Dames Citoyennes du Bataillon No 7, like their male counterparts in section 7 who had published a denunciation of Lieutaud in September 1790, expanded their political reach by publishing and sending their denunciation of d'André to both the municipal authorities and the National Assembly, adding to the "complaints, denunciations and accusation of the General Council of the Commune."[54] This publication continued to imprint the Dames citoyennes onto the revolutionary map of the city, highlighting women's parallel political engagement. However, as local and national Jacobin Club power expanded, some women realigned themselves geopolitically by moving their participation to the rue Thubaneau.

1792: Patriot Women, the Jacobin Club, and Marseille's Regional Expansion of Power

Women played an active role in the Jacobin Club, whose leadership was intertwined not only with the politics of the city but the whole of the Midi (the South of France). The Club supported women's political associations of 1790, and its *Journal des départements méridionaux, et de Débats des Amis de la Constitution de Marseille* regularly affirmed their presence and participation in Club meetings between 1792 and 1793 (the period with the most comprehensive records of the Club). Although women could not be official members and sat separately from men, they established their patriotism in parallel actions, for instance through donations to the war effort and charitable projects. Women also gave speeches but were often not recognized by name in meeting minutes or the *Journal des départements*.

Acknowledgment of their contributions and the publication of their speeches elsewhere, however, added the Jacobin Club to the map of spaces where women wielded influence and leadership.

Defense of the Revolution in 1792 led to a series of mob lynchings, and, similar to 1789, the streets provided an alternative space to those controlled by the city's government. While the violence put the vigilante crowds at odds with the new, revolutionary authorities, to punish them may have put Jacobin leaders at odds with women and men who regularly participated in Club meetings. On February 28, 1792, the flower seller and royalist, *la Cayole* (represented in the Memorial to the Marseillaise), became the first civilian victim of revolutionary lynchings, a trend that plagued Marseille's authorities throughout the spring and summer.[55] A contemporary observer, Laurent Lautard, who published his account of revolutionary events in 1848, blamed Cayole's murder, in part, on the long-standing animosity between her and a woman he called *la Fassy*, an ardent Jacobin. Elisabeth "Liberty" Fassy, whose husband was a sail maker and also a Jacobin, is said to have been at the head of a group of angry women from the Dames citoyennes who fought with Cayole at the main market place. Fassy lived in section 2 on the rue des Feuillants, and Cayole on the rue de Noailles, both near the Jacobin Club.[56] Cayole had verbally and physically fought with Fassy's group at the main market over the success two days earlier of "a force of National Guardsmen from Marseille and elsewhere" who invaded Aix-en-Provence, the center of departmental authority. "Patriots overwhelmed the [King's] Swiss d'Ernest regiment . . . As a result, most of the departmental administrators fled."[57] The victory allowed for the successful shift of geopolitical power in the region from Aix to Marseille. Later that day an angry group gathered outside Cayole's home, accusing her of being an enemy of the Revolution, speaking poorly about the constitution, and making "indecent remarks" against the nation and the volunteers returning from Aix. A municipal officer rescued her and placed her in prison for safety. But the crowd eventually forced their way in and hanged Cayole "from a lamppost at the corner of the Rue de la Prison."[58]

Marseille's Jacobin Club and the National Guard now effectively controlled the department and the military, and women contributed to departmental coalition-building. Two weeks after Cayole's lynching, the Jacobin Club sent Thérèse Gaud Cavale, a widow and member of the Dames citoyennes whose son was in the departmental army, as part of a deputation of women to the nearby, small town of Aubagne to honor its Jacobin Club, the Anti-Politiques, with a liberty bonnet.[59] *La Cavale*, who acted as a political ambassador between the Marseille and Aubagne authorities, became known for her militant activism alongside *la Fassy* and *la Boude*, and at times led crowds carrying a sword.[60] The Club employed her to reinforce the geopolitical shift of departmental authority to Marseille. Cavale reported at the March 12 meeting that she had obtained a promise from Aubagne's municipal leaders that "Marseille's mandates would be circulated there."[61] Cavale's contributions to departmental coalition-building extended to joining Jacobin political

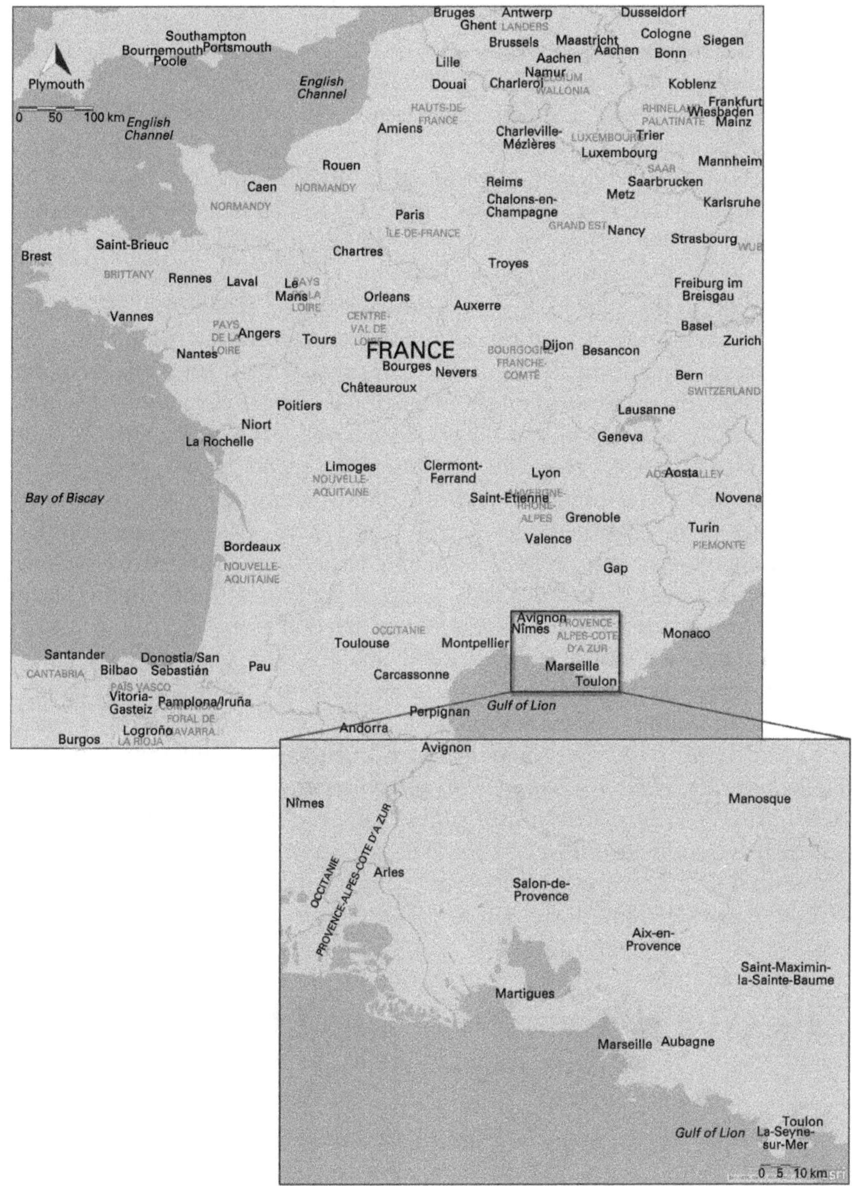

MAP 2.2: *Map of France with inset of Marseille, Aubagne, and Arles. Courtesy of Laura Talamante.*

expeditions to Arles against the counter-revolutionary Chiffonistes' rebellion, a major challenge within the region. At the March 29 meeting, Jacobin Club leaders chose Cavale to present a pike to the Marseille army preparing to enter Arles. The *Journal des départements* noted that Cavale would act as a witness to the event.[62] Cavale served as a political leader and a symbolic link between Marseille's women, the army, and Jacobin goals.

Expansion of Jacobin coalitions included women's political networks. Women at the Jacobin Club meeting on April 28 called for inclusion in plans to honor the patriots returning from Arles by sending a deputation to "offer a civic crown to the entire army." A woman obtained the floor: "[W]e want to give our recognition to these . . . courageous defenders of liberty; we too ask to participate in the honor of awarding it to them, and I request Mr. President, in the name of all the Women who hear me, and in particular the *Dames patriotes* [previously the Dames citoyennes] who regularly follow your meetings, that we join you, to present a second crown to the brave national guards, who come from Arles."[63] By placing themselves within the parameters of revolutionary leadership, the Dames patriotes successfully inserted themselves into a male-dominated space and affirmed women's contributions to the geopolitical expansion of Jacobin authority in the Midi. Furthermore, patriot women in Arles went beyond symbolic actions. As a result of the intervention of Marseille's Jacobins, "women participated in punitive expeditions carried out by Arlesian Jacobins against the moderates of the surrounding communes such as Tarascon, Saint-Rémy, Eyragues, Beaucaire, [and] Eyguière. The image of women carrying pikes and swords shocked some observers who took the opportunity to denounce revolutionary radicalism."[64] Both contemporary supporters' and critics' comments made women's geopolitical influence clear. The continuing expansion of Jacobin power in 1793, however, would lead many of these women into conflict with critics of the Club during the Federalist Revolt.

The 1793–4 Transformation of Political Space during the Federalist Revolt

By the spring of 1793, many in Marseille and the region had become critical of local Jacobin tactics for enforcing justice, leading to accusations of terrorism and the imprisonment of some Jacobins. Their campaign in Provence for war contributions, at times forced, and the disarmament of citizens alongside their attempt to levy 6,000 men for the departmental army divided citizens. The release of Jacobins accused of terrorism in April increased tensions. The interference of representatives-on-mission from Paris, who transferred cases from the Popular to the Criminal Tribunal (dominated by prominent members of the Jacobin Club), made matters worse. Section leaders reacted by expelling the representatives, rejecting the authority of the National Convention, and closing Marseille's Jacobin Club on June 3, 1793. Supporters of the section leaders joined in what became known by their political opponents as the Federalist Revolt. Proponents of the Revolt saw themselves as protectors of the republic who would save the Revolution from destruction by radical Jacobins. The period allows for analysis of how women used public spaces—section meetings, neighborhood streets, businesses, and market areas—as alternative geopolitical spaces to wield political influence during the Revolt.

Section meetings originally served as voting assemblies and were limited to active citizens. In general, records do not reveal a strong formal inclusion of women's voices prior to the Federalist Revolt, though those from sections 6 and 7 indicate that women had begun attending by 1792. Women's attendance increased significantly during the Revolt of 1793. In section 6, which housed "some of the town's wealthiest merchants" and was also "heavily committed to the sectionary cause," an anonymous and undated petition advocated that women be admitted to section meetings in every neighborhood and given entry cards, recognizing them as citizens, and that the petition be circulated to all thirty-two sections.[65] It seems likely the petition circulated since records reveal several sections addressing the question in May and June of 1793. On May 20, 1793, section 16 confronted the issue when: "The President read an address by *Citoyennes* from the section requesting permission to assist assembly meetings" and called for an examination of the pros and cons of women's presence.[66] Ten days later, section 4 decided to reserve seating in their tribunes for women.[67] On June 4, 1793, a section 8 petition requested that women be able to apply for admission cards.

Women's participation in section politics overlapped between informal and formal political spaces through familial, social, and economic networks. Jacques Guilhaumou demonstrates the strong political involvement of the Clappier family in section 4, an area that "bordered the Canebière on the side of the new quarters, devoted mainly to small-scale businesses and trades catering for a well-off clientele, and with quite a number of artists and craftsmen."[68] Joseph Clappier, a perfume maker, owned a boutique with his wife, Marie-Thérèse Brémond, a glove maker. Guilhaumou highlights the overlap of the family's social and political networks: "Marie-Thérèse received in her shop ardent republican *sectionnaires*, in particular the Maisse family; the father, Nicolas, a merchant soap maker, was guillotined in the year II as an '*enragé sectionnaire*' and the son, close to Thérèse, [the Clappier's daughter], was part of the Departmental Army levied against the Convention" during the Federalist Revolt.[69] Thérèse and a young group of women regularly attended section 4 meetings. Nineteen-year-old Sophie Maisse, daughter of Nicolas Maisse, and twenty-year-old Sabine Reboul, the daughter of a wig maker, were part of this group of politically active youth. At the August 9, 1793 section 4 meeting, as General Carteaux and his army moved closer to attacking Marseille on behalf of the Convention, Thérèse is said to have read "a petition from *citoyennes* in view 'of arousing the zeal and the ardor of the soldiers who had not joined their flag.'"[70] The petition itself originated from women in section 5, one of the richest areas of the city adjacent to sections 4 and 6.[71] By August 16, as "leaders circulated the petition to sister sections for approval . . . twenty-three of the thirty-two section assemblies had read the petition at their meetings and supported its call to action," revealing the increased political influence of female sectionnaires' interventions during the Federalist Revolt.

Proximity to formal legal and political spaces offered women opportunities to use other public spaces and their social and economic networks for political engagement. Catherine Blanc, known as the widow Garrely, ran a tobacco shop in section 18 near the Palais de Justice and the Place de la Liberté where the guillotine was located.[72] From this location, she harangued patriots passing by her shop, especially those on their way to the guillotine. Accusations in the Revolutionary Tribunal reveal how she used her business and the streets as political spaces to support the transfer of power from the Jacobin Club to the sections, which took control of the Popular Tribunal. Witnesses testified that judges from the Popular Tribunal frequented her store and discussed politics, and the space was popular for people to rejoice over "the oppression and the incarceration of the patriots." She was accused of causing others "to believe all the atrocious [accusations] hurled upon these innocents," suggesting that her words had powers of persuasion that influenced the dominant political discourse.[73] Garrely was often in the company of other women in the neighborhood, and it was in these formations that Jacobins—male and female—found themselves under attack. Garrely's case highlights how informal spaces such as shops and neighborhood streets were part of feminine territory that gave women shopkeepers "a perfect vantage-point for observing everything that went on. And, as authorities on local affairs, ever-present overseers of street life, these women had an important measure of control."[74]

Political disputes spread from male-controlled spaces, such as the Jacobin Club and the sections, to neighborhoods and other public spaces. Under the control of the sections, Jacobin leaders and their families became targets for communal political grievances. Marguerite Arnaud, for example, whose husband had participated in the disarmament that spring, testified that her husband was ordered to appear in section 18. On the way home, she encountered Garrely and a friend; they accused her husband of having stolen money during the disarmament.[75] Garrely's politicization of her boutique, the streets, and the market illustrates Martine Lapied's point that women used traditional spaces of sociability to spread political propaganda.[76] Public harassment reinforced calls for authorities to redress alleged political abuses. Magdelaine Calavery Isoard, whose son was an important Jacobin leader, told how Garrely complained at the market that Isoard should pay more for her fish "in order to restore the hundred thousand *écus* that [her] son took from the nation."[77] On another occasion, Garrely warned the woman that her son would be guillotined. Moments later she stepped outside with a pitchfork threatening to guillotine Isoard herself. For the next four months, Garrely harangued the woman who lived nearby on the rue de la Roquette in section 15.[78] David Garrioch, in his work on Parisian neighborhoods, describes the theatricality of public insults where "nearly all reported disputes follow this pattern . . . A dispute was a public performance, noisy and animated. It contained a strong element of ritual and symbol which the audience recognized and knew how to interpret."[79] Garrely's ongoing harassment of Isoard and others in public spaces served as a political and social message to the community: Jacobins and their supporters would be held accountable for their actions.

Mapping the Consequences for Women during the Federalist Revolt and the Terror, 1793–4

Women who remained devoted to Jacobin leadership during the Federalist Revolt found themselves harassed, arrested, and convicted for their continuing support. Upon their return to power, Jacobins awarded women and men indemnities as compensation for their suffering at the hands of the Federalists.[80] The records for indemnities paid to women from Marseille, Arles, and Toulon (renamed Port de la Montagne during the Terror) show that many had experienced significant persecution either as a result of their own political actions or familial ties to politically targeted males. Those for Marseille reveal that sixty-eight women received indemnities, with thirty-one records indicating women who faced repercussions, twenty of whom were forced to flee for months at a time while others had to hide for days or weeks. The beleaguered Magdelaine Isoard fled for a month, for example, due to harassment by Garrely and other sectionnaires, and received 700 livres in compensation. Women also received indemnities for their own imprisonment or the death of a husband or son at the hands of the Federalists. Of the forty-seven indemnity records selected randomly for this study of women from Toulon, eighteen records list the reason for indemnities, with being forced to flee listed eight times and the execution of a male relative also listed eight times. A random selection of women from Arles indicates that they appear to have applied for indemnities at a higher rate, but women in Marseille received overall higher indemnity amounts. Following the rise to power of section leadership in Marseille and Aix, Arles' sections followed suit on July 19, 1793. Female Arlesian Jacobins armed themselves with fusils and pikes and tried to free men imprisoned by the sections.[81] Similar to the women in Marseille who protested Jacobin leaders' imprisonment, it is likely that some of these women also received indemnities for their suffering during the Revolt. Of the 118 records selected, having to flee Arles appeared as the predominant reason women received indemnities.[82]

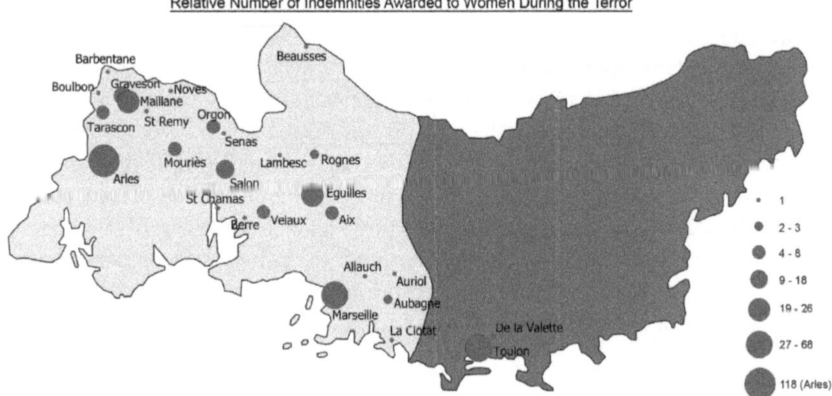

FIGURE 2.1 *Indemnities for female patriots in Marseille and selected Bouche-du-Rhône examples. Courtesy of Laura Talamante.*

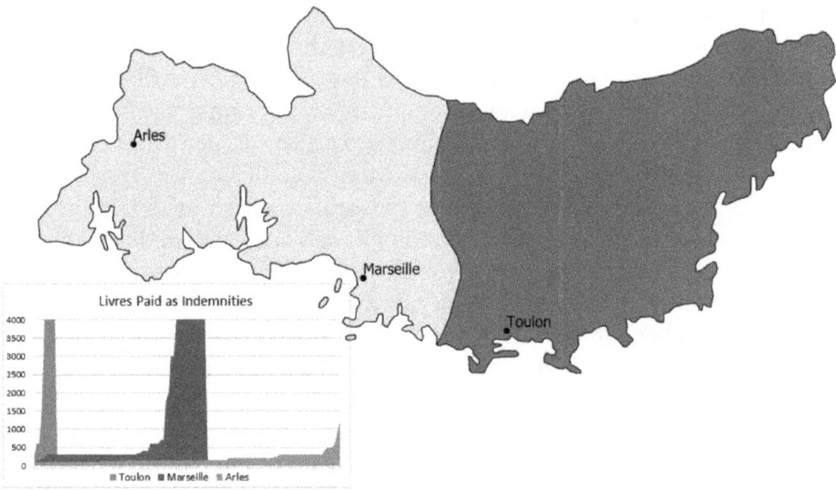

FIGURE 2.2 *Livres paid as indemnities. Courtesy of Laura Talamante.*

Indemnities might also be seen as recognition of the perceived value of female patriot commitment during a moment of crisis for the republic. Seven women received indemnities who were active in either Marseille's Dames citoyennes or their later incarnation as the Dames patriotes, revealing their long-term commitment to patriot goals.[83] In addition, Dames patriotes members Elisabeth Fassy, Thérèse Cavale, and Elisabeth Cauvière alongside nine other women in Marseille received the highest indemnity of 4000 livres because of either prolonged imprisonment, the execution of a male family member, or being forced to flee the city.

Court records for the Federalists' Military Tribunal and the subsequent Revolutionary Tribunal that tried Federalists (and others) during the Terror make clear the political value accorded to Fassy's leadership. Jacobin women challenged section dominance by rioting on July 20 and 21, 1793. The crowd swelled to around 400 people, who marched to the Committee General, yelling, "We are the sans-culottes," protesting the Club's forced closure and demanding the release of Jacobin prisoners. The Federalist Military Tribunal created four days later held Fassy responsible for instigating the riot.[84] Fassy was also indicted for her role in the August 2, 1793 food riot over the high price of commodities at the Place de la Linche. Women's takeover of the streets threatened section leaders' authority on both occasions; however, "Fassy and the other Jacobin women rioting in July exercised political militancy through their capacity to threaten and incite violence against the Federalist authorities for a purely political cause—freeing the Jacobins."[85] The Military Tribunal, operating in crisis mode as General Carteaux's troops advanced upon the city, sentenced Fassy to twelve years in chains. Once control over the city was returned to Jacobin hands, the Revolutionary Tribunal relied on Fassy's testimony against Federalist suspects and investigated those who had testified against her. Marie-Thérèse Laurent received the death penalty for testifying against Fassy and convincing others to do the same. Only seven women in total received this harsh penalty, indicating that attacks against Fassy were punished on the same level as those committed against male Jacobin leaders.[86]

The Revolutionary Tribunal's judgments of 975 people, including eighty-six women, allow another window into the consequences women faced for political engagement. Beyond the seven women sentenced to death, the court judged seventeen other women guilty (three were sent to *reclusion*, a form of imprisonment, one was sent to prison, and three were returned to prison for further consideration) and released sixty-two women.[87] However, many women spent months in jail with no trial. On March 19, 1794, Étienne-Christophe Maignet (the representative-on-mission sent from Paris to oversee regional revolutionary justice) ordered the revolutionary committees to step up arrests and to send him a list of suspects and the motives for their arrests. Records from the Prison des Ignorantins in section 20, which mainly held women, reveal 347 female suspects, the majority from Marseille. The median age of all women held here from Marseille's sections was forty, with one as young as fourteen (her stepfather was listed as absent) and another as old as seventy-eight (her son was listed as absent). Nearly 40 percent appear to have been arrested in relationship to the absence of a male relative, many of whom had fled Marseille after Carteaux's entry and were likely associated with the Federalist Revolt.[88]

Mapping reveals a difference between where Marseille men and women being held as suspects lived. Most of the male suspects were from "sections 6, 8, 9 and 18 which surrounded section 10, spokesman for the sectional movement."[89] The majority of female suspects came from "sections 1, 2 and

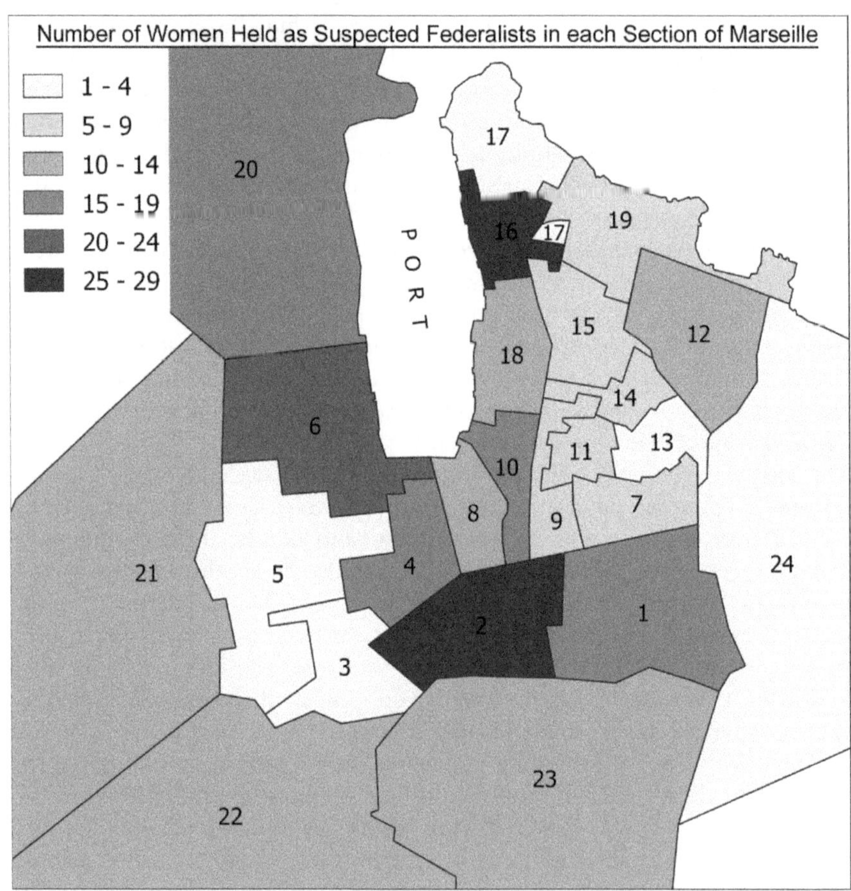

FIGURE 2.3 *Number of women held as suspected Federalists in each section of Marseille. Courtesy of Laura Talamante.*

4 corresponding to the new neighborhoods around the courts," as well as section 6 and 16, the latter where female citizens had petitioned for inclusion in their section meetings weeks before the closure of the Jacobin Club.[90] Section 12 represented women and men from the lower ranks of artisans and manufacturing workers, who were not arrested in large numbers. However, women from sections 12 and 20 were arrested at slightly higher rates than men. More male relatives of the women arrested in section 20 were listed as absent than in section 12, which may mean that women in section 12 were being arrested more often due to their direct political engagement. Suspects from section 16, like those from sections 12 and 20, stand out in that the area was not affluent, and these women were held at the Prison des Ignorantins at almost the same rate as men (44.6 percent). Mapping arrests across sections indicates that women from the elites to the

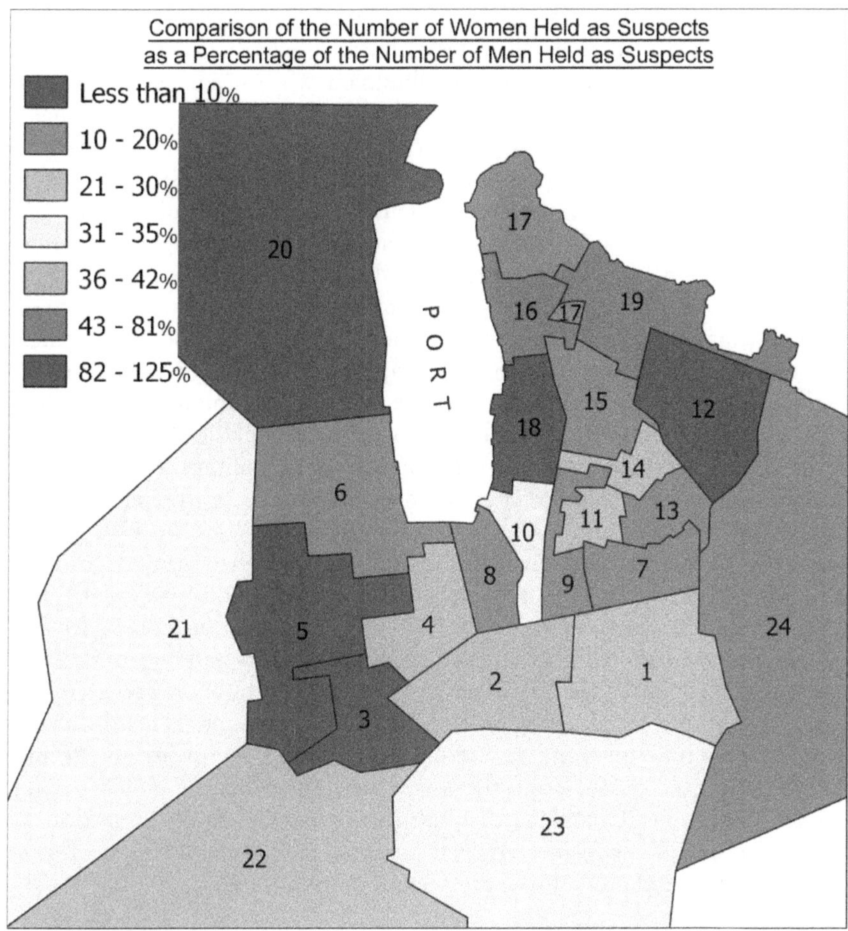

FIGURE 2.4 *Comparison of the number of women held as suspects as a percentage of the number of men held as suspects. Courtesy of Laura Talamante.*

lower orders found themselves held accountable for *sectionnaire* politics, whether they were directly involved or not, during the Federalist Revolt.

While the physical map of Marseille changed very little, the centers of power shifted during the Revolution. Women contributed to the realignment of power by modifying their existing familial, social, and economic networks. They acted as coalition builders and community enforcers of political power through everyday interactions in ordinary spaces. Old Regime spaces such as churches became central meeting places for women's political associations and section meetings. Women used the feminine spaces of the markets as geopolitical centers to organize political action. The streets and small shops served as other feminine spaces where women harassed political rivals and even meted out vigilante justice to send political and social messages to the community.

Although archival records are less abundant when it comes to women's political engagement, mapping shows the vast investment in revolutionary change by women from across the city. In 1789 the geopolitical map of revolutionary Marseille began to form. Market women, especially from section 17, become active agents of democratic change and part of the powerful coalition of patriots that brought about the municipal revolution in 1790. Women built upon more than their familial relationships, using neighborhood social networks to establish their own geopolitical centers of power through the transformation of religious spaces. Publications by women and men alike associated women's participation with specific revolutionary locations, and women inserted themselves into physical and mental spaces.

Women also contributed to the creation of new symbols of participatory political power, including their appropriation of military ranks, which emphasized parallels between women and men's participation and transformation of public space for revolutionary purposes. By 1792, some of these women joined Jacobin coalitions and contributed to their geopolitical expansion of power as ambassadors of sorts in the region that was lauded in Jacobin publications. Similarly, by 1793 other women joined the Federalist Revolt and contributed to the alliance and coalition-building of section assemblies throughout the city in efforts to save the republic. Between 1793 and 1794, women faced strong repercussions for their political involvement: harassment in the streets and the market place, arrests, imprisonment, fleeing the city, and even death. From the lower echelons of market and working women in sections 17 and 12 through the elite social ranks of section 5, women's political engagement played a crucial role in the creation of new political spaces and a revolutionary mental map of the city.

Source: Deliberation of the Dames citoyennes from the Saint-Martin district, no. 7, 7 July 1790

Today 7 July 1790, and the first year of Liberty, the *Dames Citoyennes* from District No. 7 are assembled in the Chapelle des Pénitens Bleus de Saint-Martin, with the approval of Messieurs the Mayor and Municipal Officers. Mademoiselle Louise-Françoise Raimbaud having been elected President, and Madame Marie-Jeanne Boude, Secretary, both by acclamation; Madame President said:

Citoyennes,

Animated by the sentiments of admiration, deference, and attachment to the favorable Constitution given to the French by our wise legislators; inflamed by that pure Patriotism, which has given birth in our hearts to the regeneration of the French Empire; firmly convinced that the prosperity of our country, of our spouses, of our children, of our brethren, is connected to the maintenance of these immortal decrees, of those sacred rights that the French recover, after several centuries of debasement and servitude; we must rise today to live up to these fortunate destinies, which are reserved for both sexes. It is not enough to form tacitly in our hearts a vow of devotion to the sublime work of the august Representatives of the French Nation; we must look upon it as the first and most sacred of our duties, to manifest externally our civic virtues, and to pronounce solemnly our oath of fidelity to the Constitution, the 14th of this month, joyous moment of the conquest of Liberty.

On this, the Assembly of *Citoyennes*, unanimously applauding, has stopped to participate in the mighty spectacle of this memorable day, to march rallied under the banner of Liberty, to the Altar of the Fatherland, to swear there with their citizen-husbands, their children, and their brethren, to be faithful to the Nation, the Law, and the King; to defend the Constitution with every means in their power, and to repel with a male courage the enemies of the public who would still try to plunge us back into irons.

Then the Assembly deliberated upon the costume that the *Citoyennes* should have on the day of the oath; it was decided that they would be dressed in white, with a belt in the three colors of the Nation, a national *cocarde* on the left arm, white headdress, white ribbon around it, white apron, or nothing at all, white gloves, carrying a laurel branch in hand; that they would thus walk in costume, under a flag that would be made in three colors, bearing this inscription on one side, the Nation, the Law, and the King, on the other, Strength, Union, Fidelity; that after the ceremony, the flag would be placed in the Common House, to serve as needed, and as a monument to be passed on to future generations.

The Assembly has further deliberated, to follow the order and the path, which will be indicated by *Messieurs* the Mayor and Municipal Officers, together with the Commander of the National Guard, and finally, that an Excerpt from the present Deliberation will be sent to the Municipality and to the Commander of the National Guard; and signed straightaway, the *Dames Citoyennes*, Louise-Françoise RAIMBAUD, President; Marie-Jeanne BOUDE, Secretary.

Mesdames
Martin Escalon, Wife of the Mayor; Marguerite Verdet, Jeanne-Rose Blanc, Marie-Rose Durieu, Widow Elisabeth Chevignot, Marguerite Fabre, Thérese Peron, Elisabeth Girard, Magdeleine Causimon, Anne Bonnaud, Jeanne Aubran, Claire Burle, Françoise Mauran, Françoise Roux, Elisabeth

Cauviere, Thérèse Revaute, Marie-Anne Deleuze, Elisabeth Gouirand, Marie Vernet, elder; Marie Anne Blanche-Fleur, Rosalie Vernet younger, Rose Vernet, daughter; Thérèse-Verani Jaubert, Françoise Seguiés, Marie-Roman, elder; Thérèse Roman, younger; Marguerite Vernet, mother; Marie Cauvine, Marguerite Jannolle, Marie-Jeanne Fouque, Elisabeth Beranger, Marie-Louise Tortin, Marie-Barbe Gay, Elisabeth Baudouin, Marie David, Marie Blanc, younger; Therese Maillet, Henriette Michel, Rose Matabon, Anne Begue, mother; Claire Begue, daughter-in-law; Louise Fabre, Cathérine Donjon, Adélaïde Tufreau, Victoire Lambert, Marie Suran, aînée, Marie Rousset, Elisabeth Balazard, Marie Isoard, Elisabeth Dapus, Joseph Marie Martin, Marie Reymoné, Marguerite Billaud, Adélaïde Nitard, Françoise Jourdan, Magdelaine Plassin, Adélaïde Bassi, Marguerite Fabre, Françoise Frison, Marie-Angelier Michel, Marguerite Fournier, Françoise Brard, Justine Berenguier, Françoise Berenguier, Thérèse Espagnol, Elisabeth Fabresse, Cathérine Forte, Marianne Pivau, Rose Devale, Cathérine Rey, Marie Pivau, daughter-in-law; Thérèse Hélie, Marie Chabaud, Susanne Orgon, Thérèse Vial, Thérèse Odde, Anne Arman, Marie Arnaude, Cécile Clastrier, Anne Martin, Marie Sauvane, Ursule Sauvane, Marie Sevestre, mother; Magdeleine Sevestre, daughter; Rose Maillet, Marie Monbrion, Félicité Pointié, Anne Anselme, Marie-Anne Messel, Marie-Magdeleine-Louise Daruti, Marie Ricord, Marie Michel, Marie Brun, daughter; Widow Brun, Mariane Sarrazin, Françoise Sarrazin, Benoîte Héroirt, Anne-Charle Sigaud, Elisabeth Vion, Généviève Draveton, Louise Goutenoir, Marguerite Vernet, mother; Cathérine Grece, etc.

MARSEILLE

From the Printing Press of J. Mossy, Father & Son, National Printers,

for the King & the City. 1790.

Notes

1 Thank you to the editors for their guidance and useful suggestions. Additional thanks to Jill Walshaw for critical insights and to Alexandra Morrison and Sharon MacNett for research assistance. Michelle Richards provided excellent mapping support. Maps were created using QGIS®, a project of the Open Source Geospatial Foundation (OSGeo). Please visit www.qgis.org. Additional basemaps were sourced from the ArcGIS® online resources and developed using software by Esri. ArcGIS is the intellectual property of Esri and is used herein under license. Copyright ©Esri. All rights reserved. For more information about Esri® software, please visit www.esri.com.

2 Michael Kennedy, *The Jacobin Club of Marseilles, 1790–1794* (Ithaca, NY: Cornell University Press, 1973), iv.

3 Yvonne Knibiehler, "Femmes de Provence en révolution," in *Les Femmes et la Révolution Française*, ed. Marie-Françoise Brive (Toulouse: Presses Universitaires du Mirail, 1989), 1:149–55; Jacques Guilhaumou, "Conduites politiques de Marseillaises pendant la Révolution française," *Provence historique* 186 (1996); Isabelle Brie, *Les femmes marseillaises devant la justice sous la Révolution* (Mémoire de maîtrise d'histoire moderne, Université de Provence, 1994); Laura Talamante, "Les Marseillaises: Women and Political Change during the French Revolution, 1789–1794" (Ph.D. diss., University of California Los Angeles, 2003); Martine Lapied, "Parole publique des femmes et conflictualité pendant la Révolution sud-est de la France," *Annales historiques de la Révolution française (AHRF)* 344 (2006): 47–62.

4 Michel Vovelle, *La Découverte de la Politique: Géopolitique de la Révolution Française* (Paris: Éditions La Découverte, 1993).

5 Vovelle, *La Découverte de la Politique*, 341.

6 Daniel Smail, "The Linguistic Cartography of Property and Power in Late Medieval Marseille," in *Medieval Practices of Space*, ed. Barbara Hanawalt and Michal Kobialka (Minneapolis: University of Minnesota Press, 2000), 37.

7 Smail, "The Linguistic Cartography of Property," 38.

8 The Constitution of 1791 accorded voting rights to active citizens, a category limited to males who paid annual taxes equaling the amount of local wages paid for at least three days of labor. All other males and all females held the legal status of passive citizens.

9 Kennedy, *The Jacobin Club of Marseilles*, 6; William Scott, *Terror and Repression in Revolutionary Marseilles* (New York: Macmillan, 1973), 7; Alfred Fierro, *Historical Dictionary of Paris* (Lanham, MD: Scarecrow, 1998), 238.

10 Scott, *Terror and Repression*, 4; Paul Masson, "Marseille depuis 1789. Études historiques," *Annales de la Faculté des Lettres d'Aix* 10, no. 1–2 (1917): 17–18, 19–21.

11 Masson, "Marseille depuis 1789," 35. All translations from French are my own unless otherwise noted.

12 Monique Cubells, "La place des femmes dans les émeutes populaires en Provence de 1715 à 1789," *Provence historique* 46, no. 186 (1996): 447–50, 454–5.

13 John Markoff, "Violence, Emancipation, and Democracy: The Countryside and the French Revolution," *American Historical Review* 100, no. 2 (1995): 362.

14 Kennedy, *The Jacobin Club of Marseilles*, 9. Laurent Henry credits the rioters and the work of guilds and corporations in the 1789 revolutionary transformation of Marseille, "La Politisation des corporations et les Révolutions municipales: Le Cas de Marseille en 1789," *AHRF* 370 (2012): 40.

15 Severin Vialla, *Marseille révolutionnaire. L'armée-nation (1789–1793)* (Paris: Chapelot, 1910), 7–9.

16 Vialla, *Marseille révolutionnaire*, 12–15.

17 Monique Cubells, "Marseille au printemps de 1789: Une ville en dissidence," *Annales du Midi: Revue archéologique, historique et philologique de la France méridionale* 2, no. 1 (1989): 568.

18 Interactive mapping for the chapter is available at drlauratalamante.com/Marseille-mapping-women-politics/.

19 *Journal d'un Marseillais, 1789–1793* (Marseille: Éditions, 1989), 145.

20 Georges Guibal, *Mirabeau et la Provence* (Paris: A. Fontemoing, 1891), 33 and 32 respectively.

21 *Courrier de Marseille* 4 (May 5, 1790): 27–8, Bibliothèque nationale de France, LC11-635 (94). Hereafter BN.

22 *Courrier de Marseille* 4 (May 5, 1790): 29–30.

23 Knibiehler, "Femmes de Provence," 1:149.

24 Donald Sutherland, *Murder in Aubagne: Lynching, Law, and Justice during the French Revolution* (Cambridge: Cambridge University Press, 2009), 73, 75–6.

25 Sutherland, *Murder in Aubagne*, 75.

26 Edouard Baratier, *Histoire de Marseille* (Toulouse: Privat, 1973), 72–3.

27 Vialla, *Marseille révolutionnaire*, 487–8.

28 Yves Durand's research in Paris shows the average monthly salary for day laborers at 26 sous. "Recherches sur les salaires des maçons à Paris au XVIIIe siècle," *Revue d'histoire économique et sociale* 44 (1966): 476. There were 20 sous to the livre.

29 Joseph M. de Chardon, *Tableau des noms anciens et noms nouveaux des promenades, places publiques, boulevards, rues anciennes et rues nouvelles de la ville de Marseille et de ses faubourgs, avec leurs aboutissans et leurs diverses dénominations pendant la révolution*, 2nd ed. (Marseille: Chez Chardon, 1820), 53.

30 Scott, *Terror and Repression*, 13 and 100.

31 "In the name of thirty truly respected *citoyennes*, we make a proposition worthy of patriotism to the assembly . . . The *citoyènes* [sic] Levent, Giraud Ambroise, Fabre, Moutte, Anne Richaud, Labondance, Constantin, Morland, Revotte, Icard, Roux, Bonnet, Blanchin, Antelme, Cauvière, Frison, Cazatty, Jary, Mourgand, Dauphin, Godener, etc. offer to work freely [to make] shirts, spats, and other pieces of equipment for the volunteers . . . They ask to establish their *gynécée* [female lodging] in one of the large rooms of the former convent of the Bernardines"; *Journal des départements méridionaux, et des Débats des Amis de la Constitution de Marseille* (*JDM*) 93: 380. For connections to the Dames citoyennes in 1790, Levent was likely Louise Levant; Anne, Louise, Marie and Marguerite Fabre were members; Morland may have been Françoise Morand; Revaute was probably Thérèse Revotte; and Icard was likely Clairon Icard; Françoise Roux and Françoise Frison had also been members; Anne Anselme in 1790 may have been Antelme.

32 Knibiehler, "Femmes de Provence," 1:149.

33 *Délibération des Dames Citoyennes du district de Saint-Martin, no.* 7 (Marseille: Imprimerie de J. Moissy, 1790), 3–4, *KVR 12346 New York Public Library (NYPL), http://e-mediatheque.mmsh.univ-aix.fr/Collection/imprimes/espeut/Pages/FR_MMSH_MDQ_HPE_BR_008-13.aspx.

34 Scott, *Terror and Repression*, 16.

35 Knibiehler, "Femmes de Provence," 1:149; Marie-Jeanne Barral was married to Joseph Boude, a tailor. Georges Reynaud, "CAVALE (la), Caval Thérèse épouse Agaud," in *Dictionnaire des Marseillaises*, ed. Renée Dray-Bensousan, Hélène Echinard, Catherine Marand-Fouquet, and Éliane Richard (Marseille: Éditions Gaussen, 2012), 77.

36 L320 indemnity petition 1793, Archives départementales, Bouches-du-Rhône (AD, B-du-Rh).

37 Scott, *Terror and Repression*, 15. *Bourgeois* was a legal category in France and used in the revolutionary census records. Sarah Maza notes that in eighteenth-century France the bourgeois "juridical status was usually based on some combination of fiscal privilege, hereditary rights, and enforced idleness." *The Myth of the French Bourgeoisie: An Essay on the Social Imaginary, 1750–1850* (Cambridge, MA: Harvard University Press, 2003), 22–3.

38 Archives municipales de Marseille (AMdM), 2 F 13.

39 *Discours des Dames Héroïnes de la Ville de Marseille, envoyé à l'Assemblée Nationale, concernant la Bénédiction du Drapeau du No. 11, a l'occasion du Serment Civique prêté par elles le 15 juillet* . . ., 2. * KVR 12319 NYPL.

40 *Revue de Marseille et de Provence* (Marseille: Marius Olive, 1869), 188–90, https://books.google.com/books/about/Revue_de_Marseille_et_de_Provence.html?id=7MsWAAAAYAAJ. As part of the altar for the Festival of the Federation on July 14, 1790, a statue representing Marseille was erected and two of the inscriptions on the face of the pedestal praised the taking of the *Bastille* in Paris and of Fort Notre Dame de la Garde in Marseille.

41 *Délibération des Dames Citoyennes*, 1–2. Meeting of July 7, 1790.

42 *Délibération des Dames Citoyennes*, 2. Godineau highlights that women's voting was "above all symbolic: without being illegal it did not have any legal weight and they knew it . . . they transformed a private act—the personal adhesion to the constitution by an individual excluded from [full] citizenship—into a public act from which . . . *citoyennes* inscribed themselves into the body politic," "Femmes en Citoyenneté: Pratiques et Politique," *AHRF* 300 (1995): 201–2.

43 The size of the National Guard in the processional on July 14 led authorities to schedule a second day. For a gender analysis of the Festival, see Talamante, "Les Marseillaises: Women and Political Change during the French Revolution, 1789–1794," 74–87.

44 *Serment Fédératif National Proclamation de la Municipalité* (Marseille: Mossy, 1790), 6, NYPL.

45 Felix Reynaud, "Du Comte au Royaume (1423–1596)," in *Histoire de Marseille*, ed. Edouard Baratier (Toulouse: Privat, 1973), 126.

46 *Discours des Dames Héroïnes*, 4.

47 *Discours prononcé dans l'Eglise des Dominicains, à l'occasion de la bénédiction du Drapeau du Bataillon No. 11 des Dames de Marseille, pour la cérémonie du Serment civique* (Marseille: Mossy, 1790), 6.

48 Scott, *Terror and Repression*, 79.

49 Knibiehler, "Femmes de Provence," 1:150. Struggles between Lieutaud and the municipality resulted from Lieutaud's creation of a military council, where he

issued decrees and proclamations without the approval of the municipal authorities. Kennedy, *The Jacobin Club of Marseilles*, 78.

50 Knibiehler, "Femmes de Provence," 1:150.

51 BN, *Journal de Provence* 37 (July 22, 1790): 280.

52 For details about the women's protest at the prison in section 18 on May 17, 1790, see *Journal de Provence* 8 (May 20, 1790): 63.

53 Kennedy, *The Jacobin Club of Marseilles*, 72–3.

54 "Dénonciation du Sr. André par les dames citoyennes de la section de St. Martin No 7," in *Cahiers de Doléances des Femmes en 1789 et autres textes*, ed. Paule-Marie Duhet (Paris: Des femmes, 1981), 163–7.

55 Scott, *Terror and Repression*, 72–3.

56 L. M. Lautard, *Esquisses historiques: Marseille depuis 1789 jusqu'en 1815* (Marseille: n.p., 1844), 1:128–9; Georges Reynaud, "CAYOLE, Caillol Françoise, épouse Suchon," in *Dictionnaire des Marseillaises*, 77; *JDM* 2 (March 8, 1792): 8.

57 Sutherland, *Murder in Aubagne*, 70.

58 Reynaud, "CAYOLE," *Dictionnaire des Marseillaises*, 77.

59 *JDM* 4 (March 13, 1792): 15.

60 *JDM* 4 (March 13, 1792): 15.

61 *JDM* 5 (March 15, 1792): 18.

62 *JDM* 11 (March 29, 1792): 43.

63 *JDM* 25 (May 1, 1792): 102.

64 Martine Lapied, "Peut-on considérer les femmes comme une minorité politique?," in *Minorités politiques en Révolution (1789–1799)*, ed. Christine Peyrard (Aix-en-Provence: Publications de l'Université de Provence, 2008), 134–5.

65 Scott, *Terror and Repression*, 100.

66 Quote translated from Jacques Guilhaumou's "Conduites politiques," 478.

67 Guilhaumou, "Conduites politiques," 478.

68 Scott, *Terror and Repression*, 79.

69 Scott, *Terror and Repression*, 79.

70 Jacques Guilhaumou, *Marseillaises: Vingt-six siècles d'Histoire*, ed. Renée Dray-Bensousan, Hélène Echinard, Régine Goutalier, Catherine Marand-Fouquet, Eliane Richard, and Huguette Vidalou-Latreille (Aix-en-Provence: Édisud, 1999), 74.

71 Scott, *Terror and Repression*, 100, 17, and 119 respectively.

72 AD, B-du-Rh, L3114, no. 80 (December 9, 1793) and L3110, no. 15 (October 29, 1793).

73 AD, B-du-Rh, L3114, no. 80.

74 David Garrioch, "The Everyday Lives of Parisian Women and the October Days of 1789," *Social History* 24 (1999): 241.

75 AD, B-du-Rh, L3114, no. 80.

76 Lapied, "Parole publique des femmes," 60.

77 AD, B-du-Rh, L3114, no. 80.

78 AD, B-du-Rh, L3114, no. 80.

79 David Garrioch, *Neighbourhood and Community in Paris, 1740–1790* (Cambridge: Cambridge University Press, 1986), 43.

80 AD, B-du-Rh, L307-314. L334[bis] provides names and amounts only. All women listed from Marseille are included in the data and a random selection of women from the surrounding region.

81 Lapied, "Peut-on considérer les femmes comme une minorité politique?" 135.

82 Only seventy-eight records list a reason for the indemnity, and seventy-four women listed having to flee.

83 Elisabeth Tanéron Fassy was associated with the Dames patriotes; Françoise Mauran and Victoire Marie Lambert were members of the Dames citoyennes in 1790. Thérèse Agaud Cavale, Claire Burle, Rose Maillet, and Elisabeth Cauvière were associated with both groups.

84 Scott, *Terror and Repression*, 119.

85 Talamante, "Political Divisions, Gender, and Politics: The Case of Revolutionary Marseille," *French History* 31, no. 1 (2017): 76.

86 AD, B-du-Rh, L3122 (March 18, 1794).

87 Brie, *Les femmes marseillaises devant la justice sous la Révolution*, 23.

88 Guilhaumou, "Conduites politiques," 473–5.

89 Guilhaumou, "Conduites politiques," 476.

90 Guilhaumou, "Conduites politiques," 488.

3

Emigration, Landlords, and Tenants in Revolutionary Paris

Hannah Callaway

Louis-Sébastien Mercier, an eighteenth-century author who wrote about Paris as he knew it, described the city as a giant beehive:

> At midday when the streets are crowded, you wonder how all these people are to find beds for the night. The town is like a hive, where each insect has its cell; but in these human hives the cells are by no means equally distributed. Here you see ten human insects in one; while another insect can house animals to draw him, and cooks to feed him richly, and has sixty times the amount of space to himself.[1]

These lines speak to the great inequalities in French society at the end of the Old Regime. They also point to the importance of living arrangements as an aspect of social and cultural life. Where people live, and how they live, shapes the relationships they have, their health, and their outlook on the world. The city of Paris grew rapidly in the eighteenth century: the population expanded from around 500,000 in 1700 to 1714 to roughly 600,000–700,000 in 1789; meanwhile, relentless building transformed streetscapes across the city and reconfigured interior spaces.[2] A burgeoning real estate market created opportunities for investment, and building management became professionalized with the presence of concierges in apartment buildings. How did Parisians secure lodging, and where did they stay? Who else lived around them, and what kinds of relationships did people have with neighbors, landlords, or building employees? How were the spatial inequalities that characterized housing in Old Regime Paris affected by the Revolution of 1789?

Paris was a city of renters. Among salaried, working people, 90 percent lived in rented lodgings.[3] The capital resembled many other urban centers—

and much of rural France—in the sense that the majority of peasants were tenants. But while we know about rural landholding and the tensions between tenants and landlords in those settings, relations between urban tenants and landlords have remained something of a black box.[4] Unlike in rural areas, where feudal lords and their tenants belonged to distinct social categories, landlords and tenants in the city represented a range of the social spectrum. Renting and owning were aspects of the financial strategies individuals adopted. Renting could mean finding the cheapest place to live, or it might offer greater flexibility to someone who could otherwise afford to own. Owning, for some, meant securing a place to operate a business; for others, real estate presented an investment opportunity.

The Revolution interrupted these practices, upending life in some buildings and breaking off long-standing relationships between landlords and tenants. In Paris, property seizures undertaken as part of the revolutionary political agenda had real and immediate consequences for the people who lived in buildings that were targeted. The sources of property seizure show the ways it disrupted building life and the finances of a broad array of people, some the direct targets of the seizure process, but many not. While some people were financially ruined, others found ways to gain from the chaos. As such, the sources show us the impact of the Revolution on daily life in Paris. But they do more than this. The disruption meant that people talked about issues that otherwise would have been too mundane to discuss, such as how and when to pay rent. Historical sources produced by unusual moments, such as social upheaval, can also inform us about regular, everyday life.

Information about daily life in the past can come from unexpected sources, and the records of revolutionary property seizure are a good example of this. Members of the revolutionary legislature did not intend to gather information about landlords and tenants. In fact, in February 1792 they were focused on national politics when they passed the first law calling for property to be seized from anyone who was absent from the country—a category that came to be known as the émigrés. Tensions with the Austro-Hungarian Empire were escalating, and lawmakers feared that French citizens fleeing over the border would help France's enemies.[5] Seizing property seemed like the best way to punish those who had already left and stop others from leaving. In July 1792, legislators followed this up with another law allowing seized property to be sold. In the months and years that followed, additional categories of people were subjected to the laws against émigrés, including Spaniards, Englishmen, residents of the southern French port city of Toulon, and individuals condemned by the Revolutionary Tribunal.[6] As the category of "émigré" grew more expansive and the process of actually separating people from their belongings got underway, hundreds more laws were passed. In 1802, Napoleon Bonaparte finally granted a general amnesty to everyone who had been counted as an émigré. Under the Restoration, families received an indemnity for lost assets, and about half the seized properties were returned.[7]

In the city of Paris, around 1,600 pieces of real estate were seized from roughly 900 people who had been counted as émigrés. A branch of the Ministry of Finances, the Domains bureau, oversaw administration of the seizure process. In Paris, officials in the Domains bureau worked closely with members of the municipal government to identify émigré property, secure it, and sell it at auction. The Director of Domains oversaw a staff of receivers in neighborhood offices around Paris, as well as architects, a bailiff to serve papers, and a verifier, who helped chase down important paperwork. Everyone communicated by letter, producing an extensive written record of the seizure process. Much of this material was burned in 1871 during the turmoil of the Paris Commune, which destroyed most of the Paris city archives as well as national financial records. Still, a good deal of information survives in the form of office correspondence.

The sources of revolutionary property seizure have drawbacks, just like any historical source. There is a great deal of information, but that doesn't mean that we have all of it. For example, the most problematic situations naturally attracted more attention from officials and generated more paperwork than situations where everything went according to plan.[8] This means we may get the impression that relations between landlords and tenants were more contentious than they really were. Reading the dossiers, it seems as if no one ever paid rent, and as if all kinds of people were constantly pilfering from buildings: in one case, a gardener was accused of stealing grass from the yard of a seized mansion.[9] There were probably plenty of happy tenants and harmonious buildings, but situations where something went wrong have greater archival visibility because officials spent most of their time dealing with them.

The sources highlight two central features of residential life in Paris. First, they show the diverse ways real estate could generate money, either for landlords or for others, including tenants. Many landlords owned a number of properties including Paris buildings and farmland outside the city; tenants leased entire buildings and sublet them to generate income. Administrators in the revolutionary State approached real estate in the same way, looking for ways to draw revenue out of seized properties before they could be sold. Second, the sources of property seizure show us the enduring but evolving information networks centered in residential buildings. In properties owned by émigrés, the Revolution disrupted the relationships that anchored building life, in particular by breaking up the informal relationships by which landlords and tenants negotiated leases and handled rent payments. And yet, the revolutionary State also recognized the importance of building staff as both sources of information and figures of authority in their buildings. Whereas previously information had flowed along multiple channels and various people had been responsible for aspects of building life, when the State stepped in the concierge became the central figure. In the context of the Revolution, local information such as a person's reputation in the neighborhood became extremely valuable. In many cases, officials' success in extracting revenue from seized properties depended on their ability to tap into this kind of intelligence.

The chapter is divided into three sections. First, we'll learn about living arrangements in Paris, including neighborhoods, social divisions, and the kinds of buildings and apartments people lived in. Next, we'll consider who owned residential buildings and how they were managed, looking at real estate as an asset and exploring the role of the concierge in overseeing building life. Finally, we'll examine how the Revolution intervened in the lives of tenants and building staff in properties that were subject to seizure.

Tenants, Landlords, and Building Life

The experience of being a tenant was common to the majority of Parisians, but it differed greatly depending on who a person was. Differences of wealth, region of origin, and profession distinguished how and where people lived, from servants housed in attic rooms, to seasonal laborers sharing furnished lodgings in boarding houses, to financiers occupying impressive mansions, or merchants operating their business out of the ground floor of an apartment building they owned in its entirety. Over the course of the eighteenth century, physical changes to the city and to interior spaces afforded greater anonymity and more opportunities for private retreat indoors. Still, one factor of city life held constant: personal space was slim to none, and as a result, neighbors knew a great deal about each other's lives.

The neighborhoods of Paris in the centuries preceding the Revolution had strong individual characters.[10] They differed in the types of residents, their activities, and the physical structures that could be found there. For example, the Marais, a neighborhood near the river on the northern or Right Bank of the Seine, was filled with aristocratic mansions built in the seventeenth century. Slightly to the west, in the rue de la Mortellerie, the grain merchants of Paris lived in close proximity to one another.[11] To the east, in the Faubourg Saint-Antoine, one could find furniture makers at work in their shops. Booksellers plied their trade in the area around the Sainte-Geneviève church on the Left Bank (see Map 0.2 for some of these neighborhoods of Paris).[12]

Across the city, a large proportion of residents had come to Paris from elsewhere in France. Young men and women both came to enter apprenticeships or domestic service, or to engage in seasonal labor; migrants arriving in Paris were on average twenty-two to twenty-four years old.[13] Young people did not marry until they had some financial independence (outside of the wealthiest families, daughters earned their own dowries by working), so marriages took place when couples were in their mid- to late twenties.[14] Workers arriving in Paris sought out compatriots from their home regions, creating mini-neighborhoods representing the different parts of France. Some neighborhoods had a particularly high concentration of furnished rooms for rent, where workers arriving in Paris could stay while they found something more permanent, and where seasonal workers could get temporary lodging.[15]

Many different types of lodging could be found spread through the floors of a single building.[16] Generally the first level above the ground floor had the highest ceilings, largest windows, and most elaborate decorative elements. These apartments were occupied by nobles or other wealthy elites. As one climbed higher, ceilings became lower and rooms smaller. Working people engaged as apprentices, street vendors, and laundresses might rent these apartments. In the top floor attic rooms, domestic servants lived above the families they worked for.[17] Over the course of the eighteenth century, however, social classes increasingly segregated into different neighborhoods, mostly because the wealthy moved west into newly developing areas of the city.[18]

This diversity of living arrangements was matched by an array of agreements between tenants and landlords. There were three types of possible arrangement in Paris buildings: renting an apartment directly from the landlord; renting an entire building as "principal renter" and subletting out the apartments; or subletting an apartment from a principal renter.[19] In many buildings, the principal renter was a merchant or artisan renting ground floor commercial space; landlords usually leased the entire building as a package with the ground floor. The standard lease under French common law ran for three, six, or nine years and renewed automatically. Some tenants signed a formal lease, others simply made verbal agreements.

Renters could be found at every income level, as even people with plenty of money found it more convenient to rent than to own. Wealthy nobles and financiers rented mansions rather than buying them, so as to have a house in the latest style, in the hottest neighborhood.[20] Renting gave greater flexibility than owning, though most wealthy renters likely owned real estate elsewhere. For the poor, renting meant precariousness rather than flexibility. Housing in Paris was expensive and became more so over the course of the century.[21] At the same time, people struggled to earn a stable income. Many worked seasonally, and there was little protection against being fired or injured at work. Uncertain income, rising rents, and fluctuating food prices meant that many people had to move frequently as they fell behind on rent or were evicted.

If tenants matched the diversity of the Paris population, landlords represented a much smaller group. Many buildings were owned by master craftsmen, who were successful enough in their trades to diversify their assets with a real estate investment. Particularly well-off merchants or craftsmen might own several buildings in the same neighborhood. A good number of buildings were owned by nobles, most of whom also had real estate outside of Paris. These people generally lived in a private house in a chic neighborhood, and the buildings they owned might be scattered around the city. Finally, the eighteenth century witnessed the appearance of real estate speculators, investors who put up new buildings and then either sold them off or leased them. The wave of construction that sent up a cloud of pollution over the city from about 1765 onward increased house prices overall, and also increased the spread in prices: the newest buildings were much more expensive than older buildings in the center of the city.[22]

Every building in Paris had a courtyard, and apartment buildings had an external, shared staircase. The mansions of the wealthy were situated "between courtyard and garden": they were separated from the street by a high wall with heavy wooden doors, which led into a courtyard at the front of the house. In the back, a large walled garden provided relief from the noise and smells of the city. Other buildings were made up of multiple structures distributed around a courtyard; there would be one building fronting the street and then a smaller construction behind it, across the courtyard. People entered the building through a long, narrow passageway leading back to the courtyard, and the two halves of the building would be linked by a shared staircase. Courtyards and staircases were quite public, serving as a kind of extension of the street. Visitors coming and going from the building would pass through; women might be doing laundry or hanging it up; and craftsmen might have a workbench set up in a courtyard or out in the street.

Overall, people had little privacy at home. Neighbors could easily hear disputes in other apartments, and occasionally intervened.[23] Apartments lacked interior corridors, so tenants might have to use the public corridor or staircase to get from one room of their apartment to another. One tenant might have to walk through a neighbor's room to get to their own.[24] Tenants also frequently ran shops out of rooms above street level.[25] Many people shared a single room, and daily activities, from cooking to washing to sleeping, all took place in the same space. Over the course of the century, buildings were increasingly modified to be more private, with features such as interior corridors, so that occupants no longer had to walk through one room to get to another.[26] For those wealthy enough to afford such luxury, rooms were subdivided into smaller areas to create specialized spaces for study or dressing—*cabinets* and *boudoirs*.[27] Specialized furniture such as writing desks and dressing tables might fill these spaces, or mark out an area of privacy in a larger room.[28] Still, for most people, shared spaces were the norm.

Within a single unit, households could be quite heterogeneous. Employers and their employees often shared housing; as we've seen, many servants lived in their masters' homes. It was also common for master artisans, such as seamstresses, to lodge apprentices or journeymen in their homes.[29] Though men and women both exercised trades, women were more likely to do piecework out of their homes, whereas men either lived with the master craftsman who employed them or ran their own shop.[30] Workers who couldn't afford their own apartment or who had only recently arrived in Paris shared furnished rooms in boarding houses. Households could also contain multiple generations of a family or a random assortment of relatives, as young people arriving in the city moved in with a sibling, cousin, or other family member. Intergenerational households were quite common in noble families, where young married couples often lived with the wife's family.[31] Overall, more women lived in the city than men, mostly because the majority of servants were female.[32] Young, unmarried women were more likely to live with their families as their sexuality was policed more heavily than that of young, unmarried men, who were apprenticed and lived with their employers. Older unmarried or widowed women sometimes lived alone, but also commonly shared space with other women, either employees, lodgers, or relatives, in small household arrangements.[33]

Owning and Managing Real Estate in Eighteenth-century Paris

Real estate in Paris not only provided people with a place to live, but also represented a significant financial asset. Houses and apartment buildings figured in the financial portfolios of owners among a diverse, interdependent array of assets. Even people who didn't own directly, such as tenants, found ways to profit from real estate through loans or subletting. The desire to turn a profit could put tenants and landlords at odds, leading to unpaid rent and eviction. But large assets such as real estate also linked people together in various ways, such as shared ownership of assets within a family, or credit arrangements between landlords and tenants. An apartment building was not only a place for people to live; as an economic asset, it also tied together the interests of an array of people who depended on it for shelter or for profit. Building staff who lived on site contributed to this dynamic. They assisted landlords in managing tenants, which meant knowing everything about what was going on in the building. At the same time, they lived alongside tenants and, like them, depended on the goodwill of the building owner.

Before the eighteenth century, real estate had been essentially something a person inherited. Over the course of the century, however, a market for real estate grew in parts of France.[34] This expansion occurred alongside the development and expansion of credit networks, which allowed people to invest their money and to leverage assets to raise capital. Credit and debt were an important part of many people's investment strategy, and there were many opportunities to either lend out money or borrow it. Lending at interest was illegal, but loans could be structured with fees over a fixed period. These "fees" might amount to 5 percent of the value of the loan. Real estate generated revenue and was a good place to store capital. The value of a piece of real estate, however, lay not only in the revenue it could generate, but also in the debt that it could secure. Mortgaging real assets generated capital for other investments.

Paris presented a particular opportunity for investing in real estate, because people came from across France to live there. Nobles or administrators in the royal bureaucracy chose to have a home in Paris in addition to their home in the provinces. Many nobles who left France and lost their property in the Revolution had approached real estate in just this way. Anne-Gabriel Bernard exemplifies the fate of many Parisian property owners who saw their wealth seized in the 1790s.[35] A magistrate in the Paris court, he came from an old noble family. At the time of the Revolution, his son Charles emigrated from France. This meant that when Bernard died in 1798, the family property was seized by the State, because by law émigrés could not inherit property. Bernard owned properties in the southwest of France, near Bordeaux (see Map 0.1). He also owned five buildings in Paris, all rented out, as well as two houses in the neighboring countryside. While he was alive, he lived in a home he owned in Normandy. The five houses were all seized; two were sold and three ultimately returned to Bernard's heirs.

From an accounting of his total assets, we can see that Bernard's Paris real estate was just one part of a diverse portfolio. Out of forty-two total assets, only twelve were real estate.[36] More than half of his wealth was in cash, annuities, and a noble office, which was considered property until 1789, when nobility was abolished. The value of Bernard's assets is estimated based on their revenue, which tells us something important about the property he did own. The houses and buildings were expected to earn a profit; they were not all homes he lived in. In fact, one of the buildings in Paris was a particularly large market filled with commercial and residential tenants.

Whatever a person's level of wealth, people who could afford to own in Paris generally also owned some type of land outside the city. Of course, Bernard was far wealthier than most people. He did resemble many other Parisian owners, though, in that he owned land in the provinces as well as urban real estate. Wealthy financiers who did not already have family property invested in feudal lands and châteaux in the countryside near Paris as well as in Parisian homes and, perhaps, real estate in a provincial city.[37] Successful merchants or artisans might own the building where they lived and worked, perhaps another one nearby, and some rural land as well.[38]

The capacity for real estate to generate revenue was particularly important, because in many families ownership was shared. As in the Bernard family, it was not uncommon for siblings and cousins to own real estate together. In Paris and in many parts of northern France in the Old Regime, siblings inherited from their parents equally.[39] This meant that family property was divided up every time it changed hands. Every time a new generation inherited, ownership expanded to include more brothers, sisters, and cousins. As the number of heirs grew, assets could be sold and the proceeds shared, or held onto collectively with the revenue shared over time. In some families, ownership became quite diffuse; one émigré owned one-sixteenth of two separate buildings.[40] A single building could support a variety of people in different ways. For example, a property could serve as the base for a business, while also generating rental income from upstairs apartments. Or, a parent might own a building but allow a child the right to live there with their own family. Such arrangements were often formalized in a marriage contract, where the gift of residency represented an asset among the other gifts and inheritances of cash or property settled on each of the newlyweds by their respective families.

Tenants could benefit from the financial potential of real estate in a variety of ways. Those who had a personal relationship with their landlord might be able to negotiate extra time to pay rent, which would free up their financial resources for other investments, such as a business, or allow them to survive in a period of unemployment. In other cases, though, tenants paid as much as a year in advance—a good strategy for someone who received a windfall of cash and wanted to hedge against future uncertainty. Or, a tenant might pay a large lump sum to his landlord and deduct rent from it. Unexpected opportunities could arise from the financial relations between landlord and tenant; such was the case for Anne Goislard, known by her married name as Widow Planoy, who lived in a building near the Cathedral of Notre-Dame (see Map 0.2). She loaned her landlord some money, and when he died and his estate turned out to be in debt, she leveraged her relatively small loan to buy the entire building.[41] She was the widow of a royal official and her landlord was a noble, so their relatively similar social standing may have given landlord and tenant more cause for interaction than usual. Many people, however, both lent and borrowed money to and from friends, relatives, or strangers.

Life in many apartment buildings was overseen by a live-in employee, a doorkeeper (*portier*), concierge or guardian (*gardien*). These jobs were relatively rare until the eighteenth century, when they became a fixture of building life throughout the city.[42] The concierge lived in a room or small apartment on the ground floor, generally rent-free, in exchange for managing tenants and overseeing the physical spaces of the building. Whereas concierges in large or wealthy buildings might be employed full time, *gardiens* in smaller buildings often exercised a profession alongside their duties, such as keeping a shop on the ground floor. In these situations, a married couple might share the job, with the husband running the boutique while the wife sat in the *loge*, the small apartment with a view of the courtyard assigned to the concierge. The vast majority of concierges in Paris, however, were older and single, or widowed, and many were women.

The concierge was generally the first person a prospective tenant came into contact with. The concierge might collect rent, hand over keys to a new resident, pass along requests for maintenance to the landlord, or serve as a source of information on happenings in and around the building. Until the end of the nineteenth century, the primary way to look for an apartment was to walk up and down the streets and ask the concierge in each building if there were any vacancies.[43] The concierge might size a person up before responding; this became particularly common in the nineteenth century, when the concierge had become a ubiquitous feature of urban life. Pets and children under seven were grounds for rejecting a prospective tenant; more generally, concierges might try to determine whether prospective tenants could pay the rent.[44]

Extracting revenue from a rental building necessitated keeping a close eye on building life. This meant paying attention to who left a building as much as watching who came in. Debtors could have their furniture and possessions seized, so tenants who owed rent often elected to sneak out in the middle of the night, escaping with their belongings under cover of darkness. Lienard, a concierge in the large apartment complex of the Palais-Royal (see Map 0.2), only discovered that a tenant had moved out when he went to show the apartment to the new landlord. The key was in the door and the apartment had been emptied; the tenant left behind only a pile of refuse including dirty rags, dishes, and some old furniture.[45]

Building Concierges and the Paris Information Economy

Administrators in the revolutionary government came face to face with the details of building life as they worked to carry out the property seizure laws. Officials intervened in building life as they carried out the laborious process of identifying absent citizens, locating their property, and placing it under State administration. Concierges proved to be key figures who could assist the State as it interposed itself in place of the landlord, or impede it by withholding what they knew. Officials needed information about tenants and building accounts in order to successfully take over ownership and begin collecting revenue from seized properties. As they broke up informal arrangements between landlords and tenants, and coopted concierges, they imposed more formal, impersonal arrangements in affected buildings.

In Paris, officials in the Domains bureau coordinated with representatives from the city government in seizing and managing émigré properties. When a building belonging to an émigré was found empty, municipal officials placed seals on the doors; if tenants lived there, a bailiff served them papers ordering them to start paying rent to the Domains bureau. But identifying properties and taking over their administration was just the beginning of the process. Generating revenue remained a central imperative for officials to offset the cost of the war between France and the Austro-Hungarian Empire. This meant, in particular, collecting rent from tenants during the often lengthy period that preceded the sale of a seized building.

Simply informing tenants of the new ownership of a building posed challenges. In the spring of 1793, the Domains Director noted that his staff "undertook the procedures to require the tenants who occupy [these] houses to pay their rent into the agency's coffers, but up to the present nothing has come in."[46] Some tenants had no idea their landlord had disappeared, because they did not pay rent directly to him. Inside the Domains bureau, clerks produced registers and inventories to keep track of buildings, tenants, and rent payments. Lacking knowledge about buildings and inhabitants, it was hard for them to manage the kind of detailed, personal information that anyone living in a building would easily know. When they needed to find out about a local landlord they believed had emigrated, or when they distrusted a building employee's loyalties, administrators made use of local knowledge or tapped into networks of neighborhood gossip.

The building concierge was of central importance to administrators seeking to gather local intelligence. The large building on the Left Bank owned by Anne-Gabriel Bernard, known as the Gray Musketeers Market (see Map 0.2), housed hundreds of tenants in a mixture of apartments and storefronts. The Director of the Domains hoped to appoint one of his own officials, a man named Barbié, to take charge of the building, but the existing concierge, named Petitpierre, argued that he should keep his job:

> . . . because Citizen Barbié does not have personal knowledge of the capabilities of the tenants who number more than 200, doesn't know in detail the spaces that they occupy, the necessary result will be a considerable deficit on the rentals, which also must be monitored, as a large number of tenants could move out without paying rent; also Citizen Barbié does not know the cost of the rent, and cannot manage things himself, handling arrivals and departures, or avoiding loss of revenue through vacant shops, apartments, rooms. He also can't devote himself to a slew of minute details of management. It will be better for the interests of the Republic and for the heirs of the émigré to leave [Petitpierre] in charge of the market.[47]

In seeking to justify why he should keep his job, Petitpierre gives information in his letter about the tasks handled by a concierge. First, there were administrative tasks such as finding tenants for empty apartments or handing over the keys to new arrivals. In addition, he dealt with accounting responsibilities such as tracking how much everyone owed and collecting rent. Finally, there was the critical task of general surveillance of the building, including making sure no one moved out on the sly and monitoring the "capabilities" of the tenants—this probably meant their ability to pay the coming term of rent.

Situated as they were at the center of building life, concierges were also crucial agents in the information economy of Paris. Word of mouth was central to the circulation of information, and it moved through interlocking networks of communities.[48] Tenants in a building, shopkeepers and vendors in the street, or patrons at a café were just some of the communities that circulated information through the capital. On the street, in a building staircase, at work or at leisure, conversations and exchanges were constantly observed or overheard. Rumor spurred major political events, triggering the storming of the Bastille and the September massacres, among many other popular movements. The best way to get information about what was happening was from well-informed people, such as concierges, who gained a kind of authority.

Concierges were a valuable source of information for Domains officials in regard to their own building or others in the neighborhood. When the buyer of a confiscated building stopped making payments and disappeared, an architect from the Domains bureau walked up and down the street, asking concierges, shopkeepers, and the local post office for information.[49] In another situation, the architect learned from a concierge that a confiscated building had been restored to its owner, a piece of information that even the Domains officials didn't have. Some concierges delivered up information about their absent émigré employers to Domains officials. Claude Joseph Redy, the concierge of a house belonging to an émigré, was "very known in this capacity," according to one official.[50] He was appointed to guard the seals placed on the doors and windows of the house after it was seized, to prevent anyone from entering and taking things away. When questioned by the local justice of the peace about his boss, Redy informed the official that he had left the country in September 1792 and had not been heard from since.

Just as the concierge kept tabs on his tenants and the neighborhood, the tenants monitored his activities. When officials needed information about a seized property, the best option was simply to send someone there in person to ask around. After visiting a seized building, one Domains official wrote to another about the building's *portier*, Santier: "according to the information that I gathered from the tenants of this building and from neighbors, this concierge is quite exact and very assiduous in fulfilling the duties that this place requires."[51] The use of agents to be the eyes and ears on the ground had been a well-established practice in Old Regime Paris. The city swarmed with police spies, known as *mouches* or "flies" because they were always buzzing around—in cafés, under the trees at the Palais-Royal, or anywhere people gathered and rumors circulated.[52] Surveillance took on added importance in the tense atmosphere of revolutionary Paris when saying the wrong thing could get a person arrested, and no one could be certain who was a friend and who was an enemy.

Government officials had reason to be skeptical of concierges found working in émigré buildings because they were generally loyal to their employers. In many cases where the owner of a building emigrated during the Revolution, the concierge remained on the job even after receiving no wages for several years.[53] In response to the concierge Petitpierre's letter about the Musketeers Market, the Domains director wrote to a subordinate that "the nature of this property and its revenues requires that an agent of the Police should be committed to it to watch over the tenants and the buildings."[54] In August 1798, Petitpierre was accused of furnishing faulty information to a bailiff about the number of tenants living in the building. Officials forced his wife to hand over the master register of building occupants. Yet the register in the end exonerated the concierge, as it showed that the Domains had gotten confused by tenants who were subletting, meaning they didn't pay rent directly to the landlord. The officials therefore wrote to the Director, "We think that Citizen Petitpierre can keep his duties as concierge. The knowledge he has of the place should determine the administration in his favor."[55] On the one hand, officials weren't sure if they could trust concierges in seized buildings; on the other hand, they couldn't afford to fire them, because they knew the ins and outs of life in the building like no one else.

Concierges' knowledge was especially important because so many tenants negotiated informal, oral agreements with their landlords. Officials gathered information about these arrangements, and then took steps to cancel them, placing tenants on formal leases. In one building, the widow Bryère occupied the entire second and third floors under a lease she had signed with her landlord, but was three years behind on her rent.[56] Meanwhile, her downstairs neighbor, *Citoyenne* des Jardins, lived on the first floor with no lease and paid no rent. It's possible that Jardins, who had no lease, moved into the building amidst the chaos of the Revolution and was simply squatting there. Similarly, Bryère may have stopped paying rent when her landlord disappeared. Whatever arrangements these tenants may have had with their landlord, the Revolution intervened. The Domains planned to evict Jardins when her upstairs neighbor's lease expired; since she herself had no lease, she could make no claim to stay in her apartment. Officials also began pursuing Bryère to pay her back rent.

Bryère and Jardins were women living alone, like the Widow Planoy whom we met earlier. This situation was relatively common in Old Regime Paris; Bryère and Planoy, who were both referred to as widows by Domains officials, likely already lived alone before the Revolution. The events of the Revolution, however, made it even more common for women to live alone and manage their own affairs. This was in part because many men, like Jardins' husband, volunteered or enlisted to fight in the Revolutionary Wars. In families where one or more male members emigrated, women often remained behind to manage family property. Unlike the wife of a soldier, however, the wife or mother of an émigré dealt with the revolutionary government on an adversarial basis. It was her job to protect family assets against State seizure. This could require craftiness as much as business sense. For example, the Widow Morys had the use of a house that belonged to her and her husband. Although she lived in part of it, the State had seized an interest in the house and officials wanted to collect rent on the part the widow was not occupying. Morys engaged a lawyer to sue for the whole house, but, in the meantime, she managed to prevent any new renters from moving in by behaving rudely toward a potential tenant who came to see the apartment. The would-be tenant told the Domains bureau he needed to talk to his wife before making a decision, and never came back.[57]

Simply invoking the authority of the law and transferring legal possession of a building was not enough to entirely take over the benefits of ownership, which included collecting revenue from properties. To do this, the Domains needed to talk to a building's occupants or find other ways of gathering information from the neighborhood. Still, in spite of the difficulties, the Domains imposed more formal management on the tenants in buildings it seized. This meant disrupting long-standing relationships between landlords and tenants. For example, a man named Roland rented three rooms and a storeroom spread over the first, second, and third floors of a building in the Latin Quarter.[58] He had lived in the building since he was born and collected rent for everyone on behalf of his landlord. His father had collected the rent before him, keeping track of payments in a little notebook that his son still used. Roland didn't know what had happened to his landlord, who hadn't come to count the rent in months. The landlord had been arrested and condemned to death by the Revolutionary Tribunal, which gave him the legal status of an émigré and made him subject to property confiscation. Roland wrote to the Domains asking what he should do with the rent money, suggesting he might give it to the landlord's widow and children. Administrators, however, did not plan to send any money to the wife of an émigré whom they viewed as a traitor. The Domains also ended the special arrangement Roland had with his landlord and began collecting rent from each tenant individually.

Property seizure could mean financial ruin for landlords and tenants, but it also promised financial opportunity to people who leased seized properties from the State. As we saw above, real estate offered opportunities for investment and leveraging even to people who did not actually own. Lead tenants sought to turn a profit by leasing an entire building and then renting out individual apartments. One such person, Jean Brousse, signed dozens of leases with the Domains for seized properties. He planned to rent them out for a tidy profit. Unfortunately, he ran into all the varieties of bad luck that a landlord might face. First, when taking possession of a confiscated apartment in the Palais-Royal, he discovered that the tenant had moved out in the night, leaving unpaid rent. Then it turned out the building needed repairs. The sewage ditch had overflowed into the basement, causing damage. Finally, he got embroiled in a lawsuit with a tenant who refused to pay his rent. Brousse ended up losing all his money, and his furniture was seized and sold off to satisfy his creditors. His case reveals the potential perils of investing in real estate seized by the State. Property seizure created an opportunity for Brousse to invest, but the uncertainties of the Revolution may have also magnified the risks.

Conclusion

The impact of émigré legislation on landlords and tenants reflects just how deeply the Revolution affected the lives of people who lived through it. The disruption that property seizure caused in the lives of people who were only tenuously connected to émigrés was one of the many unintended consequences of revolutionary legislation. These changes must be measured alongside the intentional changes to French society brought about by the revolutionaries.

The social fabric in confiscated buildings was torn apart when revolutionary administrators tried to insert themselves into the role of absent landlords. Domains officials needed to collect revenue from seized properties but couldn't simply insert themselves in existing landlord–tenant relationships. Imposing their own terms on tenants, they necessarily changed the status quo, imposing written leases, requiring regular payments, and gathering information from concierges. The legal capacity of the State to impose new requirements on tenants was quite extensive, and yet the success or failure of its operations still depended, at least in part, on how people in the buildings responded. Many likely felt they had no options, but small acts of resistance, like the Widow Morys' rudeness to a prospective tenant, could create problems for administrators. Even so, owners and tenants had nowhere to appeal when revolutionary officials voided their claims.

As they tried to standardize rental agreements and make building life more transparent, officials tapped into local information networks to fill in gaps in their knowledge about building life. They gathered information about landlords, tenants, and concierges; in doing so, they benefitted from information that circulated informally. The concierge, located at the center of information flow, proved a crucial figure in this respect. The ability of administrators to impose control over the building depended on how cooperative the concierge proved to be. When formalized arrangements were imposed on tenants, relationships in a building could become more anonymous. Concierges could contribute to this dynamic by informing on tenants and becoming an instrument of the State's authority. But they did not always do so reliably and continued to defend local knowledge and a sense of place when these were being eroded by the State.

At the end of the Revolution, in the early years of the nineteenth century, seized properties that hadn't been sold were returned to their owners. However, the quantity of property that had changed hands in Paris in the preceding years led to a spate of new development.[59] In addition to properties owned by people subject to the émigré laws, large parcels of land that had belonged to the Catholic Church were bought up by speculators and developed into residential blocks. Concierges and relatively distant building management became the norm in these new, large apartment buildings. The large size of new buildings and the frequency with which tenants turned over meant that residents didn't know each other as well as they had before the Revolution. Other sites of sociability, such as the workplace or bars and cafés, continued to be and became even more important in the circulation of local information. At the same time, the geographical separation of the social classes into separate areas of the city and the growing distance between landlords and tenants contributed to growing class divisions that, over the course of the nineteenth century, contributed to social conflict and a new cycle of revolution.[60]

Source: Overview of Rentals in the Boulainvilliers Market on 24 Fructidor VI (September 10, 1798)

Location	Name of Tenant	Profession	Nature of Lodging: Shops	Rooms	Bedrooms	Alcoves	Cellars	Stalls	Date of Lease	Lease term [in years]	Price [in *livres*]: Per year	Per quarter	Observations
Rue du Bac	Delarue	Hatter	1		1		1		Old lease expired 1/4/1797	3,6,9	1036	259	Holds by tacit renewal, paid Boulainvilliers 518 for 6 mo. advance, against his last 6 mo. of use
Idem [same address as above]	Morel	Grocer	1		2		1		Promised lease 24 Brum. VI	3,6,9	400	300	Paid 100 against 6 mo. advance for last 3 mo. of use
Idem	Veuve Chapy	Pin maker	1						Old lease expired 10/1/1796	"	500	125	[blank]
Idem	Rousseau	Roaster	1		2	2	2		No lease	"	800	200	[blank]
Idem	Lauvray	Wine merchant	1		1		2		Promised lease 1/26/1797	3,6,9	1400	350	Paid Boulainvilliers 700 for 6 mo. advance against last 6 mo. of use
Idem	Albert	Watchmaker	1		1		2		Lease 4/1/1795	3,6,9	400	100	Paid to same 200 for 6 mo. as above
Idem	Mussard	Grocer	1	2	1	2	2		Lease 5/10/1797	3,6,9	2000	500	Paid to same 1000 for 6 mo. as above

Rue de Verneuil	Caillot	Baker	1	1	1		1	Lease 7/1/1796	3,6,9	700	175	Paid to same 350 for 6 mo. advance as above
Idem	Baillot	Cooper	1	1	1	1	1	No lease	”	816	204	He was paid by Raillot his father-in-law 200 and by Baillot his son-in-law 75, against as above
Idem	Huin	Glass maker	1	1	2	1	2	Lease 7/1/1797	3,6,9	800	200	Paid to same 400 for 6 mo. as above
Idem	Mélot	Wig maker	1			2	2	No lease	”	200	50	
Idem	Duchemin	Fruitseller	1		1		1	No lease	”	450	112.10	Paid 112.10 to Boulainvilliers against 3 last months, which only begin 10 Vendémiaire
Idem	Verdieu	Baker	1	1	1	1	1	Lease 4/1/1797	3,6,9	800	200	Paid to same 400 for 6 mo. as above
Idem	Rachi/ Fournier femme de Verneuil	Wine merchant	2	1	2		1	Lease 7/1/1795	3,6,9	1600	400	Paid to same 500 for 6 mo. as above
Rue de Beaune	Bassin	Tanner	1				1	No lease	”	200	50	Paid to same 100 for 6 mo. as above
Idem	Faset	Wig maker	1		1	1	1	1/1/1795	3,6,9	650	162.10	Paid to same 325 for 6 mo. as above

(continued)

Location	Name of Tenant	Profession	Nature of Lodging: Shops	Rooms	Bedrooms	Alcoves	Cellars	Stalls	Date of Lease	Lease term [in years]	Price [in *livres*]: Per year	Per quarter	Observations
Idem	Strumpf	Shoemaker	1		1	1	1		Lease 7/1/1797	3,6,9	300	75	Paid to same 150 for 6 mo. as above
Idem	Gallet	Wood turner	1		1		1		No lease	"	500	125	Paid to same 200 for 3 mo. as above
Idem	Cordonnier	Locksmith	1		1		1		No lease	"	800	200	Paid to same 200 for 3 mo. as above
Idem	Humbert	Fruitseller	1		1		1		Old lease expired 7/1/1797	3,6,9	600	150	Paid to same 150 for 3 mo. as above
Idem	Marneot	Knife grinder	1		2	1	1		Old lease expired 10/1/1796	3,6,9	700	175	Paid to same 175 for 3 mo. as above
Idem	Georges	Lemonade seller	1		1		1		No lease	"	200	50	Paid to same 50 for 3 mo. as above
Idem	Rivière	Fruitseller	1		1		1		Lease 4/1/1797	3,6,9	400	1[illegible]0	Paid to same 200 for 6 mo. as above
Idem	Heuzé	Caterer	1		1	1	1		Lease 10/1/1796	3,6,9	600	1[illegible]0	Paid to same 300 for 6 mo. as above

Courtesy of Hannah Callaway.

Notes

1 Louis-Sébastien Mercier, *Panorama of Paris*, trans. Jeremy Popkin (University Park: Pennsylvania State University Press, 1999), 212.

2 Daniel Roche, *The People of Paris: An Essay in Popular Culture in the 18th Century* (Berkeley: University of California Press, 1987), 19–21. Roche notes that the rate of growth was significantly higher in the seventeenth century; the eighteenth-century expansion was thus "a less brutal and more controlled change."

3 Roche, *The People of Paris*, 104. Annik Pardailhé-Galabrun finds 77 percent of a sample of mixed socio-economic status, *The Birth of Intimacy: Privacy and Domestic Life in Early Modern Paris*, trans. Jocelyn Phelps (Oxford: Polity, 1991), 41.

4 William C. Baer, "Landlords and Tenants in London, 1550–1700," *Urban History* 38, no. 2 (2011): 234.

5 François Furet, *The French Revolution, 1770–1814*, trans. Antonia Nevill, 2nd English ed. (Oxford: Blackwell, 1996), 103.

6 Donald Greer, *The Incidence of the Emigration during the French Revolution* (Cambridge, MA: Harvard University Press, 1951); Patrice Higonnet, *Class, Ideology, and the Rights of Nobles during the French Revolution* (Oxford: Clarendon Press, 1981); see also Miranda Spieler, *Empire and Underworld: Captivity in French Guiana* (Cambridge, MA: Harvard University Press, 2012).

7 Property that had been sold was not returned. André Gain, *La restauration et les biens des émigrés; La législation concernant les biens nationaux de seconde origine et son application dans l'Est de la France (1814–1832)* (Nancy: Société d'Impressions Typographiques, 1928), 544–7.

8 Arlette Farge, *The Allure of the Archives*, trans. Thomas Scott-Railton (New Haven, CT: Yale University Press, 2013), 42–6.

9 Archives de Paris (hereafter AdP) DQ10 709 Boullogne, letter of 6 prairial II.

10 Roche, *The People of Paris*, 97–126; Daniel Roche, *France in the Enlightenment* (Cambridge, MA: Harvard University Press, 1998); David Garrioch, *The Making of Revolutionary Paris* (Berkeley: University of California Press, 2002), 15–44.

11 Steven L. Kaplan, *Provisioning Paris: Merchants and Millers in the Grain and Flour Trade during the Eighteenth Century* (Ithaca, NY: Cornell University Press, 1984), 133–5.

12 Laurence Croq and Nicolas Lyon-Caen, "La notabilité parisienne entre la police et la ville: des définitions aux usages sociaux et politiques," in *La notabilité urbaine Xe-XVIIIe siècles*, ed. Laurence Jean-Marie (Caen: Université de Caen-Basse Normandie, 2007), 135.

13 Roche, *The People of Paris*, 28.

14 Linda A. Pollock, "Parent–Child Relations," in *Family Life in Early Modern Times, 1500–1789, History of the European Family*, ed. David I. Kertzer and Marzio Barbagli (New Haven, CT: Yale University Press, 2001), 1:207–10. The age at first marriage climbed over the eighteenth century; see Jean-Louis

Flandrin, *Families in Former Times: Kinship, Household and Sexuality*, trans. Richard Southern (Ithaca, NY: Cornell University Press, 1979), 186.

15 Daniel Roche, ed., *La ville promise: mobilité et accueil à Paris (fin XVIIe–début XIXe siècle)* (Paris: Fayard, 2000), 114–41.

16 Roche, *The People of Paris*, 110–13.

17 Pierre Goubert, *The Ancien Régime*, trans. Steve Cox (London: Weidenfeld and Nicolson, 1973), 216.

18 Garrioch, *The Making of Revolutionary Paris*, 102–3; Natacha Coquéry, *L'hôtel aristocratique: le marché du luxe à Paris au XVIIIe siècle* (Paris: Publications de la Sorbonne, 1998), 194–5.

19 Roche, *The People of Paris*, 104.

20 Natacha Coquéry, *L'espace du pouvoir: de la demeure privée à l'édifice public, Paris 1700–1790* (Paris: Seli Arslan, 2000), 23–4. Some wealthy Parisians rented an apartment in the capital and a house outside the city; see Roland Mousnier, *Recherches sur la stratification sociale à Paris aux XVIIe et XVIIIe siècles* (Paris: A. Pedone, 1976), 108–10.

21 Roche, *The People of Paris*, 104–10.

22 Annik Pardaihlé-Galabrun, *La naissance de l'intime: 3000 foyers parisiens XVIIe–XVIIIe siècle* (Paris: Presses Universitaires de France, 1988), 198. The French edition is cited here for material not included in the English-language edition. On the pollution generated by building and other work in Paris, see Allan Potofsky, "Recycling the City: Paris, 1760s–1800," in *The Afterlife of Used Things: Recycling in the Long Eighteenth Century*, ed. Ariane Fennetaux, Amélie Junqua, and Sophie Vasset (New York: Routledge, 2015), 71–88.

23 Arlette Farge, *Fragile Lives: Violence, Power, and Solidarity in Eighteenth-Century Paris* (Cambridge, MA: Harvard University Press, 1993); this continued to be true in the nineteenth century: see Eliza Earle Ferguson, *Gender and Justice: Violence, Intimacy, and Community in Fin-de-Siècle Paris* (Baltimore, MD: Johns Hopkins University Press, 2010), 93–127.

24 Clare Haru Crowston, *Fabricating Women: The Seamstresses of Old Regime France, 1675–1791* (Durham, NC: Duke University Press, 2001), 364; 343–71.

25 For example, a second-hand clothing business out of the third floor of a building. AdP DQ10 89 Blottefier; Lesage fripier; previously Pierre Vilain maitre franges.

26 Youri Carbonnier, *Maisons parisiennes des lumières* (Paris: Presses Universitaires Paris-Sorbonne, 2006), 319–23.

27 Dena Goodman, *Becoming a Woman in the Age of Letters* (Ithaca, NY: Cornell University Press, 1994); Meghan Roberts, *Sentimental Savants: Philosophical Families in Enlightenment France* (Chicago: University of Chicago Press, 2016); on furnishings, see Dena Goodman and Kathryn Norberg, eds., *Furnishing the Eighteenth Century: What Furniture Can Tell Us About the European and American Past* (New York: Routledge, 2007).

28 On writing desks, see Dena Goodman, *Becoming a Woman*, 161–98.

29 Crowston, *Fabricating Women*, 343–4.

30 Garrioch, *The Making of Revolutionary Paris*, 77–8.

31 David Troyansky, *Old Age in the Old Regime: Image and Experience in Eighteenth-Century France* (Ithaca, NY: Cornell University Press, 1989), 156; Mathieu Marraud, *La noblesse de Paris au XVIIIe siècle* (Paris: Le Seuil, 2000), 135–46.

32 Scarlett Beauvalet-Boutouyrie, *Etre veuve sous l'Ancien Régime* (Paris: Belin, 2001), 170.

33 Clare Crowston cites Louis-Sébastien Mercier's observation on this score, *Fabricating Women*, 359–66; women tended to outlive men: on rates of widowhood, see Beauvalet-Boutouyrie, *Etre veuve*, 159.

34 On the development of a real estate market in the eighteenth century, see Gérard Béaur, *L'immobilier et la Révolution: Marché de la pierre et mutations urbaines 1770–1810* (Paris: Armand Colin, 1994) or, in English, "Land Markets in the Parisian Basin (17th–19th centuries): Changes over time and variation in space," in *Landholding and Land Transfer in the North Sea Area*, ed. Bas J. P. van Bavel and Peter Hoppenbrouwers (Turnhout: Brepols, 2004), 86–100. See also Fabrice Boudjaaba, *Des paysans attachés à la terre?: familles, marchés et patrimoines dans la région de Vernon (1750–1830)* (Paris: Publications Universitaires Paris-Sorbonne, 2008).

35 The first name "Anne" was also given to men in early modern France.

36 AdP DQ10 169, doss. Bernard Boulainvilliers.

37 Yves Durand, *Les fermiers généraux au XVIIIe siècle* (Paris: Presses Universitaires de France, 1971), 144–53.

38 Kaplan, *Provisioning Paris*, 135–8; Laurence H. Whinnie, *Family Dynasty, Revolutionary Society* (Westport, CT: Greenwood Press, 2002), 49–66. Merchants, in particular, might also, however, live in a rented apartment nearby; Pardaihlé-Galabrun, *La naissance de l'intime*, 199.

39 Multiple different legal regimes operated in Old Regime France, including different inheritance laws. See Suzanne Desan, *The Family on Trial in Revolutionary France* (Berkeley: University of California Press, 2004), 141–65.

40 AdP DQ10 173 Becquet. Fractional ownership was quite common in northern France, where primogeniture was not practiced.

41 AdP DQ10 751 Planoy (Bochard de Champigny); see in particular her letter dated 18 frimaire II.

42 Jean-Louis Deaucourt, *Premières loges: Paris et ses concierges au XIXe siècle* (Paris: Aubier, 1992).

43 Alexia Yates, *Selling Paris: Property and Commercial Culture in the Fin-de-Siècle Capital* (Cambridge, MA: Harvard University Press, 2015), 214.

44 Deaucourt, *Premières loges*, 134–5.

45 AdP DQ 10 Brousse.

46 AdP DQ10 709 Bernard et Delorme. 3 floréal II, Director to Administrateurs du Département.

47 Statement by Petitpierre, AdP DQ10 169 Boulainvilliers, undated, likely 1801–2.

48 Robert Darnton, *Poetry and the Police: Communication Networks in Eighteenth-Century Paris* (Cambridge, MA: Belknap Press of Harvard University Press, 2010); Arlette Farge, *The Vanishing Children of Paris: Rumor and Politics before the French Revolution* (Cambridge, MA: Harvard University Press, 1991); Arlette Farge, *Subversive Words: Public Opinion in Eighteenth-Century France* (University Park: Penn State University Press, 1995).

49 AdP DQ10 90 doss. Beaurepaire

50 AdP DQ10 709 doss. Bernard and Delorme.

51 AdP DQ10 doss. Beauharnais, visiteur des locations to Balduc, 19 pluviôse II.

52 For recent work on the subject of cafés, in particular, see Thierry Rigogne, "Readers and Reading in Cafés, 1660–1800," *French Historical Studies* 41, no. 3 (August 2018): 473–94; see also the classic, Robert Darnton, *The Forbidden Bestsellers of Pre-Revolutionary France* (New York: W.W. Norton, 1995), 187–91.

53 This was true, for example, of Guillhamont, the *portier* in a building owned by the émigré du Bois de Lauzai; see AdP DQ10 704 DuBois de Lauzai and Duvergier.

54 AdP DQ10 169 Boulainvilliers, 13 fructidor VI.

55 AdP DQ10 169 Boulainvilliers, 2e jour complémentaire an VI, Sapinault, Barbier, Radel to Director.

56 AdP DQ10 Dubois de Lauzai and Duvergier, *Visiteur des locations* to *Receveur*, no date. Bryère is also spelled Labrière; this kind of uncertainty around names is common in eighteenth-century sources.

57 AdP DQ10 170 Baraumont dossier, letter of 15 frimaire an 11.

58 AdP DQ10 89 Barré.

59 Allan Potofsky, *Constructing Paris in the Age of Revolution* (Basingstoke, UK: Palgrave, 2009), 81–2.

60 Louis Chevalier, *Labouring Classes and Dangerous Classes in Paris during the First Half of the Nineteenth Century* (London: Routledge, 1973).

4

Home Fronts and Battlefields:

The Army, Warfare, and the Revolutionary Experience

Christopher Tozzi

If warfare during the French Revolution was "becoming an anachronism," as Napoleon Bonaparte claimed in one of his more ironic statements, few people in France knew it.[1] For most of France's population—including not just soldiers who waged war but also millions of civilians whose daily lives it shaped on the home front—warfare and military institutions played a pivotal role in transforming abstract revolutionary policies into facts on the ground. In this respect, the Revolution diverged sharply from the Old Regime, during which warfare had exerted little influence on the lives of most people in France.

This chapter examines the impact of warfare and military institutions on the lives of soldiers and civilians in revolutionary France. It begins by discussing the relationship between the French army and society on the eve of the Revolution. It then examines the ways in which the Revolution radically disrupted that relationship through universal male conscription and prioritizing the needs of the army over those of civilians. The chapter also shows how the army and military affairs helped to disseminate and enact ideological principles associated with the Revolution, such as the ideas that merit rather than aristocratic birth should shape one's social standing and that army service was the duty and privilege of all French men.

Many textbooks and popular narratives treat the army and warfare as part of revolutionary "scenery." They may assume that they are important for understanding the Terror and Napoleon's eventual rise to power, but deem them otherwise peripheral to the innovations, drama, and intense personal experiences of the Revolution itself. Looking more closely reveals ways in which the army and warfare played a pivotal role in shaping the course of the Revolution —as well as permanently reshaping the way ordinary men and women experienced the military realm. Without the changes discussed below, the Revolution and its legacy might have looked quite different.

Army and Society in Old Regime France

For France, war—and specifically foreign war—was the order of the day for much of the eighteenth century. The country was involved in at least one war with foreign powers during eight of the nine decades spanning 1701 to 1790.[2] These conflicts distinguished the eighteenth century from earlier periods, when civil war inside France was at least as frequent, and certainly more devastating, than war with foreign states. The Camisard revolt of 1702–15 did divide parts of southern France, but this localized rebellion did not compare in scope to the Fronde or the Wars of Religion of the sixteenth and seventeenth centuries.[3] The nineteenth century would also entail fewer major conflicts, including civil and international war, for France and other Western European states.

What did recurring warfare mean for the home front in Old Regime France? The simple answer is "not much." Warfare during the eighteenth century exerted relatively little impact on the lives of most people in France, especially compared to earlier centuries. This was largely the result of what historians call the Military Revolution.[4] The term refers not to a specific political or military event, but rather to a series of changes in early modern Europe that reshaped the way states administered armies, with important consequences for interactions between civilians and soldiers.

Prior to the Military Revolution, most states in Europe contracted with private entrepreneurs to raise armies whenever a war broke out. Governments paid the entrepreneurs, who were in turn responsible for seeing that soldiers received pay and supplies. In the absence of State-financed barracks, soldiers typically lived in the homes of civilians, who usually were not pleased by the practice. Armies also procured most of their provisions from civilian populations. This was true not only when armies were occupying foreign territory and could obtain their sustenance at the expense of enemy subjects, but also when they were operating within the borders of the state for which they were fighting.

This system was financially expedient because it required governments to pay only contracting fees to military entrepreneurs in order to raise armies. The State also avoided the expense of maintaining permanent standing armies in peacetime. In addition, by outsourcing military organization to private individuals, the contract system minimized the administrative burden that states faced in managing armies, an important consideration at a time when most State bureaucracies remained primitive.

However, the armies that this system produced tended to be unreliable. When supplies became scarce—which happened whenever an army occupied the same territory long enough to exhaust the local population of resources—soldiers would melt away. Soldiers might also desert en masse if their officers stopped paying them, and it was not unheard of for commanders to switch sides in the midst of a conflict. The expectation that armies would live off civilian populations also resulted in predictably dismal relations between soldiers and the civilians who were supposed to house and feed them.

These problems, which resulted in disastrous performance by French armies after France's entry in 1635 into the Thirty Years' War (1618–48), prompted Louis XIV to begin building new military institutions in the later seventeenth century. The Sun King raised France's first standing armies. He dispatched royal intendants to oversee the recruitment and organization of troops. The State began supplying troops directly and constructing barracks for them to live in. Soldiers did not formally begin swearing oaths of loyalty to the French monarch until the 1760s, but the significant expansion of the role of the State in financing and supplying armies earlier in the century helped to ensure their fidelity.[5] All of these developments, which paralleled changes within other European states between the fifteenth and eighteenth centuries, led to a much larger, more effective—and more expensive—French army.

For civilians, the most important consequence of the Military Revolution was its role in making the army and its operations impinge much less on society. To be sure, civilian–military relations were not perfect. Some soldiers continued to lodge in civilian homes as the State could not afford to house all in barracks, leading to conflicts such as the one that erupted in 1712, when a soldier's misfiring weapon accidentally killed the baker in whose home he was staying. The State refused to punish the soldier because of special juridical privileges that he enjoyed.[6] But such episodes became increasingly rare as the practice of billeting troops in civilian homes declined. As the historian André Corvisier has written, soldiers came to occupy "another milieu" of society, distinct from the civilian sphere.[7] And although warfare itself could have disastrous economic consequences for civilians who were unfortunate enough to have their villages and fields become sites of battle, the operations of armies rarely resulted in physical harm to civilians once the effects of the Military Revolution had played out in the later seventeenth century.

Civilians in Old Regime France also had relatively little reason to worry about having to bear arms against their will. Although some other European states, such as Sweden and Prussia, introduced universal male conscription prior to the age of revolutions, in France the only institution that could compel young men to provide military service to the State was the *milice royale*, or royal militia. Introduced in 1688, the militia was nominally responsible for reinforcing France's professional army (often referred to as the line army) in times of military crisis. Although forcible militia service was enormously unpopular—it was a frequent subject of complaint in the *cahiers de doléances* of 1789—its actual impact was limited. Only about one out of every forty men who were eligible for militia service was actually enlisted, and various towns and provinces were exempt entirely from the requirement.[8]

In France's professional army, in contrast to the militia, enrollment was entirely voluntary under the Old Regime. Virtually without exception, the army's officers were aristocrats, whose military commissions conferred both prestige and income. Although officers received long-term leaves that allowed them to return home periodically, and many played roles in managing estates even while serving in the army, most Old Regime officers served long careers in the army. Indeed, in many cases they hailed from military families that had supplied the French army with officers for generations. Old Regime army officers thus inhabited a world mostly detached from civilian life.

The same was true of common soldiers, despite the considerably different factors that encouraged them to enlist in the army. Under the Old Regime, army life was inglorious at best, and miserable at worst, for the average soldier. Pay for non-commissioned men was meager and discipline was severe. Officers could beat and degrade their men.[9] Soldiers had little recourse against abusive officers, and new enlistees who discovered that the army was not for them had no easy way to return to civilian life: until the death penalty for desertion was outlawed in 1775, deserters were typically shot or hanged, and because recruits committed to tours of duty of around eight years, an unhappy new soldier would have to wait quite a while before he could legally leave the army.[10] And if men who bore arms expected praise from French subjects in exchange for the burden they bore, they received little; in a society where soldiering was a career of last resort, Old Regime soldiers were the subject of scorn among civilians. The Count of Saint-Germain, who served as War Minister in France during the 1770s, went so far as to remark that the army was "composed of the slime of the nation and of all that is useless to society."[11]

Given these harsh realities, it is unsurprising that most of the men who chose to enlist in the professional army under the Old Regime did so out of desperation. Individuals who lacked other employment opportunities signed up because the army offered steady food, housing, and pay, poor though it was. The fact that enlistment tended to occur at higher rates during the winter, when hunger and homelessness were particularly grave concerns, reflected the desperation that pushed many men to join the army prior to 1789.[12]

The economic forces that were at play in motivating men to enlist in the Old Regime army meant that certain demographic groups accounted for the bulk of the army's personnel. The typical Old Regime soldier was from a poor family, lacked an education and the special trades skills that might have led him to a non-military career. In addition, France's eastern provinces were significantly overrepresented within the ranks of the army, probably because most regiments were stationed along the eastern frontier and recruited from local populations.[13]

When it came to the army, then, two trends were clear during the Old Regime. First, between the reigns of Louis XIV and Louis XVI, war and the army were of little significance to the life experiences of most French men and women. Unless they served as high-level royal officials responsible for overseeing wars, as members of the armies that waged war, or as "camp followers," as some women and children were, French people under the absolutist State played virtually no role in war, and war played little direct role in their lives.

Second, among the minority of French subjects who did experience military life during the Old Regime, only certain groups—nobles on the one hand, and poor men from France's eastern frontier regions on the other—were strongly represented. The army's composition did not fully reflect the nature of the society it served.

Citizens and Citizen-soldiers in the Early Revolution

Efforts to reform military institutions, and by extension to change the way they impacted French society, had their roots in processes that began before the Revolution of 1789. The interest in army reform was the result of several factors. In one sense, it continued a series of military reforms that had begun in the closing decades of the Old Regime. Some of these, such as the Ségur Ordinance of 1781, which formally prohibited non-nobles from enlisting in most units of the army, promoted a conservative order, but also reflected a desire to restructure the military. Other changes, like those to soldiers' pay and discipline that were imposed by a military council in 1787, were more obviously innovative.[14] While the pre-revolutionary reforms to army organization did not meaningfully change the way in which soldiers or warfare impacted society, they inaugurated a spirit of military experimentation that helped to make thinkable the more momentous new military policies and institutions that emerged after 1789.[15] The role of this trend toward military reform in encouraging further change to the army was particularly important early in the Revolution, when the general focus remained on improving Old Regime institutions rather than sweeping them away, which did not happen until the Revolution took a more radical turn starting in 1792.

The army reforms of the early Revolution also reflected a concern among political leaders with reigning in the professional army of the Old Regime, which they viewed as an agent of repression. To an extent this perception was warranted; royal troops had violently confronted dissenting French subjects, and killed several people, especially during fighting in the Tuileries garden on July 12, 1789, and the famous attack on the Bastille on July 14 (see Map 0.2). On the other hand, the degree to which the king's regiments were willing to fight against civilians was limited. Some troops in Paris during the summer of 1789 vowed to destroy their own weapons if ordered to march against the people.[16] Similarly, the soldiers of the Regiment of Flanders fraternized with the largely female crowd during the Women's March on Versailles in early October 1789 and failed to stop civilians from storming the palace.[17] It is also worth noting that the troops who led the storming of the Bastille on July 14 were mutinous members of the French Guards Regiment, whose personnel had become unreliable for royal authorities starting with the Réveillon Riots of late April 1789.[18] Indeed, it was partly because of the military expertise that these troops provided to the crowd attacking the Bastille that the otherwise inexperienced revolutionaries were able to wage an effective attack on the fortress.

Despite the readiness of many troops in the professional army to support the revolutionary cause, the revolutionaries' lack of faith in the line army prompted the creation of a new military institution, the National Guard. The National Guard, which represented the first major revolutionary military experiment, differed from the army that France had previously known in several key ways. It was raised initially in a decentralized fashion, by authorities spread throughout France; only later did the national government in Paris take control. The National Guard originated with the decision by municipal authorities in Paris on July 13, 1789 to raise a new military force, which would answer to the city government rather than royal officials. Totaling 48,000 men, the Parisian National Guard was armed with weapons that the local government requisitioned or appropriated from royal depots such as the Invalides, from which a crowd removed 30,000 guns and several cannons.[19] In addition to supplying the city of Paris with a military force that it could use to defend itself in the event of royal repression, the National Guard helped to maintain public order after desertion and mutiny had decimated the ranks of the French Guards regiment, which traditionally played an important role in policing the capital.[20] During the following months, citizens throughout France emulated the Parisian example by creating National Guard forces in their own localities.[21] By the end of 1789 these units were a familiar institution across the country.

Although some observers in the fall of 1789 urged France's nascent National Assembly to combine various National Guard forces into a single army, legislators resisted such calls.[22] They instead focused on standardizing the line army, which had come under their control when the king surrendered his absolutist authority in the summer of 1789, and reorganizing the bureaucratic machinery that oversaw it. It was not until early 1791, when the revolutionaries began searching for ways to increase the number of men under arms in France to prepare for possible war with foreign powers, that the Assembly moved to centralize the National Guard. Rather than recruiting more troops into the line army, the revolutionaries ordered the levying of what they called volunteer battalions, whose ranks were filled initially by troops who had enlisted in the National Guard. By August 1791 the theoretical strength of the volunteer battalions totaled 101,000, providing the National Assembly with a formidable new military institution that answered directly to the central government in Paris, rather than the local municipalities that had organized the National Guard forces.

The men in the volunteer battalions differed from those in the line army in important respects. They wore different uniforms, represented France's various regions in relative equal proportion, received higher pay, and hailed generally from better-off families.[23] Like the National Guard, the volunteer battalions served to bring the army closer to home for many people in France. Spurred on by patriotic zeal—and encouraged further by the requirement that, initially, men in the volunteer battalions needed only to serve for one year, in comparison to the multi-year commitments required of men who enlisted in the line army—this new military institution was filled with men who might otherwise never have borne arms. In this way, the army came to exert a direct impact on the lives of a significantly broader portion of the men in French society—and, by extension, their families.

In addition to facilitating the creation of a new military institution that inducted men who would otherwise never have entered the military realm, the early years of the Revolution provided the backdrop for the formation of new ways of thinking about military service. From the first months of the Revolution, legislators made pronouncements such as "in France every citizen must be a soldier, and every soldier a citizen," as Edmond-Louis-Alexis Dubois-Crancé said in December 1789.[24] Similarly, the legislator Jacques-Pierre Brissot declared in July 1791 that France's army should be comprised of "armed citizens," rather than the "mercenary soldiers" on which foreign despots ostensibly relied for their defense.[25] Such statements reflected, in part, the revolutionaries' concern with purging the French army of foreign troops, who accounted for around 15 percent of the line army's total strength at the start of the Revolution and whom revolutionary leaders tended to associate, largely unfairly, with counter-revolution.[26]

However, French legislators' interest in encouraging all citizens to bear arms also reflected a fundamentally new conceptualization of the relationship between military personnel and the society they served. Men like Dubois-Crancé and Brissot sought to do away with the Old Regime paradigm that isolated most civilians from the military realm. In their vision, military service was no longer the province of privileged aristocratic officers and desperate enlisted men who chose to bear arms in order to avoid starvation. It became a patriotic duty of all citizens or aspiring citizens. By extension, the army was to be transformed into a mirror of society itself: purged of non-citizens and filled by men who represented all geographic and economic sectors of French society.

This was a very innovative idea in 1789. A sense of duty to the sovereign might have occasionally motivated soldiers in pre-revolutionary Europe, and the American Revolution had inspired new ways of thinking about military service as a patriotic duty—sentiments that were not lost on the French troops who served alongside the American revolutionaries.[27] By and large, however, the notion that army service constituted the duty of every able-bodied man in the polity, or that the army should be composed of the same body of citizens it served as a matter of principle, was quite foreign to most people in the modern Western world prior to the French Revolution. So was the sense that, for ordinary people, bearing arms in defense of the nation represented one of the most sacred duties that a citizen could fulfill. In transforming these ideas into a basic tenet of modern democratic societies, the revolutionaries established one of the most enduring features of the Revolution.

In practice, implementing this vision took time. Foreign regiments remained part of the French army until 1792, and foreigners were not officially barred from enrolling until the ratification of the Constitution of the Year III in 1795. More significantly, the National Guard and the line army remained officially distinct institutions until January 1794, when the National Convention ordered the "amalgamation" of the two forces. However, the government's lack of data about the forces under its command was so great that military commissioners had to draw up careful reports on each unit in the country to facilitate the amalgamation.[28] The process took thirty months to complete, and it was not until 1796 that the French State possessed a singular, uniform army that answered directly to the national government. Thus, for most of the Revolution, the French army did not mirror the society it served nearly as closely as the revolutionaries intended.

Notwithstanding these challenges, it was clear within the first years of the Revolution that the relationship between the French army and French society had changed in consequential ways. Revolutionaries initially tried to limit interactions between soldiers and civilians, and banned political clubs within the army to prevent political radicalization of the troops. But, by January 1790 the National Assembly had decreed that "all citizens, without exception, are and should be subject to the lodging of troops."[29] The decree was a response to attempts by the residents of certain towns to claim dispensation from responsibility for housing soldiers, a privilege they had enjoyed under the Old Regime. By repealing such privileges, the revolutionaries sought to make all people in France share equally in the burdens of maintaining an army and waging war. They also transformed civilian homes into a place of interaction between civilians and soldiers, a practice that had largely disappeared under the Old Regime during the reforms of the Military Revolution.

The Army and Equality

At the same time that the Revolution promulgated conceptions of military burdens as the responsibility of all of French society, the army served as a vital vehicle for putting into practice the egalitarian social philosophies of the Revolution. In this respect the army was particularly important for closing the gap separating the abstract revolutionary ideology of *égalité* (equality) from actual reality—a fact that historians have tended to overlook, focusing on legal reforms designed to increase social equality in revolutionary France rather than evidence of actual change.

That gap was large indeed at the outset of the Revolution. While the revolutionaries famously abolished France's most important feudal institutions on the night of August 4, 1789, the extent to which this legislation resulted in immediate change to the lives of ordinary French men and women was quite limited.[30] For several years after the abolition of feudalism, figures who had exercised power at a local level under the feudal regime tended to retain that power. Meanwhile, a number of the deputies in the National Assembly hailed from noble backgrounds, as did virtually every member of the French army's officer corps—from which the Ségur Ordinance of 1781 had officially barred non-nobles, as noted above. (Small numbers of non-nobles had managed to acquire or retain officer commissions after the implementation of the Ordinance, which did not extend to the artillery corps; however, non-nobles remained a very small minority among officers.)[31] Indeed, on the same day in August 1789 that the National Assembly abolished feudalism, Louis XVI named Jean-Frédéric de la Tour du Pin-Gouvernet, a nobleman and long-time army officer, as War Minister, a position he held until November 1790.[32] Thus, while the power exercised by former nobles declined gradually, it was not until the Revolution took a more radical turn following the abolition of the monarchy in September 1792 that the social, political, and economic advantages conferred by noble birth fully disappeared within most French institutions.

Yet the army also offered a very different model of change. While nobles initially remained in the ranks of the revolutionary army, any man could now become an officer, and many men of non-elite birth used the army as a vehicle for rising to social and political prestige. Napoleon Bonaparte is the most famous example; although his birth into a minor noble family in Corsica helped him to become a low-ranking officer under the Old Regime, Bonaparte almost certainly would not have become the most powerful man in France were it not for his rapid, merit-based promotions through the ranks of the revolutionary army. Other men, such as the generals Lazare Hoche and François-Joseph Westermann, both of whom were born to commoner parents of little means, rose to elite positions in the revolutionary army despite hailing from utterly ordinary backgrounds. For such individuals, military institutions played a leading role in putting the egalitarian ideology of the revolutionaries into practice.

The extent to which egalitarianism and merit-based promotion reigned within the army during the first years of the Revolution was limited, as historians such as Rafe Blaufarb have shown. Non-nobles played more important leadership roles in the National Guard, a new institution without an existing officer corps composed of nobles, than they did in the line army. And it was not until after the amalgamation of the line army and National Guard units starting in 1794 that the meritocratic principles of election and seniority became the primary basis for the selection of officers throughout the army.[33] It is worth noting, too, that to a significant extent the rapid promotion of men of non-noble birth to leadership positions in the army reflected the drastic need for new officers after thousands of aristocratic commanders abandoned their posts and fled the country; had so many noble officers not emigrated, it seems likely that fewer non-nobles would have attained commissions.

Still, the fact remains that the army, more quickly than most other institutions, became a center of social egalitarianism, helping non-noble French men (if not women) take advantage of the newfound merit-based principles that the Revolution had introduced.

It was also notable that the army became a place, to a certain extent, of religious and racial equality. Jews enlisted in significant numbers beginning early in the Revolution, a trend that was significant not just because virtually no Jews had borne arms in France prior to 1789, but also because the Old Regime State had officially regarded Jews as members of a foreign nation and forced them to pay a special tax in exchange for dispensation from militia service. Thousands of Jews enlisted as ordinary soldiers in the revolutionary line army and the National Guard. Despite some objections to Jewish troops from political leaders and some French soldiers, many rose to officers' ranks by the mid-1790s (though it was not until the later nineteenth century that France gained its first Jewish general).[34] By allowing Jews to obtain positions of prestige and power, as well as placing them in regiments where they marched and fought alongside non-Jewish citizens, the army helped to integrate into French society a religious minority that, prior to 1789, had lived largely in isolation from Christian Frenchmen.

The army did the same for some men of African descent, albeit to a less significant extent. Small numbers of black troops had enlisted under the Old Regime. Yet the Revolution witnessed the formation of the first all-black military unit to bear arms in Europe. Called the Legion of the Americans, the force was created in September 1792 and commanded by the Chevalier de Saint-Georges, a musician of partial African descent. Although the legion never saw combat prior to being reorganized in 1793 as a unit that was not exclusively comprised of black troops, it was significant as a place where blacks could serve not only as soldiers but also as officers. Given that the revolutionary government did not formally abolish slavery until February 1794, the Legion of the Americans was especially important as an effort to put the principle of racial equality into practice at a time when many French legislators hesitated to extend their concept of civil and human rights to people of color.[35]

Conscription

Despite the egalitarian qualities of the revolutionary army, not all men enlisted in it of their own volition. Although the French State did not officially implement conscription until the later 1790s, forcible enlistment within some military units began in the early years of the Revolution, marking a dramatic break with Old Regime recruitment policies.

The French revolutionaries were initially hesitant to resort to compulsory military recruitment. Aware of the resentment spawned by the Old Regime *milice*—which, despite impacting only a small portion of the population, was widely despised—the revolutionaries were careful to distance themselves from forcible military service. They abolished the *milice* in 1791, and for the first few years of the Revolution relied solely on volunteers to fill the ranks of the line army.

This strategy had proven unsatisfactory by early 1792, however, when it became clear that a manpower crisis was developing within the army. Recruitment for the line army had declined by as much as 66 percent since the start of the Revolution. At the same time, the revolutionaries had purged the line army of soldiers whom they deemed politically unreliable, and more than 2,100 officers deserted their posts because of opposition to the Revolution.[36] These changes left the line army with a serious shortage of enlisted men as well as experienced leaders, prompting fears about its inability to defend France in the event of foreign invasion.

For a time, the National Guard units that had emerged across France starting in the summer of 1789, and which were later organized into volunteer battalions, helped to alleviate these concerns. In June 1791, the national government deployed the volunteer battalions to the frontiers to provide a safeguard against the threat of foreign invasion. Yet if the revolutionaries hoped to count on the volunteer battalions to shore up the weaknesses of the line army, they had made one crucial error when organizing them. Initially, the government had required men who enlisted in these units to commit to only one year of service. As a result, in early 1792 the volunteer battalions began disintegrating. The revolutionaries responded in February 1793, by which time France was at war, by ordering the levying of an additional 300,000 men for the volunteer battalions.

When the revolutionaries raised the first volunteer battalions in 1791, they encountered few problems in filling their ranks. Many of the men whom they enlisted were already serving in the National Guard, and it was easy to find volunteers to commit to a year's worth of service at a time when France was not at war. By early 1793, however, when enrolling in the volunteer battalions very likely meant having to march into battle to fight against seasoned Prussian, Austrian, Spanish, or British troops—or fellow Frenchmen who had rebelled against the Republic—voluntary recruits proved much more elusive.

Not wanting to involve themselves directly in the messy business of raising 300,000 new troops under these circumstances, revolutionaries in Paris outsourced the problem to departmental governments across France. The national government assigned a recruitment quota to each department and charged its authorities with the task of enrolling sufficient men to meet the quota.[37] France's national leaders had not bothered to provide recommendations, let alone explicit instructions, as to how departmental authorities should go about recruiting troops. This left the door open for local authorities to resort to forcible enlistment measures, turning the nomenclature of the volunteer battalions into a cruel euphemism for some recruits. Even with this practice at their disposal, many departments struggled to meet their recruitment quotas; only about half of the 300,000 troops who were supposed to have been levied in 1793 ever appeared for duty.[38]

Not all of the "volunteers" of the February 1793 levy were raised through compulsory means, and the ad hoc policies that local authorities used to meet their enlistment quotas did not amount to conscription in the full sense of the word. However, the recruitment operations associated with the levy of the 300,000 represented an important step toward introducing universal conscription in France—and, with it, the idea that the government might demand military service from any of its citizens, with little regard to the disruption that such requirements could cause to civilian lives and families. (The one major accommodation that the State granted was permission for a conscript to hire someone else to serve in his place, a privilege that only wealthier families could afford. It was also soon outlawed and not reintroduced until 1798.)

A second major step toward universal conscription came in August 1793, when the National Convention decreed the *levée en masse* (mass levy). Conceived as an expedient for expelling foreign armies from France, the *levée*'s goal was to inspire revolutionary fervor more than to recruit troops. Its only concrete requirement regarding military enlistment was for unmarried men of between eighteen and twenty-five years of age to register for military service and practice military drill while they awaited orders to depart for battle at an unspecified time. The number of men impacted by these orders was no doubt small, and it is unclear to what extent the *levée* truly facilitated the forcible enlistment of more civilians. It did, however, officially establish the national government's power to conscript citizens if it wished. This was a major development given the hesitancy with which the revolutionaries had approached conscription earlier in the Revolution.[39]

Perhaps even more notable was that the *levée* applied not only to men who were readily eligible for military service. The decree placed all "French people" under "permanent requisition," specifying that women should perform such tasks as staffing hospitals, while old men were to deliver patriotic speeches to rouse the populace. The decree mentioned children, too, whom it charged with the task of helping to assist in the production of clothing. It even extended to horses, who could be commandeered for the service of the nation.

These dimensions of the *levée en masse* were ambiguous and not widely enforced. The law did not specify how women, children, and the elderly were to go about performing the duties imposed upon them. Nor did it establish funds to pay them for their work. Yet at a symbolic level, the *levée en masse* was tremendously important in reshaping the way civilians would experience war in France. The terms of the decree made very clear that the waging of war was not the duty of soldiers alone; it instead extended to every civilian—and even certain animals—within France's borders. This explicit subordination of civil society to the demands of the military, combined with other totalizing aspects of French revolutionary warfare, has prompted some historians to refer to the French Revolutionary Wars as the world's first "total war."[40]

It was not until September 1798, when the Directory adopted the *loi Jourdan*, that the French State granted itself complete powers to force civilians to serve in the army.[41] The law, which established universal male conscription in France for the first time, served as the basis on which France's armies would remain stocked with young men for the nearly twenty more years of warfare that followed until Napoleon's final defeat in 1815.

What is perhaps most notable about the *loi Jourdan* is not that it introduced universal conscription—as the culmination of a gradual process that had begun with the levying of the volunteer battalions, the 1798 law was predictable—but rather the circumstances of its adoption. By 1798, France was safer from foreign and domestic enemies than it had been in nearly a decade. The country remained at war, but foreign forces had been driven from France years earlier, and French troops in the later 1790s busied themselves with low-stakes campaigns in far-off locales like Italy, Ireland, and Egypt. Thus, in contrast to the levying of the volunteers and the decree of the *levée en masse* in 1793, military crisis did not serve as justification for the *loi Jourdan*.

The law instead reflected a shift in mentalities that had gradually taken place over the course of the revolutionary decade. By 1798, the idea that the government could force men to bear arms, whether or not a true military exigency existed, had become acceptable enough within French society for the State to engrave it as law. The *loi Jourdan* met with little resistance beyond individual efforts to dodge enlistment or desert at opportune moments, demonstrating how willing France's civilians had become to accept a policy that could significantly disrupt their lives. In 1793 universal conscription might have undercut the legitimacy of the national government—which is why the legislators in Paris worked so hard to keep their hands out of recruitment operations—yet by 1798 civilians exhibited relatively little concern with the fact that the government could take control of male bodies and impose hardship on the families whose members the State requisitioned for service.

Protecting Families

Although conscription created new challenges for families, the government helped to balance them with an unprecedented effort by the State to assume responsibility for the wives, children, and parents of men who served in the army, whether voluntarily or not. For the first time, the State committed to assisting families while male members were bearing arms, as well as to caring on a long-term basis for survivors of soldiers killed in war.

Such policies constituted a departure from the Old Regime. Although officers and soldiers prior to 1789 could sometimes earn pensions, and widows could sometimes claim those pensions after their husbands had died, they typically required decades of service. The monarchy's efforts to care for the families of its troops also did not extend beyond pensions.[42]

This changed during the Revolution, a fact reflected prominently in the registers that the army used to keep track of enlistees.[43] The documents, known as *contrôles de troupe*, functioned starting in the early eighteenth century as registries of every soldier who enlisted in the army. Prior to 1789, the *contrôles* served only the army's internal purposes: they recorded the names, birthplaces, physical characteristics, and service dates of soldiers, along with other miscellaneous information. The revolutionaries expanded registers to include information about soldiers' families. This data ensured that the State could administer death benefits and pensions to a soldier's survivors. In turn, it helped to forge a stronger relationship between the army and the wives and children of the men who served in it.

For soldiers' families, the payments provided by the State were not insignificant. Although pensions paid to family members varied, and the State often failed to carry through on its pension commitments due to lack of funds, the example of the survivors of Theobald Wolfe Tone, an Irish revolutionary and French army officer who died in 1798, is telling. Following Wolfe Tone's death, his wife received a pension of 1200 livres, and his three children 400 livres each.[44] These were substantial sums, given that the annual average pay of an ordinary soldier at the time was about 114 livres.[45]

Surveillance and Repression

At the same time that the revolutionaries were rethinking the treatment of soldiers' families, they were also reformulating policies on the types of surveillance and repression the State could undertake in times of war. For certain groups in France, such as foreigners and people who had been born into the nobility, the resulting measures caused some of the most dramatic disruptions to daily life during the Revolution. Here again, few historians have appreciated the extent to which the military realm and warfare sparked wide-reaching change within French society. The idea of instituting special repressive measures during wartime did not originate with the Revolution. The Old Regime monarchy had also occasionally undertaken actions such as the expulsion of some foreigners from the country when France went to war.[46] However, the revolutionaries embraced such measures with newfound fervor, applying them more broadly and with more serious consequences for people living inside the country while it was at war.

The first step toward repression by the State in the name of national defense came in February 1793, when the National Convention adopted a law that required property owners to report the names and origins of all individuals, foreign as well as French, who resided on their estates.[47] The law allowed the State to begin collecting the data that it would need to target for surveillance individuals or groups whom it deemed threatening. The following August the government took the further step of decreeing the arrest of all foreigners who had entered France since the Revolution's start. The law was not universally enforced, and various groups of foreigners were exempt, especially those working in industries that supported the war effort.[48] Nonetheless, for those foreigners living in France who were placed under arrest, the decree made the war quite consequential and personal, even if these individuals otherwise had nothing to do with the war effort.

Former nobles, too, suffered the repressive effects of the war on civilians. The law of June 19, 1790 officially abolished nobility in France, but individuals who had been born into the nobility found that the negative consequences of their birth identities outlived their titles.[49] The law of 27 Germinal Year II (April 16, 1794) prohibited nobles, along with foreigners from countries with which France was at war, from residing in Paris, anywhere on the coast, or in fortified cities. It also prevented these groups from participating in aspects of civic life in France.[50] Although these measures reflected concern that individual former nobles who remained in France might be conspiring with counter-revolutionaries abroad to help enemy armies defeat France or otherwise harm the Revolution, they targeted ex-nobles collectively.

The decree elicited a large series of petitions to the government from former nobles seeking exemption from its terms by claiming, for instance, that the ancestors from whom they inherited their noble status had falsely claimed to be nobles, or that they had acquired noble status only through marriage and therefore should not be subject to the terms of the law.[51] It is unclear whether the government ever responded favorably to such petitions, but the fact that so many were written suggests that the State did indeed enforce the law. For those former nobles who could not successfully petition for dispensation from the law and who were not members of the groups, such as the elderly, that the decree exempted, the decree placed serious restrictions on the way they could live their lives in wartime revolutionary France. It was also emblematic of the enduring idea that a democratic state, despite its rhetoric of liberty and equality, may intrude on the personal liberties of individuals if the exigencies of national security seem to require it.

"Revolutionary Until the Peace": The War and Constitutional Rights

While the repressive measures that the government promulgated in the name of national defense at first targeted specific groups, the Revolutionary War eventually became the State's official rationale for the broad suspension of constitutional rights across civilian society. This was the thinking behind the Convention's decision in October 1793 to declare the French government "revolutionary until the peace."[52] Issued following a speech by Louis-Antoine Saint-Just that accused government officials of failing to fulfill their duties, the decree spoke volumes about the role that the Revolutionary War played in reshaping civilian life in France.

That is because, in declaring the government to be in a "revolutionary" state so long as the war continued, the Convention effectively suspended efforts to establish a new constitutional, democratic government. At the time, France had no functioning constitution. The deputies had formally adopted a new constitution in 1793 to replace the Constitution of 1791. Yet despite the fact that this new framework of government received overwhelming approval in a national referendum, the Convention dragged its feet in putting it into practice, and eventually suspended it indefinitely in the name of national defense by declaring that France would remain "revolutionary"—and therefore have no constitutional basis for government—so long as the war continued.

The idea that the Revolutionary War justified extraordinary political measures began to emerge well before the Constitution of 1793 was drafted. In March 1793 an anonymous politician suggested in the Jacobin Club in Paris (see Map 0.2) that the government should cease passing new laws, as well as suspend efforts to draft a new constitution, until the war ended. "Before creating a constitution, we must silence the enemies who threaten us," he said.[53] In August another anonymous deputy, in arguing against a proposal to begin implementing the Constitution of 1793, demanded that the Convention refuse to disband so long as the war continued.[54] The next month deputies on mission in the departments began imposing prison sentences on individuals suspected of political crimes "until the peace."[55] This line of reasoning reached its most extreme state with the decree of October 1793 that declared the government revolutionary until the peace. In using the war as an excuse for suspending the constitution indefinitely, the government effectively denied to the people of France the democratic rights that the constitution was supposed to have bestowed on them. The decree also engendered a deep paradox. France was waging the Revolutionary War for the ostensible purpose of protecting the democratic rights of people in France and beyond. Yet by October 1793, the war itself became an excuse for suspending democracy indefinitely.

As it happened, the war outlived the revolutionary government. Following the Terror and the Thermidorian Reaction, which brought the Terror more or less to an end, the national government adopted the Constitution of 1795, which established the Directory (see Map 0.2). France remained at war throughout this period, showing that it was, in fact, possible to establish a democratic, constitutional government before making peace with foreign powers (even if that government failed at times to comply with democratic principles, as when it manipulated election results). Still, the effect of the war for the two years between the October, 1793 decree and the establishment of the Directory was to limit constitutional rights for everyone in France.

War and Society under Napoleon and Beyond

It was not until the Treaty of Amiens in March 1802, ten years after the Revolutionary War had begun, that France finally made peace with the last of its enemies, Great Britain. That calm did not last long, however; Britain declared war on France once again in the spring of 1803. The renewed fighting quickly expanded along with the political power of Napoleon Bonaparte, who crowned himself emperor of the French in late 1804. Warfare continued under Napoleon until his final defeat at Waterloo in 1815.

In general, the impact of warfare and the army on the French home front under Napoleon was defined by the same trends as those associated with the Revolutionary War of the 1790s. The Napoleonic regime maintained a program of surveillance and repression in the name of national defense. Conscription remained widespread. Of all of the men born in France between 1790 and 1795, no fewer than two out of five served in Napoleon's armies.[56] Despite abandoning the radical ideological messaging of the revolutionary decade, Napoleon maintained the State's commitment to supporting the families of veterans. And although he re-established noble titles, promotion in his armies remained based essentially on merit.[57]

Insofar as civilian society was concerned, perhaps the most significant change in warfare as France transitioned from the revolutionary to the Napoleonic period was the fact that French armies were waging war on increasingly distant frontiers. Whereas the first years of the Revolutionary War had entailed fighting on French soil or France's immediate borders, by the later 1790s French armies were launching campaigns in Ireland, Malta,

Egypt, and the Caribbean. Napoleon's campaigns during the first decade of the nineteenth century often took place in parts of central and eastern Europe, relatively remote from France. It was not until the final years of Napoleon's reign that foreign armies returned to French soil for the first time since the early 1790s.

As the fighting moved farther from French soil, its direct impact on French society and the French economy decreased. Notwithstanding the burdens of conscription, it became easier as the war progressed for French civilians to accept virtually unending warfare on distant frontiers as a fact of life. Warfare under Napoleon thus looked much like warfare under the Old Regime, in the respect that it was a near-constant reality, with limited consequences for many people in France.

Conclusion

Even if Napoleonic warfare came to resemble Old Regime warfare in certain ways, it also institutionalized lasting changes. One was the enduring idea that military service was the responsibility of all able-bodied men, an idea Napoleon took to heart by conscripting hundreds of thousands of his subjects. Another was the expectation that the State would care for the families of men who served it in the army, as Napoleon and his successors did, at least within the limits of financial resources. A third was the role of the army in enabling social and political advancement for men of talent, regardless of their backgrounds. A fourth was the notion that radical measures of surveillance and repression were acceptable trade-offs for national security, even if they seemed at odds with democratic principles.

All of these concepts endured long after the French Revolution. They also impacted democratic societies in other parts of Europe and beyond, whose approaches to warfare and the army during the nineteenth and twentieth centuries were frequently modeled on those of the French revolutionaries. The French revolutionary army and wars ultimately played crucial roles in helping to set the political and social standards of modern, democratic societies.

Source (a): "It should come as no surprise if I want to make a Jew into a soldier." Speech by the Abbé Henri Grégoire at the National Assembly, December 23, 1789

It should come as no surprise if I want to make a Jew into a soldier. The Jews of Paris and Bordeaux have entered eagerly into the National Guard, several of them attaining the rank of captain. Do not believe that they are required to refuse service on the day of the Sabbath. In the Talmud and the writings of Maimonides, the most preeminent of their philosophers, one finds two passages that formally permit it, and the Jewish writers of Berlin have enthusiastically cited these articles to reassure the consciences of their brothers, 3,000 of whom have enrolled in the armies of the Holy Roman Emperor . . . This Jewish nation, which has supplied a skilled general to Portugal, a commodore to England, which distinguished itself during the previous century at the sieges of Bude and Prague, which served brilliantly during the attack against Port Mahon, is it unworthy of marching beneath French battle standards?

Source (b): From the Petition of the Jews Established in France addressed to the National Assembly, January 28, 1790

[Some will say that it is a problem that Jews cannot perform military duties on the day of the Sabbath.] There is an even stronger objection, that the Law of Moses forbids military service, & that, besides, it makes Jews absolutely unfit for [service].

Before responding to each of these objections, it is important to observe that even if their religion forbade Jews from engaging in military service, that would not be grounds for refusing them the title & the rights of Citizens.

For are there not other professions than that of arms, other careers than that of war? The National Assembly has just rejected conscription, which would have made all Citizens into soldiers, without considering their temperament, their tastes, or their fortunes. Everyone is free to consecrate their life to the exercise of arms or to avoid it. One can be a good Citizen without being a soldier. Indeed, if one serves one's country well, it matters little if it is in the tumult of the encampments or the tranquil interior of the cities.

The religion of the Quakers and Anabaptists forbids them to fight; & nonetheless, they are not less good Citizens because of it.

The Quaker, in particular, is separated from the people with whom he lives by an infinity of practices, & he serves the country he inhabits as well as they do.

So even it were true that their religion barred Jews from military service, one could not refuse them the rights of Citizens on those grounds, since military service is a duty that one can be released from, and he who is released from it has other ways to be useful to the common good.

Notes

1 Jules Bertaut, *Napoleon in His Own Words*, trans. Herbert Edward Law and Charles Lincoln Rhodes (Chicago: McClurg, 1916), 133.

2 T. C. W. Blanning, *Origins of the French Revolutionary Wars* (New York: Routledge, 1986), 37.

3 On the Camisard affair, see W. Gregory Monahan's excellent book, *Let God Arise: The War and Rebellion of the Camisards* (Oxford: Oxford University Press, 2014).

4 The canonical work on the Military Revolution is Michael Roberts, "The Military Revolution, 1560–1660," in *Essays in Swedish History*, ed. Michael Roberts (Minneapolis: University of Minnesota Press, 1967), 195–225. For more recent scholarship, see Geoffrey Parker, *The Military Revolution: Military Innovation and the Rise of the West, 1500–1800* (Cambridge: Cambridge University Press, 1996); Jeremy Black, *A Military Revolution: Military Change and European Society, 1550–1800* (Cambridge: Cambridge University Press, 1997); Brian Downing, *The Military Revolution and Political Change: Origins of Democracy and Autocracy in Early Modern Europe* (Princeton, NJ: Princeton University Press, 1992); and David Parrott, *The Business of War: Military Enterprise and Military Revolution in Early Modern Europe* (Cambridge: Cambridge University Press, 2012).

5 Samuel F. Scott, *The Response of the Royal Army to the French Revolution: The Role and Development of the Line Army 1787–93* (Oxford: Clarendon Press, 1978), 27.

6 Service Historique de la Défense (hereafter SHD) Xg 31, Dec. 7, 1712.

7 André Corvisier, *L'Armée française de la fin du XVIIème siècle au ministère de Choiseul. Le soldat*, 2 vols. (Paris: Presse Universitaire de France, 1964), 1:119.

8 Alan Forrest, *Conscripts and Deserters: The Army and French Society during the Revolution and Empire* (Oxford: Oxford University Press, 1989), 9.

9 Scott, *Response*, 31.

10 Scott, *Response*, 6, 82, 91.

11 John Lynn, *Bayonets of the Republic: Motivation and Tactics in the Army of Revolutionary France, 1791–94* (Urbana: University of Illinois Press, 1984), 62–3.

12 Corvisier, *L'armée française*, 1:163.

13 Corvisier, *L'armée française*, 1:163–4.

14 Scott, *Response*, 31.

15 On military change after the Seven Years' War in particular, see Christy Pichichero, *The Military Enlightenment, War and Culture in the French Empire from Louis XIV to Napoleon* (Ithaca, NY: Cornell University Press, 2017).

16 Bernard Deschard, *L'Armée et la Révolution: Du service du roi au service de la nation* (Paris: Editions Desjonquères, 1989), 175.

17 Scott, *Response*, 74–5.

18 Alain-Jacques Czouz-Tornare, "Les formations suisses, substituts aux gardes nationales dans les capitales provinciales en 1789–1790," in *La Garde nationale entre nation et peuple en armes: Mythes et réalités, 1789–1871*, ed. Serge Bianchi and Roger Dupuy, 223–48 (Rennes: Presses Universitaires de Rennes, 2006), 224–5.

19 Albert Mathiez, *La victoire en l'an II: esquisses historiques sur la défense nationale* (Paris: Alcan, 1916), 18–19.

20 Jean-Paul Bertaud, *The Army of the French Revolution: From Citizen-Soldiers to Instrument of Power*, trans. R. R. Palmer (Princeton, NJ: Princeton University Press, 1988), 24; Czouz-Tornare, "Les formations suisses," 224–5.

21 Mathiez, *La victoire*, 19.

22 Bertaud, *Army*, 49; Lynn, *Bayonets of the Republic*, 50.

23 Scott, *Response*, 181.

24 *Archives parlementaires de 1787 à 1860. Recueil complet des débats législatifs & politiques des Chambres françaises, première série (1787–1799)*, ed. M. J. Mavidal and M. E. Laurent, 82 vols. (Paris: Paul Dupont, 1879–1913), 12:521–3.

25 François Victor Alphonse Aulard, *La Société des Jacobins: Recueil des documents pour l'histoire du Club des Jacobins de Paris*, 6 vols. (Paris: Jouaust, 1889–97), 2:619.

26 Michael Rapport, *Nationality and Citizenship in Revolutionary France* (Oxford: Oxford University Press, 2000), 50; Christopher Tozzi, *Nationalizing France's Army: Foreign, Black, and Jewish Troops in the French Military, 1715–1831* (Charlottesville: University of Virginia Press, 2016), 64.

27 Julia Osman, *Citizen Soldiers and the Key to the Bastille* (Basingstoke, UK: Palgrave Macmillan, 2015).

28 Bertaud, *Army*, 166–7.

29 Lynn, *Bayonets of the Republic*, 121; *Archives parlementaires*, 11:297.

30 Peter Jones, *The Peasantry in the French Revolution* (Cambridge: Cambridge University Press, 1988), 21, 86–8.

31 Colin Lucas, "Nobles, Bourgeois and the Origins of the French Revolution," *Past and Present* 60 (1973): 101.

32 Scott, *Response*, 73.

33 Scott, *Response*, 80–1; Rafe Blaufarb, "Démocratie et professionnalisme: l'avancement par l'élection dans l'armée française, 1760–1815," *Annales historiques de la Révolution française* 310 (1997): 601–25.

34 Christopher Tozzi, "Jews, Soldiering and Citizenship in Revolutionary and Napoleonic France," *Journal of Modern History* 86 (2014): 233–57.

35 On blacks in the revolutionary army, see Bernard Gainot, *Les officiers de couleur dans les armées de la République et de l'Empire (1792–1815): De l'esclavage à la condition militaire dans les Antilles françaises* (Paris: Editions Karthala, 2007); and Tozzi, *Nationalizing France's Army*, 106–10, 152, 158.

36 Scott, *Response*, 82, 109.

37 Scott, *Response*, 178; Bertaud, *Army*, 91.

38 Bertaud, *Army*, 91–5; Scott, *Response*, 178.

39 Alan Forrest, "'La patrie en danger': The French Revolution and the First *Levée en masse*," in *The People in Arms: Military Myth and National Mobilization since the French Revolution*, ed. Daniel Moran and Arthur Waldron (Cambridge: Cambridge University Press, 2003), 8–32.

40 David Bell, *The First Total War: Napoleon's Europe and the Birth of Warfare As We Know It* (New York: Houghton Mifflin, 2007), 11–12. Whether the term should be applied to the wars of the Revolution remains a hotly contested subject among historians.

41 Forrest, *Conscripts and Deserters*, vii.

42 For example, see the pension requirements specified in "Concordat entre le Saint-Siège et la Cour de France, Pour la restitution des Déserteurs des Troupes du Roi, qui se réfugient dans l'État d'Avignon & le Comtat Venaissin" in the Bibliothèque nationale de France 21710 (39).

43 Bertaud, *Army*, 20.

44 SHD 17Yd 14.

45 Scott, *Response*, 31.

46 Rapport, *Nationality and Citizenship*, 44–5.

47 Albert Mathiez, *La Révolution et les étrangers: Cosmopolitisme et défense nationale* (Paris: Renaissance du Livre, 1918), 122.

48 Mathiez, *La Révolution et les étrangers*, 140–1.

49 "Abolition of Nobility," *Center for History and New Media*, http://chnm.gmu.edu/revolution/d/367/.

50 *Lois, décrets, ordonnances, réglemens et avis du Conseil-d'Etat* (Paris: Guyot, 1825), 17:171–3.

51 Paris, Archives Nationales (hereafter AN) D/III/373, dossiers 313 and 591. On the law and responses to it, see Jennifer Ngaire Heuer, "Enemies of the Nation? Nobles, Foreigners, and the Constitution of National Citizenship in the French Revolution," in *Power and the Nation in European History*, ed. Oliver Zimmer and Len Scales (Cambridge: Cambridge University Press, 2005), 275–93.

52 *Archives parlementaires*, 76:312.

53 Aulard, *Société des Jacobins*, 5:83.

54 Aulard, *Société des Jacobins*, 5:343.

55 *Recueil des actes du Comité de Salut public* (Paris: CTHS, 1999), 6:453.

56 Forrest, *Conscripts and Deserters*, 20.

57 Rafe Blaufarb, *The French Army 1750–1820: Careers, Talent, Merit* (Manchester: Manchester University Press, 2002), 10.

5

Race, Freedom, and Everyday Life:

French Caribbean Prisoners of War in Britain

Abigail Coppins and Jennifer Ngaire Heuer

Dr. Johnston, commissioner for prisoners of war in and around Portsmouth in Hampshire, was in London on business when military transport ships returning from the eastern Caribbean arrived in Portsmouth Harbour in October 1796 (see Map 0.1). They brought with them several thousand prisoners captured by the British during war with revolutionary France. For several months the doctor had been preparing for their arrival. In August, he had conveyed his plans to a colleague in London, Transport Board Commissioner John Marsh, writing:

> I trust there will be time to have every article of cloathing and stores compleat before the arrival of the black corps. I have written to the Admiral stating the method I intend to adopt in washing and cloathing the prisoners—and that a certain number can only be landed in a day—to which he has promised ... to comply with whatever I may suggest to prevent infection being communicated to the fleet or the neighbourhood ... I trust matters will not prove so bad as are expected—yet too much care cannot be taken to prevent so alarming an evil.[1]

As one of a group of commissioners for the Transport Board, the department of the Royal Navy responsible for looking after prisoners of war, Dr. Johnston oversaw all matters relating to the care of prisoners captured during warfare. He was particularly concerned that the ships arriving back from the Caribbean would be carrying infectious diseases like yellow fever, which was endemic in the Caribbean and had decimated British troops.[2] As Johnston likely knew, Philadelphia had suffered a devastating outbreak three years earlier in August 1793. Contemporaries blamed this outbreak on the approximately 2,000 men and women who had fled the Caribbean for North America during the slave revolt in Saint-Domingue (modern-day Haiti).[3] Fears of yellow fever following travelers to Europe and North America thus also contained anxieties about revolutionary and racial "contagion."

In the doctor's absence it was his clerk, Richard Randall, who was on hand when the first ship, the *Hope*, entered Portsmouth Harbour with 103 prisoners of war on board. The *Hope* moored in a heavy gale, and the first seventy-four prisoners were removed in groups and taken ashore to the prison at Portchester Castle. The following morning the remaining twenty-nine prisoners disembarked. It was still raining heavily, and Randall noted that the prisoners had "scarcely any Clothing but what they had on." Another ship, the *Moore*, was waiting just outside the harbor with more prisoners, and more were expected to arrive.[4]

Johnston and Randall recount the measures taken to reduce contagious disease and give us some indication of the desperate conditions of the prisoners of war. Their letters also indicate the importance British authorities placed upon the care and containment of prisoners from the revolutionary French Caribbean. As Johnston and another colleague, William A. Otway, put it, "on the proper execution of this service depends the lives and comfort of so many persons and so materially involves the Honor of the Nation, the necessity of the most rigid attention to it is too obvious to commentate on."[5]

Johnston also specifically noted "the arrival of the black corps" among the French prisoners of war. This corps overwhelmingly outnumbered the white French captives. At the request of the Admiralty Office, authorities estimated the number of prisoners from the Caribbean in October 1797 when all ships had arrived. They counted 2,512 individuals: 333 white men, 2,080 black men (the listing including those who were potentially mixed-race), and ninety-nine women and children, whose race was not systematically noted.[6] The discovery that there were large numbers of free black soldiers (and their families) imprisoned in Britain during the Revolutionary and Napoleonic Wars challenges our understanding of race, war, and revolution. It complicates our notion of armies in the late eighteenth century as predominately white and exclusively male. It also challenges popular assumptions that the French Revolution and the wars fought on and around the European continent and British Isles can be separated from upheavals in the Caribbean.

By uncovering some of the distinctive aspects of the prisoners' daily life—most pressingly, authorities' efforts to prevent the spread of infectious disease, but also, as we will see, the attention they paid to the prisoners' clothing, shoe sizes, and diet—even prisoners' potential desire for eating potatoes—we can explore competing imperatives of care and control. Doing so can help us reimagine the experiences and status of people of color who, while prisoners in Britain, were also, in the wake of the French revolutionary abolition of slavery, free citizens of France. It therefore pushes us to rethink who was considered "French" in the midst of revolution and war, what was associated with that status, and what the "honor of the nation" might have meant in the context of the revolutionary Atlantic world.

Discovering the lives of these men, women, and children requires some creativity. Although there is a vast literature on the Revolutionary and Napoleonic Wars, much work still focuses on battles and the actions of the elite military personnel leading these campaigns. Some historians have found ways of uncovering the lives of "ordinary" soldiers, while several have begun to consider the diverse make-up of eighteenth-century armies.[7] Yet these studies are rarely incorporated into more general accounts of the French Revolution.

Conversely, historians of the French Revolution have increasingly started to treat the Revolution as a global phenomenon, or at least one with entanglements and repercussions far beyond metropolitan France or Europe.[8] There is also a growing literature on the Haitian Revolution and its relationship to events in France, especially the role of the dramatic February 1794 abolition of slavery in the French Empire—and its eventual reimposition in 1802 under Napoleon everywhere in the empire except Haiti.[9] Historians have also begun to look closely at events elsewhere in the Caribbean—including Grenada, St. Vincent, and St. Lucia, where most of the POWs brought to Portsmouth were captured—and to uncover the complicated ways that revolution and war in those islands played out.[10] But events in the West Indies are still often seen as separate from those in Europe—and especially from the experiences and concerns of people living in France and Britain. Prisoners of war, in particular, are usually assumed to have been white, European, and male.[11]

In this chapter, we look at why the prisoners of color from the French Antilles have been forgotten and the sources we can use to recover their stories. We then examine more closely how the dynamics of revolution and war in France and the Caribbean brought them to a prison in Britain. We focus most on what captivity meant for former slaves and free people of color, and how their day-to-day experiences related to those of other French prisoners of war during the Revolution. Finally, we touch on their fates after they were released to France as part of prisoner exchanges—experiencing new forms of mobility and control as they settled there, took up arms again in the Caribbean, or fought in Italy and Russia under Napoleon.

Uncovering a Lost History of Identity and Captivity

Our knowledge of the history of black prisoners of war in Britain is surprisingly recent. This chapter builds on work first undertaken in 2008 by one of the authors of this chapter, Abigail Coppins, to establish the identity of the prisoners incarcerated in Portchester Castle during the French Revolution. This research revealed that large numbers of black and mixed-race soldiers arrived alongside those of European origin at Portchester in 1796, after having been captured by British forces in the eastern Caribbean.

In many popular accounts, the beginnings of a substantial population of people of color in metropolitan Britain only dates from the arrival of the ship *Windrush*, on which about 800 migrants traveled from Jamaica to London in 1948. But scholars have shown that black people have lived in Britain since Roman times, and have called particular attention to their experiences and status during the height of British colonial slavery in the eighteenth and early nineteenth centuries.[12] Yet even these studies tend to focus on people of color in London and port cities directly involved in the slave trade, like Bristol or Liverpool, and overlook their possible presence in other places. British historians also often tend to consider stories of people of color only in relation to British history, leaving aside how the French Revolution might have changed their experiences, or how the end of slavery in the French Empire might have affected them.[13]

The challenges of this lack of attention to soldiers of color and to the reverberations of the French Revolution became apparent during research for a permanent exhibition at Portchester Castle. The exhibit, which opened in August 2017, sought to tell the story of the black soldiers, women, and children within the context of global revolution, conflict, and incarceration.[14] Yet many details proved difficult to verify. Out of the extensive literature dedicated to the uniforms of the French army during the Revolutionary and Napoleonic Wars, only one book provided useful information on what French troops in the Caribbean might have worn.[15] In the end, the exhibition team relied on an 1830 image by Vernet; while it risked being anachronistic, it helped visitors relate to the prisoners; we have reproduced it here (see Figure 5.1.).[16]

A few works specifically on prisons and POWs in Britain do allow us to glean some traces of people from the revolutionary French Caribbean. One of the most useful accounts comes from an 1845 book by W. Woodward, both a historian and an eyewitness. He particularly commented on one prominent figure among the prisoners, General Marinier, whom he presented as a "fine specimen of his race, and a thoroughly soldier-like looking fellow." Woodward reported that Marinier was taken around by the local military commander, General Pitt, who "took much pleasure in shewing him off as a lion, to the neighbouring gentry."[17] Woodward's remarks suggest both his

FIGURE 5.1 *Sketch of an unknown French soldier by Emile-Jean-Horace Vernet, c. 1830. Hickey & Robertson, Houston/The Menil Foundation.*

and Pitt's admiration for Marinier as a soldier and their simultaneous use of the prisoner as exotic spectacle.

Later scholars have also occasionally noted the presence of black POWs. They appear in Francis Abell's influential 1914 overview of prisoners of war in Britain, though he largely recycled anecdotes from Woodward.[18] More recent investigations have uncovered some archaeological evidence and passing references to imprisoned individuals, but these specialized studies have rarely made their way into more general narratives.[19] To find out who the men and women of color at Portchester were—and especially, what their stories can tell us about race and freedom in the context of the Revolutionary Wars—we need to turn back to the records from the eighteenth century.

The Sources

Much of the information about the prisoners survives in the documents of the Transport Board, which took over responsibility for the care of prisoners of war from the Sick and Hurt Board in 1795.[20] Other important sources are in the papers of the War Office and Colonial Office, including letters, dispatches, and reports from the British military campaigns in the Caribbean in the 1790s, as well as correspondence relating to colonial administration.

Despite the administrative changeover, information was recorded fairly consistently. Registers noted when individual prisoners arrived at Portchester (or other prison depots), often along with their ranks, ages, regiments, and the places and dates of their surrender or capture. Other columns record whether they died, were moved elsewhere, or were discharged via a prisoner exchange. These records reflect the ebb and flow of the military campaigns during the French Revolutionary and Napoleonic Wars.

We have relatively few sources that allow us to uncover the prisoners' own voices, though a few memoirs survive from literate officers of color. This is the case with Jean Joseph Lambert, a free soldier of color and member of the St. Lucia National Guard, who fought the British in that island and escaped temporarily to Guadeloupe before being captured and brought to Portchester. It is also the case with Magloire Pélage, a mixed-race officer who had been captured as a POW by the British once already when fighting in Martinique in 1795. He was exchanged to France, and returned to the Caribbean, where he would be captured again in Guadeloupe in 1796. Their memoirs were written several years after their imprisonment and aimed to justify their activities in the context of rapidly changing French politics and colonial dynamics, but they also give us more direct and authentic personal histories.[21]

When taken together, these sources also allow us to begin piecing together prisoners' lives and experiences. Amongst the POWs at Portchester were free black and mixed-race people, former plantation slaves, and smaller numbers of white European French soldiers. Most had been captured on the southeastern Caribbean islands of St. Lucia, St. Vincent, Grenada, and Antigua—islands, that, as we will see, were repeatedly contested by British and French forces, as well as by competing factions within the French Revolution.

Marching into Captivity

The French Revolution fueled war between France and Britain and transformed racial, political, and national relations in the Caribbean. When Britain and France went to war in February 1793, British officials hoped to expand their empire in the West Indies both to avenge earlier losses to France and compensate for American independence. British troops captured Tobago in April 1793; then Martinique, St. Lucia, where many of the French prisoners were later captured, and Guadeloupe in March and April 1794; they also took control of the south and west provinces of Saint-Domingue (later Haiti). But by the end of 1795, Guadeloupe and St. Lucia were back in French control and Saint-Domingue was embroiled in civil war. Britain had gone from dreaming of a revitalized empire to risking losing what it had.[22]

One of the biggest factors in the reversal of British fortune in the Caribbean was also one of the most dramatic events of the revolutionary era: the French abolition of slavery. Some slaves took their freedom in the northern plains of Saint-Domingue in the revolt of August 1791. Then, in August 1793, French commissioners ratified that freedom, sending delegates to Paris to announce this decision. Finally, in February 1794, the National Assembly officially decreed emancipation in all colonies under French control. In practice, abolition came only to Guadeloupe, French Guiana, and Saint-Domingue; planters in Martinique deflected the decree by ceding control to the British conquerors, while France's Indian Ocean colonists in Île Bourbon and Mauritius simply refused to comply. Yet, as Laurent Dubois has noted, emancipation fed a development that would have been almost inconceivable at the beginning of the French Revolution: black soldiers—many of them ex-slaves—as the backbone of the French army against enemies in the Caribbean theater. For free people of color, service could be a continuation of pre-revolutionary service in militias and the *maréchaussée* (a kind of police); for former slaves, it represented a radical transformation.[23]

The use of these troops changed the political and military situation in the Caribbean. They helped the recently appointed French commissioner, Victor Hugues, rally colonists to the revolutionary republican cause and challenge British control of Guadeloupe, St. Lucia, Grenada, and St. Vincent. Many of the men who would be imprisoned in Portchester were part of these struggles, like Lambert, whose memoir recounts how he fought the British in St. Lucia. Similarly, General Marinier, later shown round "like a lion" by General Pitt, had been given a commission in the French army by Lambert, and led an active campaign of resistance against the British; indeed, British authorities later acknowledged that he had "often defeated the English Generals at St. Lucia & St. Vincent."[24]

In February 1796, a large expedition set sail from southern England. Its primary objective was to bring the islands at the center of the revolutionary struggle in the eastern Caribbean back under British control. The diary of John Moore, the British military commander leading the expedition on St. Lucia, vividly depicts the surrender of the French fortress on top of Morne Fortuné, later named Fort Charlotte, and the capture of the French army, including soldiers of color, on the island.

Moore records that at the end of May 1796, he took possession of the fort from French revolutionary forces led by General Cottin and Representative Goyrand. Cottin and Goyrand negotiated a surrender which ensured that all members of the garrison, regardless of race, would be treated as prisoners of war. This was a vital condition. Soldiers from the formerly enslaved workforce on St. Lucia had been emancipated, whether through their own military service or actions or the French government's formal abolition of slavery in 1794. The terms of the surrender guaranteed that the British would consider them French citizens, not slaves.

Moore described how the entire French garrison "to the amount of 2000, marched out, laid down their arms, and were conveyed to the Vigie, and from thence on board transports." While the French garrison remained imprisoned on military transport ships, the battle for St. Lucia continued with much of the fighting turning into guerrilla warfare.[25] The forested interior of the island served as a refuge, allowing members of a renegade republican and multiracial army to hide out and regroup.[26] Some prisoners managed to escape from the ships and join the rebellion. Robert McDonall, the captain of the *Ganges*, subsequently wrote about how difficult it had been to keep the prisoners confined: they "were . . . in a very mutinous State and a great Number affected their Escape every Night . . ."[27] McDonall had also discovered that island women were carrying messages to the prisoners

> . . . in Order to enable the black prisoners on board to get on Shore with an Intention of making an Attempt to Retake the Island, which was carried on by the Means of the Women conveying Intelligence from Ship to Ship, I therefore issued an Order that no Women sho[d] be admitted to come on board any of the Transports, and that those onboard should be immediately sent on shore.

Despite McDonall's orders, women and children were among the prisoners who were taken to Britain. Their presence is surprising not just because McDonall had sought to exclude them, but also because the French National Convention had expelled all "useless" women from its armies on April 30, 1793. This officially prohibited women soldiers, wives or companions of combatants, and camp followers, allowing only a limited number of *vivandières*—women charged with providing basic foodstuffs for the troops—and laundresses.[28] Individual women sometimes escaped or circumvented the law, and the measure may not have been applied to the Caribbean and the different dynamics of its armies. Women in various circumstances could find their ways onto ships heading to British prisons, included lone travelers, those traveling on business with their husbands, and the wives of soldiers, along with their children. Their presence in the records of the Transport Board suggests the multiplicity of ways in which women and young people could experience war and incarceration during the Revolutionary and Napoleonic Wars, including in connection with male soldiers from the Caribbean.[29]

The Atlantic Crossing to Britain

The continued fighting on St. Lucia and other islands in the vicinity such as St. Vincent and Grenada probably contributed to the decision to move the prisoners out of the conflict zone to St. Kitts and, later, to Britain. Other prisoners from the region were treated with less regard. Black Caribs—

descendants of indigenous island Caribs and enslaved Africans—on St. Vincent were deported to South America. And while a few of those who participated in "Fedon's rebellion"—a 1796 revolt of enslaved workers and francophone free people of color in British-controlled Grenada—were taken to England, many others were hastily and brutally killed.[30]

On July 29, 1796, after several months in captivity, the prisoners began the long journey across the Atlantic to Britain in a convoy of 104 ships, which also carried sick British soldiers and British troops returning home.[31] Nearly two months after setting out from St. Kitts, the Atlantic convoy arrived at Crookhaven on the southern coast of Ireland to take on supplies.

Conditions were difficult throughout the voyage. As a British military commander writing from the *Acorn* wrote, "the Medical Gentlemen on Board the Hospital ships have mentioned to me that they were in want of many necessary comforts, for the sick, on the Voyage."[32] When the ships finally arrived in England, authorities tried to estimate prisoner fatalities. While there were no clear indications of yellow fever, prisoners were suffering from other serious diseases: "The Prisoners are . . . in a wretched state being in want of clothing, and very sickly: a great number are ill of the small pox, of which and other disorders 268 died on the Passage."[33]

Captain McDonall of the *Ganges* later reported other challenges: the convoy had weathered gales and fog as well as lost rudders and bowsprits. Ships had gone missing and a lack of manpower meant that "if the black prisoners had not been in the Fleet many of the Merchant Ships and Transports must have founder'd being so weakly mann'd and leakey."[34] His report suggests that prisoners helped sail the ships—a plausible scenario, given the presence of black sailors in the Atlantic world, as well as a potential and intriguing challenge to naval and wartime order.[35]

The convoy arrived at Plymouth at the beginning of October, but there was no room to land the prisoners. Some went elsewhere in England—the *London* would wreck off the coast of Devon, and surviving prisoners were taken to Stapleton prison in Bristol—but most were ordered to sail east towards Portsmouth and the prison war depot at Portchester.[36] On October 12, 1796, five months after they had been captured, the first prisoners of war arrived, in a gale, in Portsmouth Harbour.

The Gates of the Prisons

The prisoners of war the British army and Royal Navy brought to Portsmouth entered into a well-established network of prisons, or depots. These had been set up across the British Isles to receive prisoners taken during the many conflicts of the seventeenth and eighteenth centuries. This network included purpose-built prisons such as Norman Cross and Dartmoor as well as castles such as Portchester and Edinburgh.[37] At its peak during the French Revolutionary and Napoleonic Wars, Portchester Castle could hold up to

8,000 prisoners. Together with the prison at Forton some eight miles away in Gosport and the prison hulks moored close by in Portsmouth harbor, it was an important center for handling prisoners captured during warfare.[38]

The holding of prisoners of war in Britain from the seventeenth century onwards was based on two different types of captivity—imprisonment for enlisted men and parole in British towns and villages for officers. Given the expense of guarding, clothing, and for officers paroled in the local community, providing a suitable allowance, both forms of captivity were intended to be temporary measures until an exchange of prisoners could be arranged.[39] Prisoners would be returned to their home countries via *cartel* ships which operated between designated ports, like Cherbourg and Morlaix in France. By the time that war broke out between Revolutionary France and Britain in 1793, Britain had developed a system for handling prisoners of war based on nearly a century and a half of overseas military conflict.

Life in Portchester Prison

It took fifteen days to get the more than 2,500 prisoners of war from the Caribbean on shore and into Portchester Prison and its hospital.[40] All the soldiers, regardless of race, joined the French and Dutch prisoners already at the castle, as well as some Lascars, sailors from the Indian subcontinent or Southeast Asia who had been captured in Dutch East India Company vessels.[41] British authorities seemed to have viewed the Caribbean prisoners primarily as French. They were captured under French military colors, wore some sort of French uniform, and likely spoke at least some French. They were therefore placed with other French prisoners and could expect to be eventually exchanged along with them.

Authorities did not consistently record race as the Caribbean prisoners entered Portchester. Many ordinary soldiers of color were identified as "Black Soldier," but staff did not usually mention race for officers; their military rank may have appeared more salient. When Richard Randall and then Dr. Johnston first recorded the arrival of women and children, neither man noted their race. It was only once in prison that a woman was described as "white" or "Col"d" ("colored"); children's race might then also be recorded.[42] Even when they were identified in explicitly racial terms, men and women were often amalgamated under the blanket term of "colored." In the French colonial arena, the label *gens de couleur* (people of color) could include all non-white men and women or designate mixed-race people rather than those defined as black; this distinction was effaced in Britain.

Officials at Portchester and Forton prisons seem also not to have identified prisoners as slaves. This is surprising, given Britain's deep involvement in the transatlantic slave trade and clear hopes of taking advantage of the volatile situation in the French Caribbean to reinforce its own slave-based plantation economies in the region. Yet it reflects both British legal categories and the reverberations of the French Revolution. The 1772 *Somerset* case was widely understood as abolishing slavery within the British Isles. Historians have debated exactly how the judgment was interpreted and applied. "Slave" was used relatively rarely to designate men and women of color within Great Britain itself in the later eighteenth century, though contemporary newspaper advertisements for runaways suggest that neither the word—nor especially, the status—of slave had actually disappeared from the metropole.[43]

The word "slave" was also still applied to individuals in Britain during the French Revolution. In October 1796, the ship *London* wrecked off the coast of Devon. Like those arriving in Portsmouth, it contained French soldiers captured in the eastern Caribbean: in this case, an "Officer, Eight Serjeants, and Eleven Privates of the 66th Reg[t] and 106 French Prisoners (Black)." The officials at the prisoner of war depot, Stapleton Prison in Bristol, recorded the shipwrecked survivors as "Mulatto Slave" or "Negro Slave."[44] Neither description was accurate as the black prisoners from the *London* were, along with all the other prisoners in the *Ganges* convoy, free French citizens. This use of the word "slave" at Bristol likely reflects Bristol's central role in the transatlantic slave trade and the attitudes of the local workforce.[45] It may also reflect the specific brutality of the repression of the Fedon Rebellion in Grenada, where most of the prisoners on the *London* were from.

Even as legally free men and women, prisoners confronted challenging conditions. They escaped the spread of yellow fever and dysentery which Dr. Johnston had so feared. Although there were still occasional cases of smallpox, authorities also managed to contain the outbreak that had caused so many fatalities en route from the Caribbean. Yet people still died in prison, sometimes shortly after arriving in Britain, of such things as fever, wounds, ulcers and other infections, cold, and the "Itch."[46] It seems likely that their deaths were usually caused by battle and its aftermath, or the general trauma of transport and prison, including the long journey across the Atlantic with little medical assistance.

Prisoners also lacked basic necessities. As Dr. Johnston's clerk Richard Randall noted when offloading the prisoners, most had little clothing, likely because they had been captured in apparel suitable for the Caribbean rather than winter in the British Isles—and the voyage had probably worn out what they did have. Almost as soon as they had arrived, Dr. Johnston asked for more supplies to help preserve the prisoners. Many had arrived shoeless; although the prison had a stock, the shoes were designed for average European soldiers and were too small.[47] While the prison waited for new supplies to arrive, Commissioner John Marsh in London called for socks and flannel waistcoats to be issued. Dr. Johnston was pleased, but wrote that "I much fear no external covering will prove adequate—to preserve them in frosty weather."[48]

The prison surgeon also recommended changes to the prisoners' diet in the hope that it might help them cope with the British weather. Ginger was added to their beer as it was thought that the spice would give warmth. A supply of potatoes seems to have been acquired in the hope that this vegetable would be closer to the Caribbean yam and therefore more palatable.[49] Eventually the Caribbean prisoners tired of potatoes and when Commissioners Otway and Johnston visited the castle in late 1796, they reported that the prisoners had requested bread.[50] For those who had consumed a French diet in St. Lucia, bread would have been considered essential; prisoners' request for it may thus have reflected their desire for what was actually familiar to them as inhabitants of the French Caribbean instead of what commissioners thought might be appropriate.[51]

Despite the efforts of the prison staff, the prisoners continued to suffer. In the same report, both commissioners reported that some men had sold or rejected their clothing. Expressing common racist attitudes at the time, they attributed this to the "indolence and carelessness" of people of color, rather than to practical reasons prisoners might have had for selling clothing allotted to them. The commissioners noted that some POWs from the Caribbean had been robbed "by the European Prisoners, they considering themselves as a superior race of beings to the unfortunate Blacks."[52] Despite the official abolition of slavery by French revolutionaries, white French prisoners taken from the Caribbean who had grown up in a slave society were likely to view blacks as inferior, while those who had never left Europe and may never before have encountered people of color were also likely to do so. The commissioners commented further that black soldiers seemed "to have their mental and bodily faculties benumbed and stupefied by the severity of the weather";[53] their physical and psychological state may therefore also have made them targets for anyone looking to steal food and clothing.

Given these circumstances, prison staff and commissioners ultimately realized that they would have to move the Caribbean prisoners. As Dr. Johnston wrote, "he [Lord Hugh Cloberry Christian, Chairman of the Transport Board] is convinced nothing but warmth will preserve them—he gave farther instructions to hasten the ships for their reception." Two prison ships were fitted out and by January 1797 most of the Caribbean prisoners were moved out of Portchester Castle and onto these two ships, *Captivity* and *Vigilant*, in Portsmouth Harbor.

The Prison Ships

The use of ships to house prisoners of war was a response to ever-increasing numbers arriving in Britain. The *Captivity* and the *Vigilant* were the first ones to be introduced in Portsmouth Harbour in the period. They were overseen by the agent in charge of the prison at Portchester, Mr. Holmwood, and were seen as an extension of the overall prison.

Such prison ships were reputed to be "floating tombs," with conditions far worse than on the land. This reputation is based largely on the memoirs of prisoners of war held during the American Revolution and the French Revolutionary and Napoleonic Wars.[54] While these accounts vividly portray horrible conditions, recent scholarship suggests that they may be exaggerated, or only represented certain cases.[55] It is clear from Dr. Johnston's correspondence that the decision to put the Caribbean prisoners onto prison ships was made in order to save them. He wrote, "I went on board one of the ships this day and nothing can be conceived more comfortable and warm," adding that "every delay to sending the poor wretches on board is murdering them thru wanton cruelty."[56]

Dr. Johnston may have hoped not only to remove the soldiers from the conditions of an English medieval castle, but also from hostile white prisoners. However, he did so at the cost of isolating them from local British populations. Portchester encouraged contact with local communities; there was a daily prison market where the prisoners could sell objects they had made and traders could sell food and other necessities. The local church was located inside the castle grounds and accessed through the prison. Prison and community were visible to each other, and this could work in the prisoners' favor. In some cases, members of the public also called attention to unacceptable prison conditions—we know, for example, that a serving naval officer, Admiral Lord Thomas Cochrane, visited Dartmoor Prison and the prison hulks at Plymouth in about 1811 and complained to the Admiralty about their appalling conditions.[57] By contrast, fewer visitors interacted with prisoners held in ships in the deep water channel outside Portchester Castle.

The Black Officers

While Caribbean soldiers of color were moved to the prison ships, their officers remained in the prison until the Admiralty decided what to do with them. Most prisoners of war above a certain rank would be offered their parole. They would have to agree not to try to escape and in return be allowed to live in one of the parole towns distributed across the British Islands. In the 1790s, this could be controversial. Authorities worried about French prisoners spreading their revolutionary zeal to the local population and the possibility that British townspeople might help them escape to France, whether out of revolutionary sympathy or the possibility of financial gain.[58] For example, in the village of Bishop's Waltham in Hampshire, which was ten miles from Portchester and housed French officers, the local butcher William Heatrell (whose alias was "Atril") arranged escapes to France. At Alresford, another Hampshire village with a large population of French officers, the smuggler James Garret also helped them escape—for a fee.[59]

Despite official reservations and reports of escape, large numbers of French officers, as well as prisoners of other nationalities, were released to take up their parole. Over fifty communities housed paroled officers, including Ludlow in Shropshire where Napoleon's brother Lucien was paroled in 1811.[60] It is difficult to ascertain exactly how many French officers were paroled around Britain, but it likely ran into the thousands. Small villages such as Hambledon in Hampshire would probably only have had a handful of officers. Larger communities, such as Reading in Berkshire or Ashburton in Devon, would have been able to accommodate more.[61]

The black officers therefore could have expected that the offer of parole would have been extended to them, particularly as some of the white European officers who had arrived with them were paroled within a month of arrival. Unfortunately, their ranks and commissions in the French army did not protect them against racism. General Pitt, commander at Portsmouth, who had shown off General Marinier "like a lion," communicated his objections, writing that the officers were "savage in their disposition" and were "very improper persons to be turned loose in any country." Pitt went on to claim that it would be "impossible to look upon them as Gentlemen."[62]

British officials proposed instead that the black officers should be moved to Scotland. Dr. Johnston and Commissioner Otway asked that the move be deferred until "a more favourable season of the year," as the officers were too ill to make the journey. In the end, they were never sent. Within a year (by the end of 1797), many were exchanged for captured British soldiers held in France, and sent to France via cartels.[63] In the short term, they were transported to Forton Prison in Gosport, which was judged to be more comfortable.[64] It was there that the officers rejoined the women and children who had arrived with them.

Women and Young Children in Prison

When the ships from the Caribbean arrived in October 1796, staff at Portchester almost immediately discovered the ninety-nine women and children among the captured soldiers. Many of the women appear to have been wives or companions of soldiers and officers, though research verifying their status is still in its early stages. The majority are recorded as being "Col'd Woman," with one "White Woman," two listed as "Woman," and one "Marg.t Hervieux" listed as "Wife," presumably of Captain "Cha.s Hervieux." As with many officers from the Caribbean, including General Marinier, Captain Hervieux's race was not recorded.[65]

While only one of the women was recorded as *wife*, some evidence suggests that others were, or considered themselves, married. Inconsistencies in the records may simply reflect how different clerks recorded the prisoners as they arrived.[66] They likely also reflect the challenges enslaved, or formerly enslaved, people had in legally marrying, as well as potential British disregard for their familial status.[67]

Prisoners nonetheless may have hoped to appeal to general British respect for families. One indication of this comes from the exchanges of Dr.

Johnston's clerk, Richard Randall, with four women from the *Hope* transport ship; two of the women appear to have been white, and the other two black or mixed-race. Randall reported that the women "informed me they were all married—and were very solicitous to have their Husbands with them."[68] His letter also hints at the women's agency in entreating British administrators. In some senses this is surprising; we might have anticipated that male prisoners would intervene on behalf of their wives, drawing on their relative authority both as men and as military figures. On the other hand, contemporaries were more likely to expect women to solicit the benevolence of authorities. Their vocal interventions also suggest that some may have actively chosen to accompany their imprisoned spouses to Britain rather than remain in the Caribbean.

This was not the first time that British authorities had dealt with female prisoners. In a letter to John Marsh, Dr. Johnston described what had been done in the past; "When we had on a former occasion Ladies of the same description at Forton—they were indulged with their husbands, parents or children and brothers." The same procedure was followed this time; the women and children were initially held at Portchester before being sent to Forton Prison and Hospital in Gosport.[69]

Once at Forton they were given separate lodgings in the prison hospital where they "sleep in cradles [a form of bed] and have fires allowed them"; the fact that authorities emphasized these comforts suggests that they were far from a given. We still have relatively little further documentary evidence of the women's experience of captivity, but can get some glimpses through the records of young children with them. Among the women who arrived from the Caribbean in 1796 were at least five children recorded as being born in prison.[70]

One, Marie Louisa, was born around November 3, 1796 just after the Caribbean prisoners had arrived. If she was carried to term, then her mother had been pregnant through the fighting in the Caribbean, her capture and incarceration on a ship, and the grueling journey across the Atlantic to Britain. Neither Maria Louisa's parents nor her race are recorded in the prison register; her name can be found in a group of six adult women listed as women of color, one of whom may have been her mother.[71] The parents of other children are similarly unidentified, though the children's inclusion in lists of officers suggests their parentage.[72]

Older children are listed by name and designated simply as boy or girl. Their race is sometimes given, but their familial relationships (if they had any among the prisoners) were not recorded. As with the uneven identification of women as wives, this may have been due in part to a lack of clear space in the prison registers for recording familial information—but that absence itself suggests that authorities did not expect to need to record it often, or consider it important to note.

The risks involved with having children in prison and their often fleeting presence in these records is brought into sharp focus by Daniel Chanouette, identified as an "infant of color, born in prison." As with other children, there is no record of his parentage, though his name appears among the officers; his mother may have been elsewhere among the prisoners or "DD" (Declared Dead). Daniel was entered at Forton on January 30, 1797; it is unclear whether this marks his birth or when he was transferred to the prison. Regardless, he could have been no more than five months old when he died of "convulsions" on March 22, 1797.[73]

Leaving Prison

We do not yet know the fate of all of the prisoners from the Caribbean recorded in Portchester. Some, like Daniel, did not survive. Others settled in Britain; some may have changed sides and joined British regiments.[74] Many officers, ordinary soldiers, and women and children were sent to France in fall 1797 (about a year after their arrival in Portsmouth) on cartel vessels. These included the *Smallbridge*, which left England on November 3, 1797 and arrived in the port of Cherbourg (see Map 0.1) on November 7, with twenty-three of 169 prisoners on board identified as being of color, including General Marinier and Eulalie Piemont, who may have been his wife, and the *Ariel*, which left on November 9 and arrived on the 11th, with thirty-five of its 252 prisoners listed as being of color.[75]

Prisoner exchanges assumed that soldiers were being returned to their home countries, where they might be reunited with their families—if they were too injured or weakened to fight or be re-enlisted. As we have seen, British authorities sometimes treated Caribbean POWs of color differently from their European counterparts, experimenting with their diet, blaming them for particular indolence and carelessness, and denying black officers parole. But when it came to attributing a national identity to prisoners, British authorities defined them as French: they were placed with other French prisoners and removed only when white prisoners started to harass them. They were gradually released from Portchester and sent to France alongside other French prisoners.

French authorities also defined the prisoners largely as French. In the passenger manifests of cartels releasing prisoners in Cherbourg and other French ports, men were consistently identified by their military titles, whether as officers (sergeant, corporal, captain, etc.) or just as "soldier." Registers identify most as *hommes de couleur*, but military identifications were paramount. Even those designated as "slave" in the Stapleton Prison registers were exchanged to France individually, indicating that they were being treated not as slaves but free soldiers and French citizens.[76]

Yet most of the black POWs had never lived in metropolitan France. They may have been seen—and seen themselves—as French soldiers, but France itself was potentially as foreign for them as Britain had been. Returning to the Caribbean was also challenging, as it too was not necessarily "home" for many of these formerly enslaved men and women. Distances were long—a possible two-month sea voyage—and travel expensive. The islands where many of these former prisoners had lived were still under British, not French, control in the later 1790s; this was notably the case with St. Lucia. (The island would briefly return to French control with the 1802 Treaty of Amiens, after which Napoleon formally reimposed slavery; the British regained it in 1803.)

Many of the prisoners of war—like returned POWs more generally—were reintegrated into the troops. Black soldiers released from Portchester and sent to France were taken to French colonial army depots, before being brought together at Rochefort and the Île d'Aix. Some would return to the Caribbean. After Napoleon Bonaparte reinstated slavery in the colonies in 1802, the French government would seek to identify and locate all potential soldiers of color in metropolitan France.[77] This entailed a radical change in their status. The Napoleonic government ceased to treat them as citizens, viewing them instead as potential threats to be removed from metropolitan French territory. Yet they still also appeared as useful combatants for a post-revolutionary nation. Remaining troops were consolidated into Le Bataillon des Pionniers Noirs (the Battalion of Black Pioneers) and sent to fight in Naples—and for those still in the ranks when Napoleon invaded Russia in 1812, to its cold steppes.[78]

Conclusion

It is possible that the presence of large numbers of French soldiers of color in Britain—with women and young children among them—was unique to Portchester. However, there are indications of other soldiers of color, including a few Napoleonic prisoners in the Norman Cross depot and about 1,000 black Americans from Britain's 1812 War with the United States who were housed in Dartmoor Prison.[79] It seems quite likely that other men and women of color captured during the Revolutionary and Napoleonic Wars were brought to Britain as POWs; the archives have more stories to tell.

Yet even these particular archives are revealing. They show us both the potential mobility of men and women in a transatlantic world, and the lasting and global reverberations of the French Revolution. They help us rethink what the practicalities of daily life—including clothing, diet, and housing, whether prisoners were housed separately or alongside spouses, in prisons or on ships, released into towns or kept from living there—can reveal about the treatment and experiences of men, women, and children who had escaped enslavement in the French Caribbean but found themselves prisoners of war in Britain. For British authorities concerned about infectious disease, practicalities of provisions, and diplomatic and military logistics, the care of these prisoners may have "involved the Honor of the Nation." For Caribbean prisoners and soldiers it involved the honor of another nation, that of the French Republic—but what that "nation" meant would prove complicated and unstable in an Atlantic world of revolution, war, and contested freedom. Taking up arms to defend the French Republic had made most of these men and women free, or, for those who had not been enslaved before joining the troops, had helped conserve their status as free French citizens. At the same time, it had also led to their fate as captives—faced with cold, disease, unfamiliar food, and hostility from other prisoners—but captives who could hope to regain their liberty.

The story of one of these former prisoners who resumed a military career is particularly revelatory of both the power of freedom and its instability in the context of revolution and war. Captain Louis Delgrès was a professional soldier and free officer of color. Like his colleague and later enemy Magloire Pélage, he had been captured as a POW by Britain in 1795 and had been exchanged to France. Both men had returned to the Caribbean to continue with their military careers. After Delgrès' recapture and then release from Portchester Prison in 1797, he would return to Guadeloupe in 1799. There he would ultimately die—fighting this time not against the British, but against Napoleon's reinstitutionalization of slavery.[80]

Source: Undated report on the state of the prisons and hospitals of Portchester and Forton (likely from the end of 1796), TNA (The National Archives) ADM 105/44

Report of the State of the Prisons and Hospitals of Portchester and Forton.—

On our first visitation to Portchester prison we arrived when the daily allowance of Beef, soup, and potatoes were serving out to the prisoners and found them good in quality . . .

It having likewise been said that broth given to the West Indians was mere pot liquor or nothing but warm water with salt and without vegetables and that it was issued to them twice a day. We enquired into this circumstance and found that the surgeon soon after their arrival observed the climate had such an effect on their constitutions that nothing could produce a sufficient degree of heat to render them comfortable, he therefore recommended one half of their broth being given in the evening to warm them on going to bed and likewise, that as they were liable to Dysenteric Complaints, the greens might be omitted and potatoes given in lieu, which mode was adopted for two or three days, but discontinued as soon as the prisoners made known their dislike to it.

As the broth was divided, from the above recommendation, into equal parts, probably a greater quantity was made on that account consequently weaker, yet each daily allowance contained the substance of 12 oz meat . . .

It may be here necessary to observe that unless the two or three days above mentioned when the broth was without greens and served twice in the day no difference was ever made between the Diet of the West Indian and European prisoners, except the former having the grains of ginger to every quart of their beer. This was by the advice of the surgeon who likewise recommended a pound of potatoes to be allowed to each man in lieu of half a pound of bread as more nutritive and better adapted to their constitutions; partaking in some degree of the nature of yams, the food of their country, and this commutation being found to meet the wishes of the prisoners in general it was accordingly adopted: on our visitation however they had changed their opinions and requested to have Bread instead of potatoes, which we determined to comply with immediately, and gave directions accordingly . . .

The supply of clothing to every prisoner has ever been ample and liberal.

In addition to what is allowed Europeans the West Indians have each a flannel under waistcoat and a thick pair of yarn socks. These advantages have been of little avail to defend them from the inclemency of this climate.

Many of them have sold their clothing, some are so indolent and careless that they will not even take the trouble to put on what has been given them, and others have been robbed and plundered by the European Prisoners, they considering themselves as a superior race of beings to the unfortunate Blacks who in general seem to have their mental and bodily faculties benumbed and stupefied by the severity of the weather.

. . . The West Indians are universally very desirous of Tobacco and to them it may be considered, particularly in this climate, as a necessary, not a luxury of life; but as they use it chiefly for smoaking [sic] how far people of their extreme carelessness and indolence can be trusted to smoak [sic] on board the prison ships we submit to their Lordships consideration . . .

Before we quit the subject of West Indian prisoners we beg leave to recommend to their Lordships the deferring till a more favourable season of the year on account of the present bad state [of] Health of many of them, the removal of the Creole and Black Officers to Scotland, if their Lordships judge it expedient, the General with some of the principal officers may be removed to one of the buildings in the Hospital at Forton, where they will be more comfortably lodged and accommodated than at Portchester.

If their Lordships should propose admitting of any distinction of rank among this class, we take the liberty of recommending to their attention General Marinier and another person named Lambert (both blacks). The humanity of the former to his prisoners is highly spoken of and the conduct of both since their arrival in England entitles them to our recommendation. In the tower of the castle are confined the Dutch prisoners who have conducted themselves with the utmost propriety, remarkable for cleanliness, consequently healthy, and never been guilty of selling their clothes, or other irregularities in common amongst the French.

Notes

1 The National Archives, Kew, UK (henceforward TNA), ADM 105/59 letter from Dr. Johnston to John Marsh, 4th Aug. 1796.

2 David Geggus, "The Cost of Pitt's Caribbean Campaigns, 1793–1798," *Historical Journal* 26, no. 3 (1983): 699–706; and Michael Duffy, "The French Revolution and British Attitudes to the West Indian Colonies," in *A Turbulent Time: The French Revolution and the Greater Caribbean*, ed. David Barry Gaspar and David Patrick Geggus (Bloomington: Indiana University Press, 1997), 78–101.

3 J. H. Powell, *Bring Out Your Dead: The Great Plague of Yellow Fever in Philadelphia in 1793* (Philadelphia: University of Pennsylvania Press, 2014); Philip Gould, "Race, Commerce, and the Literature of Yellow Fever in Early National Philadelphia," *Early American Literature* 35, no. 2 (2000): 157–86; and Katherine Arner, "Making Yellow Fever American: The American Republic, the British Empire, and the Geopolitics of Disease in the Atlantic World," *Atlantic Studies* 7, no. 4 (2010): 447–71.

4 TNA ADM 105/59, letter from Richard Randall to Dr. Johnston, 13th Oct. 1796.

5 TNA ADM 105/44, undated "Report on the State of the Prisons and Hospitals of Portchester and Forton" by William A. Otway and Dr. J. Johnston.

6 *Account of Prisoners of War lately arrived from the West Indies, and already landed in this country, according to the last Returns.* TNA ADM 98/107, letter from Transport Office to Evan Nepean, 1st Nov. 1796.

7 For ordinary soldiers, Alan Forrest's work has been especially influential: see, for example, *The Soldiers of the French Revolution* (Durham, NC: Duke University Press, 1990). On military diversity, works include Roger Norman Buckley, *The British Army in the West Indies: Society and the Military in the Revolutionary Age* (Gainesville: University Press of Florida, 1998); Bryan Dyde, *The Empty Sleeve: The Story of the West India Regiments of the British Army* (St John's, Antigua: Hansib Caribbean, 1997); and Bernard Gainot, *Les officiers de couleur dans les armées de la République et de l'Empire, 1792–1815* (Paris: Karthala, 2007).

8 Among others, see Joseph Klaits and Michael H. Haltzel, eds., *The Global Ramifications of the French Revolution* (Cambridge: Cambridge University Press, 1994); Suzanne Desan et al., eds., *The French Revolution in Global Perspective* (Ithaca, NY: Cornell University Press, 2013); Bryan A. Banks and Erica Johnson, eds., *The French Revolution and Religion in Global Perspective: Freedom and Faith* (Basingstoke, UK: Palgrave Macmillan, 2017).

9 Key works include Alyssa Sepinwall, *Haitian History: New Perspectives* (New York: Routledge, 2012); Carolyn Fick, *The Making of Haiti: The Saint Domingue Revolution From Below* (Knoxville: University of Tennessee Press, 1990); David Geggus, *Haitian Revolutionary Studies* (Bloomington: Indiana University Press, 2002); Laurent Dubois, *Avengers of the New World: The Story of the Haitian Revolution* (Cambridge, MA: Harvard University Press, 2004); and Jeremy Popkin, *You Are All Free: The Haitian Revolution and the Abolition of Slavery* (Cambridge: Cambridge University Press, 2010).

10 See Michael Craton, *Testing the Chains: Resistance to Slavery in the British West Indies* (Ithaca, NY: Cornell University Press, 1982); David Barry Gaspar and David Geggus, eds., *A Turbulent Time: The French Revolution in the Greater Caribbean* (Bloomington: Indiana University Press, 1997); Laurent Dubois, "Citizen Soldiers: Emancipation and Military Service in the French Caribbean," in *Arming Slaves: From Classical Times to the Modern Age*, ed. Christopher Leslie Brown and Philip D. Morgan (New Haven, CT: Yale University Press, 2006), 233–54; and Paul Friedland, "Every Island is not Haiti: The French Revolution in the Windward Islands," in *Rethinking the Age of Revolutions: France and the Modern World*, ed. David Bell and Yair Mintzker (Oxford: Oxford University Press, 2018), 41–79. See also Boris Lesueur, "Les Troupes coloniales et l'échec militaire français aux Antilles, des débuts de la Révolution à 1803," *Revue d'histoire maritime* 4 (2005): 225–45; and Léo Elisabeth, "Déportés des Petites Antilles (1801–1803)," in *Rétablissement de l'esclavage dans les colonies françaises, 1802*, ed. Yves Bénot and Marcel Dorigny (Paris: Maisonneuve & Larose, 2003), 69–94.

11 Among other works, see Denis Smith, *The Prisoners of Cabrera: Napoleon's Forgotten Soldiers 1809–1814* (New York: Four Wall Eight Windows, 2001); Ian McDougall, *All Men Are Brethren: Prisoners of War in Scotland, 1803–1814* (Edinburgh: Birlinn, 2009); Peter Wilson, "Prisoners in Early Modern Warfare," in *Prisoners in War*, ed. Sybille Schiepers (Oxford: Oxford University Press, 2010), 39–56.

12 See especially Peter Fryer, *Staying Power: The History of Black People in Britain* (London: Pluto Press, 1984); David Dabydeen et al., *The Oxford Companion to Black British History* (Oxford: Oxford University Press, 2008); and Miranda Kaufman, *Black Tudors, the Untold Story* (London: Oneworld, 2017). On the late eighteenth and nineteenth century, relevant works include Gretchen Gerzina, *Black London: Life before Emancipation* (New Brunswick, NJ: Rutgers University Press, 1995); Norma Myers, *Reconstructing the Black Past: Blacks in Britain, 1780–1830* (London: Routledge, 1996); Peter King and John Carter Wood, "Black People and the Criminal Justice System: Prejudice and Practice in later eighteenth- and early nineteenth-century London," *Historical Research* 88, no. 239 (2015): 100–25; and Daniel Livesay, *Children of Uncertain Fortune: Mixed-race Jamaicans in Britain and the Atlantic Family, 1733–1833* (Chapel Hill: University of North Carolina Press, 2018).

13 Historians have considered these questions more thoroughly within Caribbean and North American contexts. See especially Rebecca Scott, *Freedom Papers: An Atlantic Odyssey in the Age of Emancipation* (Cambridge, MA: Harvard University Press, 2012), and Ada Ferrer, *Freedom's Mirror: Cuba and Haiti in the Age of Revolution* (Cambridge: Cambridge University Press, 2014).

14 The exhibit intended to promote renewed interest in Britain's war with revolutionary France, as well as the wider history of the black Atlantic, diaspora, and Caribbean studies. See https://www.english-heritage.org.uk/visit/places/portchester-castle/history-and-stories/black-prisoners-at-portchester/ and http://blog.english-heritage.org.uk/portchester-castles-black-prisoners/.

15 René Chartrand and Francis Black, *Napoleon's Overseas Army* (London: Osprey, 1989).

16 Sketch of an unknown French soldier by Emile-Jean-Horace Vernet, *c.* 1830, https://www.english-heritage.org.uk/visit/places/portchester-castle/history-and-stories/black-prisoners-at-portchester/.

17 W. Woodward, *Portchester Castle, Its Origin, Story, and Antiquities, interspersed with anecdotes of its occupation during the late French wars* (Portsea: Woodward, 1845).

18 Like Woodward's claims that Marinier had four wives and, unable to read and write, relied upon his aide-de-camp to sign his parole release. Francis Abell, *Prisoners of War in Britain 1756–1815* (London: Oxford University Press, 1914), 447. Abell's book does not provide references, making it difficult to verify information.

19 Barry Cunliffe and Beverley Garratt, *Excavations at Portchester Castle, Volume V: Post Medieval 1609–1819* (London: Society of Antiquaries, 1994), 148; Patricia K. Crimmin, "Prisoners of War and British Port Communities, 1793–1815," *The Northern Mariner/Le marin du nord* 6 (1996): 17–27, here 20; Paul Chamberlain, *Hell upon Water: Prisoners of War in Britain, 1793–1815* (Stroud, UK: History Press, 2008), 35.

20 Records for the Transport Board are in the British National Archives in Kew; those for the Sick and Hurt Board (full name "The Commissioners for taking care of Sick and Wounded Seamen and for the Care and Treatment of Prisoners of War") are in the National Maritime Museum in Greenwich, UK, with a few in Kew.

20 TNA ADM 103/133, Register of prisoners of war, Forton.

21 Jean-Joseph Lambert, *Mémoire de . . ., Délégué à Sainte-Lucie par les commissaires de la Convention Nationale Aux Isle du Vent, et présentement capitaine à la 4ième demi-brigade d'infanterie de Ligne* (Paris: Imp. Nat. des Aveugles-Travailleurs, nd); in the French Archives Nationales d'Outre-Mer, CAOM C/10C/7, and Magloire Pélage; *Mémoire pour le chef de brigade Magloire Pélage, et pour les habitants de la Guadeloupe* (Paris: Desenne Librarie, 1803).

22 Duffy, "The French Revolution and British Attitudes," 78–101.

23 Dubois, "Citizen Soldiers," 233. See also David Geggus, "The Arming of Slaves in the Haitian Revolution," in *Arming Slaves: From Classical Times to the Modern Age*, ed. Christopher Leslie Brown and Philip D. Morgan (New Haven, CT: Yale University Press, 2006), 209–32.

24 See Abigail Coppins, "Black Prisoners of War in an English Castle, 1793–1802" (Ph.D. diss., Warwick, in progress).

25 Sir J. F. Maurice, ed., *The Diary of Sir John Moore* (London: Edward Arnold, 1904), 1:219–23.

26 Friedland, "Every Island," emphasizes the multiracial nature of this army; other historians stress the importance of emancipation in filling its ranks. See especially David Barry Gaspar, "La Guerre des Bois: Revolution, War and Slavery in Saint Lucia, 1793–1838," in *A Turbulent Time: The French Revolution in the Greater Caribbean*, ed. David Barry Gaspar and David Geggus (Bloomington: Indiana University Press, 1997), 102–30.

27 See Coppins, "Black Prisoners of War."

28 See Jennifer Ngaire Heuer, "Celibacy, Courage, and Hungry Wives: Debating Military Marriage and Citizenship in Pre-revolutionary France," *European History Quarterly* 46, no. 4 (2016): 648–67.

29 For example, Elizabeth Rodrigus captured with her husband, Jacques Rodrigus, on the American vessel the *Love*, while travelling to Nantes (TNA ADM 105/59, List of all French Passengers now in the custody of Mr. Holmwood, Agent at Portchester Castle, undated); young boys incarcerated at Deal Prison (TNA ADM 105/44, Report dated 29th August 1798 from Rupert George to the Commissioners for the Transport Service); ship's boys from the *Hercule* captured at the Battle of the Raz de Seine in 1798 (TNA ADM 105/59, List of boys under 12 years on board prison ships, 8th Oct. 1798.)

30 Kit Candlin, "The Role of the Enslaved in the 'Fedon Rebellion' of 1795," *Slavery & Abolition* 39, no. 4 (2018): 665–707.

31 TNA ADM WO40/8, 26th Sept. 1796, Lt. Colonel Baldwin Leighton to William Wyndham, Secretary at War, London.

32 TNA ADM WO40/8, 26th Sept. 1796, Lt. Colonel Baldwin Leighton to William Wyndham, Secretary at War, London.

33 TNA WO 40/8, B M General Losack to Matthew Lewis Esq—9th Oct. 1796; TNA WO 40/8, Dr. Farr to B.M. General Losack—8th Oct. 1796

34 See Coppins, "Black Prisoners of War."

35 See, for example, Marcus Rediker, *Outlaws of the Atlantic: Sailors, Pirates, and Motley Crews in the Age of the Sail* (Boston: Beacon Press, 2014); Peter Linebaugh and Marcus Rediker, *The Many-Headed Hydra: Sailors, Slaves, Commoners, and the Hidden History of the Revolutionary Atlantic* (Boston: Beacon Press, 2000); and Ray Costello, *Black Salt: Seafarers of African Descent on British Ships* (Liverpool: Liverpool University Press, 2014).

36 TNA WO 40/8, Letter dated 9 Oct. 1796 from Plymouth Dock HQ to Secretary at War.

37 Chamberlain, *Hell upon Water*, and Paul Chamberlain, *The Napoleonic Prison of Norman Cross* (Stroud, UK: History Press, 2018).

38 Cunliffe and Garratt, *Excavations at Portchester Castle, Vol. V.*

39 Sibylle Scheipers, *Prisoners in War* (Oxford: Oxford University Press, 2010), 4.

40 The number of 2,512 people listed in the Portchester Prison is not a comprehensive total. There were also 830 prisoners recorded arriving at Forton Prison, although many individuals appear on both registers.

41 On Lascars in eighteenth-century Britain, see Myers, *Reconstructing the Black Past*.

42 TNA ADM 103/133, Register of prisoners of war, Forton, 1793–1797.

43 On "slave" as a category in metropolitan Britain, see Myers, *Reconstructing the Black Past*; Kathleen Chater, "Black People in England, 1660–1807," *Parliamentary History* 26, supplement (2007): 66–83; and Sue Peabody and Keila Grinberg, eds., *Slavery, Freedom, and the Law in the Atlantic World* (Boston: Bedford/Saint Martins, 2007). For newspaper advertisements, see "Runaway Slaves in Britain: bondage, freedom and race in the eighteenth century," https://www.runaways.gla.ac.uk/database/; the database currently stops in 1780.

44 https://thewreckoftheweek.wordpress.com/tag/rapparee-cove/.

45 Bristol has sought to confront aspects of this history. See, for example, https://www.bristolmuseums.org.uk/stories/bristol-transatlantic-slave-trade/

46 See Coppins, "Black Prisoners of War."

47 TNA ADM 105/59, Letter dated 8th Dec.1796—Dr. Johnston to John Marsh.

48 TNA ADM 105/59, Letter dated 6th Nov, 1796—Dr. Johnston to John Marsh.

49 TNA ADM 105/44, undated report (probably Nov./Dec. 1796)—From William Otway and Dr. Johnston.

50 TNA ADM 105/44, undated report (probably Nov./Dec. 1796)—From William Otway and Dr. Johnston.

51 Our thanks to Sue Peabody for noting the likely diet of those in St. Lucia. See also the Napoleonic watercolor by Captain Durrant of French prisoners of war baking bread at Norman Cross Prison, https://collections.hampshireculture.org.uk/object/index-number-82-painting-watercolour-painting-south-east-quadrangle-norman-cross-prison.

52 TNA ADM 105/44, undated report (probably Nov./Dec. 1796)—From William Otway and Dr. Johnston.

53 TNA ADM 105/44, undated report (probably Nov./Dec. 1796)—From William Otway and Dr. Johnston.

54 The best known is probably Louis Garneray, *The French Prisoner* (London: Merin Press, 1957), originally published in 1851 as *Mes Pontons*, multiple reissues.

55 See especially Tim Leunig, Jelle van Lottum, and Bo Poulsen, "Surprisingly Gentle Confinement: British Treatment of Danish and Napoleonic Prisoners of War during the Napoleonic Wars," *Scandinavian Economic History Review* 66, no. 3 (2018): 282–97.

56 TNA ADM 105/59, Letter from Dr. Johnston to John Marsh, 24th Nov. 1796.

57 Chamberlain, *Hell Upon Water*, 220–1, 227–8.

58 TNA WO 40/8, Letter from W. Wyngard (for General Pitt) to unknown, likely to be the Admiralty in London, 20th Oct. 1796.

59 Barbara Biddell, *Napoleonic Prisoners of War in & around Bishop's Waltham* (Dublin: Two Plus George Ltd, 2007), 55–64.

60 For details, see Marcello Simonetta and Noga Arikha, *Napoleon and the Rebel: A Story of Brotherhood, Passion, and Power* (New York: Palgrave Macmillan, 2011), 223–6.

61 Chamberlain, *Hell upon Water*, 114–37; https://historywm.com/file/historywm/e09-brother-in-exile-lucien-bonaparte-west-midlands-56302.pdf; and Biddell, *Napoleonic Prisoners of War.*

62 TNA WO/40, Letter from W. Wyngard (for General Pitt) to unknown, likely to be the Admiralty in London, 20th Oct. 1796.

63 TNA ADM 105/44, undated report from Dr. Johnston and William Otway.

64 TNA ADM 105/44, undated report from Dr. Johnston and William Otway.

65 TNA ADM 103/133, Register of prisoners of war, Forton, 1793–1797.

66 TNA ADM 103/133, Register of prisoners of war, Forton, 1793–1797.

67 Elizabeth Colwill, "Freedwomen's Familial Politics: Marriage, War and Rites of Registry in Post-Emancipation Saint-Domingue," in *Gender, War and Politics: Transatlantic Perspectives 1775–1830*, ed. Karen Hagemann et al. (Basingstoke, UK: Palgrave Macmillan, 2010), 71–89.

68 TNA ADM 105/59, Letter from Richard Randall to Dr. Johnston, 13th Oct. 1796.

69 TNA ADM 105/59, Letter from Dr. Johnston to John Marsh, 17th Oct. 1796.

70 TNA ADM 103/133, Register of prisoners of war, Forton, 1793–1797.

71 TNA ADM 103/133, Register of prisoners of war, Forton, 1793–1797.

72 TNA ADM 103/133, Register of prisoners of war, Forton, 1793–1797.

73 TNA ADM 103/133, Register of prisoners of war, Forton 1793–1797; See Coppins, "Black Prisoners of War."

74 For the case of twelve black and mixed-race French prisoners who joined the British merchant service in 1801, see Chamberlain, *The Napoleonic Prison of Norman Cross*, 174–5.

75 Coppins, "Black Prisoners of War."

76 TNA ADM 103/41, Register of prisoners of war, Bristol, 1793–1800.

77 See Michael Sibalis, "Les Noirs en France sous Napoléon: l'enquête de 1807," in *1802: le rétablissement de l'esclavage dans les colonies françaises*, ed. Marcel Dorigny and Yves Benot (Paris: Masonneuve & Larose, 2003), 95–106.

78 Gainot, *Les officiers de couleur*; Elisabeth, "Déportés des Petites Antilles," 92–3.

79 Chamberlain, *The Napoleonic Prison of Norman Cross*.

80 The French National Assembly would Pantheonize him in 1998 as part of the 150th anniversary of the second abolition of slavery in the French Empire in 1848.

PART TWO

The Right To?— Revolutionary Justice at Work

6

Crime, Law, and Justice

Claire Cage

We often associate the French Revolution with the dramatic spectacle of public executions by guillotine, but the spectacle of capital punishment had been a feature of French justice long before the Revolution. The philosopher Michel Foucault famously recounted the execution of the regicide Robert-François Damiens, a domestic servant who attempted to assassinate Louis XV. In March 1757, before a huge crowd in Paris, Damiens was brutally tortured. His flesh was burned and torn from his body, and he was drawn and quartered. But during the years following Damiens's execution, a shift in cultural sensibilities led increasing numbers of French men and women to object to criminals suffering through painful modes of execution. Foucault thus traced a gradual shift in penal practices from torture to imprisonment as the dominant form of punishment and described associated changes in how people thought about power.[1]

Shifting attitudes towards punishment also explain why the French revolutionaries adopted the guillotine, which was seen as a more humane mode of execution; and why some French citizens came to reject capital punishment altogether. Maximilien Robespierre, the revolutionary political leader most associated with the Terror, initially opposed the death penalty as barbaric, cruel, and ineffective. During the legislative debates in 1791 over the new penal code, Robespierre called upon legislators to "erase from the Code of the French the blood laws which call for judicial murder."[2] His humanitarian concerns did not sway the majority of deputies, and the revolutionary State preserved the death penalty. Robespierre himself later made clear that exceptions should be made for the king, whom he voted to execute in 1793, and for others deemed traitors to the republic. While the most famous execution of the Old Regime had been that of a regicide, years later in the Revolution, the king himself thus became a special target of the death penalty.

Robespierre's early opposition to the death penalty and his subsequent support of sentencing the king and thousands of French citizens to death reflect the inherent tensions and contradictions of revolutionary justice. In an attempt to create a more just society, the revolutionaries did away with the institutions and practices of the Old Regime that they believed perpetuated injustice, implementing sweeping changes that transformed the juridical landscape. They were able to achieve a general consensus on some issues, such as abandoning the spectacle of suffering; abolishing *lettres de cachet*, which were a means of imprisoning individuals without trial; and reorganizing the courts and introducing trials by jury. At the same time, the Revolution created new legal categories for political crimes, such as emigration (leaving the country without official permission) and *lèse-nation* (treason), resulting in thousands of imprisonments, deportations, and executions. Different understandings of what it meant to see justice done led to forms of violent, extra-legal "popular justice," including prison massacres. Both ends of the political spectrum—royalists and radical revolutionaries—exacted popular justice and vengeance on their enemies. Revolutionary legislators and ordinary men and women alike shaped the pursuit of justice in ways that profoundly affected French society as well as the course of the Revolution, and ultimately exposed the limited extent to which its liberal ideals were realized in practice. Revolutionary justice was both liberal and repressive, unifying and divisive, and the administration of justice reflected and deepened political antagonisms as well as underlying tensions between revolutionary ideals and reality.

Legal and Judicial Reforms of the Early Revolution

The revolutionaries sought to distance themselves from the judicial system of Old Regime France, which they attacked as barbaric, arbitrary, corrupt, and inegalitarian. They drew upon Enlightenment thinkers and pre-revolutionary critics in their opposition to torture. Torture under the Old Regime had served both as a tool of judicial inquiry and form of punishment. French investigators used "preparatory torture" on accused criminals in judicial chambers to elicit confessions. The State also publicly used "preliminary torture" of convicted criminals to gather the names of accomplices. In 1780, Jacques Necker ordered the end of preparatory torture, and in 1788, the French State outlawed preliminary torture.[3] However, torture persisted as a form of punishment. It had been codified by the Royal Ordinance of 1670, the last piece of criminal legislation until the Revolution. The Ordinance outlined several forms of punishment: death, varying degrees of torture, penal servitude for life or for a specified time period, whipping, branding, the *amende honorable* (which obliged the condemned to publicly confess his crime and beg forgiveness on his knees), expiation through other forms of public humiliation, and exile. The manner of execution for those facing the death penalty depended on both the nature of the crime and the social status of the condemned. Old Regime executions involved not simply the deprivation of life but also the infliction of pain. The least painful method of execution was decapitation, which was generally reserved for social elites. Executions also took the forms of hanging; dismemberment through drawing and quartering; burning at the stake; and breaking on the wheel, in which the condemned was tied to a large wheel and his limbs broken by the executioner's blows with an iron bar. Mutilation preceded death in some cases, such as cutting off the hand of those convicted of parricide.[4]

Objections to these punishments, particularly for relatively minor offenses, had become widespread by the time of the Revolution. This outcry was part of broader critiques about French criminal justice. Many French men and women resented the slow, costly, and hierarchical nature of Old Regime justice. They objected to the venality, or sale, of judgeships or other judicial offices, exorbitant judicial fees, and the arbitrary nature of some arrests and punishments.[5] These critiques found expression in the *cahiers de doléances*, grievances drawn up by local assemblies representing each of the three estates in preparation for the Estates-General of 1789. Many *cahiers* presented fully developed demands for judicial reform, calling for a more efficient, transparent, and humane judicial system. They criticized Old Regime proceedings in which judges examined the accused and witnesses in secret, and accused persons lacked access to documents, legal counsel, and information about accusers. *Cahiers* complained about seigneurial justice, particularly the multiplicity of justices and jurisdictions, absent judges, high costs, and infrequent seigneurial court sessions.[6] Some *cahiers* called for the abolition of torture, publicity for criminal proceedings, the right to defense counsel, trials by jury, freedom from arbitrary arrest and imprisonment, and the abolition of *lettres de cachet*.

Many of these demands came to fruition after the storming of the Bastille on July 14, 1789 and the transformation of the Estates-General into the National Assembly. To many French men and women, the Bastille prison symbolized despotic and arbitrary royal authority, particularly through its association with *lettres de cachet*, although only seven men were imprisoned there in 1789. Participants in the attack on the Bastille murdered the prison governor and others and displayed their severed heads on pikes through the streets of Paris. In the weeks that followed, revolutionary deputies, many of whom were lawyers or magistrates, sought to create a new legal and political order. Old Regime law and justice had emanated from the king, in whom sovereignty resided and who was the supreme judge of the land. In contrast, popular sovereignty was one of the animating principles of the Revolution, and the National Assembly represented the sovereign will of the people. On behalf of the people, the Assembly introduced dramatic legal changes. On the night of August 4, it voted unanimously to abolish seigniorial courts, feudal privileges, and venal offices, effectively transforming the judiciary and ending legal privileges.[7] It then took a crucial step in developing a new constitution based on individual liberty and legal equality by promulgating the Declaration of Rights of Man and Citizen on August 26. The Assembly adopted three articles (7 to 9) explicitly concerning legal and judicial reform, declaring that French citizens would have equality before the law, protection from arbitrary arrest and detention, the presumption of innocence, and freedom from cruel, excessive, or arbitrary punishments. The Declaration eventually became the preamble to France's first written constitution, adopted in September 1791.

The National Assembly continued to make sweeping judicial reforms, including abolishing torture and providing greater transparency, publicity, and fairness in criminal proceedings. In fall 1789, the Assembly enhanced protections for accused persons, including guaranteeing their right to legal counsel. It abolished all forms of torture and ordered that judgments be made publicly. In January 1790, the legislature decreed uniform sentencing regardless of the status of the accused, and in March 1790, it voted to reorganize the judiciary. In August 1790, the legislature decreed that judges would no longer be royal appointees but elected. The following month, it suppressed the parlements, the thirteen regional sovereign courts of law that had also served as final courts of appeal for the judicial districts of the country, and the lower Old Regime courts. The Assembly abolished the Order of Barristers in a further attack on traditional institutions, corporate bodies, and privileges in French society.[8]

Revolutionaries also tackled the problem of *lettres de cachet*. Both men and women used this legal instrument, most commonly against family members charged with financial, sexual, or moral misconduct, in order to enforce social norms surrounding the family, sexuality, spousal relationships, and parent–child relations. The monarchy also used the *lettres* against recalcitrant magistrates. The *lettres* served as an extrajudicial procedure in which the accused persons lacked legal counsel, did not appear before a judge, and were detained in various kinds of institutions, such as convents, monasteries, asylums, or prisons, depending upon their ability to pay, for a period of time ranging from several months to a lifetime. The Comte de Mirabeau led the charge against them. Mirabeau's father, outraged by his son's scandalous love affairs, had had him imprisoned by *lettres de cachet* from the late 1760s to early 1780s. After evading a death sentence for abduction and sedition, Mirabeau pursued a career in politics. He and other critics equated *lettres de cachet* with the arbitrary and despotic use of royal authority, and they fomented nearly universal hostility toward the practice. In March 1790, the National Assembly abolished the *lettres*.[9]

Most significantly in terms of judicial innovations, the Revolution introduced trial by jury, used for all serious crimes and punishments, and the participation of citizen-jurors in the administration of justice. The law of February 7, 1791 established the procedures for juries in criminal proceedings. After preliminary investigations overseen by a district judge, defendants appeared before an eight-person grand jury or *jury d'accusation*, which determined whether the evidence against the accused was strong enough for an indictment. If so, the accused then appeared before departmental criminal tribunals and a twelve-person trial jury or *jury de jugement*. Jurors came from the ranks of the voters or "active citizens," which consisted of men aged twenty-five and older who paid taxes equal to at least three days of a laborer's wage as specified in the Constitution of 1791. The introduction of juries marked a shift from the inquisitorial procedures of the Old Regime to accusatorial procedures that privileged oral testimony and debates. Revolutionaries saw trials by jury as the embodiment of revolutionary principles, including transparency, and the safeguard of liberty. Deputy Adrien Duport, who had proposed trials by jury for both civil and criminal trials, viewed them as a means to elevate humanity and cultivate ideals of freedom, equality, and fraternity. Jury duty would impart important lessons about citizenship to jurors and allow them to apply the law to their fellow citizens and participate directly in self-governance. Serving as jurors was one of the most crucial ways in which ordinary citizens shaped the justice system and were politically and civically engaged in the new revolutionary regime.[10]

Revolutionaries embraced trials by jury for criminal proceedings but had less consensus on the death penalty. Over the course of the eighteenth century, more and more French people came to view the purpose of punishment in terms of removing dangerous individuals from society rather than publicly inflicting pain upon them. By the time of the Revolution, public opinion held that the death penalty should be rarely used and be applied with the least possible amount of pain. Some objected to the death penalty altogether. Speaking on behalf of the committees charged with drafting a new penal code on May 23, 1791, Louis-Michel Lepeletier de Saint-Fargeau argued for abolishing capital punishment. In the ensuing debates from May 30 to June 1, representatives Adrien Duport, Jérôme Pétion, and Robespierre eloquently supported Lepeletier's call. They argued that the death penalty was unjust and immoral, that it did not deter crime effectively, and that judicial errors resulted in the death of innocent people. Despite their appeals, the Assembly refused to do away with the death penalty but declared that it would consist simply of the deprivation of life, effectively abolishing modes of execution involving severe pain.[11]

In the new revolutionary judicial regime, the preferred mode of punishment for most crimes was imprisonment or forced labor. The new penal code of 1791 specified fixed criminal penalties for every offense, corresponding to their severity. The total number of types of capital crimes, the most serious offenses, decreased from 115 to 32. The penal code preserved capital punishment for treason, murder, arson, poisoning, and counterfeiting.[12] Revolutionaries prescribed decapitation, which had been reserved for nobles under the Old Regime, as the mode of execution for all capital crimes for all offenders, regardless of their social status. Other punishments for felonies included forced labor; imprisonment, including *gêne* (solitary confinement);

deportation; and "civic degradation," which entailed the stripping away of full citizenship rights from "active citizens" as well as the *carcan*, an iron collar worn in public for two hours, for condemned women and others without full citizenship rights. Those condemned to hard labor with a sentence of "irons" (*fers*) worked for the profit of the State in prisons (*maisons de force*), in the navy's work prisons—or *bagnes*—in the port cities of Rochefort, Brest, and Toulon, or in other public works including draining marshes or extracting ores through mining.[13]

Deportation initially appeared a humane and practical alternative to capital punishment. Originally intended for recidivists or repeat offenders, it became more commonly used for political offenders, particularly for exiling priests to French Guiana. Due to the very high rates of mortality, this mode of punishment became known as the "dry guillotine," effectively a bloodless death sentence. A few of the first deportees in Guiana were able to avoid that fate by escaping.[14] As the Revolution progressed, maritime war made implementing the punishment of deportation overseas increasingly difficult.

The guillotine ultimately became the most visible manifestation of the new revolutionary penal regime. Under the Old Regime, those sentenced to death faced different modes of execution based on the age, sex, and status of the offender and the nature of their crime. In 1791, revolutionaries decided upon decapitation as the universal, egalitarian, and only mode of execution. At that point, the guillotine had not yet been developed. Beheadings involved the executioner wielding an axe or sword, and the condemned sometimes survived the first and even the second blow. Charles-Henri Sanson, the executioner of Paris, was concerned about the impracticality of beheadings for all capital crimes. He warned of potential accidents and "dangerous scenes" involving bloody struggles between the condemned and executioners, which would terrify the public. He sought a means of beheading by sword that would "fix the condemned in place."[15]

In response to Sanson's concerns, the prominent surgeon Antoine Louis developed plans for a decapitation machine. Louis' plans responded to an earlier proposal by Joseph-Ignace Guillotin, a physician and legislator, to the National Assembly in 1789 that capital punishment should take the form of decapitation "by means of a simple mechanism."[16] Others pursued rival plans for mechanical modes of execution. As Paul Friedland's work has shown, these plans included both a strangulation machine and a proto-gas chamber. Citizen Girardet proposed that a glass-paneled "asphyxiation booth" be placed on a scaffold and filled with charcoal, sulfur, and other fumes, which would cause the condemned to suffocate. Girardet wrote, "One will see through the panes of glass, notwithstanding the thickness of the smoke, *death by suffocation*; horrors will be concealed; and justice will be done promptly. The cadaver will be removed from the booth, it will remain for a quarter hour in the public gaze then carried to the *field of sleep*."[17] The Assembly eschewed these proposals. Insisting on decapitation, it adopted the machine that Louis had developed, which became known as the guillotine after Guillotin. Louis provided his descriptive diagram of the machine to Guidon, France's official carpenter, but his estimate was too high, so the Assembly enlisted the German harpsichord-maker Tobias Schmidt to make the device instead. The first machine built was tested using live sheep and three human cadavers on April 17, 1792. On April 25, the device performed its first execution on Nicholas-Jacques Pelletier, who was convicted of armed robbery and whose head was severed at the first stroke of the angled blade of the guillotine in Paris's Place de Grève. The government promptly ordered more guillotines to be sent to each of France's eighty-three departments beginning that month.[18] Although intended as a humane reform, the guillotine soon became associated with the repression of those deemed to be political enemies of the Revolution.

The Politics of Crime and the Search for Justice

The Revolution, as it progressed, blurred the boundaries between ordinary and political crime, between regular and political justice, and between popular, extra-legal, and extra-judicial violence and punishments based on revolutionary law. What constituted a crime changed considerably, as revolutionaries decriminalized various acts at the same time that they prosecuted new kinds of political crimes. The French State no longer prosecuted religious crimes, such as blasphemy, heresy, and sacrilege. Suicide and previously criminalized forms of consensual sex were effectively legalized as sodomy, incest, and prostitution were omitted from the Penal Code of 1791.[19] At the same time, the revolutionaries created new categories of criminal acts and put new emphasis on prosecuting a widening range of political crimes. The Penal Code of 1791 defined seventy-nine crimes against the State, thirty-one of which had a mandatory death penalty.[20] Revolutionaries replaced *lèse-majesté*, the Old Regime high crime against the State, with the crime of *lèse-nation*, treason against the nation. The court of Châtelet first judged those accused of *lèse-nation*, and the Assembly subsequently established tribunals to hear these trials.[21] Revolutionary political crimes also included espionage, sedition, emigration, contravening political exile, harboring refractory or non-juring priests (those who refused to take a legally mandated oath to the new constitution), publicly making counter-revolutionary statements, draft dodging following the introduction of mass conscription, desertion, and vandalizing symbols of the revolutionary regime, particularly liberty trees.[22] Many political offenses were capital crimes; these included treason, espionage, correspondence with the enemy, and eventually emigration.

The fall of the monarchy on August 10, 1792 ushered in a period of anxiety and uncertainty. Some feared that imprisoned counter-revolutionary suspects were awaiting a signal from abroad to break out of prisons and slaughter revolutionaries. Others feared that foreign and royalist armies at war with France would invade Paris and liberate the prisoners who would join their forces. As a result, a wave of popular violence, involving the murders of priests and suspected counter-revolutionaries, swept the countryside during the late summer of 1792 and culminated in the September prison massacres in Paris and the provinces. These claimed the lives of around 1,300 prisoners, including many non-juring priests, women, and youths, and half of all the inmates in Paris. The majority of those killed were common criminals, imprisoned for non-political crimes. Jean-Paul Marat and several other radical revolutionaries defended the perpetrators of the massacres, who were not officially investigated or tried, in the name of popular justice.[23] Later that month, the National Convention formally abolished the monarchy and France became a republic. Subsequent debates about the fate of Louis XVI led the legislators to put the former king on trial for treason. He was executed on January 21, 1793.

As Dan Edelstein has argued, the king's trial was significant not just in removing a powerful political figure, but also because it ultimately led revolutionaries to develop a new legal framework categorizing individuals as outlaws (*hors-la-loi*) who could be executed without a formal trial. Revolutionaries employed this category for men and women involved in the rebellion that broke out in the Vendée region in western France in March 1793 (see Map 0.1). On March 19, the National Convention declared that those involved in rebellions or counter-revolutionary riots were *hors-la-loi.* They would not have a trial by jury but instead be sentenced by military commissions and without appeal. Those found guilty would be executed within twenty-four hours. Scholars have noted that the March 19 law resulted in more executions than all other pieces of revolutionary legislation. Over 21,000 individuals faced criminal prosecution as *hors-la-loi*, and 13,000 were condemned to death as part of broader efforts of the revolutionary regime to eliminate its adversaries, particularly in regions of open rebellion in the west and southeast. The decree opened the door to executing thousands of those deemed enemies of the Revolution with varying degrees of judicial due process depending on whether they were categorized as *hors-la-loi*, *émigré*, *conspirateur*, *suspect*, or *ennemi du peuple*.[24]

In the context of national crisis, radicalizing politics, and new legal concepts, revolutionaries took increasingly drastic measures against those deemed enemies. The revolutionary legislature passed a flurry of laws concerning treason and crimes against the State, particularly from 1792 to 1794. Many laws targeted non-juring priests, émigrés, and aristocrats, and criminalized their existence. Revolutionaries took reprisals against priests who failed to prove their patriotism through taking an oath of loyalty to the French State or through marriage, since many viewed priests as an unnatural, alien presence in the nation because of their loyalty to a foreign power, the Pope, and their practice of celibacy. Legislators passed a number of laws aimed at priests. Citizens could request the deportation of priests beginning in May 1792, and a decree in March 1793 ordered that deported priests found in France be killed within twenty-four hours.[25] Some legislators demanded that non-juring priests be declared *hors-la-loi*.[26]

Revolutionary legislators also targeted émigrés, and in November 1791, the legislature ordered them to return to France by the end of year or be prosecuted and punished with death. Influenced by the leading Girondin and writer Jacques-Pierre Brissot, legislators deemed émigrés *hors-la-loi* and guilty of conspiracy against the State, and ordered in October 1792 that all émigrés were banished in perpetuity and would be executed if they returned.[27] In March 1793, the Convention declared émigrés "civilly dead," and the State confiscated their property.[28] Many radical revolutionaries denounced émigrés, non-juring priests, and former nobles for *incivisme*, or lack of patriotism or patriotic fervor, and the Convention made *incivisme* a capital crime of treason in June 1793.[29]

Radical revolutionaries' pursuit and punishment of those they deemed enemies and suspects intensified during the Terror (1793–4). The Law of Suspects of September 1793 decreed the arrest of anyone, particularly former nobles and relatives of émigrés, suspected of counter-revolutionary action. During the Terror, the State arrested around 300,000 suspects and officially executed 17,000 people; perhaps 30,000 to 40,000 were executed without a trial or died in prison. Civil or military commissions, particularly in regions of revolt or civil war, condemned and executed the majority of the victims of the Terror.[30] However, scholars have devoted more attention to the Revolutionary Tribunal (created in March 1793 as the Extraordinary Criminal Tribunal and renamed in October; see Map 0.2), which the National Convention tasked with judging suspected traitors, conspirators, and counter-revolutionaries without the possibility of appeal. The Revolutionary Tribunal in Paris was comprised of twelve jurors, five judges, a public prosecutor, and two assistants, all named by the Convention. The Committee of Public Safety sent deputies known as representatives on mission to enforce the policies of the Convention throughout the French provinces, where some established similar revolutionary tribunals. In May 1794, the Convention ordered that these provincial tribunals close and all trials be held in Paris. The law of 22 Prairial (June 10, 1794) later suppressed legal counsel and defense witnesses for the accused and stated that "the penalty provided for all offenses under the jurisdiction of the Revolutionary Tribunal [was] death."[31]

In the preceding thirteen months, the Tribunal had condemned about 1,200 people to death. During the six weeks between the passing of the law and Robespierre's fall, the Tribunal condemned over 1,300 persons. On average, it pronounced twenty-eight death sentences per day.[32] While recent work of historians such as Annie Jourdan and Alex Fairfax-Cholmeley has emphasized the institutional features that afforded protection and agency to the accused and led to their acquittal or liberation during the Terror, most historians have associated the operation of the Tribunal with repression.[33]

Mobilizing revolutionary laws as political weapons, radical Montagnard revolutionaries deployed the categories of "enemy of the people" and counter-revolutionary more and more broadly, including against the members of rival revolutionary factions. By the height of the Terror, Girondins, Hébertists, and Dantonists had all appeared before the Revolutionary Tribunal, and many had been executed.[34] Following their deaths, the law of 22 Prairial outlined sweeping charges that could be brought against ordinary "suspects," including those who "abuse[d] the principles of the Revolution or the laws," "disseminated false news," acted in "bad faith," or disparaged or criticized the government.[35] As Carla Hesse has argued, increasingly abstract and vague definitions of treason during the Terror were coupled with particular regulations that criminalized an array of specific actions, such as failing to wear the tricolor cockade, making flawed ropes or bad saltpeter, and manufacturing or receiving sub-standard shoes.[36]

In many cases, the boundaries between common and political crimes were porous and shifting. Throughout the Revolution, men and women exacted revenge by attacking the property and crops of political enemies. Some acts of arson also had political resonance, notably burning buildings that housed registers of births or destroying evidence of birth dates in order to evade conscription.[37] Theft, a seemingly apolitical offense, could be political when offenders stole from State officials or engaged in politicized plunder. And economic crimes, including hoarding, speculation, refusing to accept *assignats* (the revolutionary paper currency that became nearly worthless), sending money abroad, and counterfeiting were regarded as counter-revolutionary. On July 26, 1793, food speculation and hoarding food or staple goods became capital crimes. The imprint on *assignats* issued after December 1791 declared, "The law punishes counterfeiters with death. The nation rewards those who denounce them."[38] The Revolutionary Tribunal pronounced 267 sentences for economic crimes: 181 for hoarding or violating the maximum (the maximum price the National Convention set for bread, grain, and other staple goods), and eighty-six for counterfeiting money or trading in *assignats*.[39] The sometimes artificial distinctions between political and non-political offenses could make the difference between life and death for the accused.

The boundaries between judicial and extra-judicial punishment were also blurred, particularly with respect to the representative on mission Jean-Baptiste Carrier who used his sweeping powers to carry out mass executions in Nantes (see Map 0.1). Carrier imprisoned thousands of suspected royalists, counter-revolutionaries, and rebels. Due to food shortages and epidemics of typhus and dysentery, Carrier ordered that prisoners be summarily guillotined, shot, or loaded onto boats then sent into the Loire river and sunk. Mass drownings, known as *noyades*, claimed the lives of priests, women, and children among other victims. Some reported that men and women, possibly young boys and girls as well, were stripped naked, tied together, and drowned in what were termed "republican marriages." Jean-Clement Martin has estimated that at least 4,000 people died in the *noyades* and that the total number of deaths in Nantes under Carrier was approximately 10,000.[40]

News of these atrocities reached Paris, and Robespierre recalled Carrier in February 1794. Following the arrest of Robespierre on 9 Thermidor (July 27, 1794) and his execution the next day, Thermidorian leaders claimed to make justice, rather than Terror, the order of the day. Their pursuit of justice entailed the arrest of Carrier and his trial before the Revolutionary Tribunal in November 1794 for his actions in Nantes. According to one witness's deposition, Carrier had lamented that judges needed "a hundred proofs, and a hundred witnesses to guillotine a man." Carrier insisted on more immediate acts of justice without these burdens of proof: "Chuck them into the water; it's much quicker."[41] Outrage over Carrier's tactics in his ruthless pursuit of swift justice led to his execution in December. Carrier's trial was the first to raise the issue of "crimes against humanity" and of how to punish those who committed them.[42] It also put in relief the sometimes murky distinction between judicial and extra-judicial killings in the Revolution, particularly at the hands of representatives on mission.

The post-Terror search for justice was bound up with the politics of vengeance. A new wave of collective vengeance and extra-judicial violence perpetrated in the name of justice constituted the "White Terror" of 1795. Hatred and resentment towards those associated with the Terror fueled violent reprisals against Jacobins that included prison massacres and thousands of assaults, mutilations, and lynchings. Some local authorities were complicit in the violence, and the perpetrators were not always brought to justice.[43] These acts of popular justice and violence, which occurred in defiance of the law, challenged the formal judiciary and legislators who insisted on the importance of legal authorities administering rational, impartial justice. Political leaders struggled to deal with the legacy of the Terror and to put an end to popular violence during what Howard Brown and other scholars have considered a period of "transitional justice." In October 1795, the Convention granted an amnesty for "acts purely related to the revolution," excluding émigrés and priests, thus nullifying the arrests and prosecutions of accused "terrorists." This last decree of the Convention sought to bring an end to the harassment, assaults, and prison massacres directed against Jacobins and government officials throughout France.[44]

Nonetheless, the Directory (1795–9; see Map 0.2) struggled to restore law and order during a period of continuing social, economic, and political instability. Many French men and women lived in fear of criminal violence at the hands of bandits and brigands. Brigandage, or robbery by an armed band, could be both a common and a political crime. Political brigandage took the form of *chouannerie*, royalist rebellions in the west and Midi. As Alain Corbin has observed, "There was a blurring of the boundary between protest actions and popular discontent, between riots over the price of bread and theft of food, between brigandage and *chouannerie*."[45] Some brigands carried jury lists, shot witnesses, and kidnapped judges—and did so with impunity.[46] Small bands of these royalist guerrillas captured grain convoys, persecuted local officials and constitutional priests, and targeted Jacobins and those associated with the Terror.[47] Officials were wary about not only juror and witness intimidation but also counter-revolutionary jurors acquitting those who committed political crimes. After royalists won electoral victories in 1797, the government annulled the elections and scrapped the jury lists in half of the departments.[48] The Directory also overhauled the judiciary and replaced all elected judges, public prosecutors, and court presidents with government appointees.[49] In response to the problems of jurors facing or fearing reprisals and in reaction to high acquittal rates for both political and regular crimes, the Directory curtailed the power of juries. It resorted to the use of military tribunals to try civilians, particularly those involved in brigandage in areas affected by royalist revolts.[50] The government restored capital punishment for property crimes, namely highway robbery and housebreaking; when these crimes were committed by two or more persons, the accused were sent to military courts. The rate of people convicted of felonies increased, and the number of death sentences more than doubled from the first to the second half of the Directory.[51]

Judicial and Penal Policy in Practice

Various aspects of the administration of justice changed over the course of the Revolution and departed from its liberal and egalitarian ideals. The influence of class and gender on juries and the application of justice remained constant, but the nature of this influence shifted alongside institutional changes. Beginning in 1791, the prosecution and conviction of criminals in France depended upon the will of juries. Robert Allen has argued that criminal courts and particularly juries served as a source of stability and moderation over the course of the Revolution's successive political regimes, since juries frequently undermined or impeded the government's cases by refusing to indict or convict the accused, particularly for political criminal charges. While juries were reluctant to convict those who transgressed laws concerning conscription, armed rebellion, and other political crimes, they were more inclined to convict those tried for theft and other crimes against property. Some 30–60 percent of criminal trials resulted in acquittals; the highest rates were in the south and west, including the Vendée, where resistance to the Revolution was greatest. As the Directory sought to stabilize the nation and vigorously repress crime after the Terror, it increased the number of innocent votes that juries needed to acquit; however, the nationwide rate of acquittals remained about 50 percent.[52]

Despite revolutionary legislators' exclusion of women from "active citizenship," juries, and judicial and magisterial positions, women played significant roles in shaping revolutionary justice. They participated not only in acts of popular justice but also formal judicial proceedings as witnesses, plaintiffs, and defendants. Women were victims, perpetrators, and witnesses of crimes, and the pursuit of justice during the Revolution depended upon their active participation in the courts, despite their formal exclusion from politics.[53] In addition to playing active roles in criminal courts, women sought to use the newly established family tribunals to their advantage. In August 1790, the National Assembly had created family tribunals to arbitrate disputes between family members, involving inheritance, marital separation, guardianship and custody, property disputes, and marriages of minors. Increasingly egalitarian inheritance laws, a lowered age of majority, and a new divorce law provided opportunities for women to demand rights in these courts. The law of September 20, 1792, which legalized divorce, granted jurisdiction of divorce cases to these courts. The arbiters were typically relatives, neighbors, or friends, and these courts allowed ordinary people to access forms of justice that would otherwise be too expensive, public, or time-consuming. However, their existence was relatively short-lived, as the Directory suppressed family tribunals in 1796.[54]

In the criminal courts, gendered patterns of prosecutions emerged. While men and women commonly appeared before the courts for the same political and non-political offenses, some crimes were highly gendered. For example, women represented the overwhelming majority of those accused of reproductive crimes and infanticide. In contrast, sexual violence was associated with male offenders, although attempts to bring offenders to justice faced many challenges, including the underreporting of these offenses and the widespread notion advanced by medical experts that it was impossible for a single man to rape a healthy adult woman. The civil war in the Vendée, in which revolutionary soldiers raped and sexually assaulted local women, compounded these challenges.[55] Crimes concerning desertion and conscription were also gendered, although women could face prosecution for helping men evade conscription laws. Women and men at times worked alongside one another, sometimes in brigand gangs, to commit crimes, including extortion, theft, assault, or murder. When authorities broke up the *bande d'Orgères* in 1799, they indicted 118 men and women, attributed over seventy-five murders to the gang, executed twenty men and two women, and imprisoned dozens.[56] Although jurors sentenced female offenders to death in these and other trials, juries' overall rates of conviction were lower for women than men.[57]

During the Revolution, carceral institutions proliferated, and the prison population swelled. Some have estimated that there were about 400,000 prisoners in France at the peak of the Terror, and another 300,000 suspects under house arrest.[58] Paris contained over thirty prisons and over 100 provisional or temporary jails. There were additionally roughly 1,200 prisons and 40,000 provisional jails in the provinces. Many of these buildings had been schools, private houses, barracks, monasteries, or insane asylums. The confiscation of Church properties had provided physical spaces for the expansion of the French carceral system. In the wake of the 1793 law of suspects, local authorities requisitioned nearly 1,000 private establishments, including more abandoned religious buildings.[59] The Conciergerie, Paris's oldest prison, took on particular significance as the principal site of detention for those brought before the Revolutionary Tribunal (see Map 0.2). Many of the most prominent figures of the Revolution were imprisoned there before their execution. They included Marie-Antoinette, Georges Danton, Charlotte Corday, Olympe de Gouges, Robespierre, Jean-Sylvain Bailly, Manon Roland, and Jacques-René Hébert. However, many ordinary men and women of all social classes were prisoners there as well. The prolific writer Pierre-Jean-Baptiste Nougaret recounted that during the six months he spent in the Conciergerie, he saw "priests, merchants, bankers, men of letters, artisans, farmers, and *sans-culottes*."[60]

If prisoners came from varied backgrounds, their experiences, once incarcerated, also varied. The revolutionary ideal of equality did not find expression in the realities of life in prison, in which prisoners' social status and wealth determined the conditions of their detention. Prisons supplied water and bread to all inmates, but some prisoners received other food of better quality and greater quantity by working or using personal funds.[61] In the Conciergerie, prisoners were divided not by types of criminal offenses but effectively by wealth. The *pistoliers* could afford to pay for a cell with a bed. Lacking these means, the *pailleux* slept on straw. Revolutionary-era accounts depicted life in the Conciergerie in bleak terms. According to Michel-Philippe-Edme Coittant's *Almanach des prisons* (1794), the *pailleux* slept upon damp straw full of vermin, which gnawed on prisoners' clothes. At night, some prisoners covered their faces with their hands to protect their noses and ears from the rats.[62] In a March 1793 report to the Minister of the Interior on the state of the Conciergerie, the prison inspector Thierriet-Grandpré highlighted not only the problems of dampness, poor air circulation, and overcrowding, but also the appalling inequalities that contradicted France's revolutionary ideals. He contrasted the overcrowded rooms in which dozens of men or women slept amid rats with the private rooms and beds of wealthy prisoners. What is more, wealthy prisoners who lived relatively comfortably tended to be responsible for the most serious crimes, whereas indigent detainees, suffering from "the horrors of misery and hunger," were mostly charged with more minor offenses. He found this distinction "revolting" and condemned the deplorable and inhumane conditions within the prison.[63]

In many respects there was a gulf between official penal policy and actual prison conditions, which prompted calls for reform. Wretched conditions persisted even after the formal end of the Terror. In a circular from February 1796, the Minister of the Interior expressed his grave concerns about the state of prisons. He observed that the accused and convicted as well as persons of all ages and sexes were often mixed together. He decried grim conditions, observing, "Nearly everywhere detainees are reduced to bread and water, sleeping on damp straw, without linens or clothing."[64] Furthermore, there were not enough infirmaries. Ill patients with wealth were transferred to *maisons de santé*, private hospitals, where some found means of escape. The Minister also observed that dangerous criminals routinely escaped *maisons d'arrêt*, intended for pre-arraignment detention. He lamented that those condemned to long prison sentences were constantly idle and, in his estimation, this idleness bred immorality and despair and provided the impetus for prison breaks. The Minister called for an end to the provisional jails that had been proliferating and insisted that prisons must be secure and sanitary and that detained persons be divided by their type of detention, age, sex, and crime, separating those condemned of capital offenses from lesser offenders.[65]

The fates of prisoners varied. Some detainees died in prison, some succumbing to illness, others attempting suicide. For example, François Chabot, a Jacobin politician and former priest who was married to a wealthy Austrian and whom the Revolutionary Tribunal sentenced to death, tried to poison himself. The Duc de Châtelet, the army general and son of Emilie du Châtelet, who was charged with bribery and emigration, attempted suicide by banging his skull against a wall, shattering a window, and then swallowing the shards of glass. Condorcet, the writer known for promoting the rights of women and free people of color, committed suicide in prison in March 1794. Many others successfully took their own lives in order to preempt the guillotine.[66] Some women stayed, or delayed, their execution by declaring pregnancy. But thousands of prisoners were executed. Other detainees were acquitted and released, or released following the fall of Robespierre on 9 Thermidor. Some men and women published accounts of their captivity, while relatives and friends published posthumous memoirs by those guillotined.[67]

After the Terror, post-Thermidorian legislators envisioned the era of capital punishment coming to an end in the near future. On October 26, 1795, the Convention voted to abolish the death penalty as soon as France was at peace. However, France remained almost continually at war for two more decades, during which time it formally incorporated capital punishment in the 1810 Penal Code. The death penalty remained in place in France until its abolition in 1981.[68]

The Revolution's legal, penal, and judicial innovations continued to shape French justice and society after its conclusion. Under the Consulate and Napoleonic Empire, the nation moved in an increasingly authoritarian direction. While Napoleon's legal codes affirmed the revolutionary principle of equality before the law, Napoleonic law and penal policy departed from revolutionary principles in other respects. They restricted jury duty to the educated and propertied elite, replaced the election of judges with their lifetime appointment by Napoleon, and re-established harsher penalties for many non-political criminal offenses, including sentences of life imprisonment or hard labor as well as branding, mutilation, and the confiscation of property, which had been abolished by the previous Penal

Code of 1791. The Code of Criminal Instruction (*Code d'instruction criminelle*) of 1808 revived aspects of Old Regime criminal procedure, notably conducting the preliminary phase of criminal procedure in secret, in the absence of legal counsel, and in written rather than oral form. The grand jury, or the *jury d'accusation*, which decided on indictments for crimes, disappeared. While the pre-trial procedure reverted to an inquisitorial form, the actual trial was accusatorial, involving a hearing that was oral, public, before a jury, and with defense counsel. The French State retained trial by jury but modified its scope and adopted a more repressive penal code.[69]

In sum, matters of justice were central to revolutionary politics and society, and revolutionary legal and judicial reforms continued to shape French society in the years that followed. Among the most enduring legacies were the end of the spectacle of pain and suffering, the principle of equality before the law, and trial by jury. Through the adoption of trial by jury, male active citizens participated directly in the administration of justice as citizen jurors in a range of criminal proceedings, including those that involved newly created criminal categories. The most important of these somewhat amorphous categories were those of *hors-la-loi* and enemy of the people. Political leaders deployed these categories to detain and execute thousands, ranging from peasants to the most prominent political figures, including the architects of the Terror. Revolutionaries drifted from some of the liberal aspects and revolutionary ideals of the new penal and judicial regime by curtailing both the rights of the accused during the Terror and the power of juries under the Directory, and by failing to remedy inegalitarian and inhumane prison conditions. Judicial and criminal matters broadly affected the lives of large numbers of French men and women—most directly those imprisoned, executed, or engaged in the administration of justice whether through formal channels or through violent forms of "popular justice" in defiance of the law.

Source: Penal Code of 25 September 1791

FIRST PART – *OF CONVICTIONS*

FIRST TITLE – *OF SENTENCES IN GENERAL*

FIRST ARTICLE.
The sentences to be pronounced against those accused and found guilty by a jury are the death penalty, irons, imprisonment in a *maison de force*, solitary confinement, detention, deportation, civic degradation, and the stocks [*carcan*].

Article 2
The death penalty will consist of the simple deprivation of life, as no kind of torture can ever be exercised against the condemned.
Article 3
Anybody condemned to death will have their head cut off.
Article 4
Whoever will have been condemned to death for the crime of assassination, arson, or poisoning, will be brought to the execution grounds dressed in a red shirt.

The parricide will have his head and face veiled with a black cloth; he will only be uncovered at the moment of execution.
Article 5
The execution of those condemned to death will take place in the public square of the city where the jury [*juré d'accusation*] will have been convoked.
Article 6
Those condemned to irons will be employed in forced labor for the profit of the State, either inside the prisons [*maisons de force*], or in ports and arsenals, in mining, the draining of swamps, or, finally, in all other hard labor that, on request by the departments, may be determined by the legislative body.
Article 7
Those condemned to irons will drag a ball attached to one of their feet with an iron chain.
Article 8
Punishment with irons can in no case be perpetual.
Article 9
In the case where the law pronounces punishment with irons for a certain number of years, if it is a woman or a girl who is being convicted of having made herself guilty of those crimes, that woman or girl will be condemned for the same number of years to imprisonment in a *maison de force*.

. . .

Article 31
The guilty who will have been condemned to civic degradation will be brought to the center of the public square [of the town] where the tribunal that will have judged him has its seat.
The clerk of the court will address him with these words in a loud voice: *Your country has found you guilty of an infamous action: the law and the tribunal deprive you of the status of French citizen.*
The condemned will then be put in the stocks [*carcan*] in the middle of the public square; there, he will spend two hours exposed to the public eye.
On a sign will be written, in big letters, his name, address, profession, the crime he committed and the judgment passed against him.

Notes

1 Michel Foucault, *Discipline and Punish: The Birth of the Prison*, trans. Alan Sheridan (New York: Vintage, 1977); Paul Friedland, *Seeing Justice Done: The Age of Spectacular Capital Punishment in France* (New York: Oxford University Press, 2012), 176–88.

2 Friedland, *Seeing Justice Done*, 231; Dan Edelstein, *The Terror of Natural Right: Republicanism, the Cult of Nature, and the French Revolution* (Chicago: University of Chicago Press, 2009).

3 John H. Langbein, *Torture and the Law of Proof: Europe and England in the Ancien Régime* (Chicago: University of Chicago Press, 2006), 50–5; Julius R. Ruff, *Violence in Early Modern Europe, 1500–1800* (Cambridge: Cambridge University Press, 2001), 94; Lela Graybill, *The Visual Culture of Violence After the French Revolution* (New York: Routledge, 2016), 11; Sarah Maza, *Private Lives and Public Affairs: The Causes Célèbres of Prerevolutionary France* (Berkeley: University of California Press, 1993), 213.

4 Richard Mowery Andrews, *Law, Magistracy, and Crime in Old Regime Paris, 1735–1789, Vol. 1: The System of Criminal Justice* (Cambridge: Cambridge University Press, 1994), 309, 383–93.

5 William Doyle, *Venality: The Sale of Offices in Eighteenth-Century France* (Oxford: Clarendon, 1996).

6 Anthony Crubaugh, *Balancing the Scales of Justice: Local Courts and Rural Society in Southwest France, 1750–1800* (University Park: Pennsylvania State University Press, 2001), 121–30.

7 Jean-Claude Farcy, *Histoire de la justice en France: De 1789 à nos jours* (Paris: La Découverte, 2015), 7–13; Michael P. Fitzsimmons, *The Night the Old Regime Ended: August 4, 1789 and the French Revolution* (University Park: Pennsylvania State University Press, 2003).

8 Jérôme Mavidal et al., eds., *Archives parlementaires de 1787 à 1860: recueil complet des débats législatifs et politiques des chambres françaises* [AP] (Paris: Dupont; CNRS, 1862–), 12:343–9; Colin Jones, *The Longman Companion to the French Revolution* (London: Routledge, 1990), 211; Michael P. Fitzsimmons, *The Parisian Order of Barristers and the French Revolution* (Cambridge, MA: Harvard University Press, 1987), 33–64.

9 Arlette Farge and Michel Foucault, *Disorderly Families: Infamous Letters from the Bastille Archives* (Minneapolis: University of Minnesota Press, 2016); Honoré Gabriel Riqueti, comte de Mirabeau, *Des lettres de cachet et des prisons d'état* (Hamburg: n.p., 1782); Jacques-Guy Petit, "Politiques, modèles, imaginaire de la prison (1790–1875)," in *Histoire des galères, bagnes et prisons*, ed. J.-G. Petit et al. (Toulouse: Privat, 1991), 112.

10 Farcy, *Histoire de la justice*, 20–1; Emmanuel Berger, *La justice pénale sous la Révolution* (Rennes: Presses Universitaires de Rennes, 2008), 163–7; Laura Mason, "The 'Bosom of Proof': Criminal Justice and the Renewal of Oral Culture during the French Revolution," *Journal of Modern History* 76, no. 1 (2004): 29–61; Bernard Schnapper, "Le jury criminel," in *Une autre justice, 1789–1799*, ed. Robert Badinter (Paris: Fayard, 1989), 149–70; Robert Allen,

Les tribunaux criminels sous la Révolution et l'Empire: 1792–1811 (Rennes: Presses Universitaires de Rennes, 2005); James M. Donovan, *Juries and the Transformation of Criminal Justice in France in the Nineteenth and Twentieth Centuries* (Chapel Hill: University of North Carolina Press, 2010); Howard Brown, *Ending the French Revolution: Violence, Justice, and Repression from the Terror to Napoleon* (Charlottesville: University of Virginia Press, 2006), 90–118; Isser Woloch, *The New Regime: Transformation of the French Civic Order, 1789–1820s* (New York: W. W. Norton, 1995).

11 Friedland, *Seeing Justice Done*, 219–39; Jean-Claude Farcy, "La peine de mort en France: Deux siècles pour une abolition (1791–1981)," *Criminocorpus* (2006), https://criminocorpus.org/fr/expositions/peine-de-mort/la-peine-de-mort-en-france-de-la-revolution-a-labolition/complements/la-peine-de-mort-en-france-deux-siecles-pour-une-abolition-1791-/.

12 Petit, "Politiques, modèles, imaginaire de la prison," 117.

13 J.-B. Duvergier, *Collection complète des lois, décrets, ordonnances, réglemens, avis du Conseil-d'Etat* (Paris: Guyot et Scribe, 1834), 3:352–66; Petit, "Politiques, modèles, imaginaire de la prison," 115–16; Michael Rapport, "Revolution," in *The Oxford Handbook of the Ancien Régime*, ed. William Doyle (New York: Oxford University Press, 2012), 481.

14 Marc Renneville, "Les bagnes coloniaux: de l'utopie au risque du non-lieu," *Criminocorpus* (2007), http://journals.openedition.org/criminocorpus/173; Jean-Claude Vimont, *Punir autrement: Les prisons de Seine-Inférieure pendant la Révolution* (Rouen: CRDP, 1989), 38; Miranda Frances Spieler, *Empire and Underworld: Captivity in French Guiana* (Cambridge, MA: Harvard University Press, 2012).

15 As discussed and cited in Friedland, *Seeing Justice Done*, 240–2; see also Archives Nationales (AN) AA 55 dossier 1513, as cited in Friedland, *Seeing Justice Done*, 240–2.

16 AP, 11:279. See also Friedland, *Seeing Justice Done*, 221–2.

17 As discussed, translated, and cited in Friedland, *Seeing Justice Done*, 240; see also AN AA 55 dossier 1513, as cited in Friedland, *Seeing Justice Done*, 240.

18 Friedland, *Seeing Justice Done*, 247, 262; Farcy, "La peine de mort"; Michel Perrot, *Le sens des Lumières* (Geneva: Georg, 2007), 30; Laure Murat, *The Man Who Thought He Was Napoleon: Toward a Political History of Madness*, trans. Deke Dusinberre (Chicago: University of Chicago Press, 2014), 30.

19 Michael David Sibalis, "The Regulation of Male Homosexuality in Revolutionary and Napoleonic France, 1789–1815," in *Homosexuality in Modern France*, eds. Jeffrey Merrick and Bryant T. Ragan, Jr. (Oxford: Oxford University Press, 1996), 80–101.

20 Richard Mowry Andrews, "Boundaries of Citizenship: The Penal Regulation of Speech in Revolutionary France," *French Politics and Society* 7, no. 3 (1989): 93.

21 Farcy, *Histoire de la justice*, 24; Jean-Christophe Gaven, *Le crime de lèse-nation: Histoire d'une invention juridique et politique, 1789–1791* (Paris: Presses de Sciences Po, 2016).

22 Brown, *Ending the Revolution*, 366; Berger, *Justice pénale*, 249.

23 Patrice Higonnet, *Goodness Beyond Virtue: Jacobins during the French Revolution* (Cambridge, MA: Harvard University Press, 1998), 37–40; David Andress, *The Terror: The Merciless War for Freedom in Revolutionary France* (New York: Farrar, Straus & Giroux, 2006), 93–115; Donald Sutherland, "Urban Crowds, Riot, Utopia, and Massacres, 1789–92," in *A Companion to the French Revolution*, ed. Peter McPhee (Oxford: Oxford University Press, 2013), 242–3; Marisa Linton, *Choosing Terror: Virtue, Friendship, and Authenticity in the French Revolution* (Oxford: Oxford University Press, 2013), 134; Donald Sutherland, *The French Revolution and Empire: The Quest for a Civic Order* (Malden, MA: Blackwell, 2003), 142–3.

24 Edelstein, *Terror of National Right*; Eric de Mari, *La mise hors de la loi sous la Révolution française, 19 mars 1793–an III: Une étude juridictionnelle et institutionnelle* (Issy-les-Moulineaux: LGDJ, 2015); Donald Greer, *The Incidence of the Terror during the French Revolution: A Statistical Interpretation* (Cambridge, MA: Harvard University Press, 1935); Farcy, *Histoire de la justice*, 27.

25 E. Claire Cage, *Unnatural Frenchmen: The Politics of Priestly Celibacy and Marriage, 1720–1815* (Charlottesville: University of Virginia Press, 2015); Jones, *Longman Companion to the French Revolution*, 242–3; AP, 60:298.

26 Carla Hesse, "The Law of the Terror," *Modern Language Notes* 114 (1999): 702–18; Edelstein, *Terror of Natural Right*, 79.

27 Jones, *Longman Companion to the French Revolution*, 194–9.

28 AP, 60:643.

29 Hesse, "Law of the Terror."

30 Greer, *The Incidence of the Terror*; Jeremy Popkin, *A Short History of the French Revolution* (London: Routledge, 2006), 76; Paul R. Hanson, *Contesting the French Revolution* (Malden, MA: Wiley-Blackwell, 2009), 173; Brown, *Ending the Revolution*, 142.

31 See "The Law of 22 Prairial Year II (10 June 1794)," *Liberty, Equality, Fraternity*, http://chnm.gmu.edu/revolution/d/439.

32 Farcy, *Histoire de la justice*, 26; François-Alphonse Aulard, *The French Revolution: A Political History, Volume II: The Democratic Republic, 1792–1795* (New York: Charles Scribner's Sons, 1910), 286.

33 Annie Jourdan, "Les journées de Prairial an II: le tournant de la Révolution?," *La Révolution française* 10 (2016), http://lrf.revues.org/1591; Alex Fairfax-Cholmeley, "Creating and Resisting the Terror: The Paris Revolutionary Tribunal, March–June 1793," *French History* 32, no. 2 (2018): 203–25. On acquittals during the Terror, see also Anne Simonin, "Les acquittés de la Grande Terreur: Réflexions sur l'amitié dans la République," in *Les politiques de la Terreur, 1793–1794*, ed. Michel Biard (Rennes: Presses Universitaires de Rennes, 2008), 183–205.

34 Linton, *Choosing Terror*; Edelstein, *Terror of Natural Right*.

35 *Le Moniteur Universel* 264, 24 Prairial, year II (June 12, 1794), 1075.

36 Hesse, "Law of the Terror."

37 David Andress, *The French Revolution and the People* (London: Hambledon, 2006), 248.

38 Rebecca L. Spang, *Stuff and Money in the Time of the French Revolution* (Cambridge, MA: Harvard University Press, 2015), 128–9.

39 Florin Aftalion, *The French Revolution: An Economic Interpretation*, trans. Martin Thom (Cambridge: Cambridge University Press, 1990), 160.

40 Jean-Clément Martin, *Blancs et Bleus dans la Vendée déchirée* (Paris: Gallimard, 1986), 102–3, also cited in Noah Shusterman, *The French Revolution: Faith, Desire and Politics* (London: Routledge, 2013), 213.

41 *Bulletin du tribunal criminel révolutionnaire*, part 6, no. 76 (Paris: Clément, Year II), 302.

42 Jacques Dupâquier, "Le procès de Carrier," in *Le tournant de l'an III: Réaction et Terreur blanche dans la France révolutionnaire*, ed. Michel Vovelle (Paris: CTHS, 1997), 27–35.

43 Stephen Clay, "The White Terror: Factions, Reactions and the Politics of Vengeance," in *A Companion to the French Revolution*, ed. Peter McPhee (Oxford: Oxford University Press, 2013), 359–77; Howard Brown, "The Politics of Public Order," in *The Oxford Handbook of the French Revolution*, ed. David Andress (Oxford: Oxford University Press, 2015), 540; Andress, *The Terror*, 361; Donald Sutherland, *Murder in Aubagne: Lynching, Law, and Justice during the French Revolution* (Cambridge: Cambridge University Press, 2009), 214–62.

44 Brown, *Ending the Revolution*, 26–9.

45 Alain Corbin, *The Life of an Unknown: The Rediscovered World of a Clog Maker in Nineteenth-Century France* (New York: Columbia University Press, 2001), 131.

46 Brown, "The Politics of Public Order," 542.

47 Hanson, *Contesting the French Revolution*, 183; Brown, *Ending the Revolution*, 237–66.

48 Donovan, *Juries*, 39.

49 Brown, "The Politics of Public Order," 548; Brown, *Ending the Revolution*, 172–3.

50 Donovan, *Juries*, 38–9.

51 Brown, "The Politics of Public Order," 548.

52 Allen, *Les tribunaux criminels*; Brown, *Ending the Revolution*, 112, 177–8.

53 Robert Allen, "La justice pénale et les femmes, 1792–1811," *Annales historiques de la Révolution française* 350 (2007): 87–107.

54 Suzanne Desan, *The Family on Trial in Revolutionary France* (Berkeley: University of California Press, 2004).

55 Jean-Clément Martin, "Femmes et guerre civile, l'exemple de la Vendée, 1793–1796," *Clio* 5 (1997): 97–115.

56 Andress, *The French Revolution and the People*, 249–50; Brown, *Ending the Revolution*, 223; Brown, "The Politics of Public Order," 543.

57 Allen, "La justice pénale."

58 C. F. Beaulieu, *Essais historiques sur les causes et les effets de la Révolution de France* (Paris: Maradan, 1803), 5:283; Bronislaw Baczko, *Ending the Terror: The French Revolution after Robespierre* (Cambridge: Cambridge University Press, 1994), 68.

59 Vicomte Hervé de Broc, *La France pendant la Révolution* (Paris: Plon, 1891), 1:144; Jean-Claude Vimont, *La prison: À l'ombre des hauts murs* (Paris: Gallimard, 2004), 18; Petit, "Politiques, modèles, imaginaire de la prison," 118.

60 Pierre-Jean-Baptiste Nougaret, *Histoire des prisons de Paris et des départements* (Paris: Courcier, 1797), 2:39.

61 Vimont, *Punir autrement*, 43.

62 Michel-Philippe-Edme Coittant, *Almanach des prisons* (Paris: Michel, 1794), 15, 24.

63 J.-N. Thierriet-Grandpré, "Rapport au ministre de l'Intérieur sur l'état des prisons de la Conciergerie, 17 mars 1793," in *Revue rétrospective* series 2, vol. 3 (1835): 316–20.

64 Circular of 16 pluviôse year IV, cited in Vimont, *Punir autrement*, 68.

65 Circular of 16 pluviôse year IV, cited in Vimont, *Punir autrement*, 68–9.

66 Linton, *Choosing Terror*, 277, 291; Olivier Blanc, *Last Letters: Prisons and Prisoners of the French Revolution 1793–1794*, trans. Alan Sheridan (New York: Farrar, Straus & Giroux, 1987); Rémy Bijaoui, *Prisonniers et prisons de la Terreur* (Paris: Imago, 1996).

67 See, for example, Marie-Jeanne Roland, *L'Appel à l'impartiale postérité* (Paris: Louvet, 1795); Honoré-Jean Riouffe, *Mémoires d'un détenu: Pour servir à l'histoire de la tyrannie de Robespierre* (Paris: B. Mathé, 1795); Julia V. Douthwaite, *The Frankenstein of 1790 and Other Lost Chapters from Revolutionary France* (Chicago: University of Chicago Press, 2012), 180–8.

68 Farcy, "La peine de mort."

69 Rapport, "Revolution," 481; Allen, *Les tribunaux criminels*; Woloch, *The New Regime*.

7

Surveillance at Work: A Theft on the Rue du Bac

Ralph Kingston

On 7 fructidor VIII (August 25, 1800), Louis Bonnet, a clerk in the French Ministry of External Relations (the name by which the Ministry of Foreign Affairs was known between 1794 and 1814), received an official letter of termination.[1] It was delivered to him while at work in his office in the hôtel Galliffet, the Ministry building located on Paris's rue du Bac (see Map 0.2). It came from Antoine Caillard, the chief of the Archives Division and Bonnet's direct superior. In the margin, the Minister, Charles Maurice de Talleyrand-Périgord, had scribbled approval. Bonnet, the letter claimed, was a thief. He had stolen 77 gold and silver-gilt (vermeil) boxes, the little cases the archive used to protect the official wax seals on international treaties. According to the letter, the Minister had reviewed all the evidence: if the Ministry wanted to send Bonnet to a criminal tribunal, a conviction would be easy to secure. Talleyrand's sympathy for Bonnet's advanced age, however, meant that he was not going to pursue criminal proceedings. Instead, Bonnet was to turn in all his papers, cartons, and keys to cabinets. Once he had done so, he was never to set foot in the building again.[2]

Caillard had discovered the theft of the gold and silver-gilt boxes as he responded to a request for information on Old Regime treaties sent to him by First Consul Napoleon Bonaparte's Secretary of State, Hugues-Bernard Maret. During his search, Caillard realized that a treaty of alliance between France and Austria signed on May 1, 1756 was missing its seal and the box that had held it. He turned to the sub-chief of the Archives Division, Jean-François Galon-Boyer, who told him that Caillard's predecessor as chief, Louis-Pierre-Pantaléon Resnier, had had his employees draw up a detailed inventory when they moved the treaties from Versailles to Paris in July 1796.

There were, in theory, three copies of the inventory: one had been sent to the Minister, Charles Delacroix; Resnier kept another; Bonnet, who was in charge of working with the treaties within the archives, received the third. Bonnet claimed his copy was missing (somewhat suspiciously, his chief thought), but Galon-Boyer was able to secure Resnier's copy. On 3 fructidor VIII (August 21, 1800), he reinventoried the treaties in the presence of Caillard and the other members of the Archives Division. He calculated that, since 3 thermidor IV (July 21, 1796), when the archives were moved to the hôtel Galliffet, seventy-seven boxes had been stolen. There had been 123 in 1796; in 1800, there were only forty-six.

The extent of the crime discovered, Caillard established a Commission of Inquiry. It was composed of three division chiefs—Caillard himself; Emmanuel Louis Joseph d'Hermand, Chief of the Commercial Relations Division; and Jean-Baptiste Bresson, the Ministry's Budget Director. The commission met on 5 fructidor VIII (August 23, 1800). It interviewed Bonnet and Galon-Boyer, as well as other archives employees: François Jorelle and Louis-Marc Besson, the two junior clerks in the office; and Rouet, the *garçon de bureau* (office porter). All five signed formal summaries of their testimonies. According to Caillard in his report to the Minister, Bonnet, unlike the others, exhibited "evident distress." Afterwards, at least as Caillard presented it, Bonnet came to Caillard to "confess."[3] The commission decided Bonnet's guilt without further deliberation.

Robin W. Winks once compared the work of historians and detectives: "the historian must collect, interpret, and then explain his evidence, by methods which are not greatly different from those techniques employed by the detective, or at least the detective of fiction."[4] Nevertheless, it is relatively rare that historians get to step into the shoes of fictional sleuths like Sherlock Holmes, Hercule Poirot, or Nancy Drew. There are of course some similarities of method. Historians and detectives both investigate events that happened in the past and find out not just what and where, but how, when, who, and why. To close their case, they present proof—specific primary sources entered into evidence—in order to recreate what happened in an investigative and narrative reconstruction.[5] Historians, unlike fictional detectives, however, are more willing to admit that their reconstructions are inexact: that their evidence is sometimes too partial, too fragmentary. Indeed, for historians, whether someone in the past was or was not guilty is sometimes the least important element of a story told.

Complicating the theft on the rue du Bac is another, separate, and quite different, account of Bonnet's downfall in a nineteenth-century biography of Talleyrand by Charles Maxime de Villemarest. In Villemarest's account, Talleyrand, not Caillard, played the role of detective. One day, he relates, Talleyrand sent a secretary to collect information on French treaty obligations. While doing so, he discovered that several "silver boxes" had had their bottoms removed. When the secretary reported the crime, Talleyrand swore him to secrecy. It would not do, he said, for news of the crime to become public, for people to know that there was a thief working in the Ministry. Talleyrand allowed three or four days to pass. He then called into his office the employee he suspected of the crime. This employee "had always enjoyed a good reputation," but Talleyrand knew better:

> "Tell me everything," Talleyrand said to him, "because any denial is useless. For some time now, you have been the only one working in the treaty room, and only you . . ." Here the unfortunate burst into tears. "Pull yourself together," said the Minister. "I cannot keep you here, but I do not want to ruin you, as you have a wife and children. How much do you earn?" "Three thousand six hundred francs." "Very well. Here is what I can do for you, but you must promise to keep my secret as I promise to keep yours. I will give you a mission; you will not carry it out, and you will be dismissed for not carrying out the mission correctly. For the next three years though, as a form of compensation, your wife will receive half of your salary. Now, go!"[6]

According to Villemarest then, Bonnet had crumbled when subjected directly to Talleyrand's scrutiny; and, once the criminal had revealed himself, Talleyrand took care of the unfortunate affair quickly and discretely.

Although Villemarest worked as part of Talleyrand's private cabinet in the late 1790s and early 1800s, his account is a fiction. Nineteenth-century biographies are full of dubious anecdotes, and Villemarest's is no exception. That said, we must also beware of the fictions wound into the archival evidence by Caillard in the course of his detective work. A month after dismissing Bonnet, Caillard wrote up the Commission of Inquiry's formal report. He organized and labeled the various pieces of evidence he had collected, "A—I," including the testimonies and the various letters written to and by Bonnet in the process of his dismissal.[7] Though he had decided Bonnet's culpability in a matter of days, Caillard had continued to supplement his collection of evidence against Bonnet. Even after submitting the report to Talleyrand, Caillard added another document labelled "K." In an explanatory note, Caillard presented this document, a letter written by Bonnet to Talleyrand on the day Galon-Boyer inventoried the treaties, as evidence that Bonnet had tried to confuse the investigation. A literal reading of the letter, however, reveals Bonnet simply asserting his innocence. The timing of his letter suggests that he was aware, even before he was called in by the commission, that his colleagues were looking at him as the prime suspect. Bonnet's letter assured Talleyrand that "neither his colleagues nor he are capable of such infamy."[8]

In the weeks and months following Bonnet's dismissal, Caillard collected evidence of other misdeeds committed by Bonnet during his career. In germinal IX (March/April 1801), Caillard identified Bonnet as author of a wide-ranging denunciation of Ministry colleagues in 1795.[9] Another denunciation, made by Bonnet to the Revolutionary Committee in Versailles in 1793 against the duc d'Ornano, a former diplomat attached to the Ministry of Foreign Affairs in the 1780s, was also located and copied with a note in the margin accusing Bonnet of sending d'Ornano to the guillotine.[10] Adding these documents to the file, Caillard built the narrative that Bonnet had always been an untrustworthy colleague. Caillard's account did not go unchallenged, however. When Bonnet began to defend himself after his dismissal, the Archives Division also added that paperwork to his file, including a twenty-page memoir outlining his self-defense, and a letter written to First Consul Napoleon Bonaparte asking that a criminal tribunal or military commission, rather than the Ministry, should judge his guilt. It is rare that a historian happens upon a compilation of documents examining a moment in history from multiple angles and in relatively minute detail, and offering such very different stories about how the evidence should fit together.

Caillard clearly expected his compilation of evidence to lead readers to agree with his conclusion on Bonnet's guilt. That Caillard kept on adding to the dossier, however, suggests that Bonnet's "evident distress" and move to "confess" were in fact tenuous proofs. Colleagues' testimonies presented "facts" about Bonnet's behavior, but even these were not definitive. What Caillard's dossier reveals to the historian is not the certainty of a "whodunit" but the complex relationship between reality and fiction in a Revolutionary ministry's surveillance regime.

This chapter will investigate the experience of surveillance within the Ministry of External Affairs during the 1790s, using the evidence compiled by all sides. In the second half of the 1790s, French government ministries shifted away from requiring that their employees prove their political virtue as a means of ensuring transparency. They rejected denunciation. Nevertheless, they remained convinced of the need for surveillance. The testimonies of Bonnet's colleagues, as well as facts offered by the clerk in self-defense, reveal how this post-Jacobin surveillance worked in practice. This chapter will use these and geographer David Seamon's idea of "place-ballet" to explore the ways in which the physical space of the Ministry compound on the rue du Bac operated to draw attention to deviations from routine, and to expose those who stepped outside of the normal movement of people and things to suspicion. Employees were simultaneously surveillants and surveilled, disciplinarians and the objects of discipline. Solving the theft on the rue du Bac offered important assurance that this surveillance worked. The fictions constructed by Caillard and Villemarest pretended that, exposed to the scrutiny of his superiors, Bonnet's defense simply collapsed. Redoing some of the detective work in the case of the stolen seal cases also reveals, however, the limits of surveillance and transparency during the French Revolution.

The Transparency of Surveillance

Despite featuring different detectives, Villemarest's biography and Caillard's Commission of Inquiry report both claimed that Bonnet's guilt was transparent: he revealed it by bursting into tears or showing "evident distress" when called to account. Their emphasis on the power of transparency within government administration would have been familiar to anyone who had survived the dangerous years of the Terror. As Lynn Hunt has argued, revolutionary politicians constantly preached the need for transparency between citizens as an essential guarantee of the political order. The rhetoric of transparency was inseparable from the revolutionaries' emphasis on the power of publicity. Under the Old Regime, pamphleteers heralded publicity as an antidote to the secrecy and arbitrariness of royal institutions. Imperfect though they were, the proliferation of revolutionary newspapers and journals, as well as the emergence of new forums for political discussion in clubs, electoral assemblies, and Paris sections seemed to confirm the power of exposing the actions of politicians to public scrutiny, and of transparency as a means of uncovering abuses and tackling corruption. Of course, press freedom did not last. Looking to blunt the political attacks of its enemies, the government of the Terror imprisoned journalists and shut down newspapers it accused of distorting and manipulating public opinion. Nevertheless, Robespierre and others continued to cite publicity as a guarantee of transparency, and the fall of Robespierre and the Montagnards was followed by a new flourishing of newspapers and demands for freedom of the press.[11]

For clerks working in ministries during the Revolution, the rhetoric of transparency had significant consequences. During the lifetimes of the National and Legislative Assemblies, successive laws imposed an oath of allegiance on ministry clerks, mandated pay ceilings, and required the publication of their names and salaries. Ministers ordered them to set aside fixed audience hours every week to meet with members of the public. Both inside and outside the offices, politicians and ministers expected their employees to present themselves as good citizens. In 1793, they required clerks to secure certificates from their sections documenting that they were fulfilling their duties as citizens. In Versailles, clerks like Bonnet had been able to remain relatively anonymous. This was no longer possible under the new regime.[12]

Denunciations were another means of ensuring transparency. Making a denunciation, uncovering abuses of the system and acts of corruption, was an act of civic duty.[13] Bonnet's decision on 1 frimaire IV (November 22, 1795) to provide Charles Delacroix with the names of his colleagues in the archives depot in Versailles, each accompanied by an individual report on their morality and patriotism, was not random. He had been "instructed," he wrote, that the Minister wished for "particular and positive information on the morality, erudition, and civic virtues of the employees of his department."[14] Not all of his critiques of his colleagues were negative: Bonnet's chief, Geoffroy, for example, was a "man of infinitely rare merit, and as honest a patriot as he is a respected scholar." He judged others more sharply, however. His colleague Sudreau was a "musician of the former court; a mediocre subject; an ardent royalist." Tessier was a "mediocre geographer . . . hiding under a hypocritical mask an unmeasurable ambition."[15] In a second letter dated 25 frimaire IV (December 16, 1795), Bonnet did not bother to accentuate the positive. Written apparently at the urging of the Minister, who "want[ed] the truth" told with the "frankness of an honest man," it summarized his denunciation in the baldest terms. All but three of Bonnet's colleagues in the Versailles depot were "counterrevolutionaries unworthy of being salaried by the nation."[16]

Caillard's marginalia suggested that Bonnet had submitted the 1 frimaire denunciation anonymously, and that his authorship had to be deduced from his handwriting. A virtuous denunciation was necessarily a public act: the best guarantee against the use of denunciation for false purposes and the settling of private scores was for denouncers to sign their accusations.[17] Looking more closely, however, it is clear that Bonnet's first denunciation was not actually anonymous at all. Bonnet left a blank beside his own name in the list: as the only employee listed without comment, it was clear that he was the author. Bonnet signed the second denunciation at the end of frimaire. Similarly, his signature appeared at the end of his statement on d'Ornano; and the Revolutionary Committee of Versailles entered the signed document into its records.[18]

Moreover, the statement made by Bonnet to the Revolutionary Committee in Versailles in January 1793 was pretty anodyne. In the 1780s, the duc d'Ornano was a diplomat attached to the Ministry of Foreign Affairs. Bonnet witnessed that the Corsican, "who he was certain was Spanish by origin" "had the talent" to serve France's enemies. He spoke Spanish and Italian as fluently as French, and spoke English as well. According to Bonnet, d'Ornano was a mathematician, an accomplished geographer, and a knowledgeable negotiator. He had worked in the 1790s on delineating the border between France and Spain. With his knowledge of the Pyrenees in particular, "if" he was in fact conspiring with the Spanish, he "could cause the worst sort of damage." Bonnet advised that he should be "locked up and locked up a long time." The suggestion here was that d'Ornano was likely to betray France by siding with Spain, which joined the coalition fighting France the same month. The idea that this denunciation on its own sent d'Ornano to the guillotine is unlikely, however. The accusation sent by the Revolutionary Committee in Versailles to Paris in September 1793 also noted his connection to Spain and that "he knows the frontiers like his pocket." Other details provided were gleaned from somewhere other than Bonnet's statement, including a note that Louis XVI nominated d'Ornano to serve as a lieutenant general in 1790. The principal charge made against d'Ornano during his trial in Paris was that he had corresponded with foreign princes, something Bonnet had not specifically alleged. Far from precipitating d'Ornano's arrest, it is far more likely that the Revolutionary Committee called upon Bonnet to testify to particular facts in a case it was already building, and he responded as a good patriot. The denunciation was nevertheless useful evidence against Bonnet when Caillard found and copied it, because d'Ornano was a cousin of Napoleon Bonaparte.[19]

To note that Bonnet's denunciations, despite Caillard's suggestion to the contrary, conformed to revolutionary ideas of transparency and political virtue is not to say that Bonnet's denunciations were not self-interested. It seems clear from a letter Bonnet wrote to Charles Delacroix on 7 frimaire IV, to tout his own patriotism and civic virtue, that his intention in writing the denunciations was to give the Minister exactly what he wanted, and, by virtue of that, to secure the Minister's favor and his position in the government's employ.[20] It was the abuse of denunciation that led clerks, in the late 1790s, to themselves abandon political denunciations as a means of currying favor. In practice, denunciations were too disruptive, and far too indiscriminate as a means to judge employees' merits. What one employee alleged could easily be turned back on him by another; and, as Marisa Linton has noted in her account of the "Politicians' Terror," friends often ended up denouncing former friends.[21] By 1800 (as Caillard's use of Bonnet's denunciations from earlier in the decade shows), the act of denouncing one's colleagues on political grounds was treated as unacceptable by both Ministry employees and division chiefs. When he wrote them in 1795, however, Bonnet's denunciations were entirely unexceptional and were a proof of his virtue rather than his capacity for duplicity.

By 1800, the Ministry of External Relations had abandoned denunciation but not surveillance. Caillard's account of his detective work in the Commission of Inquiry's formal report, as well his careful compilation of evidence both before and after its production on paper, worked to reassure those familiar with the fact that a thief had been able to operate so easily inside the hôtel Galliffet that the Ministry was able to effectively surveille its employees. The story of Bonnet's crime lived on as a cautionary tale well after his dismissal. In January 1822, writing a report for a new Minister, the duc de Montmorency, François Jorelle (Bonnet's junior colleague) alluded to the story when arguing the need for two archives clerks to work with those treaties so that they could watch one another. He could, he promised, provide "fairly curious and infelicitous details" about what had happened to the collection in the past when a clerk (that is, Bonnet) worked with the treaties on his own.[22]

Both Villemarest and Caillard worked hard to convince their readers that surveillance worked within the walls of the Ministry compound. Although very different in some regards, they both presented the seemingly private as entirely transparent and created the fiction that surveillance could be manifested at any moment. In this regard, Caillard's and Villemarest's presentation of the power of the Commission of Inquiry or the Minister to penetrate Bonnet's duplicity and cause him to reveal his own guilt brings to mind the model of the Panopticon, made famous by Michel Foucault as a metaphor for visual surveillance as a mode of power. In Foucault's account, the Panopticon, a design for a prison imagined by philosopher Jeremy Bentham, became a means to elaborate on how the threat of surveillance is as powerful as actual surveillance. A watchman occupied the center of the building, able to see each and every individual inmate when he chose to. The inmates never knew when they were or were not being watched from the center, but their consciousness of permanent visibility functioned as an effective means of discipline and control.[23]

Yet, as Susan Maslan has noted, the rhetoric of surveillance institutionalized during the Revolution rejected the idea of centralized surveillance. Suspicious of politics and politicians, the revolutionaries' idea of transparency sprang from the notion that the people should exercise continual supervision over each other, through newspapers, political clubs and assemblies, and acts of denunciation. There was no single watchman. French men and women during the Revolution were simultaneously surveillants and surveilled.[24] As such, surveillance for those who lived through the Revolution fits better with another Foucaultian theory, that of "biopower," in which he describes how individuals engage in self-surveillance and self-discipline and thereby surveille and subjugate themselves.[25]

Unlike Caillard's report and Villemarest's story, Bonnet's self-defense articulated this more complex experience of surveillance. It demonstrates the awareness of government clerks that surveillance was something they lived with, not just in moments of high drama (being interrogated about pilfered gold and silver-gilt treaty boxes, for example) but in the most mundane moments. In his twenty-page defense, Bonnet argued that, even when the Ministry was empty of clerks, someone would still have noticed his movements. A thief's first challenge would be to escape the attention of the veterans tasked with guarding the building. The sergeant in charge had come to check on what was going on when Bonnet was in the gallery one evening conducting legitimate business. The thief's second challenge would be to avoid notice from the Minister's private apartment. A glass door connected a bedroom in the Minister's private apartment to the gallery holding the treaties. Even if the Minister did not regularly use it, and cabinets partially obscured the view from it into the gallery, the Minister, his family, or their servants, glimpsing a light through this door (or one of the gallery's windows) would surely check on it. The gallery was also close enough to the Minister's private apartments for sound to travel readily between them. The criminal would quickly be betrayed then not only by the light of his lantern, but by the sound of heavy doors opening and closing and the grating sounds made when anyone moved the gallery's rolling ladder.

Bonnet's account reveals a man who was aware not just of being under a constant threat of surveillance but also of his ability to surveille others. He was alert to the possibility and limitations of various lines of sight—thinking through them in detail, even though he was writing his self-defense after he had already been ejected from the Ministry and could no longer access the building. He had also thought through the ways in which noise traveled from one set of Ministry suites to the next. For his part, the Minister was worried enough about being peered at by his employees through the glass that he had curtains hung to block the view. The story of the stolen seal cases therefore allows us to delve deeper into government employees' awareness of how surveillance worked in practice.

In the testimonies of Bonnet's colleagues, also, surveillance worked, not because of the detective skills of the Minister or chief of the Archives Division, but because employees were conscious of their permanent visibility: they could never be sure when a superior, a colleague, a servant, or a member of the public was watching their actions. Their primary concern was therefore not to draw unnecessary attention to themselves. Bonnet's colleagues claimed that his evenings in the office made him the only one who had the opportunity to commit the crime. His break from normal Ministry practice singled him out. Bonnet's defense was that, on the contrary, the cover of darkness meant it was *more* likely a crime would be interrupted *in flagrante delicto* because it departed so radically from the normal Ministry routine.

Bonnet and his colleagues' testimonies thus reveal how surveillance operated in practice through what geographer David Seamon has described as "place-ballet." Seamon argues that, in the course of any normal day, individuals follow individual "time-space routines" which, though unchoreographed, define "place" more substantially than any physical barrier.[26] For about a year when he first moved from Versailles to Paris, Bonnet had been in the habit of returning to the Ministry in the evenings to work after everyone else had left. On some of these evenings, he had worked in the archives gallery where the seals and their case were locked away (it should be noted that Bonnet argued that this happened only twice and only with direct authorization from the Minister). Bonnet's deviation from the routine of Ministry movement helped his colleagues single him out in their testimonies to Caillard's commission. Bonnet's deviations from the "place-ballet" of normal Ministry life made him a suspect during the investigation of the theft.

In the Wrong Place at the Wrong Time

In fructidor VIII (August 1800), Caillard was still relatively new to the internal workings of the Ministry and even of his own division. Formerly a diplomat, he entered the Ministry of External Relations only eight months before the discovery of the crime, replacing the previous chief, Resnier, in nivôse VIII (December 1799) when the latter was elected senator. Caillard therefore had no personal knowledge of the period when the seals went missing. He was not even too familiar with the scene of the crime. The theft had occurred in the gallery of the hôtel Galliffet; the archives had moved to a new site, the adjacent hôtel Maurepas, between fructidor VI (September 1798) and germinal VII (April 1799) and so Caillard had never worked in the old offices. Aside from Bonnet's visible guilt and the clerk's confession (which I will return to at the end of this chapter), Caillard built his case against Bonnet out of his colleagues' testimonies. Bonnet's incrimination came down to what Caillard noted as "three principal facts." First, Bonnet was the one who was in charge of the treaties. Second, he had possession of the keys to the treaty cabinets until eighteen months previously. Third, he had a history of working with the treaties at odd hours of the evening and night, when he could (it was alleged) expect to be alone.[27]

In their accounts, junior clerks Besson and Jorelle claimed that they had had no opportunity to commit the theft. They swore that they did not have access to the keys and had never worked with the treaties. Besson noted that his only real experience of the cabinets was when he and Jorelle had helped Bonnet lift down treaty cartons (Bonnet had needed help because he suffered from a hernia). According to Besson and Jorelle, Bonnet was the only clerk in their division who worked regularly with the treaties. He had the keys to the cabinets until ventôse VII (February 1799) when, after some sort of altercation between Bonnet and his colleagues, Resnier had ordered him to return the keys to Galon-Boyer's office when he was not using them.[28]

The two younger clerks also testified that Bonnet had often worked in the Ministry in the evening on his own. Both said that he regularly returned to the archive in the late afternoon and stayed there until eight or nine o'clock. He did so through the summer of year IV (1796) and the following winter, until Resnier ordered him to stop at the end of year V (autumn 1797). Although neither Besson nor Jorelle were present during the evenings, they stated confidently that, during his nocturnal sessions, Bonnet worked not only in his office but also in the archives gallery, "for his private instruction (he claimed)."[29]

The *garçon de bureau*, Rouet, added other incriminating details. Bonnet, he claimed, had explicitly instructed Rouet to leave him on his own in the evenings. He had, he told Rouet, already "everything he needed." Rouet did as he was told and came back to the archives offices only at eight o'clock to lock the doors. The implication of Rouet's testimony was that Bonnet had had plenty of time and freedom from the normal surveillance of his colleagues to get up to mischief. Rouet had not seen Bonnet rifling through the treaties looking for gold and silver-gilt treasures, but he was happy to testify that he had seen Bonnet sleeping with a candle on his desk (a serious allegation given the fear of fire in Ministry buildings).[30]

Sub-chief Galon-Boyer's testimony strung the story together. He confirmed how Bonnet and he had organized the archives' transfer from Versailles. He detailed the making of the inventories and confirmed that Bonnet had held the key to the cabinets in which the treaties were kept until 11 ventôse VI (March 1, 1798). In the year following the treaties' move to Paris in thermidor IV (July 1796), Bonnet had, Galon-Boyer also confirmed, spent evenings in his office up to the point that Resnier ordered him to stop because it was a fire hazard. Even after Resnier took away Bonnet's keys to the treaty cabinets and placed them in Galon-Boyer's care, Galon-Boyer continued, Bonnet was still the only clerk who opened the cabinets and consulted the treaties. Galon-Boyer had himself opened the cabinets no more than twenty times in the previous five years, and then mostly to help Bonnet manhandle the big cartons. Usually, he sent Besson or Jorelle to help. This "was the order observed in the office," according to his testimony.

Galon-Boyer's role in investigating the extent of the theft also helped insulate him from suspicion. In his testimony, he outlined his response to Caillard's discovery that the seal and its case were missing from the Treaty of Versailles. He had immediately told Caillard about the existence of the inventories. He had gone to Bonnet for his copy, but the clerk declared it "missing." Galon-Boyer then launched a search for the other two copies, securing Resnier's a few days later. Jorelle confirmed his superior's account, testifying as to how Galon-Boyer had left no stone unturned in his quest to uncover the crime.[31]

The unspoken assumption in all of Bonnet's colleagues' testimonies was that the crime could not have been committed during normal office hours. The division of labor in the office defined what cabinets and cartons a particular clerk regularly accessed. The other clerks' routine work did not carry them to the end of the gallery where the treaty cabinets stood. Besson and Jorelle's testimony (confirmed by Galon-Boyer) that they never opened the cabinets on their own, and had done so only when Bonnet's hernia made it necessary that they help him, underlined that point. If Bonnet's colleagues had gone to the gallery and opened the cabinets, their deviation from the normal "place-ballet" of the offices would have stood out. There were other little observations. Besson found it suspicious that Bonnet had not noticed the missing seal boxes given he worked regularly with the treaties. He also noted that he had never seen "even the smallest disturbance in the cartons of the office that would signal that an outsider had stolen [Bonnet's] inventory of the treaties."[32] Everything added up to the same conclusion: Bonnet's deviation from the normal circulation of people and things in the Ministry made him the prime suspect.

Bonnet's colleagues' testimonies demonstrate how they lived with the same assumptions as Bonnet about how surveillance worked inside the Ministry compound. Bonnet's colleagues placed common emphasis on what was and was not routine. They played equally close attention to who did and did not go to particular places—to the extent of differentiating between one end of the archives gallery and the other. They painted a world where their day-to-day actions and movements, each unique but circumscribed by a set of rules and expectations, combined to keep the work of their office, and by extension the Ministry as a whole, running smoothly. As the circulation of people took on fixed patterns, so too did the circulation of paperwork. According to Besson, the wrong hand rifling through the wrong carton would inevitably cause a visible disturbance, something that could not escape the clerks' self-surveillance. Ministry clerks therefore deviated from the "place-ballet" they danced every day only by the failure of their physical bodies—issues like Bonnet's hernia that they documented specifically. Bonnet's evenings alone in the Ministry attracted suspicion. His colleagues' habitualness, on the other hand, was sufficient to act as their alibi.

The Scene of the Crime

In his discussion of "place-ballet," David Seamon has remarked on how the movement of people and things has a bearing on our definition of place. This might be a "neighborhood" or any other environment where users come together regularly—lounges, cafés, marketplaces, and office buildings. While Seamon is primarily interested in places defined by the unhindered movement of people, his phenomenological geography applies as well to places where movement is limited (though, for obvious reasons, not to places where there is no movement at all).[33] In the Ministry, employees lived with rules, formal and informal, about who could go where, when, and why. Mobility and immobility shaped the physical space of the compound, delimiting the stage of the employees' place-ballet (and, for us, the scene of the crime).

The physical layout of the Ministry accentuated the way any deviation from an employee's "time-space routine" would have been highly visible. Every division had its place (see Figure 7.1). A visitor entering from the rue du Bac would have walked past the lodge of the porter Jory into the first courtyard, connected to a second courtyard by an arch directly opposite. The building immediately opposite the entrance held the Division des Fonds and the apartment of the division's director. At the time of the theft, the Ministry had three "political" divisions, which divided the work of diplomatic correspondence geographically between them. Two were on the left side of the courtyard, accessed by a staircase (the ground floor was occupied by stables). The offices of the other political division, the Division du Nord, were farther into the compound, on the upper floor of the neo-classically styled hôtel Galliffet, located in the second courtyard. On the ground floor of this building was the Minister's private office and on the first floor his family's private residence. A passageway on the left of the hôtel gave access to a ceremonial staircase leading to the Minister's apartments. A door on the other side of the passageway led to the Bureau du Chiffre, the Ministry's cryptographic office. On the right past the passageway was a garden overlooked by the Minister's private apartment. A wing of the hôtel Galliffet extended on the left. The archives gallery was on the first floor of this wing.[34] The Secretariat général, which organized the flow of paper coming in and out of the Ministry, occupied the ground floor. Its members complained about the lack of light in north-facing offices and discussed the danger of the weight of the archives crashing through the floor onto their heads.[35] Each division thus had its own unique location in the Ministry. That

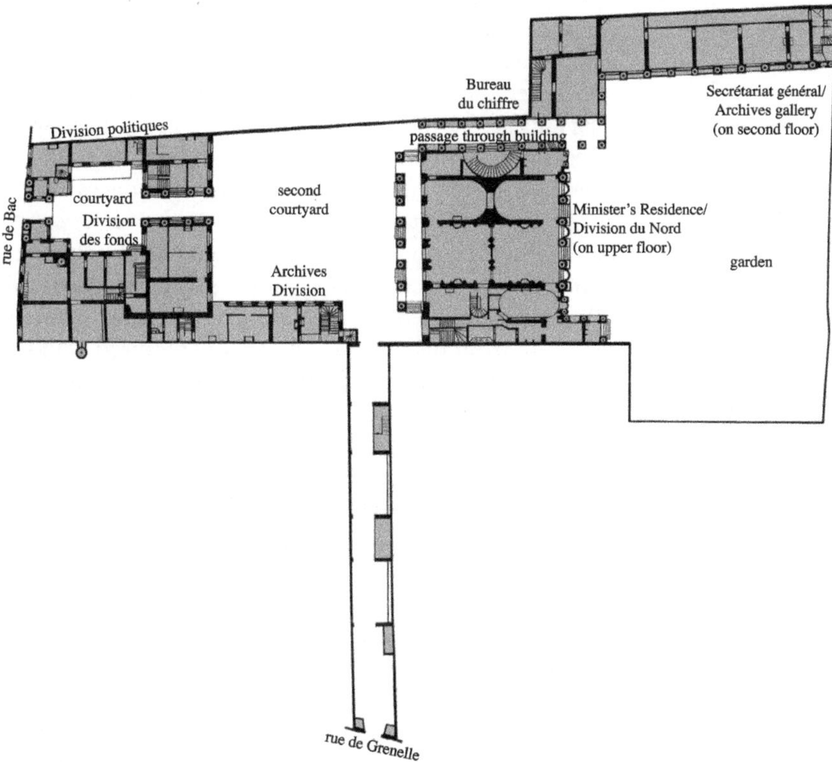

FIGURE 7.1 *Plan of the ground floor of the hôtel Galliffet in the early 1800s. Author's sketch, based on Archives Nationales f/31/3, pièce 236.*

said, lack of sufficient, suitable space in a particular building meant that sometimes bureaux were orphaned from their divisions, and several of these orphaned bureaux were located in the same wing of the hôtel where the archives gallery was located. Even in the case of orphaned offices though, a routine developed in terms of who went where, why, and when.

The clerks of the Archives Division suffered a particular spatial dislocation. A courtyard, a covered passage, and several staircases separated the archival collection from the offices of the men in charge of it. This is what Bonnet had referenced when he wrote that he would have had to pass through a small gallery, down several stairs, and open seven or eight doors in order to access the scene of the crime. It was also not easy to get from the offices into the gallery: as building maintenance invoices reveal, Ministry doors were fitted with a considerable number of locks. In year IV (1795–6), as External Affairs prepared to move into the hôtel Galliffet, it paid Citizen Toque, a locksmith, 4,103,920 in assignats (14,439 francs in hard currency), more than was paid to any other individual contractor.[36] In year V (1796–7),

Delsalte, locksmith, received 3,248 francs, 15 sous in hard currency, for services that included installing security locks on at least three different doors that Bonnet and his colleagues would have had to travel through between office and the gallery, as well as the replacement of a lock on a cabinet inside the gallery itself.[37] Unless he had the right keys, there were strict limits to what offices and cabinets an employee could access.

In the course of their day-to-day work, however, the employees of the Archives Division did not need to make regular trips to the gallery. Any journey they made there would have been remarked upon, both by their co-workers and by employees in other divisions whose offices they passed. Indeed, the fact that Bonnet mentioned opening and closing seven or eight doors suggests that the route from his office to the gallery required walking through colleagues' offices. Former eighteenth-century aristocratic mansions like the hôtel Galliffet featured few corridors: rooms opened up directly from one to the next, which meant employees had to go through rather than pass by. The subchief of the Division des Consulats, Antoine-Alexandre-Jean Butet, for example, had the office directly beside those of the archives personnel. Bonnet cited Butet as a character witness in his self-defense presumably because Butet knew everything that went on in his neighbors' rooms.[38]

Also limiting the need to move across the Ministry complex was the fact that clerks worked with copies, summaries, or excerpts kept in cartons in their offices, and not with originals. Everyone agreed, for example, that the treaties had not left the gallery since Galon-Boyer and Bonnet had installed them there in thermidor IV (July 1796). Documents did not move around the Ministry except in reproduction: reproductions could be kept in offices and did not need to be fetched and returned at the beginning and end of the workday. The immobility of original documents led Besson to cite the inventory missing from Bonnet's carton as strong proof that the theft was an inside job. Documents did not just disappear and the cartons looked otherwise undisturbed. However, Bonnet also used the immobility of documents as a proof. To show how completely his superiors trusted him, he explained how, on one occasion, division chiefs had turned over original treaties they had in their offices to him personally, sidestepping the usual paperwork process.[39] When original documents were entrusted to employees, it was exceptional. What went into the treaty cabinet stayed in the treaty cabinet.

Documents did not move around. Employees' mobility was restricted by lock and key. Surveillance was omnipresent: walking through the Ministry without being seen by someone was nearly impossible, especially when one had to walk through colleagues' offices to get there. A combination of human and material factors thus figured the steps of the Ministry's "place-ballet." The attention paid by the employees of the Archives Division to mobility and immobility, as well as to the normalcy of routine, shows the extent to which issues of access defined the Ministry compound for them.

When their workplace transformed into a crime scene, they mobilized the same understanding to claim innocence and apportion guilt.

Inviting Surveillance

Bonnet wrote his comprehensive self-defense months after his termination. Why did he not do better at defending himself during the inquiry itself? According to an appeal Bonnet later addressed to the First Consul (but which was sent by Napoleon's secretaries to the Ministry), being called before the commission to defend himself after "forty consecutive years of irreproachable service" was a "staggering blow." He found himself "drained of all sentiment on hearing the charges directed against me." In particular, Bonnet was worried that, if an accusation against him became public, it would hurt his son, Jacques-Alexis Bonnet. Jacques-Alexis, eighteen years old, was a prize-winning student in the École central de Seine et Oise. He was seeking to join, as a junior naturalist, the naval scientific expedition about to leave France under the command of the explorer Nicolas Baudin.[40] As Caillard pursued him over the theft, *père* Bonnet was trying to secure support from the Museum of Natural History for his son's ambitions.[41] On 24 floréal VIII (May 14, 1800), sixteen days after his termination, he wrote to Antoine-Laurent de Jussieu, a museum professor and one of the major forces behind the Baudin expedition. In the letter, he styled himself "*premier commis* in the External Relations archives."[42] Not only was Bonnet no longer a clerk in the Ministry of External Relations, he had never officially held the title of "*premier commis*," which had been the title given to division chiefs in the Old Regime. In his letter to Jussieu, Bonnet was hoping his position at the Ministry would encourage the professor to take a proper look at his son's credentials. His efforts were somewhat successful as Jacques-Alexis departed Le Havre in vendémiaire IX (October 1800), though not as a naturalist but as a novice sailor, second class. The evidence of Jussieu's correspondence thus backs up what Bonnet claimed in his letter to Napoleon. Bonnet's desire to avoid public controversy around his termination beyond the walls of the Ministry denied him the opportunity to mount a comprehensive self-defense before Caillard and Talleyrand decided his guilt.

In his attempts to defend himself after his termination, Bonnet, as we have already seen, argued that any evening peregrinations he was supposed to have indulged in could not have taken place without the Minister, his family, and the veterans on guard taking notice. He argued in addition that, if the Minister ordered a search in the cartons of various offices, evidence of his work product would prove his innocence. Yes, Bonnet admitted, he had worked late in his office in the evenings, but on tasks given to him by his superiors. Charles Delacroix had been in the habit of dropping by the archives office at odd hours in search of particular pieces of information.

Antoine Darbault and Jean-Claude Méhée, Division chiefs under Delacroix, had commissioned Bonnet to search for information on commercial treaties between Russia and the maritime powers of Europe and on conventions between France and Spain on the treatment of deserters. He had, he freely admitted, sent Rouet away while he worked. Checking Delcroix's files, and those of Darbault and Méhée's divisions, would show that the Ministry had profited from Bonnet's evenings in the office.[43]

Bonnet wanted the Ministry to look more closely at what he had and had not done while working for the Ministry, rather than just assuming that his departure from the routine of employee behavior was a marker of guilt. As well as paper proofs, witnesses could confirm his innocence. He had, he asserted, never been alone in the gallery at night. On the occasion when Delacroix summoned him to consult records of protocol and etiquette in advance of a meeting with a foreign power, a ministerial usher named Duverger accompanied him. He had formally notified his chief, Resnier, that the Minister had ordered him to work there that night.[44] Only one other research request had taken him to the gallery outside of normal office hours: Talleyrand, charged with negotiating peace with Portugal, had also sent him to the gallery one evening. On that occasion, Bonnet noted, Jorelle had accompanied and assisted him.[45] Bonnet expected that Duverger and Jorelle would, if questioned, confirm that they had not left him alone in the gallery.

Instead of avoiding surveillance, Bonnet embraced it. Indeed, his self-defense suggested that, even at a time when he enjoyed the full trust of the Minister, he was concerned enough about the potential dangers of transgressing routine by going into the gallery at night that he always made sure to carry a surveillant with him. Inviting surveillance, calling for more scrutiny of his life, his actions, and his character, continued to be a strategy employed by Bonnet after his termination. On 19 and 23 ventôse IX (March 10 and 14, 1801), he submitted a request to the Ministry of External Relations that it pursue criminal or military court proceedings against him. On multiple occasions, on 23 pluviôse (February 12, 1801), 16, 17, 24, and 25 ventôse (March 7, 8, 15 and 16, 1801), he formally requested to be investigated and put under surveillance by the Ministry of Police and the Paris Prefecture of Police. He requested that they apply the most rigorous examination of his conduct and his property. His contact at the Prefecture of Police was Jean Henri, chief of the second division in charge of criminal investigations (and the recruiter of the famous French criminal and criminologist, Eugène-François Vidocq). In requesting that the police investigate him, Bonnet risked much worse than the termination of his employment. He was certain a public proceeding would prove that he was not guilty, however, and left no stone unturned trying to set one up. The Ministry of Police authorized an investigation on 27 nivôse IX (January 17, 1801), but the Ministry of External Relations resisted the possibility of a public hearing.[46] The Ministry also saw off Bonnet's lawyer, Dodin, who wrote to Talleyrand on 26 pluviôse IX (February 5, 1801) asking to meet to present Bonnet's case. Instead of Talleyrand, he met Caillard, and, after this meeting, Dodin made no further inquiries.[47] On 8 germinal IX (March 29, 1801), Bonnet received a visit from a police inspector (*officier de paix*) who interviewed him about "the theft of which I was the victim," and who, Bonnet believed, would be making further enquiries. No trace of any enquiry exists in the archives, however. Calling on the power of surveillance to prove his innocence failed Bonnet at every juncture.[48]

Fictions of Surveillance

The factor that had worked most against Bonnet was the speed with which Caillard confirmed his guilt. Central to this was his "confession." According to Caillard, Bonnet had gone to talk to his co-workers after his interview and they had pressed him to confess. Having received Bonnet's "confession," Caillard disbanded the Commission of Inquiry and went to the Minister to approve the termination.[49] Talleyrand did not wait for an official report to sign off.

Talleyrand acted therefore on Caillard's word, and not a formal review of the evidence. If he had reviewed the evidence more closely, he might have seen that Caillard's account of what allowed him to determine Bonnet's guilt so quickly did not square with the evidence in Bonnet's file. Bonnet signed his official testimony on 6 fructidor VIII (August 24, 1800), the day after his appearance before the commission. He wrote a resignation letter on the same day. Neither gave any hint of a confession. In his resignation, Bonnet wrote that "I am not in any way guilty of the crime of which I am suspected." Nevertheless, "the cruel position in which I find myself has convinced me to submit my resignation," a reference perhaps to his realization that his colleagues were treating him as the prime suspect, or to his need to prioritize his son's career over his own defense. In his resignation, Bonnet continued to claim innocence. As an innocent man (albeit one under suspicion), he asked that the Minister start the paperwork for his pension.[50] Instead, a day later, he received summary dismissal without pension (and certainly not half-pay for his wife, as Villemarest alleged).

Bonnet's "visible guilt" and "confession" were therefore quite tenuous proofs of his criminality. Caillard otherwise rested his case against Bonnet on the "three principal facts" gleaned from his colleagues' testimonies. He also continued to collect other evidence against Bonnet. In particular, Caillard added the denunciations Bonnet made in 1793 and 1795 to his personnel file. Going back through the archives to look for any piece of paper that might be used to further incriminate Bonnet shows the extent of Caillard's, the Ministry's, and his former colleagues' desire to make a watertight case against him. As in the nineteenth-century detective novel, the power of the detective's gaze made the crime legible, but only through the transformation of traces and trivia into telling details ("Elementary," as Sherlock Holmes would say). In his official report, Caillard invested himself with the power of being able to see through Bonnet's account. What he deducted from the "words [Bonnet] had let slip," however, still had to be confirmed by a mass of other details, gleaned both from colleagues' testimonies, which set up means and opportunity, and from the denunciations, which confirmed Bonnet's capacity for deception and intrigue.

Caillard's reconstruction of Bonnet's criminal actions looked to prove that Ministry surveillance was operating successfully. Scholars of literature have emphasized how the conventions of detective fiction serve to confirm the power of surveillance and social control.[51] However, as Mark Seltzer has argued, nineteenth-century detective narratives were successful in presenting the ideal of an unseen but all-seeing surveillance only because readers already believed that such surveillance existed. The reader of the detective novel shared in a fantasy of surveillance and disclosure, the insistence that no area of life was invisible.[52] Caillard's case against Bonnet was imperfect. Nevertheless, the weight of details collected against him was enough for officials who worked day by day with the self-discipline of self-surveillance to deny him the benefit of the doubt. The strength of Caillard's narrative then was that, in its reconstruction of how Bonnet committed the crime, it fitted with the employees' own sense of how "place-ballet" worked as part of the Ministry's surveillance regime. Caillard's explanation of his detective work confirmed to employees their already existing assumption that self-surveillance worked.

Both his colleagues' testimonies and Bonnet's own self-defense demonstrated their willingness to play surveillant, to indulge their curiosity, and, perhaps most importantly, to remember months and years after the fact when and how their co-workers deviated from the time-space routine of the Ministry. When delivered as a cautionary tale, the story of Bonnet's crime "proved" that good employees could afford to wait for bad employees to expose themselves, as they would inevitably do. The Ministry no longer needed its employees to inform on one another. Bonnet's colleagues gave testimony that incriminated him only when questioned in an interview process that carefully treated everyone, including Bonnet, in the same way.

The retrieval of Bonnet's denunciations as a means of proving his capacity for duplicity underlined how absolutely the Ministry had abandoned by 1800 the idea of political commitment and public acts of civic virtue (like denunciation) as guarantors of transparency. Charles Delacroix's willingness to encourage Bonnet in 1795 shows that the ideology of political virtue had continued to underpin surveillance through the Thermidorian Convention and into the period of the Directory. With its abandonment, the Ministry needed new ways (like Caillard's account of his detective work) to justify that its surveillance worked.

The strength of Caillard's narrative was that it led its readers to an answer to the question—"whodunit?" Bonnet's counter narrative, on the other hand, lacked the closure of a detective story. While Bonnet, like his colleagues, asserted the omnipresence of scrutiny inside the Ministry compound, and even argued for the power of self-surveillance to penetrate the darkness of night, the conclusion he drew from this is that anyone was as likely as he was to have stolen the treaty seals and their boxes. Bonnet was aware of this weakness. In his twenty-page self-defense, he offered several different scenarios in which the theft could have taken place. Thefts were rife in the Ministry in year IV (1795–6), he claimed: during the archives' move to the hôtel Maurepas in year VII (1799), he had shown Resnier evidence of several forced locks. Or, perhaps the *garçon de bureau*, Rouet, had committed the theft: Rouet lived in the building and had access to the keys in Galon-Boyer's office as part of his job. Bonnet alleged that Rouet went missing in the evenings.[53] In his letter to Napoleon, Bonnet expanded on his Rouet theory. Fifteen months before the theft, he claimed, Resnier had discovered several books from the Ministry library in the *garçon de bureau*'s rooms. On Bonnet's urging, Resnier had pardoned Rouet, but now Bonnet wondered if this generosity was his undoing.[54]

These were both viable theories, and the latter story provided a sense of pathos, but his theories lacked the detail of Caillard's (were Rouet the perpetrator, would the *garçon de bureau* not have had the same issues of being noticed if he was in the gallery in the middle of the night?). During the Restoration, Bonnet offered his most elaborate conspiracy theory: that Caillard, the "implacable" enemy of "Charles de la Croix and his supposed favorite" (that is to say, former Minister Charles Delacroix and Bonnet himself), in fact faked the theft. It is highly unlikely that the theft was simulated (the seal boxes are missing in the collections of the Archives diplomatiques today). This wild accusation speaks more to Bonnet's frustration that Caillard's case against him, despite its errors and inconsistencies, had proved so compelling. If there never had been a crime, it removed the issue of "whodunit."

The Ministry was no Panopticon, but officials told stories as if it operated that way. The power of the center, of the officials managing the administration, was not that of surveillance but of narration, the power to explain how surveillance worked. Only Caillard and the Minister were in a position to pronounce definitively on whether Bonnet's steps (or missteps) had broken the "place-ballet" of the Ministry compound. Although they could note when someone else seemed out of place, individual clerks in practice managed only their own "time-space routines." Thus, while surveillance was something that the clerks imposed upon themselves in their daily routines, as a mode of policing it could only be wielded by the men at the top. Once Caillard and the Minister had decided on their verdict, it sealed Bonnet's fate. Talleyrand and Caillard terminated Bonnet without the right to his day in court. As Villemarest suggested, it would not do for the world to know that a thief had flourished, even if only for a short time, at the heart of the rue du Bac.

Source: Defense Statement by Citizen Bonnet, former employee of the [French Ministry of] External Relations. Written after his termination for theft on 7 Fructidor VIII (August 25, 1800)

. . . it would have been impossible not to be seen from the Minister's [apartment]; I would have had to go through a small gallery, down several stairs, and open seven or eight doors in order to commit the crime. I would have more to fear from the surveillance of the veterans guarding the archives, than from the office porter [*garçon de bureau*]; [after all,] their sergeant saw the light up in the archives gallery the evening [Minister Charles Delacroix ordered me to stay late to conduct] an impromptu search and came up to check what was happening. It is in vain to object that the Minister does not normally use the bedroom [in question] and that cabinets partially obstruct the view [from that bedroom via a glass door into the archives gallery]. It is no less true that that room is surrounded by other inhabited rooms which open into it; and that one can usually hear the family of the Minister. [Indeed, the Minister's household,] in order to not be seen [from the archives gallery], erected curtains in front of the glass door located at the extremity of the gallery and adjacent to the cabinet in which the treaties were held, and in front of which was a desk for laying out and consulting documents. And, as in the example of the sergeant I just quoted, is there anything more visible, even at a distance, than a light lit in the darkness; and, whatever the precautions, would not its rays have escaped in all directions? Even the most committed criminal would not have been so stupid to imagine that someone, in the silence of the night, would not have noticed the frequent loud noises that accompanied the opening and closing of several doors and the friction of a heavy rolling ladder; and that they would not want to know what was happening at an ungodly hour in an archive as interesting as that of [the Ministry of] External Relations. Certainly! There is no doubt that [if someone] checked, they would have been immediately assured of the truth. And, if I had been caught red-handed, what excuse could I have made in the absence of a direct order [to work there]?

"Notice justificatif du Citoyen Bonnet, ancien employé des Rélations extérieures," *Archives diplomatiques, Personnel, Volumes réliées, vol. II (Bonnet, LJA), 39rv, n.12.*

Notes

1 The author would like to thank Mette Harder, Jennifer Heuer, Rupali Mishra, and Kaitlen King, all of whom read drafts and provided thoughtful

commentary. Discussions in my spring 2018 graduate seminar, "Place and Space in Nineteenth-Century France," and in Spike Sweeting's Royal College of Art postgraduate course on the "Histories of the Material Culture of Government, 1750–1980," in summer 2018, also helped shape the piece. Finally, the author wishes to acknowledge the help given to him navigating building records in La Courneuve by Séverine Blenner-Michel and Grégoire Eldin.

2 Letter, Caillard to Bonnet, 7 fructidor VIII, Archives diplomatiques (AD), Personnel, Volumes réliées, vol. II (Bonnet, LJA) (hereafter "Bonnet personnel file"), 31rv (recto and verso).

3 "Note sur ce qui s'est passé aux Archives des Rélations extérieures lors de la découverte et la soustraction qui y avait été faite des boîtes d'argent et de vermeil renfermant les sceaux attachés aux différens actes de ratification de traités," 7 vendémiaire IX, AD, Bonnet personnel file, 65rv, 66r.

4 Robin W. Winks, *The Historian as Detective* (New York: Harper & Row, 1969), xiii.

5 On the work of the fictional detective as reconstruction, see Tzvetan Todorov, *The Poetics of Prose*, trans. Richard Howard (Ithaca, NY: Cornell University Press, 1977), 42–7.

6 [Charles Maxime Catherine de Villemarest], *Monsieur Talleyrand* (Paris: A. Roret, 1835), 3:156, 171–2.

7 "Note sur ce qui s'est passé," 7 vendémiaire IX, AD, Bonnet personnel file, 65r–66r. Documents B–I are in Bonnet's file: 32r, 45r–53r. The file does not contain document A (the 1796 inventory) and A[bis] (Galon-Boyer's inventory).

8 "Nota," AD, Bonnet personnel file, 54r; letter, Bonnet to Talleyrand, 3 fructidor VIII, AD, Bonnet personnel file, 55rv.

9 "Notice historique," 1 frimaire IV, AD, Bonnet personnel file, 22rv, 23r.

10 "Copie de la dénonciation faite au comité révolutionnaire de Versailles contre le comte d'Ornano," AD, Bonnet personnel file, 59rv.

11 On the rhetoric of publicity and transparency before and during the Revolution, see Lynn Hunt, *Politics, Culture, and Class in the French Revolution* (Berkeley: University of California Press, 1984), 44; Keith Michael Baker, *Inventing the French Revolution* (Cambridge: Cambridge University Press, 1990), 116–20; Mona Ozouf, "Public Spirit," in *A Critical Dictionary of the French Revolution*, ed. François Furet and Mona Ozouf, trans. Arthur Goldhammer (Cambridge, MA: Harvard University Press, 1989), 771–91. On the role assumed for newspapers in uncovering corruption in politics and government, see Jeremy Popkin, *Revolutionary News: The Press in France, 1789–1799* (Durham, NC: Duke University Press, 1990), 2–6; Jean-Paul Bertaud, "An Open File: The Press under the Terror," in *The French Revolution and the Creation of Modern Political Culture, Vol. IV: The Terror*, ed. Keith Michael Baker (Oxford: Pergamon, 1994), 297–308.

12 For the impact of revolutionary transparency on Ministry clerks, see Ralph Kingston, *Bureaucrats and Bourgeois Society: Office Politics and Individual Credit in France, 1789–1848* (Houndsmills, UK: Palgrave Macmillan, 2012),

32–5; Ralph Kingston, "The Bricks and Mortar of Revolutionary Administration," *French History* 20, no. 4 (2006): 405–23. For an overview of demands that administrators prove their civic virtue, see Catherine Kawa, *Les Ronds-de-Cuir: les employés du ministère de l'Intérieur sous la Première République, 1792–1800* (Paris: Éd. du CTHS, 1997), 137–61.

13 Colin Lucas, "The Theory and Practice of Denunciation in the French Revolution," *Journal of Modern History* 68, no. 4 (1996): 768–85; Jacques Guilhaumou, "Fragments of a Discourse of Denunciation (1789–1794)," in *The French Revolution and the Creation of Modern Political Culture, Vol. IV: The Terror*, ed. Keith Michael Baker (Oxford: Pergamon, 1994), 139–56.

14 Letter, Bonnet to [Charles Delacroix], 7 frimaire IV, AD, Bonnet personnel file, 24r–25r.

15 "Notice historique," 1 frimaire IV, AD, Bonnet personnel file, 22r–23r.

16 Letter, Bonnet to Delacroix, 25 frimaire IV, AD, Bonnet personnel file, 27rv.

17 Lucas, "The Theory and Practice of Denunciation," 775.

18 "Notice historique," 1 frimaire IV, AD, Bonnet personnel file, 22r. In the space left by Bonnet, someone added in different handwriting that he was a "good patriot, a good clerk, an honest man, and in fact a good father, good husband, and good friend."

19 "Copie de la dénonciation . . . contre le comte d'Ornano," AD, Bonnet personnel file, 59rv; "Dénonciation contre le nommé Ornano, Corse ou Espagnol, par le Comité de surveillance de Versailles," Archives Nationales [AN] BB/3/72; Pierre Colonna de Cesari-Rocca, *Les Maisons historiques de la Corse, Les Seigneurs d'Ornano et leurs descendants* (Paris: Jouve et Boyer, 1899), 89. Bonnet became aware that the denunciation had been found, which suggests it was used actively against him by the Ministry: letter to [duc de Richelieu], May 6, 1818, 68v.

20 Letter, Bonnet to Delacroix, 7 frimaire IV, AD, Bonnet personnel file, 24r–25r. Bonnet was hardly exceptional in looking to profit from denunciation. Marisa Linton has discussed in depth the problem of the Revolutionary men of virtue's "authenticity," arguing that their being pushed in one direction or another by private interest, personal loyalty, or individual grudges and dislikes does not negate belief in political virtue. It is important to recognize that the men of the Revolution were "complex human beings," much "as we are ourselves": Marisa Linton, *Choosing Terror: Virtue, Friendship, and Authenticity in the French Revolution* (Oxford: Oxford University Press, 2013), 20–1, 40–1, 285–6. Richard Cobb's "The Biographical Approach and the Personal Case History" describes several colorful examples of revolutionaries who progressed "from private life to public militancy and the exploitation of revolutionary chance to advantage," in *Reactions to the French Revolution* (London: Oxford University Press, 1972), 63–127 (114).

21 Linton, *Choosing Terror*, 137–61. For the move away from the use of political denunciation in government offices in the late 1790s and early 1800s, see Kingston, *Bureaucrats and Bourgeois Society*, 52–72.

22 François Jorelle, "Mémoire rédigé d'après l'ordre de Monsieur le Duc de Montmorency, sur le service des archives," January 1822, AD, 404 INVA 2, 103r.

23 Michel Foucault, *Discipline and Punish*, trans. Alan Sheridan (New York: Vintage, 1977), 195–308.

24 Susan Maslan, *Revolutionary Acts: Theater, Democracy, and the French Revolution* (Baltimore, MD: JHU Press, 2005), 127–9. In an interview titled "The Eye of Power," Foucault describes the French Revolution's "Rousseauist dream" of transparency, that each individual might be able to see (and judge) every other: Michel Foucault, *Power/Knowledge: Selected Interviews and Other Writings, 1972–1977*, ed. Colin Gordon (New York: Pantheon, 1980), 152.

25 Michel Foucault, *The History of Sexuality, Volume I: An Introduction*, trans. Robert Hurley (New York: Vintage, 1980).

26 David Seamon, *A Geography of the Lifeworld: Movement, Rest and Encounter* (New York: St. Martin's Press, 1979). See also David Seamon, "Body-Subject, Time-Space Routines, and Place-Ballets," in *The Human Experience of Space and Place*, ed. Anne Buttimer and David Seamon (London: Croom Helm, 1980), 148–65; David Seamon and Cristina Nordin, "Marketplace as Place Ballet: A Swedish Example," *Landscape* 24 (1980): 35–41.

27 Note in Caillard's handwriting, AD, Bonnet personnel file, 60r.

28 A letter, dated 11 ventôse VII, from Bonnet to Resnier, referenced this "altercation," remarking how he was "profoundly afflicted by the difficulties which have arisen between my colleagues and myself. I desire sincerely that they should be forgotten": AD, Bonnet personnel file, 30r.

29 Jorelle's testimony, 5 fructidor VIII, AD, Bonnet personnel file, 49rv. Bonnet, Jorelle said, claimed to be working in the evenings for his "private instruction." Besson's testimony, 5 fructidor VIII, AD, Bonnet personnel file, 47v.

30 Rouet's testimony, undated [5 fructidor VIII], AD, Bonnet personnel file, 51r.

31 Jorelle's testimony, 5 fructidor VIII, AD, Bonnet personnel file, 49v.

32 Besson's testimony, 5 fructidor VII, 47v–48r.

33 See especially Seamon, "Body-Subject, Time-Space Routines, and Place-Ballets," 162–3; Seamon and Nordin, "Marketplace as Place Ballet," 35–41. Seamon's work looks to inform urban and environmental planners and so his emphasis on places where movement is "free" is entirely laudable.

34 Fréderic Masson, *Le Département des Affaires étrangères pendant la Révolution, 1787–1804* (Paris: E. Plon, 1877), 413–15; M. le Comte de Garden, *Histoire générale des traités de paix et autres transactions principales entre toutes les puissances de l'Europe depuis la paix de Westphalie* (Paris: Amyot, 1851), 10:iii–v.

35 Report to Talleyrand, nivôse VI, AD 750SUP 403.

36 "État des réglemens de mémoires d'ouvrages faits par les ordres du Ministre des Rélations extérieures, dans la maison qu'il occupe rue du Bacq, et sous la direction du Cen J. A. Renard, Architect du Ministère dans le cours des 3e, 4e, et 5e années de la République française," AD, Comptabilité, Hôtels du Ministère, 750SUP/400.

37 "Mémoire des ouvrages de serrurerie faits en la maison du Ministre des Rélations extérieures, rue du Bacq, par Delsatte, serrurier même rue en l'an

5ème" and "Mémoire des ouvrages de serrurerie faits pour le Cit. de Tallerand minister des Rélations extérieures, par Delsatte, serrurier rue du Bacq, no. 479, dans le courant des mois de thermidor et fructidor de l'an 5ème de la République," AD, Comptabilité, Hôtels du Ministère, 750SUP/400.

38 "Notice justificatif du Citoyen Bonnet, ancien employé des Rélations extérieures," AD, Bonnet personnel file, 40v.

39 "Notice justificatif du Citoyen Bonnet," AD, Bonnet personnel file, 40v.

40 Bonnet to Bonaparte, undated, AD, Bonnet personnel file, 57rv, 58r.

41 On 30 floréal VIII (May 20, 1800), twenty-two days after Bonnet's termination, Versailles botanist Antoine Nicolas Duchesne also wrote to Jussieu promoting the boy's credentials: letter, Duchesne to Antoine-Laurent de Jussieu, 30 floréal VIII, AN AJ/15/569.

42 Bonnet to de Jussieu, 24 floréal VIII, AN AJ/15/569. In the body of the letter, Bonnet referred to himself more accurately as a "former" employee of the Department of External Relations. Although Jacques-Alexis did not get the position he wished, he credited Jussieu for getting him on Baudin's expedition: he wrote to Jussieu from Le Havre on 7 messidor VIII, AN AJ/15/569, to thank him. Bonnet also tried to thank Jussieu, calling on him in person on 6 prairial VIII, but he was not received.

43 "Notice justificatif du Citoyen Bonnet," AD, Bonnet personnel file, 40r.

44 "Notice justificatif du Citoyen Bonnet," AD, Bonnet personnel file, 39v.

45 "Notice justificatif du Citoyen Bonnet," AD, Bonnet personnel file, 40r.

46 Bonnet to de Richelieu, 24 May 1818, AD, Bonnet personnel file, 70r.

47 Letters, Dodin to Talleyrand, 20 pluviôse IX; Caillard to Dodin, 1 ventôse IX; Bonnet to de Richelieu, 24 May 1818, AD, Bonnet personnel file, 63r, 64r, 70r.

48 Letter, Bonnet to Bonaparte, undated, AD, Bonnet personnel file, 57v.

49 "Note sur ce qui s'est passé aux Archives des Rélations extérieurs," 7 vendémiaire IX, AD, Bonnet personnel file, 66r.

50 Letter, Bonnet to the Minister, 6 fructidor VIII, AD, Bonnet personnel file, 52r.

51 The novel reproduces social modes of surveillance and supervision through its "programmatic embodiment": D. A. Miller, *The Novel and the Police* (Berkeley: University of California Press, 1988), 28.

52 Mark Seltzer, *Henry James and the Art of Power* (Ithaca, NY: Cornell University Press, 1984), 33–9. In his analysis of Henry James's *The Princess Casamassima*, Seltzer notes that all characters in the novel were "in danger of playing the spy": 41, 46–7.

53 "Note justificatif du Citoyen Bonnet," AD, Bonnet personnel file, 38r, 40r. Caillard criticized such theories, dismissing them as attempts to muddy the waters: "Nota," AD, Bonnet personnel file, 54r.

54 Letter, Bonnet to Bonaparte, undated, AD, Bonnet personnel file, 57v.

8

Sex as Work: Public Women in Revolutionary Paris

Clyde Plumauzille

In 1791, the French revolutionaries decriminalized prostitution.[1] But they did so in an ambiguous fashion, by simply leaving it off the list of offenses in the new Penal Code and the *Code de police correctionnelle*, which dealt primarily with misdemeanor crimes not subject to corporal or specifically shaming punishments. Revolutionaries seemed to view it as a wretched but necessary part of urban life. As a departure from the politics of prohibition promoted by the *Ancien Régime*, they acknowledged the relationship of prostitutes to society, but without fully including them in the new civic community.

Yet prostitution represented an essential component of the female makeshift economy in preindustrial societies.[2] In the late eighteenth century, it was practiced by 10,000–15,000 women in the French capital, which numbered about 600,000 inhabitants at the time.[3] In her pioneering study of the subject, Érica-Marie Benabou emphasized the changing face of prostitution on the eve of the French Revolution, as the portion of occasional, clandestine, and independent prostitutes grew. Their influx made the activity more visible within the urban space.[4] The decline of the large brothels of the *Ancien Régime*, combined with economic recession affecting France since the late 1770s and decriminalization during the revolutionary period, integrated and liberalized the practice and made it more autonomous. This climate of relative police tolerance did not, however, prevent persistent demands for regulation from citizens as well as city administrators of what was still seen as scandalous in the public space. Thus, in a society increasingly obsessed with public morality but unwilling to deal with the complex causality between poverty and sex work, revolutionary police opted to manage prostitution and its visibility in the streets in order to regulate the trade and protect the public eye. Rather than fully acknowledge and legalize prostitution, officials confined marked women to the margins of the community, unraveling both the social and sexual frontiers of citizenship.

These transformations of prostitution remain a neglected area in the history of the French Revolution. Although major works dealing with prostitution have appeared over the last decades, including Jill Harsin's *Policing Prostitution in Nineteenth-Century Paris* (1985), Alain Corbin's *Les Filles de noce: misère sexuelle et prostitution au XIXe et XXe siècles* (1978), and Érica-Marie Benabou's *La prostitution et la police des mœurs au XVIIIe siècle* (1987), none of those addressed the issue of revolutionary prostitution.[5] Susan Conner was the only historian to offer a study on the topic in a 1989 article entitled "Politics, Prostitution and the Pox in Revolutionary Paris, 1789–1799."[6] Furthermore, historians usually mention prostitution only to illustrate the misery of the time or the unbridled libertinism of a society in crisis.

Prostitution, which was a moral category, pertains to the perception of a particular female use of sexuality as deviant within a given historical context.[7] For instance, we are told that during the decade between 1789 and 1799, contemporaries were alarmed by the "licentiousness of prostitution,"[8] which turned the public space into "the stage for its scandalous excesses."[9] A "prism of prejudice and emotions,"[10] this imaginary of revolutionary prostitution largely obscures the flesh-and-blood individuals who practiced this activity. In order to contest the frequent simplification of this historical subject, often referred to as "the world's oldest profession," it is crucial to unearth the *in situ* forms of women's prostitution work, by looking at their existences and experiences, and to strive to give these forgotten agents of history a voice.

One of the major problems regarding prostitution is the pursuit of the elusive voices of prostitutes, as they are usually brought into history "embedded in the histories and the contests for power of those who first fashioned their stories."[11] The world of street prostitution in revolutionary Paris constituted a space which was both dominated and denounced as deviant by the authorities and was thus only reflected in the discourses and categories of the dominant institutions (police and justice administrations, prisons or hospitals). However, the subject positions occupied by prostitutes were not simply assigned by those dominant institutions and in their records; they were also shaped by the interventions of prostitutes themselves. Hence, those records are the product of a relationship between prostitutes and police authorities that left traces. Through police reports and minutes of interrogations, it is possible to glimpse not only the circumstances that brought these women to prostitution, but also acts of female subversion and resistance in the streets of Paris.

In the tradition of feminist epistemology and women's and gender history, it is important to reconstruct these women's trajectories and their capacity for action during decriminalization in revolutionary Paris. Under certain conditions, prostitution offered relative economic and sexual independence, as demonstrated by Judith Walkowitz's study of English prostitution during the nineteenth century.[12] She applies an analysis based on power relations that takes into account the practice of stigmatizing and alienating prostitutes, as well as their resistance, most often outside of social norms and propriety. More recently, Daryl Hafter and Nina Kushner have stressed the need to explore the numerous economic practices of women that avoided the dominant model of the family economy as it was conceptualized by Joan Scott and Louise Tilly during the 1970s.[13] Simultaneously a financial resource, form of resistance, and subversive strategy of survival, prostitution should be analyzed as an economic practice in its own right for working-class women during the revolutionary period. This calls for viewing prostitutes as "female workers" or "day laborers," as fully-fledged members of the female working classes whose bodily engagement in sexual work should be emphasized. In fact, women's work in preindustrial societies "often meant selling or renting your body."[14] Highlighting this aspect denaturalizes sexuality and resituates it in the field of work. This does not entail considering it as one kind of work "among others," but rather to underscore and encourage broader reflection on the relations between sexuality and the labor market, the sexual economic exchange that ran through social relations, and the gendered division of labor during the revolutionary period.[15]

Who Were the "Public Women?"

During the *Ancien Régime*, women practicing prostitution were usually labeled by authorities as "libertines," "women of ill fame," "debauched women," *femmes du monde*, and sometimes "public women" (*femmes publiques*). The new police administration of the French Revolution introduced the exclusive use of the category of "public women" to designate and pursue women who practiced prostitution. At a time when limits were being placed on women's presence and participation in the revolutionary public sphere, this choice of words illuminates the administration's belief that prostitution constituted the transgression of women "going public."[16] The archival sources for this institution—surveillance records, arrest records, reports on the state of *esprit public* (public opinion)—reveal that supervision of prostitution was exercised in regard to a specific segment of the population determined by gender and age (exclusively young single women aged fifteen to twenty-five years old) and by lower economic position (women who were essentially unemployed). This segment of the population was also defined by sexual practices, for in selling their sexuality, they went against the norms of the new "bourgeois conjugalism" promoted by the revolutionaries.[17]

Under the Revolution, male prostitution, luxury prostitution, and the more bourgeois prostitution of courtesans, such as stage actresses, were not subject to police intervention. If a few surveillance reports mentioned those forms of prostitution over the decade it was usually to stigmatize particular individuals as lewd and immoral and, consequently, "bad citizens." By virtue of its activity and in response to the ambiguous decriminalization of prostitution, the police defined a "target population" of *femmes publiques*, consisting essentially of young single women from the working classes who practiced street prostitution.[18] The revolutionary period was characterized by the increased youth of the women who practiced prostitution. Over two-thirds of this population were under twenty-five, with the sharpest increase among the under-twenty age group. While during the 1760s this group had represented less than 20 percent of the prostitute population arrested by police, this percentage doubled during the revolutionary period, reflecting the increased precariousness of young women responsible for their means of support who, thus, joined the prostitution market at the time. It also illuminates the relative indifference of the revolutionaries, including the Jacobins, towards impoverished young women who were neither wives nor mothers of citizens and who were thus left out of the social welfare policies of the Revolution.[19]

This market consisted almost exclusively of women aged between fifteen and thirty years. The practice of prostitution thus began shortly after young working-class girls entered working life,[20] and ended at the age of thirty, a few years after the average age of marriage.[21] In fact, single women, usually unattached to families, represented almost all of the women arrested for prostitution during the revolutionary period. Prostitution was consequently a stage in the economic and sexual lives of these women, situated between their first job and their establishment within a trade or as part of a stable couple (marriage, common-law marriage), both of which offered such women rootedness and economic stabilization.[22]

In the Palais-Royal or Butte des Moulins section—a central district of the city and a sexual entertainment hot spot[23] (see Map 0.2)—interrogations conducted by police captains (*commissaires*) between 1793 and 1794 reveal a zone of social vulnerability in revolutionary Paris for young single women veering between independence and precariousness. On November 21, 1793, the seventeen-year-old Parisian fruit seller Angélique Gallant explained to a police officer that she "only had [her] mother who turned her out eight months ago."[24] Françoise Jacques, a young fourteen-year-old Polish woman who was also a fruit seller, was arrested on January 16, 1794 and stated that she "had no parents."[25] Reine Louise Vatellier, an eighteen-year-old lace worker, explained that she left her parents "a year ago, and no longer has any," adding subsequently that "nobody had ever seen to her needs, which she alone had met through her work."[26] Their statements bear witness to both the independence and isolation that affected this juvenile population. At the time Paris was the "refuge for provincial misery,"[27] and the large portion of provincial migrants among these women helps explain their isolation in the city.

As can be observed throughout the eighteenth century, migration accounted for more than 70 percent of the women working in Parisian prostitution. Like most of the migrants in the city, young women arrested for prostitution were generally from the Paris Basin and its outer limits in Picardy, Normandy, and Champagne, as well as from the regions of Nord-Pas-de-Calais, Alsace, Lorraine, and Burgundy. Another characteristic of this population was that they were generally city dwellers. This urbanity strongly nuanced the literary figure of the "perverted young peasant girl" who supposedly provided the fodder for prostitution in Paris.[28] Most often, women left their family home to escape the underemployment in their area of origin, raise a dowry, and lighten the burden weighing on the parental household.[29] Prostitution was part of this economic migration and probably represented one of the most easily available resources once in the capital. Women born in Paris during the revolutionary period also increasingly opted for this resource. This group generally possessed a more enviable economic and social situation than migrants, who were uprooted and deprived of the material and symbolic resources of their *pays* (area) of origin. Noting the unprecedented rise in women's indigence during the revolutionary decade, the historian Richard Cobb concluded, not without irony, that prostitution was certainly the leading sector for women's employment during the revolutionary period.[30] The increase in the number of Parisian women in the prostitution market should actually be seen within the context of structural unemployment affecting female labor in both the provinces and Paris, as well as the greater ease of recourse to prostitution afforded by the decriminalization of the activity. Prostitution was seen as an increasingly viable option among the economic strategies available to young women in the Parisian labor market.

Sexual "Day Laborers"

Working women were the norm in the preindustrial economy of urban France.[31] While the early modern period was clearly accompanied by the gradual withdrawal of women from official and independent participation in the occupational world, they were often situated in intermediary economic spaces that connected formal and informal economies as well as licit and illicit practices. The women accused of prostitution were no exception, as two-thirds of them asserted a professional qualification or *état* (trade). This data, however, should be used carefully, as it came as part of remarks made under duress. Did these individuals claim a trade in order to protect themselves from the accusations made against them? Was it a profession exercised in the present or the past? In any event, the data bears witness to these women's desire to assert their belonging to the working world, which represented an identity and position in early modern society. While occupation emerged as a central tool in defining individual identities, these declarations enabled these women to not only situate themselves within the Parisian working class, but to also elude the apparent simplicity of police categorization, which sought to make prostitution their only trade and *femme publique* their only identity.[32] Their narratives work as counter-narratives, and, as part of police records, try to make a case for their innocence. The data raises questions on the economic identity of the women and how it was perceived, experienced, and represented.

In a certain way, women engaging in prostitution were female laborers like any others. The professional world from which they came was that of salaried employment. Like other Parisian laborers of the time, those who engaged in prostitution were also working a series of low-skilled odd jobs.[33] Approximately 60 percent of the prostitutes listed declared a profession in textiles or the garment industry, essentially as female "production line workers" or "seamstresses," both in the category of low-skilled labor. An additional 10 percent were laundresses, and 10 to 14 percent worked odd jobs in trade or the food industry. However, with the exception of a few cooks, domestic work was underrepresented at 5 percent, at a time when it represented between 10 to 20 percent of the women working in Paris during the Revolution. The low proportion of domestic servants among the women arrested for prostitution can be explained by the supervision exercised by the master or mistress of the house. Lodging and working at their master's home, they were less free to come and go, and did not have easy access to sexual sociability outside the house. And yet this context did not prevent recourse to alternative forms of illegitimate sexuality with men from their immediate surroundings, as half of the women "seduced and abandoned" during pregnancy at the turn of the century were servants.[34]

Working conditions determined the relations between professional and prostitution activity and illustrate the porous border between licit and illicit economic practices. Most often working in the street or in their immediate surroundings, and earning their living day by day, women arrested for prostitution exhibit the daily life of the Parisian working class. While dressmakers and seamstresses often worked in shops, they were also present behind and in front of their stands, in permanent contact with the surrounding space in the street. In his chapter on fashion stores entitled "Est-ce un sérail" ("Is This a Harem"), the contemporary observer Louis-Sébastien Mercier denounced the sexual corruption in these stores, whose layout, described as that of a brothel, ensured that one "watches the saleswoman and not the merchandise."[35] Linen merchants, laundry women, and darners crossed through the city to request or deliver their work. A number of them were arrested for prostitution as they walked wearing their aprons and carrying their work through the Palais-Royal, a center for the prostitution trade, hoping to supplement their daily income. Odd jobs in the food industry also forced women of the people to earn their living with their "feet on the ground, in the middle of the street,"[36] thereby promoting both social and sexual diversity and promiscuity. Unlike those of domestic servants, the activities of these women entailed being present and visible in the street, an environment that was particularly open, fluid, and propitious to encounters, as well as to the establishment of both economic and sexual relations. The pavement was a strategic resource for these professionals of the street, with prostitution being one task among others that they could complete there.

The professional itineraries of the women were marked by change and discontinuity, as they did not have firm ties and were engaged in perpetual movement to avoid misery. Owing to the upheaval of the working world caused by the Allarde decree and the Chapelier law of June 14 to 17, 1791, which abolished guilds, three major types of work organization coexisted during the revolutionary period: domestic work; manufacturing, essentially in textiles, for which women could work at home; and "free" work, which cut across different sectors and included employees, such as laundry women, day laborers, and merchants, paid by commission or per diem.[37] The category of free work was the one in which the vast majority of women arrested as prostitutes worked. It is difficult to determine whether their declared occupation corresponded to occasional or regular work, whether they were paid by commission or per diem, and whether they were compensated in money or in kind (lodging and food). Marie Nicole Bauleu, an eighteen-year-old gold polisher who was apprehended on July 8, 1794 "with an individual she was entertaining," appears to have been in a better financial position than textile and garment workers due to her more skilled activity.[38] Nevertheless, when questioned more specifically regarding her means of subsistence, she explained that she worked for a burnisher for whom she polished metals, but, in order to earn a living, she also had to work for her mother, receive assistance from her section, and have recourse to prostitution. These women therefore generally combined a number of activities, which they carried out on a part-time and occasional basis. Having multiple jobs was a fundamental element of the survival strategies implemented by the working classes to contend with the economic uncertainty resulting from the daily fluctuation of prices as well as the preindustrial labor market.[39]

The biographical itineraries of women accused of prostitution contain numerous small jobs held either simultaneously or successively. In October 1793, Marie Dubuisson, a twenty-year-old laundry woman born in Paris, stated that she had exercised the "trade of *femme publique* for 3 months due to a lack of work."[40] Conversely, Marie Suzanne Bouillotte, who was twenty-eight years of age and arrested the same month, "was a *femme publique* for four years, and has not practiced it for 1 year" after once again working as a seamstress.[41] These remarks emphasize the instability of these women's activities in the Parisian labor market, who regularly had to change jobs and employers. The precariousness of the labor market, heightened by the revolutionary crisis, played an important role in the process leading to prostitution. Sophie Conard, a nineteen-year-old linen seamstress, laconically summarized this state of affairs upon her arrest in June 1794, when she responded to the police officer that she was doing what "all of the other women were doing, and that she had raised some savings and was seeking to establish herself."[42] Prostitution was most often occasional and temporary, and was neither an end in itself nor an irreversible fall, but rather a phase that provided a certain economic stability in anticipation of moving on to something else.

The Moral Economy of Prostitution

Recourse to prostitution was one of the economic strategies connected to the structures of a depleted and precarious Parisian market, which was rocked throughout the eighteenth century by price inflation for staples and the stagnation of salaries. It was also marked by significant disparity between the sexes, with lower salaries given to women, and the concentration of women in less skilled and subsequently less compensated sectors. Moreover, during the eighteenth century it was practically impossible for a single woman to live on her daily salary.[43] In the least skilled sectors, women's daily earnings generally represented half of the average man's salary of approximately 30 sous. Thirty sous a day was considered to be the sum needed by a single person for lodging and food. Yet during the last third of the eighteenth century, most female salaries were significantly below this threshold. This gendered division of the labor market can notably be seen in the factories of the Parisian faubourg Saint-Marcel and faubourg Saint-Antoine (see Map 0.2), where women's salaries were at the lowest levels, generally half of the male salary, or 15 sous for women compared to 30 sous for men.[44] This was accompanied by chronic underemployment, which prevented the securing of regular income, along with the high cost of living in Paris, marked by inflation in rent and staples. Rent, which cost an average of 20 livres per month, was the largest drain on income, and cost on average nearly 70 percent of a low-skilled single woman's wage.[45] The price of bread was three sous per pound, which, for an average portion of a pound and a half a day, subtracted an additional 20 percent from this average income.[46] According to this scenario, 90 percent of a young working-class woman's salary was taken up by the bare necessities of bread and lodgings. The rest of the food consumed, along with clothing and upkeep such as laundry, could not be sufficiently covered by the remaining 10 percent. The gold polisher Marie Nicole Bauleu, whom we mentioned earlier, thus explained to the police that despite her numerous jobs, she had to be a *femme publique* "to buy the clothing she could not have otherwise."[47]

In this regard, we have to take into account the growing proportion of women who not only declared themselves to the police "sans profession"—between 20 and 30 percent—but who sometimes cited prostitution as their primary employ (around 10 percent). This is a substantial transformation from the pre-revolutionary period where less than 1 percent of women had listed themselves as having no trade, an admission that was synonymous with being a prostitute.[48] This group of "declared prostitutes" usually had in common their places of birth. Most of them were Parisian or came from small towns surrounding Paris. This autochthonous capital, their claim to belong in the city, could explain the fact that they openly declared prostitution as a profession. Furthermore, these claims were allowed by the decriminalization of prostitution in 1791, which made this trade a lower-risk activity. Even if declaring oneself a prostitute remained a marginal phenomenon during the French Revolution, it certainly accords with Susan Conner's assumption that prostitution was professionalized at the turn of the eighteenth and nineteenth century. Above all, it illuminates how those women positioned themselves in relation to prostitution, which was becoming ordinary rather than infamous.

In general, the salaries reported by the women arrested for prostitution were too "inadequate to lead a decent life."[49] As prostitution was decriminalized and subject to a minimal amount of police repression, it was highly probable that, on a day-to-day basis, one lived better from the negotiation of a sexual act than from one's other work. The risk of arrest for a disturbance of the peace or lewd conduct was present, although punishments were limited. The average gain per sexual encounter was fixed at around 25 sous for working-class prostitution. As a result, the price that women could expect from prostitution generally represented a viable solution for relieving the economic pressure weighing on them. This helps explain their formulation of a "moral economy of prostitution," a system of values, norms, and obligations that served to explain and justify the recourse to prostitution.[50] This notion accounts for the lived experience of these women, as well as their capacity to act and react in a tenuous economic context. For instance, on March 15, 1794, Marie Anne Renaud responded to the police that "she preferred this occupation to stealing."[51] In similar fashion, Marie Anne Michel, who was arrested two years later as she was soliciting in the Palais-Royal, indicated "that she preferred accosting men to stealing, and that there were women much younger than she in the same trade."[52] We can see implicit in these remarks how the women understood and defined prostitution as an alternative and strategic resource that enabled them to meet their needs and even to live a little better. This was the case for an "out of work seamstress" arrested in December 1791, who said that "at this time [she] was forced to stroll about the Palais-Royal like many others,"[53] or for Augustine Remy, who, on May 21, 1794, explained to the police that "she had done what she could to live" since her recent arrival in Paris.[54]

While women said that they had to engage in prostitution, they did not necessarily present themselves as victims, subject to economic and social power relations that drove them to accost men. On July 15, 1794,

Marianne Rigeau affirmed that she had been in the *femme publique* trade "and that she has accosted very few citizens since then, currently working as a washer woman or at any other work she could find."[55] Her remarks emphasize the normality of having recourse to prostitution as one on a continuum of expedients. Prostitution was the work "she could find" alongside her occupation as a laundry woman; it was not the subject of a guilty avowal, but rather of a practical observation regarding her current situation. Under the republic, a time when options for *bienfaisance* (beneficence) were reduced, childless single women did not receive assistance. As a reflection of the revolutionary crisis, prostitution therefore bears witness to the failure of the new regime's assistance policies for women who broke with the norms of a good citizen by failing to become a spouse or a mother.[56]

When women spoke of their sexual economic practices, they inscribed prostitution within a moral economy of female precariousness, but also turned the latter into a force for taking action. The regular disputes that opposed prostitutes and their clients regarding the price of their trade can be an indication of the former's capacity to demand what they considered fair compensation for the work provided. For instance, following the complaint of Adrien Siborg on January 2, 1792, who was forced to pay 20 livres for his dinner and accommodation at Marie Lemercier's, she responded to the police that "that she had earned them and did not have to return anything."[57] In their assessment of what was good and right, these women saw prostitution as labor that could be mobilized in exchange for compensation, but also and consequently as a "right" to provide for their existence. They also asserted a moral conscience, a notion of what was just, that was specific to them and conflicted with the moral norms defined by revolutionary authorities, who valued mothers, wives, and domesticity.[58] In the face of a dominant morality that judged and condemned prostitution, these remarks bear witness to other norms and values present in revolutionary society. In other words, as these young women did not have the economic and social resources required to adhere to the bourgeois moral standards promoted by revolutionary elites, they formulated alternative standards of their own.

Second-class Citizens but Citizens Nonetheless

Even though prostitution was decriminalized in 1791, prostitutes were still condemned and discriminated against, especially as a result of police practices that played a major part from 1793 in defining and distinguishing *good* from *bad* citizens.[59] Women marked as prostitutes were considered by police administration as a dangerous and immoral class. Believed to offend republican decency within public space, they needed to be consigned to the margins of the civic community. Nevertheless, the French Revolution, by proclaiming that all public authority derived from the consent of the governed, also created new opportunities for public appeals, which women labeled as prostitutes seized. Between the end of Year II and Year III (1794–5),[60] Marie Antoinette Barthelemy, Catherine Bellot, Geneviève Challot, Gilberte Charnet, Angélique Delille, Marie Catherine François, Margueritte Grossin, Françoise Landrin, Marianne Lavale, Rose Lefèvre, Élisabeth Lenoir, Reine Leroy, Margueritte Levasseur, Marie Martin, Marie Anne Plé, Jeanne Quentin, Marie Louise Régis, Marie Catherine Rortant, and Babeth Sinard, who had all been arrested for prostitution, were able to make themselves heard by the Commission des administrations civiles, police et tribunaux (the Ministry of Justice) and its *Chargé provisoire*.[61] Incarcerated at the height of the Terror's repressiveness, they had, on average, been awaiting trial and release for at least a year. This situation was the product of the sudden and massive increase in arrests and in the systematization of arbitrary jailings following the Commune de Paris's October 4, 1793 decree.[62] Forbidding solicitation in public spaces, this decree led to the incarceration without trial of more than 700 women in the space of a single year. The fall of the revolutionary Terror government and the redefinition of repressive jurisdictions initiated after 9 thermidor Year II allowed these women to enter into a dialogue with the new authorities. Circumventing the police, who had pursued them, they submitted their cases to judicial authorities for consideration, using their own words to describe themselves and tackle the prostitution charges that led to their imprisonment.

The letters of these women illuminate the broad police definition of prostitution in Year II. Some of them were arrested in public spaces known to the police as places for sexual solicitation, usually at nightfall. Françoise Landrin, Marie Claudine Martin, and Jeanne Quentin were arrested because they were "crossing the Palais Égalité." The capital's leading open forum for social gossip and political innuendo as well as a place of entertainment, the Palais Égalité (formerly the Palais-Royal) and its environs were also famous for illicit activities such as gambling and prostitution. Other gathering places in the city were also known for their "infamous" trades, such as the boulevard du Temple, where Marie Louise Régis was arrested, or the commercial district of Les Halles (see Map 0.2) and its female "nighttime prowlers," like Elisabeth Lenoire, who could benefit from the special permission granted to surrounding taverns to remain open all night. Margueritte Gossin was arrested "at seven o'clock in the evening on the rue de la Vannerie ... at the home of a friend whose name I do not recall." Located in the Arcis Section, near City Hall, rue de la Vannerie was a popular street where many women who practiced prostitution lived and solicited (see Map 0.2).[63] Since the Police Code of 1791 allowed any police officer to proceed to a home visit in case of suspected debauchery, Margueritte and her friend were arrested as *filles publiques* for being part of what was considered a dubious gathering.[64] What was considered prostitution: actual solicitation or simply being in a place that might allow women to practice it? Both location and time shaped police perception and representation of prostitution and usually triggered their intervention: they were subject to "site effect" rather than acting on specific knowledge of particular people's activities.[65]

Besides place, manners also mattered in this broad police definition of prostitution. Another group of women arrested were those who had drunk alcohol or eaten in the company of men, practices that could be likened to prostitution. That's why Catherine Bellot introduced herself as "detained at Pelagie since 18 Germinal . . . [because of] a simple supper."[66] As for Rose Lefèvre, she explained that she was arrested for solicitation "for simply drinking a bottle of beer at a café with three defenders of the fatherland,"[67] an action that she contrived to give a patriotic aura. In both cases, sharing food and beverages between young men and women was perceived by the police as a sign of promiscuity. But how could police distinguish between a *souper galant*, specific to prostitution subculture,[68] and an ordinary gathering between persons of different sexes? Going out and having drinks was part of the common life experience of young people from all classes in revolutionary Paris.[69] Signs of ordinary delinquency like drunkenness, violence, or petty larceny were also regularly mentioned in the women's letters and their prisoners' files. They played a significant part in the practice of labeling women as prostitutes. In this context, the women's accounts of their arrest had a strategic purpose: denouncing the arbitrary nature of their imprisonment and contesting the negative judgments based on their personal and criminal histories that played a major part in defining their offense of prostitution. Relating the grounds for their charges, they emphasized the arbitrary weight of anecdotal circumstances that led to their arrest: "a simple supper," "drinking a bottle of beer," "crossing the Palais-Egalité." These references contrast sharply with descriptions of their harsh and long imprisonment. They undermine the evidence for their categorization as *filles publiques* and, in so doing, point out the disproportion between the alleged offense and its concrete punishment.

Furthermore, these letters highlight that, by granting women civil rights as well as easier access to their representatives and administrators, the Revolution fostered their ability to publicly express views and concerns, and endowed them with a new political language and practices.[70] Like countless women who addressed petitions to the National Assemblies and their representatives during the French Revolution, women imprisoned for prostitution took action and used revolutionary rhetoric to criticize police "despotism" and the arbitrariness of their own detention. Seven of the inmates wrote several letters to the commission and nine of them contributed to a collective letter, thereby using the main resource at their disposal: other inmates. By acting collectively, they were able to lower the individual price charged by a public writer for his services and to give more weight to their demands. Likewise, by regularly harassing the commission, they made clear that they did not intend to miss out on the political transition and the new opportunities it offered. Admittedly, a few of these letters used quite vindictive language. In this corpus, indeed, distress is more patent than discontent. The absence of the latter could be due to the influence of the public writer, both in regard to how he shaped the narrative and to the model letters he used. It could also be the expression of a gendered relationship between the women and those men who had the authority to decide their fates. By repeatedly referring to their unfortunate situation, the women outlined their tragic position and tried to maintain pressure on the authorities.

This pressure is all the more visible as most of the inmates proclaimed the utmost confidence in the office of the Chargé provisoire, raising him to the status of a compassionate, generous, and reachable father. The expression of filial piety is a common theme in many of those letters, such as the ones written by Marie Antoinette Barthelemy, as we can see in this citation from a letter dated 15 prairial Year III (June 3, 1795): "If I'm fortunate enough for you to deign taking an interest in my person, nothing will put an end to my respect and my gratitude. I am, with the most profound respect, your most humble servant. Marie Antoinette Barthelemy."[71]

As Lynn Hunt and Suzanne Desan have shown in their respective studies, revolutionary petitioners often drew parallels between the ideal of an egalitarian and affectionate republican family regulated by a good father and a state governed by fair and compassionate legislators.[72] In their letters, the women used a similar approach for establishing an affective or sentimental communication with the authorities, referring to a new revolutionary ethic of brotherhood, generosity, and sensitivity.[73] From amongst all the different identities that defined them, they chose to represent themselves as impoverished citizens, instead of prostitutes, and thus claimed the right to benefit from the protection and assistance of the republic. These displays of vulnerability and affection were as much gendered as political performances, in tune with revolutionary ideals.

Prostitutes' use of revolutionary rhetorical norms also manifested itself in thirteen women's auto-representation as "co-citoyennes" ("co-citizens") of the authorities to whom they were appealing. Such political performativity resulted in presenting themselves as part of the civic community, thereby virtually negating their exclusion. It is worth emphasizing that in the police records, women suspected of prostitution were never referred to as *citoyennes* by police officers. Rather, they were commonly designated by the police term *femmes de mauvaise vie* or *femmes publiques*, both of which referred to a *qualité*, an infamous condition. By taking up the pen as *co-citoyennes* to denounce the injustice done to them and to demand a review of their situation, women used the civil rights and civic dignity granted to them by the Revolution. These young single women, living "fragile lives" that did not allow them to fit into the bourgeois model of respectable womanhood were nonetheless *citoyennes* and, consequently, claimed the right to equitable justice. Hence, as Dominique Godineau explained about the Revolution's impact on the daily lives of ordinary women, the "simple fact of being called *citoyenne* is not insignificant."[74]

To further demonstrate their civic spirit, women used typical revolutionary expressions and the Revolution's new poetics of power. They ended their letters with a vigorous "farewell and fraternity," invoked the "Supreme Being" of the Montagnards' deist cult, or denounced "the chains of slavery," echoing Marat's famous book of the same title, republished in 1793, and the Herculean imagery of the Revolution.[75] In this way, they mobilized republican culture and its symbols as a way to assert their patriotism and their membership of the civic community. Besides trying to exercise their rights to justice and equality before the law, they also expressed their expectations of the French revolutionary administration. After having demonstrated in their letters their own vulnerability and the arbitrariness of the police who condemned them without any clear evidence of a crime, the letters also acted as demands for justice and humanity towards the misfortunate ones. Arbitrarily arrested and forgotten in the revolutionary prisons, even if those women had nothing left, they still believed in the republic and its representatives. The constant appeals to the humanity of the Chargé provisoire in these letters are a powerful reminder of his duty towards every human being and citizen. If women practicing, or supposedly practicing, prostitution were usually treated like second-class citizens by revolutionary authorities, they nevertheless remained citizens and, as such, acted accordingly.

Conclusion

The fragments of the lives presented here, and the precariousness they reveal, are not specific to prostitutes, as they relate to the conditions experienced by all of the working classes. Rather than posit young women's "fall" or hardship when evoking prostitution, it is instead important to emphasize and analyze the discontinuity and instability of their daily lives—a social, economic, and sexual instability connected to the fact that these women were not yet "established" in the conjugal and professional context. In these sources, young women did not "fall" into prostitution, but had recourse to it either in a temporary or prolonged manner, for a supplemental income or as a fully-fledged profession, in anticipation of assuring themselves a decent existence by becoming established. Prostitution was consequently part of a transitional and vulnerable phase in the itineraries of women from the Parisian working class. Moreover, while one could engage in prostitution, it was also possible to leave it behind. A means of action and reaction, prostitution was a strategy used by young and single female workers who had a precarious position in the Paris labor market in order to resist and accommodate the dominant social and economic order. It was part of the numerous small jobs these women did to ensure their independence, in the name of a moral economy and an ethics of subsistence. Analyzing these strategies also make it possible to grasp prostitution, and through it sexuality, as a historical subject. It was not an unchanging and universal state of affairs, but rather the result of specific social and economic processes connected to the gender system in place. Between precariousness, independence, and resourcefulness, these young women evolved alongside the great Revolution that failed to include them, in which they could not find their place, but to whose ideals they nevertheless appealed.

Source: Letters by a woman arrested for prostitution under the Terror

Marie-Antoinette Barthelemy, excerpts from the dossiers concerning prisoners detained by special police measure, department of the Seine, Year III, National Archives (France), F^7 3299[1]

1. Letter—Paris, 23 nivôse the Year III of the French Republic

Central Office
Liberty, Undying Equality or death[,]
Citizen [at the Committee of General Security],
Marie Antoinette Barthelemy, age 30, a native of Paris, washerwoman, was first arrested, taken to the Section of Bonne Nouvelle ["Good News"], then to [the prison of] La Force [see Map 0.2], where I endured all the worst possible mistreatments, having been placed in solitary confinement ... during 3 months at the end of which I was called before the Correctional Court where I was thrown before the grand jury, of which [sic.] I was told that I had made statements against the Republic, which I don't remember given that I was taken by drink at the time of my arrest and that I even struggle to believe that what I am accused of can be true, as my feelings have never approved of the conduct of those formerly known as [nobles] ...

[Together with two other female prisoners in similar circumstances, Barthelemy asks:] ... to be judged as promptly as possible or to be transferred given that we are lacking in everything having sold the little that we have to write letters from one side and the other [of the prison walls] to which we have had no response. Living in the greatest misery, we ask you to have regard for our sad position ... and to give us an immediate response ... Citizens, your co-citizenesses would be forever obliged and grateful to you
Greetings and Fraternity

2. Letter—15 prairial Year III

4th division, 2nd section, 15 prairial[,]
Citizen,
Marie Antoinette Barthelemy, washerwoman, age thirty, native of Paris, sections of Bonne nouvelle and des Droits de l'Homme ["of the Rights of Man"], accused of having cried "Long live the king," of which she has no memory, having been taken by wine, having appeared before the Correctional on 30 thermidor and sent to the Committee of General Security without appearing again anywhere, I have deprived myself of all that I owned to try to regain my liberty . . .

3. Letter—from [the prison of] la petite Force this 25 prairial Year III

Citizen,
I take for this reason the liberty to write you to assure you of my very humble respect and at the same time to beg you to please take pity on me in this cruel situation as you have had the goodness to write me that I should write to the Committee of General Security. I have written several letters and I have had no response, it is truly cruel to see that since the first messidor I have been detained without being judged and sent to the Committee of General Security on 29 thermidor having been accused of having cried "Long live the king." Knowing you as being full of goodness and humanity towards unhappy unfortunates, I dare implore your mercy. Deign to cast a commiserating glance at the trouble that I am enduring. After the Supreme Being, I have only you to ask for help . . .

4. Letter—From [the prison of] la Petite Force rue Pavés, this 21 prairial

Citizen,
I take for this reason the liberty to write to you to expose my sorrows[.] [F]or a year I suffer in chains without there having yet been a decision made on my fate. My records were transferred to your Committee on 9 fructidor . . . you sent word that I should be patient, but I cannot take this anymore . . . I prefer death to being captive as I have been for so long, reduced to the worst of miseries. Deign citizen to envision my unhappy fate, I throw myself at your feet, cover them with my tears and I expect from your goodness and your humanity, that you will have the means to end my troubles and decide at the earliest over my fate . . .
Greetings and Fraternity
Your submissive ["soumise"] co-citizeness Marie Antoinette Barthelemy

5. Letter—From [the prison of] la petite Force this 5 thermidor Year III of the one and indivisible French Republic

Citizen,
I take the liberty to write you to assure you of my very humble respects at the same time that I ask you to please have the goodness to make me appear at the earliest before you as I have something very interesting to denounce to you. I dare hope that you will not refuse me for the subject of which I speak. I cannot tell you more about it. I will have the honor of explaining myself in person before you. That is why I ask you to make me appear at the earliest . . .
With Greetings and Fraternity
Your co-citizeness Marie-Antoinette Barthelemy

Notes

1 This article draws on the findings of doctoral research published in 2016: Clyde Plumauzille, *Prostitution et Révolution: Les femmes publiques dans la cité répulicaine* (Ceyzerieux: Champ Vallon, 2016). The author would like to warmly thank the editors of the volume for their careful proofreading and help in the translation of this work.

2 Olwen Hufton, *The Poor of Eighteenth-Century France 1750–1789* (Oxford: Oxford University Press, 1974), 306–18.

3 Including 53 percent of women. See Michel Vovelle, "Le peuple de Paris en révolution," in *Paris le peuple: XVIIIe–XXe siècle*, ed. Jean-Louis Robert and Danielle Tartakowsky (Paris: Publications de la Sorbonne, 1999), 114–15.

4 Érica-Marie Benabou, *La prostitution et la police des mœurs au XVIII*[e] *siècle* (Paris: Perrin, 1987), 266.

5 Jill Harsin, *Policing Prostitution in Nineteenth-Century Paris* (Princeton, NJ: Princeton University Press, 1985); Alain Corbin, *Les Filles de noce: misère sexuelle et prostitution au XIXe et XXe siècles* (Paris: Aubier, 1978); English version: *Women for Hire: Prostitution and Sexuality in France after 1850* (Cambridge, MA: Harvard University Press, 1990); Benabou, *La prostitution.*

6 Susan Conner, "Politics, Prostitution, and the Pox in Revolutionary Paris, 1789–1799," *Journal of Social History* 22 (1989): 713–34.

7 Paola Tabet, *La grande arnaque: sexualité des femmes et échange économico-sexuel* (Paris: L'Harmattan, 2004).

8 Cahier particulier de la ville de Paris, in *Les Élections et les cahiers de Paris en 1789, L'assemblée des trois groupes et l'assemblée générale des électeurs au 14 juillet*, ed. Charles-Louis Chassin (Paris: Jouaust et Sigaux, 1888), 3:407.

9 Report from 30 nivôse year VIII (January 20, 1800), in François-Alphonse Aulard, *Paris sous le Consulat* (Paris: L. Cerf, 1903), 1:110.

10 Gail Pheterson, *The Prostitution Prism* (Amsterdam: Amsterdam University Press, 1996), 7.

11 Gail Hershatter, *Dangerous Pleasures: Prostitution and Modernity in Twentieth-Century Shanghai* (Berkeley: University of California Press, 1997), 12.

12 Judith R. Walkowitz, *Prostitution and Victorian Society: Women, Class, and the State* (Cambridge: Cambridge University Press, 1980).

13 Daryl M. Hafter and Nina Kushner, "Introduction," in *Women and Work in Eighteenth-Century France*, ed. Daryl M. Hafter and Nina Kushner (Baton Rouge: Louisiana State University Press 2015), 1–15.

14 Margaret Maruani, ed., *Les nouvelles frontières de l'inégalité: hommes et femmes sur le marché du travail* (Paris: La Découverte, 1998), 26.

15 Thierry Pastorello, "Sodome à Paris: protohistoire de l'homosexualité masculine fin XVIIIe– milieu XIXe siècle," Ph.D. thesis under the direction of André Gueslin, Paris VII, 2009 (unpublished); Michael Sibalis, "Les espaces des homosexuels dans le Paris d'avant Haussmann," in *La Modernité avant Haussmann. Formes de l'espace urbain à Paris 1801–1853*, ed. Karen Bowie (Paris: Éditions Recherches, 2001), 231–41.

16 Jennifer Heuer and Anne Verjus, "L'invention de la sphère domestique au sortir de la Révolution," *Annales historiques de la Révolution française (AHRF)* 327 (2002): 1–28; Lynn Hunt, *The Family Romance of the French Revolution* (Berkeley: University of California Press, 1992); Joan Landes, *Women and the Public Sphere in the Age of the French Revolution* (Ithaca, NY: Cornell University Press, 1988).

17 This neologism forged by the historian Anne Verjus aims to describe the ideal of the male–female relationship at the turn of the nineteenth century, legitimizing the husband's marital authority and the wife's consent; Anne Verjus, *Le bon mari: une histoire politique des hommes et des femmes à l'époque révolutionnaire* (Paris: Fayard, 2010).

18 The ensuing statistics concern a total of 3100 women arrested between 1793 and 1799 and are drawn from the official reports of police captains/superintendents (*commissaires*) from the Palais-Royal section, which are held at the Archives de la Préfecture de Police de Paris (APP), and from the Salpêtrière and the Vénériens hospitals records, which are held at the Archives de l'Assistance Publique des Hôpitaux de Paris (APHP).

19 Lisa DiCaprio, *The Origins of the Welfare State: Women, Work, and the French Revolution* (Urbana: University of Illinois Press, 2007).

20 Hufton, *The Poor*, 26.

21 Jacques Houdaille, "Les mariages à Paris de 1789 à 1803," *Population* 47 (1992): 488–92.

22 Dominique Godineau, *Citoyennes tricoteuses: les femmes du peuple à Paris pendant la Révolution française* (Paris: Perrin, 2004), 36–9.

23 The sections were administrative and political subdivisions of Paris during the French Revolution.

24 APP, A[A] 93, Section de la Butte des moulins, 1er frimaire an II(November 21, 1793).

25 APP, A^{A} 93, Section de la Butte des moulins, 27 nivôse an II (January 16, 1794).

26 APP, A^{A} 94, Section de la Butte des moulins, 18–19 messidor an II (July 6–7, 1794).

27 Christian Romon, "Le monde des pauvres à Paris au XVIIIe siècle," *Annales. Économies, Sociétés, Civilisations* 37 (1982): 729–63.

28 Pierre-Jean-Baptiste Nougaret, *La Paysanne pervertie, ou Mœurs des grandes villes, mémoires de Jeannette R*** mis au jour par Nougaret*, 4 parts in 2 vols. (Paris: J.-F. Bastien, 1777); Nicolas-Edme Rétif de La Bretonne, *La Paysane pervertie, ou les Dangers de la ville, histoire d'Ursule R***, soeur d'Edmond, le Paysan*, 1 part in 4 vols. (The Hague and Paris: Vve Duchesne, 1784).

29 Geneviève Fraisse, "Le service domestique, solitude définitive," in *Madame ou Mademoiselle? Itinéraires de la solitude féminine, XVIIIe–XXe siècles*, ed. Michèle Bordeaux, Arlette Farge, and Christiane Klapisch-Zuber (Paris: Montalba, 1984), 112.

30 Richard Cobb, *La Protestation populaire en France: 1789–1820* (Paris: Presses pocket, 1970), 157–69; Alan Forrest, *La Révolution française et les pauvres* (Paris: Perrin, 1981), 70; English version: *The French Revolution and the Poor* (Oxford: Blackwell, 1981).

31 Daniel Roche, *Le peuple de Paris: essai sur la culture populaire au XVIIIe siècle* (Paris: Fayard, 1998), 73; English version: *The People of Paris: An Essay in Popular Culture in the 18th Century*, trans. Marie Evans (Berkeley: University of California Press, 1987).

32 Clyde Plumauzille, "Du 'scandale de la prostitution' à 'l'atteinte contre les bonnes mœurs': Contrôle policier et administration des filles publiques sous la Révolution française," *Politix* 107 (2014): 9–31.

33 Arlette Farge, *Vivre dans la rue à Paris au XVIIIe siècle* (Paris: Gallimard, 1979), 130.

34 Arlette Farge, *La vie fragile: violence, pouvoirs et solidarités à Paris au XVIIIe siècle* (Paris: Éd. du Seuil, 1992), 40.

35 Cited in Laurence Mall, "Eros et labor," *Clio. Histoire, femmes et sociétés* 25 (2007): 217–47.

36 Jeffry Kaplow, *Les Noms des rois: les pauvres de Paris à la veille de la Révolution* (Paris: F. Maspero, 1974), 113.

37 Sabine Juratic, "Solitude féminine et travail des femmes à Paris à la fin du XVIIIe siècle," *Mélanges de l'Ecole française de Rome. Moyen-Age, Temps modernes* 99 (1987): 879–900.

38 APP, A^{A} 94, Section de la Butte des moulins, 20 messidor an II (July 8, 1794).

39 Laurence Fontaine and Jürgen Schlumbohm, eds., *Household Strategies for Survival, 1600–2000: Fission, Faction and Cooperation* (Cambridge: Cambridge University Press, 2000).

40 APP, A^{A} 92, Section de la Butte des moulins, October 7, 1793.

41 APP, A^{A} 92, Section de la Butte des moulins, 5 brumaire an II (October 26, 1793).

42 APP, A^{A} 94, Section de la Butte des moulins, 22 prairial year II (June 10, 1794).

43 Nicole Pellegrin and Sabine Juratic, "Femmes, villes et travail en France dans la deuxième moitié du XVIIIe siècle," *Histoire, économie et société* 13 (1994): 477–500.

44 Haim Burstin, *Une révolution à l'œuvre: le faubourg Saint-Marcel (1789–1794)* (Seyssel: Editions Champ Vallon, 2005), 190.

45 20 sous were worth one livre in the monetary system of the time. Émile Ducoudray, "Société Parisienne, 1790–1833," in *Atlas de la Révolution française. 11, Paris*, ed. Émile Ducoudray, Raymonde Monnier, Daniel Roche, and Alexandra Laclau (Paris: Éd. de l'École des hautes études en sciences sociales, 2000), 32.

46 Conner, "Politics, Prostitution, and the Pox," 713–34.

47 APP, A[A] 94, Section de la Butte des moulins, 20 messidor an II (July 8, 1794).

48 Conner, "Politics, Prostitution, and the Pox," 723.

49 Godineau, *Citoyennes tricoteuses*, 30.

50 We have borrowed the expression from E. P. Thompson, "The Moral Economy of the English Crowd in the Eighteenth Century," *Past & Present* 50 (1971): 76–136.

51 APP, A[A] 92, Section de la Butte des moulins, 25 ventôse an II (March 15, 1794).

52 APP, A[A] 93, Section de la Butte des moulins, 25 ventôse an II (March 15, 1794).

53 APP, A[A] 86, Section de la Butte des moulins, December 26, 1791.

54 APP, A[A] 94, Section de la Butte des moulins, 2 prairial an II (May 21, 1794).

55 APP, A[A] 94, Section de la Butte des moulins, 25 messidor an II (July 13, 1794).

56 DiCaprio, *The Origins*.

57 APP, A[A] 88, Section de la Butte des moulins, January 2, 1791.

58 Plumauzille, "Du 'scandale de la prostitution.'"

59 Howard Brown and Judith Miller, eds., *Taking Liberties: Problems of a New Order from the French Revolution to Napoleon* (Manchester: Manchester University Press, 2002).

60 September 1792 is considered the beginning of "Year I" of the republic as it is the founding month of the First French Republic.

61 Archives Nationales (AN), F[7]3299[1]–3299[12], Détenus pour mesure de Haute police, an II–an III. The existence of this corpus was mentioned by Jill Harsin in the appendices to her book: Harsin, *Policing*.

62 *Le Moniteur universel* 18, October 4, 1793.

63 AN, F[7] 3299[6], Lettre de Margueritte Grossin du 15 floréal an III (May 4, 1795).

64 "Décret relatif à l'organisation d'une police municipale et correctionnelle du 10–22 juillet 1791, article 10, Titre I 'Police municipale. Dispositions générale d'ordre public,'" in *Collection complète des Lois, décrets, ordonnances, réglements et avis du Conseil d'État*, ed. Jean-Baptiste Duvergier (Paris: Guyot, 1824), 3:133.

65 Deborah Cohen, "Savoir pragmatique de la police et preuves formelles de la justice: deux modes d'appréhension du crime dans le Paris du XVIIIe siècle," *Crime, Histoire & Sociétés/Crime, History & Societies* 12 (2008): 5–23.

66 AN, F^{7} 3299^{2}, Lettre de Catherine Bellot du 8 thermidor an III (July 26, 1795).

67 AN, F^{7} 32998, Lettre de Rose Lefèvre du 11 floréal an III (April 30, 1795).

68 Benabou, *La prostitution*, 231.

69 Alain Cabantous, *Histoire de la nuit: Europe occidentale. XVIIe–XVIIIe siècle* (Paris: Fayard, 2009).

70 Christine Fauré, "Doléances, déclarations et pétitions, trois formes de la parole publique des femmes sous la Révolution," *AHRF* 344 (2006): 5–25.

71 AN, F^{7} 3299^{1}, Lettre de Marie Antoinette Barthelemy du 15 Prairial year III (June 3, 1795).

72 Lynn Hunt, *Politics, Culture, and Class in the French Revolution* (Berkeley: University of California Press, 1986), 42–3, 72–4; Suzanne Desan, "Pétitions de femmes en faveur d'une réforme révolutionnaire de la famille," *AHRF* 344 (2006): 27–46.

73 Jennifer Heuer, *The Family and the Nation: Gender and Citizenship in Revolutionary France, 1789–1830* (Ithaca, NY: Cornell University Press, 2005).

74 Dominique Godineau, "Histoire sociale, histoire culturelle, histoire politique: la question du droit de cité des femmes," in *La Révolution française: au carrefour des recherches*, ed. Martine Lapied, Christine Peyrard, and Michel Vovelle (Aix-en-Provence: Publications de l'Université de Provence, 2003), 296.

75 Hunt, *Politics, Culture, and Class*, 87–122.

9

Doctors, Radicalism, and the Right to Health:

Three Visions from the French Revolution

Sean M. Quinlan

One of the striking facets of the French Revolution—beyond its immediate pathos and tragedy—remains its incessant novelty. Not just with new laws, new institutions, and new systems of government. The Revolution also generated a whole new universe of social and cultural experience: new ideas, words, rituals, symbols, manners, fashions, music, spaces, measurements, technologies, and sciences.[1] It constituted a torrent of change and innovation in ways that continue to inspire, astound, and horrify today. If the "world turned upside down" captured the shock of the American Revolution, the French Revolution did more than reverse society: it remade it from the inside out, building a new world from the debris of the old order.[2] Though counter-revolutionaries tried, they failed to turn back the clock because the measure of that time, the Old Regime itself, existed no longer. Innovation and loss went hand in hand.

Revolutionary innovation transcended politics and permeated the broader world of culture and daily life, including more erudite intellectual realms: literature, the arts, philosophy, and even the hard sciences.[3] Nowhere, arguably, was this transformation more dramatic than in the world of medicine, the art and science of healing. In a few short years, revolutionaries overturned the antiquated medical system inherited from the Middle Ages, and all the legal and philosophical traditions that supported it, and implemented a new method of studying the human body and new modes of medical practice and institutional care. Revolutionaries overhauled the old style of teaching medicine, united surgery and medicine, implemented new licensing regulations, created new areas of specialization—ranging from psychiatry to experimental physiology—and built a new institution: the modern hospital, or what contemporaries called *machines à guérir* ("healing mechanisms").[4] In this setting, doctors combined ward observation, morbid anatomy, and medical teaching, and codified a new theory of disease localization. The stethoscope, invented by Théophile de Laënnec in 1817, symbolized this revolution in medical understanding, showing how the doctor had learned to peer inside the body and find the root causes of disease and pain.[5]

However, revolutionary medicine was not only characterized by rational or objective approaches, by a hard-boiled "medical gaze" that sought to look inside the body and subjugate it to medical control. Medical science also shared many of the radical dreams and passions that appeared in so many other realms of revolutionary life. The revolutionaries wanted not only to reform the world but to make it anew and reconcile humanity's relation to itself and the world around it. Not just to improve humanity but to perfect it: to be born again in mind and body and make society more robust and beautiful.[6] Doctors did more than share this faith; they also helped shape and propagate it, providing fellow revolutionaries with critical ideas and plans to transform the world.

In this setting, several doctors, legislators, and activists articulated a stirring new idea: namely, that health was a right to which every citizen should have access. Medicine thus participated in a broader ideological development. In Europe and the Americas, as scholars have shown, eighteenth-century revolutionaries invented the idea of human rights. They believed that every person, irrespective of birth or rank or fortune, shared a universal human nature to which certain rights were attached. Societies could never alienate or deny an individual's human rights because losing them robbed the person of their status as a human being. During the French Revolution, legislators and activists applied these beliefs to groups that had been denied civil status under the Old Regime, such as African slaves, Jews, Protestants, women, actors, executioners, and the deaf and blind.[7]

However, revolutionaries extended the idea of individual rights to broader social entitlements and duties, as well: the right to education, for example, or the right to food and shelter—and, as we shall see, the right to health.[8] These ideas raised questions about social resources and how society might procure them for all citizens. For some physicians, the government had to restructure itself along more just and egalitarian lines to meet these needs and demands. Good health, in other words, required a total social and cultural revolution, one that extended into all levels of human experience—including those most associated with daily life.

At the time of the French Revolution, the health challenges that an ordinary person faced in their daily life were acute and deadly. Disease, dearth, and death were staggering realities. Now, even in the twenty-first century, everyone dies. No one escapes the final reckoning, no matter how modern society tries to postpone death's sweep. Yet life expectancy has increased, and the last moment, though never evaded, is deferred. Death is less visible. In the eighteenth century, the rate of death was much higher. Today, people not only live longer, but, in material terms, more comfortable lives. While we still suffer, better living standards and medical technology have alleviated pain markedly. In pre-modern societies, the level of suffering was on a different register. Pain and loss were everywhere more obvious. Sudden death was the norm. It burst upon life like a ruptured vein, draining whole families and communities.[9]

Contemporaries acknowledged this grim reality. In rough terms, one-third of all children died in their first year. Half were gone by age ten. Average life expectancy, once this childhood mortality was factored in, reached barely thirty years. Maternal mortality was 11.5 deaths per 1,000 births.[10] Not good odds. The great naturalist, Georges-Louis de Leclerc, the Comte de Buffon, who presided over the royal gardens in Paris, tabulated these dismal statistics:

> Half of humankind perishes before the age of eight years and a month, that is, before the age of reason and the body is developed.
>
> Two-thirds of humankind dies before age thirty-one, so that there's scarcely a third of men who can propagate the species, and that there's only a third that can take a substantive state in society.
>
> Three-fourths of humanity dies before the age of fifty-one years . . . Of nine babies born, only one attains seventy years.[11]

This super-mortality had one primary cause: infectious disease. The black death—that scourge of the Middle Ages—had disappeared from France after its last outbreak in Marseilles in 1721, though plenty of other pathogens menaced daily life, notably typhus, dysentery, and smallpox. The last of these disfigured Voltaire and Robespierre and even carried off King Louis XV. Others lurked as well: measles, mumps, rubella, rhinoviruses, gangrene, as well as more prosaic but murderous diseases such as influenza and gastroenteritis, both of which preyed upon small children.[12] With good reason, L.-A. de Caraccioli, an eloquent observer of enlightened morals and manners, wrote, "Man does not need to make an effort to think about death. It presents itself to him that he can regard it as incorporated with his very being."[13] To this theater of death, one might add an ensemble of daily sufferings and indignities, ranging from boils to warts, rashes, abscesses, gout, and toothache, as well as the fungal and low-level infections that conspired to make life miserable and unpleasant.[14]

Compounding this bleak picture were the crushing realities of poverty and hunger. Like death itself, dearth was a ubiquitous feature of daily life, feeding the cycle of infection and inequality that characterized pre-modern

France. From the early 1700s, population growth strained limited resources and forced the poor to migrate from region to region, drawing them to the towns and cities. Pauperism, beggary, prostitution, and vagrancy followed, forming a desperate "economy of makeshifts."[15] In 1707, Sébastien Le Prestre de Vauban wrote that 10 percent of the population lived by begging, while at least half lived under subsistence conditions; in 1765, Nicolas Baudeau estimated that one-sixth of the French people were paupers or vagrants.[16] These statistics worsened in times of war, recession, harvest failure, or pestilence. For many contemporaries, as historian George Rosen points out, the term "the people" was synonymous with poverty itself.[17]

Arrayed against this empire of human suffering was the learned medical trade—"corporate medicine," as scholars sometimes call the medieval system of medical guilds and schools.[18] It was a complicated state of affairs. Medicine divided itself into three different branches, each of which jealously guarded its privileges and prerogatives. There were, first, the doctors, who held university degrees, diagnosed disease and prescribed treatments, and stood at the top of the healthcare pyramid; then there were the surgeons, who trained as manual artisans and performed operations or procedures like bleeding and lancing; and lastly there were the apothecaries, schooled in *materia medica*, who mixed and sold remedies at the doctors' discretion. Some practitioners were wealthy and well respected—evidence suggests that doctors and surgeons improved their social image during the Enlightenment[19]—but many harked from the middling orders and had to eke out a living in the towns and countryside, where they met with derision and indifference.[20]

There were too few of them, as well.[21] In 1786 and 1790, official inquests suggested a ratio of one doctor for 3,242 inhabitants, a medicalization level found in the poorest countries of today, though the apprenticed barber-surgeons—whom most French people relied upon for specialized medical care—boasted a wider geographical dispersion and numbered about 40,000 in total.[22] Beyond the world of professional medicine, a vast network of irregular or itinerant healers offered their services to the masses: faith healers, amulet makers, uroscopists, mountebanks, bone setters, tooth pullers, and flat-out charlatans and cranks.[23]

Healthcare institutions provided mixed help. While welfare policies drew upon long-standing Catholic principles, modern doctors and magistrates hoped to control begging and rationalize public services. In the late 1600s, the royal government created the *hôpitaux généraux* (general hospitals) to contain vagrancy and brigandage, as well as expand its power over municipal and ecclesiastical bodies. Besides serving as internment centers, the *hôpitaux généraux* dispensed medical treatment for the poor and homeless, adding to services provided by the older hospitals and *hôtels-Dieu* (Catholic hostels). Almost 2,000 of them existed by 1790, but ordinary people viewed them as potential death factories.[24]

Above all, magistrates feared epidemics. In these crisis moments, public authorities deployed medical personnel and financial resources to affected areas. Following significant outbreaks, for instance, royal intendants in Besançon, Soissons, Champagne, and Alsace appointed permanent *médecins des épidemies* (doctors who specialized in treating epidemic outbreaks) to tend to health concerns, and like-minded physicians asked the royal government to create similar posts in their respective localities. In towns and cities, magistrates also passed laws to regulate cleanliness and dispose of waste properly, though the volume of ordinances suggests that elites couldn't enforce them.[25]

However, in the decades before the French Revolution, public opinion changed. Enlightened reformers, such as Anne-Robert-Jacques Turgot and Jacques Necker, drew upon humanitarian impulses and formed new institutions, including the innovative Royal Society of Medicine (see Map 0.2).[26] In other sectors, critics lambasted charitable institutions, above all religious hospitals and orders, as being inefficient and unable to help the poor and the sick. In the 1780s, for example, the Royal Academy of Science studied hospital care and institutions in Paris, and enlisted leading intellectuals, notably the hospital reformer Jacques Tenon and the chemist Antoine Lavoisier. They concluded that medicine and hospital care held great potential, but magistrates needed to do much more to improve both and make them useful for society.[27]

Such, in broad strokes, was the health situation in France at the end of the Old Regime. In 1789, the Revolution overturned this complete medical world and set about building something entirely new. Scientific knowledge, institutions, and politics mixed in a heady and unpredictable brew.

Doctors participated in the revolutionary fray right from the start. On July 13, 1789—the night before the Paris crowd stormed the Bastille—medical students rioted in the streets and joined public demonstrations. Doctors and surgeons composed *cahiers de doléances* (lists of grievances) to complain about medical and sanitary conditions.[28] Several were elected to the Estates-General and debated health policy and social reform, notably with the Poverty Committee (Comité de Mendicité), headed by Le Rochefoucauld-Liancourt, and the Health Committee (Comité de Salubrité), headed by Joseph-Ignace Guillotin (famed for first proposing the guillotine) and Félix Vicq d'Azyr. D'Azyr projected a sweeping reform of medical teaching and institutions in France. By 1791, with the formation of the National Assembly, the Public Assistance Committee was overwhelmed by petitions for immediate assistance and pensions, while legislators such as Lavoisier and Condorcet tried to draft national insurance schemes and assure the right of every citizen to public aid.[29]

Medical practitioners also assumed political roles. In 1792, twenty-eight doctors were elected to the National Convention and joined the radical Montagnards, including the surgeon and activist Jean-Baptiste Bô (1743–1814), who later vehemently supported the Terror. Elsewhere medical practitioners participated in the Jacobin Clubs, where they pushed for social reform and sanitary measures at the local level. When drafting the new constitution in spring and summer 1793, legislators again picked up the question of assistance, supplementing the idea of political rights outlined in the original Declaration of the Rights of Man and Citizen with a new vision of social rights: not just the right to subsistence, but the right to health as well. The Convention also adopted motions regarding free public welfare, the right to work, hospital care, insurance, and provision for children, the aged, and unwed mothers.[30]

Several intellectual trends shaped radical ideas about medicine and health. The first originated from the writings of philosopher Jean-Jacques Rousseau, and the second from the new forms of popular or countercultural science in the waning decades of the Old Regime.

In the first instance, Rousseau influenced radical doctors in essential ways.[31] He espoused an Arcadian image in which ordinary people had reconciled their needs and desires to better harmonize themselves with nature and one another. Imbuing all individuals with a moral character, Rousseau preached that personal autonomy bestowed dignity and freedom upon every person. Human problems originated not from a sinful human nature, but from a corrupt order of things, one produced by a false social contract. By rewriting the social contract and following "nature," people could rediscover their authentic selves. Rousseau did not simply believe in noble savages, as Arthur Lovejoy reminds us.[32] However, Rousseau's contemporaries often interpreted him this way, and radically inclined physicians and surgeons picked up his cause, hoping to apply Rousseau's teachings to human health and wellbeing.

Rousseau himself had broached medical issues in his famous book *Émile, or on Education* (1762). Like other enlightened philosophers, Rousseau disparaged medical personnel, criticizing their craft and scientific pretensions. However, he went farther and insisted that most sicknesses were self-inflicted, blaming "civilized" morals and manners. Medicine parasitized upon decadent and debauched habits; it treated symptoms but not the underlying moral causes. Though Rousseau dismissed medicine as corrupt and dangerous, he celebrated the new science of hygiene—though hygiene, for him, was more of a moral art than an actual science.[33] By rediscovering the virtuous and authentic self, he said, individuals could better order their desires and needs, thereby returning to a healthier way of living.

Rousseau sparked passionate disputes between his supporters and detractors, the latter, such as Alphonse Le Roy and Jacques-Louis Moreau de la Sarthe, sometimes finding his medical advice unfounded and downright dangerous (especially in how he counseled parents about child health and hygiene, as when he suggested plunging children in ice-cold water to toughen them up).[34] Nonetheless, his ideas hit a nerve. Many observers, medical men included, felt that French society was declining in demographic and economic terms, and they blamed moral factors, above all luxury and overconsumption, for physical degeneration and depopulation. Echoing Rousseau, prominent physicians sought to treat perceived "high-risk groups," notably overly nervous women, hypochondriacs, swaddled children, men of letters, grandees, libertines, and masturbating teenagers (the great scourge, it was said, of enlightened society). Often, these crusaders focused upon better hygiene and moral values amongst the aristocratic and moneyed elites. Key figures included Samuel-Auguste Tissot, a follower of Rousseau, who spoke loudly about the "people's health" and became one of the most prominent health writers of the eighteenth century, as well as Antoine Le Camus and C.-A. Vandermonde, who both looked at education and selective breeding to improve or perfect the population. In many ways, these ideas reflected a deepening mistrust of Old Regime values, habits, and institutions, offering pointed criticisms and suggesting means of reform.[35]

This Rousseauvian attitude appears also in Hugues Maret's *Memoir in which One Looks to Determine What Influence the Morals of the French Have on Their Health*, a manuscript that received top honors from the Academy of Amiens and which he published in 1772. Maret criticized Old Regime values and lifestyle yet put the relationship between disease and civilization in a broad historical sweep, starting with the late Roman Empire. Since medieval times, he said, the monarchy had served as a progressive and modernizing force, improving health and wellbeing through better laws and expanding the built environment: "This transformation in the political system has worked wonders in the physical nature of France, and the morals and manners of its inhabitants."[36]

However, progress created a paradox. Modern life solved some problems, but it also created new ones, especially in the libertine and luxurious habits found in Enlightenment society. Sexual free-living, venereal disease, overconsumption, and wet-nursing (the practice of sending babies out to nurses to feed): Maret cataloged all the abuses. Narcissism triumphed over patriotism and individual control, even amongst the noblest of hearts. As he wrote, "Because the only thing valued is riches, they think themselves on the road to glory, while actually, they are debasing themselves to acquire them."[37]

The mania for luxury, Maret complained, had contaminated everyone, not just grandees and fashionable elites; it dissipated people's vital spirits and drained energy and moral courage. Modern living had freed itself from the old scourges associated with leprosy and plague, but now individuals found themselves plagued by nervous diseases such as hysteria and hypochondria, many of which Maret attributed to women. As with many of Rousseau's followers, Maret framed resentments towards aristocratic privilege and wealth in gendered terms, scapegoating high-profile women in the salons and social networks of Old Regime France as causing social and institutional conflicts and degeneration.[38]

Beyond Rousseau's pastoral ideals, medical radicalism had a second source: popular science and the countercultural figures whom Vincenzo Ferrone has dubbed the *prophètes-philosophes*—a term derived from a book written by the radical thinker and future Girondin revolutionary,

Jean-Louis Carra (1742–93).[39] Under the Old Regime, as historians such as Robert Darnton and Simon Schaffer have shown, science obsessed the leisured and educated classes, and it influenced cultural values in powerful ways.[40] This passion extended from electrical shows to ballooning and dubious pseudo-sciences. These included Mesmerism, in which self-appointed healers explored hypnosis and magnetism as cures for disease; physiognomy, which promised to divine people's thoughts and character through facial profiling; and rhabdomancy, a technique of using pointer sticks for purposes of psychic divination. In all these events, science bordered upon spectacle, becoming a form of "showtime" rather than reasoned demonstration.

In their works, the *prophètes-philosophes* celebrated occult forces in nature, which they often derived from animistic or pantheistic doctrines, to challenge the academic establishment and conventional ideas about a divinely sanctioned social order. Rejecting rationalist approaches, these figures celebrated natural wonder and enthusiasm, offering a dynamic theory of matter and evolution. As Charles C. Gillispie has argued, they sought a more comforting view of the cosmos by trying to invest nature with personality and moral purpose, one beyond brute force and matter. These ideas emerged with philosophers such as Denis Diderot and Jean-Jacques Rousseau and were elaborated by writers such as J.-B.-R. Robinet and J.-H. Bernardin de Saint-Pierre. Significantly, this "radical science" influenced later revolutionary leaders such as Jacques-Pierre Brissot and J.-L. Carra, and elsewhere shaped Jacobin hostility towards conventional academic figures and institutions.[41]

Radical science influenced free-thinking doctors in three ways. First, the *prophètes-philosophes* advocated a form of scientific populism. Following Diderot, they argued that science should remain neither abstract nor isolated in ivory towers, something they alleged had happened under the Old Regime. Instead, science should be open to all people, not just wealthy or privileged elites, something akin to how skilled artisans exercised their handicrafts. Accordingly, radical science and medicine should remain utilitarian, in that every person should benefit from it. Knowledge should improve the world, making it more just and virtuous—just as Rousseau had written about medicine.

Second, the *prophètes-philosophes* often spoke in resentful and subversive tones. According to them, official science had become too elitist and removed from the people, entombing itself in aristocratic and monarchical academies. These institutions, they alleged, constituted privileged bastions where snobbish scientists conspired to keep the common sort from their just rewards. The swamp needed draining. Medicine, likewise, would benefit from this libertarian overhaul, freeing individual initiative and opening the public to new cures.

Lastly, the *prophètes-philosophes* grounded their populism in scientific theory. Nature, they claimed, was characterized by incessant change and progress. It legitimated a radical egalitarianism and promised to overturn injustice and intolerance. Carra wrote, "Study, then, the System of Reason and the code of natural laws. You will sense the sacred necessity of civil equality for everyone, of relative liberty, of reasonable property, and individual security for all."[42]

These opinions inspired revolutionaries in how they saw the relation between individuals, nature, and society, allowing them to proclaim that laws and institutions had corrupted human nature and needed to be swept away. Medicine did not escape this radical restructuring. Starting in 1789, politically minded doctors were willing to take up this cause.

One figure, most famously, fused medical and political radicalism: the revolutionary leader Jean-Paul Marat (1743–93). Best known for his radical populism—his newspaper, *L'Ami du Peuple*, fueled revolutionary ideas and popular activism—Marat began his professional life as a practicing physician, and later, in the 1780s, he engaged himself in experimental research and polemics over the Newtonian worldview.[43]

Born in Switzerland, Marat boasted a cosmopolitan career. He spoke several languages and immersed himself in different political and cultural settings. In 1760, he started studying in Bordeaux and continued his formal education in Paris. In 1765, Marat moved to London and practiced medicine for over a decade, attracting a large and privileged clientele, and he even joined an exclusive Masonic lodge located in Soho in 1774. It was only in 1775 that he earned his medical degree from St Andrews University in Scotland. One of the professors who signed his diploma was William Buchan, a physician who, alongside Samuel-Auguste Tissot, was one of the best-known medical writers of the Enlightenment.

In 1776, Marat returned to Paris and established himself as a fashionable doctor of high repute; one of his patrons, in fact, was the well-known socialite the Marquise de l'Aubespine. Soon afterward, in 1777, Marat received a post as a household physician to the Comte d'Artois, the younger brother of Louis XVI, who later became a redoubtable counter-revolutionary monarch of the Restoration period.

At the height of his success, Marat abruptly changed his career path. In 1783, he resigned his post as Artois's physician and abandoned medicine, choosing instead to focus upon experimental physics and scientific writing. That year, he received the top prize from the Academy of Rouen for his essay on animal electricity, and his fellow scientific colleague and political radical, Jacques-Pierre Brissot, supported his scientific contentions (though the two of them would later become deadly rivals during the Revolution proper).[44]

Clearly, Marat had larger scientific ambitions at heart. Immediately after this success, he translated Isaac Newton's seminal book on optics into French and experimented on electricity, heat, and fire. That said, his unorthodox views on Newtonian physics proved controversial and earned him the scorn of the prominent scientists in the Academy of Sciences, including Antoine Lavoisier and J.-S. Bailly, and he was denied a seat on that august body (both men were later consumed in the Terror). Many observers, then and now, suspect that Marat's political obsessions—redolent of Rousseau's paranoia—date from that time.[45]

In his works, Marat intertwined scientific, medical, and political interests. His forays into medical and social thinking began in 1772 when he composed a significant treatise in English on the mind–body problem, and in the following year he expanded this work into a two-volume opus, which he now dubbed *A Philosophical Essay on Man*. This book, which he revised in French into three full volumes in 1775, became well known in enlightened circles throughout Europe, eliciting commentary from figures such as Denis Diderot, who was the chief editor of the famous *Encyclopédie*, and Francesco Antonio Grimaldi, the enlightened Italian pioneer in the human sciences.[46]

In his medical writings, Marat followed the so-called "science of man," a scientific tradition established by Enlightenment philosophers such as John Locke and David Hume, as well as major physicians such as Albrecht von Haller, Claude-Nicolas Le Cat, and Paul-Joseph Barthez. Marat had several philosophical axes to grind. He attacked the radical materialism seen, on the one hand, with Julien Offray de La Mettrie, who had subordinated mental phenomena to internal physiological determinants, and the radical environmentalism of the philosopher Claude-Adrien Helvétius, who had seen human characteristics as products of education and milieu, on the other. Marat promoted what he considered a more integrative model of the mind–body phenomenon, one that acknowledged corporeal or materialist factors in the making of the self, but he also recognized a place for an autonomous mind and independent soul—a kind of Cartesian "ghost in the machine" at work in the human animal.

One key point emerged in this work, one which informed Marat's fundamental view of nature and society in his later writings: namely, that nature itself provided the blueprint for any understanding of the human self and society. "It is only by studying nature," he wrote, "and by penetrating its most secret recesses, that we can attain to the discovery of its arcana."[47] Science possibly prefigured a more "natural" social order itself.

Marat quickly turned from physiological thought to political questions. While staying in England, he joined the radical faction that supported the parliamentarian John Wilkes, and in 1774 he wrote a polemic to support Wilkes's crusade, entitled *The Chains of Slavery*. In this work, which drew strongly upon Rousseau, he attacked the "mixed government" system of England and denounced George III's cabinet as tyrannical and corrupt.[48] At times, he even characterized political problems as morbid pathologies in the body politic itself. In 1778, following the Italian jurist Cesare Beccaria, he turned to writing about crime and punishment, submitting a work entitled *Plan de la législation criminelle* to the Academy of Berne. Addressing his readers as "free men" (*hommes libres*), Marat averred that, "Times have changed . . . the philosophical spirit permeates all places." "Little by little," he promised, "men have recognized their rights; finally, they want to enjoy them; thus only, impatient with their chains, they want to break them."[49]

Following the insights that he gleaned from his medical science of man, Marat insisted that nature should inform human understanding, allowing people to understand themselves and the surrounding world critically. Like Carra's *prophètes-philosophes*, Marat believed that knowing nature allowed people to diagnose their social and political conditions and then to change them. "L'esprit philosophique," therefore, made people aware of their rights and social conditions, giving them a political consciousness of what they could or should be. Comprehending their rights, they could change their political and social situation.[50] Science, in this regard, constituted a consciousness-raising activity, one that prefigured concrete political involvement. And though politics ultimately consumed Marat's intellectual energies after 1789, a model had been set for other doctors and political activists.

Less known than that of Marat, but equally instructive, was the career of the doctor and revolutionary Amédée Doppet (1753–99). Doppet, like Marat and Carra, cut his teeth on the popular science and countercultural currents of the 1770s and 1780s. He belonged to the so-called literary underground of eighteenth-century culture, that bawdy and cheeky subculture of subversive philosophy, radical politics, and pornographic writings that characterize works like Jean-Baptiste de Boyer d'Argens's *Thérèse philosophe* (1748) and Mathieu-Francois Pidansat de Mairobert's *Anecdotes sur Mme. la Comtesse du Barry* (1775).[51]

A native of Savoy, Doppet studied medicine in Turin before moving to France, where, like Jean-Paul Marat, he set up a medical practice in Paris. There, in the 1780s, he became involved in polemics over Anton von Mesmer's scandalous theories and hypnotic cures. This controversy had embroiled the Royal Academy of Sciences and the Royal Society of Medicine and attracted the leading scientists of the time, including Lavoisier and Benjamin Franklin. Doppet was intrigued by Mesmerist therapeutics—how the mind could control sickness and pain—but he also dismissed Mesmer and his fellow-travelers as charlatans and quacks.[52] After having composed a satire on the subject (in verse form, no less),[53] he returned to Turin, where he presented his ideas to the royal court, assuring them that Mesmerism wasn't witchcraft or occult magic.

That said, Doppet harbored grander literary pretensions. He characterized himself as a man for all seasons, and medicine, he said, wasn't a sufficient outlet for his talent. In 1785 he published a novel, *The Memoirs of the Madame de Warens* (who was a controversial figure from Rousseau's *Confessions*), and he tried his hand at biography and sentimental fiction. The titles alone suggest his literary level: *Celestina, or the Philosopher from the Alps* (1787) and *Zélamire, or Strange Liaisons* (1788). Meanwhile, he kept publishing on sundry medical topics, including *The Doctor of Love* (1787), *Dissertation on Apparent Death* (1788)—which capitalized on large-scale anxieties about premature burial—and *Occult Medicine, or Treatise on Natural and Medical Magic* (1788).[54]

As with Marat and Bô, the French Revolution galvanized Doppet.[55] He himself underscored how medicine had propelled him into revolutionary politics. It had shaped his political values and imparted upon him a radical and egalitarian worldview. Like Carra, Doppet believed that science revealed profound moral truths about equality and justice, and this was doubly true for medicine. In his words, "Those distinctions and privileges that social pride establishes simply fall away before the observer who studies the sick person; the aspect of the same needs and the same sufferings which afflict all conditions certainly provides great and sublime lessons about equality."[56]

Doppet expanded these beliefs in his book called *The Doctor-Philosopher, a useful work for every citizen*, which he published in the midst of the economic and financial collapse of the Old Regime. Doppet's title played upon Carra's idea of the *prophète-philosophe*, but it alluded to something else as well: the figure of the *médecin-philosophe*, the so-called "doctor-philosopher." The term had come into vogue in the mid-1700s and denoted those prominent doctors who had achieved status as men of letters or engaged intellectuals in the style of Voltaire or other Enlightenment philosophers.[57] The most famous were those physicians associated with the Montpellier medical school, notably François Boissier de Sauvages, Théophile de Bordeu, and Paul-Joseph Barthez. These writers had insisted that medicine could achieve status as a bona fide empirical and experimental science, and they suggested that it could become the basis for studying human nature itself. Elsewhere, practitioners applied these insights to broader political agendas involving social reform and utopian dreams of regeneration and human perfection.[58]

Doppet also hoped that medicine could help build a more perfect polity. As he put it, "A work in which a doctor exposes the different means of combatting a species of disease is without doubt of great utility, but he who tries to prove to men that they can save themselves from disease and return the human species to its original vitality, would be most useful to humanity: such is the goal of the Doctor-Philosopher."[59]

Following Rousseau, Doppet insisted on the relationship between individuals, health, and nature. The closer people hewed to nature, he said, the healthier and more virtuous they became.[60] Unfortunately, modern life had disrupted real needs and wants and had spawned moral and physical degeneracy. "The population grows," he wrote, "and needs expand; from there, men assume a new way of life and this change must influence health." This "new way of life" influenced both the haves and the have-nots: "The first find a source of infirmity in the pleasures they procure from the social state; the others are prey to diseases that are caused by forced labor."

In this manner, both "opulence and poverty transform the constitution of mankind."[61]

The doctor-philosopher understood that medicine had social utility, but also liabilities for patients. Revealing a strong libertarian streak, Doppet claimed that every person could be his or her own doctor, but one must always be wary of quacks and charlatans, both of whom exploited the poor and desperate. At the same time, he lambasted doctors and surgeons for catering only to their wealthy and privileged clientele. Like other self-appointed elites, doctors needed to reclaim their moral duties and build a healthier and more just community.

Throughout, Doppet told his readers that good health was within every person's grasp. Though people needed greater social and political equality, they could take private initiatives for themselves. Following insights gleaned from the Mesmerist controversy, he insisted that the mind ruled over physical and emotional experiences, including sickness and suffering. The key was self-control, which constituted a stronger remedy than anything concocted by doctors and apothecaries. He gave concrete examples of how the mind could master the body: how a toothache stopped once someone sat in the dentist's chair; how fear and suffering empowered the patient to submit to the surgeon's blade; and how patients sometimes cured themselves because they believed in the prowess of their physician. In these passages, Doppet harked back to the world of the *prophètes-philosophes*, all who had taught that will and intuition were crucial to mastering nature.

From here, Doppet turned to education and discipline, the two means by which free-minded individuals could master their bodies and minds. Gymnastics, as developed by ancient Greek masters such as Iccus and Herodotus, could better control the "animal spirits" (the vital forces in the nerves and fibers) and promote individual health and wellbeing. He celebrated the traditional Greek sports, ranging from wrestling to javelin and discus-throwing, but he also added contemporary forms of exercise and leisure, including dancing, running, horseback riding, and even swimming.[62]

There were reasons for this Spartan idealism. Humans, he insisted, needed physical exercise; it was an innate drive they shared with all other animal types. He lambasted what he called an "effeminate education" and insisted that good physical conditioning helped make strong and morally virtuous citizens. Anticipating the post-1789 discussions of citizenship, Doppet said that physical education was the first step towards creating independent and self-possessed individuals, all based upon autonomous self-control.[63]

Doppet's comments culminated in a sweeping critique of contemporary morals and manners. For him, the greatest danger remained excess. He decried libertinism and nervous diseases, and he cautioned, like Samuel-Auguste Tissot and Achille Le Bègue du Presle (who had served as Rousseau's personal physician), against the evils of masturbation.[64] Elsewhere, he followed the advice dispensed in traditional health manuals, using the Galenic/Arabic "six things non-natural" as his guide to ameliorating people's lifestyles: air, food and drink, work and rest, sleep and waking, excretion, and the unstable passions of the mind. Such views appeared in other hygienic books from the revolutionary period, notably with Ambroise Ganne and L.-C.-H. Macquart.[65] Individual citizens, these authors emphasized, were the architects of their own good health or sicknesses. Doppet wrote, "In following the rays of reason, the virtuous man has no reason to fear being taken away by excesses . . . through virtue, he will always be moderate, and moderation will give and assure him his health."[66]

Nonetheless, Doppet was not a puritanical figure obsessed with Rousseau's cult of virtue. His other writings veered more directly into pornography and radical politics, undercutting his tone of moral rectitude. In 1788, he published a salacious book, *A Treatise on the Whip, and its effects on the physics of love or external aphrodisiacs*, a work that served as a harbinger for an entire literature on medicine and sex that appeared in the later stages of the French Revolution, notably with figures such as J.-A. Millot and Louis Robert.[67]

In this short book, based upon an earlier Latin text published in the German city of Lübeck, Doppet analyzed how and why certain people were drawn to "truly depraved tastes"—specifically, why they became sexually aroused when they were whipped or beaten on their undersides.[68] Doppet assured readers, with a wink of his eye, that he "only had . . . the intention of being useful"—and promoted a new sexual ethos, a vision in which people glorified the body's natural wonders and stripped themselves of prudery and superstition.[69] In the style of his *The Doctor-Philosopher*, readers could use natural knowledge to improve and modernize daily life.

According to Doppet, nature inscribed sexual desire on the human heart. This instinct formed an essential part of personal experience, providing the means by which the species propagated itself. Both men and women possessed "normal" sexual appetites, but when they denied themselves outlets, they developed bizarre and unhealthy sex lives—a point made in Denis Diderot's scathing critique of abstinence in his novel *La Religieuse*, which told the story of a young nun who tried to escape her forced celibacy.[70] In such circumstances, said Doppet, natural impulses became complicated and overwrought, impeding a healthy lifestyle. At the same time, he warned, people should avoid succumbing to their passions, as this debased their strength, beauty, and vitality, rendering them less than human. Sex was healthy, but it should not be abused.

Throughout, Doppet sought to explain aberrant sexual proclivities in scientific terms. Flagellation, he said, had entirely natural causes, rooted in education and biological penchants. Here again, Doppet turned from medicine to social and political critique. According to him, young people often learned sadistic sex in religious schools and communities, a pleasure that nuns and monks inflicted upon one another because of their repressed sexual desires. This noxious miasma spread, contagion-like, through entire communities of young people, encouraging masturbation and nocturnal emissions. Anticipating the revolutionary rhetoric of de-Christianization, Doppet's ideas became increasingly anticlerical and irreverent, not just aimed at religious authority and institutions, but at all religion itself, which he dismissed as crass superstition.[71] Like Carra, he hoped for that "happy age," that "age of reform," when religious beliefs and practices, so inimical to modern civilization, had been swept away—and that young men and women weren't buried alive in convents and monasteries.[72]

Shifting from religious critique, Doppet turned to corporal punishment in educational institutions more generally, where he saw spanking and caning children as a clear case of misplaced sexual aggression. Teachers were dispensing more than punishment, he thought, as they often disciplined handsome or pretty students, forcing them to strip down and expose themselves. Worse yet, this abusive behavior inculcated a taste for sexual depravity within their victims, deforming their normal romantic relations. Parents and magistrates, he begged, should interest themselves in disciplinary reform, lest their children become habitual masturbators or slaves to "the Jesuit vice"—presumably sodomy.

In his conclusion, Doppet reiterated that he wanted to promote more natural libidinal impulses amongst his readers, a new sexual ethos stripped of perversion or debauched behavior. He finished his book with a long list of remedies or recipes that readers could use to promote a healthier sexual attitude and avoid moral degeneracy. "So that people don't misunderstand, my goal isn't to promote libertinism," he insisted. "I only want to unveil the secrets of my craft for the utility of several frosty hands and so many spouses who complain on the marriage bed."[73]

One revolutionary, more than any other, embodied the figure of the radical physician: François-Xavier Lanthenas (1754–99). Lanthenas put his experience as a doctor in the service of an explicit political and social agenda. As with Doppet, he imagined medical science as a means for building a healthier society, but he argued that this healthy society must also be a just society, one that eradicated social injustice and the roots of poverty and disease. In fact, he argued, these two things—health and social justice—were ineluctably connected.

Having started his medical studies in Paris, Lanthenas finished his degree at the University of Rheims, where he submitted a medical dissertation on the relationship between health and education in 1783. Upon the outbreak of the French Revolution, he associated with the *Cercle Social*, a radical coterie of legislators, activists, and editors who advocated for wide-ranging political agendas, including female emancipation, the abolition of slavery, and even the redistribution of private property.[74] To these radical ideas, Lanthenas added another: healthcare and public relief for all French citizens.

Like Marat and Doppet, Lanthenas had an extraordinary political trajectory. A cosmopolitan and confirmed democrat, he joined the Girondin faction, which included figures such as the *philosophe* and mathematician

Condorcet, as well as more countercultural scientific figures such as Brissot and Carra. In 1792, after the fall of the monarchy, Lanthenas was elected to the National Convention. There he befriended that icon of the American Revolution, Thomas Paine, and even translated Paine's most radical books, *Common Sense* and *The Age of Reason*, into French. Notably, Paine, like Lanthenas, had also explored questions of health and public welfare in the second part of his *Rights of Man*, a book on "principle and practice" which he published in 1792.[75]

However, politics soon turned dangerous for Lanthenas. In January 1793, he voted for Louis XVI's execution but, like other moderates, moved to suspend the sentence and instead imprison the king for life. Consequently, Lanthenas, ran afoul of the radical Montagnards, and only Marat's appeal saved him from dying, alongside his Girondin colleagues Carra and Brissot, on the guillotine.

In Lanthenas, the figure of the *médecin-philosophe* dovetailed, in extraordinary ways, with that of the radical *prophète-philosophe*. Strikingly, medical experience helped shape Lanthenas's politically opinionated activities. He had started his professional life by studying disease and society, emphasizing how environment and education shaped good health for people. Egalitarian values marked his medical approach.

When the Revolution broke out, Lanthenas put these radical impulses in the service of a legislative agenda, seeing public instruction as a critical element in the physical and moral regeneration of the French nation. For him, public welfare and instruction ought to abolish, as much as possible, "the inequality that results from the difference of spirit, in giving to everyone the greatest facilities for instruction of one's self."[76]

For Lanthenas, a more profound principle was at stake. Accordingly, education comprised "the entire physical and moral development of man." All human experience—ranging from literacy to civics to private hygiene—fell within its purview, constituting a key part of the "regeneration of the species." However, it was something that took time and effort, an undertaking that was not individual but collective, encompassing "the progress of virtue, enlightenment, and our new institutions."[77]

For Lanthenas, the French Revolution had empowered citizens to control better their public and private lives, improving themselves in body and spirit. Medicine, he insisted, could build this more perfect polity by helping citizens attain their freedom and happiness. He had long believed, like Carra's *prophète-philosophe*, that science undermined despotism by promoting more egalitarian sentiments. No science, however, had better potential to do so than medicine, but doctors needed to reformulate their principles and mission and focus upon their chief responsibility: the patient.

Herein lay the great challenge. The doctor, by virtue of his intimate relationship with patients, had witnessed the most extreme states of disease and despair, giving him penetrating insights into the human condition. Universal human joys and suffering taught him the fundamental equality between all people, irrespective of their background or social standing. Consequently, doctors must acknowledge democratic and egalitarian principles, assuming the mantle of social justice. Medicine could potentially assure liberty and justice for all.[78]

Lanthenas expanded these views in his extraordinary text, *De l'influence de la liberté sur la santé*, which he published through the *Cercle Social* in 1792. In this short work, he underscored that "health is the primary good."[79] For him, doctors must embrace a larger moral mission, using their science to regenerate the nation. To do so, however, they must purge society of shady charlatans and greedy mountebanks, making doctors and surgeons into useful and patriotic citizens.

According to Lanthenas, two groups had constituted themselves as agents of monarchical-aristocratic oppression: priests and magistrates, both of whom sowed superstition and bigotry amongst the masses so as to maintain their power. Medicine, Lanthenas regretted, participated in this grand conspiracy and it made the situation worse by only giving the rich and privileged classes the fruits of its craft.[80]

Beyond perfidious elites, other factors menaced the body politic: dirt and dearth amongst the popular classes, on the one hand, and decadent and debauched behavior amongst the affluent classes, on the other. Going beyond earlier doctors such as Hugues Maret, Lanthenas insisted that an unjust social and political system fomented both causes. "Yes, indeed!" he wrote. "It is despotism whose negligence, ignorance, and often perverse designs have spread those legions of diseases that disfigure society and particularly afflict the poor man and the artisan."[81]

In some ways, Lanthenas fulminated, the rich and privileged expropriated not just the working person's labor but also their health and wellbeing, crushing them with their avarice and egoism. As a boon for their labor, the elite classes proffered to the people those two factories of death: the prison and the hospital. Worse yet, doctors supported, in direct or indirect ways, this corrupt state of things. Lanthenas complained:

> [E]ither doctors are stupid, to the point of not perceiving the sensible causes and real remedies for the evils to which they are witnesses, or else they've betrayed the interests of humanity, to which they pretended to pledge themselves, because, in seeking only the false reputation of being a healer . . . they fail to perceive . . . the first causes of disease.[82]

For Lanthenas, these "first causes" were clear: tyranny and slavery, both of which blinded people to their true potential as human beings. Freedom was the antidote and prophylactic to all diseases. It was the first cure before all other cures. "True liberty, enlightenment, and philosophy," he wrote, "alone can guide humanity to the point of ameliorating his being, in the body and mind . . . bodily cleanliness and happiness of mind are the characteristics, as the primary advantages of true freedom."[83]

Accordingly, health was not an individual concern, isolated from community and nature. Instead, it embraced the entire human condition, involving concrete questions about material resources and social justice. "Society," Lanthenas insisted, "must provide to humankind the means of staying outside the influence of the elements . . . without suffering from their vicissitudes, their shocks, or their alterations. The enlightened insights that society procures ought to return humankind, the most quickly as possible, to the laws of nature and to the simple and pure lifestyle which she prescribes it."[84]

In his more powerful passages, Lanthenas sketched out this more just society. Freedom, individual rights, self-government: these things would redeem humanity and make it pure and healthy again. He imagined, foremost, a system of national education, one that taught citizens basic hygiene, physical exercise and proper diet, and moral principles. As one of Lanthenas's colleagues wrote elsewhere, medicine might provide knowledge and instruction, but it needed a stronger partner in the government itself.[85]

For Lanthenas, health required more than political and social revolution; it mandated a whole shift in cultural sentiment and behavior. He proclaimed, "Order our morals and manners by good laws, our customs by instruction and public festivals. Change our fashions; watch over our nutrition; act by persuasion and reason; know the force, the extent and strength of your influence; but above all, PREACH BY EXAMPLE."[86]

With these words, Lanthenas returned to the basic sermon, as inherited from Rousseau and the *prophètes-philosophes*, of human innocence and nature's healing powers. By reclaiming these two things, humanity could regenerate itself and build a more just and healthy society. However, it was the revolutionary moment itself, which had empowered citizens and legislators, that would rouse the French government to cure underlying social pathologies and allow the people to reclaim their primeval health and nature.

In the end, revolutionary legislators and activists articulated powerful new political ideas—such as the right to health—but struggled to turn them into actual social policies. Abstract laws and ideals, based on principles of liberty, equality, and fraternity, failed to alleviate the distress experienced by large segments of the French populace, a distress rendered more acute by the realities of war and terror, the significant accomplishments of the post-1794 "medical revolution" notwithstanding. The challenges were mostly structural. Anticlerical and anti-feudal laws undercut traditional revenue sources for sick and poor relief. Furthermore, the government lacked a stable and efficient bureaucratic system to implement its laws and policies; nor did it possess a national culture or communications system that could support large-scale programs such as pensions or sickness insurance. Lastly, revolutionary legislators, inspired by the Jacobin vision of the unitary nation, tended to favor centralized bureaucratic policies that undermined or ignored local prerogatives and needs.[87] Some historians, particularly those who are ambivalent or hostile to the Revolution's legacy, go so far as to say that the utopian schemes of the Constituent Assembly and the Convention created an unmitigated disaster for the sick and needy—a clear case of what happens when citizens value "liberty" over duty and "obligation."[88]

That said, despite the failures of post-1789 public aid, revolutionaries did bravely face the problems of health and poverty and tried to solve both in new terms, recognizing that the old system of private and religious charity no longer addressed actual needs. In truth, revolutionary France simply lacked the economic resources to implement a national health and welfare system. The "right to health" was not an empty slogan, and this is why the radical doctors of the French Revolution matter. The message that physicians and radicals such as Doppet and Lanthenas sent was clear. Under monarchical and aristocratic dominion, French society had become corrupt and decadent, and it was only by reclaiming civic values and individual moral virtues that citizens could recover their primal liberty and regenerate their nation. At the same time, however, these physicians also placed health and wellbeing in a broader social setting. Foremost, they argued, health was a fundamental right, something upon which all citizens had a claim; this legislators and medical personnel alike must recognize as a fundamentally moral equation. Though individuals could control hygienic regimen and exercise autonomy over their personal lives, doctors such as Lanthenas emphasized that social status, wealth, and born privilege also impacted how people experienced sickness and health; these structural forces, in essence, perpetuated the cycle of disease in society and made health unattainable for many. Both physicians and government officials must take steps, through law and public instruction, to provide citizens with more equal opportunities for healthcare and make medical services more equitable and available to all. Nature, as always, provided the model. Liberty would return people to their more virtuous selves and allow them to celebrate their communal and egalitarian sentiments. Citizens would not just reclaim their rights and liberties, but gain power and autonomy over their bodies, finding in the French Revolution the keys to health and wellbeing in their daily lives.

Source: The French doctor and legislator François Lanthenas on freedom, health, and hygiene: *De l'influence de la liberté sur la santé* (1792)

Today, is there anything one should not expect from liberty as it applies to the health of our citizens and the perfection of future races? All those sciences, which once spent their treasures to profit a few individuals, will finally fulfill their destiny when they apply their results to the well-being of the greatest number of people.

Public prosperity, which will be established by good laws that repress the desire for wealth, will drive indigence away. Poor people will no longer vegetate sadly in the cramped and dirty housing to which they have been reduced. Education will teach them the cost of WATER, AIR, LIGHT, and CLEANLINESS. Their food will be pure and sufficient. A paternal police will guard them against those innumerable evils to which despotism had exposed them with indifference. Prisons and hospitals, those eternal stores of all corruption, will be reformed, guided by those principles which humanity had vainly demanded under the Old Regime. These places will stop spreading disease and death amongst thousands of victims that the consequences of the vices which remain with us still cause.

The well-being of our citizens; the sense of fraternity amongst them; the charm and allure of public festivals and assemblies; those of the education to which all people will have access; finally, honest and praiseworthy impulses: all of these will correct our depraved tastes and with them will disappear the immense cohort of diseases to which [these tastes] give birth.

Liberty will annihilate the vain and greedy calculations that alone determined the union between the sexes. Love will reclaim its power. Laws, and the most sacred rights of nature, will be respected. Future generations will be born more happily. Under the rule of liberty, they will no longer degenerate, as under despotism, but will tend towards the perfection that the human race can attain. A masculine education will strengthen the bodies and minds of young people. Hygiene, that is, the art of conserving one's health, and the moral values that constitute part of it, will shape new men, freed from all disease. Finally, medicine will become what it should be—the knowledge of natural and social man—and not the arid and gloomy analysis of the millions of infirmities that he should not have, and which the loss of one's self and one's dignity alone has spread over the whole of the human race.

Notes

1 Lynn Hunt, *Politics, Culture, and Class in the French Revolution* (Berkeley: University of California Press, 1984); Antoine de Baecque, *Le Corps de l'histoire: Métaphores et politique* (Paris: Calmann-Lévy, 1993); and Jonathan Israel, *Revolutionary Ideas: An Intellectual History of the French Revolution from The Rights of Man to Robespierre* (Princeton, NJ: Princeton University Press, 2014).

2 Jonathan Israel, *The Expanding Blaze: How the American Revolution Ignited the World, 1775–1848* (Princeton, NJ: Princeton University Press, 2017).

3 Emmet Kennedy, *A Cultural History of the French Revolution* (New Haven, CT: Yale University Press, 1989); Michel Serres, "Paris 1800," in *A History of Scientific Thought: Elements of a History of Science*, ed. Michele Serres (Oxford: Blackwell, 1995).

4 Michel Foucault, Blandine Barret Kriegel, Anne Thalamy, and François Beguin, *Les Machines à guérir* (Paris: Institut de l'environnement, 1976).

5 Michel Foucault, *Naissance de la clinique: une archéologie du regard médical* (Paris: Presses Universitaires de France, 1963); Erwin Ackerknecht, *Medicine at the Paris Hospital 1794–1848* (Baltimore, MD: Johns Hopkins University Press, 1967); David M. Vess, *Medical Revolution in France: 1789–1796* (Gainesville: University of Florida Press, 1975); and for a historiographical assessment, see Caroline Hannaway and Anne La Berge, eds., *Constructing Paris Medicine* (Amsterdam and Atlanta: Rodopi, 1998).

6 Mona Ozouf, *L'Homme régénéré: Essais sur la Révolution française* (Paris: Gallimard, 1989).

7 Lynn Hunt, *Inventing Human Rights: A History* (New York: W.W. Norton, 2007).

8 Dora B. Weiner, "Le Droit de l'homme à la santé: une belle idée devant l'Assemblée Constituante, 1790–91," *Clio Medica* 5 (1970): 209–23; George Rosen, "Hospitals, Medical Care, and Social Policy in the French Revolution," in *From Medical Police to Social Medicine: Essays on the History of Health Care* (New York: Science History Publication, 1974), 220–45.

9 Robert Favre, *La Mort dans la littérature et la pensée françaises au siècle des Lumières* (Lyons: Presses Universitaires de Lyon, 1978); John McManners, *Death and the Enlightenment: Changing Attitudes to Death Among Christians and Unbelievers in Eighteenth-Century France* (Oxford: Oxford University Press, 1985).

10 Alain Bideau, Jacques Dupâquier, and Hector Gutierrez, "La mortalité," in *Histoire de la population française: de la renaissance à 1789*, ed. Jacques Dupâquier (Paris: Presses universitaires de France, 1988), 238–9.

11 G.-L. de Leclerc de Buffon, *Oeuvres complètes* (Paris: Dunénil, 1836–7), 4: 298, qtd. in Favre, *La Mort dans la littérature*, 44.

12 Dr. Massie, "Mémoire sur l'état présent de la médecine dans les campagnes," July 23, 1776, Archives de la Société Royale de Médecine, carton 116, dos. 5; Dr. Dufau, "Mémoire concernant l'établissement d'un médecin-inspecteur des épidémies," n.d., Archives de la Société Royale de Médecine, carton 169, dos. 11.

13 Louis-Antoine de Caraccioli, *Le Tableau de la mort ... nouvelle édition, revue, augmentée, & corrigée* (Francfort: Bassompierre, 1761), 50.

14 Robert Darnton, *George Washington's False Teeth: An Unconventional Guide to the Eighteenth Century* (New York: W.W. Norton, 2003).

15 Olwen H. Hufton, *The Poor of Eighteenth-Century France, 1750–1789* (Oxford: Clarendon, 1974).

16 On these figures, see Rosen, "Hospitals, Medical Care, and Social Policy," 221–2.

17 Rosen, "Hospitals, Medical Care, and Social Policy."

18 N. D. Jewson, "The Disappearance of the Sick-Man from Medical Cosmology," *Sociology* 10 (1976): 225–44; François Lebrun, *Se soigner autrefois: Médecins, saints et sorciers aux XVIIe et XVIIIe siècles* (Paris: Seuil, 1995); see also Jan Goldstein, *Console and Classify: The French Psychiatric Profession in the Nineteenth Century* (New York: Cambridge University Press, 1987), 8–40.

19 Kathleen A. Wellman, "Medicine as a Key to Defining Enlightenment Issues: The Case of Julien Offray de La Mettrie," *Studies in Eighteenth-Century Culture* 17 (1987): 75–89.

20 Harvey Mitchell, "Rationality and Control in French Eighteenth-Century Medical Views of the Peasantry," *Comparative Studies in Society and History* 21 (1979): 81–112.

21 "État des médecins et chirurgiens de la province" (n.d.), Bibliothèque de la Faculté de Médecine de Paris, ms. 221.

22 Toby Gelfand, "The Decline of the Ordinary Practitioner and the Rise of a Modern Medical Profession," in *Doctors, Patients, and Society: Power and Authority in Medical Care*, ed. Martin S. Staum and Donald E. Larson (Waterloo, Ont.: Wilfrid Laurier University Press, 1981).

23 Matthew Ramsey, *Professional and Popular Medicine in France: The Social World of Medical Practice* (New York: Cambridge University Press, 1987).

24 Robert M. Schwartz, *Policing the Poor in Eighteenth-Century France* (Chapel Hill: University of North Carolina Press, 1988); Thomas McStay Adams, *Bureaucrats and Beggars: French Social Policy in the Age of the Enlightenment* (New York: Oxford University Press, 1991).

25 L. J. Jordanova, "Policing Public Health in France 1780–1815," in *Public Health*, ed. Teizo Ogawa (Tokyo: Saikon, 1980), 12–32; Jean-Pierre Peter, "Les mots et les objets de la malade: remarques sur les épidémies et la médecine dans la société française de la fin du XVIIIe siècle," *Revue historique* 246 (1971): 13–38.

26 Caroline C. Hannaway, "Medicine, Public Welfare, and the State in Eighteenth-Century France: The Société Royale de Médecine de Paris (1776–1793)," Ph.D. thesis, Johns Hopkins University, 1974.

27 Louis Greenbaum, "Tempest in the Academy: Jean-Baptiste Le Roy, the Paris Academy of Sciences and the Project of a New Hôtel-Dieu," *Archives internationales d'histoire des sciences* 24 (1974): 122–40; Harvey Mitchell, "Politics in the Service of Knowledge: The Debate Over the Administration of Medicine and Welfare in Late Eighteenth-Century France," *Social History* 6 (1981): 185–207.

28 Vess, *Medical Revolution*, 40–4.

29 Dora B. Weiner, *The Citizen-Patient in Revolutionary and Imperial Paris* (Baltimore, MD: Johns Hopkins University Press, 1993), chaps. 3–4.

30 See Weiner, "Le Droit de l'homme"; and Rosen, "Hospitals, Medical Care, and Social Policy."

31 Gilbert Py, *Rousseau et les éducateurs: Étude sur la fortune des idées pédagogiques de Jean-Jacques Rousseau en France et en Europe au XVIIIe siècle* (Oxford: Voltaire, 1997), chap. 7; Rudy Le Menthéour, *La Manufacture de maladies: La dissidence hygiénique de Jean-Jacques Rousseau* (Paris: Garnier, 2012).

32 Arthur O. Lovejoy, "The Supposed Primitivism of Rousseau's *Discourse on Inequality*," in *Essays in the History of Ideas* (Baltimore, MD: Johns Hopkins University Press, 1948).

33 J.-J. Rousseau, *Émile, ou de l'éducation* (Paris: Flammarion, 2009), 60, 99, 100–1.

34 Py, *Rousseau*, 269–70.

35 Anne C. Vila, *Enlightenment and Pathology: Sensibility in the Literature and Medicine of Eighteenth-Century France* (Baltimore, MD: Johns Hopkins University Press, 1998), chaps. 6–7; Michael Winston, *From Perfectibility to Perversion: Meliorism in Eighteenth-Century France* (New York: Peter Lang, 2005), esp. chaps. 1–2; and Sean M. Quinlan, *The Great Nation in Decline: Sex, Modernity, and Health Crises in Revolutionary France, Ca. 1750–1850* (Aldershot: Ashgate, 2007), chap. 1.

36 Hugues Maret, *Mémoire dans lequel on cherche à déterminer quelle influence les moeurs des françois ont sur leur santé* (Amiens: Godard, 1772), 25.

37 Maret, *Mémoire*, 59–60.

38 Maret, *Mémoire*, 90 et seq.

39 Vincenzo Ferrone, *I profeti dell'illuminismo: le metamorphosi della ragione nel tardo settecento italiano* (Bari: Laterza, 1989).

40 See Robert Darnton, *Mesmerism and the End of the Enlightenment in France* (Cambridge, MA: Harvard University Press, 1968); Simon Schaffer, "Natural Philosophy and Public Spectacle in the Eighteenth Century," *History of Science* 21 (1983): 1–43.

41 Charles C. Gillispie, "The *Encyclopédie* and the Jacobin Philosophy of Science: A Study in Ideas and Consequences," in *Critical Problems in the History of Science*, ed. M. Clagett (Madison: University of Wisconsin Press, 1969); Charles C. Gillispie, "Science in the French Revolution," *Behavioral Science* 4 (1959): 67–73.

42 J.-L. Carra, *Système de la raison, ou le prophète philosophe*, 3rd ed. (Paris: Buisson, 1791), vii–viii.

43 Louis Gottschalk, *Jean Paul Marat: A Study in Radicalism* (Chicago: University of Chicago Press, 1967).

44 Clifford D. Conner, *Jean Paul Marat: Scientist and Revolutionary* (Atlantic Highlands, NJ: Humanities Press, 1997), chaps. 5–7.

45 For debates on this point, see Conner, *Jean-Paul Marat*, 42–65.

46 Jean-Paul Marat, *De l'homme, ou Des principes et des loix de l'influence de l'âme sur le corps et du corps sur l'âme*, 3 vols. (Amsterdam: M.-M. Rey, 1775–6).

47 Jean-Paul Marat, *A Philosophical Essay on Man, Being an Attempt to Investigate the Principles and Laws of the Reciprocal Influence of the Soul on the Body*, 2 vols. (London: J. Ridley, 1773), I:xxvi.

48 Clifford D. Conner, *Jean-Paul Marat: Tribune of the French Revolution* (London: Pluto, 2012), 12–16.

49 Jean-Paul Marat, *Plan de législation criminelle*, 3rd ed. (Paris: Imprimerie de la Veuve Marat, n.d.), 3, 5–6.

50 Marat, *Plan de législation*, 11–13.

51 Margaret C. Jacob, "The Materialist World of Pornography," in *The Invention of Pornography, 1500–1800: Obscenity and the Origins of Modernity*, ed. Lynn

Hunt (New York: Zone, 1993), 157–202; Robert Darnton, *The Forbidden Best-Sellers of Pre-Revolutionary France* (New York: W.W. Norton, 1996).

52 Amédée Doppet, *Traité théorique et pratique du magnétisme animal* (Turin: Jean-Michel Briolo, 1784).

53 Amédée Doppet, *La mesmériade, ou Le triomphe du Magnétisme animal, poëme en trois chants, dédié à la Lune* (Geneva and Paris: Couturier, 1784).

54 For this bibliography, see "Notice sur la vie et les ouvrages du général Doppet," in Amédée Doppet, *Mémoires politiques et militaires* (Paris: Baudouin frères, 1824), i–vii.

55 Vincenzo Ferrone, "Medicina naturale e mentalità rivoluzionaria: il caso di François-Amédée Duppet, medico e giacobino savoiardo," in *Una scienza per l'uomo: Illuminismo e Rivoluzione scientifica nell'Europa del Settecento* (Turin: UTET Libreria, 2007), 262–77.

56 Doppet, *Mémoires*, 5.

57 John H. Zammito, "Médecin-Philosophe: Persona for Radical Enlightenment," *Intellectual History Review* 18 (2008): 427–40.

58 Elizabeth A. Williams, *The Physical and the Moral: Anthropology, Physiology, and Philosophical Medicine in France, 1750–1850* (New York: Cambridge University Press, 1994), chap. 1; and Vila, *Enlightenment and Pathology*, chap. 2.

59 Amédée Doppet, *Le Médecin philosophe* (Turin and Paris: Leroy, 1787), xiv–xv.

60 Doppet, *Le Médecin philosophe*, 15–19.

61 Doppet, *Le Médecin philosophe*, v–vi.

62 Doppet, *Le Médecin philosophe*, 19–33.

63 Doppet, *Le Médecin philosophe*, 48.

64 See Samuel-Auguste-André Tissot, *L'Onanisme, ou Dissertation physique sur les maladies produites par la masturbation* (Lausanne: Chapuis, 1760); Achille-Guillaume Le Bègue de Presle, *Le Conservateur de la santé, ou Avis sur les dangers qu'il importe à chacun d'éviter, pour se conserver en bonne santé & prolonger la vie* (Paris: Didot, 1763).

65 Ambroise Ganne, *L'Homme physique et moral, ou recherches sur les moyens de rendre l'homme plus sage* (Strasbourg: Treuttel, 1791); Louis-Charles-Henri Macquart, *Dictionnaire de la conservation de l'homme*, 2 vols. (Paris: Bidault, 1798).

66 Doppet, *Le Médecin philosophe*, 19.

67 Sean M. Quinlan, "Sex and the Citizen: Reproductive Manuals and Fashionable Readers in Napoleonic France, 1799–1808," in *Views from the Margins: Creating Identities in Modern France*, ed. Kevin J. Callahan and Sarah Ann Curtis (Lincoln: University of Nebraska Press, 2008), 189–208.

68 Amédée Doppet, *Traité du fouet et de ses effets sur le physique de l'amour, ou Aphrodisiaque externe: Ouvrage médico-philosophique, suivi d'une dissertation sur tous les moyens capables d'exciter aux plaisirs de l'amour* (n.p.p.: n.p., 1788), 72.

69 Doppet, *Traité du fouet*, iv.

70 Denis Diderot, *La Religieuse* (Paris: Flammarion, 2009).

71 Doppet, *Traité du fouet*, 53.

72 Doppet, *Traité du fouet*, 57.

73 Doppet, *Traité du fouet*, 74.

74 Gary Kates, *The Cercle Social, the Girondins, and the French Revolution* (Princeton, NJ: Princeton University Press, 1985).

75 See *Théorie et pratique des droits de l'homme, par Th. Paine . . . traduit en françois par F. Lanthenas* (Paris: Cercle Social, 1792–95); and *Le siècle de la raison . . . traduit de l'anglais de Thomas Paine . . . par F. Lanthenas* (Paris: Gueffier, 1793–4).

76 François-Xavier Lanthenas, *Rapport et projet de décret sur l'organisation des écoles primaires* (Paris: Imprimerie nationale, n.d.), 3.

77 François-Xavier Lanthenas, *L'Éducation, cause éloignée et souvent même prochaine de toutes les maladies* (Paris: Imprimerie nationale, 1793), 3, 6, 7–8.

78 Lanthenas, *L'Éducation*, 60.

79 François-Xavier Lanthenas, *De l'influence de la liberté sur la santé, la morale et le bonheur* (Paris: Cercle Social, 1792), 23.

80 Lanthenas, *De l'influence*, 3.

81 Lanthenas, *De l'influence*, 5.

82 Lanthenas, *De l'influence*, 6.

83 Lanthenas, *De l'influence*, 9.

84 Lanthenas, *De l'influence*, 13.

85 A. Bacher, *De la Médecine considérée politiquement* (Paris: Huzard, Year XI), 4.

86 Lanthenas, *De l'influence*, 22.

87 On these challenges, see the nuanced remarks in Alan Forrest, *The French Revolution and the Poor* (New York: St. Martin's Press, 1981), 169–76.

88 Léon Lallemand, *La Révolution et les pauvres* (Paris: Picard, 1898), 6, 393.

PART THREE

Revolutionary Experiences, Practices, Sensations

10

Tasting Liberty: Food and Revolution

E. C. Spary

What is the first thing anyone learns about the French Revolution? Usually, that it was a political event driven by hunger. According to a 2010 article in the *Smithsonian Magazine*, the Revolution features among the "landmark food-related moments in history."[1] Although research on the revolutionaries has shown that those who assumed power probably lacked much personal experience of hunger, the causal connection continues to be made in both popular and scholarly accounts of the Revolution.[2] Yet food riots were an intermittent if recurrent feature of French life from 1709 onwards. Why, then, the historian might well ask, did it take eighty years before French subjects came to see the overthrow of the reigning monarch and the dismantling of an entire social order as appropriate responses to a food crisis? The causal argument linking hunger to revolution does not explain why hunger caused a different outcome in 1789 than it had before, why it led to political change rather than charitable relief, nor why the response in France diverged from that elsewhere in Europe. Harvest failures leading to food shortages occurred around Europe during the 1780s; yet only in France did a Revolution with a capital R ensue, hailed as the "creation of modern political culture" and a foretaste of modern democracy.[3] Still, this marshalling of hunger to explain the events of the Revolution is not new. It dates back to the Revolution itself and was consecrated in canonical histories written soon after the event, such as those of Jules Michelet or Hippolyte Taine.[4]

Food, then, bears a heavy explanatory burden in accounts of the French Revolution. Yet its history was long limited to the study of food prices and commerce, to the neglect of the conversations over food that took place between publics and politicians. The purpose of this chapter is not to deny the reality of French hunger before, during, or after 1789. Rather, it seeks to explore some of the ways in which eating and drinking featured in revolutionary debate, both figuratively and literally. For at this time, food, and some foods in particular, took on a heuristic role that extended well beyond ordinary understandings of need and consumption. It would be wrong to suppose that in political debates over food, those who hungered were compelled by irresistible biological urges and lacked the capacity for political reflexivity.[5] Rather, for all groups caught up in the Revolution, whether its architects or its victims, its supporters or its opponents, the practices of eating and drinking that were so central to everyday life would become implicated in the production of new definitions of sovereignty and public order. In the process, they would become moralized and politicized in ways that still affect us today. Precisely because an *absence* of food was a core legitimation for overthrowing the Old Regime, taking control of the food supply—and being seen to manage it more effectively than the previous administration—was a priority for each of the regimes that succeeded one another between 1789 and 1799, including the monarch. As the government officials who shaped French food policy through the 1790s would discover, and as this chapter argues, determining need and allocating resources was no easy task. Different factions profoundly disagreed over both the symbolic and scientific meanings of nourishment. Discussion centered upon the very subject of this volume: life in revolutionary France. Or rather, life and death—big questions that were especially provoked by the chaos of revolutionary events, both in the obvious sense of how to get enough to eat, but also in less obvious ways: questions about exactly *which* foods were necessary to sustain life, and about the moral significance of death and violence. In this chapter, I will argue that food stood as a symbol of the relationship between power and the people, while political violence was narrated, in both a positive and a negative sense, through the language of butchery.

Butchers of the Revolution

In school textbooks, popular histories, and newspapers, the French Revolution tends to be portrayed in two very specific ways where food is concerned. Firstly, it is seen as literally *provoked by* hunger: appetites in the social body are implicitly taken to cause and justify radical political change. Secondly, it is seen as figuratively *cannibalistic*: an entire people consuming itself. Words like "bloodthirsty" or "butchers" and anthropophagic imagery are generically applied to the Terror and other famous events of the Revolution like the prison massacres of September 1792 or the guillotining of the monarch in January 1793. In just one recent example, an article in the *New Yorker* magazine shudderingly frames "Robespierre and his group" as "revolutionary butchers, but they were butchers surrounded by vampires."[6] Since the 1790s, the Revolution has been written in the language of meat. Such figures echo through the historiography from the very first event that is usually taken to mark the start of the Revolution: "After storming the Bastille [see Map 0.2], the crowd killed the prison's governor, the Marquis de Launay, and a butcher named Desnot cut off his head with a pocket knife."[7] Cutting off a human head is no easy task, as anyone who has ever attempted it will know. When the thirty-three-year-old François-Félix Desnot confessed to his role in the governor's famous death, in January 1790, he declared himself in fact to be a cook rather than a butcher, formerly employed by the widow of the Marquis de Breteuil, but jobless since July 1789 and dependent upon his seamstress wife.[8] He had not himself dispatched de Launay, who had kicked him in the groin during the brawl, but was handed a sabre to cut off the dead man's head. Struggling with this implement, "he drew a knife with a black handle from his pocket, and finished off the operation ... the head, thus separated from the body, was placed on the end of a pikestaff." Desnot was again on the scene—coincidentally or not—when Louis-Bénigne Bertier de Sauvigny, royal *intendant* of Paris, was murdered eight days later by a "furious Soldier," after which someone had "torn out Mr Berthier's heart, and put it in [Desnot's] hand." In company with the soldier, Desnot proceeded to the town hall to listen to Lafayette giving a speech, and then, with the heart spitted on the soldier's sabre, the two men "walked through Paris along the streets to the Palais Royal ... As [Desnot] was having supper in a cabaret with the soldier, in a street off the rue St-Honoré, the People arrived and demanded the heart. So he tossed it to them out of the window, and has no idea what became of it."[9]

The processing of the bodies of these early victims of revolutionary violence indicates a prolonged period of contact, as well as butchery skills. Like decapitation, removal of the heart is a comparatively complex process that must have entailed either removing Bertier's other organs first, or else an instrument capable of opening the ribcage. Desnot's interrogators at the Châtelet, Paris's main police court, initially doubted he could have decapitated de Launay "with such a small and weak instrument." To this he responded "that thanks to his job as a cook, he knew how to work with meat."[10] Whatever truth remains in the old story of revolutionary cooks leaving aristocratic households and opening restaurants, it is clear that not all of them responded so peaceably to the exigencies of the Revolution.[11] Ever since 1790, accounts of this episode have identified Desnot as a butcher, reflecting the shock value of someone skilled in the handling of meat for nourishment turning to the dismemberment of a human body, and not just any body but a figure of authority.[12] At one level, the conversion of de Launay and Bertier's bodies into meat figuratively recast them—specifically in their guise as representatives of Royal power—as potential food, a juxtaposition evident in Desnot's ensuing leisurely dinner with the *intendant*'s butchered heart ready to hand. The dispassionate quality of Desnot's narration of his own actions is striking. To his interrogators, "he replied that he wanted no reward, that he had acted out of patriotism and in hopes of a medal, and that he was not short of food."[13]

FIGURE 10.1 *Duchemin, "Tremble, aristocrats, here come the butchers," engraved by Hurard, Paris, 1790. Bibliothèque nationale de France, département Estampes et photographie, RESERVE QB-370 (29)-FT 4.*

The (mis)identification of Desnot as a butcher in the historiography is more than mere sensationalism. Both real and figurative butchers regularly figured in the annals of revolutionary events. Butchers were among the wealthier city merchants nationwide, and in the 1780s they inhabited an increasingly articulate, literate, and politically engaged artisanal stratum of French society.[14] Olympe de Gouges, the author of the famous feminist riposte to the Declaration of the Rights of Man, was the daughter of a butcher. The Paris butcher Louis Legendre rose to become, first, deputy for the *département* of the Seine, and subsequently president of the National Convention after Thermidor.[15] The appellation "butcher" hovered somewhere between a respected urban trade and a metaphor for animal excesses of violence. In revolutionary language and imagery, butchers appeared as symbols of socially sanctioned bloodshed coupled with skill, or as plebeians who nonetheless had access to life-sustaining resources.

During the early republic, where the title was bestowed positively or even appropriated—as with two generals dispatched to quell the Vendée uprising in Year II (see Map 0.1), Florent-Joseph Duquesnoy, self-titled "butcher of the Convention," and François-Joseph Westermann, "butcher of the Vendée"—it cast their actions as needful killing, serving the common good.[16] Counter-revolutionaries, conversely, often figured the entire Revolution as an act of butchery gone wrong. The term continues to be used in connection with the Revolution's more violent episodes. According to Wikipedia for Schools, during the September Massacres, "the [Paris] Commune sent gangs into the prisons to try arbitrarily and butcher 1400 victims, and addressed a circular letter to the other cities of France inviting them to follow this example."[17] References to butchers undermined not only deputies' moral character but also their political legitimacy: the title cast them both as sanguinary monsters and as tradesmen unfit for high governmental office.[18] When Lord John Russell, a member of the British government, sought in 1833 to explain where the Old Regime had gone wrong, one of his telling examples was the fact that Louis XV had stooped to sexual relations with a butcher's daughter, Madame de Pompadour.[19]

Meat-eating in general, and butchery in particular, were thus ambiguous practices throughout the period, and nowhere more so than in the political domain. In the two decades before the Revolution, an expanding French vegetarian movement had amplified Jean-Jacques Rousseau's claim that meat-eaters were inured to pity and incapable of compassion towards fellow human beings. These associations of meat-eating with moral insensibility, articulated by one of the most-cited philosophical authors, led some revolutionaries to trial a vegetarian diet.[20] When one contemporary writing in Year VI noted "that a savage brought to Paris would admire nothing so much as Butchers' Row," this was not entirely complimentary to Parisians.[21]

Butchers and Pigs

One reason why patriotism slipped so readily into literal butchery after 1789 was that the figure of nourishment was threaded through political discourse before, during, and after the Revolution. In accounts of events, revolutionary protagonists were turn by turn addressed as providers and as sources of nourishment. This is most clearly apparent if we turn from Desnot to the king himself.

There is evidence that, when it came to food, Parisian crowds shared the same understanding of the monarch's role as their English counterparts, a view termed by the British Marxist historian E. P. Thompson as the "moral economy."[22] In moral-economic politics, the king's key role was as provider for his people. Even before Louis XVI had ascended the throne, his nourishing tendencies were portrayed in just such terms by images of him at the ploughshare.[23] Crown administrators kept close tabs on the national flour and bread supply throughout the eighteenth century, imposing price caps at times of dearth.[24] But Louis' reign was marked from the outset by experimentation with alternative policies, including the liberalization of the grain trade, justified on the grounds that monarchical intervention actually harmed the stabilization of the food supply: economic laws—apparent only to scientific minds—would ensure that resources always reached areas of the country at greatest need.[25] The king and many noble reformers took an interest in agricultural improvers and chemists who promised to enhance the national food supply. Old Regime ministers, with the king's backing, lent financial and institutional support to such programs, from Anne-Robert-Jacques Turgot's exchanges with the chemist Antoine-Laurent de Lavoisier over the best machine for boiling animal bones down into nutritive substance for the poor, to the pharmacist Antoine-Augustin Parmentier's elaborate, failed project for making bread entirely out of potatoes.[26]

These ardent efforts could not however shore up the king's reputation during the Revolution. After the royal family's abortive flight to Varennes in 1791, caricaturists flocked to portray them as pigs, animals at once humanoid and edible. Many images, like that reproduced in Figure 10.2, particularly stressed the king's personal gluttony. The notion that, beneath his nurturing mask, the king was no more than a greedy pig fits well with Claude Fischler's thesis that the abuse of societal resources is often metaphorically figured as an aberration of individual appetite.[27]

If kings were greedy pigs, revolutionaries would be their butchers. The pig has greater political significance here than it might appear. As Reynald Abad has shown, pork was a meat found only on the tables of the poor.[28] Although their identity remains largely unknown, the semi-literate artists who produced these images were thus framing the king specifically as food for themselves. In this sense we can see the series of porcine portraits as a kind of running commentary upon the character of political power.[29]

After the king was guillotined on January 21, 1793, representations of his nourishing role shifted registers from comic to sinister. In a striking and widely-distributed image (see Figure 10.3), the king appeared as a mere severed head, whose blood would fertilize the nation's soil. His only residual value to the polity now lay in the material recycling of his body to provide nourishment for the people.

FIGURE 10.2 *"You knew me too late." Anonymous caricature of 1791, featuring Louis XVI as a pig eating a pie while seated on a gilded chair, one of several similar images of this date. Bibliothèque nationale de France, département Estampes et photographie, RESERVE QB-370 (23)-FT 4 [detail].*

A gory scene was reported to have transpired at the king's execution, when those present were purposely sprayed with "the blood of a tyrant" as if it were holy water. A media-savvy witness to this scene supposedly cried out, "'Friends, what are we doing? This will all be reported; we'll be depicted internationally as a ferocious and bloodthirsty people!' Someone replied: yes, thirsting for the blood of a despot. Let them report that worldwide, if they want." As predicted, the émigré noble Alexandre du Tilly vividly described these "flows of blood poured with cannibal barbarity" to English high society.[30] Whether such events were true or not—the question would divide royalists and republicans for decades—the dialogue between ruler

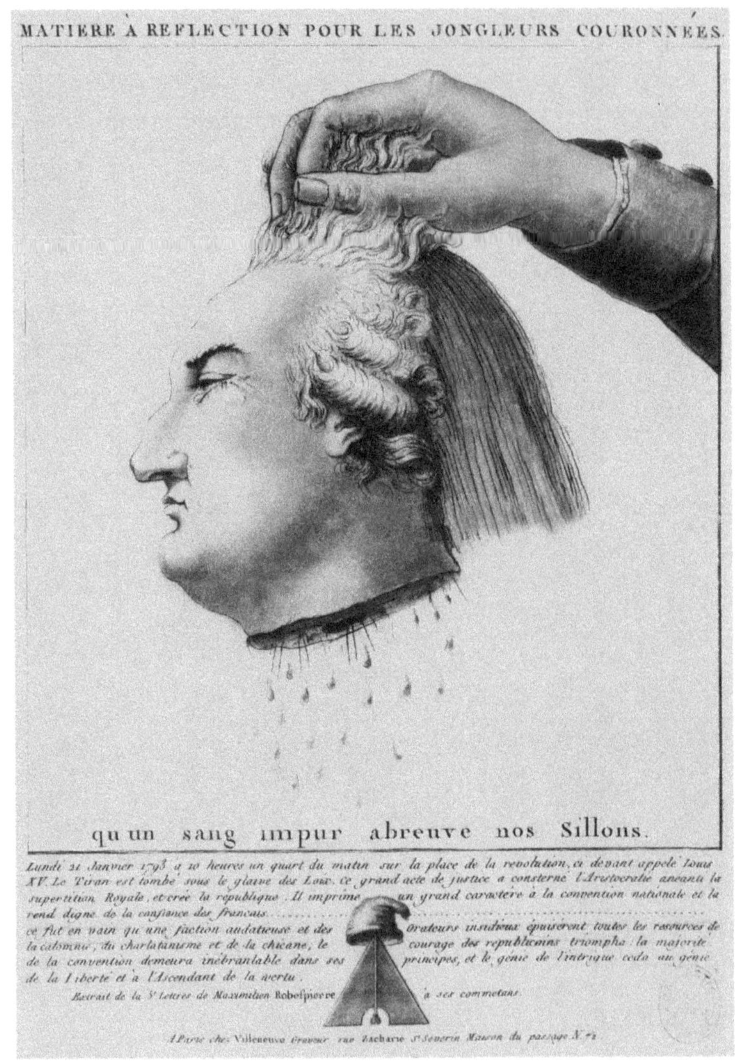

FIGURE 10.3 *Royal blood fertilizing French fields: Anon., "Matière à reflection pour les jongleurs couronnées: qu'un sang impur abreuve nos Sillons," [Paris?: n.p.], 1793. Bibliothèque nationale de France. Getty Images.*

and population was now being written in blood, mediated by the printing press, and structured by the figure of eating and drinking.

Anthropophagic themes also resonated among opponents of the Revolution. In the wake of the September massacres, the English caricaturist James Gillray portrayed sans-culottes gorging themselves on human flesh (see Figure 10.4).[31] For anti-Jacobins in both England and France, the revolutionary crowd seemed driven by a hunger beyond the bounds of need,

FIGURE 10.4 *James Gillray, "Un petit soupèr a la Parisiènne: or—A Family of Sans Culotts refreshing after the fatigues of the day." Etching with hand coloring 1792. The Fitzwilliam Museum, Cambridge.*

reason, or comprehension. At the king's trial, the Gironde deputy Alexandre Deleyre saw quite clearly the horns of the republican dilemma: "If you sacrifice Louis, you'll have countless enemies abroad; but if you keep him alive, how many more at home?" Extended starvation under monarchical rule might, he contended, have altered the blood of the people so as to turn them into ravening, carnivorous beasts, devoid of any capacity for political judgment. If Louis were kept alive, "once [the people] has devoured the remains of the prey we seem to be saving for their fury, they'll end up devouring each another, not differentiating friends from enemies."[32] The ultimate fate of the Revolution was to devour itself.[33]

This motif of the bloodthirsty, carnivorous political actor recurred time and again. It was used with particular effectiveness against the Montagnards, the radical wing of the Convention. Georges Couthon, Robespierre's close associate, complained after Marat's assassination that journalists "said, after I'd defended the interests of the people particularly energetically one day, that I needed a glass of blood to refresh myself, I who am afraid of blood, and repelled by the sight of a dead body . . . Really? People who are murderers are accusing us of being blood-drinkers?"[34] After Robespierre's fall, a pamphlet appeared advertising a "Leopard-Barrère" for sale for 150,9870,617 francs, which, despite an externally sociable manner, possessed a "character of ferocity, cruelty, atrocity through weakness," although "he hasn't yet been seen to eat human flesh."[35] The leopard's namesake was Bertrand Barère, an outspoken member of the Committee of Public Safety. In January 1795, motions were passed against Jacobin "terrorists and blood-drinkers" at the café de Chartres, while at the café des Canonniers someone was arrested as a "Jacobin blood-drinker."[36]

The Revolution's opponents forged links between democratic political action and mindless savagery. Yet nearly identical rhetorical figures were mobilized by its supporters to legitimate the grievances provoking revolutionary violence. The king, ministers, nobles, and tax farmers were frequently depicted feeding upon the body and blood of the nation (see Figure 10.6 in the source section for this chapter). In the view of Thuau-Granville, editor of the *Moniteur* in year IV, the *intendants*, Crown officials who had governed France's provinces, were "pashas . . . who grew fat on the flesh of peoples and weakened them with forced labor, taxation, misery and hunger in order to keep them obedient . . . that troupe of contractors, quenching its thirst in the shadows upon the blood of human victims, trembled with rage."[37] At the king's trial, the Moselle deputy François-Paul-Nicolas Anthoine declared that the monarch "allowed the purest of men's blood to be sucked by horrible vampires. Louis deserves to die." His words were echoed by other deputies, like Pierre-Charles-François Dupont, deputy of the Hautes-Pyrénées.[38]

Ironically, it was a real butcher, Louis Legendre, who, as president of the National Convention, oversaw the trial of the "butcher of Nantes," Jean-Baptiste Carrier, so named for his role in the deaths of counter-revolutionaries, 132 of them literally killed inside the town's butchery. A 1795 account of these inglorious episodes from the Vendée uprising framed Carrier and his agents as "cannibals" moved by the "instinct of a tiger."[39] Yet Carrier himself had resorted to the language of cannibalism in a pamphlet published the previous year by order of the Convention, the assembly which had dispatched him to handle the uprising. Here he accused the Vendée rebels in exactly the same terms: they were, according to him, "fanatical tigers" and "cannibals," who had cut body parts off loyal republicans before throwing them into "their black dungeons."[40] With such linguistic convergence characterizing the debate over sovereignty and violence in government, it was increasingly difficult for ordinary readers to distinguish the good guys from the bad. Who should eat whom? Clearly, themes of eating and drinking extended far more deeply into French political culture than the pragmatic question of filling the empty bellies of the poor. Good and legitimate governance was marked by right eating practices, but the French disagreed fundamentally over what those were.

Feeding the Nation

The Englishwoman Charlotte West and her friend and husband were in Châlons-sur-Marne when the royal family passed through on their humiliatingly public return to Paris after the flight to Varennes.[41] She and her friend waited upon Marie-Antoinette and the royal children under guard.

Later, West watched troops coming through the town, en route to and from the besieged frontier. The town being short of food, she noted an important difference between British and French eaters: "Potatoes was a vegetable very little known, and less used by the French." Although she and her family used potatoes whenever possible, "my [French] *servants* would not *eat them*, and asked me if I took them for *pigs*! but *pigs*, or not *pigs*, they were obliged to eat them, at that time, or go without any thing in the shape of bread."[42] Revolutionary shortages brought lurking worries about the relationship between food production and consumption, as well as the role of the ruling authority in underwriting that relationship, to the fore in public debate. These centered upon particular iconic foods.

If revolutionary interventions in the food supply were predicated on a promise to relieve the lot of the hungry, government projects for accomplishing that end proved less than successful. Problems continued for nearly a decade, so the main way most people experienced the French Revolution, where food was concerned, was as a time of want and frugality, with food frequently lacking or in short supply. Attempts to replace the Crown administration with a new centralized and rationalized system of food production and trade, so far from ending hunger, would exacerbate the supply crisis around France, even in the normally affluent capital. Successive regimes struggled to establish a legislative framework capable of producing a dependable national food supply. The National Assembly began from the standpoint that liberalizing the grain trade would allow supply and demand for foods to balance naturally. Yet by 1793, the situation looked, if anything, worse than it had in 1789.[43] Ordinary people were marching in the streets for bread, and raiding grocers' shops for coffee and sugar.[44] In Year II, the newly-founded Committee of Public Safety reverted to a paternalistic approach similar to the monarchical era, implementing a price cap upon bread and other goods, known as the General Maximum. Throughout the revolutionary decade, successive regimes swung back and forth between commitments, respectively, to free trade and to moral-economy price controls; yet none could agree as to which foods counted as legitimate cause for public unrest.[45]

In the political debate, bread was paramount before 1794. At least in Paris, a daily supply of white, wheaten bread was the sign, for the city's poor, that society was functioning as it should: as one advisor warned the Committee of Public Safety, bread was "an electric spark in popular crises."[46] Some radical Jacobins, interpreting this public demand as the "will of the people," called for enforced wheat cultivation on all areas of cultivatable land, and even sent to the scaffold landowners found to have replaced wheat with other crops.[47] Others radically reappraised the very definition of dietary "needs," worrying that government programs would merely habituate new groups of consumers around the country to luxurious white bread, creating needs where before there were none. Numerous trials of substitutes like rice, acorns, nuts, and potatoes, suitable for succoring the virtuous republican, were conducted. The deputy Jacques-Michel Coupé harangued the National

Convention for a return to a primitive Gallic patriarchalism, characterized by economy, sobriety, and frugality, and exhorted cultivators to exploit local resources, such as beech mast and acorns to replace olive oil.[48] Good republicans should prioritize foods provided by nature to the territory of France. The accent on primitivism was also to be found in individual deputies' practices of conspicuously frugal consumption.[49]

Jacobin disagreements expressed not only the opposition between carnivore and herbivore, but also enduring public suspicion over official attempts to provide substitutes for bread, although some of those were familiar staples in other European cultures. As Charlotte West's remarks indicate, the potato was one such contentious vegetable, rejected by many Old Regime French consumers. During the republic's most radical phase in 1793–4, this humble tuber would be taken up by authorities as "one of the greatest presents of Nature" and the "food of the free man." By 1796 there were no fewer than five nationally-funded potato mills in operation, converting millions of potatoes to dried product for year-round use. Industrialization and political idealism converged in the promotion of the potato.[50]

The symbolic rupture in the nourishing relationship between monarch and subjects that had characterized the moral economy was addressed in republican symbolic culture by replacing the figure of the monarch-provider with that of nature or providence. Many educated reformers took it as axiomatic that nature was benevolently inclined towards the Revolution and would provide for the needs of all, provided every republican acted with austere self-restraint and fraternal equity. Artists portrayed nature as Diana of Ephesus, the goddess at whose many breasts republicans might feed (see Figure 10.5). In connection with what Lynn Hunt has memorably termed the "family romance" of the French Revolution, such images evoked both a contestation of different styles of sovereignty—the male monarch versus the female nation—and contemporary debates over the legitimacy of wet-nursing, a practice that separated élite from poor parents.[51] The paternalist moral contract was to yield to faith in nature as provider.

The retreat from radicalism during the Directory period and beyond correlated with a retreat from the dietary Utopianism of the years between 1792 and 1794. The deputy Antoine-François Fourcroy had served in the government after Marat's assassination, but in the wake of Robespierre's discredit, he sought to distance himself from his radical past: "In my household, five people and I lived on potatoes; I have seen what no-one had seen up to then, what perhaps no-one will ever see again, an entire government . . . living in such privation." Although touted as a favored food of republicans a few years before, the potato could now be used as a marker for shortage and thus as proof that political radicalism was bad government.[52]

Much political importance was attached to the settlement of food crises. It was not merely a matter of providing the entire country with food, but, first and foremost, of deciding what counted *as* food, let alone the quantities an individual body required to survive—and lastly, who was empowered to

FIGURE 10.5 *Louis-Charles Ruotte, "La Liberté et l'Egalité unies par la Nature," Paris: Potrelle, Year IV [1795–6]. Nature, as the goddess Diana of Ephesus, is shown enthroned above the heads of Liberty and Equality, with milk-filled breasts ready to nourish her Republican children. Bibliothèque nationale de France, département Estampes et photographie, RESERVE FOL-QB-201 (139).*

decide such matters. Around the country, republican administrators and popular societies struggled to account for food shortages. Some relied on reason, using quantitative measures to evaluate and regulate the distribution of food resources; others promoted the cultivation of substitute foodstuffs vetted by doctors and chemists, or proselytized about household economy.[53] Many such initiatives and the experts who promoted them had been supported by the monarchy before 1789, but the Revolution afforded unparalleled opportunities for reformers to make direct and sometimes radical contributions to national food policy. After Thermidor, however, government views on the ideal diet shifted, and officials, chemists, and publics began to show more interest in meat. Dominique Godineau notes that when food complaints on the streets of Paris increased again from January 1794 onwards, they were now directed at butchers rather than bakers: "the lines before butcher shops began in the middle of the night."[54] And by 1802, a Napoleonic Minister could argue that "since the Revolution, meat has almost become the ordinary food of the people: which was not formerly true."[55]

Food riots might have served a useful political purpose in toppling royal rule and justifying revolutionary government. But in light of the fragile hold on sovereignty experienced by successive republican regimes, bread marches—one of the main ways women engaged with national food policy—increasingly appeared a threat to social order.[56] The public domain was rife with rumors concerning famine plots, which testified eloquently to the profound insecurities produced by the dismantling of moral-economic structures for famine relief. Up to 1794, marchers were seen as having political legitimacy for their grievances, and administrators scrambled to be seen to be addressing problems with the food supply.[57] Later, the National Convention applied more repressive measures, sending mounted troops out to drive hunger marchers back to their homes, for example during the so-called "Hunger Insurrection" of 1 prairial, Year III (May 20, 1795). Such actions generated ironic responses to the whole principle of revolution. As the revolutionary anthem "Ça ira" ("It'll be fine") was being played in August 1795, a man in the crowd called out "It'll be even finer when you give us our pound of bread."[58] Bitter reproaches over the price of bread were leveled against the government in public spaces; women threatened suicide if the ration were not increased.[59] If the Revolution was undertaken on a platform of addressing hunger, some eaters felt distinctly cheated, and they responded to attempts at quantification and centralization by recollecting the old political order more charitably. In the spring of Year III (1795), one disaffected citizen wandering down Paris's rue Jacob was arrested for shouting "We need a king, long live the king! If we had a king, at least we'd have bread."[60] Food shortages posed a significant risk to political support for the republic among ordinary people, as well as to the principle that the popular will was the source of sovereign legitimacy. It is clear therefore that public violence over food-related issues was neither mindless nor uncontrollable. Rather, it was problematic precisely because it had previously served as a legitimate premise for challenges to political sovereignty.

Increasingly, administrators began to pose questions about *when* food riots were legitimate. Did the French public *need* meat, and was rioting for it legitimate? Did meat generate violence? Should true republicans prefer vegetables? How indispensable was white bread for human health? Was the State obliged to guarantee the supply of *all* foods for which people rioted, like sugar or coffee?[61] These were essential questions of governance, since they had a bearing on whether food-related bloodshed was deemed legitimate or illegitimate, the justifiable outcome of genuine want or mob rule. Political attempts to address food shortages faltered partly because practical interventions could only be deemed a success once such questions had been answered. The problem of managing the food supply was dietetic, political, and ethical as well as logistical. By the later 1790s, attempts to manage public need were often mediated in a top-down manner, through institutions which prescribed diet, such as the "poor soup" program for (often incarcerated) poor people.[62] Meanwhile, the middling sort celebrated the return of dietary choice and plenty with the invention of gastronomy and national alimentary patrimony, and gastronomic authors began to celebrate regional foods as a political cornerstone of French identity.[63] Directory France also hosted the world's first industrial exhibitions, showcasing scientific and technological novelties like chemically-produced gelatin, stock cubes, and canning. These early technoscientific interventions into the food supply tell us what the French thought food *was*, but also what they thought it was *for*, and how far the new state was considered to be responsible for providing it.

State-supported scientific research into diet took new directions after Thermidor. The later 1790s marked a retreat from direct State intervention into the food supply of the sort that had characterized both the monarchical regime and, paradoxically, its political opposite, the Jacobin government of the year II. Instead, from this time onwards, French regimes of knowledge and politics would explore ways of calibrating the body's needs, while research into human dietary requirements would be undertaken specifically to shed light on whether certain foods were actually necessary, as opposed to being addictions formed by repeated exposure.[64] This close relationship between scientific experts, government, and the management of the public food supply has become so normalized, thanks to subsequent historical phenomena such as the two World Wars and the rise of modern nutrition science, that we forget that one of its points of origin lay in the need of revolutionary regimes to stabilize public discourse over food.[65] A quantified and rationalized diet is an integral part of a much broader phenomenon of regulation producing our bodies as we understand them today.[66] We cannot see the Revolution as *responsible for* this modern complex of the quantified body with disciplined tastes, but it is possible to see the contestations of sovereignty that characterized it as creating a political space for scientific advisors who sought to rethink the body in new ways, assessing human dietary needs in light of laboratory experiments.[67]

Conclusion: In Retrospect

At the heart of the food crises of the French Revolution were profound disagreements over what food was and who controlled its production and meaning. Conversely, food could manifest the political legitimacy of a regime in multiple ways. The political concerns that surrounded eating and diet are still alive today, which is why the French Revolution remains a "landmark food-related moment in history." On July 14, 2011, the British newspaper the *Daily Mail* carried the headline "Bastille Day: in honour of butchers and murderers." Typical of this tabloid's xenophobic stance, the journalist hit out at the French for celebrating July 14 as the originary moment of their nation: "Today France celebrates its revolution with Bastille Day parades and parties. Me, I reckon that 18th century slaughter-fest should merit only a national day of mourning . . . But the French see it otherwise."[68] The journalist was unaware that she was mobilizing a 200-year-old tradition of the use of butchery metaphors by the right-wing British press, yet again to cast doubt on the political legitimacy of the French Revolution. Yet this perspective was not wholly alien to the French themselves. A century earlier, the historian Hippolyte Taine had already asked how, in pursuit of liberty, "politicians, legislators, statesmen, and even ministers and heads of government" could have ended up "in an abattoir . . . how within the confines of that national butchery, they were by turns slaughterers and cattle."[69]

Between 1789 and 1799, the relationship between food and revolution had, however, been far more multifarious than these commentators suggested. The butcher motif would briefly be mobilized in positive ways, to denote the revenge of skilled plebeians upon a cannibalistic government, literally cutting authority down to size. But in appropriating the consuming/ruling role for themselves, sans-culottes and Jacobin leaders attracted charges of anthropophagy in their turn. Where Jacobins had attacked calculating, tyrannical Old Regime vampires, the Revolution's opponents leveled charges of bestial, irrational violence against ordinary people protesting in city streets and the legislators who represented them. At the heart of this debate lay an important question over whether popular manifestations, and in particular popular violence, were legitimate means of political self-expression.[70] The fact that public hunger is so widely cited as the cause of the French Revolution—indeed of revolution in general—shows that this claim was never fully silenced by moves to contain popular political expression after 1794. Étienne Cabet's socialist history of the Revolution, written in the 1830s, made the left-wing political equation clear: "When the People are dying of hunger, they will gather in crowds; then the *cause of the riots* must be addressed in order to appease them."[71]

Yet the problem of hunger remained. Scientific accounts of the proper diet for human bodies were not stable. Government policies for managing the food supply shifted between promoting frugality and a plant-based diet as more "natural" to the French, and representing meat as essential to national wellbeing and public order. This dialectic which cast the French by turns as vegetarians or carnivores, eaters or prey, held sway in revolutionary discourse throughout the decade. These dietary opposites were recognized by contemporaries, even outside France, as equally undesirable extremes that served to illustrate the consequences of radical politics. So much is evident from two of Gillray's most famous caricatures—both, not coincidentally, published in 1792, the year the republic was founded. "French Liberty—British Slavery" and "Un petit soupèr a la Parisiènne" show sans-culottes eating onions in one image, and babies in another (see Figure 10.4 above). Both vegetarian and cannibalistic outcomes were held up as equally undesirable consequences of bad government.

The issue of how politics perverted appetites, hinted at in Gillray's images, remained unresolved, partly because it continued to be impossible to develop either a scientific or a political solution to the question of food needs and entitlement.[72] Through the lens of food metaphors, we can see that a history of food in the French Revolution must address debates about entitlement and responsibility; about rights; and about right government. Such political-metaphorical uses of food continued well beyond the revolutionary decade, for example in the set of engravings—published in different European languages—which censured the French general and future emperor Napoleon Bonaparte for his territorial conquests in the Revolutionary Wars by caricaturing him as a "world-eater."[73] Historians, as James Vernon shows, can never afford to understand hunger as a mere biological urge.[74] To do so is to take sides with just one of the many groups of eaters who made the Revolution.

Source: Anon., "L'Hydre aristocratique," Paris, 1789

FIGURE 10.6 *Anon., "L'Hydre aristocratique," Paris, 1789. "This male and female monster has nothing human about it but its heads; its nature is ferocious, barbarous and bloodthirsty; it feeds only on the blood, tears and subsistence of the unhappy people." Bibliothèque nationale de France, département Estampes et photographie, RESERVE QB-370 (10)-FT 4 [detail].*

Notes

1 https://www.smithsonianmag.com/arts-culture/when-food-changed-history-the-french-revolution-93598442/, accessed March 22, 2018.

2 Even in the Revolution's most extreme phase, members of the legal profession predominated in government. Edna Hindie Lemay, "La Composition de l'Assemblée nationale constituante: les hommes de la continuité?," *Revue d'histoire moderne et contemporaine* 24 (1977): 341–63; Timothy Tackett, *Becoming a Revolutionary: The Deputies of the French National Assembly and the Emergence of a Revolutionary Culture (1789–1790)* (Princeton, NJ: Princeton University Press, 1996), chap. 1; Malcolm Crook, *Elections in the French Revolution: An Apprenticeship in Democracy, 1789–1799* (Cambridge: Cambridge University Press, 1996), 80–1; Melvin Edelstein, *The French Revolution and the Birth of Electoral Democracy* (Farnham, UK: Ashgate, 2014), 269ff.; Lynn Hunt, *Politics, Culture and Class in the French Revolution*, new ed. (Berkeley: University of California Press, 2004), chap. 8; Alison Patrick, *The Men of the First French Republic: Political Alignments in the National Convention of 1792* (Baltimore, MD: Johns Hopkins University Press, 1972), 365.

3 Keith Michael Baker, Colin Lucas, François Furet, and Mona Ozouf, eds., *The French Revolution and the Creation of Modern Political Culture*, 4 vols. (Oxford: Pergamon, 1987–94). On harvest failures, see, e.g., Joerg Baten, "Climate, Grain Production and Nutritional Status in Southern Germany during the 18th Century," *Journal of European Economic History* 30, no. 1 (2001): 9–48, 26; Robert A. Dodgshon, "Coping with Risk: Subsistence Crises in the Scottish Highlands and Islands 1600–1800," *Rural History* 15, no. 1 (2004): 1–25, 3; James Kelly, "Scarcity and Poor Relief in Eighteenth-Century Ireland: The Subsistence Crisis of 1782–4," *Irish Historical Studies* 28, no. 109 (1992): 38–62; Leslie F. Musk, "Glacial and Post-Glacial Climatic Conditions in North-West England," in *Geomorphology of North-West England*, ed. R. H. Johnson (Manchester: Manchester University Press, 1986), chap. 4, 77; Charles R. Ritcheson, *Aftermath of Revolution: British Policy Toward the United States, 1783–1795* (Dallas, TX: Southern Methodist University Press, 1969), 199–203; Gustaf Utterström, "Some Population Problems in pre-Industrial Sweden," *Scandinavian Economic History Review* 2, no. 2 (1954): 103–65, 111; Walter Bodmer, "Die Bewegungen einiger Lebensmittelpreise zwischen 1610 und 1821 verglichen mit denjenigen in Luzern und Zürich," *Schweizerische Zeitschrift für Geschichte* 34, no. 4 (1984): 449–67, 462; Oiva Turpeinen, "Les causes des fluctuations annuelles du taux de mortalité finlandais entre 1750 et 1806," *Annales de démographie historique* (January 1980): 287–96; Klemens Kaps, "Creating Differences for Integration: Enlightened Reforms and Civilizing Missions in the Eastern Europe Missions of the Habsburg Monarchy (1750–1815)," in *Enlightened Colonialism: Civilization Narratives and Imperial Politics in the Age of Reason*, ed. Damien Tricoire (Cham: Palgrave Macmillan 2017), 111–55. Several states in fact experienced more severe famine in the early 1770s; see, e.g., Michel Morineau, "Budgets populaires en France au XVIIIe siècle," *Revue d'histoire économique et sociale* 50, no. 4 (1972): 449–81, 452–3; Martin Dribe, Mats Olsson, and

Patrick Svensson, "Nordic Europe," in *Famine in European History*, ed. Guido Alfani and Cormac Ó Gráda (Cambridge: Cambridge University Press, 2017), 187–212.

4 Jules Michelet, *Histoire de la Révolution française*, in *Œuvres complètes*, 40 vols. (Paris: Ernest Flammarion, 1893), 17:297; Hippolyte Taine, *Les origines de la France contemporaine*, 4 vols. (Paris: Hachette, 1901–4), passim.

5 The British Marxist historian E. P. Thompson characterized this as "the spasmodic view of popular history." See E. P. Thompson, "The Moral Economy of the English Crowd in the Eighteenth Century," *Past & Present* 50 (1971): 71–136, 71.

6 "Headless Horseman," *New Yorker*, June 5, 2006, https://www.newyorker.com/magazine/2006/06/05/headless-horseman, accessed March 23, 2018.

7 Philip Fisher, "Art and the Future's Past," in *Museum Studies: An Anthology of Contexts*, ed. Bettina M. Carbonell, 2nd ed. (Chichester: Wiley-Blackwell, 2012), 457–72, 467.

8 [Jules Guiffrey,] "Documents inédits sur le mouvement populaire du 14 juillet 1789 et le supplice de M. de Launay, gouverneur de la Bastille, et de Berthier de Sauvigni," *Revue historique* 1, no. 497–508 (1876): 501.

9 *Supplément au Journal de Paris*, January 26, 1790. The soldier's name was Soudin. See [Guiffrey,] Documents inédits," 498, note 1.

10 [Guiffrey,] "Documents inédits," 500. This particular expertise suggests Desnot had worked as a *rôtisseur*, a cook specializing in roast meats.

11 For an archivally-grounded revision of the restaurant myth, see Rebecca L. Spang, *The Invention of the Restaurant: Paris and Modern Gastronomic Culture* (Cambridge, MA: Harvard University Press, 2000). On cooks in the eighteenth century, see especially the work of Jennifer Davis, *Defining Culinary Authority: The Transformation of Cooking in France, 1650–1830* (Baton Rouge: Louisiana State University Press, 2013); Jennifer Davis, "To Make a Revolutionary Cuisine: Gender and Politics in French Kitchens, 1789–1815," *Gender & History* 23, no. 2 (2011): 301–20; Sean Takats, *The Expert Cook in Enlightenment France* (Baltimore, MD: Johns Hopkins University Press, 2011).

12 As, for example, in a recent "Awesome Story" of the French Revolution, https://www.awesomestories.com/asset/view/French-Revolution-Storming-the-Bastille, accessed January 20, 2018.

13 [Guiffrey,] "Documents inédits," 505.

14 On the butchery trade, see especially Sydney Watts, *Meat Matters: Butchers, Politics and Market Culture in Eighteenth-Century Paris* (Rochester, NY: University of Rochester Press, 2006); on the guilds, see, most recently, Michael P. Fitzsimmons, *From Artisan to Worker: Guilds, the French State, and the Organization of Labor, 1776–1821* (Cambridge: Cambridge University Press, 2010), 73–6, 92–3.

15 On one memorable occasion, Legendre threatened to "brain" a fellow deputy, Jean-Denis Lanjuinais. François Victor Alphonse Aulard, *Les orateurs de la Legislative et de la Convention*, 2 vols. (Paris: Hachette, 1885–6), 2:99; see also August Kuscinski, *Dictionnaire des Conventionnels* (Yvelines: Brueil-en-Vexin, 1973), 392–4.

16 "Extraits de l'ouvrage intitulé *la Loire vengée, ou Recueil historique des crimes de Carrier et du Comité révolutionnaire de Nantes*," in *Archives curieuses de la ville de Nantes et des départements de l'Ouest*, ed. François-Joseph Verger (Nantes: Forest, 1837), I:219–36; 227; Louis Mayeul de Chaudon, ed., *Dictionnaire universel, historique, critique et bibliographique*, 9th ed. (Paris: Prudhomme fils, 1812), 18:217–18.

17 http://schools-wikipedia.org/wp/f/French_Revolution.htm, accessed March 22, 2018.

18 For an interesting reflection upon the continued use of these themes, see Maxime Carvin [pseud.], "Deux siècles de calomnies: Robespierre sans masque," *Le monde diplomatique*, November 2015, 3.

19 John Russell, 1st Earl Russell, *The Causes of the French Revolution* (London: Longman et al., 1832), 12–18.

20 On French vegetarianism, see Tristram Stuart, *Bloodless Revolution: Vegetarianism and the Discovery of India* (London: HarperPress, 2006); Colin Spencer, *The Heretic's Feast: A History of Vegetarianism* (London: Fourth Estate, 1993), chaps. 9–10; E. C. Spary, *Eating Beyond Reason* (forthcoming), introduction; Pierre Serna, *Comme des bêtes: Histoire politique de l'animal en révolution* (Paris: Fayard, 2017). For the British case, see especially Timothy Morton, *Shelley and the Revolution in Taste: The Body and the Natural World* (Cambridge: Cambridge University Press, 1994); Anita Guerrini, "A Diet for a Sensitive Soul: Vegetarianism in Eighteenth-Century Britain," *Eighteenth-Century Life* 23, no. 2 (1999): 34–42; Anita Guerrini, "Health, National Character and the English Diet in 1700," *Studies in History and Philosophy of Biological and Biomedical Sciences* 43, no. 2 (2012): 349–56.

21 Alphonse Leroy, *De la nutrition, et de son influence sur la forme et la fécondité des animaux sauvages et domestiques* (Paris: Crapelet, Year VI/1797–8), 25.

22 Thompson, "Moral Economy of the English Crowd"; more recently, John Bohstedt, *The Politics of Provisions: Food Riots, Moral Economy, and Market Transition in England, c. 1550–1850* (Aldershot: Ashgate, 2010). For France, see especially Louise A. Tilly, "The Food Riot as a Form of Political Conflict in France," *Journal of Interdisciplinary History* 2 (1971): 23–57; Louise A. Tilly, "Food Entitlement, Famine and Conflict," *Journal of Interdisciplinary History* 14 (1983): 333–49; Cynthia A. Bouton, "Les mouvements de subsistance et le problème de l'économie morale sous l'ancien régime et la Révolution française," *Annales historiques de la Révolution française (AHRF)* (2000): 71–100.

23 Bibliothèque nationale de France, RESERVE QB-201 (170)-FT 4. On royal support for agricultural reform, see John Shovlin, *The Political Economy of Virtue: Luxury, Patriotism, and the Origins of the French Revolution* (Ithaca, NY: Cornell University Press, 2006); Octave Festy, *L'agriculture pendant la Révolution française: L'utilisation des jachères 1789–1795* (Paris: Librairie Marcel Rivière et Cie., 1950); Jean Boulaine, *Histoire de l'agronomie en France* (Paris: Lavoisier Tec & Doc, 1992).

24 Steven L. Kaplan, *Bread, Politics and Political Economy in the Reign of Louis XV*, 2 vols. (The Hague: Nijhoff, 1976); Steven L. Kaplan, *Provisioning Paris: Merchants and Millers in the Grain and Flour Trade During the Eighteenth Century* (Ithaca, NY: Cornell University Press, 1984); Robert Darnton, "Le

lieutenant de police J.-P. Lenoir, la guerre des farines et l'approvisionnement de Paris à la veille de la Révolution," *Revue d'histoire moderne et contemporaine* 16 (1969): 611–24.

25 Cynthia A. Bouton, *The Flour War: Gender, Class and Community in Late Ancien Régime French Society* (University Park: Pennsylvania State University Press, 1993).

26 On these and other initiatives, see E. C. Spary, *Feeding France: New Sciences of Food* (Cambridge: Cambridge University Press, 2014).

27 Claude Fischler, *L'homnivore. Le goût, la cuisine et le corps* (Paris: Editions Odile Jacob, 1993). On gluttony and the royal family, see especially Spang, *The Invention of the Restaurant*, chaps. 4–5.

28 Reynald Abad, *Le grand marché: L'approvisionnement alimentaire de Paris sous l'Ancien Régime* (Paris: Fayard, 2002), part I, chap. 8.

29 See Joan B. Landes, "Revolutionary Anatomies," in *Monstrous Bodies/Political Monstrosities in Early Modern Europe*, ed. Laura Lunger Knoppers and Joan B. Landes (Ithaca, NY: Cornell University Press, 2004), 148–78, 155; Annie Duprat, "Le langage des signes: Le bestiaire dans la caricature révolutionnaire," *History of European Ideas* 17, no. 1 (1993): 201–5; also, in general, Annie Duprat, "Louis XVI condamné par les images," *Information historique* 54, no. 4 (1992): 133–41. On French caricature, see James Cuno, ed., *French Caricature and the French Revolution, 1789–1799* (Chicago: University of Chicago Press, 1988); Annie Duprat, *Histoire de France par la caricature* (Paris: Larousse, 1999); Annie Duprat, "Le Regard d'un royaliste sur la Révolution: Jacques-Marie Boyer de Nîmes," *AHRF* 337 (2004): 21–39; Claude Langlois, *La caricature contre-révolutionnaire* (Paris: Presses du CNRS, 1988).

30 Louis Prudhomme, *Révolutions de Paris, dédiées à la Nation* 1, no. 15, 205, quoted in *Histoire parlementaire de la Révolution française*, ed. Philippe-Joseph-Benjamin Buchez and P.-C. Roux (Paris: Paulin, 1836), 23:325; *Mémoires du comte Alexandre de Tilly pour servir à l'histoire des moeurs de la fin du XVIIIe siècle* (Paris: Mercure de France, 1986), 591.

31 On English caricatures and the Revolution, see Pascal Dupuy, *Face à la Révolution et l'Empire. Caricatures anglaises (1789–1815)* (Paris: Paris-Musées, 2008).

32 *Le Procès de Louis XVI, ou Collection complette, des Opinions, Discours et Mémoires des Membres de la Convention nationale, sur les crimes de Louis XVI* (Paris: Debarle, year III/1795), 309–19.

33 See Maggie Kilgour, *From Communion to Cannibalism: An Anatomy of Metaphors of Incorporation* (Princeton, NJ: Princeton University Press, 1990).

34 Jérôme Mavidal et al., eds., *Archives parlementaires de 1787 à 1860: recueil complet des débats législatifs et politiques des chambres françaises*, series 1, 2nd ed. (Paris: Dupont; CNRS, 1862–) [henceforth *AP*], 69:18, session of July 15, 1793.

35 [Martin?], *Description et Vente Curieuse des animaux féroces mâles et femelles, de la ménagerie du cabinet d'histoire naturelle des ci-devant Jacobins, les cris et les hurlemens de chaque heure, et leur utilité* (Paris: Gaulemeriti, n.d.), 8.

36 François-Victor-Alphonse Aulard, ed., *Paris pendant la réaction thermidorienne et sous le Directoire. Recueil de documents pour l'histoire de l'esprit public à*

Paris (Paris: Librairie Léopold Cerf, Librairie Noblet et Maison Quantin, n.d.), 1:415, 438–40; Marisa Linton and Mette Harder, "'Come and Dine': The Dangers of Conspicuous Consumption in French Revolutionary Politics, 1789–95," *European History Quarterly* 45 (2015): 615–27.

37 *AP*, 1:23. On Thuau-Granville, see Joseph-Marie Quérard, *La France littéraire*, 9:466.

38 *Le Procès de Louis XVI*, 4:176, 112; Antoine de Baecque, "Le discours anti-noble (1787–1792) aux origines d'un slogan: 'Le Peuple contre les gros'," *Revue d'histoire moderne et contemporaine* 36, no. 1 (1989): 3–28. Similarly, *AP*, 53:401, opinion of Claude Fauchet (Calvados), session of November 13, 1792 (appendix).

39 "Extraits de l'ouvrage intitulé *la Loire vengée*," originally published 1795.

40 *Convention Nationale. Rapport de Carrier, représentant du Peuple Français, sur les différentes missions qui lui ont été déléguées* (Paris: Imprimerie Nationale, year III), 28.

41 Timothy Tackett, *When the King Took Flight* (Cambridge, MA: Harvard University Press, 2003).

42 Charlotte West, *A Ten Years' Residence in France, During the Severest Part of the Revolution; From the Year 1787 to 1797, Containing Various Anecdotes of some of the Most Remarkable Personages of That Period* (London: William Sams and Robert Jennings, 1821), 46–7.

43 Another traveler, Helen Maria Williams, noted in March 1795 that "a man's daily wages, instead of purchasing four or five pounds of meat, as they would before the revolution, now only purchase one," *A Residence in France, During the Years 1792, 1793, 1794, and 1795; Described in a Series of Letters from an English Lady* (New York: Cornelius Davis, 1798), 461.

44 Olwen Hufton, "Women in Revolution, 1789–1796," *Past & Present* 53 (1971): 90–108; Olwen Hufton, "Social Conflict and the Grain Supply in Eighteenth-Century France," *Journal of Interdisciplinary History* 14 (1983): 303–31; Olwen Hufton, *Women and the Limits of Citizenship in the French Revolution* (Toronto: University of Toronto Press, 1999), chap. 1; Rebecca L. Spang and Colin Jones, "Sans-Culottes, Sans Café, Sans Tabac: Shifting Realms of Necessity and Luxury in Eighteenth-Century France," in *Consumers and Luxury: Consumer Culture in Europe 1650–1850*, ed. Maxine Berg and Helen Clifford (Manchester: Manchester University Press, 1999), 37–62; E. C. Spary, *Feeding France*. Bouton, *The Flour War*, 110–12, notes that, even on such marches, it was rarely the poorest in society who took part.

45 Albert Mathiez, *La vie chère et le mouvement social sous la Terreur* (Paris: Payot, 1927), part II; Michael L. Kennedy, *The Jacobin Clubs in the French Revolution, 1793–1795* (New York: Berghahn Books, 2000), chap. 7.

46 Archives Nationales de Paris, F^{11} 435–436: Antoine-Alexis Cadet de Vaux, "Rapport au Comité de Salut public," [before 21] Frimaire, Year III/December 11, 1794; Kaplan, *Bread, Politics and Political Economy*; Steven L. Kaplan, *The Bakers of Paris and the Bread Question, 1700–1775* (Durham, NC: Duke University Press, 1996).

47 E.g. [Louis-Pharamond Pandin], *Vues patriotiques d'un cultivateur, dont l'objet est de rendre le pain de froment commun à tous les citoyens de la République sans distinction* (Paris: Fr. Buisson, Year III/1794).

48 Jacques-Michel Coupé, *Rapport et projet de decret présentés au nom des Comités d'agriculture et des domaines, sur la récolte des Faînes, Glands & Fruits sauvages des bois* ([Paris]: Imprimerie nationale, [Year II/1794]); Henri Wallon, *Histoire du tribunal révolutionnaire de Paris avec le journal de ses actes*, 6 vols. (Paris: Hachette, 1881–2), 2: chap. 23; also Spary, *Eating Beyond Reason* (forthcoming), chap. 2.

49 Linton and Harder, "Come and Dine," 618–21.

50 Spary, *Feeding France*, chap. 5, with quotes 180, uttered by the Paris Commune and the Subsistence Commission respectively.

51 Lynn Hunt, *The Family Romance of the French Revolution* (London: Routledge, 1992). On Diana of Ephesus, see Madelyn Gutwirth, *The Twilight of the Goddesses: Women and Representation in the French Revolutionary Era* (New Brunswick, NJ: Rutgers University Press, 1992), "Imageries of the Breast"; Marina Warner, *Monuments and Maidens: The Allegory of the Female Form* (Berkeley: University of California Press, 2000/1985), chap. 12; Londa Schiebinger, *Nature's Body: Gender in the Making of Modern Science* (Boston: Beacon Press, 1993). On the late eighteenth-century campaign against wet-nursing, see especially Mary Jacobus, "Incorruptible Milk: Breastfeeding and the French Revolution," in *Rebel Daughters: Women and the French Revolution*, ed. Sara E. Melzer and Leslie W. Rabine (New York: Oxford University Press, 1992), 54–75; Lindsay Wilson, *Women and Medicine in the French Enlightenment* (Baltimore, MD: Johns Hopkins University Press, 1993), 111–12; George D. Sussman, *Selling Mothers' Milk: The Wet-Nursing Business in France, 1715–1914* (Champaign: University of Illinois Press, 1982); Sean M. Quinlan, *The Great Nation in Decline: Sex, Modernity, and Health Crises in Revolutionary France, c. 1750–1850* (Aldershot: Ashgate, 2008), 26–33. On milk as a food, cf. especially Barbara Orland, "Enlightened Milk: Reshaping a Bodily Substance into a Chemical Object," in *Materials and Expertise in Early Modern Europe: Between Market and Laboratory*, ed. Ursula Klein and E. C. Spary (Chicago: University of Chicago Press, 2010), 163–97.

52 Georges Kersaint, *Antoine-François de Fourcroy (1755–1809). Sa vie et son oeuvre* (Paris: Editions du Muséum, 1966), 32; Linton and Harder, "Come and Dine," 620–9.

53 Spary, *Feeding France*, passim.

54 *The Women of Paris and their French Revolution* (Berkeley, Los Angeles, and London: University of California Press, 1998/1988), 175. The struggle faced by the republican authorities to micro-manage the meat supply following the introduction of rationing is vividly described by Adolphe Thiers, *The History of the French Revolution* (Auburn, NY: J. C. Derby & Co., 1847), 3:39.

55 Archives nationales de France, F[11] 1147, pièce 6. For later developments, see Vincent J. Knapp, "The Democratization of Meat and Protein in Late Eighteenth- and Nineteenth-Century Europe," *The Historian* 59, no. 3 (1997): 541–51, 544; Deborah Neill, "Of Carnivores and Conquerors: French Nutritional Debates in the Age of Empire, 1890–1914," in *Setting Nutritional*

Standards: Theory, Policies, Practices, ed. Elizabeth Neswald, David F. Smith, and Ulrike Thoms (Rochester, NY: University of Rochester Press/Woodbridge, UK: Boydell and Brewer, 2017), 74–96.

56 This "transfer of sovereignty" argument stems from François Furet's classic *Penser la Révolution française*, translated as *Interpreting the French Revolution* (Paris: Editions du Maison des Sciences de l'Homme and Cambridge: Cambridge University Press, 1988). On female hunger protests, see Olwen Hufton, "Women in Revolution 1789–1796," *Past & Present* 53 (1971): 90–108; David Garrioch, "The Everyday Lives of Parisian Women and the October Days of 1789," *Social History* 24, no. 3 (1999): 231–49; Dominique Godineau, *The Women of Paris and Their French Revolution*, trans. Katherine Streip (Berkeley, Los Angeles, and London: University of California Press, 1998).

57 On the "language of virtue," which took public discourse as the expression of the general will, and therefore the proper foundation for the new civic order, see especially Marisa Linton, *Choosing Terror: Virtue, Friendship and Authenticity in the French Revolution* (Oxford: Oxford University Press, 2013); Mary Ashburn Miller, *A Natural History of Revolution: Violence and Nature in the French Revolutionary Imagination, 1789–1794* (Ithaca, NY: Cornell University Press, 2011). On famine plots, see especially Haim Burstin, *Révolutionnaires: Pour une anthropologie politique de la Révolution française* (Paris: Vendémiarie, 2013); Cynthia A. Bouton, "Gendered Behavior in Subsistence Riots: The French Flour War of 1775," *Journal of Social History* 23 (1990): 735–54; Steven Kaplan, *The Famine Plot Persuasion in Eighteenth-Century France* (Darby, PA: Diane Publishing Co., 1982); Lindsay Porter, *Popular Rumour in Revolutionary Paris, 1792–1794* (Cham: Palgrave Macmillan, 2017), chap. 4.

58 Cited in Adolf Schmidt, *Paris pendant la Révolution d'après les rapports de la police secrète, 1789–1800*, 4 vols. (Paris: Champion, 1880–94), 3:17ff.; Morris Slavin, *The French Revolution in Miniature: Section Droits-de-l'Homme, 1789–1795* (Princeton, NJ: Princeton University Press, 1984), 163–6.

59 Spary, *Feeding France*, 312.

60 Report of the policemen Barbarin and Beurlier on public order, 27 floréal Year III/May 16, 1795, quoted in *Tableaux de la Révolution Française*, ed. Adolphe Schmidt, 3 vols. (Leipzig: Veit & Co., 1869), 2:337.

61 Rebecca L. Spang, "The Frivolous French: 'Liberty of Pleasure' and the End of Luxury," in *Taking Liberties: Problems of a New Order from the French Revolution to Napoleon*, ed. Howard G. Brown and Judith A. Miller (Manchester: Manchester University Press, 2002), chap. 5.

62 Sandra Sherman, *Imagining Poverty: Quantification and the Decline of Paternalism* (Columbus: Ohio State University Press, 2001).

63 Julia Csergo, "La constitution de la spécialité gastronomique comme objet patrimonial en France (fin XVIIIe–XXe siècle)," in *L'esprit des lieux. Le patrimoine et la cité*, ed. Daniel J. Grange and Dominique Poulot (Grenoble: Presses Universitaires de Grenoble, 1997), 183–93; Julia Csergo, "La modernité alimentaire au XIXe siècle," in *À table au XIXe siècle* (Paris: Flammarion, 2001), 42–69; Julia Abramson, "Legitimacy and Nationalism in the *Almanach*

des Gourmands (1803–1812)," *Journal for Early Modern Cultural Studies* 3, no. 2 (2003): 101–35.

64 Spary, *Feeding France*, chap. 8.

65 Harmke Kamminga and Andrew Cunningham, eds., *The Science and Culture of Nutrition, 1840–1940* (Amsterdam: Rodopi, 1995); Frederic L. Holmes, "The Transformation of the Science of Nutrition," *Journal of the History of Biology* 8, no. 1 (1975): 135–44; Nick Cullather, "The Foreign Policy of the Calorie," *American Historical Review* 112, no. 2 (2007): 337–64; Lizzie Collingham, *The Taste of War: World War Two and the Battle for Food* (London: Allen Lane, 2012); L. M. Barnett, *British Food Policy during the First World War* (Boston: Allen & Unwin, 1985).

66 John Coveney, *Food, Morals and Meaning: The Pleasure and Anxiety of Eating*, 2nd ed. (London: Routledge, 2006); Ina Zweiniger-Bargielowska, *Managing the Body: Beauty, Fitness and Health in Britain 1880–1939* (Oxford: Oxford University Press, 2010); Peter N. Stearns, *Fat History: Bodies and Beauty in the Modern West* (New York: New York University Press, 2002); Tim Armstrong, ed., *American Bodies: Cultural Histories of the Physique* (Sheffield: Sheffield Academic Press, 1996).

67 Dana Simmons, *Vital Minimum: Need, Science, and Politics in Modern France* (Chicago: University of Chicago Press, 2015); Frank Stahnisch, "Den Hunger standardisieren: François Magendies Fütterungsversuche zur Gelatinekost 1831–1841," *Medizinhistorisches Journal* 39 (2004): 103–34.

68 Mary Ellen Synon, "Bastille Day: In Honour of Butchers and Murderers," *Mail Online*, July 14, 2011, http://synonblog.dailymail.co.uk/2011/07/bastille-day-in-honour-of-butchers-and-murderers.html, accessed February 28, 2018.

69 Taine, *Origines de la France contemporaine*, 5:10–11.

70 Micah Alpaugh, *Non-Violence and the French Revolution: Political Demonstrations in Paris, 1787–1795* (Cambridge: Cambridge University Press, 2014), though scarcely mentioning hunger as a reason for revolutionary marches, notes that the majority elapsed without violence.

71 *Histoire populaire de la Révolution française de 1789 à 1830, précédée d'une introduction contenant le précis de l'histoire des Français depuis leur origine jusqu'aux États-généraux*, 4 vols. (Paris: Pagnerre, 1839), 1:332 (original emphasis). On Cabet, see Nathalie Brémand, "Etienne Cabet jusqu'en 1840," *Les premiers socialismes—Bibliothèque virtuelle de l'Université de Poitiers*, 2010, http://premierssocialismes.edel.univ-poitiers.fr/collection/etiennecabetjusquen1840>, accessed July 17, 2018.

72 Simmons, *Vital Minimum*.

73 Rolf Reichardt, "Napoleon der 'Weltfresser'? Die europäische Karriere eines anti-revolutionären Bildmotivs," in *Napoleonische Expansionspolitik: Okkupation oder Integration?*, ed. Guido Braun et al. (Berlin: Walter de Gruyter, 2013), 241–70.

74 James Vernon, *Hunger: A Modern History* (Cambridge, MA: Belknap Press of Harvard University Press, 2007).

11

Spectacles of French Revolutionary Violence in the Atlantic World

Ashli White

Madame Tussaud, whose wax museums attract millions of visitors today, got her start during the French Revolution. She apprenticed under her uncle, Philippe Curtius, who ran one of the most stylish wax museums in Paris (see Map 0.2). While there, she was a frequent witness to the political violence of the late 1780s and early 1790s: she crossed riots in the streets, she watched as crowds attacked the Bastille, and she saw the guillotine fall again, and again. Tussaud also claimed that the government called upon her, whenever someone notable died, to cast that person's head. In her capacity as a wax artist, she supposedly held Maximilien Robespierre's "severed head in her lap," handled Jean-Paul Marat's "still warm . . . and bleeding body," and modeled a likeness of the Princesse de Lamballe from her decapitated head, "whilst surrounded by the brutal monsters, whose hands were bathed in the blood of the innocent."[1]

Tussaud took a good deal of license with her past, and so the details of her memoirs, including the grisly conditions under which she fashioned her figures, are suspect. However, we do know that in 1802 she arrived in England with several wax heads of famous individuals who had died between 1793 and 1794: Louis XVI, Marie-Antoinette, and Robespierre, among others. Although Tussaud's fantastic success and longevity as a wax artist are exceptional, her choice of subjects for exhibition was part of a broader trend. In the last quarter of the eighteenth century, artists throughout the Atlantic world staged shows of life-sized wax figures that featured French revolutionary deaths prominently.

How do we explain this, from our perspective, unexpected cultural phenomenon during the French Revolution? This chapter recovers these forgotten, but at the time widespread, exhibitions in order to understand how people made sense of revolutionary-era violence. Although violence in the Revolution took on various forms, wax artists highlighted the Terror (1793–4) and those of its features that were most striking to Atlantic observers: what became its iconic instrument (the guillotine), its volume and pace, and the high profile of some victims (aristocrats, royals, and self-avowed revolutionaries).[2] From the moment it began, the Terror was a source of debate. Even revolutionaries recognized the contrast between "our virtues" and the "horrors that we committed," and, ever since, scholars have tried to account for it, too.[3] The explanations run the gamut. Some historians see the Terror as the inevitable product of revolutionary ideology and the political culture of the Revolution; others interpret it as a response to the specific circumstances of 1793–4— either a consequence of fear and paranoia among revolutionaries, or an effort to prevent further popular violence.[4]

While its roots were many, the Terror's impact on France is undeniable. But it also resonated in the broader Atlantic world, especially in Britain and the United States. Observers there learned about the violence in France through various means. Newspapers, periodicals, and first-hand reports were influential sources of information, and engravings translated written accounts into eye-catching scenes. Scholars have emphasized that these accounts and images mapped onto existing political debates in Britain and the United States and contributed to polarization in each place. The Terror drove some Britons and North Americans to oppose the Revolution, and those who continued to be sympathetic to the French project faced increasing pressure at home.[5]

The exhibitions of wax figures related to French revolutionary events, however, suggest that this is only part of the story. By transforming news into spectacles, the wax figures elicited from audiences a range of cognitive and emotional responses, ones that defy tidy categorization as "for" or "against" the French Revolution. As the first section of this chapter establishes, the conventions of the medium aimed to transfix viewers with its intense realism. When wax artists applied these standards to their depictions of French revolutionary deaths, they offered viewers a powerful and unique experience of the Terror. To explore the dynamics of these experiences, we will analyze two often-reproduced deaths—those of Louis XVI and Jean-Paul Marat—that bring to light different aspects of the Terror's influence abroad. With the execution of Louis XVI, viewers wrestled with the implications of the death of this particular monarch and with the use of the guillotine. In the case of Marat's assassination, attention focused less on the target of violence than on its perpetrator, Charlotte Corday, and, as a result, visitors were confronted with the question of women's participation in revolutionary violence.

Together, these examples allow us to see how the political violence of the French Revolution entered the everyday lives of people far removed from the center of action. The wax displays took the conversation out of the realms of rarefied intellectual debate and party politics and into entertainment halls. With this change of venue, the exhibitions created what we might think of as a "virtual" experience of violence. Clearly, visitors to US and British wax museums did not observe the actual deaths of these individuals; yet, they did have potent encounters with French revolutionary violence—ones that for some viewers felt remarkably "real." In this way, Atlantic audiences engaged actively with the consequences of witnessing French political violence in an enlightened age.

When Madame Tussaud arrived in England, she was just one of the latest practitioners of a familiar art that was centuries old. The Egyptians and ancient Greeks and Romans produced wax figures for both religious and secular purposes, and the practice persisted in medieval and early modern Europe with funeral effigies for royals and other dignitaries.[6] In the eighteenth century, scientists and doctors used wax figures for anatomical study, celebrating them as vehicles of reform.[7]

Significantly, for our purposes, displays of life-sized wax figures also emerged as a popular entertainment throughout the Atlantic world in the decades before the French Revolution. These shows were "popular" in both senses of the term: they were trendy and affordable. Wax figures appeared in amusement halls in London and Paris and in their smaller-scale incarnations in North America and the Caribbean.[8] Some were grand like Philippe Curtius's *salon de cire* at the Palais-Royal, complete with expensive furniture and props, ornate architectural detail, and dramatic lighting.[9] Others were more modest traveling shows staged in rented rooms, taverns, hotels, and other places.[10]

Whatever their scale, eighteenth-century wax exhibitions featured an array of notables. Artists portrayed historical, literary, and biblical characters, but in order to lure audiences to visit repeatedly, they relied on introducing renditions of individuals who had lately captured the public interest. These luminaries, one advertisement proclaimed, "must be highly gratifying to all, who, having heard of the fame of their characters, wish to see . . . their persons."[11] People could "see" these "characters" in prints too; however, wax artists prided themselves on producing representations closest to life. Not only were they life-sized, but wax has the uncanny capacity to imitate human flesh. This quality, along with accessories such as actual hair and clothing, intensified the realism of the wax figure.[12] Promotional copy highlighted the provenance of clothing especially, sometimes noting that the real person had worn the clothes that appeared on the wax figure.[13]

The hyper-realism of wax sculpture created a compelling viewing experience. Eighteenth-century spectators frequently professed that they had mistaken a wax figure for a living person. In a letter to his local paper, "Columbus" described his visit to an artist's studio in New York, where he thought a wax figure of the Virgin Mary was an actual woman. Not until he, at the artist's urging, touched the woman's "solid, cold" hand did "the curtain of delusion disappear."[14] Unlike other visual deceptions of this era that were offered up as puzzles to delight audiences, wax figures were less about ferreting out the ruse and more about giving oneself over to the encounter.[15] When a spectator did so, practitioners maintained that he or she would discover important truths through, as one artist put it, "the most agreeable sensations."[16] These "sensations," according to performance historian Joseph Roach, amounted to a "vivid intimacy" in which viewers connected with the person portrayed as well as the qualities, events, and other attributes with which that person was associated.[17] By gazing on individuals, even in simulacrum, one could identify various virtues (or vices) in their very faces. What's more, a spectator could look at a wax figure with an intensity that civility, status, and other factors prohibited in interactions with a living person. As a result of this ability to scrutinize, encounters with wax figures, artists argued, could prove even more instructive than those with the actual individuals portrayed.

In light of these practices and notions about wax figures, it is not surprising that late eighteenth-century revolutionaries from across the Atlantic world appeared in wax displays. Some wax artists saw their inclusion as an opportunity for visitors to participate in the political debates of the day.[18] In the 1770s, the wax artist Patience Wright produced a series of figures sympathetic to the patriot cause in North America for her London showroom. When anyone complimented her republican figures, she remarked, "My good friend, you may behold those men's hearts in their faces."[19] Their very visages reflected their principles, and in Wright's estimation, her art helped people to understand republican ideology in a way that was easier to access and more persuasive than any treatise or text.

For all their vaunted rhetoric, however, wax artists had few qualms about using the unique characteristics of their medium for another purpose: to probe the macabre.[20] When visiting a gallery of wax figures in Philadelphia, John Adams felt as if he were "walking among a group of corpses."[21] He found unnerving the suspended motion of the figures—some laughed, others cried, and still others walked, sat, or stood. Their poses, combined with their hyper-realistic features, created a morbid experience, and for some visitors, this creepiness was part of the allure. They enjoyed the thrill of dabbling safely in dark matters, and, aware of these less lofty impulses, wax artists regularly staged wax recreations of infamous murders, replete with gore.[22]

Given the conventions of the genre, wax figure exhibitions were almost ready-made venues for exploring the violence of the Terror. They traded on the timely, with the twin aims of instruction and entertainment, and they evoked both life and death. When the Terror began in earnest, wax artists were quick to recreate some of the most controversial deaths for visitors. The execution of Louis XVI in January 1793 initiated the trend. In this era, public executions of criminals were commonplace in the Atlantic world. In New York alone, almost 70 people were hanged between 1776 and 1796 for crimes ranging from arson, counterfeiting, and forgery to rape, murder, and robbery.[23] These were massive events, drawing large crowds comprised of all sectors of the population. The novelty of Louis's death, then, was not that it was an execution *per se*—rather, that it was the execution of a king by guillotine. Wax artists sought to capitalize on the public's fascination, and in their renditions of the scene, they amplified two thorny aspects of the subject at hand: who was being executed and how. These issues had broader political significance in the United States and Britain, albeit in different ways.

During his trial and execution, the French revolutionary regime insisted on calling Louis XVI, Louis Capet. It was crucial to the government's endeavor to desacralize and delegitimize monarchy. But wax displays of the execution still referred to him as "king." Such a stance is expected in Britain, where the defense of monarchy was central to denunciations of the French Revolution.[24] Perhaps more interestingly, it persisted in the United States as well. Reuben Moulthrop, for example, notified the New Haven public "That he has modeled [*sic*] in Wax, a striking Likeness of the KING OF FRANCE in the Act of losing his Head under the GUILLOTINE, preserving every Circumstance which can give the Eye of the Spectator a realizing View of that momentous and interesting Event."[25] Employing the monarch's title—in capital letters, no less—was, in part, a marketing ploy, for Moulthrop and other wax artists understood that what was extraordinary about this execution, compared to others, was the status of the victim. But the choice betrays some political ambivalence, too. After all, Louis XVI was a familiar face in the United States from its own revolution. The visual culture of the American Revolution had celebrated the US–French alliance, and the king was a key figure in those homages. Even after independence, Americans continued to honor the French monarchy with a pair of magnificent state portraits of the king and queen that hung in the congressional assembly room.[26] Given this recent past, it was hard for Americans—even the most radical among them—not to see Louis XVI as a king.

In both the United States and Britain, the insistence on the title was instrumental to the drama of the scene. It played up the disjuncture between the traditional treatment of a monarch and the circumstances of his death. First, there was the question of his appearance. Thanks to widely circulated, written accounts, Moulthrop and other artists knew that Louis did not wear monarchical trappings at his execution. Reports noted that before ascending the scaffold, he removed his coat and met his fate "with his neck and breast bare," wearing only "a clean shirt and stock, white waistcoat, black florentine silk breeches, black silk stockings, and his shoes were tied with black silk strings."[27] This state of undress—in public—was unthinkable for an eighteenth-century monarch and contributed to signaling just how revolutionary the event was. With their faithful recreations, the wax displays made this visible for audiences.

Then there was the effect of the execution on Louis's body. On this score, Daniel Bowen's waxwork reveals how far artists were willing to go to present the episode in all its gruesome detail. An advertisement for his

Philadelphia show describes what visitors could expect from his version of Louis XVI's death:

> When the last signal is given . . . the king lays himself on the block, where he is secured. The executioner then turns and prepares to do his duty, and, when the second signal is given, the executioner drops the knife and severs the head from the body in one second. The head falls in a basket, and the lips, which are first red [*sic*], turn blue.[28]

Automata formed at least part of Bowen's display, and while this was unusual, his attention to detail (of lips turning from red to blue, for example) is in keeping with the overall impulse of this medium and its adherents: to bring hyper-specificity to the death of this man.

By reconstructing Louis's execution so meticulously, wax artists invited viewers to deliberate whether the punishment fit his alleged crime. This debate was already raging in print. Many Britons decried Louis's fate, and even Thomas Paine, who had made such a mockery of monarchy in *Common Sense* (1776), claimed that his death was unjust because of his endorsement of the American Revolution.[29] But the wax displays made the execution an emotional experience for visitors, and their visceral reactions informed their political appraisals. Critics were worried that audiences' conclusions would not be condemnatory—that they would see the execution of Louis XVI as a cause for celebration or as an amusement like the others in museums. William Cobbett, an outspoken opponent of the French Revolution, complained in a local paper of Bowen's exhibition:

> The queen of France, the calumniated Antoinette, was the first foreigner . . . that advanced a shilling in the American cause. Have I ever abused her memory? . . . It was not I that guillotined her husband, in an automaton, every day, from nine in the morning till nine at night, for the diversion of the citizens of Philadelphia.[30]

Cobbett argued that the distasteful exhibition desensitized audiences; the relentless repetition (twelve hours each day) and its placement among other diversions made Americans forget that they owed, to a certain extent, their independence and citizenship to the French king and queen.

Others defended the didactic potential of visual representations of the execution. At his London office, the printer William Lane offered an engraving of the "Massacre of the King of France" for three pence. The "very cheap" price was intentional so "that this horrid and unjust Sacrifice . . . should be known to all classes of People, and in particular to the honest and industrious Artisan and Manufacturer, who might be deluded by the false and specious pretences of artful and designing persons." He felt it his duty to make sure that "the conduct of France, in their destruction of Monarchy . . . be publicly and universally known."[31] Lane emphasized that people needed to see the carnage for themselves—if only in simulacrum—in order to comprehend the terrible price of political revolution. If Lane thought that prints had the power to make the horror more real, wax tableaux were even more convincing in this respect.

The reactions of audiences, however, were hard to shape consistently—even within the same crowd. A London newspaper recounted an episode where a woman, upon seeing a Louis XVI wax figure guillotined at a local show, "could express her feelings only by broad unfeeling laughter." Whether this laughter was gleeful or nervous is unclear, but this ambiguity is the problem; emotional reactions to the displays were unpredictable and hence, in the minds of some, politically dangerous. In this instance, the woman was censured by other spectators, and as the newspaper was careful to note, some women in attendance "were so distressed at the bare representation of such an outrage to human nature, as to leave the room in tears"—a response that the editor felt was more fitting for an "Englishwoman."[32] The comment suggests, though, that a reliable response was difficult to ensure.

The instability of reactions points to a central tension with the shows: that they were amusements. As such, some critics felt that their instructive potential was at odds with the need to entertain. This tension surfaced not only around the question of Louis XVI's execution, but also around his mode of death. Hangings were the typical means of execution throughout the Atlantic world; guillotine-like machines had been employed in Europe in the past, but they were rare.[33] With their prominent and recurring use in revolutionary France, people were eager to see this technology in action. One English newspaper summed it up bluntly: "[I]t is presumed the curiosity of the Public will be gratified by the View and the Effect of an Instrument like that by which [Louis XVI] suffered."[34]

There was an ideological aspect to the guillotine as well. Its adoption in France had resulted from an extended campaign among self-proclaimed enlightened individuals who touted the humanity of the machine. Penal reform movements in Britain and the United States got their start during this era, too, and in light of French arguments, the issue arose as to whether the guillotine might be a less cruel form of capital punishment.[35] Proponents contended that the criminal died swiftly—a mercy for the subject and the crowd, as both experienced less anguish. Moreover, mechanization spared the executioner the stigma traditionally associated with his profession.[36] These claims had Atlantic resonance, and guillotine displays of Louis XVI were a chance for individuals to weigh the benefits and drawbacks of the machine for themselves.

Consider the impressions of John DePeyster, a member of the New York elite, who saw a guillotine at the Tammany Society's museum in 1794. He wrote to his brother-in-law, Charles Willson Peale, that the guillotine had "a figure on it, of a Man who has his head Severed from his Body,—Verry Natural—but the most frightfull-awfull sight that can be Imagined."[37] His revulsion stemmed less from the act of execution and more from the method:

"I . . . Coencide in opinion with every Man, who condem's the publick Exhibition of such a Machien in a Country where it is hoped it will never be put in Use,—Especially when it has a Corpse on it, in the Attitude and appearance of Reallity."[38] The mere sight of the guillotine at work, even in a wax simulation, endorsed violence by the same means.

In the early 1790s, Peale was debating whether he should acquire a guillotine for his museum in Philadelphia, and DePeyster discouraged him in the strongest of terms. A guillotine in a museum was like stopping in "a Summer House" only to find "five or Six hooks to it, to hang Men on by the Neck."[39] Men like Charles Willson Peale saw a museum as a place where people could better themselves by what they encountered there, becoming more virtuous citizens to sustain the US republican experiment.[40] A guillotine in such a setting, DePeyster made clear, transformed a site of uplift into a killing field. The other exhibitions could not temper the guillotine's impact: DePeyster claimed that during his visit, the guillotine "drove every other Consideration from me."[41]

Others must have thought similarly because the caretaker of the Tammany Society's museum tried to mitigate negative reactions by keeping the guillotine separate from the rest of the exhibitions and by offering to show it with or without the body. The advertisement explained almost apologetically, "when the Machine is seen alone, nothing appears horrible."[42] Yet for some, the problem was not the body—it was the machine itself. The replacement of human with mechanical action—one of the merits of the guillotine—heightened anxiety.[43] Early modern capital punishment relied on lengthy spectacle as a clear demonstration of State power. The scaffold was the stage for a drama that took some time to perform, including speeches, appeals, and other rituals.[44] While gruesome, this prolonged practice was essential for crowd catharsis, a sense of justice achieved. With the guillotine, the pace of the executions accelerated exponentially. In the case of Louis XVI, the *London Magazine* reported, "the short length of time in which he appeared on the scaffold, and the interval of the fatal blow, was no more than two minutes."[45] The deadly speed, accuracy, and durability of the guillotine encouraged repetition. One English observer named Mary Russell noted with horror that it took only thirteen minutes to decapitate sixteen men.[46] Critics claimed that such tempo and volume numbed onlookers: "The Parisians have been too long familiarized to the sight of blood, to be affected by seeing it stream from *only* twenty-one bodies at a time!"[47] The machine's bloodlust seemed insatiable, as did that of the crowds who attended the executions, and some wondered if the killings would ever stop.[48]

The guillotine's association with Louis XVI's execution and with the Terror more generally discouraged penal reformers outside of France from adopting it for use. Without doubt, graphic wax displays also convinced elite men like DePeyster, Cobbett, and Lane to reproach the Revolution that embraced it. Some may have reached the same conclusions without ever seeing the tableaux, but the exhibitions, more than newspaper accounts or engravings, brought mixed and wider audiences closer to the experience of Louis XVI's execution. In the process, they opened up a Pandora's box of reactions, as visitors laughed, cried, were curious, or revolted. These emotional and physical responses introduced greater uncertainty into Atlantic observers' impressions of the Revolution that had produced such a spectacle in the first place.

Some of the same factors were at work in the second wax tableau under consideration: the assassination of Jean-Paul Marat by Charlotte Corday. In contrast to Louis XVI, Corday captured public interest from a position of obscurity, but her case became the first in a series of high-profile trials, and subsequent executions, of eminent women with various political associations. The year 1793 saw the guillotining of Olympe de Gouges, Madame Roland, Madame du Barry, and Marie-Antoinette, among others. These deaths were reported in the US and British press; however, only Corday's example was transformed into a wax display in North America. At first glance, the choice of Corday over, say, Marie-Antoinette is surprising: Marie-Antoinette was a queen, and so the aspects that made her husband's death noteworthy applied to her as well. But from the perspective of wax artists, the similarities were a drawback: Marie-Antoinette's execution lacked novelty, whereas Corday's death had it in spades. What made Corday a prime candidate for a wax figure was her murder of Jean-Paul Marat. The wax displays staged the assassination, and because Corday was an agent rather than a victim of violence, these exhibitions brought to the fore the provocative question of women's participation in revolutionary violence.

The standard account of Marat's assassination goes something like this: in early July 1793, Corday, a twenty-four-year-old woman from Caen (see Map 0.1), traveled to Paris, with the goal of killing the man whom she blamed for what she saw as the Revolution's errant path. Marat was a vocal mouthpiece for the rising tide of radical sentiment; self-styled as "the friend of the people," he published a newspaper of the same name, in which he denounced those whom he felt had betrayed the Revolution. As a deputy in the National Convention, Marat had the power to convert words into action and under his influence more and more of his political enemies were imprisoned or, if lucky, fled. Corday intended to kill Marat at the national festivities on July 14, but, on reaching Paris, she learned that illness confined him to his apartment. On July 13, Corday visited his building twice and was denied entry. Not easily thwarted, she sent a note to Marat, claiming that she had information worth his time. Falling for the ruse, Marat agreed to see Corday, whom he received while soaking in a rented bathtub to relieve a skin condition. She took out a knife she had purchased earlier and stabbed him in the chest. He died almost instantly, and Corday was seized by neighbors, arrested by officials, and taken to prison. She stood trial on July 17 and was beheaded the same day.[49]

The murder and trial captivated publics at home and abroad, and French officials tried to make Marat the focal point. Marat's funeral, orchestrated by the artist Jacques-Louis David, was an elaborate affair that venerated him as a republican martyr.[50] But for all the pomp and ceremony surrounding Marat in Paris, Corday upstaged him outside of France. Audiences were curious about this heretofore unheard-of woman, and newspapers throughout the Atlantic world rehearsed whatever details they could learn about her story.

Popular visual representations emphasized the assassination scene, and wax artists did the same. In the United States, wax renditions of "the unparalleled murder of Marat, by Miss Cordie, in France" soon appeared.[51] At Bowen's Museum in Boston, she was depicted "holding the bloody Dagger over the dead Body of MARAT." According to accounts, Corday's single blow had gone straight to the heart, resulting in torrents of blood, so for wax artists the opportunity for reproducing gore was high. Advertisements suggest that artists indulged in this vein: the assassination was "placed in a separate Apartment, and may be viewed or not, at the pleasure of the Company."[52] As with the guillotine, squeamish visitors could avoid the scene, while those who braved it could luxuriate in the lurid representation.

Wax recreations of Corday relied on the same dynamics that were at work in representations of Louis XVI: hyper-realism, the spectator's ability to linger, and the relationship between pleasure and horror. But in this instance a woman stood at the center of action, one who transgressed gendered expectations by perpetrating a violent and political crime. On one level, Corday offered yet another example for the lively trade in crime fiction and "true crime" stories that found an eager readership in the eighteenth-century Anglophone world. Of these narratives, those of "[a] female Offender," one period commentator declared, "excites our curiosity more than a male."[53] At times, female killers could be cast sympathetically. At their most radical, authors critiqued patriarchy and its social, economic, and legal supremacy that left women with few options.[54]

In general, however, accounts of female murderers were cautionary tales, meant to warn female readers to safeguard their virtue through vigilant conduct. During the Age of Revolutions, republicanism became part of the definition of that virtue. Although war and lawmaking were allegedly a man's business, the rhetoric of revolution opened up possibilities for women to act. In France, the vocal and sometimes very physical participation of white women in politics was initially celebrated, but around the time of Marat's assassination, some revolutionaries worked to rein in women's political activity and sequester their contributions to the home.[55] Their efforts were never entirely successful, and their rhetoric became increasingly shrill, as evidenced by the harsh denunciations of prominent women.[56] Officials subjected Corday to damning accusations, yet these stubbornly refused to stick—in large part because of the way she managed her narrative in the aftermath of her crime.

The influence of gender in interpretations of Marat's assassination is apparent in US wax displays. Despite the universal condemnation of murder across the Atlantic world and attempts by some republicans to check women's political action, exhibition promoters described Corday as "beautiful" and "tragical." The juxtaposition of these adjectives with the vivid recreation of the assassination scene created a cognitive tension between the sympathetic actor and her heinous deed. It is worth examining each term closely to see how it shaped audiences' understandings of this instance of revolutionary violence. First, Corday the "beautiful." While Louis XVI's face was recognizable throughout the Atlantic world long before his execution, Corday's was not, and she sought to change that by requesting, from prison, that an artist take her portrait. She couched her appeal in clever terms: "I would like to leave this token of my memory to my friends. Indeed, just as one cherishes the image of good citizens, curiosity sometimes seeks out those of great criminals, which serves to perpetuate horror at their crimes."[57] Corday played to the regime's desire to stress the "horror" of her act, but the resulting portrait by Jean-Jacques Hauer undercut that "horror" by highlighting her beauty.

Although there was some variation in staging and detail, a few tropes recur frequently enough to suggest how Charlotte Corday looked—in wax and other media. Most show her as young and slim, with long locks, a serene face, and elegant stature. Madame Tussaud, who claimed that she visited Corday in jail, described her as "tall and finely formed; her countenance had quite a noble expression; she had a beautiful color, and her complexion was remarkably clear; her manners were extremely pleasing, and her deportment particularly graceful."[58] Her clothing accentuated her beauty. On the day of the murder, she wore a stylish, but sensible striped dress, a tall black hat decorated with jaunty green ribbons, a pink scarf, and gloves.[59] In Hauer's prison portrait she wears a different set of clothes—a white bonnet and simple dress, which showed her good taste and modesty. In both scenarios, her dress is appropriate for a woman of her background and rank.[60]

Since wax artists adhered as faithfully as possible to written accounts, their recreations of the assassination no doubt reproduced these features of Corday's appearance. Rather than an enraged or deranged murderess, spectators saw a self-possessed, lovely, and young woman—with knife in hand. For the French revolutionary regime, Corday's beauty was a political problem. It stood in stark contrast to Marat's physical deformity: the reason Corday had found him in the bathtub was to seek relief for a chronic skin ailment that compromised his body and health. In an age when outward appearance was thought to manifest one's inner character, Corday's beauty and Marat's disease muddied the waters of culpability.[61] His bodily corruption could be interpreted as an external manifestation of perverted principles, and although she was caught red-handed, her beauty, in contrast to his malady, hinted that perhaps not all was as straightforward as it seemed.

French authorities tried to counteract this interpretive tendency in two ways: they attempted to characterize Corday in negative terms, and they focused public attention on Marat. At a time when marriage was expected for women of Corday's age, officials cast her as an "old maid" to insinuate that she was deviant, and some suggested that she was not a woman at all. The Marquis de Sade described her as one of "those mixed beings to which one cannot assign a sex, vomited up from Hell to the despair of both sexes."[62] He insisted that "all those who have dared to present her as an enchanting symbol of beauty should be stopped."[63]

But these negative textual descriptions did not translate into an outpouring of unflattering visual portrayals, and so, some revolutionaries directed audiences to ignore Corday altogether. After Robespierre visited Philippe Curtius's wax tableau of Marat and Corday, he entreated the crowds in line outside to concentrate on Marat, "our departed friend, snatched from us by an assassin's hand, guided by the demon of aristocracy."[64] Jacques-Louis David, in his *The Death of Marat*, painted three months after the assassination, removed Corday completely in an effort, as art historian Helen Weston has persuasively contended, to negate her power. He also reinvigorated Marat's body, giving him a manly torso, strong arms, smooth skin, and saintly aura.[65]

In most portrayals, though, the erasure of Corday was impossible to sustain. It is telling that even Curtius, in the heart of revolutionary Paris, felt compelled to include Corday in the scene. Marat and Corday were inextricably linked in the public eye, and people wanted to see the woman who had managed such a feat. The demand meant that her beauty was replicated, including in North American waxworks, introducing seeds of doubt into what the French revolutionary regime had hoped to make into a simple morality play.

In wax displays and elsewhere, Corday was cast as "beautiful," but beauty alone was not enough to make her, rather than Marat, the "tragical" figure in the scenario. While the definition of "tragedy" is a moving target, changing over time and by context, the term designates, at its most basic, a sad event that precipitates a feeling of loss. In drama, the tragic mode encourages sympathy for the sufferer from the audience, which experiences catharsis at the play's conclusion.[66] The case of Corday and Marat draws on both the event definition (the assassination occurred) as well as the dramatic one (its reproduction in wax tableaux). Despite all Jacobin propaganda to the contrary, Corday, instead of Marat, emerged as the object of sympathy for many in the Atlantic world, and this had political repercussions.

Wax displays of Corday and Marat were shaped by her actions in the immediate aftermath of the assassination. Newspapers in Britain and the United States reported extensively on her trial and execution. A few early articles were unflattering, but they were the exception in the Anglophone press, where her conduct was portrayed positively. Observers at her trial remarked that she "struck every person with respectful awe, and the idea of her as an assassin was removed from every mind."[67] Corday maintained the same poise before the guillotine: "You would have said, when she was conducted to the scaffold, that she was marching to a nuptial feast; she appeared with a gay air and smile on her lips, and a modest deportment without affectation." Even the executioner "appeared profoundly penetrated with grief at the mission he had to fulfill."[68] The specific circumstances of her decapitation were the stuff of legend: when the executioner showed her head to the crowd, he allegedly slapped a cheek. Onlookers recoiled from the disrespectful treatment, but it also "restored to her cheeks their former animated glow," a reanimation reminiscent of tales of saints and martyrs. Although people cried "vive la république," some accounts concluded that "the spectators dispersed less impressed with the recollection of her crime, than of her courage and beauty."[69]

Corday could not have performed better had she been following a script. Her actions were beyond reproach—so much so that they hinted that the assassination was justified, too. Thanks to her impeccable behavior, Corday managed to cast doubt on whether her murder of Marat was truly criminal. In the United States, Corday's conduct struck a chord, and she was held up as an exemplar, although an imperfect one. A 1798 "sketch" of Corday began with a preface, which pointed out that "even though she stopped the impious breath of the diabolical Marat, [she] cannot be praised for her deed. Let us look only at the brighter parts of her picture, and draw a veil over the images of terror and blood." The article speaks of Corday in effusive terms, revisiting accounts of her fortitude and calm. It closes with a reflection on the assassination, declaring it as wrong, but insisting that Corday's was "the least culpable and most disinterested instance that can be imagined; and the whole behavior of Marie Charlotte Corde exhibits a benevolence of intention and heroic firmness of mind, that perhaps has never been surpassed by woman or by man."[70] This was not exactly a scathing condemnation.

Among others, the praise was even less qualified. In 1796 a "party of Ladies" in Newburyport, Massachusetts celebrated President Washington's birthday by raising "a few glasses" with five "truly sentimental and highly republican toasts." The first two were for Washington and his wife, and the fifth had religious overtones. However, the third and the fourth reveal the power of Corday's example. The third appealed to "the fair patriots of America" who shall "never fail to assert their Independence which nature equally dispenses," while the fourth was for Charlotte Corday, with the hope that "each Columbian daughter, like her, be ready to sacrifice their life to liberty."[71] The toasts celebrate women's capacity for "independence" and cite Corday as a model for how to act on that independence. Such sentiment is easy to express when the threat is distant; after all, they were not in France. Nevertheless, there was a radicalism in the appropriation of Corday as a model, one that involved exceptional public action.

In light of these admiring stories about Corday's execution, the promotional language of "tragical" for the wax displays predisposed viewers to sympathize with the assassin rather than the assassin's victim. In so doing, wax displays critiqued the Jacobin government of the French Revolution. But there was another way to read the "tragic" aspect to Corday's story, one that neutralized Corday as a political actor: France did not witness the immediate peace that she hoped to inaugurate. Convinced that France was awash in counter-revolutionary conspiracies, the Jacobins pursued their enemies with ferocity, using the memory of Marat to justify, in part, their efforts. As a few reports pointed out at the time, Marat's assassination was disastrous for the so-called Girondins, a group of revolutionary politicians Corday had supported. Unlike Corday, "the leaders of the Girondists" (all men) knew better than to let "their passions so far . . . blind their judgments, as to encourage a murder that must excite odium against themselves and strengthen the hands of their opponents."[72] This appraisal rested on long-standing notions about how women fell prey to their emotions, resulting in poor decisions, and perhaps for some spectators at US wax exhibitions, this explanation tempered the radical nature of her act. From this perspective, wax displays of the assassination implied that if Corday, for all her virtue, beauty, and fortitude, fell short in her grand venture into public politics, then it was impossible for other women to achieve better through similar means. For some, Corday was the ultimate cautionary tale, showing just how awful the consequences could be should women in the Atlantic world engage in politics.

The wax exhibitions of the execution of Louis XVI and the assassination of Marat shed light on the many ways that audiences in the United States and Britain tried to make sense of the violence of the French Revolution. The wax displays relied on detailed written accounts and evocative prints to stage their tableaux as precisely as possible. Yet unlike first-hand reports or engravings, the exhibitions had a visceral, three-dimensional quality. This characteristic made the violence much more "real," and it put these political events in conversation with other macabre amusements—renditions of murderers, crimes, and other tragedies that played with the fraught line between pleasure and horror. According to some observers, this presentation was politically volatile in an age of revolutions, as audiences' reactions ranged from repulsion to inspiration, and they sometimes empathized with the "wrong" individuals.

The case of French revolutionary wax figures points to even larger questions of portrayals of violence and their influence on viewers. Similar to commentators today, eighteenth-century actors worried about the effects of violent depictions on the public. Would they promote violence or discourage it? Would their repetition cheapen individuals' respect for human life? And most importantly in this era, what were the political repercussions of these violent renditions? These issues plagued French revolutionaries, their opponents, and spectators in the broader Atlantic world, as they tried to gauge the costs of translating ambitious and supposedly enlightened political ideals—or, at least, their contested understandings of them—into action. This is part of the ambiguous legacy of the French revolutionary age. Although the means through which we consume violence has changed, we still wrestle with similar questions regarding its various renderings and their impact on people and politics in our present time.

Source: *Massachusetts Mercury* (Boston), December 25, 1795, page 3: This Evening—Advert for Bowen's Museum

THIS EVENING—*Dec.* 25.

Bowen's Muſeum.

AT THE HEAD OF THE MALL,
Will be open and elegantly illuminated:
With the ADDITION OF MUSIC,
On the Grand Piano Forte,
By the celebrated Dr. BERKENHEAD,
(For this Evening only.)

THE MUSEUM contains a large Collection of PAINTINGS, Hiſtorical, Theatrical, and Portraits of ſeveral of the moſt diſtinguiſhed Characters in the United States.

A large Collection of Wax-Work,

Among which are the following FIGURES, viz.

A Likeneſs of the late Rev. Dr. Ezra Stiles Preſident of Yale College, Connecticut.

Maternal Affection; or, a Lady with two beautiful Children.

A young Lady, repreſented as a ſpectator, viewing a Glaſs Ship.

A tea party of LITTLE MISSES.

Two Greenwich Penſioners, drinking and ſmoaking.

The beautiful Miſs CHARLOTTE CORDE, holding the bloody Dagger over the dead Body of MARAT, whom ſhe had aſſaſſinated.

The GUILLOTINE, with a perfect repreſentation of a Man beheaded;--with the Executioner holding up the head to public view.

BARON TRENCK, in Priſon, loaded with Chains of great weight.

Two Happy Cottagers; or, Darby and Joan, ſelling Fruit, drinking and ſmoaking.- Negroes, &c. &c. &c.

Among the NATURAL and ARTIFICIAL CURIOSITIES, are, an elegant GLASS SHIP.—A Collection of beautiful BIRDS, preſerved to the life.

An INDIAN's SCALP.--A perfect model of a 74 GUN SHIP, ſix feet in length.--With a great Variety of other pleaſing and curious Articles, in the Muſeum Hall.

☞ The GUILLOTINE and TRAGICAL WAX FIGURES, are all placed in a ſeparate Apartment, and may be viewed or not, at the pleaſure of the Company.

TICKETS of admiſſion (for that Evening only) 4s. 6d.

ANNUAL TICKETS, not transferable, FIVE DOLLARS, may be had at the Muſeum.

Mr. BOWEN reſpectfully requeſts the preſence of his ANNUAL SUBSCRIBERS on that Evening.

*** The ſtated Times for opening the Muſeum, will be, during the winter Seaſon, On every TUESDAY, THURSDAY and SATURDAY, untill Sun-ſet: And on every TUESDAY and THURSDAY EVENING from 6 'till 9 o'Clock.

Boſton, December 25.

FIGURE 11.1 Massachusetts Mercury *(Boston), December 25, 1795, page 3: This Evening—Advert for Bowen's Museum. America's Historical Newspapers, NewsBank.*

Notes

1 Francis Hervé, ed., *Madame Tussaud's Memoirs and Reminiscences of France, forming an Abridged History of the French Revolution* (London: Saunders and Otley, 1838), 96, 198, 273; Uta Kornmeier, "Almost Alive: The Spectacle of Verisimilitude in Madame Tussaud's Waxworks," in *Ephemeral Bodies: Wax Sculpture and the Human Figure*, ed. Roberta Panzanelli (Los Angeles: Getty Research Institute, 2008), 67–81.

2 On the question of the Terror as myth, see Jean Clément Martin, *Violence et Révolution: Essai sur la Naissance d'un Mythe National* (Paris: Seuil, 2006), and Martin, *Les Echos de la Terreur. Vérités d'un Mensonge d'Etat, 1794–2001* (Paris: Editions Belin, 2018).

3 Dominique-Joseph Garat, *Mémoires sur la Révolution*, quoted in Timothy Tackett, *The Coming of the Terror in the French Revolution* (Cambridge, MA: Harvard University Press, 2015), 2.

4 For classic and more recent interpretations of the Terror, see Michel Biard, ed., *Les Politiques de la Terreur, 1793–1794* (Rennes: Presses Universitaires de Rennes; Société des Etudes Robespierristes, 2008); Keith Michael Baker, ed., *The French Revolution and the Creation of Modern Political Culture, Vol. 4: The Terror* (Oxford: Pergamon, 1994); Dan Edelstein, *The Terror of Natural Right: Republicanism, the Cult of Nature, and the French Revolution* (Chicago: University of Chicago Press, 2009); Marisa Linton, *Choosing Terror: Virtue, Friendship, and Authenticity in the French Revolution* (Oxford: Oxford University Press, 2015); R. R. Palmer, *Twelve Who Ruled: The Year of the Terror in the French Revolution* (this ed., Princeton, NJ: Princeton University Press, 2017); Tackett, *The Coming of the Terror*; Sophie Wahnich, *In Defence of the Terror: Liberty or Death in the French Revolution*, trans. David Fernbach (London: Verso, 2015).

5 There is a long literature but a few important works include John Barrell, *Imagining the King's Death: Figurative Treason, Fantasies of Regicide, 1793–1796* (Oxford: Oxford University Press, 2000); David Bindman, *The Shadow of the Guillotine: Britain and the French Revolution* (London: British Museum Publications, 1989); Rachel Hope Cleves, *The Reign of Terror in America: Visions of Violence from Anti-Jacobinism to Antislavery* (New York: Cambridge University Press, 2009); and Simon P. Newman, *Parades and the Politics of the Street: Festive Culture in the Early American Republic* (Philadelphia: University of Pennsylvania Press, 1997), chap. 4.

6 Thelma R. Newman, *Wax as Art Form* (South Brunswick, NJ: Thomas Yoseloff, 1966), 84–5; Joseph Roach, *It* (Ann Arbor: University of Michigan Press, 2007), 46, 48.

7 Anna Maerker, *Model Experts: Wax Anatomies and Enlightenment in Florence and Vienna, 1775–1815* (Manchester: Manchester University Press, 2011).

8 Richard D. Altick, *The Shows of London* (Cambridge, MA: Harvard University Press, 1978), 50–6; David R. Brigham, *Public Culture in the Early Republic: Peale's Museum and Its Audience* (Washington: Smithsonian Institution Press, 1995); James T. McClellan, *Colonialism and Science: Saint-Domingue in the Old Regime* (Baltimore, MD: Johns Hopkins University Press, 1992), 97.

9 Pamela Pilbeam, *Madame Tussaud and the History of Waxworks* (London: Hambledon and London, 2003), 25.

10 Charles Coleman Sellers, *Patience Wright: American Artist and Spy in George III's London* (Middletown, CT: Wesleyan University Press, 1976), 47–9.

11 *Columbian Centinel* (Boston), September 7, 1791.

12 Roach, *It*, 84, 87.

13 *New-York Daily Gazette*, September 19, 1789; *Federal Gazette* (Philadelphia), May 14, 1793; *Massachusetts Mercury* (Boston), January 15, 1799; *Gazette* (Portland, ME), April 5, 1802; *Connecticut Journal* (New Haven), September 2, 1802; *Republican Gazetteer* (Boston), October 20, 1802; *The Democrat* (Boston), February 25, 1804.

14 *Commercial Advertiser* (New York), December 13, 1803.

15 On visual deceptions in the early republic, see Wendy Bellion, *Citizen Spectator: Art, Illusion, and Visual Perception in Early National America* (Chapel Hill: University of North Carolina Press, 2011).

16 *Massachusetts Mercury* (Boston), February 24, 1797.

17 Roach, *It*, 55.

18 Catherine E. Kelly, *Republic of Taste: Art, Politics, and Everyday Life in Early America* (Philadelphia: University of Pennsylvania Press, 2016), 159–94.

19 Reported in *Freeman's Oracle* (Exeter, NH), July 1, 1786.

20 Michelle E. Bloom, *Waxworks: A Cultural Obsession* (Minneapolis: University of Minnesota Press, 2003).

21 Quoted in Wendy Bellion, "Patience Wright's Transatlantic Bodies," in *Shaping the Body Politic: Art and Political Formation in Early America*, ed. Maurie D. McInnis and Louis P. Nelson (Charlottesville: University of Virginia Press, 2011), 31.

22 Karen Halttunen, "Humanitarianism and the Pornography of Pain in Anglo-American Culture," *American Historical Review* 100, no. 2 (1995): 303–34.

23 Philip English Mackey, *Hanging in the Balance: The Anti-Capital Punishment Movement in New York State, 1776–1861* (New York: Garland Publishing, Inc., 1982), 42.

24 Barrell, *Imagining the King's Death*, 49–86.

25 *Connecticut Journal* (New Haven), September 4, 1793.

26 T. Lawrence Larkin, "A 'Gift' Strategically Solicited and Magnanimously Conferred: The American Congress, the French Monarchy, and the State Portraits of Louis XVI and Marie-Antoinette," *Winterthur Portfolio* 44, no. 1 (2010): 31–76.

27 *London Magazine* (February 1793), 68.

28 J. Thomas Scharf and Thompson Westcott, *History of Philadelphia 1609–1884* (Philadelphia: L. H. Everts & Co., 1884), 2:950.

29 Thomas Paine, "Preserving the Life of Louis Capet" (1793), in *The Thomas Paine Reader*, ed. Michael Foot and Isaac Kramnick (New York: Penguin Books, 1987), 396.

30 Scharf and Westcott, *History of Philadelphia*, 2:950.

31 *Morning Post* (London), February 9, 1793.

32 *St. James's Chronicle* (London), March 28–30, 1793.

33 Daniel Arasse, *The Guillotine and the Terror*, trans. Christopher Miller (London: Allen Lane, Penguin Press, 1989), 4, 9.

34 *Diary or Woodfall's Register* (London), March 19, 1793.

35 V. A. C. Gatrell, *The Hanging Tree: Execution and the English People* (New York: Oxford University Press, 1994), 46–7, Louis P. Masur, *Rites of Execution: Capital Punishment and the Transformation of American Culture, 1776–1865* (New York: Oxford University Press, 1989), esp. chaps. 3 and 4.

36 Arasse, *The Guillotine and the Terror*, 15–17.

37 John DePeyster to Charles Willson Peale, March 22, 1794, in *The Selected Papers of Charles Willson Peale and his Family*, ed. Lillian Miller (New Haven, CT: Yale University Press, 1988), vol. 2, part 1:85.

38 John DePeyster to Charles Wilson Peale, April 15, 1794, in *The Selected Papers of Charles Willson Peale*, vol. 2, part 1:88–9.

39 John DePeyster to Charles Wilson Peale, April 15, 1794, in *The Selected Papers of Charles Willson Peale*, vol. 2, part 1:88–9.

40 Brigham, *Public Culture in the Early Republic*, 5–10; Robert I. Goler, "'Here the Book of Nature is Unfolded': The American Museum and the Diffusion of Scientific Knowledge in the Early Republic," *Museum Studies Journal* (1986): 10–21; and Kelly, *Republic of Taste*, 159–94.

41 John DePeyster to Charles Willson Peale, April 15, 1794, in *The Selected Papers of Charles Willson Peale*, vol. 2, part 1:89.

42 *Columbian Gazetter* (New York), March 24, 1794.

43 Barbara Maria Stafford, *Artful Science: Enlightenment Entertainment and the Eclipse of Visual Education* (Cambridge, MA: MIT Press, 1994), 195.

44 Gatrell, *The Hanging Tree*; Richard J. Evans, *Rituals of Retribution: Capital Punishment in Germany, 1600–1987* (Oxford: Oxford University Press, 1996), especially part I; and Paul Friedland, *Seeing Justice Done: The Age of Spectacular Capital Punishment in France* (Oxford: Oxford University Press, 2014).

45 *London Magazine* (February 1793), 68.

46 S. H. Jeyes, *The Russells of Birmingham in the French Revolution and in America, 1791–1814* (London: George Allen and Co., Ltd., 1911), 134.

47 *St. James's Chronicle* (London), November 12–14, 1793.

48 Minsoo Kang, *Sublime Dreams of Living Machines: The Automaton in the European Imagination* (Cambridge, MA: Harvard University Press, 2011), 185–222.

49 Nina Rattner Gelbart, "Death in the Bathtub: Charlotte Corday and Jean-Paul Marat," in *The Human Tradition in Modern France*, ed. K. Steven Vincent and Alison Klairmont-Lingo (Wilmington, DE: SR Books, 2000), 18–23.

50 Guillaume Mazeau, *Le bain de l'histoire: Charlotte Corday et l'attentat contre Marat, 1793–2009* (Seyssel: Champ Valon, 2009), 140–3; Tony Halliday,

"David's *Marat* as Posthumous Portrait," in *Jacques-Louis David's* Marat, ed. William Vaughan and Helen Weston (Cambridge: Cambridge University Press, 2000), 62–6; Marie-Hélène Huet, *Rehearsing the Revolution: The Staging of Marat's Death, 1793–7*, trans. Robert Hurley (Berkeley: University of California Press, 1982), chap. 4; Antoine de Baecque, *The Body Politic: Corporeal Metaphor in Revolutionary France, 1770–1800*, trans. Charlotte Mandell (Stanford, CA: Stanford University Press, 1997).

51 *American Minerva* (New York), April 10, 1795.

52 *Massachusetts Mercury* (Boston), December 25, 1795; William Vaughan and Helen Weston, "Introduction," in *Jacques-Louis David's* Marat, 5.

53 Quoted in Kirsten T. Saxton, *Narratives of Women and Murder in England, 1680–1760: Deadly Plots* (Farnham, UK: Ashgate, 2009), 19.

54 For examples of this critique, see Saxton, *Narratives*.

55 Chantal Thomas, "Heroism in the Feminine: The Examples of Charlotte Corday and Madame Roland," in *The French Revolution 1789–1989: Two Hundred Years of Rethinking*, ed. Sandy Petrey (Lubbock: Texas Tech University Press, 1989), 67–9; Denise Davidson, "Feminism and Abolitionism: Transatlantic Trajectories," in *The French Revolution in Global Perspective*, ed. Suzanne Desan, Lynn Hunt, and William Max Nelson (Ithaca, NY: Cornell University Press, 2013), 102.

56 Historians have found evidence of efforts to check women's political participation as well as of their continued participation in spite of those attempts. Suzanne Desan, *The Family on Trial in Revolutionary France* (Berkeley: University of California Press, 2004); Jennifer Heuer, *The Family and the Nation: Gender and Citizenship in Revolutionary France, 1789–1830* (Ithaca, NY: Cornell University Press, 2005); Lynn Hunt, *The Family Romance of the French Revolution* (Berkeley: University of California Press, 1992), 116–21; and Joan B. Landes, *Visualizing the Nation: Gender, Representation, and Revolution in Eighteenth-Century France* (Ithaca, NY: Cornell University Press, 2001), 90.

57 Quoted in Nina Rattner Gelbart, "The Blonding of Charlotte Corday," *Eighteenth-Century Studies* 38, no. 1 (2004): 205.

58 Hervé, *Madame Tussaud's Memoirs*, 340.

59 Gelbart, "Death in the Bathtub," 21.

60 Gelbart, "The Blonding of Charlotte Corday," 211.

61 Elizabeth Kindleberger, "Charlotte Corday in Text and Image: A Case Study in the French Revolution and Women's History," *French Historical Studies* 18, no. 4 (1994): 978–9.

62 Sade quoted in Adriana Craciun, "The New Cordays: Helen Craik and British Representations of Charlotte Corday, 1793–1800," in *Rebellious Hearts: British Women Writers and the French Revolution*, ed. Adriana Craciun and Kari E. Lokke (Albany: State University of New York Press, 2001), 201.

63 Quoted in Helen Weston, "The Corday–Marat Affair: No Place for a Woman," in *Jacques-Louis David's* Marat, 129.

64 Gelbart, "Death in the Bathtub," 25.

65 Weston, "The Corday–Marat Affair," 128–52.

66 *Oxford English Dictionary*, entries for "tragedy" and "tragic."

67 *Oracle of the Day* (Portsmouth, NH), October 26, 1793.

68 *City Gazette and Daily Advertiser* (Charleston, SC), October 4, 1793.

69 *Providence Gazette* (RI), October 5, 1793.

70 *Farmer's Weekly Museum* (Walpole, NH), September 24, 1798.

71 *The Moral and Political Telegraphe, or Brookfield Advertiser* (Brookfield, MA), March 16, 1796. On how elite US women were inspired by the French Revolution, see Susan Branson, *These Fiery Frenchified Dames: Women and Political Culture in Early National Philadelphia* (Philadelphia: University of Pennsylvania Press, 2001).

72 *Morning Chronicle* (London), July 26, 1793.

12

Practice and Belief: Religion in the Revolution

Jonathan Smyth

The aim of this chapter is to give a brief overview of the place and influence of religion in the Revolution. This is important to understanding both the Revolution in general and how attitudes towards religious practice and belief could affect political decision-making.

There is often confusion as to the extent of the importance of religion and of religious life in revolutionary France. If one looks at the Revolution as presented in popular fictional accounts, such as Charles Dickens's *A Tale of Two Cities* or the Baroness Orczy's *Scarlet Pimpernel*, there is a clear impression that religion disappeared from the life of the nation after the events of 1789. Even in more recent novels dealing with real figures of the Revolution, such as Hilary Mantel's *A Place of Greater Safety*, religion has only a marginal place. In fact, religion and religious practice were a permanent undercurrent to the politics of the Revolution and, for many ordinary citizens of France, especially those living in the provinces, were very much part of their daily existence.

The earliest history of the Revolution, published by Buchez and Roux[1] between 1834 and 1838, took a liberal view of the problem of the relations between Church and State, but this viewpoint was dismissed by the great classical literary historians of the nineteenth century, such as Michelet and Quinet,[2] who, although they accepted that religion was one of the major elements at the beginning of the Revolution, downgraded its importance after 1790, considering any form of religion to be essentially anti-revolutionary. The socialist historians of the end of the nineteenth and the beginning of the twentieth century, led by Jaurès, Aulard, and Mathiez,[3] continued this tendency, as did the work of the holders of the Chair of

Revolutionary Studies in Paris in the twentieth century—Lefebvre, Soboul, and Vovelle[4]—who embraced the Marxist view of the Revolution. This view of the Revolution as a class struggle was challenged, in the 1960s, firstly in England by Cobban,[5] then in France originally by Plongeron,[6] followed by Furet[7] and Ozouf.[8]

Although modern historians, such as Tackett, Desan, Banks, and Dean, have offered new thinking on many aspects of the problem of religion in the Revolution, it still tends to play only a minor role in general studies of the period, often confined to discussions of specific aspects, such as the divisive effect of the Civil Constitution of the Clergy in 1790, the enfranchisement of the Jews in 1791, the horrors of the de-Christianizing campaigns of 1792 and 1793, or the unsuccessful attempt to impose some form of State-sponsored religion under the Directory in 1796 and 1797.[9] They do, however, demonstrate some of the challenges men and women faced when confronting or rethinking the power of the Catholic Church during the period of the Revolution and invite us to try to understand how and why religion survived all attempts to remove it from daily life.

The Church in the *Ancien Régime*

To understand why religion did not completely disappear after 1789, we need to look both at how the Church was involved in politics and the court and also its importance in the general life of the nation. "The Church" is the Roman Catholic Church; there was a relatively small Protestant Calvinist Church, but after the Revocation of the Edict of Nantes in 1685, many of its members had chosen emigration to other nations, particularly England and the Netherlands. Calvinism, which once had a strong presence in the professional classes, had lost most of its followers and all its political influence. The Church was everywhere; no official occasion was conceivable without the presence of the clergy. This was as true of great State occasions attended by a bishop, as it was for a village fête, attended by the parish priest. This not only reflected the importance of the Church as the national religion, but also the fact that the Church had three other important functions: it was the national record keeper and the main source of both education and health and welfare.

Before the introduction of the national system of record keeping in 1792, all records of birth, marriage, and death were the responsibility of the Church and were kept in parish, not municipal, records. Since in eighteenth-century France many people were illiterate or only partially literate, particularly in the countryside, the parish church was often the only place where records could be kept. A further important function of the Church was to be, in effect, the national calendar. In a largely agricultural economy, the year was measured by the great feast days of the Church, starting at the spring equinox with Lady Day (Feast of the Annunciation) on March 25 to begin the sowing season, continuing through Easter, then in the summer with Pentecost in May or early June, the Fête-Dieu (Corpus Christi) later in June, through to the Feast of the Assumption on August 15, marking the beginning of harvest, and finally the end of the active agricultural year on Michaelmas (St. Michael's Day) on September 29, when the major markets and hiring fairs were held. These religious feast days were also the official national holidays, although each town and village held its own special celebration on its patron saint's day, and in the cities the guilds and confraternities of tradesmen and artisans celebrated the feast of their patron saint.

Another area in which the Church had major influence was education. There was little education available for the lower classes in the towns, and effectively none in the countryside. Even in the major cities, the rare parish schools, such as those established by Charles Démia in Lyons in the seventeenth century, were chiefly designed to teach the catechism, with a basic level of reading and writing for boys, and, for the girls, more practical studies such as needlework. In the countryside, a conscientious village priest might teach some basics of reading and arithmetic to selected boys, with the view of enabling them to serve the Church in some way. Formal secondary education was the exclusive province of the middle and upper classes. The establishment of the great Lycées, the equivalent of an American high school or British public or grammar school, by the Jesuits in the sixteenth century, with Latin, Greek, and Rhetoric as the mainstays of the system, and daily Mass the norm, ensured that the Church effectively controlled the education of the sons of the professional classes. After the expulsion of the Jesuits in 1764, their place was taken by another religious order, the Oratorians, who added republican works by Livy, Cicero, and Tacitus to the syllabus.

Madame de Maintenon, Louis XIV's mistress and later wife, attempted to do the same for girls with the establishment in 1686 of the *Maison Royale* at St. Cyr, but the experiment was never a success. There were some girls' schools in the larger towns, but these were run by nuns, whose syllabus was strongly devotional and practical in preparation for a life as wife and mother. The sons and daughters of the aristocracy and the daughters of the upper merchant classes would usually be educated at home, by tutors and masters-at-arms in the case of the boys. In some households, girls might join their brothers to learn the basics of reading and writing, but for the most part, female education was firmly based on their eventual responsibilities in the management of a household.

The Church was equally present in all aspects of the provision of health and welfare services. During the Renaissance, the teaching and practice of medicine had broken away from the restraints of the clergy, and in France the Wars of Religion of the sixteenth century had firmly laicized the medical profession, yet the hospitals to which the sick were admitted were still under the control of the Church. The nursing profession was composed almost entirely of nuns from the nursing orders. Even in the nominally lay charitable establishments for the care of orphans, the blind, or injured veterans, the day-to-day administration was the province of clergymen and nursing was in the hands of nuns. The Church was not only concerned with the sick; welfare was also her exclusive field, although here the burden was shared between professed religious and pious lay people, particularly women. The welfare scene covered a very wide area, from the down-and-outs of the street to the aged and infirm in alms-houses, but everything was based, if not directly on the Church, at least on the practice of Christian charity. There were many charitable fraternities in the towns and cities, but, even where these were organized by lay people, they all had their roots in religion, and each had its chaplain or almoner. Charitable work was also one of the very few things a woman, of any social class, could undertake with full approval from both her family and society. In the event, the overall national need for health and welfare was far greater than even the best efforts of the charitable foundations could cope with, and the sight of wounded ex-soldiers and handicapped persons begging in the streets was commonplace.

The early revolutionary period was particularly notable for the development of both Christian and non-Christian sects or cults. In addition to the emergence of several Christian prophetic sects, the period between 1770 and the actual Revolution saw the flourishing of several semi-religious bodies. The fashionable world flocked to demonstrations of hypnotism by the German Dr. Mesmer and of "psychic healing" and "magic" by the Italian adventurer Cagliostro. Some practitioners offered miracle cures using "animal magnetism" or the application of electricity.[10] The prophecies of medieval and Renaissance figures like Nostradamus, Jean de Roquetaillarde, and Thomas-Joseph Moult were once again the subject of popular examination. The development of Freemasonry was another element in the decline of the influence of the Church. In France, Freemasonry, because of its opposition by the Catholic Church, developed both as an anti-religious and an anti-establishment movement with strong international connections with similar movements in Europe. Although the influence of the Enlightenment writers, particularly Voltaire, was strong among the educated classes, their attacks, which were mainly directed against hypocrisy in the Church rather than at the faith itself, are generally agreed to have had little effect on the actual level of practice of the Catholic faith in France.[11]

One of the most remarkable facets of religion in the years immediately before the Revolution itself was the emergence, within the Church, of groups of visionaries. Three women, Jacqueline-Aimée Brohon, Catherine Théot, and Suzette Labrousse, established considerable followings as prophets. The Bonjour brothers established in 1783 a Millenarian sect, the Fareinistes, which, inspired by the approaching Millennium, looked for the coming of the Messiah to bring about a political revolution and the spiritual regeneration of mankind.[12] All of them prophesied the coming of a great revolution which would totally change the nation: Brohon in 1772, Théot in 1778, and Labrousse and the Fareinistes in 1779.[13] Claude Fauchet, later a bishop of the Constitutional Church, preached a form of evangelical socialism based on an egalitarian and fraternal vision of the Gospels.[14] Brohon died in 1776, and though the other groups carried on through the early years of the Revolution, by 1793 they had become fringe movements. Théot died in 1794, while Labrousse was imprisoned in Rome in 1793 and disappeared from active life after her return to France in 1798. The Fareinistes lost all influence when 1800 came and went without the expected Second Coming.

Religion in the Early Revolution

Louis XVI was forced to call together the Three Estates for 1789, for the first time since 1614, officially to give him advice on how to deal with the financial disaster which threatened France. It was expected that the Second Estate, the clergy, would be made up of the most senior, and therefore most conservative, Churchmen, primarily bishops and heads of religious foundations. Their nature was often less that of religious leaders than of administrators of large amounts of the nation's wealth, a wealth which was never made available to the administration or to the people. The lower clergy, whether parish priests, monks, or friars, saw the world very differently from their overlords. They lived with the people of France, they shared their poverty, their anger at the injustice of the system, and their dissatisfaction at the place of the Church within it. In the end, of the 305 selected representatives of the clergy, 205 were from this lower clergy. The democratic tendencies of these priests were already in evidence before the elections to the Estates. One parish priest from Brittany forcefully warned his bishop, "Do not stand against that natural force which is driving men on towards Liberty. Do not try to argue against the wishes of the Creator who made no man to be a slave."[15] With this inbuilt majority against the hierarchy it was clear that the lower clergy would be able to impose its will. They argued that everyone should have an equal vote, and when the king attempted to end their discussions by locking them out of their meeting place, it was these members of the lower orders who followed Sieyès, the author of the polemic *What is the Third Estate?*, to join with Mirabeau and the Third Estate at the meeting which culminated in the Tennis Court Oath on June 20, 1789 and the creation of the National Assembly.

The new alliance between lower priesthood members of the Second Estate and representatives of the Third Estate had far-reaching consequences which few of the revolutionary clergy would have expected. The first major event in the crisis of the Church occurred on the night of August 4, 1789 when the newly constituted National Assembly voted for the abolition of the three things which were effectively the bases of the economic existence of the Church in France, and without which its whole infrastructure was inevitably to collapse. The first was the abolition of all existing and future feudal or seigniorial rights. This effectively cut the ground from under the whole of the Church's financial structure, since these rights were the basis of her monetary strength. Even more important and radical were the decisions to abolish the *dîmes*, the tithes, and the *casuel*, the system of perquisites or fees which clergy received for baptisms, weddings, or funerals, income on which the parish clergy relied for the upkeep both of themselves and their church buildings. These were the decisions which most directly affected all the lower orders, since with this vote the lower clergy lost its regular sources of income. There was no question, at that time, however, of any attack on religion as such; indeed when the Assembly adopted the Declaration of the Rights of Man and of the Citizen on August 26, 1789, the preamble stated that it was agreed "in the presence and under the auspices of the Supreme Being," while Article 10 guaranteed freedom of worship.[16]

The final act in the sequence of events leading to the destruction of any form of Church independent of the executive was taken on November 2, 1789 when the Assembly voted for the confiscation of all Church property in an attempt to respond to France's ongoing financial crisis. It was then faced with the question of how the priests were to live and how the buildings could be maintained if the Church was without any form of income. The logical outcome was that the State should bear the responsibility and that priests should receive an annual salary, paid by the State. This reform drew a variety of reactions. The more radical priests, led by Grégoire, who had voted wholeheartedly for the decrees of August, believed that the result would not only be good politically but would also revitalize the Church spiritually, leading it back to the Jansenist concept of primitive purity. The more moderate majority, including the democrats among the clergy, led by Sieyès, foresaw the serious organizational and spiritual difficulties which would arise from any attempt to meld Church and State economically while trying to maintain spiritual distance between them.

There is evidence in the *Cahiers de Doléances* (lists of grievances) for 1789–90 that some members of the French public regarded the measures affecting the Church and clergy critically. According to Perrard, almost half (47 percent) of the complaints to the king opposed the suppression of the *casuel*. Only 4 percent were in favor of the suppression of the regular (monastic) clergy, a proposition that was to become one of the flagship reforms suggested by the Constitutional Church, and even fewer, only 2 percent, supported the majority view in the Assembly that both bishops and parish priests should be elected by lay suffrage.[17] At the same time, Arthur Young, who was in Clermont-Ferrand on his tour around France in 1789, commented on the apparent disinterest of the inhabitants of provincial France in what was happening in Paris at that time:

> The abolition of tythes, the destruction of the gabelle, game made property, and feudal rights destroyed, are French topics, that are translated into English within six days after they happen, and their consequences, combinations, results, and modifications, become the disquisition and

> entertainment of the grocers, chandlers, drapers, and shoemakers, of all the towns of England; yet the same people in France do not think them worth their conversation.[18]

The problems that Mirabeau, Sieyès, and the moderates had foreseen happened far more quickly than anyone would have expected. Unlike the majority of the Assembly, those who, like Sieyès, had experience of the actual administration of the Church, understood that if ecclesiastics no longer had the financial means to pursue their primary function, which was the cure of souls, then an unacceptable vacuum would inevitably ensue, and something would either have to be created or would create itself to fill this space.

The non-clerical members of the Assembly decided that this problem should be solved by a complete reorganization of the Church. They would establish a new Constitutional Church, which would combine the practice of religion with subservience to the political leaders of the nation. The aim was to create a State-funded and thus State-controlled religious organization, which would be specifically French, with no input from such external sources as the Papacy. Originally most Catholic laymen, and many clergy, hoped that there could be some coming together of the old and new systems, maintaining the Church's effective position as the national religion, while simultaneously bringing in reforms intended to purify its practices. The reorganization of the old episcopal areas and their replacement by sees formed by the new *Départements*, which got rid of the scandal of absentee bishops who lived in Paris or Versailles rather than in their sees, was generally approved. The problem was that the new Constitutional Church incorporated some radical reforms which the majority of those practicing the Catholic faith could not accept. The more extreme elements in the Assembly proposed that parish priests would be chosen by an electorate made up not of believers or regular church-goers, but by a selection of "active republicans" whose only qualification was that they were taxpayers. In the end, the legislators agreed to restrict the number of non-believers who would be allowed to take part in the elections. As a result, while it enjoyed the unlikely approval of both the *philosophes* and atheist factions in the Assembly, the new Church was met with distrust by both opposing sets of committed clergy. It was approved neither by those who combined the desire for the pursuit of their faith with an acceptance of the need for constitutional reform, nor by those who opposed any reform.

Such major changes in France needed the approval of the Pope as Head of the Church, and Louis XVI hoped that Pius VI, having accepted a similar type of constitution imposed on the clergy of the Holy Roman Empire by his brother-in-law, the Austrian Emperor Joseph II, would agree. In the absence of any clear statement from Rome, he grudgingly signed the decree establishing the new Church on August 24, 1790. The Assembly proceeded to formalize the situation by drawing up the Ecclesiastical Oath of November 27, 1790, which became law on December 26, and which all clergy were required to sign. The Oath stated:

> I swear to watch over the Faithful of the Parish (or the See) which is given to me, to be faithful to the Nation, to the Law, to the King, and to uphold with all my strength the Constitution decreed by the National Assembly and accepted by the King.

Grégoire led 105 members of the Assembly in signing the new Oath, in the hope that this would lead to a general acceptance of the new constitution, but it caused even more division. Only seven bishops and approximately half the lower clergy swore the Oath, many of them with the caveat that they reserved the right to retract depending on the final position of the Papacy.[19] According to Tackett, the incidence of oath-taking was highest in France's center, the Île-de-France and the southeast. In areas later noted for the continuation of religious practices—the northwest, northeast and the Massif Central—well over half of the clergy, led by their bishops, refused the oath.[20] Pope Pius VI finally clarified the Church's official position by issuing two Papal Bulls, *Quod aliquantum*, on March 10, and *Caritas*, on April 13, 1791. He ordered all clergymen to refuse the Oath, and any who had signed were ordered to recant within forty days. The Assembly forbade the publication of these documents, but they were widely circulated clandestinely.

The Civil Constitution is one of the most discussed aspects of the Revolution among historians. The major work on the causes and effects of the Ecclesiastical Oath of 1791 is unequivocally Tackett's original and magisterial study, published in 1986, with a more recent work on the events of 1790 provided by Rodney Dean.[21] There have also been studies of the wider effects of the split by Van Kley and others,[22] while Desan argues that the requirement of the Oath was one of the critical errors of the Revolution, provoking, as it did, unending controversies among the clergy and laity alike and persuading many in the countryside to oppose the Revolution.[23] With this considerable difference in attitude in various parts of France, the Church was irrevocably split between the jurors, who accepted the new structures, and the "non-jurors," whose conscience would not permit them to swear the Oath. It should be emphasized that although the new Constitutional Church accepted the essence of political control, all its priests and bishops also firmly defended their right to be considered as true Catholics following the rites and practices of the Roman Church.

The religious problems in France continued after the end of the Assembly and the election of the new parliamentary body, the Legislative Assembly, following the Constitution of 1791. None of the members of the new body had served as revolutionary legislators before, and previous, relatively moderate members were replaced by more radical politicians, linked to the emerging, powerful political clubs of the Cordeliers and Jacobins.[24] As the influence of the clubs grew, especially after France went to war against its

European enemies in April 1792, so did the influence of the anti-religious faction. Each of the clubs included moderate or semi-moderate members on religious issues, such as Danton, Robespierre, and Desmoulins, but also extremist de-Christianizers such as Hébert, Chaumette, Lequinio, and Fouché. In the meantime, the Church inside France still had more non-jurors than constitutional priests, and religious practice remained strong in many areas outside Paris.

The combination of a weak constitution, the inability of successive administrations to manage the increasing economic and social problems, and the increasing intransigence of the king brought matters to a head. On June 20, 1792 the leaders of the Paris *sections* called the people of Paris to arms. On August 10, the army of the people of Paris, led by National Guard units, attacked the Tuileries Palace. The royal family took refuge in the building of the Legislative Assembly where a rump of deputies voted for the suppression of all royal powers. The royal family were taken as prisoners to the Temple.

Patriots assumed that both the Catholic clergy and the practicing laity were automatically royalist and counter-revolutionary. The defeat of the revolutionary army at Longwy on August 23 and, on September 2, the capitulation of Verdun, the only remaining major fortress defending Paris (see Map 0.1), increased popular fears of a counter-revolution led by political prisoners, including refractory priests, in Paris. Wall posters invited the public to "cleanse the nation before marching to the frontiers,"[25] and Marat and Fréron used their newspapers to call for the massacre of the enemies of the Revolution.[26] Between September 2 and 6, the sans-culottes of Paris stormed the prisons and massacred some 1,300 people, including a large number of refractory priests and several hundred other prisoners.

Among the last acts of the Legislative Assembly was to pass two laws which would finally remove the last official functions of the Church. The first of these was the vote to allow divorce, which removed from the Church its control of marriages. This was followed on September 20, 1792 by the establishment of the *Etat civil*, by which all records of birth, marriage, and death were removed from the Church and transferred to the civil power. On the same day that the Legislative Assembly disbanded, the French army halted the Austro-Prussian advance at Valmy.[27] The next day, September 21, the new National Convention proclaimed the abolition of the monarchy, and, on 22nd, the establishment of the French republic, which heralded the most difficult period for those still following any type of religious life.

The Rise of De-Christianization

After the creation of the republic, the relationship between the Catholic Church and the revolutionary government entered a new and more difficult phase. There had already been opposition to the religious policies of 1790 and 1791 in large areas of France, particularly the center and the east. The new assembly saw the arrival of more radical members as well as the return of members of the original National Assembly. Its radical deputies no longer viewed the Church as either a potential ally or as an unimportant sideshow. They considered any form of religious practice as a dangerous counter-revolutionary political and cultural system, one which would prevent the citizen from carrying out his civic duties as a member of the republic. This was the beginning of the era of active de-Christianization, a policy which, although never formally adopted by any of the successive regimes between 1792 and 1794, became the norm in much of France.

The outbreak of counter-revolution in the provinces, and the introduction, in March 1793, of the system of appointing deputies as traveling *Représentants en Mission* (representatives on mission) to ensure that the decrees of the Convention were properly observed outside Paris, created the possibility for ardent de-Christianizers to impose their personal brands of de-Christianization on the areas under their control. In Nantes (see Map 0.1), Carrier rounded up non-juror priests and nuns, incarcerated them in specially prepared barges, and drowned them in the River Loire. Fouché in the Nièvre and Lequinio in the Charente (see Map 0.1) forced priests and nuns to marry, and pillaged the churches of any precious metals, which were melted down, officially to provide funds for the war effort. In La Rochelle, Lequinio took charge of some 800 prisoners from the revolt in the Vendée, executed sixty of them and condemned the rest to forced labor; over 500 of them died of disease or starvation.[28]

In the west, Brittany and the Vendée had long been strongly Catholic and, since the Church and the former nobility lived more closely with the people than in many other parts of the country, there was far less revolutionary fervor. Things came to a head in the Vendée when, in March 1793, commissioners arrived from Paris to impose conscription on the area. The local population resisted vigorously and, when troops sent from Paris with the commissioners fired on the crowds, the people rioted and massacred the forces from the capital. The riot became an insurrection headed by the former local nobility, with the formation of the Royal and Catholic Army and the beginning of a bloody civil war. There was a separate rising in Brittany, where an army of peasants, called Chouans, fought for religion and independence.

The rebels had some early success, despite Paris sending General Kléber with experienced troops from the Army of the Rhine. The war dragged on until 1796 when, in a final move to exterminate the rebels, General Turreau led the *colonnes infernales* (infernal columns) through the area, burning and destroying as they went. When this didn't finish off the rebellion, later in the same year, the Directory sent General Hoche from Paris with instructions to offer conciliatory terms, and a peace formula was agreed.

It should not be assumed that this type of event was the norm throughout France; many *Représentants en Mission* were far less fanatical and there were many areas away from Paris where the Church maintained its position. Most of the Convention were not avid de-Christianizers; many, including Danton and Robespierre, felt that if religion was ignored, it would quietly disappear on its own, and that there were more pressing needs for the nation than the pursuit of a moribund belief system. As Tackett and others have shown, in multiple areas of central and eastern France, there was also little or no sign of revolt against the republic, and the Church, with the quiet help of much of the population, managed to maintain both a low profile and much of its influence in daily life.

Among the revolutionary measures taken to remove all traces of the previous political and religious regime was the decision in 1793 to reorganize the calendar. The stated aim was to eliminate all references to classical and religious nomenclature, although some modern scholars have suggested that there was a deeper philosophical significance in the Revolution's attempted reorganization of the measurement of time.[29] A commission under the mathematician Romme produced a proposal for a new republican calendar, based on an idea originally put forward by the prominent atheist Sylvain Maréchal in 1788.[30] The year would still have twelve months, each of thirty days, with each month divided into three weeks of ten days, thus eliminating Sunday as a traditional day of worship and rest for Christians. This left five days at the end of each year, which would be called *journées sans culottides* and be public holidays. Each month and day was given a new revolutionary name, suggested by the republican poet Fabre d'Eglantine. The new calendar was supposed to have begun with the establishment of the republic on September 22, 1792, although it only actually came into use a year later, so September 22, 1793 became 1 Vendémiaire, Year II. The months were named after the seasons and their associated tasks and characteristics; for example, misty November became Brumaire, rainy February Pluviôse, and hot July Thermidor. The new names of the months were the subject of considerable satire outside France; the British cartoonist, Cruickshank, lampooned the republican calendar, renaming the months from September to November as Wheezy, Sneezy, and Breezy.[31] The proposed names for the days of the week never took hold at all, but were simply known—from Primédi through to the tenth day, Décadi.

Towards a Republican Religion

It was always clear to most revolutionaries that if the Church were to be removed from public life, some other form of national festivals, celebrations of nationality, and particularly of solidarity with the Revolution would be needed. The result was the series of Fêtes Nationales which continued throughout the Revolution and the Empire. The first of these was the Festival of Federation, held in Paris on July 14, 1790. The government had decreed that the date of the storming of the Bastille in 1789 would be the National

Day and proposed a great celebration on the Champ de Mars in Paris. Ambitious proposals were made for the design of the festival, but little practical work was carried out, so much so that in the weeks before the day of the festival, the people of Paris had to turn out and do the hard work preparing the site. What is remarkable is the enthusiasm which the population showed, as people of every class and profession worked together to make sure that the site would be ready on time.[32] Sadly, despite this general enthusiasm, there was practically no public input to the celebrations on the actual day. It was a very formal affair, strongly reminiscent of those under the *Ancien Régime*. The king and court attended, Mass was said, the banners of the newly-formed *Garde Nationale* were formally blessed, and the music throughout was highly reminiscent of a Church celebration.[33] This was unfavorably commented on in the Parisian press: the *Chronique de Paris* suggested that "a people who celebrate Liberty should be given a new form of language"[34] and that a celebration of the Revolution should have involved the people.

Once the idea of celebratory festivals took hold, many smaller local and national festivals were celebrated. They were, however, in the main limited to the celebration of political events, and although they did to some extent take the place of the old Church celebrations, with a tree of liberty replacing the Christian symbols, there was no positive drive towards a national form of morality. In some areas the festivals openly occupied the space previously filled by the great festivals of the Church. In Angers, for example, the festival in 1791 strongly resembled the procession previously associated with the Festival of Corpus Christi, when, in place of the display of the Sacrament surrounded by priests, there were the tablets of the Rights of Man, surrounded by the municipal officers.[35]

The great national festivals continued in Paris, with a celebration in 1791 very similar to that of 1790. Because of the political situation and the beginning of the war in 1792, there was no great national festival in that year. By 1793, the ethos of the national festivals had gone well beyond the simple replacement of previous Church feast days. In that year the Convention decided that it would have a completely new type of civic festival to be held exclusively in the capital—to celebrate the proclamation of the new republic and to promote loyalty to the new constitution. A great procession, representing the entire nation, would cross the whole of Paris, starting at the site of the Bastille, where an oath of fidelity would be sworn to the new constitution, and finishing with speeches at a triumphal arch on the Champ de Mars. This procession included all the members of the Convention, representatives from each *Département*, the National Guard and the army, and delegates from each of the forty-eight sections of Paris. There was still some echo of the old Church festivals in that the procession was to stop at selected points on the route to pay homage to memorials to the heroes of the early Revolution, as though they were the wayside shrines of saints.

Throughout the whole of this period, the struggle for the de-Christianization of the nation was continuing in both Paris and the provinces. It was, however, in no sense a national occurrence since it depended on the personal views of the *Représentant en Mission* to any particular area. In the more distant parts of France it was almost non-existent. The Catholic religion continued to play a considerable part in the daily lives of the population either through constitutional priests or, in some places, non-juror priests who had stayed in France clandestinely or semi-clandestinely, but were still holding services, baptizing, marrying, and burying people, and carrying on the same ministry as before the Revolution. Later in 1793, the Convention agreed to the proposal of the de-Christianizer, Chaumette, to rid France of any vestiges of religion by requiring that each church be renamed a "Temple of Reason." He also proposed a special festival to be held in Notre-Dame de Paris on 20 Brumaire (November 10, 1793). Originally this was to be a purely Parisian celebration, but, with the support of other de-Christianizers in the Convention, it was decided to make it a national event. Instructions went out from Paris to rename all churches and to hold a Festival of Reason in the new temples. Unfortunately, this decision was taken so near the proposed date of the festival that, by the time the detailed instructions reached the provinces, it was usually too late to coordinate with the events in Paris and only a few of the major cities actually held a festival. In Notre-Dame de Paris a small mountain was erected in the nave on which was a Grecian temple, the home of the goddess of reason. Speeches were made by Chaumette and the ex-Archbishop of Paris, Gobel. Unfortunately, after Chaumette and his entourage had left, according to contemporary sources, the celebrations were anything but edifying, descending instead into scenes of drunkenness and public immorality.[36]

With the exception of the Festival of Reason, national festivals initially avoided any emphasis either on de-Christianization or on public morality, concentrating instead on strengthening national solidarity with the basic concepts of Revolution and republic. This was to change completely, as Robespierre's distaste of Chaumette's attempt to destroy any traces of religion or morality drove him to decide that what was needed was a new national morality to replace the old faith-based system, one which would offer a way of life that would be both republican and moral.[37] His first act after the Festival of Reason was to make a speech on 1 Frimaire (November 21, 1793) in the Jacobin Club attacking Chaumette and his followers for peddling atheism, which he asserted was both aristocratic and unrepublican. Robespierre continued his search for public morality in a series of speeches over the next six months. The best known of these is the speech of 17 Pluviôse (February 5, 1794) to the Convention on the principles of political morality which should guide the republic. His conclusion was that the only acceptable government was that of a democratic republic based on the practice of public virtue. He maintained that since, sadly, virtue alone could not guard the republic from the combined onslaught of both external enemies and internal traitors, virtue must be given arms to defend itself. This drove him to the logical but terrible conclusion that the only way to arm virtue was to join it to the implacable force of terror:

> If the mainspring of popular government during peace is virtue[,] the mainspring of popular government in revolution is both virtue and terror; virtue without which terror is a disaster, terror without which virtue is powerless. Terror is nothing but justice, fast, hard and remorseless . . .[38]

Throughout the speech, Robespierre hammered home the point that it was up to the members of the Convention to ensure the purification of the republic. The tone of his speech is as inflexible as the Terror itself. His further public speeches during the spring of 1794 continued on this theme as the Terror took hold of France, especially in Paris, where the victims included Chaumette, Danton, and Desmoulins. The day after Danton's execution, Couthon announced that the Committee of Public Safety intended to present various proposals to the Convention, one of which was for a great festival dedicated to the Eternal, stressing that despite the attempts of the de-Christianizers, nothing had managed to remove from the population their need for some form of spiritual consolation. On 18 Floréal (May 7, 1794), Robespierre presented his ideas for the re-establishment of an acceptable code of public morality throughout France. In this speech, he invited his fellow revolutionaries to reconsider their opposition to religion by demonstrating how he had examined the problem of establishing an acceptable belief system in the context of the Revolution. Discarding the claims of both the classical philosophers and the Church to be the sole arbiters on civic virtue, he proposed to establish, in the name of the Republic of Virtue, a system of public morality under the benign watchfulness of the same Supreme Being. The latter, he reminded his listeners, was specifically mentioned in both the preambles to the Declaration of the Rights of Man and to the republican Constitution of 1793. To crown this new dawn in the morality of the Revolution, he proposed that there should be a great festival in honor of the Supreme Being on 20 Prairial (June 8, 1794).

There were several aspects to Robespierre's festival which clearly distinguishes it from every previous revolutionary festival. It was to be dedicated not only to solidarity within the nation but to a specific idea of civic virtue overseen by the presence of a Supreme Being. It was also to be a truly national festival which would be held in every city, town, village, and even hamlet throughout the whole of France on the same day at the same time, so that the entire nation would be joined together in a unique act of solidarity. Even though there was very little preparation time available between his speech and the day set aside for the festival, it was a great national success. It was celebrated in every part of France, not always exactly as Robespierre had required in the detailed instructions which accompanied his speech, but always with the same underlying theme. The many detailed records available from both the capital and the provinces also indicate strongly the overall national feeling of joy as well as unity. There was a widely held hope, reported by several contemporary commentators, that the day would mark not only the beginning of the Republic of Virtue but also the proclamation of a general amnesty and the end of the Terror, a hope supported by the demolition of the guillotine in Paris two days before the festival.[39] Sadly, these hopes were dashed two days later when the infamous Law of 22 Prairial was published and the Terror resumed, more implacable and bloodier than ever.

Robespierre's ideas about civic morality were not universally popular in the Convention. During the festival, several members, including Lecointre, Baudot, and Thirion, were heard to refer to Robespierre as a dictator and tyrant,[40] and Lecointre was plotting to assassinate him.[41] A group headed by Vadier, of the Committee for General Security, supported by Barère and Billaud-Varenne of the Committee of Public Safety, was also already conspiring to bring about Robespierre's downfall. They needed to present some believable accusation of treason, so they sought to implicate Robespierre in the activities of one of the extreme prophetic sects, led by the prophetess Catherine Théot and Dom Gerle. Théot claimed that she had been told in a vision that she would be given power to rule the world with the Chosen One at her side.[42] She never named the Chosen One, but popular rumor, carefully nurtured by his opponents, suggested that it was Robespierre. On 27 Prairial (June 15, 1794), a week after the Festival of the Supreme Being, a report by Barère, entitled *Actions of the false prophetess Catherine Theos* (sic), was presented to the Convention by Vadier. The Convention voted to have Théot and Gerle sent to the Revolutionary Tribunal on a charge of treason. Although he firmly denied any involvement with the Théot sect, on 8 Messidor (June 26, 1794) Robespierre personally ordered the Chief Prosecutor, Fouquier-Tinville, to drop the case against Théot and Gerle. [43]

Religion Under the Directory

Robespierre's great festival seems to have marked the beginning of the disappearance of active de-Christianization throughout France. During Prairial and Messidor (May–July 1794), leading up to the fall of Robespierre on 9 Thermidor (July 27, 1794), the power of the more extreme de-Christianizers was noticeably curtailed. After Thermidor and the fall of the Jacobin government, a new and more moderate set of politicians took over the government of France. Several extremists, notably Carrier, were summoned to Paris to answer for their crimes and, by early 1795, a return to a more generalized form of religious practice was beginning to take shape. A law passed on February 21, 1795 legalized public worship, although it still forbade the ringing of church bells, religious processions, and any public display of the crucifix. The problem of establishing some form of acceptable national morality combining the populism of the Revolution and the Catholic faith, which was still strong throughout France, continued to bedevil successive administrations. The government of the Directory was very conscious of the fact that religion remained an important factor and various attempts were made between 1795 and 1797 to try to provide some form of State-controlled religion. In 1796, the Directory, under the guidance of La Révellière-Lépeaux, proposed to continue Robespierre's search for a system of public morality outside the Christian faith by actively supporting the Theophilanthropy movement, a semi-deist belief system put forward by a Paris printer, Chemin Despontès.[44] This attempted to reconcile many of Robespierre's ideas expressed in the cult of the Supreme Being, especially its emphasis on internationalism and family harmony, while maintaining complete opposition to the practice of the Catholic faith. Despite official approval, this awkward mixture of deism, populist Rousseauvian philosophy, and patriotism offered no real response to the religious aspirations of the bulk of the nation. Even with extensive financial support from the Directory, by the end of 1797 the new "religion" had control of only fifteen parishes, all in central Paris. Theophilanthropy had no success at all outside Paris, and had disappeared completely by the end of 1798.

Napoleon and the Concordat of 1801

After 1796 there continued to be strong signs of a Catholic revival, and things began to change markedly after Napoleon Bonaparte seized power on 18 Brumaire Year VIII (November 9, 1799). It is a measure of his political acumen that he appreciated the enormous advantage to be gained by solving this apparently intractable problem. Although he was personally indifferent to religion, Bonaparte was well aware of the political importance of a religious revival in France. His experiences with the potential strength of the Church in his foreign campaigns, especially his struggles with the Papacy in Italy, had shown him that, to be successful, he would need the support of the greater majority, including those still practicing their faith. Napoleon also understood the political necessity of a strong Church in France, which would be at once a force for unity and social harmony and a reliable support of his administration and his objective of becoming the sole ruler. Once in power, he began to allow churches to reopen and granted amnesties to some exiled priests. After difficult negotiations, a Concordat was signed on July 15, 1801 with Pope Pius VII, re-establishing the Catholic Church as the official religion of France. The Concordat retained many of the original reforms of 1789, including salaries for the priesthood paid by the State and the confirmation that the State had the right to nominate bishops. It also allowed the State the right to permit the practice of other religions. The map of Church geography was rewritten, with altered parishes and bishoprics, based on the reforms of 1791, and seminaries again became legal. The reluctant presence of Pius VII at Napoleon's coronation as emperor in December 1804 effectively confirmed that Napoleon had succeeded where Robespierre had failed: he had legitimized the national desire for a State-approved morality based on religious ethics and had satisfied the need for the temporal power to control it.

Conclusion

This chapter shows how, despite the best efforts of the reformers of 1789–91, the de-Christianizers of 1793–4, and the attempts to replace the Christian faith by some combination of deism and republican philosophy, the Church survived all efforts to remove it from the public and private life of France. Against all odds, religion in France also survived the changes from the anachronistic Church of the *Ancien Régime* to the State-sponsored Church of the Napoleonic Concordat. The revolutionaries did, however, leave two major legacies: the Concordat confirmed the decision of the Assembly in 1789 that there would be no single State religion, which ensured that in the future all faiths could be openly practiced in France. On the other hand, the Church's opposition to reform both fueled the de-Christianization of 1793 and 1794, and led to a general anticlericalism, which has been a part of French intellectual culture ever since. The Concordat itself lasted for more than a century and was only finally abrogated by the government of the Third Republic, which passed the Law of December 9, 1905, establishing the formal and final separation of Church and State.

Source: Extract from Robespierre's speech on Freedom of Worship, made at the Jacobin Club, Paris, on November 21, 1793 (1 Frimaire Year 2 of the Revolution)

By what right do aristocrats and hypocrites try to insinuate their standards into those of patriotism and civic virtue? By what right do men unknown up to now in the history of the Revolution, try to seek a false popularity in the middle of all these events, even trying to lead patriots into bad actions, and to sow confusion and discord in our ranks? By what right do they attack freedom of worship in the name of Liberty and attack bigotry with their own bigotry? By what right do they denigrate the genuine homage paid to truth by a continuous and ridiculous farce? Why should they be allowed to diminish the dignity of the nation by hanging a jester's bells on the scepter of philosophy?

Some people believed that, by accepting civic gifts, the Convention had proscribed the Catholic faith. No, the Convention has taken no such rash action. The Convention will never do so. Her intention is to maintain the freedom of worship, which she has proclaimed, while, at the same time, punishing anyone who dares abuse this privilege in order to disturb public order: she will not permit the persecution of peaceful ministers of religion but she will punish them severely should they dare overstep their proper function, deceive citizens and spread royalism and opposition to the Republic. Priests have been denounced for holding services: they will hold even more of them if we forbid it. He who wants to stop them is more bigoted than the one holding the service.

There are those who want to go further, who, under the pretext of wanting to destroy superstition, want to make atheism itself a sort of religion. Every philosopher, every person is free to adopt whatever view they like. Anybody who would make a crime of it is stupid; but the public servant, the legislator, would be even more stupid to adopt it as a system. The national Convention detests it. The Convention is not a writer of books, or an inventor of metaphysical concepts: it is the political body of the people charged with ensuring that not only the rights, but also the character of the people of France are honored. It is not by chance that the Declaration of the Rights of Man was issued in the presence of the Supreme Being.

Some will say that I am narrow-minded, a man of prejudices, perhaps even a fanatic. I have already said that I am speaking neither as an individual nor on behalf of a specific philosophy, but as a representative of the people. Atheism is aristocratic. The idea of a Great Being who watches over the oppressed and the innocent is democratic. The people, the downtrodden will be with me. If there were any against me, it would be the rich and the oppressors. Since my schooldays I have been a fairly lukewarm Catholic; I have never been a lukewarm defender of humanity. This makes me even more attached to the moral and political ideas which I have suggested. If God did not exist, we would have to invent Him.[45]

Œuvres de Maximilien Robespierre, ed. Marc Bouloiseau et al. (Paris: Phénix, 2000), 10:196–7.

Notes

1 Philippe-Joseph-Benjamin Buchez and Pierre-Célestin Roux-Lavergne, *Histoire parlementaire de la Révolution Française, ou, Journal des assemblées nationales, depuis 1789 jusqu'en 1815*, 40 vols. (Paris: Paulin, 1834–8).

2 Jules Michelet, *History of the French Revolution*, trans. Charles Cocks (London: Bohn, 1864); Edgar Quinet, *La Révolution* (Paris: A. Lacroix, Verboeckhoven, 1865).

3 Jean Jaurès, *A Socialist History of the French Revolution*, trans. Mitchell Abidor (Paris: n.p., 1901; this ed. London: Pluto, 2015); Alphonse Aulard, *Histoire politique de la Révolution française* (Paris: Armand Colin, 1901); Albert Mathiez, *The French Revolution* (London: Grosset & Dunlap, 1964).

4 Georges Lefebvre, *La Révolution française* (Paris: Presses Universitaires de France, 1951); Albert Soboul, *A Short History of the French Revolution, 1789–1799*, trans. Geoffrey Symcox (Berkeley: University of California Press, 1977); Michel Vovelle, *Religion et Révolution* (Paris: Hachette, 1976).

5 Alfred Cobban, *A History of Modern France, Vol. 1: 1715–1799* (London: Pelican, 1961).

6 Bernard Plongeron, *Conscience religieuse en Révolution* (Paris: Picard, 1969).

7 François Furet and Denis Richet, *The French Revolution*, trans. Stephen Hardman (London: Weidenfeld and Nicholson, 1972).

8 François Furet and Mona Ozouf, *Dictionnaire critique de la Révolution française, Vol. 5: Interprètes et historiens* (Paris: Flammarion, 1988).

9 Relevant works include Suzanne Desan, *Reclaiming the Sacred: Lay Religion and Popular Politics in Revolutionary France* (Ithaca, NY: Cornell University Press, 1990); Timothy Tackett, *Religion, Revolution, and Regional Culture in Eighteenth-Century France: The Ecclesiastical Oath of 1791* (Princeton, NJ: Princeton University Press, 1996); Nigel Aston, *Religion and Revolution in France, 1780–1804* (Washington, DC: Catholic University of America Press, 2000); Rodney Dean, *L'Église Constitutionelle, Napoléon et le Concordat de 1801* (Paris: Picard, 2004); Jonathan Smyth, *Robespierre and the Festival of the Supreme Being: The Search for a Republican Morality* (Manchester: Manchester University Press, 2016); and Bryan A. Banks and Erica Johnson, eds., *The French Revolution and Religion in Global Perspective: Freedom and Faith* (Basingstoke, UK: Palgrave Macmillan, 2017).

10 Robert Darnton, *Mesmerism and the End of the Enlightenment in France* (Cambridge, MA: Harvard University Press, 1995).

11 Plongeron, *Conscience religieuse.*

12 Claude Hau, *Le Messie de l'An XIII et les Fareinistes* (Paris: Denoël, 1955).

13 In 1779, Suzette Labrousse prophesied to Dom Gerle that a National Assembly would be established and that he would be a member of it.

14 Fauchet founded the patriotic *Cercle Social* and edited the left-wing journal *La bouche de fer*.

15 Plongeron, *Conscience religieuse*, 195.

16 Article 10: "No one may be penalized for his opinions, even religious ones, provided that their expression does not disturb the public order as established by law."

17 Pierre Perrard, *L'Église et la Révolution: 1789–1889* (Paris: Editions Nouvelle Cité, 1988); Laura Mason and Tracey Rizzo, "Cahiers De Doléances," in *The French Revolution: A Document Collection* (Boston: Houghton Mifflin, 1999).

18 Arthur Young, *Travels in France During the Years 1787, 1788, 1789*, ed. Constantia Maxwell (Cambridge: Cambridge University Press, 1929), 210.

19 Of the 125 bishops, only four took the oath: "Talleyrand of Autun, Brienne of Sens, Jarente of Orléans, and Lafond de Savine, of Viviers, three coadjutors or bishops *in partibus*, Gobel, Coadjutor Bishop of Bâle; Martial de Brienne, Coadjutor of Sens; and Dubourg-Miraudet, Bishop of Babylon." Charles G. Herbermann et al., *The Catholic Encyclopedia* (New York: Robert Appleton Co., 1912), 13:11.

20 Tackett, *Religion, Revolution, and Regional Culture.*

21 Tackett, *Religion, Revolution, and Regional Culture*; Rodney Dean, *L'Assemblée constituante et la réforme ecclésiastique, 1790: La constitution civile du Clergé du 12 juillet et le serment ecclésiastique du 27 novembre* (Paris and London: Picard, 2014).

22 Dale Van Kley, *The Religious Origins of the French Revolution* (New Haven, CT: Yale University Press, 1996); François Furet and Mona Ozouf, *Dictionnaire Critique de la Révolution Française* (Paris: Flammarion, 1988).

23 Desan, *Reclaiming the Sacred.*

24 The two clubs took their names from their meeting places. The Cordeliers met at the Convent of the Franciscans (called Cordeliers because of the knotted cord they wore over their robes) and the Jacobins at the Convent of the Dominicans, whose chief convent was in the rue Saint-Jacques.

25 "Purger la Nation avant de courir aux frontières."

26 In *L'Ami du Peuple*, Marat called for a massacre of all "enemies of the Revolution." In *L'Orateur du Peuple*, Fréron denounced the inertia of the elected authorities against the fifth column of royalists in the Paris prisons.

27 Battle of Valmy: September 20, 1792.

28 Jacques Hussenet, ed., *Détruisez la Vendée! Regards croisés sur les victimes et destruction de la guerre de Vendée* (La Roche-sur-Yon: Centre vendéen de recherches historiques, 2007), 462.

29 Matthew Shaw, *Time and the French Revolution: The Republican Calendar, 1789–Year XIV* (London: Royal Historical Society, 2011); Sonja Perovic, *The Calendar in Revolutionary France: Perceptions of Time in Literature, Culture, Politics* (Cambridge: Cambridge University Press, 2012).

30 Sylvain Maréchal, *Almanach des Honnêtes Gens* (Paris: n.p., 1788), 14–15.

31 The full list is: Vendémiaire, Brumaire, Frimaire, Nivôse, Pluviôse, Ventôse, Germinal, Floréal, Prairial, Messidor, Thermidor, and Fructidor. Cruickshank lampooned them as Wheezy, Sneezy, and Breezy; Slippy, Drippy, and Nippy; Showery, Flowery, and Bowery; and Wheaty, Heaty, and Sweety.

32 Mona Ozouf, *Festivals and the French Revolution*, trans. Alan Sheridan (Cambridge, MA: Harvard University Press, 1991).

33 Mass was said by the Bishop of Autun, Talleyrand, who was so out of practice that he had to ask his friend Mirabeau to rehearse it with him the day before. A special Te Deum was composed by Gossec for the occasion.

34 *La Chronique de Paris*, July 8, 1790, 753.

35 Benjamin Bois, *Les Fêtes révolutionnaires à Angers de l'an II à l'an VIII* (Paris: Alcan, 1929).

36 Louis-Sébastien Mercier, *Le Nouveau Paris* (Paris: n.p., 1798).

37 Smyth, *Robespierre and the Festival of the Supreme Being.*

38 Marc Bouloiseau et al., eds., *Œuvres complètes de Maximilien Robespierre* (Paris: Phénix, 2000), 10:357.

39 See Smyth, *Robespierre and the Festival of the Supreme Being*, chap. 6, on contemporary commentators on the Festival.

40 Marc-Antoine Baudot, *Notes historiques sur la Convention Nationale, le Directoire, l'Empire et l'Exil des Votants par Marc-Antoine Baudot, ex-Membre de la Convention Nationale* (Paris: D. Jouaust; I. Cerf, 1893), 5.

41 Laurent Lecointre, *Conjuration formée dès le 5 préréal (sic) par neuf représentants du peuple contre Maximilien Robespierre pour l'immoler en plein Sénat* (Paris: n.p., An II).

42 Joachim Vilate, *Les mystères de la mère de Dieu dévoilés* (Paris: n.p., An II).

43 Gérard Walter, *Maximilien de Robespierre* (Paris: Gallimard, 1961), 449–53; Françoise Brunel, *Thermidor: La chute de Robespierre* (Brussels: Complexe, 1989).

44 Jean-Baptiste Chemin Despontès, *Manuel des Théophilanthrophiles ou adorateurs de Dieu et amis des hommes* (Paris: n.p., An III).

45 This is Voltaire's famous dictum: "Si Dieu n'existait pas, il faudrait l'inventer."

13

Facing the Unknown:

The Private Lives of Miniatures in the French Revolutionary Prison

Sophie Matthiesson

The miniature portrait may have been the most successful and widely consumed form of portraiture in eighteenth-century Europe, but nowhere more so than in Paris, where the art form could be found in luxury shopping streets and around the wrists of princesses from the early decades of the century, and in the homes and clothing of working people by the century's end.[1] Produced in a dazzlingly wide range of formats, small portraits were fixed into costly settings, such as jewel-encrusted rings and gold lockets, on the surfaces of enameled *étuis* (little cases) and snuff and sweet boxes (*tabatières* and *bonbonnières*), or sandwiched between glass and cardboard in cheaper medallions. Viewed today in museums or antique shops, typically unsigned and with no indication of their subjects' identities, we usually encounter them alienated from the personal histories of their original owners and shorn of the contexts that once animated them. They have become instead aesthetic artifacts, to be valued by connoisseurs only for their qualities of execution. It is difficult therefore for the modern viewer to imagine the power that such tiny effigies exerted over the people who acquired them, exchanged them, and preserved them for future generations. Their histories need to be recovered. What was it about miniatures that made them so popular in this period, and, more specifically, what can the miniature portrait tell us about the experience of the French Revolution?

The social significance of miniatures was celebrated in French paintings of the second half of the century. Pre-revolutionary images depicting the use of miniature portraits repeatedly link them in delightful ways with sensual love and romance, showing the flushed transfer of amorous feelings for absent lovers onto the small tokens that bore their image, alongside the letters that accompanied them, within the privacy of silk-furnished boudoirs or masculine libraries (see Figure 13.1). In such images a focus upon miniatures as the erotic coin of aristocratic courtship conceals, however, the other important social and emotional functions that they also served.

FIGURE 13.1 *Louis-Marin Bonnet (1743–93),* Le portrait chéri, *n.d., after Jean-Frédéric Schall (1752–1825),* Le bien-aimé *(The Beloved Portrait), c. 1783. Engraving, 23.5 × 17.5 cm. Bibliothèque nationale de France, département Estampes et photographie.*

Miniatures were vehicles for the condensed expression of many types of love that were increasingly valorized over the eighteenth century: friendship, the love between parents and children, the brotherly love of Freemasons, the love of king or nation, and melancholic love.[2] In an age of frequent separations for education or work, and early death from natural causes, miniature portraits helped mitigate the experience of loss, serving both as proxies for absent loved ones, and as material and enduring tokens of intangible dynamic relationships formed over time. It was miniatures' capacity to meet so many emotional needs that drove a burgeoning demand for them among ordinary people by the close of the century. By this time miniature portraits, like watches, were owned in large numbers by members of the servant classes, an indication of how integral these personal items had become to the daily lives of people in eighteenth-century France.[3] Far from rejoicing in this democratization, the eminent painter Peter Adolf Hall ascribed the widespread consumption of miniatures to fashion, which in his view had led to the trivialization of the once-élite art form and its skilled creators. Hall wrote bitterly in 1788 that "the miniature painter no longer has any rights today to immortality. Nowadays his art form is only treated as a trifle of fashion, and we are in the Age of Enlightenment."[4] The advent of the Terror would soon cast doubt on Hall's assessment, but his emigration to Belgium in 1791 meant that he was not present to witness the new roles that political events would create for miniatures in everyday lives.

It was not until the end of the eighteenth century, in the most radical years of the French Revolution (1793–5), that the value of the miniature portrait as a social artifact was most fully put to the test and revealed. In this period, fears of sudden absences or death acquired an altogether more frightening dimension, in the form of new, politically-generated threats that affected the population as a whole. These threats took the specific forms of mass conscription (*levée en masse*), civil and foreign wars that drove thousands to emigrate, and laws allowing for the arrest, imprisonment, and execution of civilians. Taken together, they formed the impetus behind a new demand for miniature portraits.

Portraits of Consolation

The capacity of miniature portraits to assist their owners negotiate loss and separations beyond their control arguably became their primary function in the Terror. Miniature painters and other artists who had lost traditional forms of patronage soon found themselves servicing a new market of consumers: ordinary people who feared the personal losses that the rapidly changing political situation entailed. In the early days of the Revolution, the painter Jean-Baptiste Isabey recorded how prospective customers, sometimes in pairs, approached him for miniatures of themselves that could be exchanged as keepsakes in the event of a separation: "A new vein of work emerges," he reflected, and:

> . . . it arises from the misfortunes of the time. I go on a campaign [of painting], offering my services to all souls in pain. I baptize my new works with the title of portraits of consolation. Sometimes a mother, an emigrant, brings together the features of her children in a single medallion; often too, in a short session, a double memory would be exchanged. How many times did I attend this mutual gift of love, followed by a cruel separation! The absence should not last more than a month, one would say. Alas! except that it is not always an eternal farewell![5]

The sudden demand for miniatures created commercial openings for women artists, especially genteel amateurs, who found themselves the family breadwinners during the Terror. This was the case for Mme Jeanne Doucet de Suriny, whose husband was in prison, and Sophie de Grouchy, the young wife of the Marquis de Condorcet, who was in hiding following an arrest warrant for him in October 1793. De Grouchy rented a lingerie shop where she set up a portrait studio and worked incognito, making cameos and miniatures for outlawed citizens (*proscrits*) and members of the revolutionary armies.[6] For many of these artists' clients who fell into a proscribed category of citizen, it was only a matter of time before they would find themselves in prison.

In fact, it was not long before the revolutionary prison would become the unexpected and premier locus of separation. In autumn 1793 the newly-fledged republic of France faced a crisis of survival, attacked by foreign powers without, and by defenders of Church and monarchy within. In a bid to consolidate its recent gains, to protect its economy and war effort, and to discourage popular justice, the Convention voted to grant the Committee of Public Safety extraordinary powers of surveillance and detention.[7] The decree known as the Law of Suspects, passed on September 17, 1793, ordered the arrest of anyone who, by their conduct or their relations, or by their words or writings, revealed themselves as enemies of the Revolution. Although aimed at certain categories of people—rebellious former nobles, émigrés, officials removed or suspended from office, treasonous officers, and hoarders of goods—the terms of the new law were sufficiently vague that it was applied to ever-increasing numbers of people. Over the next ten months an estimated 500,000 civilians were sent to prisons, of whom the more serious cases were referred to a newly-created Revolutionary Tribunal for trial, in a period now known as "the Terror."[8] The aim of imprisonment was not to punish suspects but rather to suspend their economic and political activities until the evidence against them could be assessed, or (somewhat more vaguely) "until the peace." While the great majority of people who were imprisoned were eventually released, those found guilty were usually, although not invariably, sentenced to death.[9] In the meantime, suspects faced weeks or possibly months of confinement in political prisons, uncertain of the charges against them, uncertain of their fates, and away from their families.

Undertaking the arrests were revolutionary committees and officers of the local electoral section, who comprised men from the neighborhood.[10] Once they decided to act on a denunciation, they employed an element of surprise, often visiting suspects at night and summoning them from their beds. There was little certainty as to which prison an arrested citizen would end up in. With the capacity of existing prisons rapidly overwhelmed, new provisional prisons were hastily created by municipal authorities out of nationalized properties: religious buildings, colleges, and palaces, as well as requisitioned mansions belonging to émigrés and suspects. These makeshift prisons (the more luxurious of which were known as *maisons de santé*) were often gracious establishments, but they too would soon become overcrowded. Ideally suspects would be escorted to the closest establishment, but if that prison was too full, they would be turned away and forced to make a wearying circuit of prisons in quest of one with space to accept them. Instructed in the first instance to take with them only "personal belongings of absolute necessity," suspects hurried to dress themselves and gather money and essentials, while the authorities set about fixing seals across the desks and valuables in their homes in order to freeze their targets' assets for the duration of an investigation and to secure any written evidence against them.[11] It is striking, therefore, that in these anxious moments so many suspects managed to locate and bring with them little portraits of many kinds. Portraits on chains were slipped around a neck, others into pockets and writing cases, or between the leaves of books. These small likenesses, either worn or carried, served as substitutes for the loved ones that suspects were leaving behind. The typical formats of miniatures—rounded, lightweight, and diminutive—made them easy to encompass in the hand, to wear on the body, or to keep in a pocket away from prying eyes, creating for their owners a sense of physical and emotional closeness to the person depicted wherever they might find themselves. The capacity of such miniatures to accompany their owners wherever they went, and to become in the process virtual extensions of their wearers' bodies, has led the art historian Marcia Pointon to describe them as "ambulant" portraits.[12]

Ambulant Portraits

For all the modest comforts that political prisoners with means were allowed to arrange for themselves once inside prison, and the friendships that were renewed or formed between suspects with members of their own class, professions, or neighborhoods, political detention was full of unknowns over which suspects had little control. The comfort that they derived from small items they brought with them, such as portraits, thus highlights the genuine vulnerability of their situations. In 1794 the arrested banker Pierre-Raphaël Doucet de Suriny wrote proudly of wearing a ring into prison which contained a little painting that was "at once the work and portrait of my wife," the miniaturist Jeanne Doucet de Suriny.[13] Small, and discreet, the capacity of such objects to provide private consolation was apparently in inverse relation to their size.[14] In the case of Doucet de Suriny, the portrait-miniature worn on his finger seemed endowed with a near-talismanic character, as if psychologically shielding its owner wherever fate might take him.[15]

A sense of guardianship and surveillance is more explicitly inscribed into a miniature painted by Louise Marie Thérèse Bathilde, the former Duchesse d'Orléans, for her young nephews who were imprisoned with her at Fort Saint-Jean in Marseilles (see Figure 13.2; see also Map 0.1). With their father, Philippe Égalité, transferred from the prison to Paris for execution in November 1793, and their mother confined at the Luxembourg prison in

FIGURE 13.2 *Bathilde d'Orléans, Antoine-Philippe d'Orléans duc de Montpensier (1775–1807) and Louis-Charles d'Orléans, comte de Beaujolais (1779–1808), 1793. Miniature on ivory, 7.6 × 9 cm, framed in 1847. Musée Condé, Chantilly. RMN-Grand Palais/Art Resource, NY.*

Paris (see Map 0.2), the children had only their aunt to protect them. A member of the mystic Martinist order, the former duchess shows herself as a guardian angel hovering over the boys in their cell, a comforting but nonetheless unorthodox image which may owe something to Martinism's faith in serial reincarnation by means of occult ritual and the intercession of good spirits and angels.[16]

There was little prospect of stability once inside prison. In the politically febrile climate of Year II (1793–4), military reports, factional feuds, or even common rumor could suddenly alter the government's attitude to its interned populations and their presumed right to judicial protections. For the first months of the Terror there was no official pathway for arrested suspects to mount a defense from prison and exonerate themselves in order to be released before trial. Even when the deputy Saint-Just finally established a process on February 26, 1794, suspects were not informed of the reasons for their arrest, or of who had denounced them, leaving them ill-equipped to refute charges and in a state of doubt and often bewilderment.[17] Meanwhile, new suspects arrived at prisons each day and others departed just as suddenly, released or transferred to another prison or called to the Tribunal. Amid such uncertainty, every abrupt change was viewed with apprehension.

The prospect of a sudden transfer between prisons filled the famous poet Jean-Antoine Roucher with dread. On a freezing night in January 1794, he and fellow detainees at the prison of Sainte-Pélagie on the Left Bank were ordered to prepare for a journey by open cart across the Seine to a newly-opened prison at the former religious establishment of Saint-Lazare in north Paris (see Map 0.2). Roucher had to steel himself at the prospect, as the transfer carried him miles away from his wife and children, who had been visiting him regularly. Roucher's prison companion, the equally-famous artist Hubert Robert, made an oil painting recording the last moments that the poet spent alone in his cell staring at a framed portrait of his wife on his desk, having just written to tell her of this latest calamitous development. "I know that I am leaving," he wrote in one of his letters, "and I don't know what I will find"[18] (see Figure 13.6 in the source section for this chapter).

Not worn, but framed, the portrait of his wife that Roucher brought with him nevertheless served a similar function to Doucet de Suriny's ring. Carried in a briefcase, it could be set up in the relatively private setting of a cell, looking out at its occupant and projecting a sense of spousal concern and companionship into a potentially hostile environment where Roucher's social identity as a known intellectual carried little weight with prison authorities. It is possible to speculate that Robert's painting was in fact destined for the poet's wife, along with other pictures that Robert regularly made for his friend's family as a visual chronicle of the poet's life behind bars. If so, the picture might also have been intended to convey to Mme Roucher the consoling influence that her portrait had for her husband in his prison.[19]

The political prisons of the Terror brought many people of the élite social classes temporarily together into what historian Barbara Rosenwein has called "emotional communities." These were groups in which people adhered to the same norms of emotional expression, and valued (or devalued) the same or related emotions.[20] It is evident from Robert's picture of Roucher, and the moment that it records, that the two men shared an emotional understanding of their common predicament. Old friends, who once belonged to the same Masonic lodge (*Neuf Sœurs*), their classical educations instilled in them a common set of Stoic values that would determine their disciplined approach to life in prison. They were not the only ones. The future statesman Etienne-Denis Pasquier confirmed the existence of such an "emotional community" at Saint-Lazare where he befriended Robert and Roucher and joined the painter's rugged sporting team. He later reflected on the camaraderie of the prison, noting that "behind bars you re-entered society, as it were. You were surrounded by your relatives and friends and could converse freely with them."[21] Indeed, Pasquier's surprisingly positive description of Saint-Lazare—as a social environment that offered freedom of individual expression away from the paranoid atmosphere of Paris—corresponds to what cultural anthropologist William M. Reddy might call an "emotional refuge," which is to say, a place or group that provides safe release from prevailing emotional norms.[22] A number of collective portraits, made by Hubert Robert in prison, appear to record the emotional community at Saint-Lazare that Pasquier described. He showed suspects sitting closely together in the evening, reading, conversing, and playing music, or with jackets removed playing the high contact sport *ballon* in the exercise yard in the afternoons.[23] Both types of prison image, interior and exterior, show the walls as almost protective barriers, as if to imply that imprisonment offered some elements of refuge.

Within the social environment of the prison, differences of political opinion among suspects could to some degree be overcome by commonalities of class, education, and sensibility. Despite the shortfalls of their prison setting, for example, suspects continued to observe the civilities of their class, such as dressing for dinner and holding musical soirées, pressing into service the many talents and instruments in the prison community. Some aristocrats went so far as to continue using the formal address "vous" and formal titles in greeting fellow prisoners, a practice that preserved social rank and distance and which was for this precise reason discouraged by authorities. Extravagant displays of emotion were not acceptable in the political prisons, especially not among men, and perhaps not among women either, particularly in the presence of strangers and people of lower classes, including prison staff.

Unwritten codes governed the way in which small portraits were to be engaged with and required that the imprisoned guardians of miniatures master the emotions for which these images were such potent catalysts. Typically gifted in trust by the person they represented, there was an assumption that miniature portraits would be treasured, protected, and consumed appropriately; contemplated in private, perhaps in conjunction with the reading and writing of letters, and shown only to trusted confidantes. This was a significant point in the congested setting of revolutionary prisons, through which a constant flow of strangers passed. That understanding is implicitly confirmed in the way that prison-made images show miniatures being viewed in ideal conditions of privacy even though such conditions did not in reality exist, as most cells had a minimum of three occupants.

In a large, almost life-sized pastel self-portrait by the former academician and painter Jean-Bernard Restout, made at the prison of Saint-Lazare, Restout shows himself alone with a *tabatière*, the lid of which is adorned with a miniature portrait of a woman (see Figure 13.3). He tilts the box toward the viewer with one hand, while covering his heart with the other. The intended viewer is presumably the artist's long-term companion Anne Maréchal, who campaigned faithfully for his release and to whom he later left part of his estate.[24] As with the scene of Roucher alone in his cell, the demonstrated value of the miniature to its owner is central to the picture's meaning, and a sign of reciprocated tenderness. Both pictures vouch for

FIGURE 13.3 *Jean-Bernard Restout (1732–97),* Self-portrait holding a miniature, *1794. Pastel, 46.5 × 37.5 cm. Signed and dated* Restout l'an 1794. 3ème de la Rép. Fran. 5ème de la Liberté à Saint-Lazare. *Rouen, Musée des Beaux-Arts (since 1938). Alamy Stock Photo.*

their featured miniatures' proper use: cherished and viewed in private, with a solemnity appropriate to the situation.

Not everyone, however, could restrain their feelings with regard to their beloved portraits. At the prison of Port-Libre, one Mme de la Chabeaussière was said to be in pitiable health and spirits, and prone to tears. A fellow prisoner noted that the distressed woman "showed us a portrait of her daughter made by [the miniaturist] Isabey, which is of an exquisite finish . . . she hopes to get permission to have her daughter brought in with her."[25] Sympathetic as her witnesses may have been, whether they actually approved of her extravagant surrender to her own emotions is another matter. In a prison context where everyone else had private sorrows to contend with, decorum may have restrained most suspects from regaling relative strangers with portraits of their loved ones.

Prison employees more frankly disapproved of flamboyant displays of emotion around miniatures. One administrator at Saint-Lazare was said to have snatched a *tabatière* from a prisoner that was adorned with a portrait of his wife. Exasperated, it seems, by the undisciplined conduct such tokens appeared to produce among his charges, Jean-Baptiste Bergot apparently exclaimed that "These monsters console themselves with these portraits, for the absence of the originals, and forget that they are in prison."[26] Bergot's response suggests that open shows of dependence upon such love-objects in prison may have risked the confiscation of the very items that their owners prized most. The historical value of such anecdotes is sometimes dismissed by scholars as Thermidorian propaganda designed to impute gratuitous cruelty to jailors during the Terror. But they are nevertheless revealing for what they can tell us about wider social norms and regimes around the consumption of miniatures and about what was, from an official viewpoint, an appropriate relationship between prisoners and their miniatures in the prison context.

For all that miniature portraits ostensibly belonged to the Age of Enlightenment and the secular realm, the degree of emotion or *sentiment* invested in these keepsakes set them outside rational frameworks. It placed them beyond hierarchies of monetary and aesthetic value. In his 1999 study of revolutionary portraiture, Tony Halliday observed that during the eighteenth century, portraits were the images "least likely to be viewed as aesthetic objects. Their significance was overwhelmingly private and depended on the identity of their individual subjects."[27] Miniatures are arguably the most extreme example of portraits that were valued according to non-objective criteria. Marcia Pointon attributes this subjective dimension to the proximity that miniatures had to the body, noting how they "stand on a continuum that at once connects them to full-scale publicly displayed portraiture and at the other ties them into an economy of the body that is intimate, and private even if it is much discoursed upon."[28]

Unlike large portraits, miniatures were easily assimilated to the owner's body through their characteristics of portability and concealability. Their small scale and fragility demanded protection. They were susceptible to touching and kissing. They conjured up the presence of the person they depicted both visually, through an artistic likeness, and often also in a haptic sense, through fragments of hair, fabric, and handwriting fitted to their undersides, which were both kept from view and worn next to their wearers' skin. In fact, miniature portraits had more in common with *objets de piété*, talismans and holy "touch" relics, worn on the body or carried, than they did with conventional works of art hanging on walls, and it was in a prison context that this intrinsic significance came to the fore.

Protection and Guardianship of Miniatures

The prospect of a prisoner's physical separation from his or her miniature was intolerable, in part because it entailed another layer of loss, and in part because the miniature morally belonged to someone else. In this latter respect, miniatures qualify as a type of commodity that anthropologists have called "inalienable possessions," a concept famously formulated by Annette Weiner through her research on the material culture of the Trobriand Islands for objects embodying kinship, family history, and ritual power.[29] Although inalienable objects cannot be sold, such items may be bestowed as gifts on the understanding that they still retain a tie to their owners. Bestowed or—more properly—*loaned* on trust, they are understood by giver and recipient as transcendent treasures and heirlooms that must be guarded from all exigencies. This was also true of the eighteenth-century miniature, which was a proxy for a particular person and a symbol of a relationship involving mutual solicitude. Taboos existed around the careless guardianship of the miniature. As Marcia Pointon has observed, "miniature portraits unsecured, neither worn nor kept safely stored are part of a European iconography of abandoned morals and scandalous behaviour."[30] The protection of miniatures in prison became something of a trope of Thermidorian literature, a way of signaling the threat that the revolutionary prison posed to objects of love and by extension posed to their virtuous owners who tried valiantly to defend them. It is in this context that one memoir describes a female suspect at Le Plessis who had slipped a medallion portrait and lock of hair to a gendarme for safekeeping during a prison search. The sympathetic soldier was observed discreetly returning it to her and was punished for his efforts by being placed under arrest for conspiracy.[31]

Return of Miniatures

Many suspects arrested after the decree of September 1793 at first believed themselves relatively safe in prison. Statistics support their belief. Of the approximately half a million people imprisoned during the Terror, only 17,000 (or 3.5 percent) were condemned by Revolutionary Tribunals, with the majority of death sentences passed after the notorious Law of 22 Prairial on June 10, 1794, which did away with suspects' right to a defense and limited the outcomes to release or execution.[32] After 8 Ventôse (February 26, 1794), many placed their hopes in their defense lawyers or any papers that proved their patriotism (*pièces justificatives*) that they had managed to assemble from their prison cells. Such papers might in theory be sent to the Public Prosecutor and trigger a preliminary investigation by the *chambre de conseil* (a smaller working group of the Revolutionary Tribunal), which *might* result in release and thus bypass the need for a formal trial. As Alex Fairfax-Cholmeley has recently noted, much more remains to be known about these preliminary investigations, which could result in the highly desirable "pre-trial releases." Statistically, this approach did in fact often pay off, with pre-trial releases making up a quarter of all Tribunal judgments in early 1794.[33]

But by early April 1794 there was growing cause for pessimism. Public sentiment was hardening against the suspect population, amid rumors that prisoners were plotting to break out, slaughter the Committee of Public Safety, and instate the child Louis XVII on the throne.[34] Security was stepped up, with new prohibitions on communications with the outside that sometimes lasted for weeks. Cell searches were conducted, and money, sharp implements, and valuables confiscated. Locks and grills were retro-fitted onto the once-elegant buildings that served as prisons (or *maisons de suspicion*, as they were sometimes called). Paling fences were constructed around their perimeters, blocking prisoners' glimpses of relatives in the streets outside, and guards were set to patrol the new boundaries, forcing back those who refused to be deterred.[35] It had become depressingly apparent to detainees that their written appeals addressed to the Public Prosecutor were going unread.[36] Most worrying of all, though, was a sudden increase in the death sentences handed down by the Revolutionary Tribunal. April 20, 1794 marked the first of the batches of suspects to be sent to the guillotine, grimly known as *fournées* (a term for bakers' trays holding multiple loaves for the oven). By this point it had become impossible for prisoners to ignore the precarious phase into which they had entered.

With the odds against them clearly growing, suspects began thinking of ways to return the miniatures in their possession to their rightful owners. At Port-Libre prison in mid-May, one suspect, Philippe-Edmé Coittant, heard his name called from the lists of those ordered before the Revolutionary Tribunal. He immediately fetched a portrait of his wife Hélène from his room and asked a friend to see that it was returned to her.[37] Coittant's summons was an administrative error, but the priorities he revealed through his actions when his name was called are revealing. The unspoken pacts that existed between prisoners to see their companions' mementos safely restored to relatives were hardly foolproof. Those who accepted that doleful responsibility could just as easily be called to the Revolutionary Tribunal themselves. Inevitably, therefore, many portraits and personal mementos went astray, alienated from their original owners, and, in some cases, ending up in the Public Prosecutor's office.[38]

In one such case, the twenty-one-year-old widow of a prisoner named L'Herbette was emboldened to take matters into her own hands, writing to the Public Prosecutor, Fouquier-Tinville, to request the return of a miniature of herself that her husband had carried with him before his death.[39] She told him frankly that "since I think my face can be of interest only to those who know me, I dare to hope that you will not refuse to return it to me," and she offered to pay the value of the gold frame to the republic.[40] In this instance, Mme L'Herbette was attempting to retrieve her own portrait from the illegitimate hands into which it had fallen and restore it to the private emotional economy to which it belonged. But the significance of the object that she was reclaiming had in the meantime changed by virtue of its wearer's death. The object now related intrinsically not just to herself, but to the person who had last owned and touched it, compounding its value as an inalienable possession, and making the urgency of its return all the greater.

The *Avant-décès* Portrait

As the Terror intensified by the spring of 1794, it grew apparent to many prisoners that they would soon no longer need portraits for their own consolation. Instead, their loved ones would. The prison-made portrait was a new phenomenon that first emerged in the unique framework of the French revolutionary justice system, in the prisons which sprung up after the Law of Suspects in September 1793, and which vanished again with the effective dismantling of that system by October 1795. But for all its poignant originality, the prison-made portrait did not emerge in a vacuum. It came into being as part of an economy of portraits and letters through which people conducted their relationships across the eighteenth century. Unlike the "portraits of consolation" produced and described by J.-B. Isabey that were made in the hope of an eventual reunion between owners, portraits made in the "shadow of the guillotine" were produced in the knowledge of their finality, and as markers of the end of an exchange of portraits. *Avant-décès*, or pre-death, portraits signaled ultimate closure, just as the final letters written from prison that often accompanied them signaled the conclusion of all correspondence.

It remains to be determined how individual prisoners, detained alongside hundreds of others in essentially the same predicament, could conceive of procuring a portrait of themselves in prison, especially at a time when their contact with the outside world was being gradually shut off? The answer lies in the demographic breadth of prisoners swept into the prison system as the Terror progressed. Artists, architects, and luxury craftsmen were no safer from the Law of Suspects than anyone else, and many were placed under arrest, suspected of allegiances to their former patrons in the court, loyalty to the Church, or alignments with the wrong political faction. Artistic skills could also be found throughout the wider population of most prisons. Soldiers, engineers, and doctors acquired drawing skills in the course of their vocational training. The imprisoned nobility also included many skilled amateurs, privileged beneficiaries of an Enlightenment education that included practical instruction in the fine arts.

Professional artists, who relied on their work for survival, and whose assets were under seal and frozen, soon found (perhaps to their surprise, and no doubt to their relief) that their talents were keenly sought by their fellow prisoners. Indeed, noted art collectors can be identified in the *écrous* (prison registers) of most prisons of the Terror, the most conspicuous example being perhaps Hubert Robert's main patron, the wealthy financier Jean-Joseph de Laborde, confined at the former palais du Luxembourg. Many artists proved willing or eager to put their talents to the service of the captive markets they encountered behind prison walls and took steps to have their artistic equipment delivered to them in order to do so.

One such artist was the former court miniature painter Pierre-Maurice Bénard, imprisoned at the Luxembourg since November 1793. In January 1794, Bénard explained his dire circumstances to the authorities, stating that "I am the father of two children, I have a wife and old man to support and I have no fortune other than my work."[41] Although he was not released, Bénard managed to obtain his painting materials and immediately undertook a commission from a co-prisoner, the politician François Chabot. Accused of financial corruption in relation to the French East India Company, Chabot was under no illusion as to his fate. By all accounts he had a suspicious amount of money in prison and was rumored to be dining sumptuously on luxuries delivered to him by a local restaurateur.[42]

Chabot placed an order with Bénard for nine small portraits of himself: five ordinary miniatures, three rings with tiny inset portraits, and a tortoiseshell *bonbonnière* with a portrait fitted on its lid. Upon their completion, Chabot paid the painter Bénard 545 livres, according to a surviving receipt in the artist's hand.[43] Chabot then arranged for the dispatch of his jewel-like keepsakes to their recipients, most likely his wife, mother, and sisters, before he drank poison in mid-March. But he failed to die and was guillotined in early April.[44]

Other prisoners also took steps to acquire their portraits early, not knowing what tomorrow would bring and possibly anxious to obtain an artist's services ahead of fellow prisoners. It may have been Chabot's monopolization of Bénard's time at the Luxembourg that caused some prisoners to look elsewhere. The wife of an inmate discovered the unmet need for miniatures and took to holding portrait sittings during her visits. "La femme Goust," as she was known, was, in fact, Julie Pourvoyeur, possibly a member of the Paris family of pastellists and miniature painters.[45] The demand for her talents soon became such that in May 1794, as the dangers for prisoners kept rising, the artist defied the risks and made the extraordinary decision to join her husband, Charles Goust de Longpré, at his prison full time. Mme Pourvoyeur was thus almost certainly the unnamed woman who was said to have set up painting equipment in the gallery of the Luxembourg, where she worked in "permanent session" making portraits.[46]

The royalist journalist Claude François Beaulieu wrote appreciatively of the presence of a young painter, whom he described as "assez gentille" (quite well-bred) at the Luxembourg, observing that "it was at a time when everyone of us regarded his death as certain; in this sad belief, it was yet more of a pleasure to cut off a section of our hair and twist it around medallions, portraits, and to have them sent to our wives, to our mothers, to our children, to loved ones that we would not see again."[47]

Five surviving portraits made in the Luxembourg prison and bearing similarities of format and inscription can cautiously be ascribed to Julie Pourvoyeur, based on their correspondence to the assembly-line mode of production that she was reported to have established. One pair of portraits, set on the lids of tortoiseshell boxes, shows the marquis and marquise Chambon d'Arbouville, aged fifty-nine and forty-seven respectively, who had been transported to Paris from their estates in Eure-et-Loire (see Figures 13.4

FIGURE 13.4 *Attributed to Julie de Pourvoyeur (femme Goust de Longpré),* Marquis Gaspard Louis du Chambon d'Arbouville, Chevalier de Saint Louis *(July 17, 1735–July 9, 1794). Watercolour and gouache on ivory; tortoiseshell box, copper, 8 × 8 × 2.3 cm. Inscribed:* fait a la Maison du Luxembourg le 24 Ventos l'an deux de la République *(March 14, 1794). Charles Vatel Bequest, 1883, Musée Lambinet, Ville de Versailles.*

FIGURE 13.5 *Attributed to Julie de Pourvoyeur (femme Goust de Longpré),* Marquise Félicité-Françoise-Sophie d'Arbouville née Frétau *(1747–July 9, 1794). Watercolour and gouache on ivory, tortoiseshell box, copper, 8 × 8 × 2.3 cm. Inscribed:* fait a la Maison du Luxembourg le 24 Ventos l'an deux de la République *(March 14, 1794). Charles Vatel Bequest, 1883 (inv. 788), Musée Lambinet, Ville de Versailles.*

and 13.5). They are portrayed against a grey stone wall and a grilled window (emblematic details which little resembled the actual palace setting in which they were confined). The inscription around the edge of each roundel dates their manufacture to March 14, 1794, before the general downturn of April. Despite the relatively stable moment in which they were painted, the d'Arbouvilles' worst fears were eventually realized. They died on the guillotine four months later, in July. The early acquisition of their portraits ahead of the rush was doubtless a source of reassurance in the meantime. With portraits secured well in advance, prisoners had, as Beaulieu notes, the pleasure of being able to embellish their reverse sides with interlaced initials or other "devices" made from their own woven hair, a time-consuming skill that some gentlewomen possessed. Alternatively, the task may have been entrusted to imprisoned *perruquiers* (wigmakers), who often specialized in "hairwork" for miniatures after the fashion for wigs faded in the Revolution, and whose presence in prisons can also be traced in the *écrous*.[48]

The acquisition of a portrait in prison was something of a triumph. The artists upon whom a prison population relied could, like anyone else, be suddenly whisked away, never to be seen again. At Port-Libre prison, where professional artists were in short supply, Philippe-Edmé Coittant arranged to have his portrait made by an amateur, Jean Fougeret. An aristocrat and former *receveur général des finances* (a high-level, profit-making tax collector in the Old Regime), the popular Fougeret was imprisoned with his wife and daughters, surrounded by friends of similar rank. Fougeret set a up a small atelier in the family's cell in which he produced miniature portraits from memory for his imprisoned friends and acquaintances. To everyone's horror, the amiable artist was called away to the Revolutionary Tribunal and guillotined on May 12, 1794. After a tactful period of mourning, Coittant called on the family's cell where he had an opportunity to inspect his miniature whose progress had been interrupted by the calamity. "I have just been this morning to see my portrait, painted from memory by the citizen Fougeret at the same time as several other cameos, which seem to breathe of the misfortune of this estimable artist's family."[49] Remarkably for the prisoners concerned, Fougeret's daughter Angélique, herself an amateur artist, appears to have stepped into the breach and completed her father's much-valued work. Her memoirs state that in due course she obtained a small space in the prison's attic, where she and another female artist held portrait sessions for fellow detainees, who were, with few exceptions, royalists.[50]

In the event that a prisoner was suddenly called away to the Paris Tribunal without having had a portrait made, all was not yet lost. The Conciergerie prison (see Map 0.2), to which all prisoners were briefly transferred prior to trial, offered one final chance for the acquisition of an *avant-décès* portrait. The famous court portraitist Joseph Boze, a royalist accused of conspiracy, was confined at the overcrowded prison from October 1793 to August 1794, where he shared a cell with five other men.[51] Boze soon obtained his painting equipment and appears at times to have worked in virtual "permanent session," meeting the needs of each day's new arrivals. In this he received crucial assistance from the prison's superintendent, Toussaint Richard, and his wife Marie Anne Barassin, who were fellow royalists and old acquaintances. The couple solved the problem of the artist's lack of a working space by arranging for him "to go often to their private quarters in order to paint their children and some prisoners or friends."[52]

Like Bénard and Mme Pourvoyeur, Boze was methodical. He appears to have provided rapid sketches for those with no time to spare, or more developed pictures at a higher price for prisoners who felt they could wait for a more sophisticated end product. Choosing a more elaborate portrait carried risks, however, as becomes apparent in the case of one prisoner named Vendeuil. Vendeuil (who was most likely Louis-Marie-Athanase de Loménie, Comte de Brienne, marquis de Möy, and seigneur de Vendeuil), found himself suddenly called to the Revolutionary Tribunal and hit complications in organizing payment for his picture via proxies. In a panic, Vendeuil wrote to a friend, "I ask you to hurry [the payment] so that he [Boze] can finish the portrait and send it." In due course another friend paid the artist's wife 100 livres, for which she issued a receipt on May 7, 1794, and the painting was released, but just in the nick of time, as Vendeuil was guillotined three days later.

Some prisoners were not so lucky. On March 29, 1794, Jean Valery Harelle, a thirty-year-old cotton manufacturer from Alençon, sent his wife an incomplete portrait from the Conciergerie, possibly also by Boze, writing apologetically:

> My dearest, my last moments have come. I have been condemned to death by the Revolutionary Tribunal. I am innocent of what I am accused of; but no matter, it is settled, and at least I die well, rest assured. Be consoled. This is the only happiness I can hope for during the brief moments remaining to me. My sister-in-law Houdouard, to whom this paper is addressed, will hand you my portrait, taken here. It is not very good, because I had to start for trial just when the painter was taking it. This testimony of my remembrance will be a sure guarantee to you of that affection which I have ever cherished for thee, and which will not end, but which I shall gladly carry away with me.[53]

The *Après-décès* Portrait

Even less fortunate than Harelle was Claude-Guillaume Lambert, Baron de Chamerolles and comte d'Auverse at Saint-Lazare, who missed out altogether on having a portrait made. In late June 1794, during the weeks known as the "Great Terror" when the guillotine was working at its fastest pace, Lambert was summoned to the Conciergerie and guillotined the next day. Back at Saint-Lazare, his distraught son, Paul-Augustin-Joseph Lambert du Fresne, sought out Jean-Bernard Restout and asked him for a posthumous portrait of his father. Unable to recollect clearly the features of the deceased man, the sympathetic painter turned to the victim's "emotional community" for information. One prisoner recalled how "this artist did me the honor of consulting me, [and] interrogated the memories of people who had been close to him. He united and founded, so to speak, their precious information in his memory." The result was proclaimed to be a great success. "This portrait," the narrator wrote, "which friendship seemed to dictate to that skillful artist, is drawn with superiority, and has moreover, the merit of a perfect resemblance."[54]

The notorious Law of 22 Prairial, which marked the onset of the Great Terror, coincided with a state of continual lockdown in the prison system. The Law encouraged the exposure of so-called "prison conspiracies" as a means to more quickly liquidate larger groups of suspects in the overflowing system. It thus paved the way for much higher numbers of executions in the last six weeks of the Terror than had been seen in the previous nine months. The same law also significantly diminished the chances of last portraits ever reaching their intended recipients. At Saint-Lazare, the painter Charles-Louis Trudaine de Montigny wrote, in a letter that may never have reached his sister, that "It is very true that I work ... I have made two little medallions; there is no opportunity for me to send them to you."[55] Paranoid about being implicated in alleged prison plots, suspects became too fearful to speak to one another and jailers too nervous to perform any errands for them. The royalist journalist Claude François Beaulieu had noted months earlier that at the Luxembourg prison it had become "necessary to take the greatest care in getting these sad presents out. The jailers would only take responsibility for them under the toughest conditions; even more would not."[56] With no one left to ask, one young mother, Antoinette Paisac (or Paysac), who had been called to the Revolutionary Tribunal with her husband on June 25, 1794, was forced to write to the Public Prosecutor to ask him to convey her portrait to her son, saying, "I beg you, citizen public prosecutor, to be so kind as to send my son, a young child of ten, staying in the rue de Berry, my portrait, which you will find on a portfolio in my red morocco writing set, which must have been handed over to you," adding "You are taking from him a mother whose image, at least, must remain with him.[57]

Personal portraits in the eighteenth century have histories intrinsically bound up with the emotional lives of the people that they represented and of those to whom they were given. Unwritten laws governed how they should be kept, shown, and looked upon. In a prison context full of potential threats, the burden of their guardianship and protection was compounded, but their consolatory power grew correspondingly. In the cases of portraits brought into prison or made there, their value never resided primarily in their qualities of artistic execution, or the reputation of the artist who made them, or in their cost. The true value was emotional and only fully revealed at times of existential threat. In the prison context, portraits served as a poignant physical interface between people who found themselves separated against their wills and provided enduring proof of a suspect's existence, beliefs, and affections beyond the anonymity of a mass grave.

The political events of the French Revolution thus brought about a remarkable change in people's understanding of the significance of the portraits that they owned, viewed, and commissioned. They moved from being purely aesthetic and commercial objects to playing a crucial part in people's emotional and political responses to the violence and disruption of the Terror. The new value that they acquired is attested by the way that such portraits were later retained in families, displayed in reliquaries and shrine-like settings, or collected by sympathetic historians in the nineteenth century, who were intrigued by their dual function as tangible relics of, and mute witnesses to, an extraordinary moment in modern history.[58] Although produced within the secular framework of eighteenth-century art, these small portraits, which were so closely connected to life, death, and the body in the French Revolution, came to have much more in common with the objects and rituals of piety and even martyrdom. If miniatures had, according to Peter Adolf Hall, sunk to being mere "trifles of fashion" in 1788, they were far from simply that by 1794.

Source: Hubert Robert (1733–1808), *Jean-Antoine Roucher (1745–1794) as he prepares to be transferred from Sainte-Pélagie to Saint-Lazare*, 1794

For the locations of the prisons, see Map 0.2.

FIGURE 13.6 *Hubert Robert (1733–1808),* Jean-Antoine Roucher (1745–1794) as he prepares to be transferred from Sainte-Pélagie to Saint-Lazare, *1794. Oil on canvas, 32 × 40 cm. Signed on bed frame: H. Robert Pinxit. The Ella Gallup Sumner and Mary Catlin Sumner Collection Fund 1937.1, Wadsworth Atheneum, Hartford CT.*

Notes

1 I would like to thank the editors Mette Harder and Jennifer Heuer, and Alex Fairfax-Cholmeley, Matthew Martin, and Joseph Baillio, who have read drafts or otherwise provided assistance with aspects of this chapter.

2 William M. Reddy, *The Navigation of Feeling: A Framework for the History of Emotions* (Cambridge: Cambridge University Press, 2001), 145–6.

3 Matthew Shaw, *Time and the French Revolution: The Republican Calendar, 1789–year XIV* (Rochester, NY: Royal Historical Society/Boydell Press, 2011), 126–7. On the democratization of luxury goods such as watches and snuff boxes through the second-hand market, see Laurence Fontaine, "The Circulation of Luxury Goods in Eighteenth-Century Paris: Social Redistribution and an Alternative Currency," in *Luxury in the Eighteenth Century: Debates, Desires and Delectable Goods*, ed. Maxine Berg and Elizabeth Eger, trans. Vicky Wittaker (London: Palgrave Macmillan, 2003), 89–102.

4 Pierre Nicolas Violet, *Traité élémentaire sur l'art de peindre en miniature* (Paris: chez l'auteur Guillot, 1788), 68. Quoted in Nathalie Lemoine-Bouchard, *Les Peintres en miniature 1650–1850* (Paris: Les Éditions de l'Amateur, 2008), 31: "Au surplus, le peintre en miniature n'a plus aujourd'hui de droits à l'immortalité. On ne traite plus ces formes d'ouvrages, que comme une bagatelle de mode, & nous sommes dans l'âge des Lumières."

5 Edmond Taigny, *J.-B. Isabey: sa vie et ses oeuvres. Extrait de la Revue européenne* (Paris: E. Panckoucke, 1859), 18. "Une veine nouvelle de travaux se rencontra: elle surgit des malheurs mêmes de l'époque. Je me mis en campagne, offrant mes services à toutes les âmes en peine. Je baptisai ainsi mes œuvres nouvelles du titre de «portraits de consolation». Tantôt une mère voulait, en émigrant, rassembler dans un seul médaillon les traits de ses chers enfants; souvent aussi, dans une courte séance, un double souvenir devait être échangé. Que de fois j'assistai à ce don mutuel de l'amour, suivi d'une cruelle séparation! L'absence ne devait durer qu'un mois, disait-on. Hélas! n'étaient-ce pas toujours d'éternels adieux!"

6 Eliza O'Connor, "Notes biographiques sur Mme de Condorcet et sur Mme Vernet, par Mme O'Connor (remises à M. Arago, mars 1841)," in Jean-François Eugène Robinet, *Condorcet sa vie, son œuvre 1743–1794* (Paris: Ancienne Maison Quantin, 1893), 370.

7 Timothy Tackett, *The Coming of the Terror in the French Revolution* (Cambridge, MA: Harvard University Press, 2015), 303–5.

8 Donald Greer, *The Incidence of the Terror during the French Revolution: A Statistical Interpretation* (Cambridge, MA: Harvard University Press, 1935/1966), 27.

9 Anne Simonin, "Les acquittés de la Grande Terreur. Réflexions sur l'amitié dans la République," in *Les Politiques de la Terreur 1793–1794*, ed. Michel Biard (Rennes: Presses Universitaires de Rennes; Paris: Société des études robespierristes, 2008), 183–205.

10 For a complete history of the revolutionary justice system, see James Logan Godfrey, *Revolutionary Justice: A Study of the Organization, Personnel, and*

Procedure of the Paris Tribunal, 1793–1795 (Chapel Hill: University of North Carolina Press, 1951).

11 Décret du 17 septembre 1793 relatif aux gens suspects: Art. 7: "Les détenus pourront faire transporter dans ces bâtimens [nationaux] les meubles qui leur seront d'une absolue nécessité; ils y resteront gardés jusqu'à la paix." Antoine Auguste Carette, *Lois annotées ou Lois, décrets, ordonnances, avis du conseil* (Paris: Bureaux de l'administration, 1845), 2:269.

12 Marcia Pointon, "'Surrounded with Brilliants': Miniature Portraits in Eighteenth Century England," *Art Bulletin* 83, no. 1 (2001), 48–71, 48.

13 Raphaël-Pierre Doucet-Suriny, *Mémoire sur trois arrestations consécutives, exécutées par le gouvernement de Robespierre et compagnie* (Paris: chez l'auteur, 20 Prairial an III), 691.

14 Susan Stewart, *On Longing: Narratives of the Miniature, the Gigantic, the Souvenir, the Collection* (Durham, NC: Duke University Press, 1984/2003), 53.

15 On eighteenth-century miniatures with apotropaic functions, see Hanneke Grootenboer, *Treasuring the Gaze: Intimate Vision in Late Eighteenth-Century Eye Miniatures* (Chicago: University of Chicago Press, 2012), 6.

16 On the vitalistic cult of Martinism and its leader, Louis Claude de Saint-Martin (the "unknown philosopher"), to whom the duchess was attached, see David Allen Harvey, *Beyond Enlightenment: Occultism and Politics in Modern France* (DeKalb: Northern Illinois University Press, 2005), 9–24.

17 On 8 Ventôse l'an II (February 26, 1794) the National Convention deputy Saint-Just publicly confirmed that the Committee of General Security was invested with powers to release detained patriots and stated that anyone wishing to reclaim freedom should give an account of his conduct since May 1, 1789.

18 Antoine Guillois, *Pendant la Terreur. Le poète Roucher 1745–1794* (Paris: Calmann Lévy, 1890), 248. "Je sais ce que je quitte, me disais-je, et j'ignore ce que je vais chercher."

19 For Robert's gifts of drawings and paintings to Roucher's family, a number of which have remained in the family and never been published, see Guillois, *Pendant la Terreur*, passim.

20 Barbara H. Rosenwein, *Emotional Communities in the Early Middle Ages* (Ithaca, NY: Cornell University Press, 2007), 2.

21 Etienne-Denis, Duc de Pasquier, *Histoire de mon temps, mémoires* (Paris: Plon, 1893), 92. "Derrière les verrous, au contraire, on se trouvait en quelque sorte rentré dans la vie sociale; on était entouré de ses parents, de ses amis; on les voyait sans contrainte, on causait librement avec eux."

22 Reddy, *The Navigation of Feeling*, 129 and 150–4.

23 See, for example, Robert's *Ball game in the courtyard of Saint-Lazare*. Oil on canvas, 35 x 41 cm. Musée Carnavalet, Paris and Interior of the Saint-Lazare prison, "concert au réfectoire." Black chalk sketch on paper, 28 x 33 cm. Signed: H. Robert S. L. Current whereabouts unknown. Reproduced in Jean Robiquet, *Daily Life in the French Revolution*, trans. James Kirkup (London: Weidenfeld and Nicholson, 1964).

24 Abbé Estournet, *La Famille des Hallé* (Paris: Plon-Nourrit, 1905), 167.

25 Philippe Coittant, 13 Pluviôse l'an II (February 1, 1794). In Pierre Jean Baptiste Nougaret, *Histoire des prisons de Paris et des départements* (Paris: chez Courcier, 1797), 2:241.

26 Émile Campardon, *Le Tribunal révolutionnaire de Paris* (Paris: Henri Plon, 1866), 3:404. "Ces monstres, disait-il pour justifier sa cruauté, se consolent avec les portraits d'être privés des originaux, et ils ne s'aperçoivent plus qu'ils sont en prison!"

27 Tony Halliday, *Facing the Public: Portraiture in the Aftermath of the French Revolution* (Manchester: Manchester University Press, 1999), 2.

28 Marcia Pointon, "The Portrait Miniature as an Intimate Object," in *European Portrait Miniatures: Artists, Functions and Collections*, ed. Bernd Pappe, Juliane Schmieglitz-Otten, and Gerrit Walczak (Petersberg: Michael Imhof Verlag, 2014), 16–26, 16.

29 Annette B. Weiner, *Inalienable Possessions: The Paradox of Keeping-While-Giving* (Berkeley: University of California Press, 1992), 33.

30 Pointon, "The Portrait Miniature," 25.

31 *Reign of Terror: Authentic Narratives of the Horrors Committed by the Revolutionary Government of France* (London: W. Simpkin and R. Marshall, 1826), 144.

32 Greer, *The Incidence of the Terror*, 29, and Simonin, "Les acquittés."

33 Alex Fairfax-Chomeley, "Creating and Resisting the Terror: the Paris Revolutionary Tribunal, March–June 1793," *French History* 32, no. 2 (2018), 203–25.

34 Alphonse Dunoyer, *The Public Prosecutor of the Terror: Antoine Fouquier-Tinville*, trans. A. W. Evans (London: Herbert Jenkins, 1913), 57–67.

35 Jean de Laurencie, *Une Maison de détention sous la Terreur: L'hôtel des Bénédictins anglais* (Paris: Schola, 1905), 4. Laurencie notes a locksmith's bill for the Bénédictins anglais from the months of Floréal, Prairial, and Messidor, l'an II (April to July 1794), consisting of "a long enumeration" of large and small grills and bolts for the prison wicket gate, the courtyard, and the guard-house.

36 On prisoners' appeals being ignored, see Louise Henriette Charlotte Philippine de Noailles de Durfort Duras (Duchesse de Duras), *Prison Journals During the French Revolution by the Duchesse de Duras née Noailles*, trans. Martha Ward Carey (New York: Dodd, Mead and Company, 1892), 76, and Ben Kafka, "The Demon of Writing; Paperwork, Public Safety and the Reign of Terror," *Representations* 98, no. 1 (2007): 1–24, 3–6.

37 Prairial l'an II (June 14, 1794). Philippe Coittant's journal, quoted in Charles Dauban, *Les Prisons de Paris sous la Révolution*, 1870 (Geneva: reprint Slatkine-Megariotis, 1977), 356–7.

38 Following a decree of March 3, 1793, the property of all condemned prisoners was confiscated by the State, and so prisoners often distributed their personal effects to their companions before leaving for the Revolutionary Tribunal. What happened to the items after falling into official hands varied. Clothes

were sent to the Hôtel-Dieu or Hospice de l'Humanité, and victims' effects were inventoried by prison concierges and sold. See Richard Wrigley, *The Politics of Appearance: Representations of Dress in Revolutionary France* (Oxford: Berg, 2002), 28–9. On 21 Prairial year III (June 9, 1795), the National Convention ordered the return of unsold confiscated property to victims' relatives.

39 This was presumably the stockbroker Antoine Charles L'Herbette, executed as a counter-revolutionary on 13 Prairial l'an II (June 1, 1794).

40 Olivier Blanc, *Last Letters: Prisons and Prisoners of the French Revolution, 1793–1794*, trans. Alan Sheridan (London: A. Deutsch, 1987), 6.

41 Archives Nationales F^{7}4637, p. 87. 1 Pluviôse an II (January 20, 1794): "Citoyens, je suis père de deux enfans, j'ai une femme et un vieillard a soutenir et je n'ai d'autre fortune que mon travail."

42 Georges Lenôtre, *A Gascon Royalist in Revolutionary Paris: The Baron de Batz 1792–1795*, trans. Mrs. R. Stawell (London: Heinemann, 1910), 136–7 and 137, n. 1.

43 Archives Nationales, F^{7}4637, p. 87. Invoice dated February 12, 1794.

44 Joseph de Bonald, *François Chabot, membre de la Convention Française, 1756–1794* (Paris: E. Paul, 1908), 320–1.

45 These were the master oil painter and pastellist Jean-Baptiste Pourvoyeur, former member of the Académie de Saint-Luc, and his son, the miniature painter Jean-Baptiste Pourvoyeur *fils*. Further details about Julie Pourvoyeur are discussed in a forthcoming publication by the author.

46 Rémy Bijaoui, *Prisonniers et prisons de la Terreur* (Paris: Imago, 1996), 71.

47 Dauban, *Les Prisons*, 214. "II fut un temps où chacun de nous regardait sa mort comme certaine; dans cette triste persuasion, c'était encore une jouissance de couper une portion de nos cheveux, d'en entourer des médaillons, des portraits, et de les faire passer à nos femmes, à nos mères, à nos enfants, aux personnes chères, enfin, que nous ne devions plus revoir."

48 On hair in jewelry, see Cynthia Amnéus, "The Art of Ornamental Hairwork," in *Perfect Likeness: European and American Portrait Miniatures from the Cincinnati Art Museum*, eds. Julie Aronson and Marjorie E. Weisman (New Haven, CT: Yale University Press, 2006), 63–76, 65. See also Marcia Pointon, "Materializing Mourning: Hair, Jewellery and the Body," in *Material Memories*, ed. Marius Kwint (Oxford: Berg, 1999), 39–57.

49 2 Messidor an II (June 20, 1794). Philippe Coittant's journal, quoted in Dauban, *Les Prisons*, 359. "J'ai été voir ce matin mon portrait, peint de mémoire par le citoyen Fougeret, ainsi que plusieurs camées où semblait respirer la malheureuse famille de cet artiste estimable."

50 Angélique de Maussion, née Fougeret, *Rescapés de Thermidor* (Paris: Nouvelles éditions latines, 1975), 69. Angélique Fougeret appears to have made an exception for Victor de Broglie, chief of staff of the republican army, who, according to Coittant, sat for his portrait on June 26, 1794, two hours before departing for the Revolutionary Tribunal, which was then placed with his friends. "Memoirs of Philippe Coittant," in Dauban, *Les Prisons*, 359–60.

51 Boze's cellmates were the constitutional Bishop Lamourette, a prior named Saumenil, a tailor called Parisian, the ex-Minister of Finance Clavières, and the comte Jacques-Claude Beugnot. Beugnot recalled the atmosphere of their cell as unusual for its serenity and noted the men's different outlooks: "Clavières was a materialist, the bishop and the prior a very pious priest, the tailor was a Protestant and the painter nothing at all." Jacques-Claude Beugnot, comte, *Life and Adventures of Count Beugnot, Minister of State under Napoleon I*, trans. and ed. Charlotte Yonge (London: Hurst and Blackett, 1871), 1:188.

52 Gaspard Louis Lafont d'Aussonne, *Mémoires secrets et universels des malheurs et de la mort de la Reine de France* (Paris: Petit, 1824), 347–8.

53 9 Germinal l'an II (March 29, 1794). See John Goldworth Alger, *Paris in 1789–94: Farewell Letters of Victims of the Guillotine* (London: G. Allen, 1902; AMS Press, 1970), 425.

54 François Simon Aved de Loizerolles, *La mort de Loizerolles: Poème* (Paris: Dondey-Dupré, 1828), 84. "Quelques jours après cet horrible événement, il pria M. Restout, digne héritier d'un nom illustre dans les arts, et qui partageait notre détention, de dessiner les traits de son infortuné père. M. Restout se rappelait à la vérité la figure de M. Lambert; mais il ne l'avait jamais fixée comme ayant l'intention de la peindre. Cet artiste me fit l'honneur de me consulter, interrogea la mémoire des personnes qui avaient vécu dans l'intimité avec M. Lambert. Il réunit, et fondit, pour ainsi dire, leurs précieux renseignemens dans sa mémoire. Ce portrait, que l'amitié semblait dicter à cet habile artiste, est supérieurement dessiné, et a en outré, le merite d'une parfaite ressemblance."

55 Ernest Chouillier, "Les Trudaine," *Revue de Champagne et de Brie* 14 (1882): 14–15. "Il est très vrai que je travaille . . . J'ai fait un tableau et deux petits médaillons; il ne me manque qu'une occasion de te les envoyer."

56 Dauban, *Les Prisons*, 214. "Encore fallait-il les plus grandes précautions pour faire sortir ces tristes présents. Les guichetiers ne voulaient s'en charger qu'à des conditions très-dures; plusieurs même ne le voulaient pas."

57 Olivier Blanc, *La dernière lettre: prisons et condamnés de la Révolution, 1793–1794* (Paris: Robert Laffont, 1984), 127. "Je vous prie . . . de vouloir bien envoyer à mon fils, jeune enfant de dix ans, en pension rue de Berry, mon portrait que vous trouverez sur une portefeuille dans mon écritoire de maroquin rouge qui a dû vous être remise. Vous lui arrachez une mère dont l'image, au moins, doit lui rester." 7 Messidor an II (June 25, 1794).

58 These mostly amateur historians and collectors include the lawyer Charles Vatel (1816–85), who once owned the miniatures of the Darbouvilles, illustrated here, and the geologist and former Jacobin politician Jean-Louis Soulavie (1752–1813), who owned a group of prison portraits on paper, now in the Louvre. On the key role of these private collectors, described as "central actors in heritage politics," see Tom Stammers, "The Homeless Heritage of the French Revolution, c.1789–1889," *International Journal of Heritage Studies* 25, no. 5 (2018): 478–90, DOI: 10.1080/13527258.2018.1431688.

14

Revolutionary Parents and Children: Everyday Lives in Times of Stress

Siân Reynolds

No more scary stories from our wet-nurses
Equality of right and left hand . . .
Not forced to sleep in the same bed
No more Latin, much more French
No nasty stiff clothes
Equal inheritance[1]

This *cahier des bambins* (toddlers' list of grievances) was written, probably by a teacher as a joke, in the spring of 1789, when *cahiers de doléances* (lists of grievances) were being sent to the Estates-General. It hints at everyday family matters relating to young children—wet-nursing, overcrowding—but also touches on education and ends with the important adult demand for equal inheritance among siblings, one that the revolutionary assemblies later took seriously. Although light-hearted, the document seems to be rooted in everyday reality. But how much is known about the real-life experiences of children during the Revolution, in particular the children of the revolutionaries themselves, those with politically involved parents? It is not a question that has hitherto attracted very much attention. Some themes bearing on families and children during the French Revolution have been well explored in recent years: notably education and family law.[2] But literature on the actual experiences of the generation that grew up during the Revolution is sparse, no doubt because of the scattered nature of the sources and the plurality of possible approaches. Emmanuel Fureix recently pointed out that:

> We still do not have a genuine sociography of the sons and daughters of the revolutionary participants, enabling us to trace both their relation to the past and their political trajectories in the early nineteenth century. Such a study . . .—despite all the difficulties, especially relating to archive sources—would be particularly fruitful.[3]

This chapter aims to suggest some initial lines of inquiry, taking a biographical approach and drawing on a sample of revolutionaries and their families.

Revolutionary parents are defined here as a couple where the father (occasionally the mother) played an active part in national politics between 1789 and 1795, while the family was bringing up children. There are three possible definitions of the polysemic word "children": it can refer to young human beings; to the offspring of particular parents—("children of X"); or to an entire generation. All three definitions need to be kept in mind. What was it like to spend one's early childhood in a revolutionary family? What did it mean to carry the name of a known politician? Or of an executed revolutionary? What effect did it have on a child's education and later development? How did a generation of such children look back as adults on their parents and the Revolution?

The sample drawn on here consists of twenty-three political families: almost all the fathers were deputies to the assemblies, in particular the Convention (1792–5). (For full details, see the source accompanying this chapter.) Most leading revolutionaries came from a cohesive age cohort, born in the 1750s and 1760s, and aged roughly between twenty-five and forty when the Revolution began. In this sample, ten of the fathers were in their twenties in 1789, nine in their thirties, and only four were forty or over. It is possible to see their children too as belonging to a particular generation, since about half of them were born in the 1780s, half in the early 1790s. They shared, to a degree, background and origins. With some variations, especially in income, these families were mostly of the "middling sort": from moderately comfortable and well-educated urban milieux. Many of these politicians, like their colleagues in the Convention, had some legal training. Their wives usually came from similar families. Their material circumstances were often adversely affected by the Revolution, but they were originally from fairly established backgrounds.[4]

I have picked examples from different factions across the political chequerboard, including faithful companions of Robespierre (Couthon and Le Bas), Dantonists (Danton and Desmoulins), Girondists (Brissot, Barbaroux, plus three deputies from the Gironde—see Map 0.1), and Thermidorians (Tallien and Fouché), adding to them some non-deputies such as the Rolands and the journalist Hébert. What they have in common is that they had young—sometimes very young—children. And since many leading revolutionaries met a violent death (execution, suicide, or other) during or after the Terror, most of the children in our sample lost their fathers at an early age: this affected eighteen of the twenty-three families; three of the children lost both parents during the Terror.

Secondary and biographical sources are readily available on most of the children's fathers. Their political lives have often been thoroughly explored, precisely because they seem so dramatic and unusual. But their private lives were not necessarily "extraordinary." Reference works, such as biographical dictionaries of the assemblies, though a good starting point, often deal cursorily with personal matters.[5] To go further into families means drawing on a disparate range of sources, including parents' memoirs, dossiers in official archives, private papers, early narratives with access to sources now lost, diligent exploration by local historians, and so on.[6] Few children of revolutionaries, it seems, wrote memoirs themselves, and their papers have rarely been explored. The aim cannot be to provide a definitive survey, but to pull together some scattered data and identify certain factors shared by this sample, as a contribution to the picture of the everyday life of revolutionary families.

Some key themes ask to be explored: the children's birth and early upbringing; their education, where gender difference is most noticeable; their family circumstances during the Revolution, in particular the presence or absence of supportive networks during difficult times (imprisonment, clandestinity, or death of parents); the children's later lives, including material conditions; and finally, the longer-term impact of the Revolution, intellectual, political, or psychological.

Children of the Enlightenment

Historians of childhood have suggested that attitudes to children were shifting in a positive direction by the late eighteenth century: parents were increasingly likely to see children as an investment in the future and a sign of hope. Rousseau's view of the child as innocent and open to natural development was particularly influential.[7]

Children's given names can be a guide to such changing parental attitudes. During the *Ancien Régime*, almost all French children, given the dominance of the Catholic Church, would have been baptized within days or even hours of their birth, and given traditional saints' names by their godparents. By the 1780s, some parents were already tending to invest children with abstract properties, a trend more obvious during the Revolution. Fashionable or ideological first names appear during the Enlightenment, influenced by the Greek and Roman classics or by modern literature. For girls, names from novels—in particular by Rousseau—were popular: examples are Sophie, Julie, Héloïse, Virginie, Zélia, Zoé (= Life). Jean-Jacques and Émile were favorites for boys. For children born *during* the Revolution, some parents made quite radical statements through naming their children. There is now a considerable literature on revolutionary given names.[8] Once the revolutionary calendar had replaced saints' days with ideas, flowers, fruit, and everyday objects, some babies were given names like Liberté, Montagne, Gentiane, and Floréal (usually prudently combined with more traditional Pierres and Maries). Roman heroes, especially Brutus, were much in favor.

Our sample contains numerous examples of deliberate idealistic naming: Jean-Marie Roland, Minister of the Interior (1792–3) and his more famous wife, Marie-Jeanne (Madame Roland), baptized their daughter (b. 1781) conventionally, after her grandmother, Marie-Thérèse, but she was always known by her Greek-influenced name, Eudora.[9] Jacques-Pierre Brissot, a leader of the Girondist group, called his eldest son Félix (b. 1784) to indicate happiness; the second, Sylvain (b. 1786), a name relating to trees and woods, "to vow him to a rural life from the cradle";[10] and the third Anacharsis (b. 1791), after a fashionable book, *The Travels of Anacharsis the Younger in Greece* (1788). Gracchus Babeuf, the future insurrectionary activist under the Directory (who changed his own name from François-Noël to that of a Roman tribune), also changed the name of his oldest son Robert (b. 1785)—to Émile, after Rousseau's novel. Similarly, the Girondin deputy Jean-François Ducos called his son (b. 1791) Jean-Jacques Émile. Camille and Lucile Desmoulins's son, born in July 1792, was one of the first children to be civilly registered. His father stated that he did not wish his son to reproach him in later life for committing him to a religious identity, and named him Horace, explicitly after the Horatii represented in J.-L. David's painting, *Le Serment des Horaces* (1785).[11] The daughter (b. 1793) of Jacques Hébert, editor of the combative newspaper *Le Père Duchesne*, was registered as Scipion-Virginie.[12] The son (b. 1792) of Girondist Charles Barbaroux was named Ogé, after Vincent Ogé, the free man of color who had instigated the revolt of 1790 in Saint Domingue. Foreign Minister Henri Lebrun-Tondu named his fifth child, born in autumn 1792, Isabelle-Civilis-Victoire-Jemappes-Dumouriez, in honor both of the recent battle and the commanding general. The centrist deputy Louis La Révellière called his son (b. 1797) Ossian, after the Europe-wide craze for the Scottish "bard," while the daughter (b. 1795) of the Thermidorian Jean-Lambert Tallien received the name Rose-Thermidor.[13]

Once they were born, the babies had to be reared. We might expect this generation of middle-class parents, at least in Paris and other cities, to be influenced by Rousseau's ideas on child-rearing, especially his encouragement of maternal breastfeeding.[14] The Revolution, with the sanction of Le Peletier de Saint-Fargeau and later Robespierre, encouraged mothers to feed their own babies rather than take a wet nurse.[15] In practice, it seems that only a minority of parents followed this advice, given the prevalence of wet-nursing in France, particularly in larger cities. In our sample, Desmoulins and Danton, for instance, sent their babies out simultaneously to the same wet nurse in 1792, as a letter by Desmoulins tells us: "I've called my son Horace, and he went at once to a wet-nurse in L'Isle Adam [Seine-et-Oise] with the little Danton boy."[16]

At least two of the mothers in the sample, however, were committed to nursing their babies. Marie-Jeanne Roland is the best documented case (having been wet-nursed herself for two years, far from home, like other parents in the sample). She persisted in feeding Eudora, despite many difficulties, recorded in her letters and papers. When the milk failed, her husband made an expedition to the foundlings' home in Paris to investigate advice about bottle-feeding.[17] La Révellière was married to a fellow botanist, Jeanne Boyleau de Chandoiseau, and we know that she herself nursed their daughter Clémentine (b. 1782), Ossian's elder sister.[18]

Babies' wellbeing could not be taken for granted and child mortality remained high in this period. Many infants died young, with wet-nursing a likely factor. Even children who survived their first years were still being lost before the age of ten.[19] Danton, Babeuf, Couthon, La Révellière, Guadet, and Valazé, among others, all lost one or more children at birth or in early infancy. One particularly agonizing choice, new for this generation of parents, was whether or not to inoculate the child against smallpox, then a risky procedure.[20] In 1788, Mme Roland set out very clearly how the dilemma presented itself:

> We are trying to decide whether to have her inoculated or not. This is really preoccupying and affecting me. If it was for a stranger, I would be in favor, since it seems the probability lies that way, but I would never forgive myself if my child was to be one of the exceptions. If she were to be a victim, I would prefer it was the effect of a natural cause than my doing.[21]

They decided against, and Eudora did get smallpox in later life. She survived but with noticeable scarring.[22]

In their early years, children would normally be educated at home by family members. Most of these parents were concerned about their children's upbringing in a new way, sometimes explicitly turning to Rousseau for advice. Mme Roland is a notable witness here, too. She wrote to her husband in 1787:

> I re-read Julie's plan [in *La Nouvelle Héloïse*] and I found we have got too far away from it . . . We have been paying too much or too little attention to our child [aged six]. Being extremely busy, in the kind of work that requires peace and quiet, we have expected her to do lessons without taking the time to allow her to develop a taste for them . . . Then if there is a tantrum, we do everything to obtain silence, because without it we can't get on with our work. What makes children whine, *Julie says*, is the attention one pays to them . . . but if one takes no notice, they soon stop [crying].[23]

Eudora's early childhood is well documented, but in other cases, we have only glimpses of children at home. When Jérome Pétion became mayor of Paris in 1791, he moved his wife Suzanne and nine-year-old son Étienne from Chartres to an apartment near the Tuileries. The inventory later made of its contents includes a three-volume *Théorie de l'éducation* by Guillaume Grivel, inspired by Rousseau, as well as twenty-four volumes of *L'Ami des enfants*, a Rousseau-influenced periodical of 1782–3 published by Arnaud Berquin, indicating an interest in child-rearing. Étienne was learning English, and his parents bought him dictionaries and novels (*Tom Jones* and *Robinson Crusoe*). "The child could also play at being a defender of the fatherland, thanks to a little gun, provided with a bayonet, and two little swords he had been given," so it is perhaps not surprising that he later went into the army.[24]

Children born to future revolutionary parents in the 1780s might have attended school, lay or clerical, for a while, but many in our sample had an episodic or interrupted education. Depending on their parents' circumstances, they might move to Paris from the provinces and back, especially in the period 1792–4. The revolutionaries cared desperately about education and saw the child "as the cornerstone of future society."[25] But the actual provision of schools became uneven, as most clerical schools, in particular the *collèges* (secondary schools for boys), progressively closed from 1792 and were not easily replaced in the short run.[26] Parents worried about how their children would fare. In Brissot's last letter to his wife (October 1793) he bitterly regrets his absences from home:

> Embrace my Félix [aged nine] for me and tell him his father's only regret is to be leaving him without having been able to concern myself with his education. Ask him to make haste to get instruction so as to be of help to his brother and his mother. Alas, I have cost him much pain.[27]

Gender was undoubtedly "the key organizing principle of education in the eighteenth century."[28] It is much easier to discover recorded data about the formal education of the boys. As they reached their teens in the later 1790s, they were often sent to public colleges, military or otherwise. Like others in their age cohort, many ended up in the revolutionary or Napoleonic armies, leaving a readable career trail. Girls were more likely to be educated at home: we have to guess at their level of achievement, and their itineraries were usually shaped by marriage, their choices being affected by factors such as the political and social complexion of the family.[29]

We can glimpse a little of how things might develop, including from very unpromising circumstances, by looking at the educational histories of some individuals of both sexes from the cohort. Three of the boys had a tragic start but acquired a solid secondary education. Two-year-old Horace Desmoulins, suddenly orphaned in April 1794 when both his parents, Camille and Lucile, were guillotined, was brought up by his maternal grandmother, Anne Duplessis. Aged eight in 1800, Horace was granted a scholarship to the

Prytanée français, by that time a State-run school for boys under the temporary wing of the former famous collège, Louis-le-Grand (attended by his father and Robespierre; see Map 0.2).[30] Several other boys in the sample passed through its doors in the late 1790s–1800s. Young Horace spent two years there, before his family was helped to obtain further grants by sympathetic political friends of his father. He was redirected to the Lycée de Bordeaux, but, following his grandmother's pleas, was accepted as a non-paying pupil at the Parisian Collège Sainte-Barbe. Finally, he graduated in law (his father's profession) in 1813.

Philippe Le Bas was only six weeks old when his father, also Philippe, committed suicide, having been arrested alongside Robespierre on 9 Thermidor (July 27, 1794). His mother was Elisabeth née Duplay, the daughter of Robespierre's landlord. The whole Duplay family was pursued after Thermidor for their connection to Robespierre, so the baby spent several months with his mother in a series of prisons—La Petite Force, Talaru, Saint-Lazare, and the Luxembourg—before she was freed. Young Philippe was brought up in the Duplay family to revere Robespierre's memory as well as his father's. By 1806, aged twelve, he was attending the Collège de Juilly under the wing of a cleric, Le Père Ballard, whose life the elder Le Bas had saved during the Revolution. This ex-Oratorian college had been closed but reopened in 1796. Philippe Le Bas thus had a solid education before signing up at eighteen, first to the navy, then the imperial army.[31]

Éléonor-Zoa Dufriche de Valazé was thirteen when his father died by his own hand during the trial of the Girondins in 1793. The elder Valazé had said, "Ah, if I could only hope my son might one day be a Captain in the *génie* [engineers], I would have some consolation before dying."[32] The family took refuge with relations until after Thermidor, and Éléonor first embarked on drawing and sculpture. In October 1795, he too was awarded a scholarship to the Prytanée français, and finally entered Polytechnique on December 29, 1798, aged eighteen, exiting as a *sous-lieutenant de génie*, thus meeting his father's wish.[33]

We know much less about the education of the daughters in the sample. Those old enough to have been schooled before the Revolution might have been taught by nuns in a convent (the experience, briefly, of both Madame Roland and her daughter). The educational context from 1792 was more problematic for girls than for boys, since there were few dedicated girls' schools beyond primary level, and even that provision was fragmentary. After the closure of most religious foundations from 1792, primary education was supposed to be free and compulsory for all children, boys and girls (law of frimaire Year II, prolonged by the law of Year IV until the end of the Directory). In theory, the State schools were to teach girls to read and write; to train them in domestic accomplishments like sewing; but also to inculcate a new republican morality. In practice, it proved hard to find schoolmistresses who were both competent and willing to combine the latter requirement with the previous ones. Private schools sprang up again, and fees were charged even in the public schools.[34] In her pioneering thesis, Caroline Fayolle gives a glimpse of civic education for girls in the republican schools:

> The People's society in LePelletier section [sic] Paris organizes every 7 days a recitation during which one girl pupil of the republican schools recites a passage from the Declaration of the Rights of Man and the Citizen. The little girl is rewarded by a "fraternal kiss" from the president.
>
> (Spring 1794)[35]

The daughters in our sample, however, seem mostly to have been educated at home by mothers or governesses, or in private establishments.

Eudora Roland's education was much disrupted despite her parents' concern: she was sent from the age of nine to friends, then to a convent school, next to another boarding school, and finally lived at home, entrusted to a governess. After her parents' deaths in the same week in 1793, she was hidden, incognito, in other people's households, where between the ages of twelve and fourteen, her education must have been entirely haphazard. We have documentary evidence of her distress, at having so little solid education, in a melancholy letter written to her first guardian, Louis Bosc, in April 1796. It is partly a desperate cry for help, but can also be read as a desire for learning and a reflection of the disarray of her young life. Eudora had tried music and painting, as her mother had urged her, in order to earn a living, but, without adequate resources, felt lost:

> I've been here 4 months [in Rouen, with two elderly ladies] . . . If only I could have the consolation of a friendship! But I'm absolutely isolated and abandoned, and my only consolation has to be my own courage and the idea that it might make you happy one day. I don't have any paper, or books to read. I wish, I wish, I don't know what I would wish for. I shed tears because I'm not better educated and I don't seem to have the heart for anything. I need you to give me a plan for my studies like for a child, and tell me the books I should read . . .[36]

Just over a year later, Eudora, having run away to Paris, found herself married, at fifteen, to Léon, the son of her second guardian, Luc-Antoine de Champagneux, a friend of her parents in Lyon (see Map 0.1).[37]

Another girl about whom something is known, almost exactly Eudora's contemporary, was Suzanne (b. 1782), daughter of Michel Le Peletier de Saint-Fargeau. This revolutionary nobleman, assassinated by a royalist in January 1793, following his vote for the death of the king, was consequently heralded as a martyr for liberty. In the emotionally charged atmosphere after his death, Suzanne, aged eleven, was presented to the Convention by her uncle Félix, and made a "daughter of the nation," the first such but not the last. Living under the tutelage of her uncle and a governess, Madame Halm, Suzanne applied at the age of fifteen to marry a connection of her governess's, Jean-François de

Witt. The request was controversial and gave rise to a lawsuit, both because of Suzanne's unusual status as the ward of the nation, and because De Witt was an impoverished foreigner opposed by her uncles.[38] In both these examples, a fatherless daughter married, or *was* married—very young—to a relative or contact of those charged with caring for her, indicating perhaps that her immediate circle saw this as the most satisfactory end-point of any education for a girl, and a way of solving an apparent problem of guardianship.[39]

Sometimes we catch rare glimpses of girls who had an occupation. For a gifted girl, the arts were a possibility. Thérèse-Clémentine (1781–1862), the daughter of centrist deputy Jacques-Antoine Creuzé-Latouche, took up painting. Married to Pierre-François Martinet, deputy and mayor of Châtellerault, she is described as an "amateur painter, but not without talent."[40] Scipion-Virginie Hébert, daughter of the fiery journalist Jacques Hébert, was only one year old when both her parents were guillotined. At first cared for by an uncle, she was the subject of a *conseil de famille* (a frequent policy in all these bereaved families)[41] and made a ward of her father's associate, the printer Jacques-Christophe Marquet, probably a Protestant, and his young wife. Scipion-Virginie appears to have been educated in this obviously literate household to the point where as a young teenager she was a "sous-maîtresse de pension," a junior teacher in a Protestant boarding school. But by age sixteen, she too was married—to Frederic-Léon Née, a Protestant pastor. They had four children and became integrated into the Protestant community near Dreux.[42]

When Things Went Wrong: Networks of Support

From these examples, it is clear that networks of family and friends could make a large difference to revolutionaries' children's lives in difficult times. If their fathers had been executed, their mothers—who come into public focus much more in these circumstances—might be exposed to persecution or obliged to hide, and in some cases were imprisoned or under house arrest with their children for months at a time (as was the case for Félicité Brissot, Suzanne Pétion, and Elisabeth Duplay). Initially, these widowed mothers depended on family and friends, especially since any personal property would have been confiscated. In some cases, they married again, occasionally within the family, which presumably created even stronger ties. In Paris, Elisabeth Le Bas, née Duplay, married her husband's younger brother in 1799, and had two more children. In Bordeaux (see Map 0.1), Agathe Lavaud, widow of Girondin deputy Jean-François Ducos, later married his younger brother, Henri;[43] Ducos's sister, Jeanne-Justine, was the widow of another Girondin, Jean-Baptiste Boyer-Fonfrède, so these families were close. Between them, the two widows had six young children.[44]

In an immediate crisis, grandparents were often the first to be called upon, as we saw with Horace Desmoulins. The young sons, Antoine and François-Georges, of revolutionary leader Georges-Jacques Danton had already lost their mother in childbirth before he was guillotined in April 1794. A *conseil de famille* on 22 messidor Year II (July 10, 1794), soon after Danton's execution, arranged guardianship of the two boys, who had been cared for temporarily by his second wife. They were taken under the wing of their maternal grandfather, Jérôme Charpentier, a café proprietor in Paris, aided by uncles from the same family, with frequent trips back to Arcis sur Aube, their father's birthplace, where their paternal grandmother lived (see Map 0.1). Finally, in 1805, as they wrote, "we came back to Arci [sic] never to leave it. We spent these years with our father's mother."[45]

Sometimes tensions marked grandparental intervention, revealing political disagreements. Georges-Auguste Couthon, who was executed as Robespierre's associate, came from Orcet, a small town near Clermont-Ferrand. He had married a childhood friend, Marie Brunel, whose father was mayor of Orcet. After Thermidor, her family literally expunged Couthon's name: the revolutionary's brother changed his surname to Lafond, while the mayor insisted that Couthon's surviving seven-year-old child, Antoine (b. 1787), become "Antoine Brunel." Couthon's wife also changed her name by remarrying.[46]

In addition to family help, it became possible eventually to receive various kinds of official aid and compensation, usually requiring some lobbying by sympathetic politicians. The property (houses, moveable goods, money) of deputies who had been executed or imprisoned was normally confiscated by law, like that of émigré nobles. Post-Thermidor, the assemblies debated restoring the property of victims of the Revolutionary Tribunal. François Boissy d'Anglas, in response to many demands by widows requesting the return of their husbands' confiscated property (*biens des condamnés*), argued that this was a moral and political duty. The government finally passed a decree on restitution in June 1795. Similarly, some of the wives of executed deputies were granted a pension by the assembly, backdated and lasting till the dissolution of the Convention.[47]

One documented instance from the sample is that of Suzanne Pétion, whose husband had killed himself in Saint-Émilion in 1794 to escape execution. She successfully petitioned for return of property, receiving 34,036 livres capital, 64,503 livres for furniture, plus the 547 books in their library. At the time, she and her son were living with a relative in Paris. In spring 1796, Suzanne, along with widows of Brissot, Gorsas, Carra, and Valazé, also appealed to the Council of Five Hundred for further assistance and, following a report by Bailleul, they were granted 2,000 livres, plus 1,000 per child up to age fifteen. At the request of the deputy Goupilleau, Desmoulins's son Horace, "who is in poverty," was added to the list and in fact received 2,000 francs until the age of eighteen.[48]

Horace Desmoulins is an obvious example of a child who benefited from a network of his parents' political friendships: Goupilleau along with Brune and Fréron, who had been close to Camille Desmoulins, were active in finding help for his son in the form of grants and scholarships.[49] Émile, the son of Gracchus Babeuf, the radical later implicated in the Conspiracy of Equals of 1795, was another beneficiary of outside help. Émile had a militant upbringing, helping his mother fold and dispatch his father's newspapers. As a twelve-year-old, he had also apparently brought his father the knife with which he unsuccessfully tried to kill himself in prison. After Babeuf's execution in 1797, Émile was adopted by the wealthy Félix Lepeletier (brother of Michel, uncle of Suzanne, and a sympathizer and financial supporter of the Conspiracy). The boy's adoptive father sent him to boarding school, though Lepeletier's assistance lapsed in 1801, when he was deported as a former Jacobin.[50]

Some children and their families found themselves more or less abandoned. Botanist Louis Bosc, the Girondist sympathizer who himself helped shelter several wanted politicians, visited Bordeaux in 1796 and observed that the families of the executed Girondins were not popular. He may have been thinking of the particularly tragic case of Marie-Thérèse Guadet, whose father, aunt, sister, and brother-in-law had all been guillotined in 1794 alongside her husband, the Conventionnel Marguerite-Élie Guadet, for sheltering him while he was in hiding. Her circumstances, under house arrest at first, with her two surviving children, were difficult, and she was obliged to move to Saint-Émilion because of hostility from other in-laws.[51] In the cases of other Girondin dynasties in the city, such as the wealthy Fonfrède, Grangeneuve, and Ducos families, survivors were probably not in financial hardship, but Bosc implies that they were socially ostracized and obliged to fall back on each other's moral support.

The family of Fouquier-Tinville, the former Public Prosecutor at the Revolutionary Tribunal, could expect little sympathy after Thermidor from either political side. Fouquier had several grown-up children from his first marriage in Saint-Quentin, including Pierre-Quentin, now a serving soldier (see below). Fouquier's second wife Henriette had given birth to twins in 1793 while the couple lived in the building housing the Revolutionary Tribunal (the Conciergerie). The boy died in infancy; the girl, also Henriette, and her mother fell on hard times after Fouquier-Tinville was executed in 1795. No network seems to have helped them, and they ended in extreme poverty and tragic circumstances.[52]

Growing Up after the Revolution: Delayed Impact?

This entire generation of French children born between *circa* 1780 and 1795, whatever their personal circumstances, and whether or not their parents were involved in the Revolution, lived through times that could be called both exhilarating and traumatic. In these children's formative years, political turmoil was accompanied by civil and foreign warfare from 1792 and then throughout the Napoleonic era. The children of politicians, however, were statistically likely to be most affected. Prosopographical studies of the assemblies, such as those by Michel Biard, have concluded that over eighty deputies of the National Convention—mainly the more prominent ones—died violent deaths (at the guillotine, or by suicide or assassination), while many others spent time in prison or in hiding.[53] Alain Dieuleveult has estimated that of the Conventionnels, about one-third either died or suffered some tragedy or extreme distress during the Revolution, which will have had an impact on their immediate family.[54] How did their children process these events as they grew up and became adults? This chapter concludes by considering two aspects of the afterlife of the Revolution: emotional impact and potential trauma, and the political attitudes of children later to their own parents and/or to the Revolution in general.

The Terror and Trauma

Trauma is a hard subject to research and an anachronistic word. Is there any way of gauging the impact that fear and bereavement at a time of crisis would have on children's later lives? In recent years, historians have opened a productive line of enquiry about the long-term effect of major events on people's lives, in particular in relation to twentieth-century wars.[55] Looking back over 200 years is far more difficult, but studies of the concept of trauma in this period have begun in the work of Barry Shapiro, Ronen Steinberg, and others. They caution against random application of the term to the revolutionary period.[56] Nevertheless it is worth following Katherine Astbury, who quotes one twentieth-century definition of trauma in this context: "an event in the subject's life defined by its intensity, by the subject's incapacity to respond adequately to it, and by the upheaval and long-lasting effects that it brings about in the psychic organization."[57] With due caveats, this might apply to adult experience during the Revolution, but what about children?

Pierquin de Gembloux, writer of a pamphlet against the death penalty in 1830, argued that the Terror had left an indelible imprint on the psyche of an entire generation. He claimed that "if you calculated the number of individuals charged with murder in the last few years, you would see that they are precisely those *whose childhood* was surrounded by the scaffolds of the Terror."[58] This is an unsupported assertion, but it shows at least that people were aware of emotional turmoil during the years of war and revolution, and the possibility that the young might be particularly affected. And the guillotine ("the scaffolds of the Terror"), despite being introduced as a "humane" form of execution, has a special place in the history of trauma.[59] Brissot's wife, Félicité, wrote strikingly, in a letter after his death,

"How many times has his bloody image appeared to me. It freezes me with terror. He suffered for only a second, but my mind goes over and over his ordeal, prolonging it every day."[60] Even those who had not experienced the Revolution were subject to fantasies about the guillotine, as evidenced by the dream recounted in 1852 by the historian Alfred Maury, born only in 1817. He had heard accounts of executions from his royalist mother, and his childhood was a time when "everyday objects, jewels, knives and children's toys were in the form of miniature guillotines."[61]

We can only speculate about how their experiences affected children living in the 1790s.[62] Many of the children in the sample were too young to have any direct memory of the events of 1793 to 1795. We now know, however, that even very young babies are capable of responding to emotional distress in those surrounding them. Revolutionaries' children would certainly not have witnessed executions but could have been told many times about them by surviving mothers and relations. In December 1794, a delegation of widows and orphans came to the Convention to reiterate "the painful cries of thousands of wives and children whose husbands and fathers had been dragged inhumanely to the scaffold."[63] There was also a possible lack of what would today be called closure, since executed bodies were not released to families but buried in mass graves. This was not new during the Terror, but quickly became one of its particular features—hence the later establishment of memorial sites such as that at Picpus, the location of several mass graves.[64]

We have as yet little primary testimony from this sample, for want of letters and memoirs by these children in later life: we might cautiously try to deduce their attitudes from their later itineraries (see below). Some children undoubtedly felt the shadow of the Terror hanging over them, and there is occasional evidence of their possibly being quite disturbed by the experience. Most of the mothers in the sample were faced with bringing up fatherless children. Louis Bosc, when he visited the families of executed Girondins, was critical of certain mothers, Mme Guadet and Félicité Brissot, for example, for smothering and spoiling their children through overprotectiveness, something that might be regarded as explicable in the circumstances.[65] The result, in any case, might have been either restlessness or extreme prudence. All three of Brissot's sons, despite their mother's best efforts, seem to have found it difficult to settle to anything, and all left France at some time: Félix died young at sea off Saint-Domingue; Sylvain died relatively young in the United States, after a succession of teaching posts; Anacharsis, who was probably the most troubled, according to Félicité, spent some time in Mexico, but moved about a lot in France. Others in the sample also went abroad, usually westward, perhaps to escape into voluntary exile. Horace Desmoulins went first to England to learn commerce and then to Haiti to take up the coffee trade. He died there of yellow fever, aged thirty-three, leaving a wife and four young children. Danton's two sons, by contrast, appear to have reacted to their tumultuous early life by seeking security back in Arcis-sur-Aube, and apparently did their best not to respond to historians' enquiries about their father: if they sent private letters, it was to defend him from charges of corruption (often levied against him in the nineteenth century and still unresolved).[66] The evidence of their correspondence suggests a retreat into private life, at odds with their inherited name.[67]

Attitudes to Parents and the Revolution

The Danton children's defensive correspondence is but one example of the dilemma faced by revolutionaries' children: to defend their parents and the Revolution or not? The Napoleonic interlude sometimes provides pointers. As noted above, many boys in the sample, like others in their generation, went into the army or navy in the 1800s, usually after attending an academy: the military roll-call includes all three of Brissot's sons; Antoine Couthon; both of Grangeneuve's sons; Quentin Fouquier-Tinville; Philippe Le Bas; Étienne Pétion and Eleonor Valazé. (Fouché's sons, though too young to fight by the end of the wars, all received military training.) Valazé's son had a particularly brilliant career, ending up as a general. Pétion's son, too, had considerable success, finishing as a cavalry commander (*chef d'escadron*), and receiving the Légion d'honneur.[68] We must assume that these two young men accepted Napoleonic authority, but there is evidence that some of the others rejected it, or fell foul of the emperor. Sylvain Brissot, for example, attended Saint-Cyr, then enrolled at Polytechnique aged seventeen in 1803. He had to leave the next year, for refusing to take the oath to the Empire, citing as a reason that his father had died on the scaffold a republican, and that he was one too. His younger brother, Anacharsis, resigned his commission as *sous-lieutenant* in the dragoons in May 1815 just before Waterloo (for a reason unknown).[69] Antoine Couthon was apparently denied promotion by Napoleon in person, since he refused to change his surname (which he had by then reclaimed).[70] Pierre-Quentin Fouquier-Tinville soldiered through several campaigns during and after the Revolution, but in Year XI voted against Napoleon becoming consul for life, so was demoted, suspended for two years, then "dragged his gaiters round Europe, as a poor devil in the ranks." After the Restoration, he was forbidden to live in Paris and realized that his identity made him a pariah.[71]

If they did not go into the army, or after leaving it, some revolutionaries' sons, like their fathers, went into the legal profession, the choice of Grangeneuve's two sons, Henri-Etienne and Maurice, who returned to Bordeaux. Some entered politics, administration, or other professions, where their sympathies can sometimes be traced. Henri Boyer-Fonfrède became a liberal journalist at a Bordeaux newspaper, before moving to the political right. Philippe Le Bas had received a classical education, before serving as a very young soldier until 1814. In 1820, Hortense de Beauharnais (Napoleon's adopted daughter and sister-in-law) invited him to tutor her son, the future Napoleon III, a post he held until 1827, when his firmly-held republican sympathies became too unacceptable. Le Bas went on to forge a distinguished academic career as a Hellenist. While he disapproved of the 1851 coup d'état, he remained on good terms with his former pupil.[72] Surprisingly, the sample contains another important Hellenist, Jules David, son of the famous painter and ex-député. Receiving a good education from 1795 on, and no doubt helped by Napoleon's favor towards his father, Jules held several administrative posts from 1805 to 1815, latterly being made a prefect, but was never able to take up the appointment, because of the return of the Bourbons.[73]

Jules David, along with Fouché's children, falls into a particular group of children whose fathers were surviving regicides when the monarchy was restored. In 1816, under Louis XVIII, former deputies of the Convention who had voted for the death of Louis XVI in January 1793, especially if they had been compromised during the 100 Days, were sentenced to exile.[74] The painter David was exiled to Brussels (see Map 0.1), where his son Jules joined him at first. Joseph Fouché died in exile in Trieste, after one too many twists to his sinuous career. Neither Fouché's nor David's children suffered greatly in material terms: the four David children had their father's artistic inheritance, while Fouché had amassed a fortune to be passed on.[75] But there is a bulging set of files in the Archives Nationales of appeals, usually written by the widows and children of regicides, requesting clemency for other former revolutionaries now getting on in years and often in poor health. Substantial military service by deputies' sons is often cited as grounds for special treatment (though this could be a two-edged weapon depending on their career in the Napoleonic years). Only four of the fathers in our sample survived to 1816, but this set of papers is a major resource for the afterlife of other revolutionary families.[76]

We have a more explicit indication of the attitudes of children of revolutionaries in the case of those who published their parents' memoirs. Thanks to the pioneering work of Sergio Luzzatto, we know a great deal about some of these: he cites the memoirs of Barbaroux, Levasseur, Brissot, Courtois, Lanjuinais, Pontécoulant, Carnot, and La Révellière, all published on the initiative of a son.[77] Ogé Barbaroux, who can have had no memory of his father, studied law and was briefly a prosecutor in Nîmes under the Restoration. Obliged to leave for the inevitable political reasons, he then set about "devouring" all he could find about the Revolution, before editing his father's memoirs in 1822 with such an enthusiastically republican biographical preface that the editors subsequently suppressed it. Ogé, like several others in the cohort, became a warm supporter of the July Monarchy.[78] Ossian La Révellière similarly was a "very convinced partisan" of the Orléanist regime, but did not allow his father's memoirs to appear at this time, arguing that it was inopportune to publish something that could be used by the regime's enemies, since it "was seeking with good faith and courage to make order and liberty live alongside each other."[79] These sons clearly gave the régime of Louis-Philippe and Guizot the benefit of the doubt, in contrast to their entrenched hostility to the Bourbons. The case of Anacharsis Brissot is a little different. The last survivor of his family, he owned a copy of his father's hastily written prison memoirs. He allowed the publisher to pad them out with other material in the interest of receiving some royalties and remedying his very poor financial situation (not that it helped).[80] Eudora Roland was in her teens when her mother's prison memoirs, published in various editions by her two guardians, became a bestseller. She knew that they had provided an income for her during the 1790s, when she was without resources or living relations. In later life, she regretted however that her mother's celebrity had overshadowed that of her father: "Nothing in the world . . . is dearer or more sacred to me than the memory of my father," she wrote in October 1822. At this time, her father's actions as Minister of the Interior in 1792 and 1793 had either been forgotten or, if remembered, were the subject of highly partisan judgments (of both kinds). It appears that what she wished to remember was his honor and honesty.[81]

Suzanne Lepeletier on the other hand appears to have wanted to eliminate all memories of her father's radical life, possibly as a result of her second marriage to a royalist cousin, Léon Le Peletier de Mortefontaine. When her uncle Félix published an edition of her father's writings in Brussels in the 1820s, she bought up all the copies so that the book could not be propagated. More notoriously, when David's children offered for public sale all the unsold paintings by their father in the 1820s, she bought for 100,000 francs his famous painting of her father on his deathbed. Thereafter, the picture disappeared, as have virtually all images or engravings reflecting it. It is assumed that Suzanne either destroyed it or hid it.[82]

If we consider the questions raised at the start of this chapter, firm answers are hard to put forward. But some points emerge from the fragmentary knowledge we have. To most revolutionary parents, their children were intensely important. At least half of the children had been raised during the 1780s, and their early childhood may have been stable and protected. The Revolution introduced upheaval and frequently distress into their young lives, sometimes leading to an existence under threat, in hiding, in prison, or on the run. Family ties appear in most cases to have remained very strong, indeed essential. When both parents had died, grandparents and family friends rallied round to protect infants and minors. Mothers left alone had to devise strategies of survival and appear to have fought hard to see that their children were properly educated, at least in the case of the boys. There is a book yet to be written about the wives and widows of revolutionaries.

Politically, these children were often marked out. While in later years, to be descended from a member of the Convention might be regarded as a source of pride, in the immediate aftermath of the Revolution, and in particular under the Bourbon Restoration, it was a disadvantage, if not a ball and chain. Even Charlotte Robespierre, sister of Maximilien, changed her surname for a time. Depending on the politics of their fathers, the family name might, at different times and in different quarters, be identified with treason/federalism (the Girondins), the Terror (the Robespierrists), corruption (Danton), or self-serving (Tallien and Fouché). After 1830, the climate changed radically. Where we know of the children's politics, they seem, like the elderly regicides flocking back from exile, to have warmly welcomed the July Revolution and Louis-Philippe's regime, at least at first, some being committed to political office or public service. As distinct from either Napoleon or the Orléans dynasty, the Bourbons were their real enemy.

In most cases, throughout the years of eclipse, the children in this sample honored their family name and defended it, a few in public, most in private. In our sample, Suzanne Lepeletier appears to be an exception (though she may well not have been so in the generation as a whole). More typical of the sample perhaps is the testimony by Antoine Couthon. Whatever the overall verdict on Georges-Auguste, his son's account of bearing his name is moving:

> The son of a *bleu*, I am a *bleu* myself from head to toe; for ten years I fought for France [*c.* 1804 to 1814] and shed my blood in a dozen wounds ... during the Restoration, I retreated into private life, and these were bad days for me. Thanks to the émigrés ... a wave of outrageous judgments was hurled at the men of the Revolution ... But at last the sun of July shone. Slightly better days began to dawn for the memory of my father: history was rewritten by going back to authentic sources and it is proving that these men who were so discredited, at whom so much mud was slung, can emerge triumphant from the test, like a group of antique sculpture from the lava of a dead volcano.[83]

Source: The families of revolutionaries

Material in this chapter is drawn from the families of the following (some dates approximate or contested):

François-Noël (Gracchus) Babeuf (1760–97), activist, journalist, m. Marie-Anne Victoire Langlet (*c.* 1756–after 1817)
Children: two daughters, both called Catherine (b. 1783 and 1785), died in childhood; three sons, Robert-Émile (1785–1842), bookseller, publisher; Camille (1790–1815) and Caïus Gracchus (1797–1814), both died in youth, from suicide and a war-related accident respectively

Charles-J.-M. Barbaroux (1767–94), Girondist *député* at Convention, unmarried
Children: one son, Charles-Ogé (1792–1867), lawyer, *député* for Réunion in 1849, senator 1858

Jean-Baptiste Boyer-Fonfrède (1765–93), *député* for the Gironde at Convention, m. Jeanne-Justine Ducos (1767–1820)
Children: three daughters, Zoë (b. 1786); Clémentine (1792–1876); Camille (b. 1793 posthumous); one son, Henri (1788–1841), liberal journalist at Bordeaux, briefly *député* in 1831

Jacques-Pierre Brissot [de Warville] (1754–93), Girondist *député* at Législative and Convention, m. Félicité Dupont (1759–1818)
Children: three sons, Félix (1784–1803), naval cadet; Sylvain (1786–1819), Polytechnique, then tutor in United States; Anacharsis (1791–*c.* 1859), Imperial army, then various occupations

Georges-Auguste Couthon (1755–94), Jacobin *député* at Legislative and Convention, m. Marie Brunel (1765–?1843)
Children: one surviving son, Antoine (1787–1867), career soldier

Jacques-Antoine Creuzé-Latouche (1749–1800), member of Constituent Assembly, centrist *député* at Convention, member of Conseil des 500, m. Jeanne Creuzé (1754–1810)
Children: two daughters, Thérèse-Clémentine (1781–1862), painter and femme de lettres; Laure (1783–after 1815)

Georges-Jacques Danton (1759–94), "Indulgent" *député* at Convention, m. (1) Gabrielle Charpentier (1760–93); m. (2) Louise Gély (1776–1856)
Children: two surviving sons, Antoine (1790–1858); François-Georges (1792–1848), both *propriétaires*

Jacques-Louis David (1748–1825), *député* at Convention and painter, m. Charlotte Pecoul (1764–1826)
Children: two sons, Charles-Jules (1783–1854), diplomat, Greek scholar; Eugène (1784–1830); two daughters, Laure and Pauline, twins (b. 1786), both married generals

L.-Simplice-Camille-Benoît Desmoulins (1760–94), "Indulgent" *député* at Convention, m. Lucile Duplessis (1770–94)
Children: one son, Horace-Camille (1792–1825), law degree, then coffee trader, Haiti

Jean-François Ducos (1765–93), *député* for the Gironde at Convention, m. Jeanne-Agathe Lavaud (1772–1831)
Children: one son, Jean-Jacques Émile (1791–1816); one daughter, Adèle, aka Minette (1792–1804)

Joseph Fouché, duc d'Otrante (1763–1820), *député* at Convention, Thermidorian, later Minister of Police under Napoleon, m. (1) Bonne Jeanne

Coiquaud (1763–1812); m. (2) Ernestine Castellane-Majastre (*c.* 1788–1850)
Children: four surviving children from first marriage: three sons, Joseph-Liberté (1796–1862); Armand (1800–78); Athanase (1801–86), all of whom inherited in turn Fouché's title duc d'Otrante; one daughter, Joséphine (1803–93); all later protected by Bernadotte in Sweden

Antoine-Quentin Fouquier-Tinville (1746–95), Public Prosecutor at Revolutionary Tribunal, m. (1) Dorothée Saugnier (d. 1782); m. (2) Henriette d'Aucourt (1762–1827)
Children: from first marriage: one surviving son, Pierre-Quentin (1776–1826), career soldier; two surviving daughters, Geneviève and Émilie (b. before 1782, d. after 1830), the latter a *demoiselle de comptoir*; from second marriage, one surviving daughter, Henriette (1793–1813), seamstress and domestic servant, murdered by her husband (?)

J.-Antoine [Lafargue de] Grangeneuve (1751–93), *député* for the Gironde at Législative and Convention, m. Marie Disnematin-Dorat (1753–1819)
Children: one daughter, Marie (b. 1788); two surviving sons, Henri-Étienne (1788–1874), career soldier, then *juge de paix* at Bordeaux; Maurice (1794–1868), lawyer at Bordeaux

Marguerite-Élie Guadet (1755–94), *député* for the Gironde at Législative and Convention, m. Marie-Thérèse Dupeyrat (*c.* 1760–1810)
Children: two daughters, Zélia (1785–?); Catherine (1786–95); two sons, Jean-Michel (1782–?); Jean-Baptiste Prosper (1790–1864), *juge de paix* at Libourne

Jacques-René Hébert (1757–94), journalist/publisher, m. Marie-Marguerite-Françoise Goupil (1756–94)
Children: one daughter, Scipion-Virginie (1793–1830), briefly a schoolteacher before marrying a Protestant pastor

Louis-Marie de La Révellière-Lépeaux (1753–1824), member of Estates-General and centrist *député* at Convention, Director; m. Jeanne Boyleau de Chandoiseau (1754–1824)
Children: one surviving daughter, Clémentine (1782–1824); one son, Ossian (1797–1876), journalist, writer

Philippe-F.-Joseph Le Bas or Lebas (1765–94), Robespierrist *député* at Convention, m. Elisabeth Duplay (1772–1859)
Children: one son, Philippe (1794–1860), military career, tutor to future Louis-Napoleon, later Hellenist scholar and librarian

P.-Henri Lebrun-Tondu (1754–93), Foreign Minister, m. Marie-Jeanne-Adrienne Cherette or Cheret (1762–1848)

Children: two sons, Jean-Pierre-Louis (1784–1852); Théodore Charles-Joseph Gilbert (1788–61), artist, légion d'honneur; three surviving daughters, Marie-Françoise-Charlotte-Henriette (1789–1871); Isabelle-Civilis-Victoire-Jemmapes-Dumouriez (1792–after 1813); Sophie-Minerve (posthumous, 1794–1883)

L-Michel Lepeletier de Saint-Fargeau (1760–93), member of Estates-General and *député* at Convention, m. Louise-Adelaide Joly de Fleury (1762–1823?)
Children: one daughter, Suzanne (1782–1829)

Jérome Pétion [de Villeneuve] (1756–94), member of Estates-General, mayor of Paris, Girondist *député* at Convention, m. Louise-Anne-Suzanne Lefebvre (1760–1820)
Children: one son, Étienne (1783–1847), successful military career

Jean-Marie Roland de la Platière (1734–93), Minister of the Interior, m. Marie-Jeanne Phlipon (1754–93)
Children: one daughter, Marie-Thérèse-Eudora (1781–1858)

Jean-Lambert Tallien (1767–1820), *député* to Convention, Thermidorian, m. Thérésia Cabarrus (1773–1835), divorced
Children: one daughter, Rose-Thermidor-Thérésia (aka Joséphine or Laure, 1795–1862), m. Comte Félix de Narbonne-Pelet

Ch.-Éléonore [Dufriche-de] Valazé (1751–93), Girondist *député* to Convention, m. Anne-Charlotte-J.-B. de Broe (1752–1814)
Children: one son, Éléonor-Zoa (1780–1838), career soldier, ends as general, name on Arc de Triomphe, *député* de l'Orne 1834–7; one daughter, Charlotte (1785–after 1809)

Notes

1 Extract from "Doléances des bambins de France à présenter aux États-généraux," reproduced in Claire Gaspard, "Le cahier de doléances des enfants," *Annales Historiques de la Révolution Française* (hereafter *AHRF*) 278 (1989): 476–86. Original document (April 1789) in Bibliothèque historique de la ville de Paris, cote: 8884. All translations from the French, unless otherwise indicated, are my own.

2 From a considerable literature, see, for example, Marie-Françoise Lévy, ed., *L'Enfant, la famille et la Révolution française* (Paris: Orban, 1990); Suzanne Desan, *The Family on Trial in Revolutionary France* (Berkeley: University of California Press, 2004); Colin Heywood, *Growing up in France* (Cambridge: Cambridge University Press, 2007); Jennifer Heuer, *The Family and the Nation: Gender and Citizenship in Revolutionary France, 1789–1830* (Ithaca, NY: Cornell University Press, 2005); Anne Verjus and Denise Davidson, *Le Roman*

conjugal: Chronique de la vie familiale à l'époque de la Révolution et de l'Empire (Seyssel: Champ Vallon, 2011); Suzanne Desan, "The French Revolution and the Family," in *A Companion to the French Revolution*, ed. Peter McPhee (Oxford: Wiley-Blackwell, 2013), 470–85; Caroline Fayolle, *La Femme nouvelle: genre, éducation, révolution 1789–1830* (Paris: CTHS, 2017), based on her thesis "Genre, savoir et citoyenneté. Les enjeux politiques de l'éducation des filles (de 1789 aux années 1820)," University of Paris 8 (2013).

3 Emmanuel Fureix, "Une transmission discontinue: présences sensibles de la Révolution Française, de la Restauration aux années 1830," in *Histoire d'un trésor perdu: transmettre la Révolution francaise*, ed. Sophie Wahnich (Paris: Les Prairies ordinaires/Belles lettres, 2013), 169–70. On "experience" of the Revolution, see Peter McPhee, *Living the French Revolution* (London: Palgrave Macmillan, 2006); David Andress, ed., *Experiencing the French Revolution* (Oxford: Voltaire Foundation, 2013).

4 See Colin Jones, *The Longman Companion to the French Revolution* (London: Longman, 1988), 313–400, for biographical summaries with dates. Several prominent politicians, including Robespierre, Saint-Just, and Marat, had no recorded children.

5 Dictionaries include Auguste Kuscinski, *Dictionnaire des conventionnels* (Paris: Société de l'histoire de la Révolution française/F. Rieder, 1916); Edna Hindie Lemay, *Dictionnaire des Constituants (1789–1791)* (Oxford: Voltaire Foundation, 1991) and *Dictionnaire des Législateurs (1791–1792)* (Ferney-Voltaire: Centre international d'étude du XVIIIe siècle, 2007); Bernard Gainot, ed., *Dictionnaire des membres du Comité de Salut Public* (Paris: Tallandier, 1990). A new biographical dictionary of the Conventionnels is in preparation.

6 The Paris *état civil* records having been lost in 1871, Auguste Jal's *Dictionnaire critique de biographie et d'histoire* (Paris: Plon, 1867) is valuable. The French edition of Wikipedia, and the umbrella genealogical website Geneanet provide useful initial data about names and dates. Wherever possible, these have been checked against other sources.

7 Heywood, *Growing up in France*; Larry Wolff, "Children and the Enlightenment," in *The Routledge History of Childhood in the Western World*, ed. Paula S. Fass (New York: Routledge, 2013), 78–100.

8 See *AHRF* 322 (2000), special number, *Les Prénoms*, containing several articles; McPhee: *Living the French Revolution*, 149–50, 153.

9 For details, see Siân Reynolds, *Marriage and Revolution: Monsieur and Madame Roland* (Oxford: Oxford University Press, 2012), 73.

10 J. P. Brissot, *Mémoires* (Paris: Ladvocat, 1830–2), 2:36, quoted by Sergio Luzzatto, *Mémoire de la Terreur*, trans. Simone Carpentari-Messina (Lyon: Presses Universitaires de Lyon, 1988), 146.

11 Jules Claretie, *Camille Desmoulins, Lucile Desmoulins: étude sur les dantonistes* (Paris: Plon, 1875), 183.

12 Scipio(n) was a Roman hero but Hébert's daughter was probably named after her "godfather," Scipion Duroure, a friend of her father's, witness to her *acte de naissance*. See Paul Nicolle, "La fille d'Hébert; son parrain—la descendance du Père Duchesne," *AHRF* 108 (1947): 326–32.

13 Several of these names are cited in Luzzatto, *Mémoire de la Terreur*, 146–7. I am grateful to Michelle Zancarini-Fournel for alerting me to this book, a major inspiration for this study.

14 Jennifer J. Popiel, *Rousseau's Daughters: Domesticity, Education, and Autonomy in Modern France* (Hanover: University of New Hampshire Press, 2008); Meghan K. Roberts *Sentimental Savants: Philosophical Families in Enlightenment France* (Chicago: University of Chicago Press, 2016); Wolff, "Children and the Enlightenment."

15 Maximilien Robespierre, picking up on Le Peletier de Saint-Fargeau, proposed that mothers with breastfeeding certification get a grant. *Projet de décret sur l'éducation publique*, July 29, 1793, 4, BNF Gallica.

16 See E. Campagnac, "Les fils de Danton," *AHRF* 105 (1947): 37–63, and 106 (1947): 141–65; Claretie, *Camille Desmoulins*, 183. Lucile Desmoulins was distressed that Horace was sent away at three days old. Hervé Leuwers, *Camille et Lucile Desmoulins* (Paris: Fayard, 2018), 228. On this topic, see Mary Jacobus, "Incorruptible Milk: Breast-feeding and the French Revolution," in *Rebel Daughters: Women and the French Revolution*, ed. Sara E. Melzer and Leslie W. Rabine (New York and London, Oxford University Press, 1992), 54–78.

17 Reynolds, *Marriage and Revolution*, 75ff. See also Marie-Jeanne Roland, "Avis à ma fille en âge et dans le cas de devenir mère," in *Oeuvres de J.-M.Ph. Roland* [sic] *femme de l'ex-ministre de l'intérieur*, ed. L.-A. Champagneux (Paris: Bideault, An VIII/1799–1800), 1:301–44, and the many references in her correspondence from 1781 to 1782. Cf. Dorinda Outram, *The Body in the French Revolution* (New Haven, CT: Yale University Press, 1989), chaps. 8 and 9, featuring Mme Roland as a case study.

18 *Mémoires de Louis-Marie de La Révellière-Lépeaux* (Paris: Plon, 1895/1873), 1:51.

19 François Lebrun, "La famille en France à la fin de l'ancien régime," in *L'Enfant, la famille et la Révolution française*, ed. Marie-Françoise Lévy (Paris: Orban, 1990), 38–9.

20 See Roberts, *Sentimental Savants*, chap. 4.

21 Marie-Jeanne Roland to Louis Bosc, April 6, 1788, in *Lettres de Madame Roland (1788–1793)*, ed. Claude Perroud (Paris: Imprimerie Nationale, 1902), 2:7.

22 According to Louis Bosc, her ex-guardian, letter of 1799 on meeting Eudora again, she had had two attacks of smallpox: quoted in Antoine da Sylva, *De Rousseau à Hugo: Bosc, l'enfant des Lumières* (Ermont: Edition Le Chemin du philosophe, 2008), 179.

23 My italics. The letter, written on December 1, 1787, in *Lettres de Madame Roland (1780–1787)*, ed. Claude Perroud (Paris: Imprimerie Nationale, 1900), 1:716, is quoted at length in Reynolds, *Marriage and Revolution*, 79.

24 Pierre Casselle, *L'Anti-Robespierre: Jérôme Pétion ou la Révolution pacifique* (Paris: Vendémiaire, 2016), 128, 452–3. On *L'Ami des enfants* as a magazine that combined "Rousseauism and academic ambition," see Pierre de Vargas, "L'éducation du 'petit Jullien', agent du Comité de Salut Public," in *L'Enfant, la*

famille et la Révolution française, ed. Marie-Françoise Lévy (Paris: Orban, 1990), 227–8. The Jullien family had a subscription too.

25 Jacques Gélis, "L'enfant et la conception de la vie sous la Révolution," in *L'Enfant, la famille et la Révolution française*, ed. Marie-Françoise Lévy (Paris: Orban, 1990), 73.

26 The history of education under the Revolution, usually approached through projects rather than by attendance records, is beyond the scope of this study. Primary education was less affected, but evidence of school attendance for our sample is either before 1791–2 or after 1795. See Dominique Julia, "L'Institution du citoyen: instruction publique et éducation nationale dans les projets de la période révolutionnaire," in *L'Enfant, la famille et la Révolution française*, ed. Marie-Françoise Lévy (Paris: Orban, 1990).

27 Brissot papers, Archives Nationales, 446AP, file 14, letter dated October 29, 1793.

28 Roberts, *Sentimental Savants*, 109, quoting Popiel, *Rousseau's Daughters*, 14.

29 Fayolle, *La Femme nouvelle*, is a rich source on this subject; see pp. 225–6 for a complaint in Year VIII that there were no national schools for girls.

30 Claretie, *Camille Desmoulins*, 375–81, for details of Horace's education; R. R. Palmer, *The School of the French Revolution: A Documentary History of the Collège of Louis le Grand and its Director, J.-F. Champagne* (Princeton, NJ: Princeton University Press, 2015/1975); R. R. Palmer and Dominique Julia, "Le Prytanée français et les écoles de Paris 1798–1802," *AHRF* 243 (1981): 123–52. The Prytaneum, unlike its prestigious predecessor, taught only introductory subjects and was more like a residence hall. Reduced in size in 1800, it became the Lycée de Paris in 1803, then the Imperial Lycée in 1804.

31 He later had an academic career: Alexandre Cousin, *Philippe Lebas et Augustin Robespierre: deux météores dans la Révolution française* (Paris: Bérénice, 2010); Stéfane-Pol, *Autour de Robespierre: le Conventionnel Le Bas, d'après des documents inédits et les mémoires de sa veuve* (Paris: Flammarion, 1901).

32 [R. D. G.] Desgenettes: *Souvenirs de la fin du XVIIIe siècle et du commencement du XIXe, ou mémoires de R.D.G* (Paris: Didot, 1835–6), 2:232.

33 See Paul Nicolle, *Valazé, député de l'Orne à la Convention nationale*, preface G. Lefebvre (Paris: Alcan, 1933).

34 For details, see Elke Harten and Hans-Christian Harten, *Femmes, Culture et Révolution* (Paris: des femmes, 1988), 96.

35 Fayolle, "Genre, savoir et citoyenneté," 188.

36 Letter reproduced in Claude Perroud, *Le Roman d'un girondin: le naturaliste Bosc* (Paris: Hachette, 1916), 23–4, originally published as three articles in *Revue du dix-huitième siècle* (1916). This is one of the few documents from a child (teenager).

37 Details in Paul Feuga, *Luc-Antoine [de Rosière] de Champagneux, ou le destin d'un rolandin fidèle* (Lyon: Éditions lyonnaises d'art et d'histoire, 1991).

38 See Jennifer Heuer, "Adopted Daughter of the French People: Suzanne Lepeletier and Her Father, the National Assembly," *French Politics, Culture and Society* 17, no. 3/4, (1999): 31–51.

39 Condorcet's daughter Alexandr[in]e-Louise Sophie—known as Élisa—was also married as a teenager to a much older man.

40 On the Musée de Châtellerault website, see http://www.alienor.org/collections-des-musees/fiche-personne-33853-creuze-clementine for a list of works held there. See also Marcel Marion, "Un révolutionnaire très conservateur, Creuzé-Latouche," *Revue d'Histoire Moderne et Contemporaine* 11–22 (1936): 101–34.

41 See, for example, the papers relating to the *conseil de famille* for Eudora Roland on 8 nivôse Year III (December 28, 1794) in Bibliothèque Nationale de France, Manuscrits, NAF 22424.

42 Nicolle, "La fille d'Hébert," and Philippe Bourdin, "L'inventaire des biens de l'imprimerie de Jacques-René Hébert," *AHRF* 368 (2012): 155–62.

43 This would have been impossible later under the Code Napoléon of 1804, art. 162.

44 See Bernardine Melchior-Bonnet, *Les Girondins* (Paris: Tallandier, 1989/1969), epilogue.

45 Le docteur Robinet, *Danton, Mémoire sur sa vie privée* (Paris: Charavay, 1884; 2nd ed. 1865), 290–1.

46 In later life, Antoine reverted to his paternal surname. See Pascal Cedan, "Orcet à la veille de la Révolution et la famille de G. Couthon," *AHRF* 252 (1983): 228–37.

47 For details, see Ronen Steinberg, "Reckoning with Terror: Retribution, Redress and Remembrance in Post-Revolutionary France," in *The Oxford Handbook of the French Revolution*, ed. David Andress (Oxford: Oxford University Press, 2015), 493–4.

48 Casselle, *L'Anti-Robespierre*, 569ff.; Bailleul, Conseil des Cinq-Cents, 21 Germinal IV, *Moniteur* 28, no. 206, 26 germinal IV, 207.

49 Claretie, *Camille Desmoulins*, 378. See also Claretie, *Camille Desmoulins*, 376–7: letter to Mme Duplessis from Brune, who was in touch with Fréron, and recommending she apply for Desmoulins's papers and books to be restored, for Horace's instruction.

50 Laurence Constant-Ancet, "Félix Lepeletier de Saint-Fargeau: un personnage ambigu de l'histoire," *AHRF* 308 (1997): 321–31. He was later amnestied but restricted in activity. Émile became a bookseller; on his eventful life and that of his brothers, see entries on "Babeuf" in Antoine-Vincent Arnault, *Biographie nouvelle des contemporains (1787–1820)* (Paris: Dufour & Cie, 1827), vol. 2 (B–Bez), 7ff.

51 Perroud, *Le Roman d'un girondin*, 41–2.

52 Papers in Bibliothèque Historique de la Ville de Paris. The secondary source for details of the Fouquier-Tinville family is G. Lenôtre [pseudonym of T. Gosselin], *Paris révolutionnaire: vieilles maisons, vieux papiers* (Paris: Perrin, 1903), 2:esp. 233–89. Lenôtre's anecdotal histories are, however, based on

documentary sources. The only Fouquier-Tinville child still living in 1830 was Émilie, a *demoiselle de comptoir*; the youngest daughter, Henriette, after sewing for a living, went into service, married young, and was possibly murdered by a violent husband; Lenôtre, *Paris révolutionnaire*, 2:259–60.

53 Michel Biard, "La mort à la Convention: des représentants dans l'oeil du cyclone (1793–1794)," in *Visages de la Terreur, l'exception politique de l'An II*, ed. Michel Biard and Hervé Leuwers (Paris: Armand Colin, 2014), 186; of eighty-six "people's representatives" who suffered a non-natural death between 1793 and 1795, sixty-seven died between early October 1793 and Thermidor, i.e. late July 1794. For a fuller account, see Michel Biard, *La Liberté ou la mort. Mourir en député (1792–1795)* (Paris: Tallandier, 2015).

54 Alain de Dieuleveult, "Mort des conventionnels," *AHRF* 251 (1983): 157–66.

55 There is much literature on the effects of the Second World War on children, families, and later generations, in various countries. In France, children of parents involved in the events of May 1968 have recently published childhood memories, not always happy ones, marking anniversaries in 2008 and 2018. Cf. Ludivine Bantigny and Arnaud Bauberot, eds., *Hériter en politique: filiations, générations et transmissions politiques (Allemagne. France et Italie, XIXe–XXIe siècles)* (Paris: PUF, 2011).

56 See Steinberg, "Reckoning with Terror"; Barry Shapiro, "The Impact of Terror in the Early French Revolution," *Proceedings of the Western Society for French History* 34 (2006): 73–98; Ronen Steinberg, "Trauma before Trauma: Imagining the Effects of the Terror in the Revolutionary Era," in *Experiencing the French Revolution*, ed. David Andress (Oxford: Voltaire Foundation, 2013), 177–99; and Ronen Steinberg, "Trauma and the Effects of Mass Violence in Revolutionary France: A Critical Inquiry," *Historical Reflections* 41, no. 3 (2015): 28–46, esp. 30.

57 Definition from Laplanche's *Vocabulaire de la Psychanalyse* (1973) quoted by Katherine Astbury, *Narrative Responses to the French Revolution* (Oxford: Legenda, 2012), 5.

58 My italics. Quoted in Steinberg, "Trauma before Trauma," 196. Jeremy Popkin has commented that many personal memoirs demonstrated "the profoundly disturbing impact of [the Revolution] on notions of personal identity." Jeremy Popkin, "Facing Racial Revolution: Captivity Narratives and Identity in the Saint-Domingue Insurrection," *Eighteenth-Century Studies* 36, no. 4 (2003): 527.

59 Daniel Arasse, *The Guillotine and the Terror*, trans. Christopher Miller (London: Penguin, 1991); Nathalie Richard, "Rêver à la guillotine. Souvenirs révolutionnaires, psychologie et politique en France au XIXe siècle," in *Histoire d'un trésor perdu: transmettre la Révolution francaise*, ed. Sophie Wahnich (Paris: Les Prairies ordinaires/Belles lettres, 2013), 195–224.

60 Brissot papers AN 446AP, file 14; see also a description of physical terror in a speech by Tallien, quoted by Steinberg, "Trauma and the Effects of Mass Violence," 34, and in Mette Harder, "Reacting to Revolution: The Political Career of J.-L. Tallien," in *Experiencing the French Revolution*, ed. David Andress (Oxford: Voltaire Foundation, 2013), 99.

61 Richard, "Rêver à la guillotine," 197.

62 Erin Corber suggests that historians concerned with "the impact of violence, persecution, dislocation, war, and ethnic cleansing on populations must consider not only the experiences and memories of adults, but of children, as well as their children and grandchildren," Review of Ivan Jablonka, ed., *L'Enfant-Shoah* (Paris: Presses Universitaires de France, 2014), *H-France Review* 15, no. 159 (November 2015).

63 "France awaits a cure for the deep wounds inflicted by the barbarity of tyrants," *Moniteur* 22, no. 83, 23 Frimaire III, 721, quoted by Steinberg "Reckoning with Terror," 192–3.

64 See Ronen Steinberg, "Spaces of Mourning: the Cemetery of Picpus and the Memory of Terror in Post-revolutionary France," *Proceedings of the Western Society for French history* 36 (2008): 133–47, and the project on Picpus at http://picpus.mmlc.northwestern.edu/cgi-bin/WebObjects/Picpus.woa/wa/overView.

65 Perroud, *Le Roman d'un girondin*, 42.

66 For a recent discussion, see Richard Flamein, "Un corrompu?," in *Danton: Le mythe et l'histoire*, ed. Michel Biard and Hervé Leuwers (Paris: Armand Colin, 2016), 127–41.

67 On Brissot's sons, see Suzanne d'Huart, *Brissot: la Gironde au pouvoir* (Paris: Robert Laffont, 1986), 225–8. On Danton's, see Edmond Campagnac, "Les fils de Danton," and Edmond Campagnac, "Comment s'est formée la légende dantonienne," *AHRF* 113 (1949): 1–53.

68 Casselle, *L'Anti-Robespierre*, 573: Étienne Pétion de Villeneuve was an officer in the 21st Regiment of Dragoons, fought at Austerlitz, Iena, and Eylau, and in Spain, became *Officier* in the Légion d'honneur in Napoleon's last days, and later Chevalier de Saint-Louis.

69 Huart, *Brissot*, 225–8.

70 Francisque Mège, ed., *Correspondance inédite de Georges Couthon* (Paris: Aubrey, 1872), 336, quoted by Luzzatto, *Mémoire de la Terreur*, 173.

71 Lenôtre, *Paris Révolutionnaire*, 256.

72 On Le Bas, see Cousin, *Philippe Lebas*, and Stéfane-Pol, *Autour de Robespierre*; cf. Fureix, "Une transmission discontinue," 170.

73 Jean Caravolas, "L'Helléniste français Jules David (1783–1854)," *Historical Review/La Revue Historique* 2 (2005): 129–51; see also Luzzatto, *Mémoire de la Terreur*, 159–60, on both these men, sons of fervent Robespierrists, whose paths crossed in later life.

74 On the exiles, see François Antoine, Michel Biard, Philippe Bourdin, Hervé Leuwers, and Côme Simien, eds., *Déportations et exils des Conventionnels* (Paris: Société des Études Robespierristes, 2018).

75 On Fouché's relations with his children, see Emmanuel de Waresquiel, *Fouché, dossiers secrets* (Paris: Tallandier, 2017), chap. 1, "Dans le cercle de la famille," 30–64.

76 Archives Nationales, F7: 6709–6715. Some 84 percent of surviving regicides were sentenced to lifelong banishment. Apart from Fouché and David, the only

two in our sample are Tallien—who was exempted from exile (see Harder, "Reacting to Revolution," 109)—and La Révellière-Lépeaux, who appears not to have been exiled, but cf. Luzzatto, *Mémoire de la Terreur*, 66, on his son's problems in 1816.

77 Luzzatto, *Memoire de la Terreur*, 153. See also Anna Karla, "Éditer la Révolution sous la Restauration: la collection 'Barrière et Berville,'" in *Histoire d'un trésor perdu: transmettre la Révolution francaise*, ed. Sophie Wahnich (Paris: Les Prairies ordinaires/Belles lettres, 2013), 129–48.

78 Luzzatto, *Mémoire de la Terreur*, 166–7. He later moved to the right, became deputy for Réunion in 1849, and supported the 1851 coup, having in 1841 written a work querying the wisdom of slave emancipation; Luzzatto, *Mémoire de la Terreur*, 68, n. 129.

79 *Mémoires de La Revellière-Lépeaux, . . . publiés par son fils sur le manuscrit autographe de l'auteur et suivis des pièces justificatives et de correspondances inédites* (Paris: E. Plon 1895/2003 facsimile), 1:xx.

80 Luzzatto, *Mémoire de la Terreur*, 166.

81 BNF MSS naf, 22422, fo 468, October 24, 1822. Her father had intended to write his memoirs but on the prompting of his wife burnt his papers while in hiding.

82 Luzzatto, *Mémoire de la Terreur*, 150–1.

83 Luzzatto, *Mémoire de la Terreur*, 57, quoting from *Correspondance inédite de Georges Couthon*, ed. Francisque Mège (Paris: Aubrey, 1872), 337.

NOTES ON CONTRIBUTORS

Claire Cage is Associate Professor at the University of South Alabama, USA. She is the author of *Unnatural Frenchmen: The Politics of Priestly Celibacy and Marriage, 1720–1815* (2015).

Hannah Callaway is a Lecturer in Social Studies at Harvard University, USA. She is completing a book manuscript about property seizure in Revolutionary Paris.

Abigail Coppins is a public historian and archaeologist in the UK and is pursuing a Ph.D. in French Studies at the University of Warwick, UK. She has worked as a curator and researcher for English Heritage and has produced exhibitions on the history of people of color and prisoners of war at Portchester Castle.

Mette Harder is Associate Professor of History at the State University of New York at Oneonta, USA. She is working on a book on parliamentary violence in revolutionary France and has published with AHRF, French Historical Studies, Studies on Voltaire & the Eighteenth Century, and CNRS. Her next project explores private and political visions of fatherhood in the Revolution.

Jennifer Ngaire Heuer is Associate Professor of History at the University of Massachusetts Amherst, USA. She is the author of *The Family and the Nation: Gender and Citizenship in Revolutionary France* (2005) and of articles in journals such as *French History*, the *Journal of Military History*, *Law and History*, *Gender and History*, and the *European History Quarterly*.

Ralph Kingston is Associate Professor of European History at Auburn University, USA. His research interests lie at the intersections of the cultural, intellectual, and social histories of eighteenth- and nineteenth-century France. He is the author of *Bureaucrats and Bourgeois Society: Office Politics and Individual Credit in France, 1789–1848* (2012).

Sophie Matthiesson was Curator of International Paintings and Sculpture, 1100–1980 at the National Gallery of Victoria (NGV) in Melbourne,

Australia until 2019. In 2020, she became Senior Curator of International Art at the Auckland Art Gallery Toi o Tāmaki. She is completing a book on prison art in Revolutionary France, 1793–1795.

Clyde Plumauzille is Chargée de Recherches at the Centre National de la Recherche Scientifique (CNRS), France. A member of the Centre Roland Mousnier (Sorbonne Université), she specializes in social and gender history. She is the author of *Prostitution et Révolution: Les femmes publiques dans la cité républicaine, 1789–1804* (2016). Her current research project focuses on wet nurses and carework in eighteenth- and nineteenth-century France.

Sean M. Quinlan is Dean of the College of Letters, Arts and Social Sciences, and Professor of History at the University of Idaho, USA. He is the author of *The Great Nation in Decline: Sex, Modernity, and Health Crises in Revolutionary France, 1750–1850* (2007) and *Morbid Undercurrents: Medical Subcultures in Post-Revolutionary France* (forthcoming).

Siân Reynolds is Emerita Professor of French at the University of Stirling, UK. She is a historian of France and Scotland, specializing in women's and gender history. Her most recent book is *Marriage and Revolution: Monsieur and Madame Roland* (2012, winner R.H. Gapper Prize).

Jonathan Smyth is an Honorary Research Fellow at Birkbeck, University of London, UK. He is the author of *Robespierre and the Festival of the Supreme Being: The Search for a Republican Morality* (2016).

E. C. Spary is a Reader in the History of Modern European Knowledge at the University of Cambridge, UK. She is the author of *Utopia's Garden: French Natural History from Old Regime to Revolution* (2000), *Eating the Enlightenment* (2012), and *Feeding France, New Sciences of Food, 1760–1815* (2014).

Laura Talamante is Professor of History at California State University, Dominguez Hills, USA. She specializes in eighteenth-century Enlightenment and French revolutionary women's and gender history. Her publications include a recent essay in the journal *French History* and a forthcoming chapter in *Transgresser, une voie pour les femmes*.

Christopher Tozzi is a Senior Lecturer in Science and Technology Studies at Rensselaer Polytechnic Institute, USA. He is the author of *Nationalizing France's Army: Foreigners, Jews, and Blacks in the French Military, 1715–1831* (2016).

Jill Maciak Walshaw is Associate Professor at the University of Victoria, Canada. She has published in the area of communication, rural political culture, and criminality in early modern and revolutionary France, including the book *A Show of Hands for the Republic: Opinion, Information, and Repression in Eighteenth-Century Rural France* (2014). Her current research focuses on the counterfeiting of money in France from 1670 to 1800.

Ashli White is Associate Professor of History at the University of Miami, USA. She is the author of *Encountering Revolution: Haiti and the Making of the Early Republic* (2010) and was Associate Curator of *Antillean Visions: Maps and the Making of the Caribbean* (2018) at Lowe Art Museum.

RECOMMENDED READING

We recommend the following list as a starting point on life in revolutionary France. The literature on the French Revolution is so vast that we could not possibly include every important work; please consult the notes to the Introduction and to individual chapters for some further ideas. We have organized this list by themes closely related to this collection, but also encourage readers to think about other possible themes and connections.

Introductions, Overviews, and Reference Works

Anderson, James M., ed. *Daily Life in the French Revolution.* Westport, CT: Greenwood, 2007.

Andress, David. *The French Revolution and the People.* London: Hambledon and London, 2004.

Andress, David, ed. *Experiencing the French Revolution.* Oxford: Studies on Voltaire & the Eighteenth Century, 2013.

Andress, David, ed. *The Oxford Handbook of the French Revolution.* Oxford: Oxford University Press, 2015.

Baker, Keith Michael. *The French Revolution and the Creation of Modern Political Culture.* 4 vols. Oxford: Pergamon Press, 1987–94.

Bertaud, Jean-Paul. *La vie quotidienne en France au temps de la Révolution: 1789–1795.* Paris: Hachette, 1983.

Biard, Michel. *Parlez-vous sans-culotte? Dictionnaire du Père Duchesne (1790–1794).* Paris: Tallandier, 2009.

Brown, Howard and Judith Miller, eds. *Taking Liberties: Problems of a New Order from the French Revolution to Napoleon.* Manchester: Manchester University Press, 2002.

Desan, Suzanne. "Recent Historiography on the French Revolution and Gender." *Journal of Social History* 52, no. 3 (2019): 566–74.

Desan, Suzanne, Lynn Hunt, and William Max Nelson, eds. *The French Revolution in Global Perspective.* Ithaca, NY: Cornell University Press, 2013.

Doyle, William. *The Oxford History of the French Revolution.* Oxford: Oxford University Press, 1989/2002.

Forrest, Alan and Matthias Middell, eds. *The Routledge Companion to the French Revolution in World History.* London: Routledge, 2015.

Fremont-Barnes, Gregory. *The Encyclopedia of the French Revolutionary and Napoleonic Wars.* 3 vols. Santa Barbara, CA: ABC-CLIO, 2006.

Furet, François and Mona Ozouf. *A Critical Dictionary of the French Revolution*. Translated by Arthur Goldhammer. Cambridge, MA: Belknap Press of Harvard University Press, 1989.

Jones, Colin. *The Longman Companion to the French Revolution*. London: Longman, 1988.

Lyons, Martyn. *France under the Directory*. Cambridge: Cambridge University Press, 1975.

Marsh, Ben and Mike Rapport, eds. *Understanding and Teaching the Age of Revolutions*. Madison: University of Wisconsin Press, 2017.

McPhee, Peter. *Living the French Revolution*. Basingstoke, UK: Palgrave Macmillan, 2006.

McPhee, Peter. *A Companion to the French Revolution*. Oxford: Wiley-Blackwell, 2013.

Robiquet, Jean. *Daily Life in the French Revolution*. New York: Macmillan, 1965.

Woloch, Isser. *The New Regime: Transformations of the French Civic Order, 1789–1820s*. New York: W.W. Norton, 1994.

Primary Source Collections

French Revolution Digital Archive: https://frda.stanford.edu/en/.

Liberté, Egalité, Fraternité: Exploring the French Revolution: http://chnm.gmu.edu/revolution/.

Alpaugh, Micah, ed. *The French Revolution: A History in Documents*. London: Bloomsbury, forthcoming 2021.

Baker, Keith Michael et al., eds. *The Old Regime and the French Revolution. Vol. 7 of University of Chicago Readings in Western Civilization*. Chicago: University of Chicago Press, 1987.

Beik, Paul H., ed. *The French Revolution*. New York: Walker, 1971.

Dawson, Philip, ed. *The French Revolution*. Englewood Cliffs, NJ: Prentice-Hall, 1967.

Dubois, Laurent and John Garrigus, eds. *Slave Revolution in the Caribbean, 1789–1804: A Brief History with Documents*. Boston: Bedford/St. Martins, 2006.

Dwyer, Philip G. and Peter McPhee, eds. *The French Revolution and Napoleon: A Sourcebook*. London: Routledge, 2002.

Geggus, David P., ed. *The Haitian Revolution: A Documentary History*. Indianapolis, IN: Hackett Publishing Company, 2014.

Gilchrist, John T. and William J. Murray, eds. *The Press in the French Revolution: A Selection of Documents taken from the Press of the Revolution for the Years 1789–1794*. New York: St. Martin's Press, 1971.

Goldstein, Marc Allan, ed. *Social and Political Thought of the French Revolution, 1788–1797: An Anthology of Original Texts*. New York: Lang, 1997.

Hunt, Lynn, ed. *The French Revolution and Human Rights: A Brief Documentary History*. New York: Bedford/St. Martins, 1996.

Hyslop, Beatrice F., ed. *A Guide to the General Cahiers of 1789, with the Texts of Unedited Cahiers*. New York: Octagon Books, 1968.

Levy, Darline et al., eds. *Women in Revolutionary Paris, 1789–1795: Selected Documents Translated with Notes and Commentary*. Urbana: University of Illinois Press, 1979.

Mason, Laura and Tracey Rizzo, eds. *The French Revolution: A Document Collection*. New York: Houghton Mifflin, 1999.

Palmer, R. R., ed. and trans. *The School of the French Revolution: A Documentary History of the College of Louis-Le-Grand and its Director, Jean-François Champagne, 1762–1814*. Princeton, NJ: Princeton University Press, 1975.

Popkin, Jeremy D., ed. *Facing Racial Revolution: Eyewitness Accounts of the Haitian Insurrection*. Chicago: University of Chicago Press, 2007.

Stewart, John Hall, ed. *A Documentary Survey of the French Revolution*. New York: Macmillan, 1951.

Tannahill, Reay, ed. *Paris in the Revolution: A Collection of Eye-Witness Accounts*. London: Folio Society, 1966.

Revolutionary Identities, Choices, and Engagement

Alpaugh, Micah. *Non-Violence and the French Revolution: Political Demonstrations in Paris, 1787–1795*. Cambridge: Cambridge University Press, 2015.

Caiani, Ambrogio A. *Louis XVI and the French Revolution*. Cambridge: Cambridge University Press, 2012.

Candlin, Kit and Cassandra Pybus. *Enterprising Women: Gender, Race, and Power in the Revolutionary Atlantic*. Athens, GA: University of Georgia Press, 2015.

Cobb, Richard. *The Police and the People: French Popular Protest, 1789–1820*. Oxford: Clarendon, 1970.

Cobb, Richard. *Death in Paris: The Records of the Basse-Geôle de la Seine, October 1795–September 1801, Vendémiaire Year IV–Fructidor Year IX*. Oxford: Oxford University Press, 1978.

Coller, Ian. "Citizen Chawich: Arabs, Islam and Rights in the French Revolution." *French History and Civilization* 5 (2014): 42–52.

Crook, Malcolm. *Elections in the French Revolution: An Apprenticeship in Democracy, 1789–1799*. Cambridge: Cambridge University Press, 1996.

Desan, Suzanne. "'Constitutional Amazons': Jacobin Women's Clubs in the French Revolution." In *Re-creating Authority in Revolutionary France*, edited by Bryant T. Ragan and Elizabeth A. Williams, 11–35. New Brunswick, NJ: Rutgers University Press, 1992.

Doyle, William. *Aristocracy and its Enemies in the Age of Revolution*. Oxford: Oxford University Press, 2009.

Foster, Thomas A. "Recovering Washington's Body-Double: Disability and Manliness in the Life and Legacy of a Founding Father." *Disability Studies Quarterly* 32, no. 1 (2012). http://dx.doi.org/10.18061/dsq.v32i1.3028.

Garrigus, John D. *Before Haiti: Race and Citizenship in French Saint-Domingue*. New York: Palgrave Macmillan, 2006.

Garrioch, David. "The Everyday Lives of Parisian Women and the October Days of 1789." *Social History* 24, no. 3 (1999): 231–50.

Gendron, François. *The Gilded Youth of Thermidor*. Translated by James Cookson. Montreal: McGill-Queen's University Press, 1993.

Gershoy, Leo. *Bertrand Barère: A Reluctant Terrorist*. Princeton, NJ: Princeton University Press, 1962.

Godineau, Dominique. *The Women of Paris and their French Revolution*. Translated by Katherine Streip. Berkeley: University of California Press, 1998.

Goldstein Sepinwall, Alyssa. "Eliminating Race, Eliminating Difference: Blacks, Jews, and the Abbé Grégoire." In *The Color of Liberty: Histories of Race in France*, edited by Sue Peabody and Tyler Stovall, 28–41. Durham, NC: Duke University Press, 2003.

Hampson, Norman. *Will & Circumstance: Montesquieu, Rousseau and the French Revolution*. London: Duckworth, 1983.

Harder, Mette. "Reacting to Revolution: The Political Career of J.-L. Tallien." In *Experiencing the French Revolution*, edited by David Andress, 92–9. Oxford: Studies on Voltaire & the Eighteenth Century, 2013.

Hardman, John. *Louis XVI*. London: Arnold, 2000.

Harten, Elke and Hans-Christian Harten. *Femmes, Culture et Révolution*. Paris: des femmes, 1988.

Heuer, Jennifer Ngaire. *The Family and the Nation: Gender and Citizenship in Revolutionary France, 1789–1830*. Ithaca, NY: Cornell University Press, 2005.

Higonnet, Patrice. *Class, Ideology, and the Rights of Nobles during the French Revolution*. Oxford: Clarendon Press, 1981.

Hufton, Olwen. *Women and the Limits of Citizenship in the French Revolution*. Toronto: University of Toronto Press, 1992.

Kennedy, Michael L. *The Jacobin Clubs in the French Revolution*. 2 vols. (1. *The First Years*; 2. *The Middle Years*). Princeton, NJ: Princeton University Press, 1982–8.

Linton, Marisa. *Choosing Terror: Virtue, Friendship, and Authenticity in the French Revolution*. Oxford: Oxford University Press, 2013.

McPhee, Peter. *Robespierre: A Revolutionary Life*. New Haven, CT: Yale University Press, 2012.

Melzer, Sara and Leslie Rabine, eds. *Rebel Daughters: Women and the French Revolution*. Oxford: Oxford University Press, 1992.

Palmer, R. R. *Twelve Who Ruled: The Year of the Terror in the French Revolution*. Princeton, NJ: Princeton University Press, 2005.

Plumauzille, Clyde and Guillaume Mazeau. "Penser avec le genre: trouble dans la citoyenneté révolutionnaire." *La Révolution française* (2015). http://lrf.revues.org/1458.

Popkin, Jeremy D. *Revolutionary News: The Press in France, 1789–1799*. Durham, NC: Duke University Press, 1990.

Rapport, Michael. *Nationality and Citizenship in Revolutionary France: The Treatment of Foreigners 1789–1799*. Oxford: Oxford University Press, 2000.

Reiss, Tom. *The Black Count: Glory, Revolution, and the Real Count of Monte Cristo*. New York: Crown Trade, 2012.

Rose, Robert B. *The Making of the Sans-Culottes: Democratic Ideas and Institutions in Paris, 1789–92*. Manchester: Manchester University Press, 1983.

Roudinesco, Élisabeth. *Théroigne de Méricourt: Une femme mélancholique sous la Révolution*. Paris: Albin Michel, 2010.

Schechter, Ronald. *Obstinate Hebrews: Representations of Jews in France, 1715–1815*. Berkeley: University of California Press, 2003.

Soboul, Albert. *The Parisian Sans-Culottes and the French Revolution, 1793–1794*. Translated by Gwynne Lewis. Oxford: Clarendon Press, 1964.

Sydenham, Michael J. *Leonard Bourdon: The Career of a Revolutionary, 1754–1807*. Waterloo, ON: Wilfrid Laurier University Press, 1999.

Tackett, Timothy. *Becoming a Revolutionary: The Deputies of the French National Assembly and the Emergence of a Revolutionary Culture (1789–1790)*. Princeton, NJ: Princeton University Press, 1996.

Waldinger, Renée, Philip Dawson, and Isser Woloch, eds. *The French Revolution and the Meaning of Citizenship*. Westport, CT: Greenwood Press, 1993.

Revolutionary Spaces (Domestic to Atlantic)

Ampilova-Tuil, Louise and Catherine Gosselin, "Les logements parisiens de Saint-Just." *Société des Etudes Robespierristes* (2017). http://etudesrobespierristes.com/recherche

Bell, David. "Questioning the Global Turn: The Case of the French Revolution." *French Historical Studies* 37, no. 1 (2014): 1–24.

Bell, David. "Global Conceptual Legacies." In *Oxford Handbook of the French Revolution*, edited by David Andress, 642–68. Oxford: Oxford University Press, 2015.

Blanc, Olivier. *Last Letters: Prisons and Prisoners of the French Revolution, 1793–1794*. Translated by Alan Sheridan. London: A. Deutsch, 1987.

Desan, Suzanne. "Transatlantic Spaces of Revolution: The French Revolution, Sciotamanie, and American Lands." *Journal of Early Modern History* 12, no. 6 (2008): 467–505.

Desan, Suzanne et al., eds. *The French Revolution in Global Perspective*. Ithaca, NY: Cornell University Press, 2013.

Dubois, Laurent. "An Enslaved Enlightenment: Rethinking the Intellectual History of the French Atlantic." *Social History* 31, no. 1 (2006): 1–14.

Forrest, Alan. "Re-imagining Space and Power." In *A Companion to the French Revolution*, ed. Peter McPhee, 91–106. Chichester: Wiley-Blackwell, 2013.

Forrest, Alan and Peter Jones, eds. *Reshaping France: Town, Country and Region during the French Revolution*. Manchester: Manchester University Press, 1991.

Friedland, Paul. *Seeing Justice Done: The Age of Spectacular Capital Punishment in France*. New York: Oxford University Press, 2012.

Garrioch, David. *The Making of Revolutionary Paris*. Berkeley: University of California Press, 2002.

Geggus, David and David Gaspar, eds. *A Turbulent Time: The French Revolution and the Greater Caribbean*. Bloomington: Indiana University Press, 1997.

Goodman, Dena and Thomas Kaiser, eds. *Marie-Antoinette: Writings on the Body of a Queen*. New York: Routledge, 2003.

Hunt, Lynn. "The Unstable Boundaries of the French Revolution." In *A History of Private Life*, ed. by Michelle Perrot, 13–45. Cambridge, MA: Belknap Press, 1990.

Jarvis, Katie. *Politics in the Marketplace: Work, Gender, and Citizenship in Revolutionary France*. Oxford: Oxford University Press, 2019.

Jones, Peter. *The Peasantry in the French Revolution*. Cambridge: Cambridge University Press, 1988.

Jones, Peter. *Liberty and Locality in Revolutionary France: Six Villages Compared, 1760–1820*. Cambridge: Cambridge University Press, 2003.

Klooster, Wim. *Revolutions in the Atlantic World, New Edition: A Comparative History*. New York: New York University Press, 2018.

Landes, Joan B. *Women and the Public Sphere in the Age of the French Revolution*. Ithaca, NY: Cornell University Press, 1988.

Lefebvre, Georges. "The Place of the Revolution in the Agrarian History of France." In *Rural Society in France: Selections from the "Annales, économies, sociétés, civilisations,"* edited by Robert Forster and Orest Ranum, translated by Elborg Forster and Patricia M. Ranum, 31–49. Baltimore, MD: Johns Hopkins University Press, 1977.

Legacey, Erin-Marie. *Making Space for the Dead: Catacombs, Cemeteries, and the Reimaging of Paris, 1780–1830*. Ithaca, NY: Cornell University Press, 2019.

Leith, James. *Space and Revolution: Projects for Monuments, Squares, and Public Buildings in France, 1789–1799*. Montreal: McGill-Queen's University Press, 1991.

Livesey, James. *Making Democracy in the French Revolution*. Cambridge, MA: Harvard University Press, 2001.

O'Connor, Adrian. *In Pursuit of Politics: Education and Revolution in Eighteenth-Century France*. Manchester: Manchester University Press, 2017.

Outram, Dorinda. *The Body in the French Revolution: Sex, Class, and Political Culture*. New Haven, CT: Yale University Press, 1989.

Ozouf, Mona. "Space and Time in the Festivals of the French Revolution." In *The French Revolution and Intellectual History*, edited by Jack Censer, 186–200. Chicago: Dorsey Press, 1989.

Polasky, Janet. *Revolutions without Borders: The Call to Liberty in the Atlantic World*. New Haven, CT: Yale University Press, 2015.

Popiel, Jennifer J. *Rousseau's Daughters: Domesticity, Education, and Autonomy in Modern France*. Hanover: University of New Hampshire Press, 2008.

Potofsky, Allan. *Constructing Paris in the Age of Revolution*. Basingstoke, UK: Palgrave Macmillan, 2009.

Rapport, Mike. *The Unruly City: Paris, London, and New York in the Age of Revolution*. New York: Basic Books, 2017.

Spieler, Miranda. *Empire and Underworld: Captivity in French Guiana*. Cambridge, MA: Harvard University Press, 2012.

Talamante, Laura. "Political Divisions, Gender and Politics: The Case of Revolutionary Marseille." *French History* 31, no. 1 (2017): 63–84.

Walshaw, Jill Maciak. *A Show of Hands for the Republic: Opinion, Information, and Repression in Eighteenth-Century Rural France*. Rochester, NY: University of Rochester Press, 2014.

Making a Living

Blaufarb, Rafe. *The Great Demarcation: The French Revolution and the Creation of Modern Property*. Oxford: Oxford University Press, 2016.

DiCaprio, Lisa. *The Origins of the Welfare State: Women, Work, and the French Revolution*. Urbana: University of Illinois Press, 2007.

Farge, Arlette. *Fragile Lives: Violence, Power and Solidarity in Eighteenth-Century Paris*. Translated by Carol Shelton. Cambridge, MA: Harvard University Press, 1993.
Forrest, Alan. *The French Revolution and the Poor*. Oxford: Basil Blackwell, 1981.
Horn, Jeff. *Economic Development in Early Modern France: The Privilege of Liberty, 1650–1820*. Cambridge: Cambridge University Press, 2017.
Jarvis, Katie. "Exacting Change: Money, Market Women, and the Crumbling Corporate World of the French Revolution." *Journal of Social History* 51, no. 4 (2017): 837–68.
Jones, Colin. *Charity and Bienfaisance: The Treatment of the Poor in the Montpellier Region, 1740–1815*. Cambridge: Cambridge University Press, 1982.
Kingston, Ralph. *Bureaucrats and Bourgeois Society: Office Politics and Individual Credit in France, 1789–1848*. London: Palgrave Macmillan, 2012.
Plumauzille, Clyde. *Prostitution et Révolution: Les femmes publiques dans la cité républicaine (1789–1804)*. Paris: Champ Vallon, 2016.
Vardi, Liana. *The Land and the Loom: Peasants and Profit in Northern France 1680–1800*. Durham, NC: Duke University Press, 1993.

Material Culture: Revolutionary Art, Objects, and Machines

Arasse, Daniel. *The Guillotine and the Terror*. Translated by Christopher Miller. London: Penguin, 1991.
Auslander, Leora. *Cultural Revolutions: The Politics of Everyday Life in Britain, North America and France*. Oxford: Berg, 2009.
Berg, Maxine and Elizabeth Eger. *Luxury in the Eighteenth Century: Debates, Desires and Delectable Goods*. Basingstoke, UK: Palgrave Macmillan, 2003.
Freund, Amy. *Portraiture and Politics in Revolutionary France*. University Park: Pennsylvania State University Press, 2014.
Spang, Rebecca. *Stuff and Money in the Time of the French Revolution*. Cambridge, MA: Harvard University Press, 2015.
Taws, Richard. *The Politics of the Provisional: Art and Ephemera in Revolutionary France*. University Park: Pennsylvania State University Press, 2013.
Wrigley, Richard. *The Politics of Appearance: The Symbolism and Representation of Dress in Revolutionary France*. Oxford: Berg, 2002.

Living with War

Bell, David. *The First Total War: Napoleon's Europe and the Birth of Warfare as We Know It*. Boston: Houghton Mifflin, 2007.
Bertaud, Jean-Paul. *The Army of the French Revolution: From Citizen-Soldiers to Instrument of Power*. Translated by R. R. Palmer. Princeton, NJ: Princeton University Press, 1988.
Dubois, Laurent. "Gendered Freedom: Citoyennes and War in the Revolutionary French Caribbean." In *Gender, War, and Politics: The Wars of Revolution and*

Liberation—Transatlantic Comparisons, 1775–1820, edited by Karen Hagemann, Gisela Mettele, and Jane Rendall, 58–70. New York: Palgrave Macmillan, 2010.

Forrest, Alan. *The Soldiers of the French Revolution.* Durham, NC: Duke University Press, 1990.

Hagemann, Karen, Alan Forrest, and Jane Rendall, eds. *Soldiers, Citizens and Civilians: Experiences and Perceptions of the French Wars, 1790–1820.* Basingstoke, UK: Palgrave Macmillan, 2009.

Heuer, Jennifer Ngaire. "Citizenship, the French Revolution, and the Limits of Martial Masculinity." In *Gender and Citizenship in Historical and Transnational Perspective*, edited by Rachel Fuchs and Anne Epstein, 19–38. Basingstoke, UK: Palgrave Macmillan, 2016.

Kaiser, Thomas E. "Who's Afraid of Marie-Antoinette? Diplomacy, Austrophobia and the Queen." *French History* 14 (2000): 241–71.

Mainz, Valerie. *Days of Glory? Imaging Military Recruitment and the French Revolution.* Basingstoke, UK: Palgrave Macmillan, 2016.

Morieux, Renaud. *The Society of Prisoners: Anglo-French Wars and Incarceration in the Eighteenth-Century.* Oxford: Oxford University Press, 2019.

Pichichero, Christy Lauren. *The Military Enlightenment: War and Culture from Louis XIV to Napoleon.* Ithaca, NY: Cornell University Press, 2017.

Serna, Pierre, Antonino de Francesco, and Judith A. Miller, eds. *Republics at War, 1776–1840: Revolutions, Conflicts and Geopolitics in Europe and the Atlantic World.* Basingstoke, UK: Palgrave Macmillan, 2013.

Tozzi, Christopher. *Nationalizing France's Army: Foreigners, Jews, and Blacks in the French Military, 1715–1831.* Charlottesville: University of Virginia Press, 2016.

Woloch, Isser. *The French Veteran: From the Revolution to the Restoration.* Chapel Hill: University of North Carolina Press, 1979.

Forms of Revolutionary Justice

Andress, David. *The Terror: The Merciless War for Freedom in Revolutionary France.* New York: Farrar, Strauss & Giroux, 2006.

Berger, Emmanuel. *La justice pénale sous la Révolution.* Rennes: PUR, 2008.

Brinton, Crane. *French Revolutionary Legislation on Illegitimacy, 1789–1804.* Cambridge, MA: Harvard University Press, 1936.

Brown, Howard. *Ending the French Revolution: Violence, Justice, and Repression from the Terror to Napoleon.* Charlottesville: University of Virginia Press, 2006.

Clay, Stephen. "Vengeance, Justice and the Reactions in the Revolutionary Midi." *French History* 23, no. 1 (2009): 22–46.

Desan, Suzanne. *The Family on Trial in Revolutionary France.* Berkeley: University of California Press, 2004.

Dubois, Laurent. *A Colony of Citizens: Revolution and Slave Emancipation in the French Caribbean, 1787–1804.* Chapel Hill: University of North Carolina Press, 2004.

Edelstein, Dan. *The Terror of Natural Right: Republicanism, the Cult of Nature, and the French Revolution.* Chicago: University of Chicago Press, 2009.

Fairfax-Cholmeley, Alex. "Creating and Resisting the Terror: The Paris Revolutionary Tribunal, March–June 1793." *French History* 32 no. 2 (2018): 203–25.

Gough, Hugh. *The Terror in the French Revolution*. Basingstoke, UK: Macmillan, 1998.

Greer, Donald. *The Incidence of the Terror during the French Revolution: A Statistical Interpretation*. Cambridge, MA: Harvard University Press, 1935.

Hunt, Lynn. *Inventing Human Rights*. New York: W. W. Norton, 2007.

Jordan, David. *The King's Trial: The French Revolution against Louis XVI*. Berkeley: University of California Press, 1979.

Lucas, Colin. *The Structure of the Terror: The Example of Javogues and the Loire*. Oxford: Oxford University Press, 1973.

Lyons, Martyn. *Revolution in Toulouse: An Essay on Provincial Terrorism*. Bern: Peter Lang, 1978.

Markoff, John. *The Abolition of Feudalism: Peasants, Lords, and Legislators in the French Revolution*. University Park: Pennsylvania State University Press, 1996.

Martin, Jean-Clément. *Violence et Révolution: essai sur la naissance d'un mythe national*. Paris: Seuil, 2006.

Mason, Laura. "The 'Bosom of Proof': Criminal Justice and the Renewal of Oral Culture during the French Revolution." *Journal of Modern History* 76, no. 1 (2004): 29–61.

Popkin, Jeremy D. *You Are All Free: The Haitian Revolution and the Abolition of Slavery*. Cambridge: Cambridge University Press, 2010.

Ragan, Bryant T. "Rural Political Activism and Fiscal Equality in the Revolutionary Somme." In *Re-creating Authority in Revolutionary France*, edited by Bryant T. Ragan and Elizabeth A. Williams, 36–56. New Brunswick, NJ: Rutgers University Press, 1992.

Ragan, Bryant T. "Same-Sex Sexual Relations and the French Revolution: The Decriminalization of Sodomy in 1791." In *From Sodomy Laws to Same-Sex Marriage: International Perspectives Since 1789*, edited by Sean Brady and Mark Seymour, 13–30. London: Bloomsbury, 2019.

Schechter, Ronald. *A Genealogy of Terror in Eighteenth-Century France*. Chicago: University of Chicago Press, 2018.

Shapiro, Barry. *Revolutionary Justice in Paris, 1789–1890*. Cambridge: Cambridge University Press, 2002.

Spieler, Miranda. "The Destruction of Liberty in French Guiana: Law, Identity and the Meaning of Legal Space, 1794–1830." *Social History* 32, no. 3 (2011): 260–79.

Sutherland, D. M. G. *Murder in Aubagne: Lynching, Law, and Justice during the French Revolution*. Cambridge: Cambridge University Press, 2009.

Tackett, Timothy. *The Coming of the Terror in the French Revolution*. Cambridge, MA: Belknap Press, 2015.

Walton, Charles. *Policing Public Opinion in the French Revolution: The Culture of Calumny and the Problem of Free Speech*. New York: Oxford University Press, 2009.

Waresquiel, Emmanuel de. *Juger la reine: 14, 15, 16 octobre 1793*. Paris: Tallandier, 2016.

Family, Friendship, and Love in Revolution

Darrow, Margaret. *Revolution in the House: Family, Class and Inheritance in Southern France, 1775–1825*. Princeton, NJ: Princeton University Press, 1989.

Desan, Suzanne. "The French Revolution and the Family." In *A Companion to the French Revolution*, edited by Peter McPhee, 470–85. Oxford: Wiley-Blackwell, 2013.

Dupre, Huntley. *Two Brothers in the French Revolution: Robert and Thomas Lindet*. London: Archon Books, 1967.

Fass, Paula S., ed. *The Routledge History of Childhood in the Western World*. London: Routledge, 2013.

Fauve-Chamoux, Antoinette. "Beyond Adoption: Orphans and Family Strategies in Pre-Industrial France." *History of the Family* 1, no. 1 (1996): 1–13.

Gager, Kristin Elizabeth. *Blood Ties and Fictive Ties: Adoption and Family Life in Early Modern France*. Princeton, NJ: Princeton University Press, 1996.

Gerber, Matthew. "Bastardy, Race, and Law in the Eighteenth-Century French Atlantic: The Evidence of Litigation." *French Historical Studies* 36, no. 4 (2013): 371–600.

Heywood, Colin. *Growing up in France*. Cambridge: Cambridge University Press, 2007.

Hunt, Lynn. *The Family Romance of the French Revolution*. Berkeley: University of California Press, 1992.

Leuwers, Hervé. *Camille et Lucile Desmoulins: un rêve de république*. Paris: Fayard, 2018.

Lévy, Marie-Françoise, ed. *L'enfant, la famille et la Révolution française*. Paris: O. Orban, 1990.

Linton, Marisa. "Fatal Friendships: The Politics of Jacobin Friendship." *French Historical Studies* 31, no. 1 (2008): 51–76.

Palmer, Jennifer. *Intimate Bonds: Family and Slavery in the French Atlantic*. Philadelphia: University of Pennsylvania Press, 2016.

Parker, Lindsay. *Writing the Revolution: A French Woman's History in Letters*. New York: Oxford University Press, 2012.

Phillips, Roderick. *Family Breakdown in Late-Eighteenth Century France: Divorces in Rouen, 1792–1803*. Oxford: Clarendon Press, 1980.

Reynolds, Siân. *Marriage and Revolution: Monsieur and Madame Roland*. Oxford: Oxford University Press, 2012.

Roberts, Meghan K. *Sentimental Savants: Philosophical Families in Enlightenment France*. Chicago: University of Chicago Press, 2016.

Sibalis, Michael David. "The Regulation of Male Homosexuality in Revolutionary and Napoleonic France, 1789–1815." In *Homosexuality in Modern France*, edited by Jeffrey Merrick and Bryant T. Ragan, 80–101. Oxford: Oxford University Press, 1996.

Stéfane-Pol. *Autour de Robespierre: le conventionnel Le Bas d'après des documents inédits et les mémoires de sa veuve*. Paris: Ernest Flammarion, 1900.

Steinberg, Sylvie. "Et les bâtards devinrent citoyens: La privatisation d'une condition d'infamie sous la Révolution française." *Genèses* 108 (2017): 9–28.

Théry, Irène and Christian Biet, eds. *La Famille, la loi, l'état de la Révolution au Code Civil*. Paris: Imprimerie nationale, 1989.

Trouille, Mary. *Wife-Abuse in Eighteenth-Century France*. Oxford: Studies on Voltaire & the Eighteenth Century, 2009.

Verjus, Anne. *Le bon mari: Une histoire politique des hommes et des femmes à l'époque révolutionnaire*. Paris: Fayard, 2010.

Verjus, Anne and Denise Zara Davidson. *Le roman conjugal: chroniques de la vie familiale à l'époque de la Révolution et de l'Empire*. Paris: Champ Vallon, 2011.

Viallaneix, Paul and Jean Ehrard. *Aimer en France 1760–1860*. 2 vols. Clermont-Ferrand: Publications de la Faculté des Lettres et Sciences humaines de l'Université de Clermont-Ferrand, 1980.

Wolff, Larry. "Children and the Enlightenment." In *The Routledge History of Childhood in the Western World*, edited by Paula S. Fass, 78–100. New York: Routledge, 2013.

Food, Health, and the Natural Environment

Arnaud, Sabine. *On Hysteria: The Invention of a Medical Category between 1670 and 1820*. Chicago: University of Chicago Press, 2015.

Chappey, Jean-Luc and Julien Vincent. "Republican Ecology? Citizenship, Nature, and the French Revolution, 1795–1799." *Past & Present* 243, no. 1 (2019): 109–40.

Easterby-Smith, Sarah. *Cultivating Commerce: Cultures of Botany in Britain and France, 1760–1815*. Cambridge: Cambridge University Press, 2018.

Jones, Colin. *The Smile Revolution in Eighteenth-Century Paris*. Oxford: Oxford University Press, 2014.

Kaplan, Steven L. *The Famine Plot Persuasion in Eighteenth-Century France*. Philadelphia: American Philosophical Society, 1982.

Linton, Marisa and Mette Harder. "Come and Dine: The Dangers of Conspicuous Consumption in French Revolutionary Politics." *European History Quarterly* 45, no. 4 (2015): 615–37.

Matteson, Kieko. *Forests in Revolutionary France: Conservation, Community, and Conflict, 1669–1848*. Cambridge: Cambridge University Press, 2015.

McPhee, Peter. *Revolution and Environment in Southern France: Peasants, Lords, and Murder in the Corbières, 1780–1830*. Oxford: Oxford University Press, 1999.

Miller, Mary Ashburn. *A Natural History of Revolution: Violence and Nature in the French Revolutionary Imagination, 1789–1794*. Ithaca, NY: Cornell University Press, 2011.

Quinlan, Sean. *The Great Nation in Decline: Sex, Modernity, and Health Crises in Revolutionary France, 1750–1850*. Aldershot: Ashgate, 2007.

Serna, Pierre. *L'animal en république, 1789–1802: Genèse du droit des bêtes*. Toulouse: Anarchis, 2016.

Spang, Rebecca. *The Invention of the Restaurant: Paris and Modern Gastronomic Culture*. Cambridge, MA: Harvard University Press, 2001.

Spary, Emma. *Feeding France, New Sciences of Food, 1760–1815*. Cambridge: Cambridge University Press, 2014.

Religion and Spirituality

Banks, Bryan A. and Erica Johnson, eds. *The French Revolution and Religion in Global Perspective: Freedom and Faith*. Basingstoke, UK: Palgrave Macmillan, 2017.

Cage, E. Claire. *Unnatural Frenchmen: The Politics of Priestly Celibacy and Marriage, 1720–1815*. Charlottesville: University of Virginia Press, 2015.

Clarke, Joseph. "'The Rage of their Enemies': Religious Fanaticism and the Making of Revolutionary Violence." *French History* 33, no. 2 (2019): 236–58.

Coller, Ian. *Arab France: Islam and the Making of Modern Europe 1798–1831*. Berkeley: University of California Press, 2010.

Livesey, James. "Theophilanthropy and the Politics of the Directory 1795–99." In *Religion and Rebellion: Papers read before the 22nd Irish Conference of Historians, held at University College Dublin, 18–22 May 1995*. Dublin: University College Dublin Press, 1997.

Mathiez, Albert. "New Evidence about Catherine Théot." In *The Fall of Robespierre and other Essays*, 119–25. London: Williams and Norgate, 1927.

Smyth, Jonathan. *Robespierre and the Festival of the Supreme Being: The Search for a Republican Morality*. Manchester: Manchester University Press, 2016.

Tackett, Timothy. *Religion, Revolution, and Regional Culture in Eighteenth-Century France: The Ecclesiastical Oath of 1791*. Princeton, NJ: Princeton University Press, 1996.

Vovelle, Michel. *The Revolution against the Church: From Reason to the Supreme Being*. Translated by Alan José. Cambridge: Polity, 1991.

Experiences, Emotions, and Reactions to Revolution

Baecque, Antoine de. *Glory and Terror: Seven Deaths under the French Revolution*. Translated by Charlotte Mandell. New York: Routledge, 2001.

Campbell, Peter R., Thomas E. Kaiser, and Marisa Linton, eds. *Conspiracy in the French Revolution*. Manchester: Manchester University Press, 2007.

Cobb, Richard. *Reactions to the French Revolution*. London: Oxford University Press, 1972.

Dodman, Thomas. *What Nostalgia Was: War, Empire, and the Time of a Deadly Emotion*. Chicago: Chicago University Press, 2018.

Hunt, Lynn. "The Experience of Revolution." *French Historical Studies* 32, no. 4 (2009): 671–8.

Lucas, Colin. "The Theory and Practice of Denunciation in the French Revolution." *Journal of Modern History* 68, no. 4 (1996): 768–85.

Mazeau, Guillaume. "Emotions politiques: la Révolution française." In *Histoire des émotions: Des Lumières à la fin de XIXième siècle*, edited by Alain Corbin and Jean-Jacques Courtine, 98–142. Paris: Seuil, 2016.

Parker, Lindsay. "Veiled Emotions: Rosalie Jullien and the Politics of Feeling in the French Revolution." *Journal of Historical Biography* 13 (2013): 208–30.

Porter, Lindsay. *Popular Rumour in Revolutionary Paris, 1792–1794*. Basingstoke, UK: Palgrave Macmillan, 2017.

Reddy, William M. *The Navigation of Feeling: A Framework for the History of Emotions*. Cambridge: Cambridge University Press, 2001.

Valade, Pauline. "Public Celebrations and Public Joy at the Beginning of the French Revolution (1788–1791)." *French History* 29, no. 2 (2015): 182–203.

Representations, Legacies, and Memories of the Revolutionary Era

Biard, Michel, Philippe Bourdin, Hervé Leuwers, and Yoshiaki Ômi, eds. *L'écriture d'une expérience: Révolution, histoire et mémoires de Conventionnels*. Paris: Société des études robespierristes, 2015.

Clarke, Joseph. *Commemorating the Dead in Revolutionary France: Revolution and Remembrance, 1789–1799*. Cambridge: Cambridge University Press, 2007.

Fritzsche, Peter. *Stranded in the Present: Modern Time and the Melancholy of History*. Cambridge, MA: Harvard University Press, 2004.

Hazareesingh, Sudhir. *The Jacobin Legacy in Modern France*. New York: Oxford University Press, 2002.

Heuer, Jennifer Ngaire. "Did Everything Change? Rethinking Revolutionary Legacies." In *The Oxford Handbook of the French Revolution*, edited by David Andress, 625–41. Oxford: Oxford University Press, 2015.

Kaplan, Steven L. *Farewell, Revolution: The Historians' Feud: France, 1789/1989*. Ithaca, NY: Cornell University Press, 1995.

Luzzatto, Sergio. *Mémoire de la Terreur: Vieux Montagnards et jeunes républicains au 19e siècle*. Lyon: Presses Universitaires de Lyon, 1991.

Lyons, Martyn. *Napoleon Bonaparte and the Legacy of the French Revolution*. Basingstoke, UK: Palgrave Macmillan, 1994.

Stammers, Tom. "The Homeless Heritage of the French Revolution, c. 1789–1889." *International Journal of Heritage Studies* 25, no. 5 (2018): 478–90.

Steinberg, Ronen. *The Afterlives of the Terror: Facing the Legacies of Mass Violence in Post-Revolutionary France*. Ithaca, NY: Cornell University Press, 2019.

Vovelle, Michel. *1789: L'héritage et la mémoire*. Toulouse: Privat, 2007.

Wahnich, Sophie. *Histoire d'un trésor perdu: transmettre la Révolution française*. Paris: Les Prairies ordinaires/Belles lettres, 2013.

INDEX

Page numbers in *italics* indicate illustrations. All locations are in France unless otherwise specified.